FUNDAMENTALS OF DATA PROCESSING

second edition

S. J. Wanous — Professor Emeritus of Education
University of California
Los Angeles, California

Gerald E. Wagner — Professor of Information Systems
School of Business Administration
California State Polytechnic University
Pomona, California

Judith J. Lambrecht — Associate Professor of
Business Education
University of Minnesota
Minneapolis, Minnesota

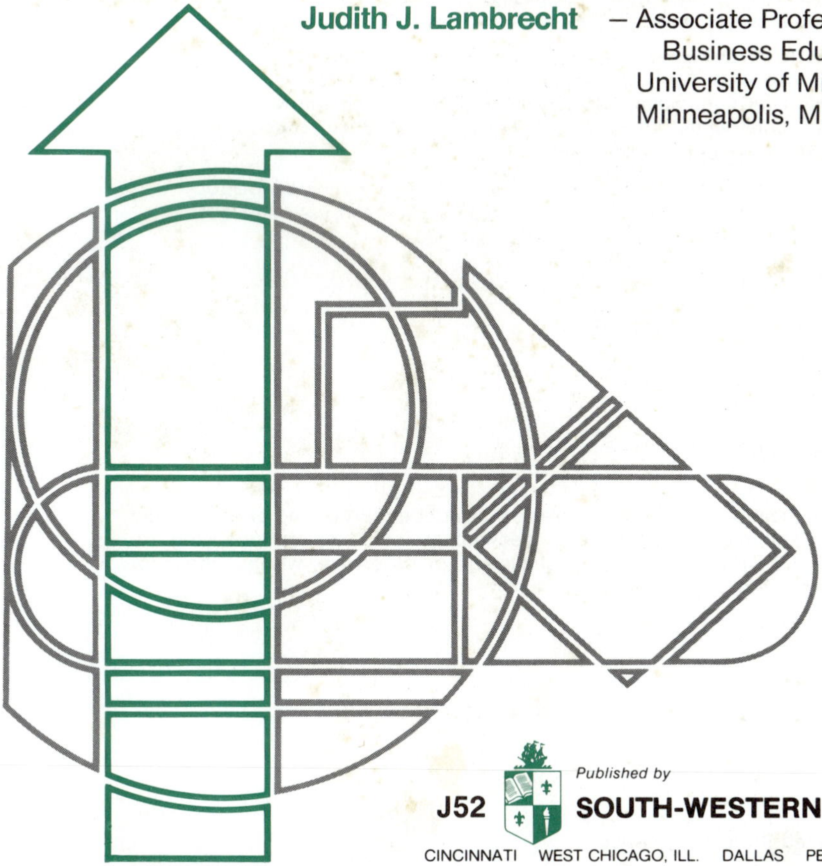

Published by

J52 **SOUTH-WESTERN PUBLISHING CO.**

CINCINNATI WEST CHICAGO, ILL. DALLAS PELHAM MANOR, N.Y. PALO ALTO, CALIF.

COBOL ACKNOWLEDGMENT

The following acknowledgment is reprinted from COBOL Edition 1965, published by the Conference on Data Systems Languages (CODSSYL) and printed by the U.S. Government Printing Office:

Any organization interested in reproducing the COBOL report and specifications in whole or in part, using ideas taken from this report as the basis for an instruction manual or for any other purpose, is free to do so. However, all such organizations are requested to reproduce this section as part of the introduction to the document. Those using a short passage, as in a book review, are requested to mention "COBOL" in acknowledgment of the source, but need not quote this entire section.

COBOL is an industry language and is not the property of any company or group of companies, or of any organization or group of organizations.

No warranty, expressed or implied is made by any contributor or by the COBOL Committee as to the accuracy and functioning of the programming system and language. Moreover, no responsibility is assumed by any contributor, or by the committee, in connection therewith.

Procedures have been established for the maintenance of COBOL. Inquiries concerning the procedures for proposing changes should be directed to the Executive Committee of the Conference on Data Systems Languages.

The authors and copyright holders of the copyrighted materials used herein

FLOW-MATIC (Trademark of Sperry Rand Corporation), Programming for the Univac (R) I and II, Data Automation Systems copyrighted 1958, 1959, by Sperry Rand Corporation; IBM Commercial Translator Form No. F-28-8013, copyrighted 1959 by IBM; FACT, DSI 27A5260, copyrighted 1960 by Minneapolis-Honeywell

have specially authorized the use of this material in whole or in part, in the COBOL specifications. Such authorization extends to the reproduction and use of COBOL specifications in programming manuals of similar publications.

ISBN: 0-538-10520-8

Library of Congress Catalog Card Number: 79-67205

1 2 3 4 5 6 7 8 K 8 7 6 5 4 3 2 1

Printed in the United States of America

PREFACE

Understanding computers is no longer a matter of choice in today's society. It is almost a necessity. We need to know how computers affect our lives because their effect is felt in every area.

Advances in computer technology have made it possible to use the computer in virtually all fields of endeavor. Computers are used in medicine, business, communications, science, engineering, law enforcement, traffic control, and nearly all career fields. Computers address and process much of our mail. They route telephone calls, calculate bills we receive, and even keep track of our money in the banks. Tiny computers or microprocessors are used in many ways to increase the efficiency of familiar appliances and machines. Computers are even used in automobiles and in homes to help save fuel and energy costs.

A basic knowledge of computers is an asset to any person wishing to be a productive member of modern society. FUNDAMENTALS OF DATA PROCESSING, Second Edition, is written to give the beginner a general understanding of data processing. This introductory text is designed to provide background knowledge needed in order to function as an intelligent user of computer resources in an electronic society. In addition, a foundation is provided that will enable students to go on to more advanced studies of a specific programming language or phase of data processing.

Objectives of this Book

1. To provide students with an understanding of the terminology used in the computer industry.
2. To explain to students how the computer can and does affect their daily lives.
3. To educate students who wish to know how data are processed by computers.
4. To help students develop a pattern of logical thinking by analyzing problems and planning step-by-step solutions.
5. To prepare students for careers in which they need to understand the computer even though their jobs may not be in the data processing field.
6. To give students a broad-based understanding of information processing in order to prepare for further education leading to careers in the field of computerized data processing.
7. To give students a basic foundation in one or both of the most frequently used computer programming languages, BASIC and COBOL.
8. To acquaint students with computer-related occupations as well as the qualities and education needed to succeed in these positions.

Concepts

The material is presented in a step-by-step manner that is easy to follow. A building-block approach is used, in which students are introduced to simple, easy-to-see concepts. These concepts are well illustrated and are reinforced as more data processing principles are introduced.

Related to the computer from the start, the text contains an overview of the component parts and function of the computer. Students are taught basic data processing operations in connection with the manual system first. These operations then are immediately related to a computer system.

Because the magnetic spots on tapes and disks cannot be seen or understood, the punched card is used as a visible medium for helping the students gain a beginning knowledge of data processing operations and record planning. All knowledge is immediately applied to magnetic tape and magnetic disk systems. Students understand the planning and layout of punched card data records first. This knowledge is then applied to magnetic tapes and disks.

New to this edition: information systems are explained in simple, easy-to-understand terms. The need for maintaining various data processing systems within the total operation of a company is first emphasized. Then, establishing goals for a system is discussed, along with determining the input, operations, and output needed to meet these goals.

The problem-solving approach is stressed. The importance of first understanding the objective (output) is taught as the initial step in the solution. After a problem has been defined, students learn to develop a logical approach to the entire problem. Solutions are first developed in English, and the English-language solutions are converted to computer programs.

Programming Principles

General programming concepts are briefly explained in Chapter 9, *Human-Language Programs and Flowcharts*. Differences between machine language, assembly language, and higher-level language are explained. Students learn about conditional and unconditional branches, loops, and various types of logical decisions. This chapter provides a background for the programming languages presented in the next four chapters.

Programming Languages

The BASIC and COBOL languages are introduced in this text. Students may study either one or both of the languages. Program instructions are applied to simple problems that are explained and illustrated. Problem solutions include flowcharts and accompanying explanations. The numbered explanations correlate with the numbered steps in the flowcharts and help students to develop a logical approach to problem solving. Samples of input records, output records, and programs are included, providing a complete learning package.

Specialized Equipment Not Needed

The example programs presented in the text and those in the projects booklet have been run on a computer. However, it is possible to work the projects without a computer. Emphasis is on the development of logic rather than on the use of equipment. Although specialized equipment does motivate students, it is not an essential element in meeting the goals of an introductory course.

Outstanding Features

1. Numerous photographs and line drawings are used throughout the text to explain the concepts presented. Color is used to clarify illustrations and to enhance the appearance of the book.
2. All new terms are italicized and defined when used for the first time. They are then repeated at the end of each chapter in the list of *New Terms* and are also listed in a *Glossary of Special Terms*.
3. Review questions are placed in the text at points at which students should check their knowledge before proceeding further.
4. Advanced concepts are introduced by building on simpler ones presented earlier.
5. Computer programming material is presented in a manner that permits the introduction of either BASIC or COBOL in any sequence after Chapter 9, *Human-Language Programs and Flowcharts*. The BASIC and COBOL chapters are self-contained. Students can study either language or both. However, the text can be used without studying either language, by skipping from Chapter 9 to Chapter 14.
6. Chapter 14, *Social Impact of the Computer*, and Chapter 15, *A Look into the Future*, provide a brief look at many different applications of computers in our society. Some of the legislated safeguards against invasion of personal privacy are discussed. Many different computer-related positions are described, together with duties involved, educational background, and training required.
7. School activities and common business transactions are used as examples to which students can relate.

Teaching Materials Available

The text is self-contained and can be used without additional materials. However, a number of supplementary aids are available.

A kit of materials, titled DATA PROCESSING APPLICATIONS, includes the following:

1. Projects booklet that includes directions and forms for working many of the projects.
2. Punched cards, card layout forms, printer spacing charts, programming sheets, and other working papers needed to complete the projects.
3. Flowcharting template.
4. Study guides booklet containing objective questions, accompanied by an answers key card that permits students to check the accuracy of responses in a programmed approach by checking each answer before progressing further. All answers on the answers key card include page references that direct students to the correct answers.

Two objective examinations are available, one covering the first half of the text and another covering the second half.

An instructor's manual contains objectives for each chapter in the textbook, answers to review questions appearing in the chapters, solutions to all projects, and solutions to the two examinations.

The authors express their thanks to the teachers, students, and data processing specialists who have helped in writing this book, especially to the organizations that generously provided so many of the illustrations.

S. J. Wanous/G. E. Wagner/J. J. Lambrecht

CONTENTS

1

GROWTH and IMPORTANCE of DATA PROCESSING

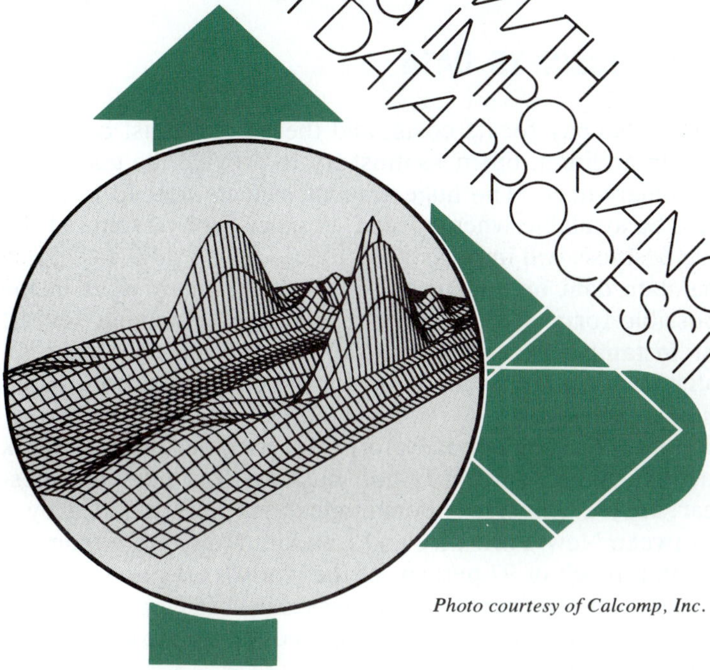

Photo courtesy of Calcomp, Inc.

Data is a term that means facts of all kinds. The date of your birth is a fact. Your school grades, your address, and your health records are also facts. Your personal data start accumulating the day you are born, and they multiply at a rapid rate as you grow older. The number of facts needed by a business to carry on its affairs and to serve its customers is even more impressive.

IMPORTANCE OF PERSONAL DATA

You need look no further than yourself to realize the important part that data play in today's world. You may prepare a resume to get a job. The resume will contain many personal facts. If you get the job, you will receive paychecks showing the number of hours worked, rate of pay, gross earnings, deductions for taxes, and net earnings. You will deposit all or part of the check in a bank. Then, you will write checks to pay bills for rent, food, car payments, telephone, gas, lights, and water.

You may use credit cards to buy gasoline for a car or to make many other purchases. Sooner or later, these bills must be paid, too. Insurance and income tax records must be kept, and these payments must be made on time.

All your bills must be paid when they are due. Just as important, expenses must be kept in line with income. To meet these two goals, you will need many kinds of data, and the data must be well managed.

IMPORTANCE OF BUSINESS DATA

Business must also pay for its costs, and these costs must be in line with its income. In addition, business must try to provide the goods and services its customers need. The huge amount of facts needed to reach these goals must be available when needed. A quick look at some of the ways data serve business will impress you.

Airlines maintain data on vacancies for all flights many days in the future. It is possible for a user to make reservations involving several airlines almost instantly. Investors can call stock brokers' offices all over the country and in a few seconds obtain the daily quotations listed on the major stock exchanges.

More than 185 million telephones form a communication network over which are exchanged several billion business and personal messages each year. In 1927, overseas communications were handled by a single circuit between New York City and London. Now, more than 200 countries are within reach of 97 percent of the world's telephones. Telephone calls can be made to friends or businesses in foreign countries by direct dialing. The costs of the calls are figured automatically and included in the monthly bill.

Facts are also transmitted by mail — 90 billion pieces a year in this country alone. These are only indications of the importance of the data that are generated, communicated, and used by business.

WHAT IS DATA PROCESSING?

Collecting facts is one thing; putting them into usable form is another. That's the job of data processing. Names of students are facts. Arranging the names in alphabetic order so a certain name can be found quickly is a form of data processing. Recording test scores made by students, preparing a bill for a customer, or classifying the kinds of jobs obtained by high school graduates are other examples of data processing. *Data processing* may be defined as converting facts into usable form. See Figure 1-1.

The foregoing definition of data processing is true whether the data are handled mentally, manually (with or without the aid of machines), or automatically (by a computer or other device.)

PROCESSING DATA ELECTRONICALLY

Business managers, space engineers, scientists, homemakers, technicians, school administrators, teachers, and students — all of these and many more are busy creating data or searching for and using data al-

Data	Processed Data
ALEXANDER, DARLENE	ABELL, GEORGE
BEGULIA, ROSE	ALEXANDER, DARLENE
ABELL, GEORGE	BEGULIA, ROSE
HALL, KEITH	HALL, KEITH
WILSON, PETER	KNIGHT, NANCY
KNIGHT, NANCY	WILSON, PETER

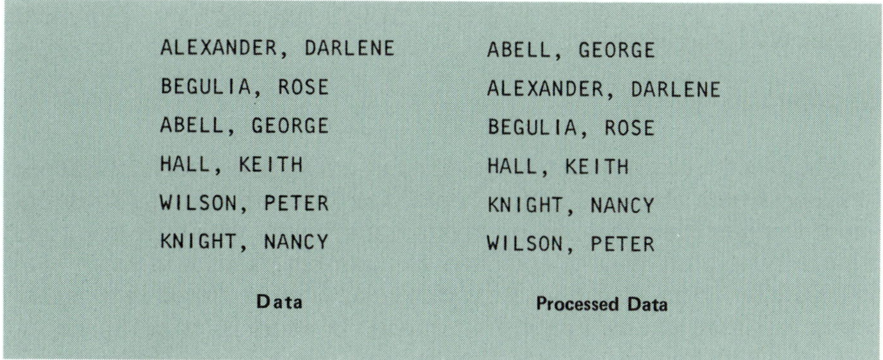

Figure 1-1. *Data processing is converting facts into usable form.*

ready created. The search is endless. The perfect car has not been invented. The risks of operating a business have not been eliminated. No cure for cancer has been found. Perfect school papers are rare. And, detergents do not make all clothes snowy white! There is need for more factual information, for better ways of storing it so it can be located when needed, and for better ways of using it. As a result, people throughout the ages have tried to devise tools to make data handling easier.

First mechanical adding machine

The first mechanical adding machine, invented in 1642 by Blaise Pascal, was a step in the right direction. It could carry tens automatically.

Pascal's machine consisted of wheels with cogs or teeth, on which were engraved the numbers 0–9. See Figure 1-2. The first wheel on the right represented units; the second, tens; the third, hundreds; and so on. As the wheels were turned, the numbers would appear in a window at the top of the machine. When the units wheel was turned beyond the Digit 9, the tens wheel at the left would reflect the carry. This procedure was accomplished by a series of gears arranged in such a way that they turned the next wheel.

Figure 1-2. *Pascal's adding machine consisted of wheels with cogs on which were engraved numbers.*

Courtesy of Planning Research Corporation

In time, even Pascal's landmark invention was too slow. New tools were needed and invented.

Electronic computer

The electronic computer is the latest in a long list of tools developed to process data. Here, at last, is a machine that can store information, find it when needed, and make computations rapidly with little help from a human operator. A large computer can store in its main memory over 500,000 characters. It can locate a particular number stored in its memory in less than one-millionth of a second. In addition, it can make six million calculations a second. Reports say that a large computer can work faster than 500,000 men and women with desk calculators. Figure 1-3 shows a modern computer in action.

Honeywell, Inc.

Figure 1-3. *Computers process data.*

Computers are radically different from mechanical adding machines. The adding machines process numeric data with cog wheels, gears, and levers. Processing is quite slow. On the other hand, computers convert both numeric and alphabetic data to electronic codes. These codes representing data are processed by electric current. There are no moving mechanical parts. Processing becomes lightning fast. Moreover, these electronic codes or impulses can be stored in the computer in compact form and used as needed.

When the data have been processed, the results can be converted to numeric and alphabetic characters as they leave the computer so that a human reader can understand them. The computer can store the data as well as the instructions for processing the data. (See Figure 1-4.)

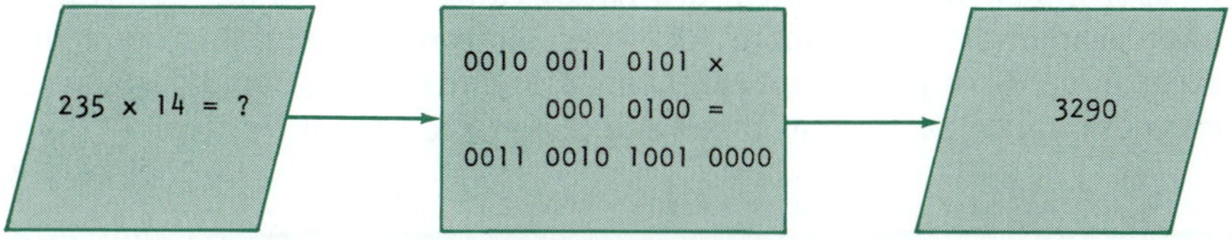

Figure 1-4. *Computers convert data to electronic codes. After processing, the data are converted to numeric or alphabetic characters as they leave the computer.*

A *computer* may be defined as an information device in which data and the instructions for processing these data are represented as electronic codes or impulses. There is much more to computers, but for the time being the explanation given is enough to get you started. You will take a closer look at computers later.

How knowing about computers can help you

So widespread is the use of computers that a good argument can be made for introducing everyone to the computer. Every person now comes under its daily influence. A personal knowledge of computers is needed in most professions and businesses. In addition, many authorities believe that there are three important reasons for introducing students to a computer:

(1) It shows how to solve problems by paying attention to detail and by using a process of logical thinking.
(2) It gives instructions on a tool that may be used all through life no matter what a future job may be.
(3) It makes it possible to work on creative, complex problems that would be impossible to solve by manual methods.

DATA PROCESSING OPERATIONS

Data processing includes one or more of the following operations:

Recording	Summarizing
Coding	Communicating
Sorting	Storing
Calculating	Retrieving

All data processing includes at least one of these operations. The number and order depend upon the problem being solved. Some operations may be repeated. Some may be omitted.

Recording

Recording deals with the process of writing, rewriting, or reproducing data by hand or by machine. Recording includes a very broad range of operations. Some of them are handwriting, typewriting, duplicating, photographing, microfilming, drawing, embossing, painting, punching holes in cards or paper tape, stenciling, and inscribing data or sounds on magnetic surfaces, such as tapes and disks. See Figure 1-5.

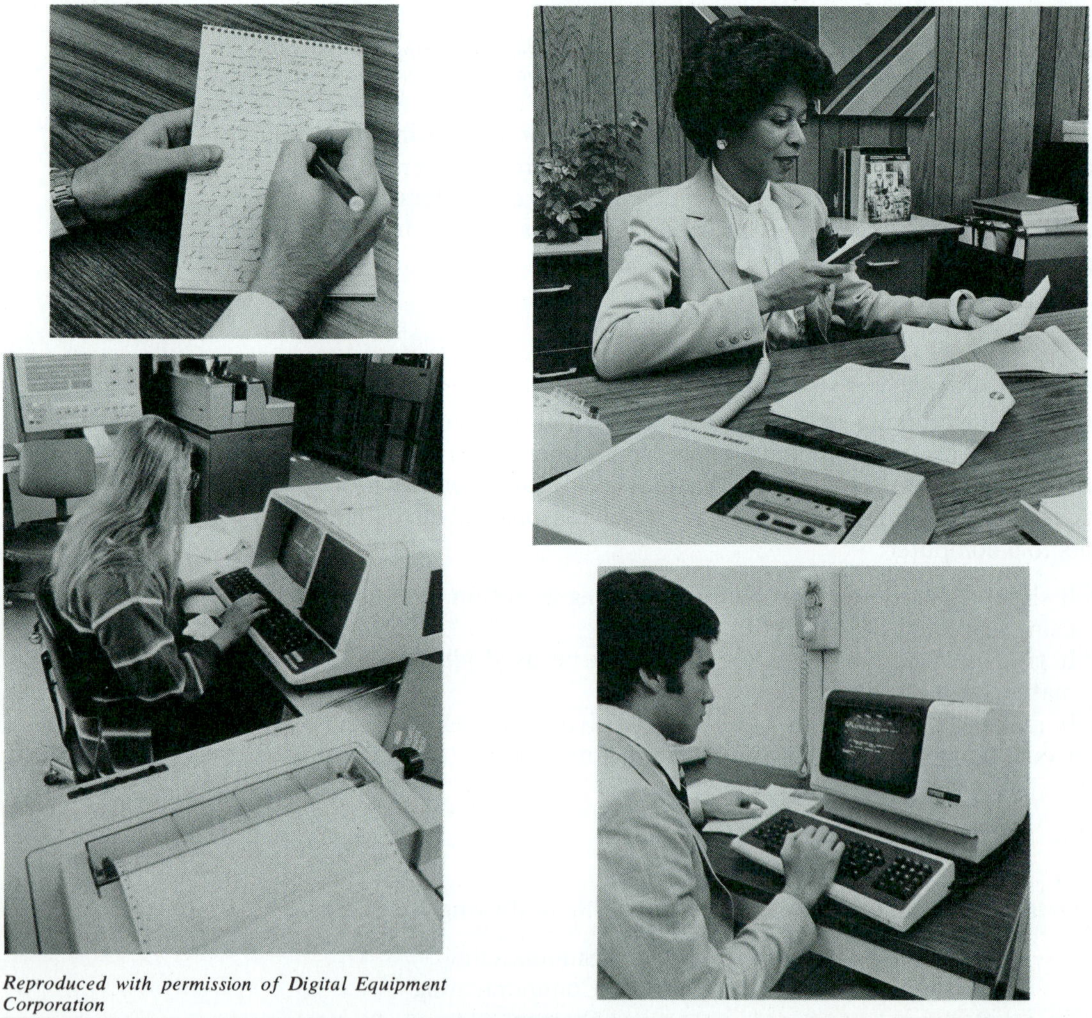

Reproduced with permission of Digital Equipment Corporation

Figure 1-5. *Recording deals with all reproducing of data, by hand or by machine.*

Records have become a way of life in today's complex world. The number of devices designed to aid in recording operations is almost limitless. Some examples are typewriters, check writers, duplicators, cameras, card and paper punches, and rubber stamps. Other recording devices are printing machines, tape recorders, and common pens and pencils. Recording, by any means, is an important part of data processing.

All original recordings of data must be checked or verified for accuracy. Verification is important, but it is regarded as part of the recording process.

Coding (Classifying)

Coding is the process of assigning a system of symbols, letters, or words to data in accordance with a set of rules. For example, *1* often stands for freshmen, *2* for sophomores, etc. Similar codes may be assigned to major programs of study, names of courses, and job preferences of students.

Stores identify items of stock by codes in order to keep accurate sales and inventory records. Items appearing in catalogs have code numbers. ZIP codes on letters are used to sort the letters by cities and various locations in the cities. Names of the states have two-letter abbreviations. A single sales slip may contain several codes. One may be for the salesperson and another for the department. One code may be for the account number of the customer and another code for the article sold. A telephone number is a code in which some of the numbers stand for a geographic area (the area code), some for a city or part of a city, and some for a particular telephone. A date may be coded with numbers.

Codes speed up processing. They aid in selecting the data needed to solve a given problem. They also save space in a computer. Note the codes used in the partial enrollment summary in Figure 1-6.

NAME	CLASS	MAJOR	SEX	BIRTHDATE			NUMBER
				MO	DAY	YEAR	
EARLE, TIMOTHY	1	1	M	7	5	67	750
EBER, LESLIE	2	3	F	12	14	66	313
EDELMAN, ARTHUR	1	2	M	3	12	66	485
EDWARDS, ANN	4	1	F	5	6	64	484
EIDUSON, KAREN	1	4	F	4	11	65	749
ENG, MICHAEL	3	1	M	9	7	65	751

Figure 1-6. *Codes make processing easier.*

With the codes shown, the following are some of the facts that could be listed:

(1) Number of students in each class.
(2) Number of students in each major.
(3) Number of female students.
(4) Number of male students.
(5) Average age of female students.
(6) Average age of male students.

Sorting

Sorting is the process of arranging information in order or of separating it into similar groups according to some predetermined plan. It includes:

(1) The sequencing of names or other data in alphabetic or numeric order.
(2) The grouping of data by date, product, department, state, or some other classification.
(3) The selecting of a certain record from a group of similar records.

An example of sequencing is the arranging of students' names in numeric order according to the student numbers assigned to each student. An example of grouping is the bringing together of all the names according to the class of the students. An example of selecting is the extraction of a specific record from a group of similar records. See Figure 1-7 for an example of sequencing, grouping, and selecting data.

EBER, LESLIE	313	
EDWARDS, ANN	484	
EDELMAN, ARTHUR	485	
EIDUSON, KAREN	749	Sequencing records by number
EARLE, TIMOTHY	750	
ENG, MICHAEL	751	
EARLE, TIMOTHY	1	
EDELMAN, ARTHUR	1	Grouping records by class
EIDUSON, KAREN	1	
ENG, MICHAEL	751	Selecting a particular record

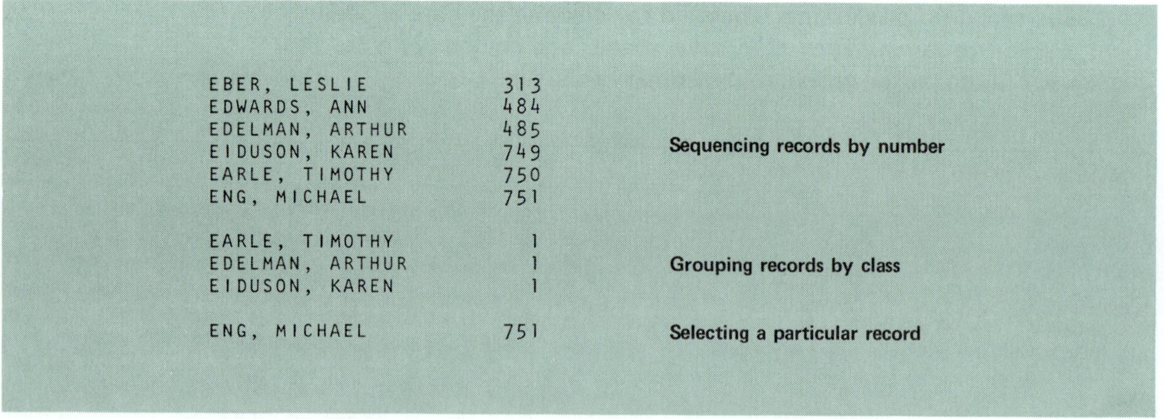

Figure 1-7. *Sorting consists of sequencing, grouping, and selecting data.*

Often the sole objective of data processing is the arranging of a list of names in alphabetic order or the grouping of records into separate categories. More often than not, however, sorting speeds up further processing. Before recording course grades on student record forms, for example, the grade reports for each student would have to be grouped together. This is a sorting operation.

The sorting of data by hand is quite common. Mechanical and electronic methods sort data faster and usually are more exact. If the volume of work is great, mechanical and electronic methods do the sorting more economically.

Calculating

Calculating is the process of computing in order to arrive at a mathematical result. It includes adding, subtracting, multiplying, and dividing. There are many calculations needed to arrive at the wages earned by an employee, for example. Note these calculations in the paycheck shown in Figure 1-8.

PERIOD ENDING 11 16 19--
EARNINGS $ 180 00
REG. $ 160.00
O.T. $ 20.00
DEDUCTIONS $ 36 03
INC TAX $ 23.01
FICA TAX $ 10.02
GROUP INS $
MED INS $ 3.00
OTHER $
NET PAY $ 143 97

GRANT COMPANY
PAYROLL ACCOUNT
No. 298
90-0307
1222
November 21 19--
Pay to the order of Karen Bell $ 143.97
One hundred forty-three and 97/100 — Dollars
FIRST TRUST BANK
Pomona, CA 91767-1035
GRANT COMPANY
J. Anderson Meyer
⑆122203073⑆ 2670025040⑈

Figure 1-8. *Calculating of wages and deductions must be made in order to produce a paycheck*

The regular hours worked must be added and multiplied by the hourly rate. The overtime hours worked must be added and multiplied by 1½ to arrive at the overtime pay. The two amounts must be added to arrive at the total earnings. Then, all deductions are added together and subtracted from the total earnings to arrive at the amount of the paycheck.

Many calculations are made mentally. However, a wide variety of mechanical and electronic machines have been designed to perform calculations. The machines range from the common ten-key adding-listing machine to sophisticated computers.

Summarizing

Summarizing is the process of converting the processed data into concise, meaningful form. All printed reports are summaries. As already explained, many calculations must be made to prepare paychecks for employees of a company. These data can be summarized to make them more useful to a business. For example, summaries can list some of the following:

(1) Total wages paid.
(2) Total deductions for social security taxes.
(3) Total number of employees on the payroll.
(4) Total earnings for each employee from the beginning of the calendar year to the date of the last check.

Summaries can also consist of such things as percentages, averages, and comparisons of one year's operations with those of another year. For example, the average score on a test is useful in figuring whether a particular score is high, average, or low. Figure 1-9 shows a financial summary.

FINANCIAL SUMMARY

SUMMARY OF OPERATIONS	1982	1981	1980
NET SALES	$1,777,108	$158,635	$140,162
COST OF SALES AND OPERATING EXPENSES	146,147	140,173	123,244
NET EARNINGS	30,861	18,462	16,918
NET EARNINGS PER COMMON SHARE BASED ON AVERAGE SHARES OUTSTANDING	3.01	2.51	1.63

Figure 1-9. *Financial data are summarized to make them more meaningful.*

Communicating

Communicating is the process of transmitting information to the point of use. This operation covers both oral and written transmission. Often communicating consists of nothing more than the transfer of reports from one desk to another. Communicating includes such activities as the transmission of information by mail, telephone, telegraph, radio, and television.

The computer is also used in communications.

For a number of years, computers have kept us in touch by pictures and messages with the moon and several of the planets in the solar system. Almost every day we are learning more about our world. And almost every day we are adding new improvements to the computer to help us in these discoveries.

A "nerve center" has been established that connects one company with another on a world-wide basis. The center handles the transmission of messages, charts, graphs, or other documents. Figure 1-10 shows a computer being used in a TV station to monitor the programs.

Figure 1-10. *Computers aid communications.*

Storing

Storing is the orderly safekeeping of information so that it may be used later. The storing operation should allow for prompt filing of data, for strict adherence to rules about the checking out of filed materials, and for destruction of records when they are no longer needed.

The storing of data, such as letters and memoranda, is largely a manual operation. However, a great deal more information can be stored in a computer, in punched cards, or on magnetic tapes and disks than in ordinary file folders. When data are stored on punched cards, magnetic tapes, and disks, the data can be processed or converted to printed copy by the computer as needed.

Computer output microfilm (COM) is a recent development in the storing of information produced by a computer. Images of complete documents, such as invoices, bank statements to depositors, canceled checks, and pages of reports can be stored in compact form on microfilm. The information can be retrieved and read from microfilm readers which magnify the copy. See Figure 1-11.

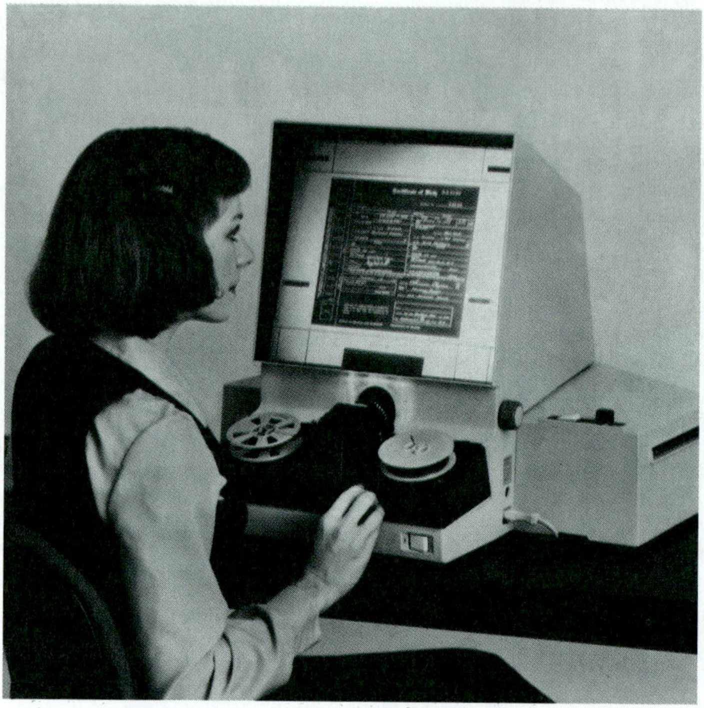

Eastman Kodak Company

Figure 1-11. *Data can be stored on microfilm.*

Retrieving

Retrieving is the process of making stored information available when needed. If information is properly stored, it can be obtained by a search of filed records. Records stored in file folders must be retrieved manually. This is a common operation in all offices.

Records stored in punched cards can be retrieved by running the cards through a sorter, a machine that selects the desired cards on the basis of a code punched into them.

Records stored in a computer or on magnetic tapes or disks can be retrieved by the computer only if the information is properly coded. The computer can find it almost instantly and make it available to the user in print, on a television screen, on microfilm, or in other ways that will be explained later. See Figure 1-12.

Eastman Kodak Company

Figure 1-12. *When the correct code is keyed into the retrieval terminal, the desired record appears on the reader in seconds.*

REVIEW QUESTIONS

1. What is meant by the term *data*?
2. What is meant by the term *data processing*?
3. What is meant by the statement that data are processed electronically by computers?
4. What three reasons are generally given for introducing students to computers?
5. What eight operations are included in processing data?
6. Name five recording operations.
7. Give three reasons for coding data to be processed.
8. What three functions does the sorting operation include?
9. What calculations must be made in preparing a paycheck?
10. What essential must be kept in mind in retrieving information stored in a computer?

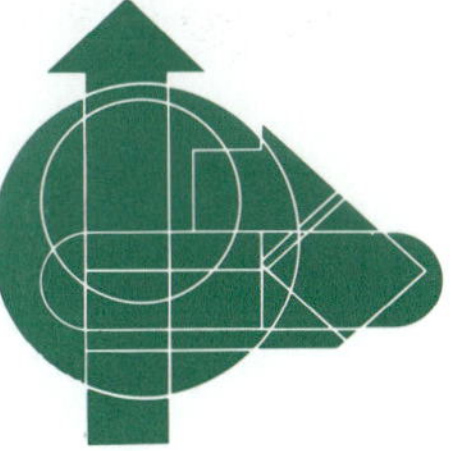

AUTOMATED DATA PROCESSING

Automated data processing is a process, largely self-regulating, in which information is handled with a minimum of human effort and intervention. The process depends upon original data that have been recorded in such a way that future use can be made of them without later manual rerecording and duplicate handling.

Automation is a process, not a machine. However, machines capable of handling data with very little human help are often used in the process. At the very heart of the process is an attempt to cut out the duplicate recording and handling of data in order to make them available to the user.

Automation as applied to data processing is never completely automatic. Quite often the original record must be created with a pencil, a typewriter, or a cash register. Generally, too, the data must be entered in code form on some material that is acceptable to the computer. While there are some exceptions, depending upon the system being used, these operations are *manual* in character (done by hand). To put it simply, some person must start the action before automation can take over. Someone must operate a keypunching device, must record marks or other data for optical reading, or must in some other way start the processing of data before automation can proceed.

FUNCTION OF DATA PROCESSING

The function of data processing is to turn data into usable or storable form. In other words, raw data enter the processing system; useful information leaves it. In the language of automation, the data that enter a system for processing are known as *input*. The form or material on which these data are recorded for processing is known as the *input medium*. The processed information is known as *output*. The form or material on which the processed information appears is known as the *output medium*. In the paragraphs that follow, these terms are often used to describe data processing functions whether the data are processed with or without a computer.

ORIGIN OF DATA

What is the origin of the data that processing systems handle? They come from many sources. Information about students in a school, for example, comes from registration forms, grade reports, and other similar forms. Data regarding hours worked by an employee are taken from time tickets. Information on test scores is obtained from the scored tests. The data to be processed are referred to as *raw* or *original data*, and the forms on which the raw data appear are referred to as source documents. A *source document* is thus the document from which raw or original data are obtained.

Figure 1-13 shows the relationship of the source document to input, input media, output, and output media. The source document is a receipt, prepared manually, for a contribution received to a camp fund. The data taken from the receipt for processing are the name of the contributor and the amount given. These data are the input. The input medium is a punched card, which will be described in detail in Chapter 3.

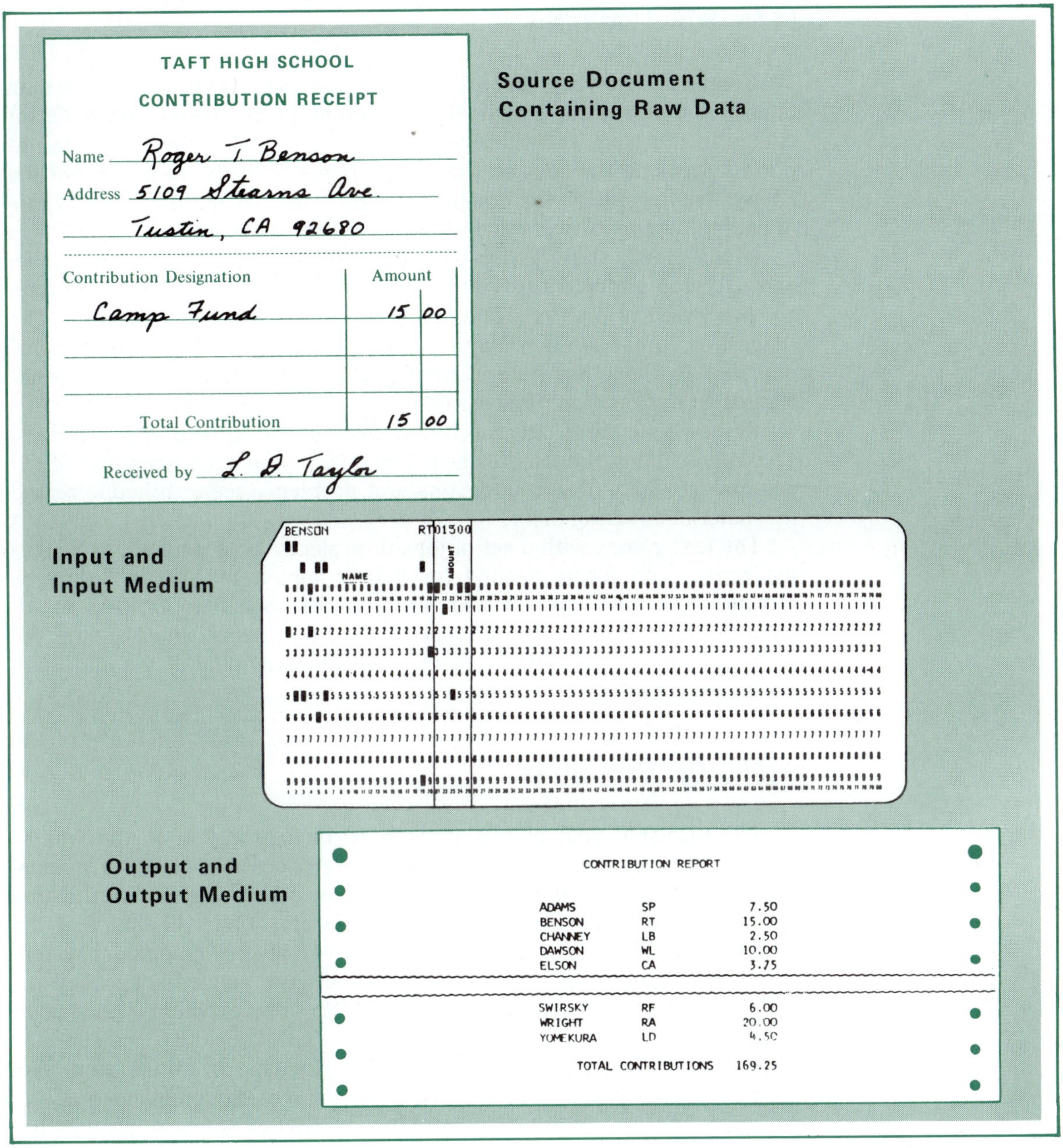

Figure 1-13. *Selected data (input) are taken from the receipt (source document) and punched into a card (input medium). A list of contributors (output) is printed on a printed report form (output medium).*

Data will be read from the punched card into a computer for processing. The output is an alphabetic listing of the names of contributors, the amount each gave, and the total contributions. The output medium is the report form.

PLAN FOR LEARNING

Computers solve problems in much the same way that the human mind does. For both, every step important to the answer must be included in the plan, and these steps must be in logical order. When important steps are left out or when logic is not followed in laying out the answer to a problem, the computer won't work. When the same is true of people, wrong answers and wrong decisions are made.

In this book, step-by-step explanations are given for solving a problem. No step important to your understanding of the way in which data are processed is omitted. The steps are arranged in logical order. The suggestion is made that you understand each step and the relationship of one step to the other before moving ahead. Read, think, understand. Reread an explanation if necessary.

Review questions and problems appear throughout the chapters. These aids should be used to help you check your understanding of the material covered. If the questions and problems seem difficult, reread the material covering them.

The text comes with a set of jobs or projects to be worked, as well as the papers and forms needed for their completion. You will thus be brought into close contact with some of the special tools used in automated data processing. In addition to the projects, study guides for each chapter are included to check your understanding of the important points covered.

SCOPE OF THIS BOOK

The principal goal of this book is to introduce you to the way in which computers process data. Some references are made to manual means of processing data for the purpose of comparing and contrasting the manual system with the computer system. You will find that the steps followed by both methods are very much alike. The manual system of processing data for a given problem will give you a background for understanding the processing of data for the same problem with a computer.

You will learn to speak and read the language of automation. Not only is this language used in business, but it is becoming popular in everyday life. All new terms introduced and defined in a chapter are listed in color at the end of that chapter.

You will learn how to communicate with computers. You will also learn how to write directions for computers in order to solve many kinds of problems. Computers can be used in so many ways that only a small number of their applications can be covered in this book. Still, you should be able to understand the ways in which computers are being used in today's world to make this journey into the Computer Age worthwhile.

SUMMARY

Data may be defined as facts of all kinds. *Data processing*, then, is the converting of facts into usable form. Data processing generally includes one or more of the following operations: recording, coding, sorting, calculating, summarizing, communicating, storing, and retrieving. The number and order of the operations depend upon the problem to be solved. Some operations may be repeated. Some may not be used.

The electronic computer is the latest in a long list of tools developed to process data. It converts both numeric and alphabetic data to electronic codes. These codes are processed by electric current. Processing is lightning fast. The codes can be stored in the computer and used as needed. When the processed data leave the computer, they can be printed or displayed in a manner that a person can read and understand.

Automated data processing is a process, largely self-regulating, in which information is handled with a minimum of human effort. Automation is a process, not a machine. However, machines are often used in the process.

The function of data processing is to turn data into usable form. Raw data enter the processing system; useful information leaves it. Raw data enter the processing system as *input*. The form or material on which input is recorded is known as the *input medium*. Processed information leaving the system is known as *output*. The form or material on which output is made available is known as the *output medium*.

The principal goal of this book is to introduce you to the way in which computers process data. You will learn to speak and read the language of automation. In addition, you will learn to communicate with computers.

REVIEW QUESTIONS

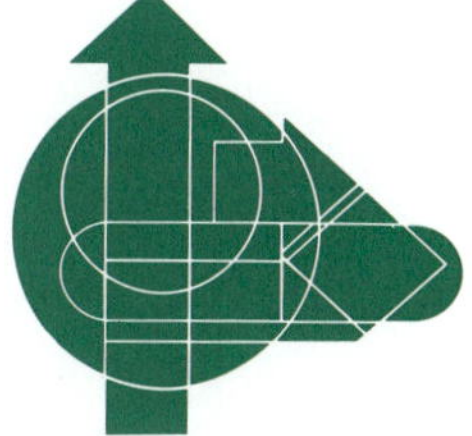

1. What is *automated data processing*?
2. Does the use of a computer by a business firm eliminate all manual operations? Explain.
3. What is the purpose of data processing?
4. What is meant by *input*? *Input medium*?
5. What is meant by *output*? *Output medium*?
6. Which one of the terms used in Questions 4 and 5 would you use to refer to the data that must be processed to produce a paycheck?
7. Which one of the terms in Questions 4 and 5 would you use to refer to the form or material on which the data in Question 6 are recorded in order to make them available for processing?
8. Which one of the terms would you use to refer to the processed data leaving the processing system?
9. Which one of the terms would you use to refer to the form or material on which processed information is recorded?

NEW TERMS

- Automated data processing
- Calculating
- Coding (classifying)
- Communicating
- Computer
- Data
- Data processing
- Input
- Input medium
- Manual
- Original data
- Output
- Output medium
- Raw data
- Recording
- Retrieving
- Sorting
- Source document
- Storing
- Summarizing

STUDY GUIDE

Complete Study Guide 1 by following the instructions in your STUDY GUIDES booklet.

PROJECTS

Complete Projects 1-1 and 1-2 by following the instructions in your PROJECTS booklet.

2

DATA PROCESSING FRAMEWORK and SYSTEMS

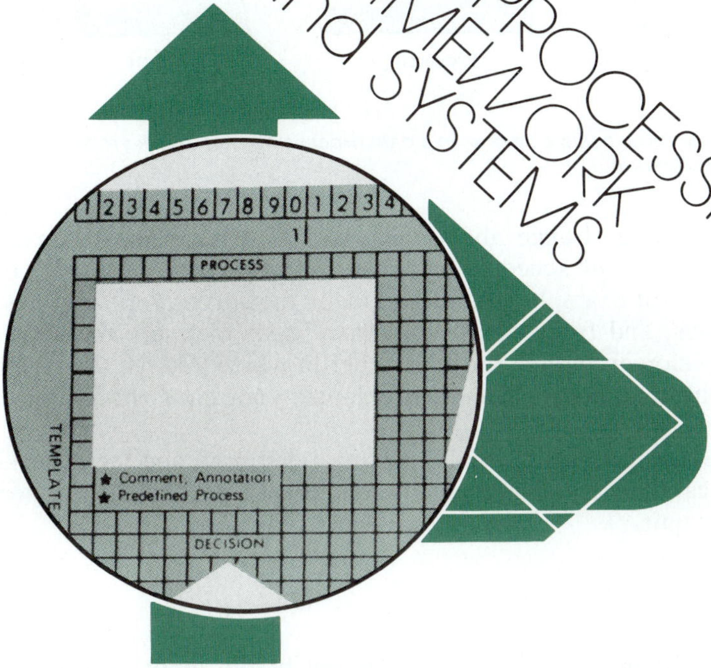

Data processing problems can be solved by two approaches or methods and usually both are used. One is by planning a system to solve the entire problem. The other is by writing computer programs to solve the different parts of the problem. The two approaches are closely related. This chapter will deal mainly with solving problems by setting up systems. Later in the book, solving problems by computer programs will be explored.

DATA PROCESSING FRAMEWORK

In the systems approach, raw data are collected and enter the framework as input. Useful information leaves it as output. What happens in between these two points? The data are processed. A number of steps are set up to make sure that everything that should be done to the data is done. The data pass through these steps in order. The action that should be taken at each step is taken. Each action and often the form or forms on which the data appear are specified. This is the basic framework or plan followed to turn raw data into useful output. Figure 2-1 illustrates this basic plan. Note that the three basic elements in a data processing framework are input, processing, and output.

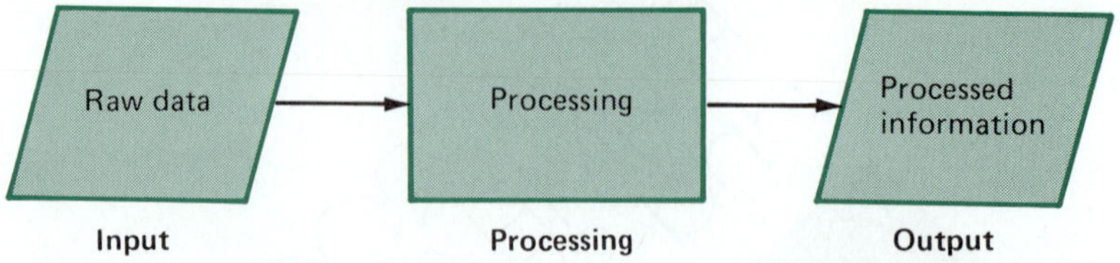

Figure 2-1. *The three basic elements in a data processing framework are input, processing, and output.*

There is nothing strange about this plan. You have used it many times in arranging your schedule of classes or writing a term paper. In writing a paper, for example, you collect many facts from your readings, from interviews, and from expert opinions. These facts are the input. Next, you develop an outline for your paper in which you list the major points you expect to cover. Then you organize your facts around these points.

The processing plan also includes writing a first draft and then checking it for logical development, accuracy, and good English. The finished paper is the output.

Input

As you noted in Figure 2-1, the function of the input part of the framework is to bring raw data into it. Input may also be made up of data that have been collected and processed for an earlier period. You have used this framework, too, when you bring a report that you have already written up to date. The data in the original report plus the new facts you collect enter the processing part of the framework as input. Output consists of the updated report.

Figure 2-2 shows the data processing framework when previously processed data enter the system along with new facts, to produce a new or updated report.

Processing

Processing is the nitty-gritty part of the framework. The raw data pass through the steps that have been set up to produce the finished product. In the example given earlier, these steps consist of the following:

(1) Developing an outline for the paper.
(2) Organizing the facts around major points in the outline.
(3) Writing a first draft.
(4) Checking the draft for logical development, accuracy, and good English.
(5) Writing the final paper.

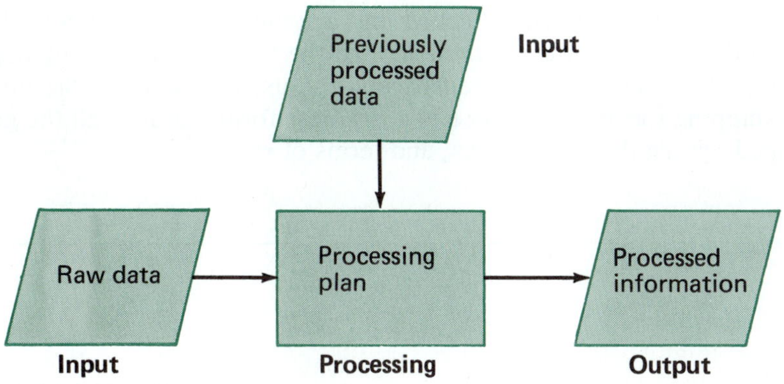

Figure 2-2. *Input may be made up of previously processed data as well as raw data.*

The foregoing steps in the plan are basic. Other steps may be added. The kind and number of operations required depend upon the report to be prepared.

Output

The output part of the framework receives the finished paper from the processing unit. In business, output consists of many different kinds of reports. These include transaction documents, such as tax statements, end-of-the month statements, payrolls, and sales forms (invoices). Included also are operating reports, special reports, and updated records of all kinds.

Data Processing framework for business

In business, the framework for processing data is the same as the one illustrated in Figure 2-1. For example, in processing an order from a customer, input consists of the data appearing on the customer's order form. This data would include the date, order number, customer's name and address, shipping information, quantity, catalog number, and description of items ordered.

Steps or procedures are set up to process the order by an order clerk, as follows:

(1) An account is opened for a new customer.
(2) The status of an old customer's account is checked.
(3) The order is edited to make sure that catalog numbers and descriptions are accurate.
(4) Stock on hand is checked to make sure that items ordered are available.
(5) The price is checked for each item of stock ordered.
(6) The total amount for each item is computed, and all the totals are added.

Output consists of the checked and approved order, which is shown in Figure 2-3. This order is then sent to the billing and shipping departments, where additional systems would be used to produce the invoice and shipping forms. An *invoice* is a business form that lists all the goods shipped, giving the date, prices, and terms of sale.

Tower
Advertising Company
Lincoln Square
Worcester, MA 01608-0746

PURCHASE ORDER

OHIO CAMERA SUPPLY CO
45 CLIFTON AV
SPRINGFIELD, OH 45504-0952

Purchase order No. 68903
Date MAY 10, 19--
Terms NET 30 DAYS
Ship Via EXPRESS

Quantity	Cat. No.	Description	Price	Total
12	781-C	LUCITE PHOTO FRAMES	2.15	25.80
8	858-G	INSTAMATIC LENS ATTACHMENTS	11.90	95.20
5	775-C	MOVIE REEL ALBUMS	4.25	21.25
10	554-L	POSTER MOUNTS, BLACK	.89	8.90
				151.15

Rec'd. 5/12/--

NEW ACC'T OK ✓
OLD ACC'T OK
EDIT ✓
STOCK CHECK ✓
PRICE ✓
TOTAL ✓

By ______________________ Purchasing Agent

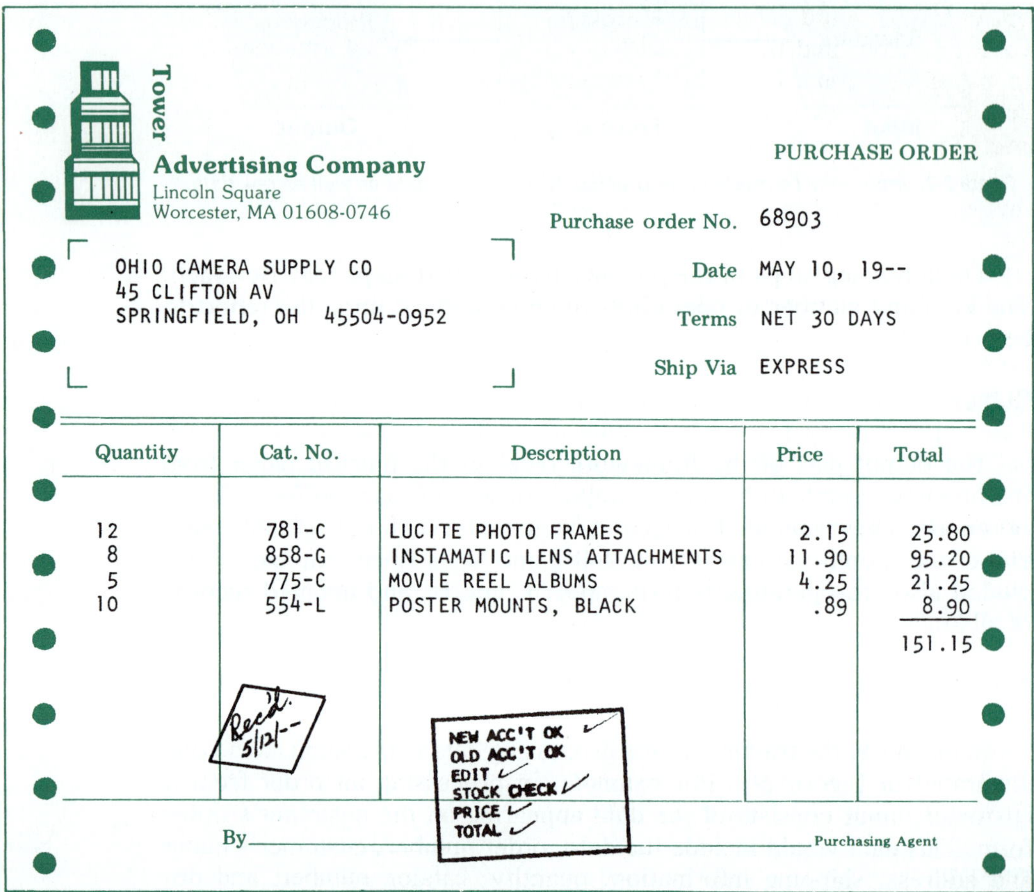

Figure 2-3. *Input is the data on the customer's order form. The order clerk checks off processing steps as they are finished. Output is the checked and approved order.*

SYSTEMS AND PROGRAMS

A *system* is a group of items or actions that work together to perform a certain function. For example, you can speak of the nervous system, the digestive system, and the hearing (auditory) system. You can also speak of a communication system, a recreation system, a school system, and a data processing system. The discussion that follows is about data processing systems.

Data Processing system

A *data processing system* is a plan for making information available to the user. Before a system can be designed, the end product must be kept clearly in mind. Then the system spells out the inputs needed, the processing plan, and the outputs that will be produced. The data entering the system must be carefully selected and identified. The different parts of the processing plan must be worked out and placed in proper order. The output must give the information desired.

The operation of almost any organization is so complex that a number of systems must be established to handle the whole operation. For example, a school enrolls students and keeps records of courses completed for each student. It also prepares class schedules, hires teachers, keeps attendance records, and maintains records of its graduates. It buys supplies and keeps a record of them. It engages in sports, music, and a great many other programs. While it is best to have one overall information handling system in mind, for practical reasons the operation of an organization is broken down into a number of major operations. A system is then set up for each operation.

The various parts of a system for handling incoming orders from customers were listed on p. 21. Some of these parts could be considered systems. For example, the inputs, plan, and outputs needed to open an account for a new customer might be a system. Inputs would consist of a completed credit application form, bank references, and credit references furnished by the customer. Processing would consist of moving the data through the steps set up to study each of these inputs in order to arrive at a decision about the credit status of the customer. Output would contain this decision.

The goal of a system is to make sure that all the steps needed for the efficient handling of an operation are taken.

Program

Whereas a system is an overall plan adopted to process data, a program spells out in detail the steps meeded to do a specific job or jobs in the system. The program includes these steps in proper order. These detailed steps are usually not included in a system. A *program* can be defined as a detailed set of instructions for solving a problem.

When a computer is used to process data, a program is written and stored in the computer first. The data to be processed then enter the computer, and the program tells the computer what to do with the data, step by step. While the practice is not common, a similar program could be written to direct a human operator to do the work.

The framework for processing data by an electronic computer is shown in Figure 2-4. Raw data and program instructions enter the computer as input. The data are processed according to the instructions. Processed data leave the computer as output. In Figure 2-4, the processing instructions are shown as input, but in the illustrations that follow in the early part of this book, the processing instructions will not be shown. It will be understood that processing instructions are part of the input for every system.

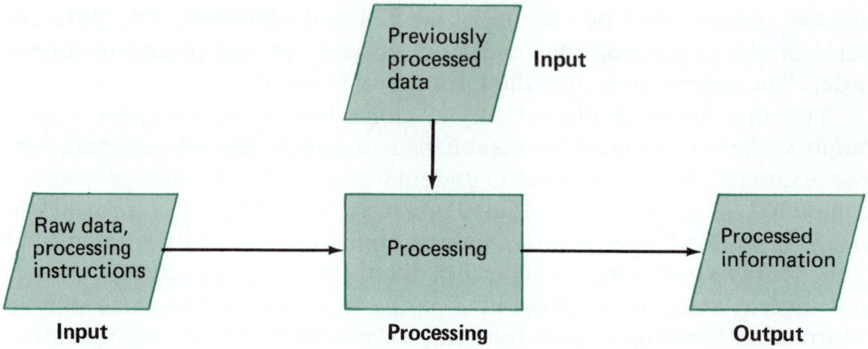

Figure 2-4. *The basic framework of a program for processing data includes processing instructions as well as raw data as input.*

Input may also consist of data that have been processed for an earlier period, such as a report of customers' names and their account balances. These balances, the new charges made, and the payments received on account all enter the computer as input. The data are processed in accordance with the program instructions. That is. charges are added and payments received are subtracted from earlier balances. Output consists of an updated report, such as a list of customers and their account balances at the end of the new period. See Figure 2-5.

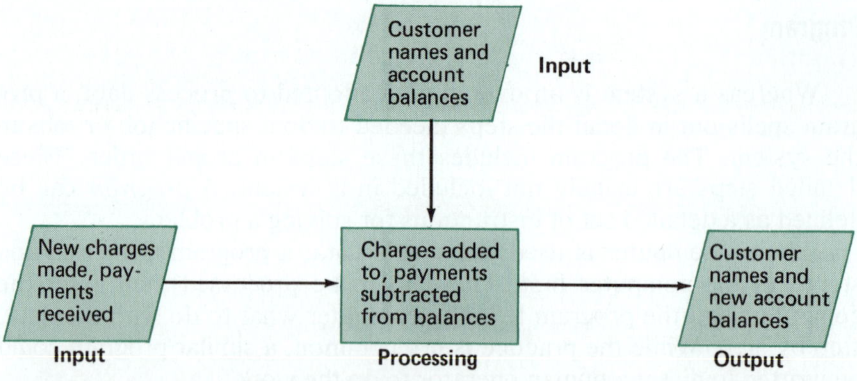

Figure 2-5. *Keeping customers' accounts up to date requires merging (combining) new and old input to produce new output.*

SYSTEM FOR UPDATING A MASTER ENROLLMENT FILE DUE TO NEW ENROLLMENTS

In the system described here, the school keeps a master file of enrollment forms for all its students. Each form contains the name of a student, the address, telephone number, name of parent or guardian, and other important information. The forms are in alphabetic order according to the last names of the students.

As the term is used in data processing, a *file* is a collection of related records treated as a unit. A collection of forms, a deck of punched cards, or a printed report is a file. A *master file* is a file that contains relatively permanent records. These records must be updated from time to time.

As new students enter the school, they are required to fill out enrollment forms. These forms are placed for a time in a new student enrollment file. An enrollment form is illustrated in Figure 2-6.

SCHOOL ENROLLMENT FORM

South High School

Name Findl, Marci M ___ F X Birthdate 5/15/--
(Last) (First)

Address 489 Wade Ct. Ogden, UT 84403-1042 Phone 677-4344

Name of Parent or Guardian Henry Findl

Date of Enrollment 10/7/19-- Grade 12

Approved X yes ___ no

Counselor Chris Corbin

Figure 2-6. *The student enrollment form is placed in a new student file.*

From time to time, the forms in this file are manually placed in alphabetic order. The records from the master file and the records from the new student file then enter the system as input. Processing consists of combining (merging) the records from the two files. The merged file will be in alphabetic order.

Output will consist of an updated master student enrollment file. Output will also consist of a printed updated enrollment report and such other reports as the administration may require. The word *update* as used in this book means the act of changing a file or a program with current data according to a specified plan.

Merging

Merging is the process by which two or more files of records, each of which is in sequential order, are combined into one file. Figure 2-7 illustrates this operation.

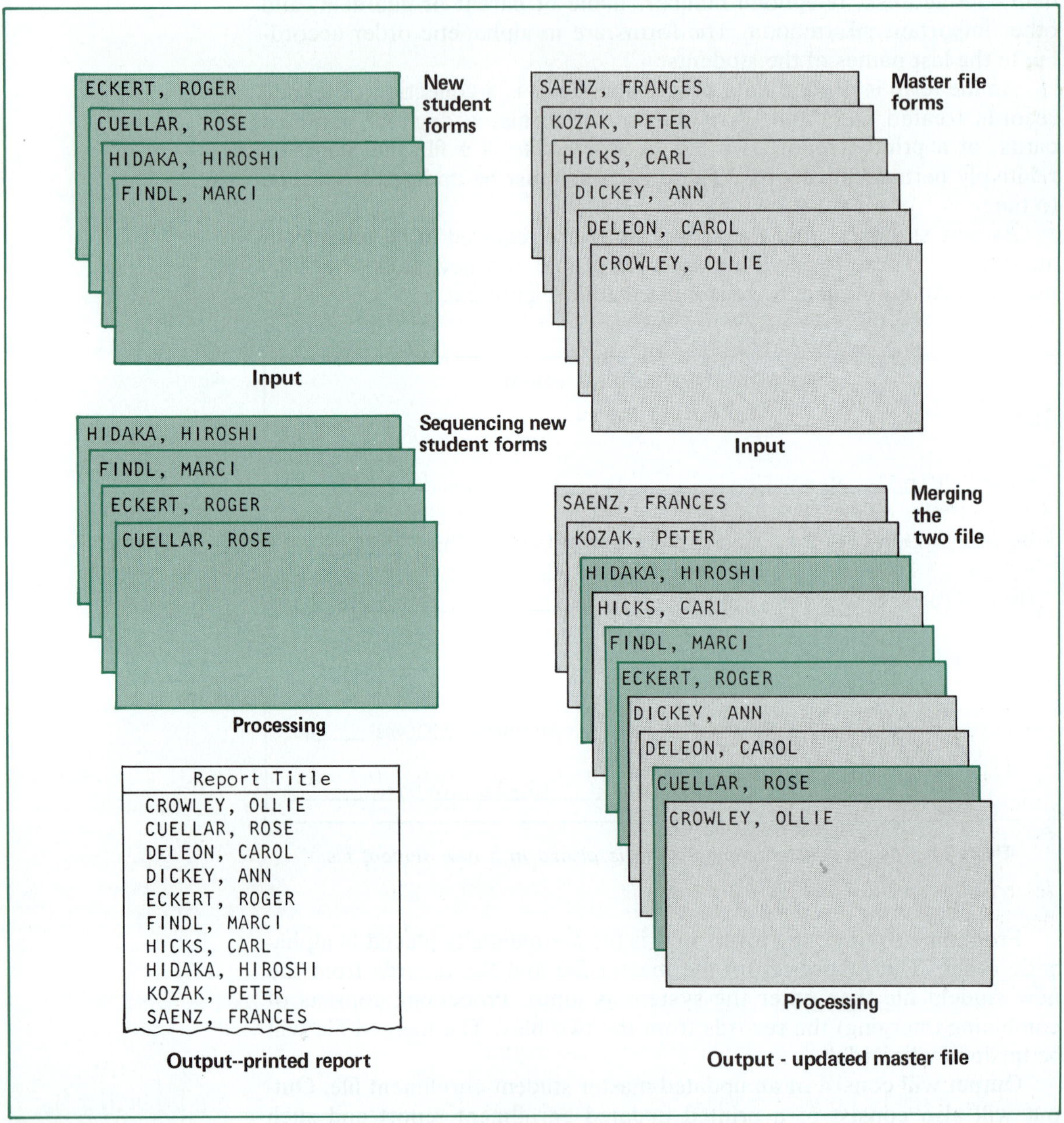

Figure 2-7. *The student enrollment file is updated by placing the new student forms in alphabetic order and then merging them with the master student file, which is also in alphabetic order. Output includes an updated student file and a printed report of all students.*

The steps in the system for updating a student enrollment file are shown in Figure 2-8.

STEP 1: THE COMPLETED FORMS FOR NEW ENROLLMENTS ARE RECEIVED.
STEP 2: THE FORMS ARE STORED IN A TEMPORARY STUDENT ENROLLMENT FILE AS THEY ARE RECEIVED.
STEP 3: FROM TIME TO TIME, THE FORMS IN THE FILE ARE ARRANGED ALPHABETICALLY ACCORDING TO THE LAST NAMES OF STUDENTS, MAKING A TEMPORARY ALPHABETIZED STUDENT ENROLLMENT FILE.
STEP 4: THE FORMS IN THE NEW ENROLLMENT FILE ARE MERGED WITH THE FORMS IN THE MASTER FILE.
STEP 5: A TYPEWRITTEN REPORT IS MADE OF ALL STUDENTS' NAMES IN THE UPDATED MASTER FILE.
STEP 6: THE UPDATED MASTER FILE IS STORED UNTIL IT IS NEEDED AGAIN.

Figure 2-8. *Steps in the system for updating a master student enrollment file are carried out in order.*

Testing systems

Systems are often tested before they are installed to see if they work. The system is applied to a limited number of cases. Samples of all the papers and records used in the system are used in the test. The test should provide answers to these questions:

(1) Does the system handle the different kinds of cases that are met in processing the data?
(2) Is there a logical flow of information from input to processing to output?
(3) Does the system clearly describe the plan set up to process the data?

These questions apply to systems. Computer programs are tested in much the same way. The process is known as "debugging." It is described in a later chapter.

When a system for handling a certain operation is worked out and tested, as described, the various steps are written out in detail. No step needed in processing the data should be left out.

REVIEW QUESTIONS

1. What three elements are included in the basic framework for processing data?
2. What is the function of the input part of the framework?
3. What two types of information are included in an updated report?
4. What output is produced when an order form from a customer is processed by an order clerk?

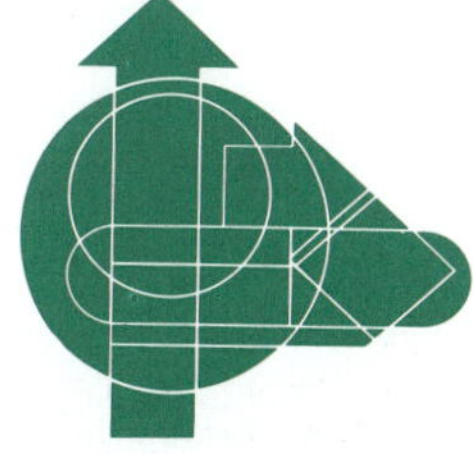

(Continued)

5. What is a *system*?
6. What is a *data processing system*?
7. What is the goal of a system?
8. What is a *program*? How do programs differ from systems?
9. What types of data enter the system as input in order to update a master student file due to new enrollments?
10. The test of a system should give answers to three questions. What are they?

FLOWCHARTS

A *flowchart* is a graphic representation of the order of operations in a data processing system or program, in which symbols are used to represent processing operations, media, equipment, and data flow. There are two types of flowcharts. One type shows the media used for input and output and the flow of data through the various steps in a data processing system. It is known as a *systems flowchart*. The other flowchart outlines the step-by-step instructions in a program to solve a problem with a computer and is called a *program flowchart*. Systems flowcharts will be described here. Program flowcharts will be described in Chapter 9.

Systems flowcharts

A systems flowchart is like a road map. Through it, in a matter of minutes, you can trace the steps in a plan set up to process data. You can trace information backward to its source. You can see the relationship of one step in the plan to another.

A systems flowchart shows what media bring data into the system, the steps through which the data pass, and the output produced. Media and operations are emphasized rather than detailed instructions. Little is shown on this flowchart of the instructions used to process data. This is the function of program flowcharts.

Some of the symbols specifically designed for systems flowcharting are illustrated and explained in this chapter. All of these symbols are shown and explained on the flap of the large envelope containing the kit of materials. With few exceptions, these symbols conform to the American National Standard Draft Recommendation on Flowchart Symbols for Information Processing and are consistent with the newer symbols adopted by the American National Standards Institute, Inc. (ANSI).[1]

Basic symbols. A *symbol* in flowcharting is a shape or outline that is drawn to represent a certain medium, operation, piece of equipment, or direction of data flow. Look at Figure 2-9. Note that there are six basic symbols: input/output, process, annotation, connector, off-page connec-

[1]The off-page connector, in the basic group of symbols shown in Figure 2-9, and the transmittal tape and keying symbols, shown on the large envelope housing the kit of materials, were designed by the IBM Corporation and are widely used in flowcharting.

tor, and arrowheads and flowlines. The basic symbols are common to both systems flowcharting and program flowcharting. These symbols are used in diagramming both systems and programs.

Input/Output

In systems flowcharting in this book, the input/output symbol refers to any type of medium bringing data into the system for processing or to any type of medium on which processed information is recorded. The types of media are not shown.

Process

This symbol refers to the processing operations or stations through which data must pass to produce the desired output. The processing operations are not always shown. The basic symbol covers all operations.

Annotation

This symbol is used to provide additional notes or comments. The broken line shows the symbol being explained. Brief notes are often included in a flowchart, however, without the annotation symbol.

Connector

This symbol shows an exit to, or entry from, another part of the flowchart. The connection between the two is marked by a number placed in the circle that marks the end of a flowline. The same number is then placed in another circle marking the continuation of that flowline.

Off-page Connector

This symbol marks the exit from and the entry to a flowline from one page to the next. A number placed in the symbol marking a flowline at the end of a page is the same as the number placed in the symbol showing the continuation of the flowline on the next page.

Arrowheads and Flowlines

Arrowheads and flowlines are used to show the order of operations and direction of data flow. The arrowheads are required if the path of any flowline does not follow the normal direction, which is left-to-right or top-to-bottom. However, the arrowheads may also be used to show normal flow.

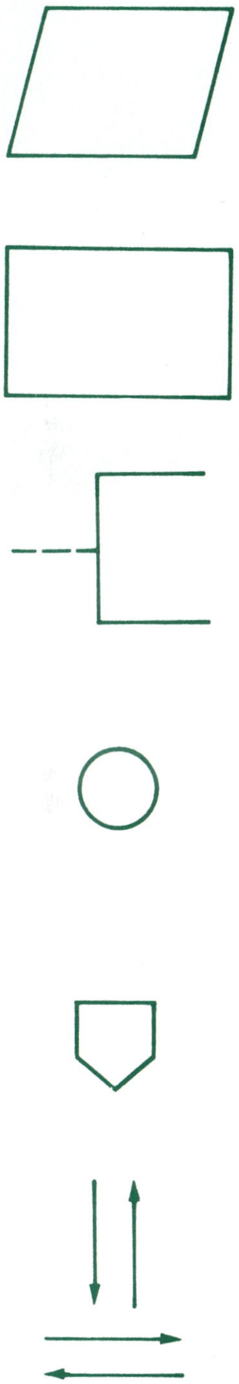

Figure 2-9. *Basic flowcharting symbols are used for both systems and programs.*

Specialized symbols. Systems flowcharts may be drawn, using only the basic symbols. There are also specialized symbols, however, that show:

(1) The type of input and output media being used.
(2) Whether storage of data is on-line or off-line (terms that will be defined later in the text).
(3) The kind of processing operations used in a system. Where proper, these specialized symbols may be used instead of the basic symbols.

Look at Figure 2-10. It shows the specialized symbols that will be used in this chapter. The full range of specialized symbols is illustrated and explained on the envelope for the kit of materials. In addition, as each new symbol is used in this book, it is illustrated and explained.

Drawing flowcharts is an individual matter. No two people will draw them alike because operations may be viewed differently. One person may show more detail than another. The goal is clear expression. Using standardized symbols will help you reach this goal.

Flowcharting practices

Templates are available for drawing flowchart symbols. A *template* is a device used to draw symbols of different sizes and shapes in a flowchart. The symbols appear as cut-out forms, and the symbols for systems and program flowcharts appear on the same template. The template itself is made of plastic or metallic material.[2]

For the most part, flowcharts are drawn so that they read from left to right and from top to bottom. The symbols are connected by lines. Arrowheads and flowlines are often used to show the flow of data. If the data flow is in a reverse direction, arrowheads must be used to indicate the direction of the flow. However, you may also use the arrowheads to show normal flow. This takes more time, but sometimes makes the data flow easier to follow when you check over the flowchart.

A short statement identifying the form, file, or process is usually written inside the symbol. If more detailed explanations are needed, the annotation symbol is used.

A systems flowchart may start with a symbol that shows the medium used for the input of data into the system. However, it can start with an identification of the source document on which the data are recorded. The flowchart may end with a symbol showing the output medium. It can, however, end with a symbol showing the final disposition of the processed information. The procedure followed in each case is largely a matter of choice on the part of the person who is describing the system.

As explained earlier, systems flowcharts may be drawn using only the basic symbols. The specialized symbols give a more detailed picture of a system and should be used in describing complex arrangements.

[2]A template is included in the kit of materials that comes with this textbook.

Document

Input/output using documents and reports of all kinds.

Sort

Arranging a set of items into some kind of sequence, manual or computer methods.

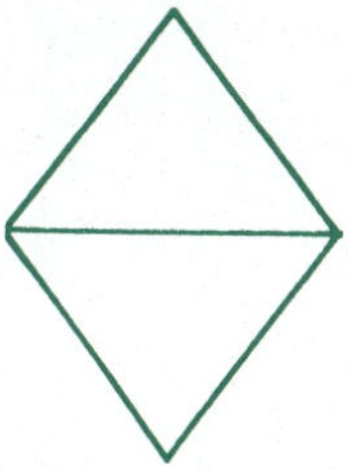

Keying

An operation using a key-driven device — such as punching, verifying, typing.

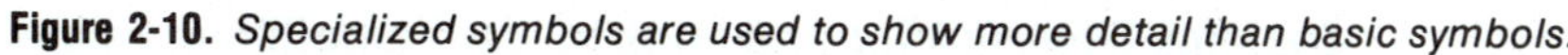

Off-Line Storage

Storage of data off-line, regardless of the medium used. Not directly accessible to the computer.

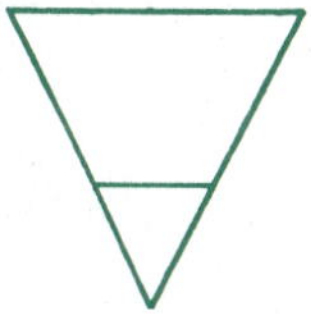

Merge

Combining two or more sets of items into one set.

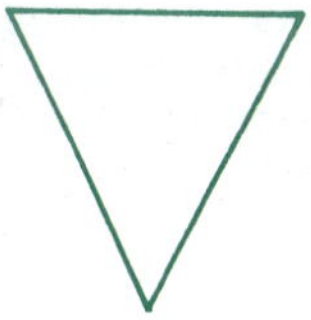

Manual Operation

Any off-line process (at human speed) without mechanical aid.

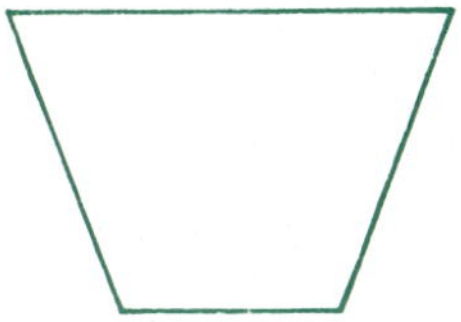

Figure 2-10. *Specialized symbols are used to show more detail than basic symbols.*

Systems flowchart for updating master student enrollment file using basic symbols

Figure 2-11 shows a systems flowchart for updating the master student enrollment file and for preparing a printed student enrollment report. The flowchart is based on the system described in statement form in Figure 2-8, page 27. Only basic symbols are used in this flowchart. Data about new students enter the system from a temporary file of unsequenced enrollment forms. Information about previously enrolled students also enters the system from the master student file, which is in alphabetic order. Note that the input/output symbol is used for both of these inputs. The medium used is not named.

The processing symbol shows the operations through which the input data pass:

(1) Arranging the forms in the temporary student enrollment file in alphabetic order.
(2) Merging the new enrollment forms with the forms in the master file.
(3) Preparing a printed report of the names of students in the updated master file.

Output consists of the updated master student enrollment file and the printed report. The flowlines in the illustration show the order of operations. The arrowheads indicate the direction of flow. The reversed, broken flowline on the right is used to show that the updated master file becomes the new master file for the next time new students are added.

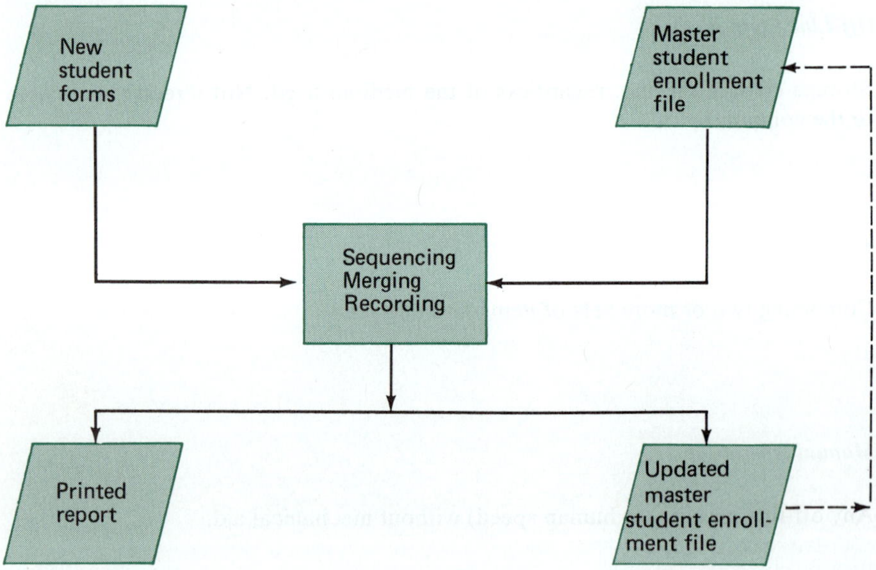

Figure 2-11. *This flowchart for updating the master student enrollment file uses basic symbols.*

Systems flowchart for preparing student enrollment report using specialized symbols

Figure 2-12 shows the flowchart for a manual system for processing a student enrollment report. The system charted is the same as the one described in Figure 2-8, p. 27. In Figure 2-12, however, a number of specialized symbols are used. The advantage of using specialized symbols is that the flowchart is more detailed and clearer.

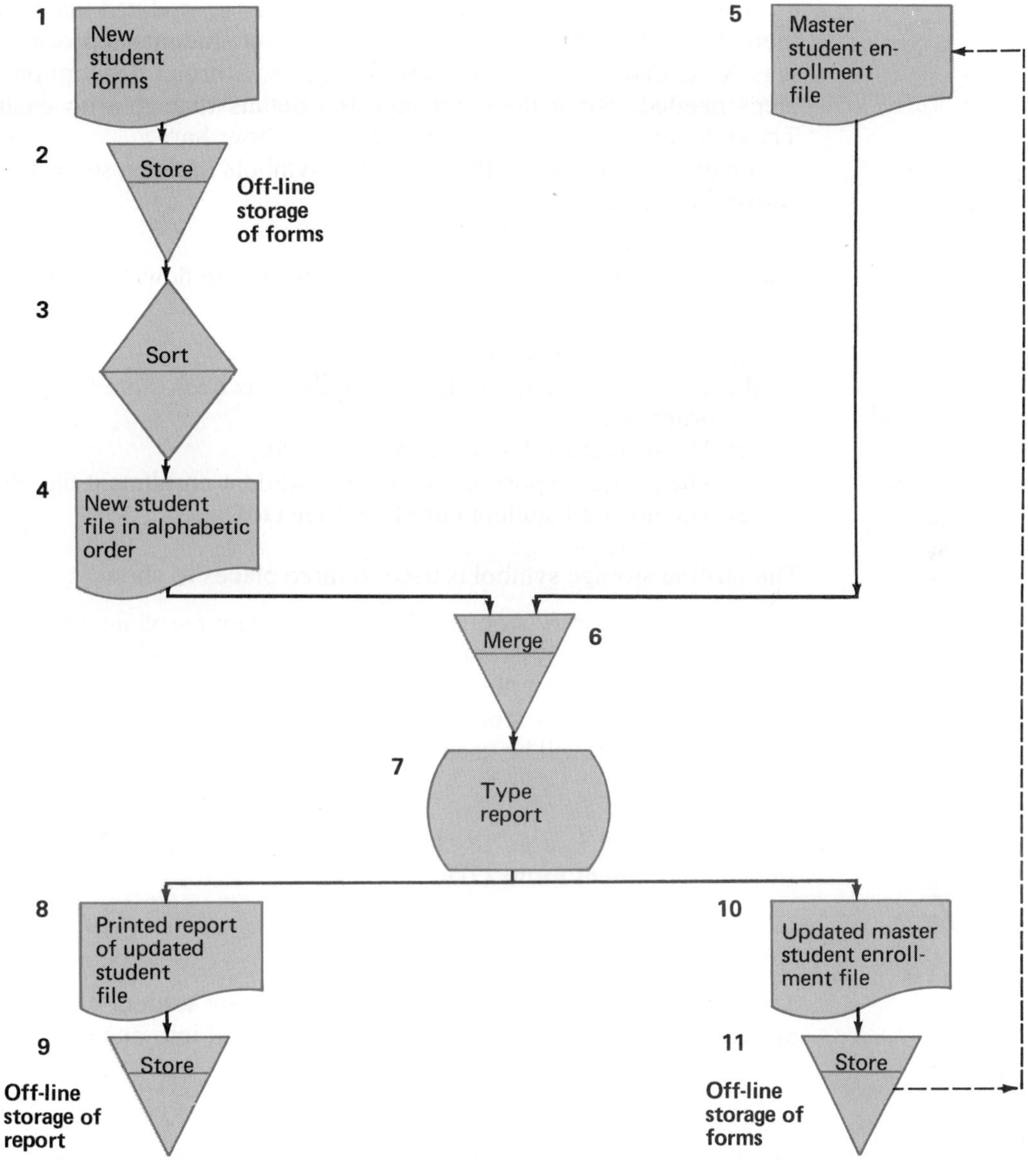

EXPLANATION

1. The forms for updating the master file are received and
2. filed temporarily.
3. The forms are sequenced alphabetically,
4. making a new student file that is in alphabetic order.
5. The forms in the master student enrollment file and those in the new student file
6. are merged.
7. A report is typed from the merged student enrollment file.
8. Output includes a printed report of the updated master student enrollment file,
9. which is stored temporarily.
10. Output also includes an updated master student enrollment file,
11. which is stored temporarily, and which becomes the master file for the next period.

Figure 2-12. *This flowchart for updating the student enrollment file uses specialized symbols.*

The system shown in Figure 2-12 produces an updated master enrollment file as well as a typed list of the names of students appearing in that file. Note that this systems flowchart gives a broad description of the steps needed, but it does not give the details that go with each step. These details would be shown in a program flowchart.

Figure 2-13 describes the use of the symbols in the systems flowchart shown in Figure 2-12.

The document symbol is used in five places in the flowchart to represent the following:

(a) The new student enrollment forms (1).
(b) The new student enrollment file that has been stored in alphabetic order (4).
(c) The master student enrollment file (5).
(d) The printed report of the updated student enrollment file (8).
(e) The updated student enrollment file (10).

The off-line storage symbol is used in three places to show:

(a) The temporary storage of the new student enrollment forms (2).
(b) The temporary storage of the printed report of the updated student enrollment file (9).
(c) The temporary storage of the updated master student enrollment file, which will be used as the master file for the next period (11).

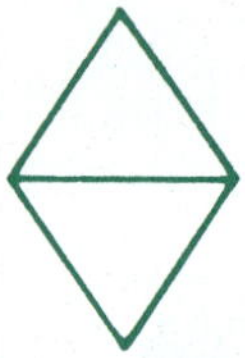

The sort symbol is used to show the alphabetic sequencing of the new student enrollment forms (3).

The merge symbol is used to show that the new student enrollment file and the master student enrollment file are merged into one file (6).

The keying symbol is used to show that a report of the updated student file is prepared manually on a typewriter (7).

Figure 2-13. *The reasons for choosing the symbols for Figure 2-12 are explained.*

If you are asked to flowchart a system, ask yourself what data come in and on what types of media the data appear. Go over in your own mind the steps the data must pass through in order to become useful information. Determine, too, what the output will be and also on what media it will appear. Draw the correct flowcharting symbols for the input and output, whenever possible, and for the processing steps. Place these symbols in proper order and indicate the flow of data through the system by using flowlines and arrows.

SYSTEM FOR PROCESSING A PAYROLL

The goals of the payroll system described here are:

(1) To pay employees for the work they do.
(2) To provide to employees and management records of earnings and deductions from these earnings.
(3) To update individual employees' records at the end of each pay period.[3] (These records make up the master earnings file.)

The steps in the system to meet these goals are basic and can be used with either manual or computer procedures. These steps are as follows:

STEP 1: EACH EMPLOYEE OF THE COMPANY RECORDS ON A TIME CARD THE BEGINNING AND ENDING TIMES OF WORK FOR EACH DAY. A TIME CLOCK IS USED. THE TIME CARD IS THE SOURCE DOCUMENT. (A time card is illustrated in Figure 2-14.)

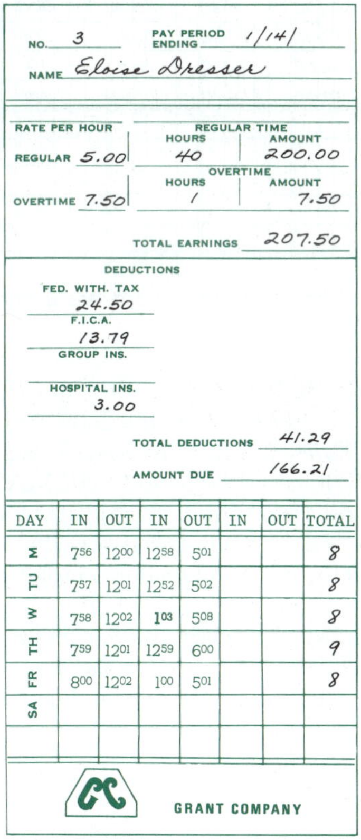

NO. 3 PAY PERIOD ENDING 1/14/

NAME Eloise Dresser

RATE PER HOUR
REGULAR 5.00
OVERTIME 7.50

REGULAR TIME: HOURS 40 AMOUNT 200.00
OVERTIME: HOURS 1 AMOUNT 7.50

TOTAL EARNINGS 207.50

DEDUCTIONS
FED. WITH. TAX 24.50
F.I.C.A. 13.79
GROUP INS.
HOSPITAL INS. 3.00

TOTAL DEDUCTIONS 41.29
AMOUNT DUE 166.21

DAY	IN	OUT	IN	OUT	IN	OUT	TOTAL
M	7^{56}	12^{00}	12^{58}	5^{01}			8
TU	7^{57}	12^{01}	12^{52}	5^{02}			8
W	7^{58}	12^{02}	1^{03}	5^{08}			8
TH	7^{59}	12^{01}	12^{59}	6^{00}			9
FR	8^{00}	12^{02}	1^{00}	5^{01}			8
SA							

GRANT COMPANY

Figure 2-14. *Calculations of total earnings have been made on the time card.*

[3]Payroll reports required by government agencies are handled by another system.

STEP 2: EACH WEEK THE TIME CARDS ARE COLLECTED FROM THE TIME CARD RACK. THE TOTAL HOURS WORKED BY EACH EMPLOYEE FOR THE WEEK ARE CALCULATED AND RECORDED ON THE TIME CARD.

STEP 3: THE CARDS ARE SORTED IN ALPHABETIC ORDER BY EMPLOYEES' NAMES.

STEP 4: FROM THE TIME CARDS, THE EMPLOYEES' NAMES AND THEIR NUMBERS ARE RECORDED IN THE APPROPRIATE COLUMNS OF A PAYROLL REGISTER. ALSO RECORDED IN THE PAYROLL REGISTER ARE THE NUMBER OF HOURS WORKED, RATES PER HOUR, AND TOTAL EARNINGS.

STEP 5: IN ADDITION, DEDUCTIONS FOR SUCH ITEMS AS GROUP INSURANCE PREMIUMS AND WITHHOLDING TAXES ARE TAKEN FROM EACH EMPLOYEE'S RECORDS AND ENTERED IN THE CORRECT COLUMNS OF THE PAYROLL REGISTER. (A payroll register is shown in Figure 2-15.)

PAYROLL REGISTER

WEEK ENDED *January 14, 19--* DATE OF PAYMENT *January 19, 19--*

EMPL. NO.	EMPLOYEE'S NAME	MARITAL STATUS	NO. OF ALLOWANCES	EARNINGS: REGULAR	EARNINGS: OVERTIME	EARNINGS: TOTAL	DEDUCTIONS: FEDERAL INCOME TAX	DEDUCTIONS: FICA TAX	DEDUCTIONS: HOSP. INS.	DEDUCTIONS: OTHER	DEDUCTIONS: TOTAL	NET PAY	CK. NO.
4	Art Avedon	M	2	144 00		144 00	8 70	9 57	3 00		21 27	122 73	355
6	Glenda Beggs	S	1	168 00	6 30	174 30	22 80	11 59	3 00		37 39	136 91	356
3	Eloise Dresser	M	1	200 00	7 50	207 50	24 50	13 79	3 00		41 29	166 21	357
1	Mark Gomez	M	4	152 00	5 70	157 70	4 80	10 48	3 00		18 28	139 42	358
5	Jane Cheng	S	1	180 00	13 50	193 50	27 00	12 86	3 00		42 86	150 64	359
2	Bert Cowman	S	1	200 00		200 00	29 10	13 30	3 00		45 40	154 60	360
	Totals			1044 00	33 00	1077 00	116 90	71 59	18 00		206 49	870 51	

Figure 2-15. *Data from the time card and employee's earning record are entered on the payroll register.*

STEP 6: DEDUCTIONS ARE TOTALED AND SUBTRACTED FROM EARNINGS TO ARRIVE AT THE NET EARNINGS. THE NET EARNINGS ARE THEN RECORDED IN THE PROPER COLUMN OF THE PAYROLL REGISTER.

STEP 7: SUMMARIES OF EARNINGS AND DEDUCTIONS FROM EACH EMPLOYEE ARE PREPARED AND RECORDED IN THE INDIVIDUAL EMPLOYEE'S EARNINGS RECORD IN THE MASTER EMPLOYEE FILE, THUS BRINGING THESE RECORDS UP TO DATE. (An individual employee's earnings record is shown in Figure 2-16.)

STEP 8: PAYCHECKS AND STATEMENTS OF EARNINGS AND DEDUCTIONS FOR EMPLOYEES ARE PREPARED. (A paycheck with an attached record of earnings and deductions is shown in Figure 2-17.)

STEP 9: THE PAYCHECKS ARE STORED UNTIL SUCH TIME AS THEY ARE PASSED OUT TO THE EMPLOYEES.

STEP 10: THE TIME CARDS AND PAYROLL REGISTER ARE STORED FOR FUTURE USE.

STEP 11: THE UPDATED INDIVIDUAL EMPLOYEES' EARNINGS FILE BECOMES THE MASTER EARNINGS FILE FOR THE NEXT PERIOD.

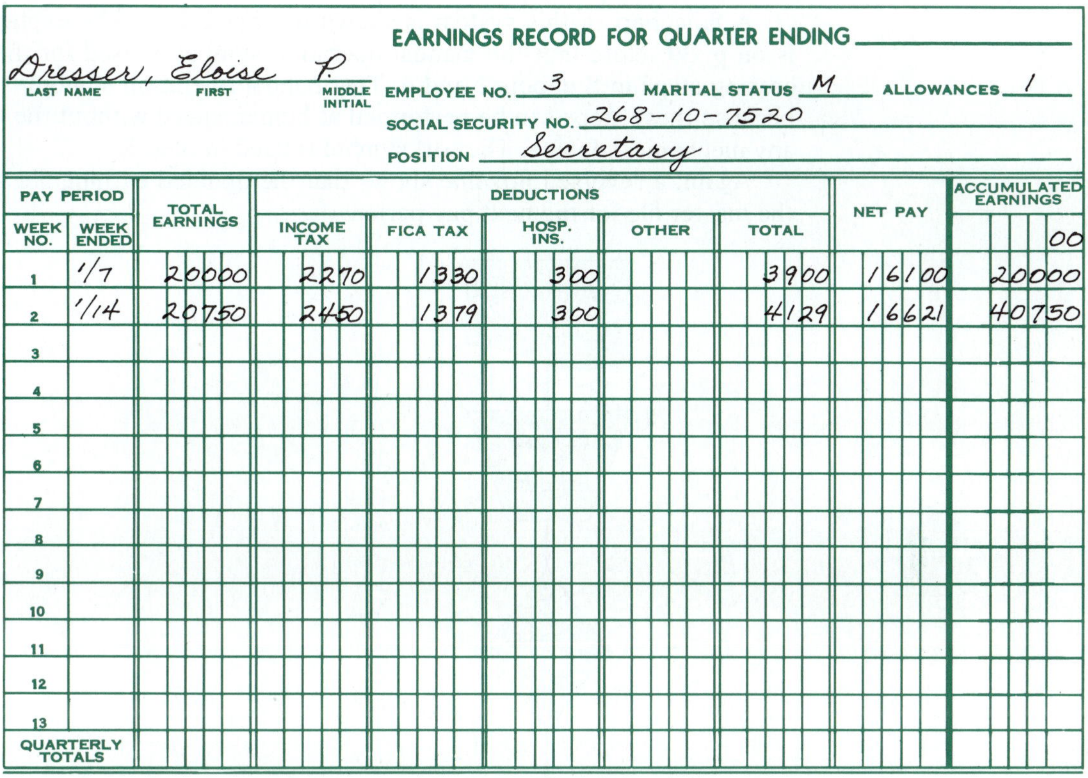

EARNINGS RECORD FOR QUARTER ENDING ______

Dresser, Eloise P.
LAST NAME FIRST MIDDLE INITIAL

EMPLOYEE NO. 3 MARITAL STATUS M ALLOWANCES 1

SOCIAL SECURITY NO. 268-10-7520

POSITION Secretary

PAY PERIOD WEEK NO.	WEEK ENDED	TOTAL EARNINGS	DEDUCTIONS INCOME TAX	FICA TAX	HOSP. INS.	OTHER	TOTAL	NET PAY	ACCUMULATED EARNINGS
									00
1	1/7	200 00	22 70	13 30	3 00		39 00	161 00	200 00
2	1/14	207 50	24 50	13 79	3 00		41 29	166 21	407 50
3									
4									
5									
6									
7									
8									
9									
10									
11									
12									
13									
QUARTERLY TOTALS									

Figure 2-16. *A separate earnings record is kept for each employee.*

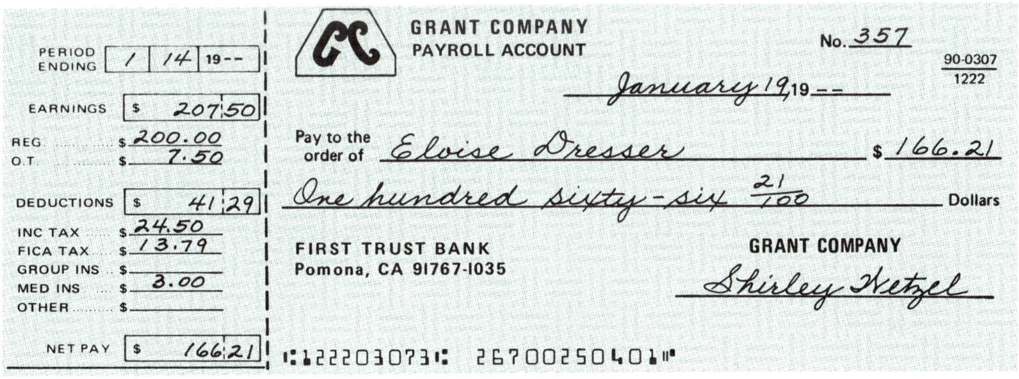

Figure 2-17. *The employee receives a paycheck with an attached record of earnings and deductions.*

Output from the system consists of:

(1) The payroll register.
(2) The paychecks with statements of earnings and deductions for employees.
(3) An updated earnings record for each employee.
(4) The time card file that will be kept temporarily.

A flowchart of this system is shown in Figure 2-18. The explanation is on p. 39. Note that the manual operation symbol is used for the processing steps in Symbols 2 and 6. The manual operation symbol is used because these steps can be performed at human speed without the use of any mechanical device. The sort symbol is used in Step 3.

Again, a reversed flowline shows that the updated earning file will be the master file for the next pay period.

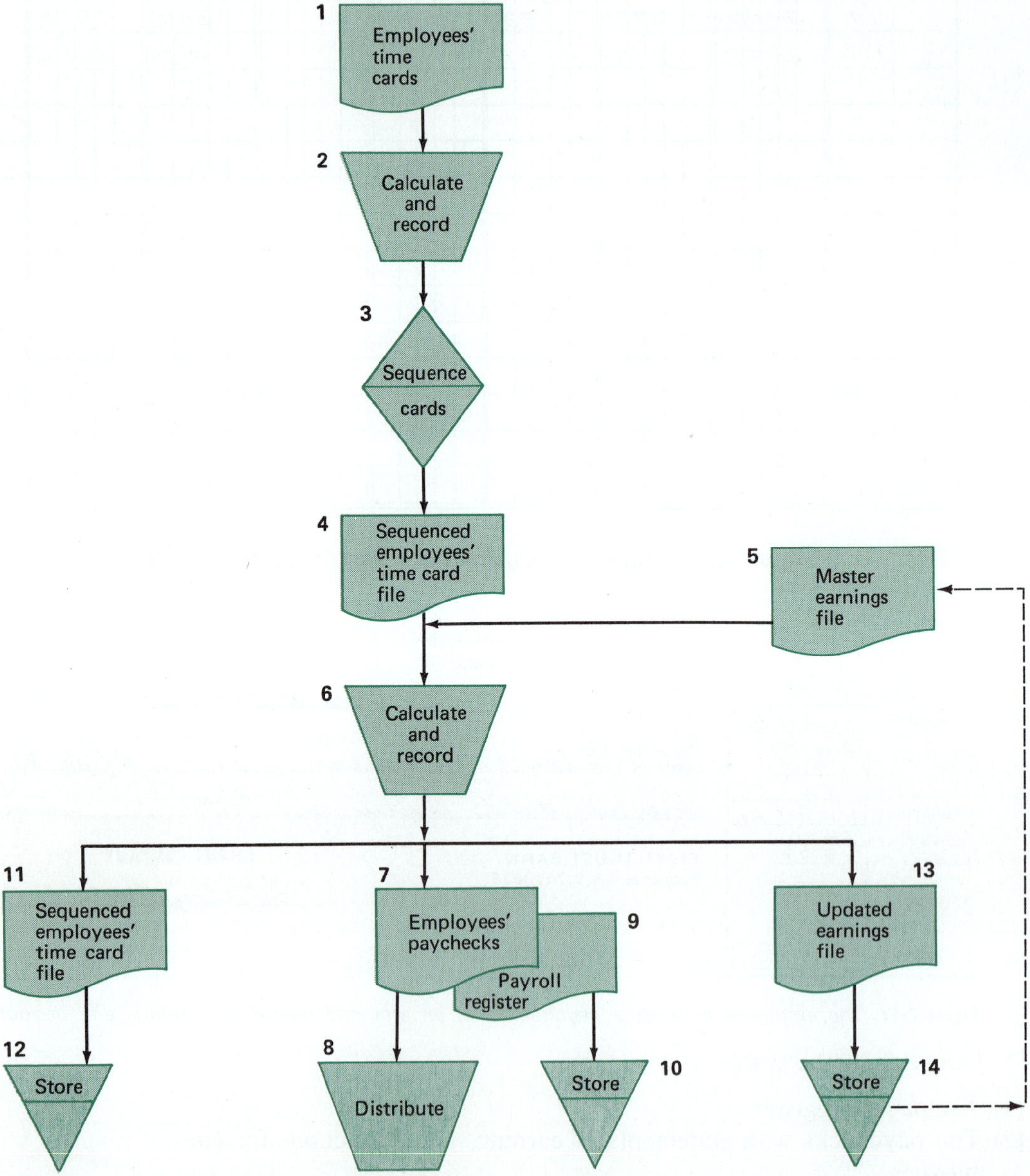

Figure 2-18. *The employees' time cards and the master earnings file are used for input to the system that produces as output the paychecks, payroll register, and updated master earnings file.*

EXPLANATION

1. The employees' time cards enter the system as source documents.
2. The number of hours worked each day, the total hours worked for the payroll period, and total earnings for the period are calculated and entered manually on the time cards.
3. The time cards are sequenced alphabetically by employee names,
4. making a file of sequenced employees' time cards.
5. The data from the employees' earnings records in the master earnings file and the data from the time cards
6. are manually recorded in the payroll register. Columns are added and checked. Data from the payroll register are then recorded in the employees' earnings records. Calculations are made to bring the earnings records up to date.
7. Output from the system is the employees' paychecks,
8. which are distributed to the employees.
9. Output also includes the payroll register,
10. which is stored temporarily.
11. The employees' time card file
12. is stored temporarily.
13. The updated earnings file also leaves the system as output.
14. This updated earnings file is stored temporarily and becomes the master earnings file for the next payroll period.

SUMMARY

Raw data come into the data processing system. Useful information leaves it. Between these two points, the data go through a number of processing operations, such as recording, coding, sorting, and calculating. This is the basic framework or plan within which input becomes useful output.

The job of the input part of the system is to bring raw data into the system. Input may also be made up of the data that have been processed before. When the new data are combined with the old data that have been collected, a new or updated report is prepared.

Processing is the heart of the system and takes in those operations needed to produce the desired result. Output is made up of many different kinds of reports, such as transaction documents, payrolls, and sales forms. Included, also, are operating reports, special reports, and updated records.

A data processing system is a plan for making information available to the user. The plan must be based on order. The inputs must be carefully chosen and identified. The changes that must take place in the inputs must be worked out and understood. The output must supply the information needed in the form in which it is needed.

Systems differ from programs. A system is an overall plan adopted to process data. A program, on the other hand, spells out the detailed steps needed to do a specific job in the system.

Systems flowcharts are drawn. They usually show the media used for input and output, as well as the steps through which the data must pass in order to become useful information. In a flowchart, standardized symbols are used to show media and operations. Brief statements may accompany the symbols to explain clearly the data flow through the system.

Generally, flowcharts are drawn so they read from left to right and from top to bottom. The symbols are connected by lines and arrowheads to explain the flow of information.

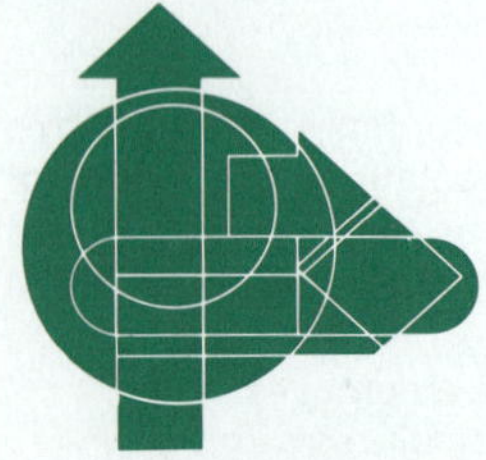

REVIEW QUESTIONS

1. What is a flowchart?
2. What is the difference between a systems flowchart and a program flowchart?
3. What is the purpose of the basic input/output symbol in systems flowcharts?
4. What is the purpose of specialized symbols when used in a flowchart?
5. What are the normal directions in which flowcharts are drawn? If these directions are reversed, what practice must be observed in drawing the flowlines?
6. What is a template?
7. What is the purpose of the sort symbol in Figure 2-12? Of the merge symbol?
8. Does the systems flowchart in Figure 2-12 spell out exactly each step in a program to put the students' names in alphabetic order?
9. What is the advantage of using specialized symbols in a systems flowchart?
10. In the payroll register in Figure 2-15, what data were taken from the time card shown in Figure 2-14? What data were taken from the employee earnings records in Figure 2-16?
11. What three outputs are produced by the system described in the flowchart in Figure 2-18?

NEW TERMS

- Annotation symbol
- Arrowheads and flowlines
- Document symbol
- File
- Flowchart
- Input/output symbol
- Keying symbol
- Manual operation symbol
- Master file
- Merge symbol
- Merging
- On-page connector symbol
- Off-line storage symbol
- Off-page connector symbol
- Process symbol
- Program
- Program flowchart
- Sort symbol
- Symbol (flowcharting)
- System
- Systems flowchart
- Template
- Update

STUDY GUIDE

Complete Study Guide 2 by following the instructions in your STUDY GUIDES booklet.

PROJECT

Complete Projects 2-1 through 2-4 by following the instructions in your PROJECTS booklet.

3

PUNCHED CARD as INPUT MEDIUM for COMPUTERS

A *punched card* is a card in which a pattern of holes is punched to represent data to be processed or stored. All the digits (0 through 9), all the letters of the alphabet, and a number of special characters can be recorded in a single card. See Figure 3-1, p. 42.

A computer that is equipped with a card reader can read the punched data in a card and translate these data into its own language system for processing. After the data are processed, a computer that is equipped with a punching and a printing unit can punch the results into a new set of cards and also print a report.

Even though the punched card has lost some of its popularity, it is still used widely in applications that will be explained later in this chapter. Because the data punched into a card can be seen, the card still remains the best medium to use when learning the concepts of data processing. These concepts can later be applied to other input/output media, such as magnetic tapes and disks.

ADVANTAGES OF THE PUNCHED CARD

The advantages of the punched card in processing data may be listed as follows:

(1) The data can be seen and read by anyone knowing the Hollerith code. Besides, most keypunching machines print the interpretation (meaning) of the punched holes above the card columns in which the holes appear while the holes are punched. In this case, the data can be read by anyone knowing the English language.
(2) The data in the punched card cannot be accidentally erased or destroyed unless, of course, the card is mutilated.
(3) The data can be first recorded in the cards. Then the cards can be sequenced, selected, or grouped by fairly inexpensive equipment before they are processed by a computer.
(4) Once the data have been recorded and verified in a punched card, the card may be used again and again without having to record the information again.
(5) The punched cards can serve as business documents, such as checks and statements. They can be mailed, written on, typed on, and filed. This feature of the punched card makes it a very versatile business form.
(6) Each card record is physically separated from the other records. For this reason, a record can be added, deleted, or changed by adding a new card, taking one out, or replacing an old record with a new one without disturbing the other records in the file.
(7) Punched card records are similar in format to magnetic tape and disk records. Anyone who knows how to record data into cards can adapt to the recording of data on tapes and disks without any trouble.

DISADVANTAGES OF THE PUNCHED CARD

The punched card has a number of limitations, which may be listed as follows:

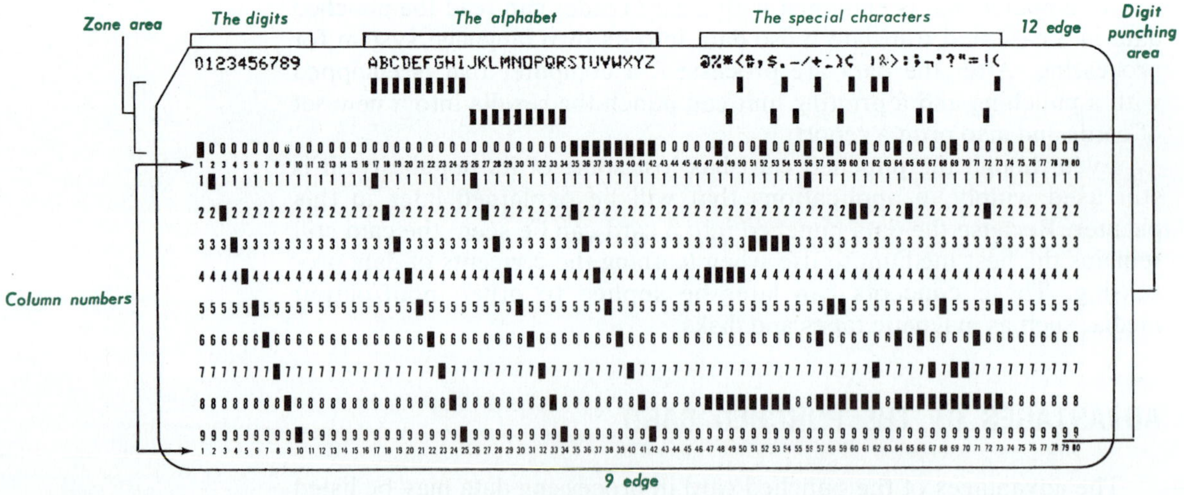

Figure 3-1. *This card represents all the digits, all the letters of the alphabet, and some special characters.*

(1) Punched cards are not reusable except to process the data already punched into them. This is not true of some of the other input media used. A magnetic tape or disk can be erased and used again.
(2) The cards are bulky and require a large amount of storage space, particularly if great numbers of cards are used.
(3) A mechanical device is needed to move cards into place so that the computer can read the data punched into them. This is a time-consuming operation that does not make the best use of the computer's high speed. Other media, such as magnetic tape and disks, are much faster and are being used more and more as replacements for cards.
(4) Unlike magnetic tapes or disks, punched cards are of fixed length — either 80 or 96 columns. This means that punched cards cannot hold as much information as magnetic tapes or disks.

STANDARD 80-COLUMN CARD

Look at the card in Figure 3-2. Note that it is divided into 80 vertical columns. A scale at the bottom of the card and another near the top designate each of the 80 columns. A *column* in a punched card is a vertical division of a card that is marked with a numbered scale above and below it. A column can hold one or more punches that stand for a single number, letter of the alphabet, or special character.

Card design

In this book, the term *digit* is used to refer to any of the numbers from 0 through 9. Note that the digits 0 through 9 are shown in each

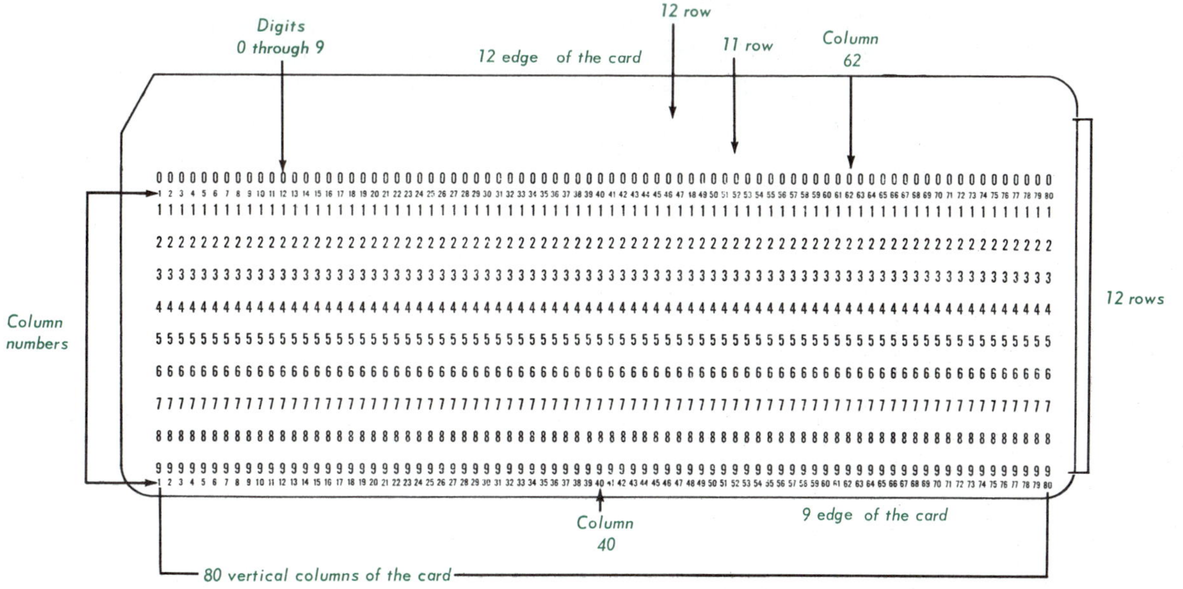

Figure 3-2. *The standard card has 80 columns and 12 rows.*

column and that the 12 and 11 positions, which appear at the top of the card, are not actually shown with numbers. Each vertical column is divided into 12 punching positions. Each horizontal line of punching positions across the card is referred to as a *row*. There are 12 horizontal rows.

Each single digit, 0 through 9, may be punched into any one of the 80 columns. When a digit punch, 1 through 9, in any one of the columns is combined with a 12, 11, or zero punch in the same column, a letter of the alphabet is recorded. The alphabetic code will be described later.

The top of the card is referred to as the *12 edge*. The bottom is the *9 edge*. These designations are made to identify how the cards are fed into machines, because either edge may be fed first.

Zone and digit positions

The 12 location on a card is also referred to as the *Y position*; the 11 location, as the *X position*. Punches in either of these two locations are referred to as *zone punches*. Punches in the 1 through 9 locations are referred to as digit punches. A punch in the zero position may be either a zone punch or a digit punch. It is a zone punch when it is used with another punch in the same column to represent a letter or special character. It is a digit punch when it stands alone in a column to represent zero.

Limited length

Each vertical column of the card will accommodate a punched hole or holes, to stand for a single number, letter, or special character. Thus, the card can contain no more than 80 single pieces of information. All 80-column cards are of the same size. Because there are only 80 columns on the card, information must often be condensed to fit into the spaces available. You can use abbreviations or special numeric codes, in which figures are used to represent alphabetic information.

Card variations

Note that the upper left corner in the card in Figure 3-2 has been cut off. This has been done to make sure that all cards in a group are stacked in the same way. Either of the two upper corners and the right lower corner may be cut. Corner cuts may be used to identify the different kinds of cards. For example, master cards could have the right upper corner cut, while detail cards might have the left upper corner cut. Master and detail cards will be explained fully later.

Numeric code

The card shown in Figure 3-3 has the digits 0 through 9 printed in each vertical column. The card also shows the digits 0 through 9

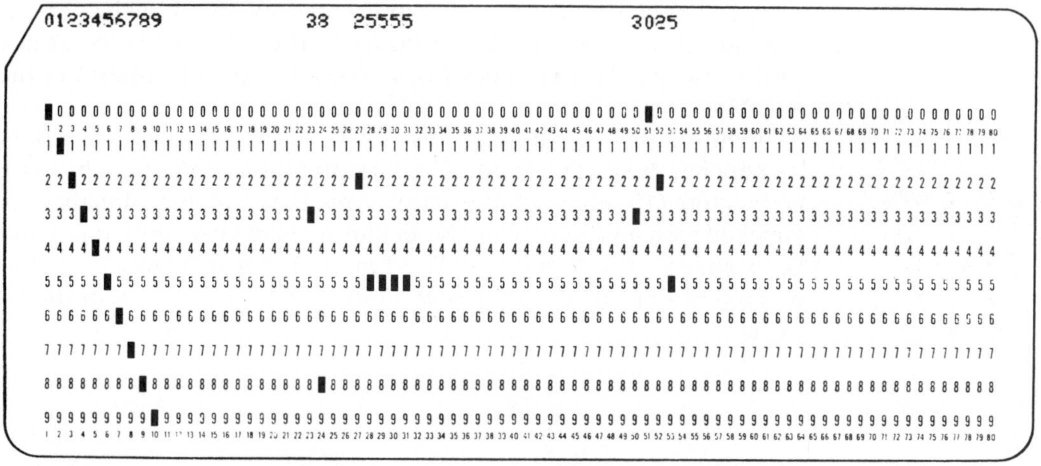

Figure 3-3. *This card contains digit punches.*

punched in Columns 1 through 10. The interpretation of each punched hole is printed at the top of the card. A single digit can be punched in any one of the 80 columns on the card. For example, the Digit 2 in Column 27 could have been punched in any one of the 80 columns. It will be recognized by the computer as the Digit 2.

When a two-digit number is to be recorded, two columns of the card must be used. A multidigit number must take up as many columns as there are digits in that number. For example, the Number 38 appears in Columns 23 and 24 of Figure 3-3. One could not punch both of these digits in the same column. The processing machines would not interpret the information correctly.

Refer to Figure 3-3 again. What number is punched in Columns 27–31? In what columns is 3025 recorded? How many vertical columns would be needed to record 471090?

Meanings assigned to figures

What do the figures in the different columns represent? They represent what you want them to represent. There is no way of knowing what the number 3025 in Figure 3-3 means. It could mean the number of cars bought, sold, or on hand. It could mean $3,025 or $30.25. It could be the code name of a city or sales representative. The number means nothing until you know what it is intended to mean. Decimal points may be punched in the card, or they may be understood. The information to be recorded in cards must be decided and meanings must be given to this information.

Alphabetic code

Just as holes punched in a card represent different digits and numbers, punched holes may also stand for the letters of the alphabet.

Each letter of the alphabet is represented by two punches in any one column. One of the punches appears in the zone punching area of the card — the 12, 11, and 0 positions. The other punch appears in the digit punching area.

Figure 3-4 shows how all the letters of the alphabet are represented by punched holes in a card. The interpretation of the punches is shown at the top (12 edge) of the card. Any letter of the alphabet may be punched into any one of the 80 columns. However, only one letter may be represented in a column. The Letter A, for example, is represented by punches in the 12 and 1 rows. Letter Z uses punches in the 0 and 9 rows.

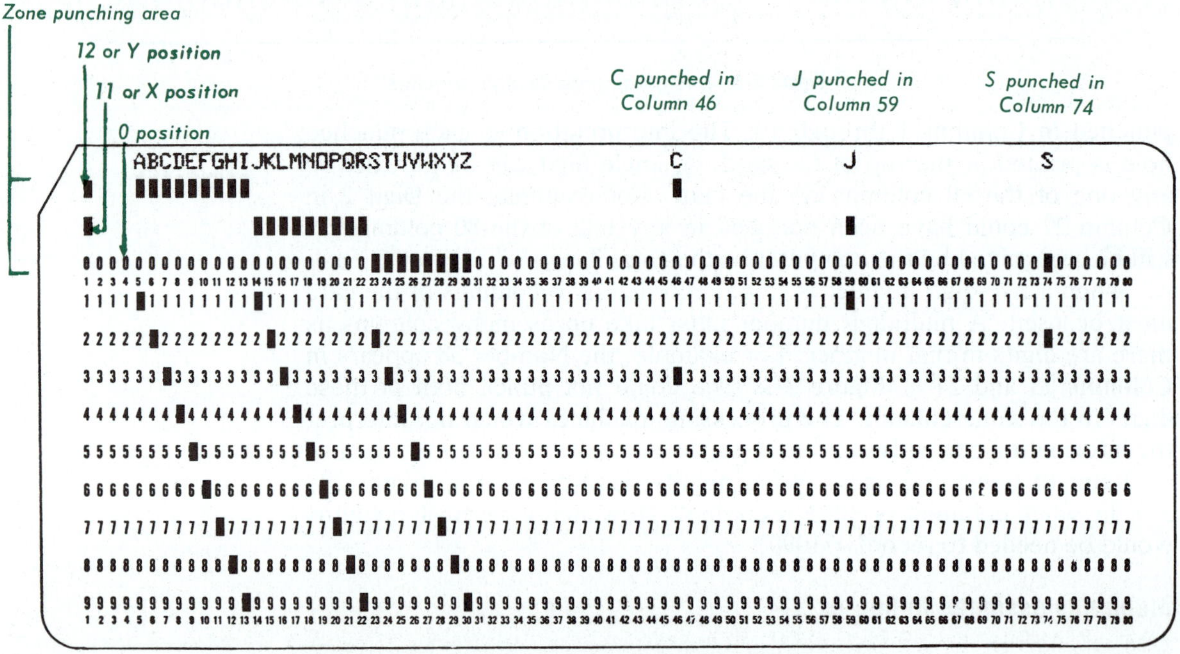

Figure 3-4. *This card contains all the letters of the alphabet.*

Code for special characters

Besides the codes that have been devised to stand for numbers and letters of the alphabet, codes have been developed to stand for a few special characters such as (&#.$,-/@/''?=!). These special characters are represented by one, two, and sometimes three punches in any one column of the card. Some of the characters are used in mathematical formulas. Some are used for transmitting messages over long distance equipment. Some are also used in computer programming.

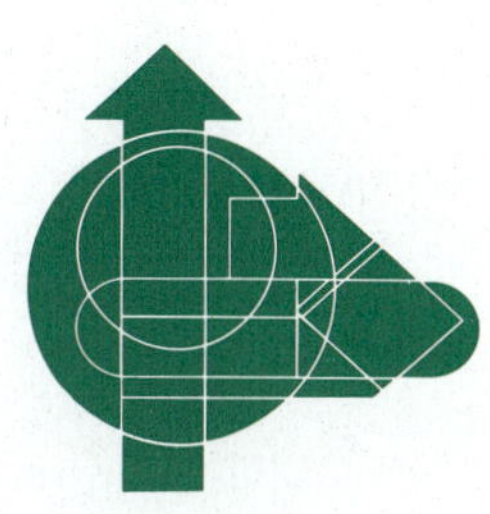

REVIEW QUESTIONS

1. How are data represented in a punched card?
2. What kinds of data are represented in the punched card shown in Figure 3-1, page 42?
3. What feature of the punched card makes it a good medium for learning the concepts of data processing?
4. What is meant by the statement that punched cards can be used as business documents?
5. Do punched cards bring data to the computer as fast as magnetic tape or disks? Why, or why not?
6. How many vertical columns are in a standard punched card? How many horizontal rows are there?
7. What is the top edge of a punched card called? The bottom edge of the card?
8. How many columns are needed to record a single digit? Can a multiple-digit number be recorded in a single column?
9. How many columns are needed to record a single letter of the alphabet?
10. How many vertical columns are needed to record A4590B?

CARD FIELDS

The different items of information in a punched card are recorded in fields. A *card field* is a vertical column or group of consecutive columns in a punched card set aside to record a single fact. A field could contain a date, an amount, a name, an address, or a code. A card may contain many fields. A field may vary in length. It could be as small as one column. However, the number of columns allowed for a given field depends upon the number of columns needed for the largest item to be recorded in that field. A field could be as large as 80 columns, but this would not be likely.

The vertical columns used for a particular field in a card must be the same in number for that field in all the cards in a file. (If a customer number is allowed five columns in the first card in the file, that field must have five columns in all the cards in the file.) Also, the fields must be in the same order for each of the cards in a file. (If the name follows the number in the first card, the name would follow the number in all the cards in the file.) The same type of data must be recorded in a particular field in all the cards in the file. (If a two-column field is used to represent a sales person in one card, the same field should be used for sales persons in all the cards in the file.)

In Figure 3-5, note that these rules are used in planning the two cards selected from the customer data file.

(1) The number of vertical columns in the different fields in a card may vary in length. The length depends upon the number of columns

needed to record the longest item in that field. Note that the customer number field has seven columns while the name field has 20.

(2) The number of columns allowed for a particular field must be the same in all the cards in a file. Note that in both cards the customer number field has seven columns and the name field has 20.

(3) The fields must be in the same order in all the cards. Note that this is true in the two cards shown in Figure 3-5.

(4) The same type of data must be recorded in the fields allowed for that data in all the cards in a file. Note that the first field in each card is a customer number field and the last field is for the zip code. Both cards contain exactly the same kind of data.

The same four rules apply when planning fields for records on magnetic tapes or disks.

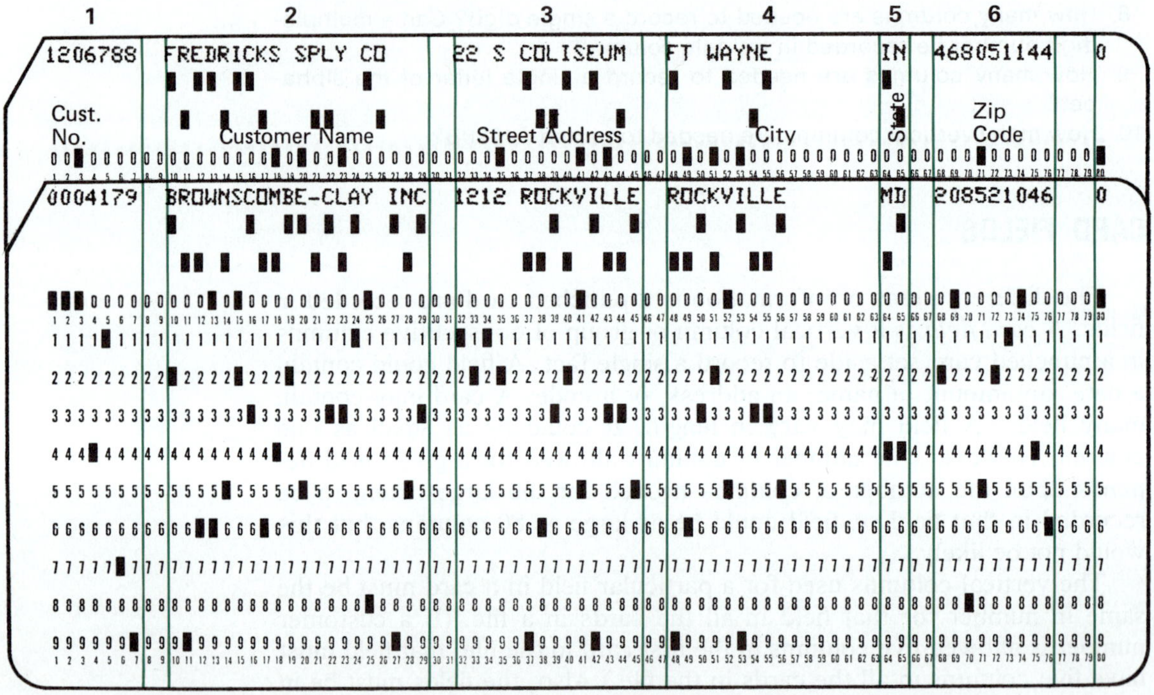

Figure 3-5. *These two cards are part of a punched card file containing customer data.*

Planning card fields

Fields for both numeric and alphabetic data may be planned in a single card. The number of columns in which data may be recorded cannot be more than 80 in a standard card. For this reason, care must be used in laying out card fields. No card column should be wasted by poor planning. You must be sure, however, to allow enough columns in a field to take care of the longest name or longest number of digits that may be needed in that field.

Whenever possible, a number is used as a code to stand for alphabetic data. Such a code saves space, is easier to record, and takes less time to process. Dates, names of states, names of students, names of courses, and names of customers are often identified by number.

The arrangement of fields on a card does not matter to the computer as long as all the cards in a file are consistent. The computer can read data anywhere on a card. If possible, however, the fields should appear on the card in the same order as the information appears on the source document. This arrangement speeds up the keypunching process because the operator is able to read and record the information in order.

Abbreviations are used to save space whenever possible. Standard abbreviations need not be used. Except in those forms in which legal names are important, such as payrolls, tax forms, and student enrollments, initials are commonly used for given names. When space is limited, the first and second initials may be run together.

Periods need not be used after abbreviations. Commas are not used between the last and given names or between cities and states. Dollar signs are not used. Decimal points can be omitted.

In Figure 3-5, two blank columns separate the fields of data. This is not always done. If space is available, however, separating the fields makes for easier reading of the printed interpretations at the top of the card.

Numeric fields

In Figure 3-5, note that customer numbers are right-justified (aligned at the right). The last digit in the customer number must be punched in the right-most column in the field (Column 7). If fewer than the maximum number of columns planned for a numeric field are used, zeros must be added at the left to fill all the columns in the field. Note that zeros are punched in the top card (0004179). The zeros are punched into the card by the keypunch operator. Some new keypunch machines have devices for suppressing "leading zeros" so that they do not print at the top of the card, but the zeros are always punched into the card.

Alphabetic fields

Zeros are not used in alphabetic fields to fill the unused columns. Spaces or blank columns are used instead. Alphabetic lists, addresses, and other information are usually aligned on the left in printed reports. For this reason, alphabetic data in a card are normally aligned on the left also (left-justified). When the alphabetic items require less than the number of columns allowed in the field, the blank columns appear to the right of the items. Look again at Figure 3-5. Note that in both cards the customer names, street addresses, and cities have blank columns on the right.

Printed matter on cards

Standard cards are printed as shown in Figure 3-2, p. 43. That is, the digits 0 through 9 are printed in each of the 80 card columns. However, the user of cards may have other information printed on the cards. An example of such a card, which is used as a statement, appears in Figure 3-6. When punched cards are used as the input medium, the computer will recognize only the punched holes. The printed matter will not be recognized.

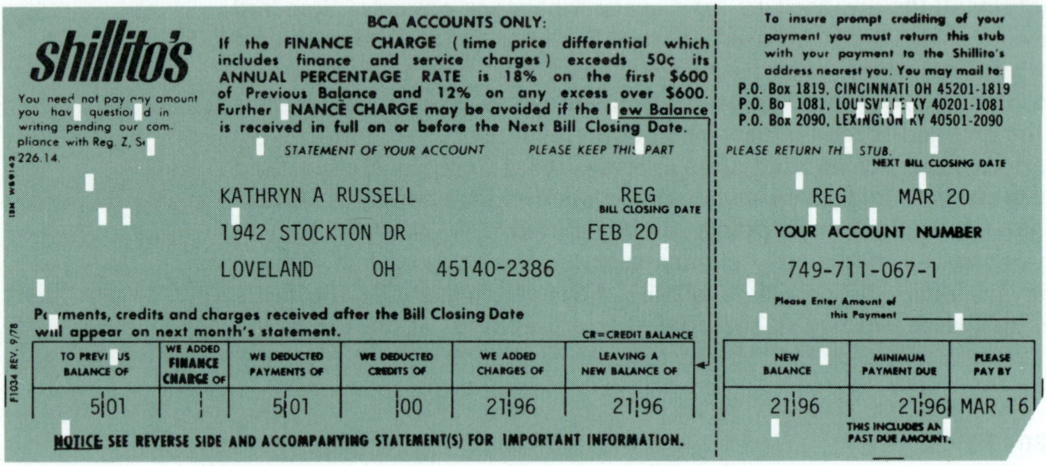

Figure 3-6. *This punched card is used as a monthly statement.*

BASIC RULES FOR RECORDING DATA IN PUNCHED CARDS

Standardization is an important requirement for processing data automatically. All data must be recorded in the same language. This language must be "understood" by the various machines in a computer system.

There must be uniform organization of all data keyed from a source document into an input device. In the case of punched cards, no machine can identify data except by the location of the data on the card. As stated earlier in this chapter, the different pieces of information about transactions of a particular type must appear in uniform places on the card.

Besides the principles stated earlier, each punched card in a file must be of the same size and shape. With magnetic tapes and disks, however, the length of the single records in a file is not limited. These media are continuous and need not be restricted to 80 or 96 spaces for each record.

Each item in a transaction should be identified fully and recorded as a separate record. This requirement allows the records to be grouped and processed according to the different categories of information included in the record. With punched cards, for example, a separate card must be prepared for each customer in a customer data file. Each card must contain the same kinds of information about the customer. Look again at Figure 3-5, p. 48. Using these cards, printed reports could be prepared that would list customers as follows:

(1) In alphabetic order according to customers' names.
(2) In numeric order according to customers' numbers.
(3) According to cities.
(4) According to zip codes (postal zones).

By regrouping the cards after each listing, entirely different types of reports could be prepared.

The use of a standard set of rules is thus an important requirement for processing data when punched cards are used. The same rules are true with magnetic tapes and disks.

96-COLUMN CARD

The IBM Corporation has developed a 96-column card for its System/3 computer. This computer was designed for small businesses. The card is one-third the size of the 80-column card, but it holds 20 percent more information. See Figure 3-7.

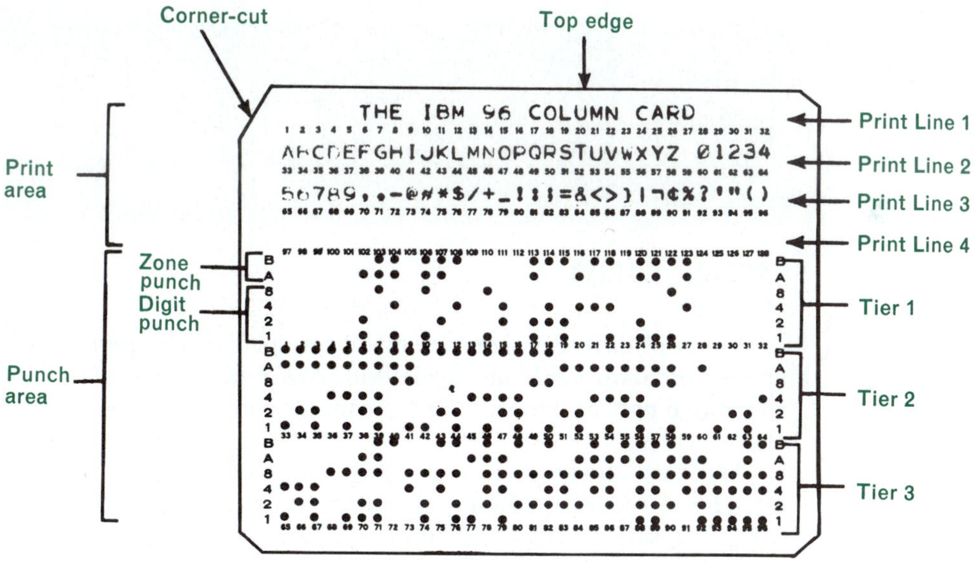

Figure 3-7. *This 96-column card contains letters of the alphabet, numbers, and special characters.*

Punching positions in this card are based on a two-digit numbering system known as the *binary code*. The numbering system using this code has a base of 2. This means that the value of a digit increases two times with each move of one space. Note how the digits are shown in the 96-column card in Figure 3-8.

Figure 3-8 shows a 96-column card with all the digits 0 through 9 punched in it. Zero is recorded by a punch in the A position of Column 1. Digits 1, 2, 4, and 8 are recorded by a single punch in these digit positions in each of the following columns: 3, 5, 9, and 17. The remaining digits require a combination of punches. Digit 3 in Column 7, for example, has punches in the 1 and 2 positions. Digit 5 in Column 11 has punches in the 1 and 4 positions. Digit 7 in Column 15 has punches in the 1, 2, and 4 positions. Any digit can be punched in any one of the columns. The same holds true of letters of the alphabet and special characters.

Letters and special characters can be recorded by combining punches in the digit positions with punches in the A and B positions. (See Figure 3-7.) The letter A, in the second row at Column 33 has punches in the B, A, and 1 positions. The letter Z in the second row at Column 58 has punches in the A, 8, and 1 positions.

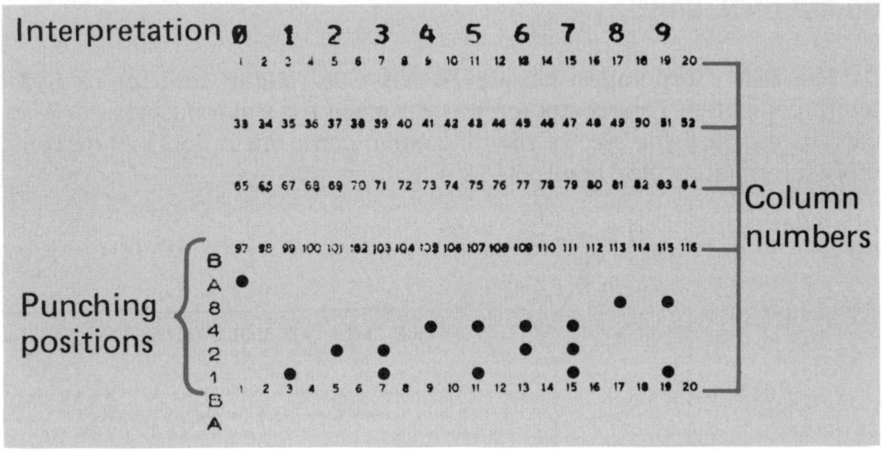

Figure 3-8. *Part of a 96-column card shows the numbers 0–9.*

SPECIAL CARDS

Cards of different sizes are made for specialized operations. For example, standard cards are made with perforations that make it possible to remove part of the card. The computer can be adapted to process the shorter card.

The card shown in Figure 3-9 is one that is used in keeping school attendance records. When a student returns to school after an absence, it is necessary to report to the attendance office. This office gives the student the right side of the card, which has been prepared in advance by the data processing office. (The data processing office punches the student's name and number in the card and sends the card to the attendance office.) The attendance office marks on the card the months and days the student has been absent and if the absence is excused or unexcused. The left part of the card, which contains 39 columns, is then sent back to the data processing office for processing. The student uses the right side as a reentry pass into classes.

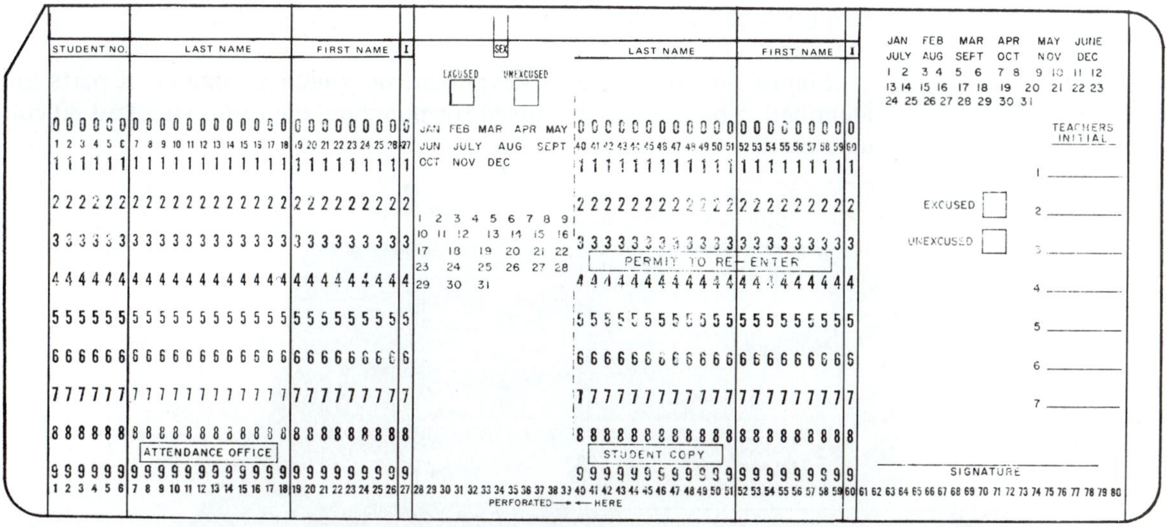

Figure 3-9. *This student's attendance card is perforated between Columns 39 and 40.*

REVIEW QUESTIONS

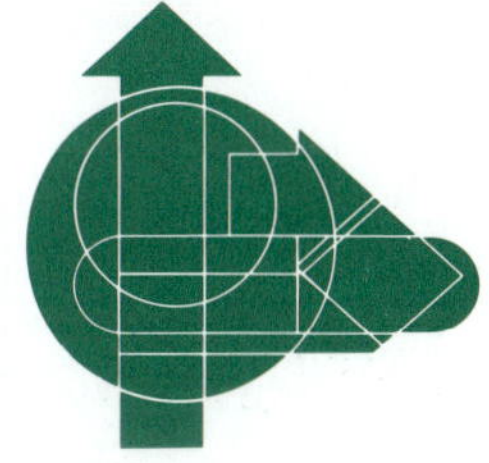

1. What is a card field?
2. How many vertical columns are there in a card field?
3. May the different fields on a single card vary in length? May the vertical columns in a given field vary in number for that field in the cards in a file?
4. May the date field, for example, vary in location on the different cards in a file? May it vary in length?
5. May a numeric field consisting of six columns be used to record an account number in some but not all of the cards in a file?
6. Should numeric data be right- or left-justified?
7. What digit must be punched in the unused columns of a numeric field?
8. Should alphabetic data be right- or left-justified? How are unused columns shown?
9. Can the computer interpret the printed matter on a punched card?
10. On what numbering system are punching positions in the 96-column card based?

CARD PUNCH (KEYPUNCH) MACHINES

A *keypunch* is a machine that records data in cards by punching holes to represent numbers, letters of the alphabet, and special characters. Typically, keypunch machines punch data into cards as punched holes and print the meaning of the punched holes at the top of the cards. Also, some provision is made for checking the accuracy of the punched holes — either by a separate machine or by special features built into the keypunch machine itself.

Keypunch components

Figure 3-10 illustrates a keypunch, on which a number of parts are identified. The keypunch is used for punching data into standard 80-column cards.

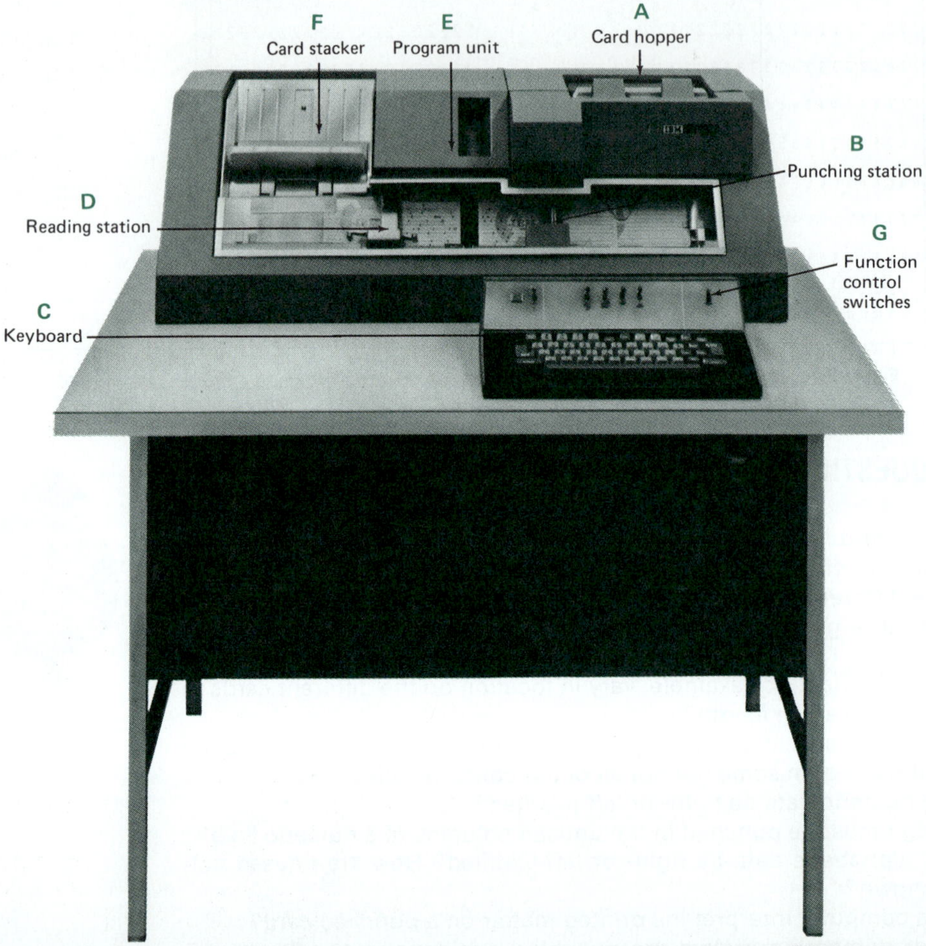

Photo courtesy of IBM Corporation

A. Card hopper for cards to be punched.
B. Punching station where cards are moved for punching.
C. Keyboard for recording the punches in the cards.
D. Reading station where punched cards move for reproduction of punches in a new card.
E. Program unit for automatic control of skipping, spacing, repeating, and shifting from numeric to alphabetic positions.
F. Card stacker for output cards.
G. Switches for controlling machine operations.

Figure 3-10. *The IBM 29 key-operated card punch is a typical keypunch machine.*

Cards to be punched are placed in the card hopper and pass through the machine one card at a time from right to left. A card that is to be punched moves from the card hopper to the punching station, where punching takes place. After a card is punched, it moves ahead to the reading station. At the same time, a new card from the hopper enters the punching station. While the new card is being punched, the card in the reading station advances through this station, column-for-column, with the card in the punching station. When a card in the punching station is completed, it moves to the reading station. Then the card in the reading station moves to the stacker. This action is repeated until all the cards are punched.

The punched cards enter the stacker, one at a time, and are added to at the bottom of the deck. This feature keeps the cards in order — first card on top, last card on the bottom.

Because the cards in the reading and punching stations move ahead through these stations column for column, automatic duplication is possible. If the machine is properly programmed, any data punched into a card in the reading station can be duplicated in another card in the punching station. This is done by just depressing the duplicate (DUP) key. A sensing device, together with connecting cables, reads the data in the first card and punches it into the second card.

Repeated data in the first card in the file, such as the date, customer number, and invoice number, may be automatically duplicated in all the rest of the cards relating to a given transaction. The duplication of data stops when the duplicate key is released. With this feature, only the common data in a group of cards will be duplicated. The common data are the same on all the cards. Variable data can be punched into the cards manually by the operator. Variable data change from card to card. Note the repeated and variable data in the punched card in Figure 3-11. The stock number, quantity, unit price, and total price are variable. Other data in the card are repeated.

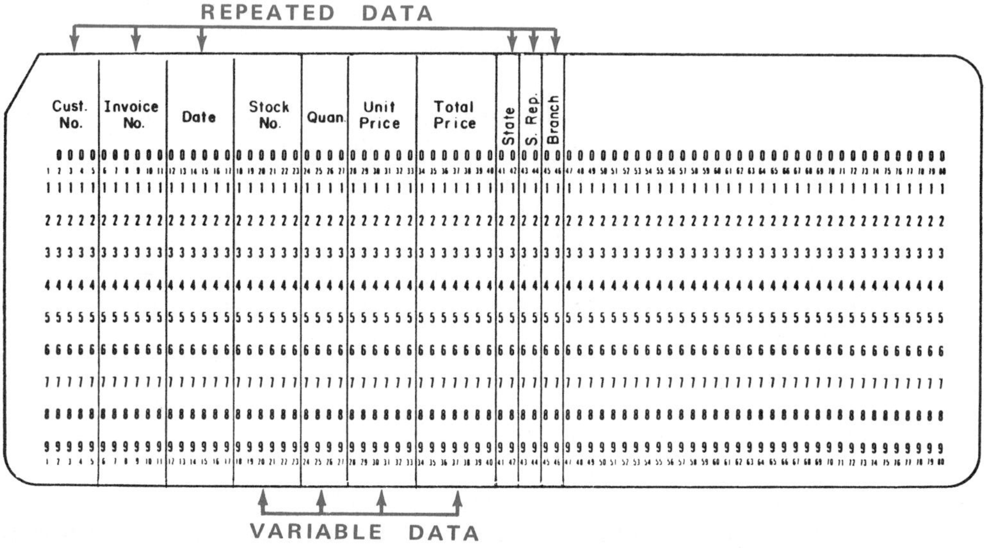

Figure 3-11. *This card contains repeated and variable data.*

The location of the duplicate key (DUP) on one of the machines is shown in the shaded part of the keyboard in Figure 3-12.

Keyboard of the keypunch

Note that the alphabetic keyboard in Figure 3-12 is the same as that of a standard typewriter. The keys in the shaded area are used by the right hand and are for punching both letters and numbers. For example, the U key will print both U and Number 1. The letter is printed by depressing the indicated key; the number, by depressing the left shift key (NUMERIC) along with the indicated right-hand key. Note the keys that are used to punch Digits 0 through 9. Note, too, the letters on these keys.

The keyboard shown in Figure 3-12 is almost the same as the keyboards of the keying devices that are used with magnetic tapes or disks. The idea of keying input data is much the same. It is thus quite easy for a keypunch operator to make the change to keying devices used for magnetic tape or disk recorders.

Figure 3-12. *The keyboard of an IBM 29 keypunch machine combines alphabetic and numeric keys.*

VERIFYING INFORMATION IN CARDS

When only a small number of cards needs to be verified for accuracy, the punches can be checked visually. With a large number of cards, however, a card verifier is used. Cards punched on a printing key machine are not often verified by proofreading because the type is too hard to read. Visual checking is not as accurate as verification by machine.

The *card verifier* is a machine much like the keypunch and is used for checking the accuracy of previously punched data in standard 80-column cards. A verifier is shown in Figure 3-13.

The operator of the verifier takes the cards that have already been punched on the keypunch and feeds the cards into the verifier. Using the same source documents from which the original cards were punched, the operator strikes the same keys on the verifier that should have been struck when the cards were originally punched. If the verifier finds an incorrectly punched column, an error is noted and a notch is punched at the top of the incorrectly punched column. A card with an error usually is punched over again on the keypunch machine.

When keypunch machines with built-in verifiers are used, all the data are first keyed into electronic memory units (buffers) rather than into the cards as punched holes. When the operator catches a mistake before the cards are actually punched, he or she just strikes the correct key at the point at which the mistake was made.

All the data punched into a card can then be verified by rekeying the data into memory. The rekeyed data are compared with the data in memory, and additional errors, if any, are noted by the keypunch machine. To make the corrections, the operator just keys the correct data over the incorrect data. The corrected data are then automatically punched into a new card.

Photo courtesy of IBM Corporation

Figure 3-13. *The IBM 59 card verifier is used to check the accuracy of data punched into cards.*

HOW PROCESSING MACHINES READ THE PUNCHED HOLES IN CARDS

As a punched card is fed into an input device or processing machine, each card column passes over or under a sensing device. If there is no hole in a column, no electrical contact is made and no electrical impulse is created. If there is a hole, however, the sensing device senses the hole and causes a *timed electrical impulse* to be created. For instance, a punched hole in Row 6 on a card will create an impulse at a different time than a punched hole in Row 8. If there is more than one hole in a column, two or more impulses are created. Each impulse has a meaning to the machine that reads the card. These impulses may also be used to punch holes in another card, to sort cards and group them as desired, or to print lines of information. The 80-column card contains the Hollerith Code. The 96-column card contains a variation of the binary code.

Data on magnetic tapes and disks are sensed in a different manner, but the idea is the same. Coded matter on the input records are read and processed. Usable information is produced as it is needed.

PUNCHED CARD APPLICATIONS

Punched cards are often used as an input medium for computers. They contain the data to be processed by a computer. The processed data can be printed, punched into a new set of cards, displayed on a picture tube, or made available in many other ways. The applications that follow are typical examples.

Processing student enrollment cards

Generally, students enrolling in a school are expected to fill out an enrollment form. The data are recorded manually on the form by each student. This form, as a source document, is shown in Figure 3-14.

Name ______________________________ Number __________
Last name First name Initial

Address ______________________________ Birthdate __________
Street City State Zip

Name of Parent or Guardian ______________________ Phone __________

Date of Enrollment ______________________ Class Sr __ Jr __ So __ Fr __

Major ______________________________ Sex M ____ F ____

Figure 3-14. *An enrollment form is filled out by all students.*

The data processing department punches a separate card for each student. A card for one of the students is shown in Figure 3-15. This card is the input medium for the computer. Note that only selected data are punched into the card. The cards are alphabetized by a sequencing operation described in Chapter 6, after which they are stored in a Student Enrollment File.

The card may be described as follows:

Columns 1–20 Student name
Columns 22–36 Street
Columns 38–49 City address
Columns 51–52 State address
(2-letter abbreviation)
Columns 54–62 ZIP code
Column 65 Major
(1-digit code)
1 — academic
2 — special
3 — general
4 — business
5 — arts
6 — mechanical

Columns 67–72 Birth date
Column 74 Class
(1-digit code)
1 — freshman
2 — sophomore
3 — junior
4 — senior
Column 76 Sex
(1-digit code)
1 — female
2 — male

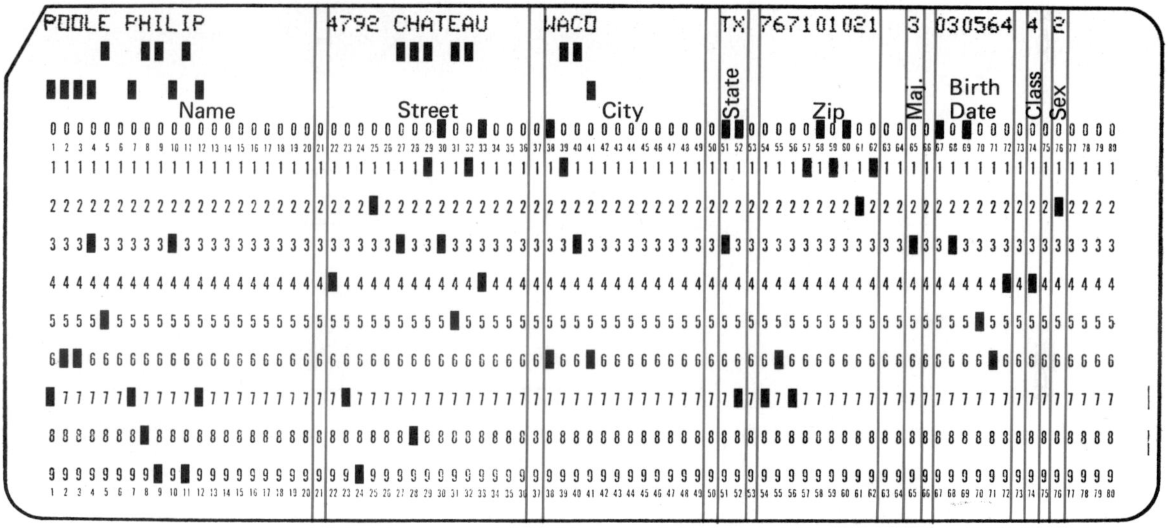

Figure 3-15. *This punched card is used for processing student enrollment data.*

Many reports could be processed from these records. However, the problem in this case is to print a report in alphabetic order of the names of senior students only and of their addresses. The cards for senior students are selected (extracted) from the file by a sorting operation described in Chapter 6. The cards will be in alphabetic order.

A program is stored in the computer to read the data from these cards and to print the desired data as output. When the report is completed, the processed cards and the cards remaining in the Student Enrollment File are merged again and returned to the Student Enrollment File.

The flowchart to solve this problem appears in Figure 3-16. The explanation is on the next page. Three new symbols are introduced at this time. They are shown in Figure 3-17. A portion of the printed report is shown in Figure 3-18.

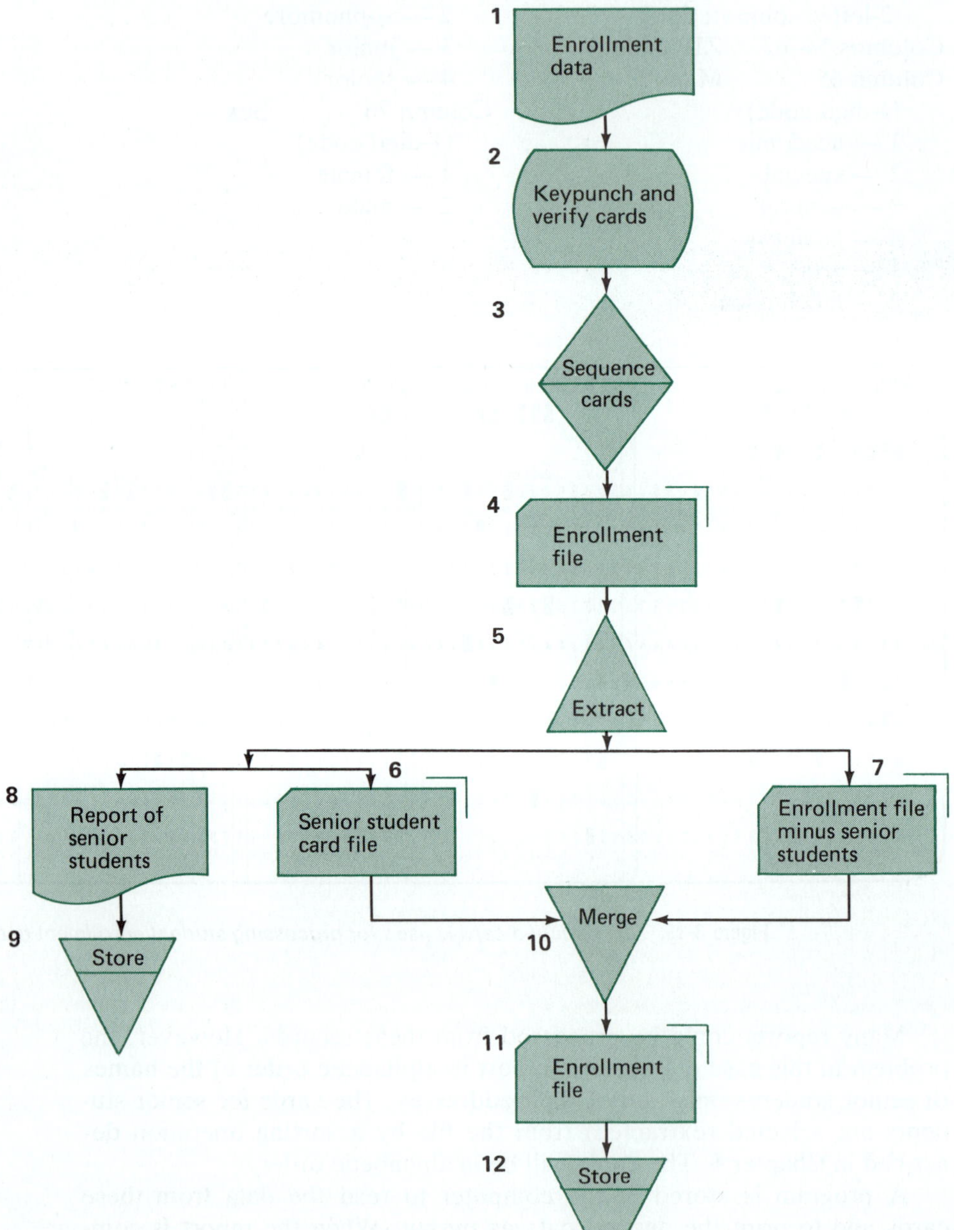

Figure 3-16. *The above flowchart is for preparing a report of senior students only.*

EXPLANATION

1. Each student manually completes an enrollment form,
2. from which selected data are keyed and verified in cards.
3. The cards are alphabetized by a sequencing operation, resulting in a
4. student enrollment file.
5. From the student enrollment file are extracted
6. the cards for senior students only, making a senior student card file,
7. leaving an enrollment file of all but senior students.
8. Selected data from the senior student cards are printed as a report,
9. which is filed.
10. The processed cards of senior students and the cards remaining in the student enrollment file are merged.
11. A complete student enrollment card file is again created
12. and is stored temporarily until needed.

Punched Card

Represents input/output to computers using any kind of punched card, including stubs.

Card File

Collection of related punched card records.

Extract

Removal of one or more sets of items from a set.

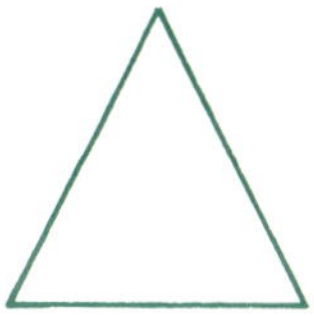

Figure 3-17. *New symbols are the punched card, punched card file, and extract symbols.*

POOLE PHILIP	4792 CHATEAU	WACO TX	76710-1021
PORCHE MARCELLA	1416 BECKWITH	WACO TX	76710-1023
POSADA MARIE	1863 CLAREMONT	WACO TX	76705-1067
POWAZEK ALBERT	498 CAROL CT	WACO TX	76711-1045
RAMOS LUISA	895 ARNOLD	WACO TX	76704-1062
SUMIDA JOHN	922 CARMEN AV	WACO TX	76711-1039
WANG JOSEPH	5536 ABBEY PL	WACO TX	76710-1035
WEINER ANITA	501 LINDA LN	WACO TX	76710-1045
WILLIAMSON JH	455 HAVEN AV	WACO TX	76710-1035

Figure 3-18. *Above is a portion of a printed report of senior students and their addresses.*

A different program can be written and stored in a computer to read the data in all the cards in the file. The computer will print only the selected data in cards for senior students, without separating their cards from the rest of the file. When the report is finished, all the cards are in the file in the same order. This processing method, which is described later in this book, does away with the selecting and removing of the cards for senior students from the file. It also eliminates the merging of the cards when the report is completed.

System for processing proxies

A *proxy* is a document or form that gives one person the power to act for another person. Corporations hold annual meetings, at which time directors are elected by the stockholders. The stockholders are also asked to vote for or against other matters that are properly brought before the stockholders for action.

Proxies are sent to all stockholders so those who cannot attend the meeting may vote by mail. The reverse side of the proxy used in this discussion is shown in Figure 3-19. The front side has boxes in which the stockholders can record their votes on the different issues covered in the proxy. This proxy is an example of a punched card used as a business form.

The reverse side of the proxy, shown in Figure 3-19, includes the stockholder's account number (238951), which is prepunched in the card. The number of shares owned (600) is not punched in the card.

When the proxy is sent back by the stockholder, properly dated and signed, the stockholder's voting choices on the issues are keypunched into the card. A vote FOR the election of directors is punched as 1 in a specified column, for example. A vote AGAINST is punched as 2 in the same column. A vote FOR the appointment of an accounting firm is punched as 1 in a certain column. A vote AGAINST is punched as 2 in the same column. If no choice is given for either proposal, a FOR vote

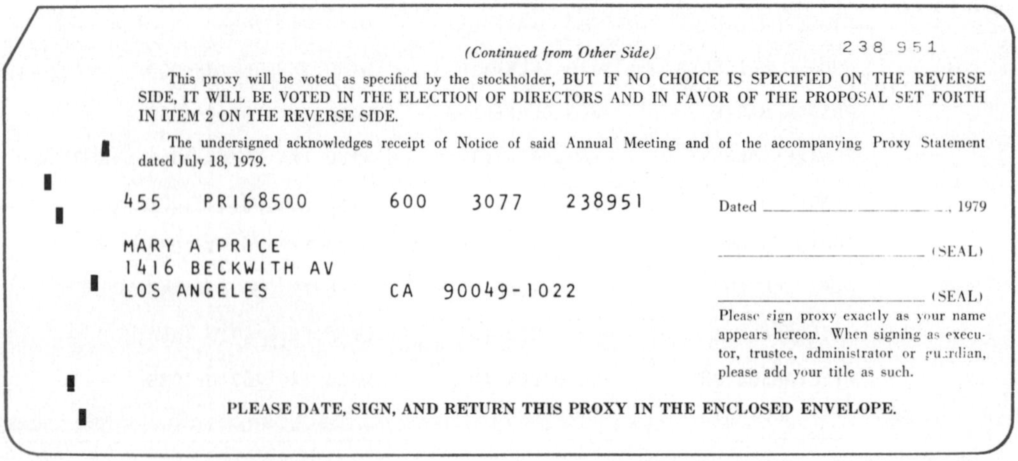

(Continued from Other Side) 238 951

This proxy will be voted as specified by the stockholder, BUT IF NO CHOICE IS SPECIFIED ON THE REVERSE SIDE, IT WILL BE VOTED IN THE ELECTION OF DIRECTORS AND IN FAVOR OF THE PROPOSAL SET FORTH IN ITEM 2 ON THE REVERSE SIDE.

The undersigned acknowledges receipt of Notice of said Annual Meeting and of the accompanying Proxy Statement dated July 18, 1979.

455 PR168500 600 3077 238951

Dated ______________, 1979

MARY A PRICE
1416 BECKWITH AV
LOS ANGELES CA 90049-1022

______________ (SEAL)

______________ (SEAL)

Please sign proxy exactly as your name appears hereon. When signing as executor, trustee, administrator or guardian, please add your title as such.

PLEASE DATE, SIGN, AND RETURN THIS PROXY IN THE ENCLOSED ENVELOPE.

Figure 3-19. *A punched card can be used as a proxy.*

(1 punch) is recorded. The number of shares owned by the stockholder are punched in the card at this time.

Proxy votes are counted before the meeting and are added to the votes cast by the stockholders who are present at the meeting. Stockholders are allowed one vote for each share of stock held. The results of the balloting are given at the meeting.

The system described here begins with the receipt of the proxy cards from the stockholders. It ends with a printed report of the number of proxies received, the number of shares represented by these proxies, the number of FOR votes for each proposal, and the number of AGAINST votes for each proposal. A program is stored in the computer to read the data in the cards, to perform the calculations, and to print a report of the results. The goal of the system is to produce the report.

The flowchart of a system for preparing the proxy voting report is shown in Figure 3-20. The explanation with the flowchart describes the steps in the system. An example copy of the report produced by the system is illustrated in Figure 3-21.

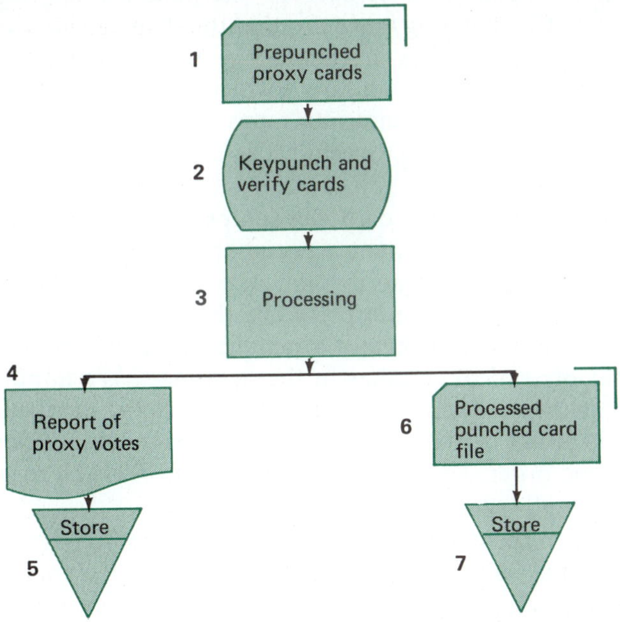

EXPLANATION

1. The prepunched proxy cards are received into the system, and the
2. voting preferences for each of the proposals and number of shares of stock are punched and verified in the proxy cards.
3. A count is made of the number of cards received. The number of shares represented are counted. The number of votes cast FOR and AGAINST each proposal are also counted. The count is based on the number of shares held by each stockholder.
4. The results are printed in the proper form as a report, which is
5. stored until needed.
6. The processed file of cards is
7. stored until needed.

Figure 3-20. *The above flowchart is for a system for preparing a proxy voting report with a computer.*

TOTAL PROXIES RECEIVED	1,200
TOTAL SHARES REPRESENTED BY PROXIES	50,000
FOR VOTES FOR ELECTION OF DIRECTORS	40,000
AGAINST VOTES FOR ELECTION OF DIRECTORS	10,000
FOR VOTES FOR APPOINTMENT OF ACCOUNTING FIRM	48,000
AGAINST VOTES FOR APPOINTMENT OF ACCOUNTING FIRM	2,000

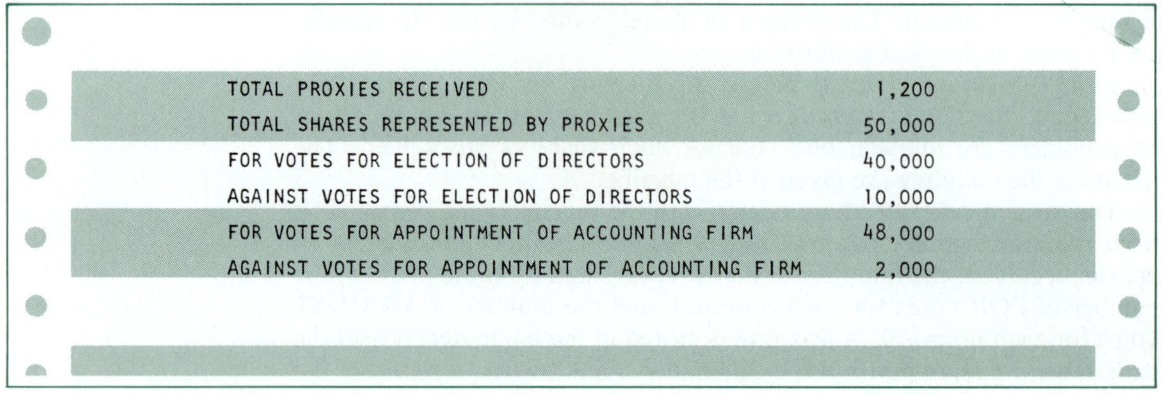

Figure 3-21. *Above is a copy of the proxy report produced by the system.*

SUMMARY

As an input medium for computers, the punched card has a number of advantages. Chief among these are that the data can be seen and read. Also, punched card records are similar in format to magnetic tape and disk records. Anyone knowing how to record data in cards can readily change to the recording of data into tapes and disks. The punched card is not as popular as it once was, but it is still used a great deal in computer applications.

The standard 80-column card can represent all digits 0 through 9, all letters of the alphabet, and many special characters. Only one character can be punched into a single column of a card, however. The printed matter on a card cannot be interpreted by the processing machines.

The different items of data in a punched card are recorded in fields. The number of vertical columns in the field may vary in number. However, the number of columns for a particular field, such as a customer number field, must be the same in all the cards in a file. The fields must be in the same order, and the same type of data must be recorded in the same fields for all the cards in a file.

If fewer than the maximum number of columns in a numeric field are used, zeros must be added at the left to fill the field. Zeros are not used in alphabetic fields to fill unused columns. Spaces are used at the right instead.

Standardization is important in planning input records. The processing machines identify information by its location on a record. Each item in a transaction must be fully identified. Each must appear on a separate record.

The punching positions on a 96-column card are based on a two-digit numbering system. The card is smaller, but it can hold 20 percent more data than the 80-column card.

A keypunch is used to record data in cards. The keyboard is like that found on a typewriter. Repeated data in cards can be punched in succeeding cards automatically. Only variable data need to be manually recorded.

Punched data can be verified in several ways. The most common method is to rekey the data with a card verifier. If the punches in the card match in the rekeying operation, it is assumed that no mistake has been made. If the punches do not match, a mistake has been made, which is corrected by punching an entirely new card. Keypunches with memory units allow the correction of errors as data are rekeyed into a buffer. When the data for a complete card are keyed into memory, the corrected data, if any, are automatically punched into the card.

REVIEW QUESTIONS

1. What feature of the keypunch makes it unnecessary to key repeated data manually into succeeding cards?
2. How are variable data punched into a card?
3. What is the chief difference in the arrangement of the number of keys on a keypunch as compared with the same keys on a standard typewriter?
4. How are punching mistakes found and corrected when a card verifier is used?
5. What is the chief advantage of using keypunch machines with built-in memory units?
6. What source document is used in the application problem explained and illustrated in this chapter on processing student enrollments?
7. What are the input and the input medium for the problem in Question 6?
8. In addition to the processed cards, what is the output in Question 6?
9. What is the input for the application problem explained in this chapter for processing proxies by management?
10. What output is produced by the system in the problem in Question 9?

NEW TERMS

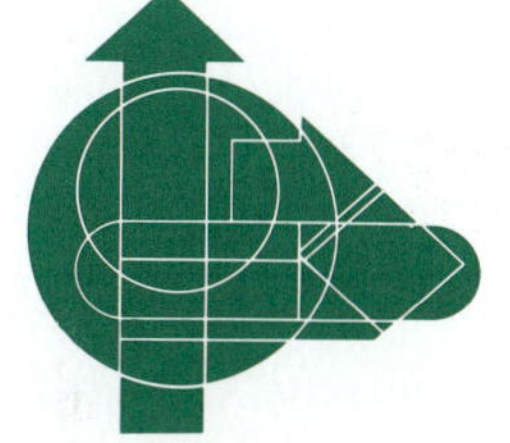

- Binary code
- Column (card)
- Digit
- 11 position
- Field (card)
- Keypunch
- 9 edge
- Proxy
- Punched card
- Row (card)
- 12 edge
- 12 position
- Verifier (card)
- X position
- Y position
- Zone punch

STUDY GUIDE

Complete Study Guide 3 by following the instructions in your STUDY GUIDES booklet.

PROJECTS

Complete Projects 3-1 and 3-2 by following the instructions in your PROJECTS booklet.

4

DESIGNING RECORDS for AUTOMATED EQUIPMENT

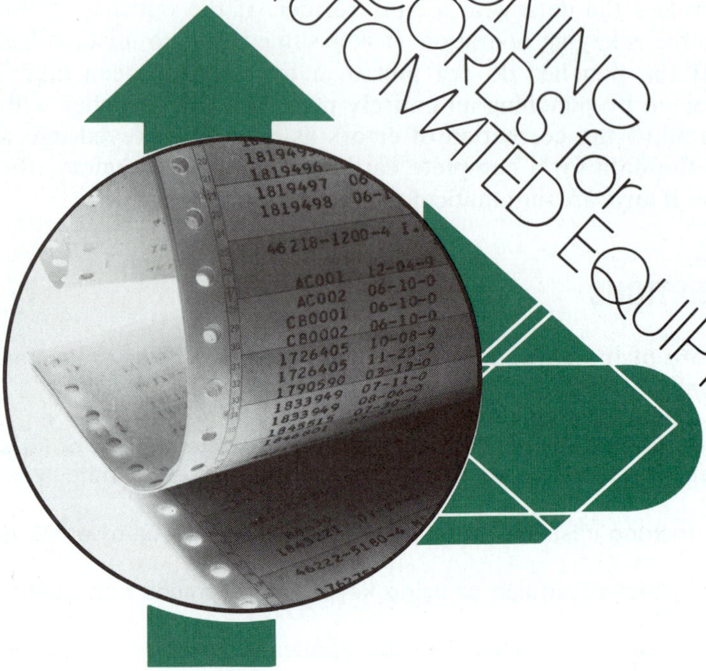

In data processing, creating and using records is the goal. Records take the guesswork out of decision making. Because wrong decisions can ruin a business, it is very important that correct records be ready when and where they are needed.

For example, a florist must know how many flowers and plants will be needed for the Christmas holidays. If too many are ordered, the florist loses money. If too few are stocked, business is lost. Last year's records of purchases and sales will help the florist make decisions.

An insurance company needs to know when to send out premium notices (bills) to its policyholders. A teacher needs to know what final grades have been earned by students in each class. A taxpayer needs to keep careful records of earnings and deductible expenses. In these cases and many more, records play a vital part in the decisions that must be made.

DATA ORGANIZATION

The data needed to produce the kinds of information a business or a person needs are logically organized into files, records, and data fields or *items*.

Files

You have already learned that a file is a collection of related records treated as a unit. A file may be a manila folder holding a number of related records like the names of customers and their addresses. In electronic data processing, a file may be made up of a deck of punched cards, a reel of magnetic tape, a magnetic disk, or data recorded on some other medium acceptable to the computer.

See Figure 4-1 for the cards in a partial illustration of a file of information about customers. Note that the file is made up of many records. Note, also, that all the records contain the same kinds of data. The file contains customers' numbers, names, addresses, and, in this case, their credit limits. Note that each record contains the name of a different customer. Also, the different fields of information in each record appear in the same columns.

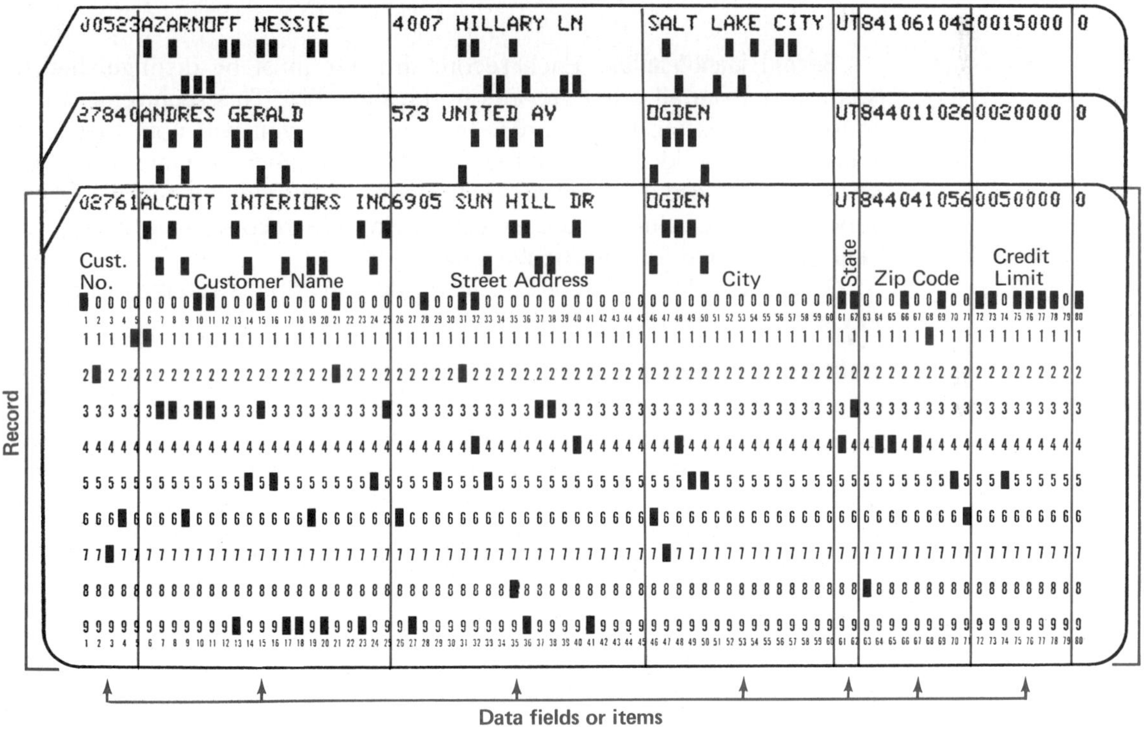

Figure 4-1. *All the records in a file are made up of fields of similar data.*

Records

A *record* is a group of related data items treated as a unit. In Figure 4-1, each punched card in the file is a record. Each card holds data about a customer. Each card is a single unit in a file. As you already know, a group of similar records make up a file.

The same kinds of data could also be entered on segments of magnetic tapes or disks. Each segment would be considered a record, and all similar records entered on a magnetic tape or disk would make up a file.

The word *magnetic* in this book is used to refer to an input, output, or storage medium that holds data in code form as positive or negative electric charges.

Unit record principle. A *unit record* is a record in which all data about a single person or transaction are entered on a separate record. A punched card is a unit record. As you noted in Figure 4-1, each punched card contains information about only one customer.

Later you will learn that each card in a sales file, for example, may contain data about a single item sold to a customer. A separate card must be punched for each item sold. However, each card must contain all the information needed about the item. The customer name or number, the date of sale, the name and number of the item sold, its price per unit, and the total price are examples of items or fields in a unit record.

Record identification. Each record in a file must be distinguished in some way from all other records in the same file. This requirement is a must in processing the records. In Figure 4-1, you will note that each record could be identified by the customer's number or name. The data in these fields are different on each record. The identification is used in processing operations, such as sequencing the records in a file or for searching the file for a particular record.

The data field in a record used for identification is referred to as the *key* or the *key field*.

Data fields or items

Card fields were discussed in Chapter 3, so this explanation will not be new to you. In a punched card, the vertical column or group of consecutive columns set aside to record a single fact is known as a field. On magnetic tapes or disks, a single space or group of consecutive spaces needed to record a single fact is known as a *field*. A field in a record is often referred to as a *data item*.

Note that each punched card in Figure 4-1 contains seven data fields. Can you name them? Finally, look at Figure 4-1 again. Note the relationship between a file, a record, and a field or data item.

KINDS OF FILES

The records in files are used to solve data processing problems. Rarely are all the data needed in solving a particular problem in a single file. The records in several files must be brought together and used. Four kinds of files are in common use. They are master, detail, balance, and summary files.

Master files

Master files are files that contain relatively permanent records. Figure 4-1, p. 67, shows a part of a master file. It contains the records of customers that are updated whenever there is a change, such as a new address or a change in credit limit. The punch in Column 80 of the card is a zero punch. This punch is a transaction code, which will be explained later in this chapter. Any record from a master file is a *master record*.

Some reports may be prepared from only the master records. For example, an alphabetized list of customers for a certain state may be prepared. Records for that state are first selected from the file and placed in alphabetic order. The customers' names are then printed. All these steps can be automatic. More often than not, however, records from other files will also be needed.

Detail files

A *detail file* contains records of day-to-day transactions. A *sales detail file* contains records of sales to customers. A separate record is needed for each item sold. A *payments detail file* contains records of payments on accounts received from customers. A separate record is needed for each payment received. There are other detail files, such as a file of stock received or a file of stock shipped out. Any record from a detail file is called a *detail record*.

Sales detail records. Figure 4-2 shows sales detail records that are used in preparing an invoice. An *invoice* is a business form that lists all the goods shipped, giving the date, price, terms of sale, and other important information. Note that there are three sales detail records with the invoice in Figure 4-2. Note also that a separate record is prepared for each item sold. Figure 4-2 is shown on p. 70.

Note the fields or data items included in each record (card) in Figure 4-2. They are (1) customer number, (2) invoice number, (3) salesperson code, (4) date, (5) stock number of items sold, (6) quantity, (7) price per unit, and (8) total amount. Each punched card in Figure 4-2 has eight fields. From the data in these fields, a great many reports important to management can be prepared. The 2 punch in Column 80 of the sales detail card is a transaction code, which will be explained later in this chapter.

Payments detail records. A payments detail record is used to process payments received from a customer. Note the payments record shown in Figure 4-3. It has the customer number, date payment was received, and the amount received. A similar detail record is prepared each time the customer makes another payment on account.

The 4 punch in Column 80 of the card is a transaction code, which will be explained later.

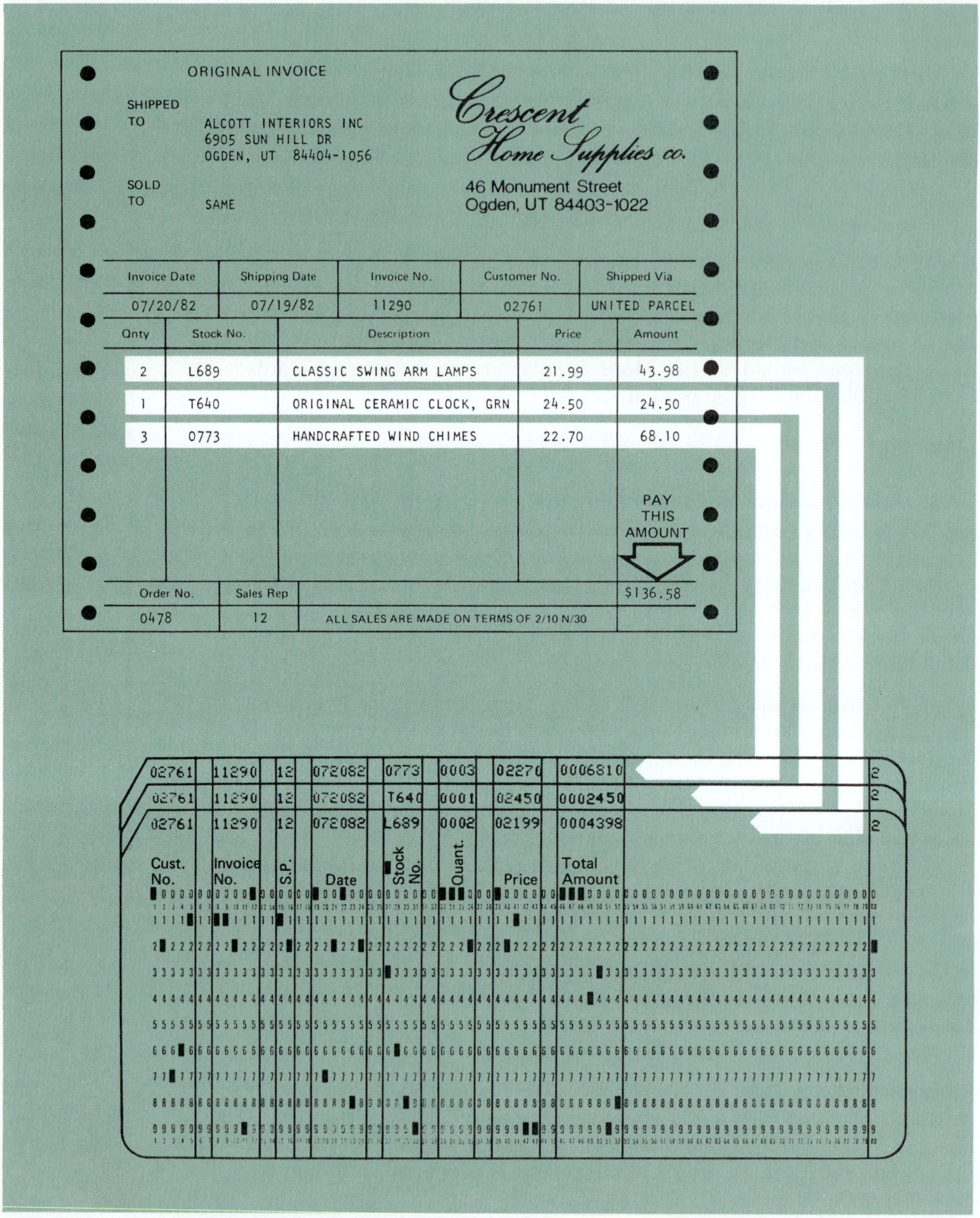

Figure 4-2. *Sales detail records are used to prepare an invoice.*

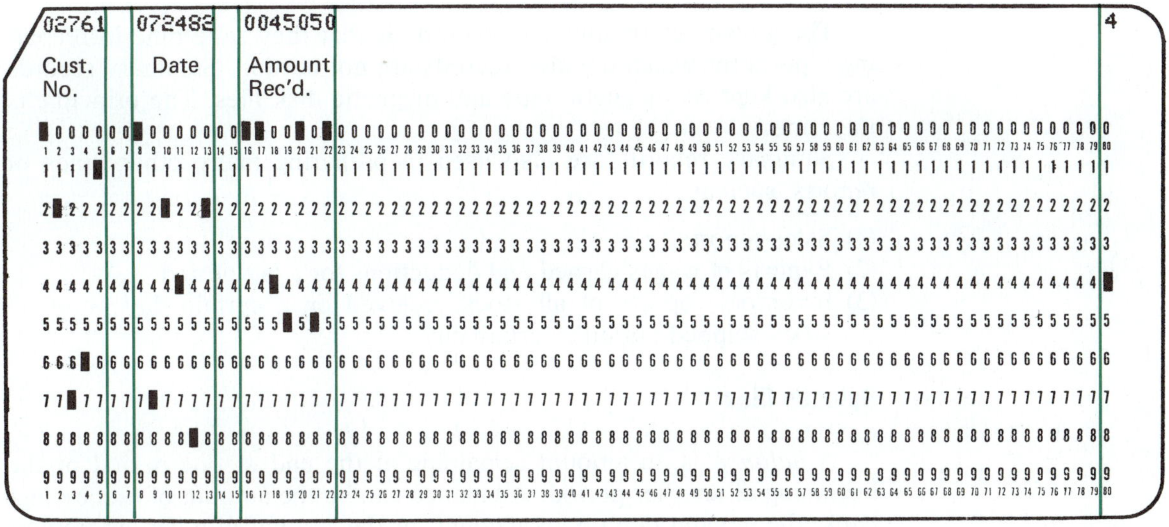

Figure 4-3. *A payments detail record shows the payment made on a certain date.*

Summary files

A *summary file record* or *summary record* summarizes the transactions of similar detail records. The punched card in Figure 4-4 summarizes the data in the sales detail cards listed in the invoice in Figure 4-2. It shows the customer number, date of the invoice, invoice number, and total amount of all the sales shown in Figure 4-2. These data are used in preparing end-of-the-month statements to customers. The statements show all the sales for a certain invoice, but each item is not listed separately.

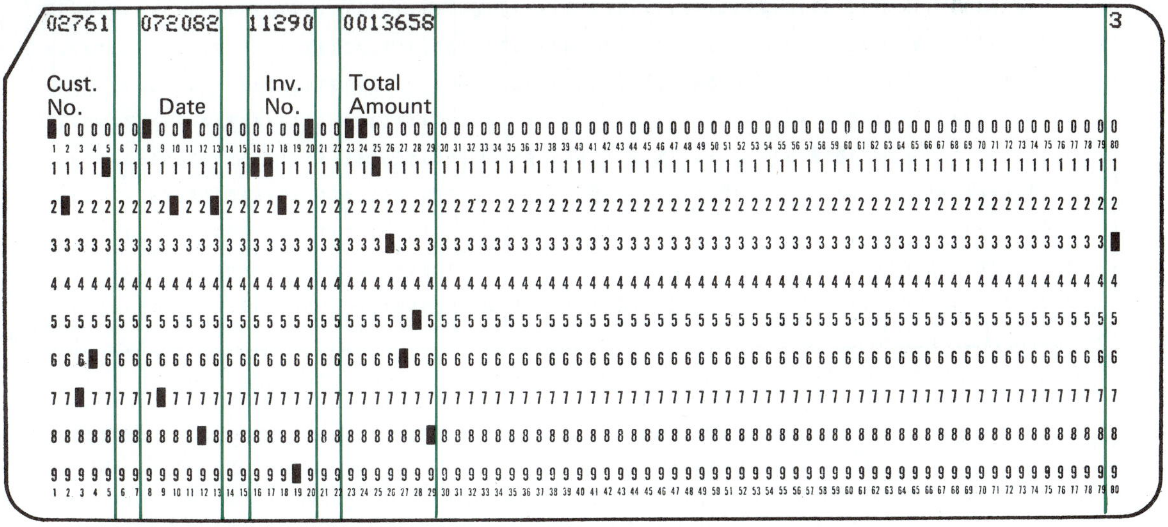

Figure 4-4. *The sales summary record summarizes all sales transactions on a given date.*

The advantage of summary records is that they save time in preparing reports for which detailed records are not needed. Summary records are also kept on magnetic tape and magnetic disk files. The principle is the same.

Summary records are also used in preparing many other kinds of reports, such as:

(1) Sales reports.
(2) Reports of wages earned and deductions for a tax period.
(3) Inventory reports of all stock received on a certain day or of all stock shipped out on a certain day.

Balance files

A *balance* is an amount remaining at the end of one period or the beginning of another period. A balance can be the amount of money in a bank, the amount due on an account, or the amount of a certain item of stock on hand on a certain date. A *balance file* is made up of records that show a balance of some kind for a certain date. The punched card in Figure 4-5, for example, shows the amount owed by the customer on the date shown on the card. The card contains the customer's number, date at the end of the period, the amount owed by the customer at that time, and the branch number. The same balance card can be used to show the amount owed by the customer at the beginning of the next period. A *balance record* is a record in a balance file.

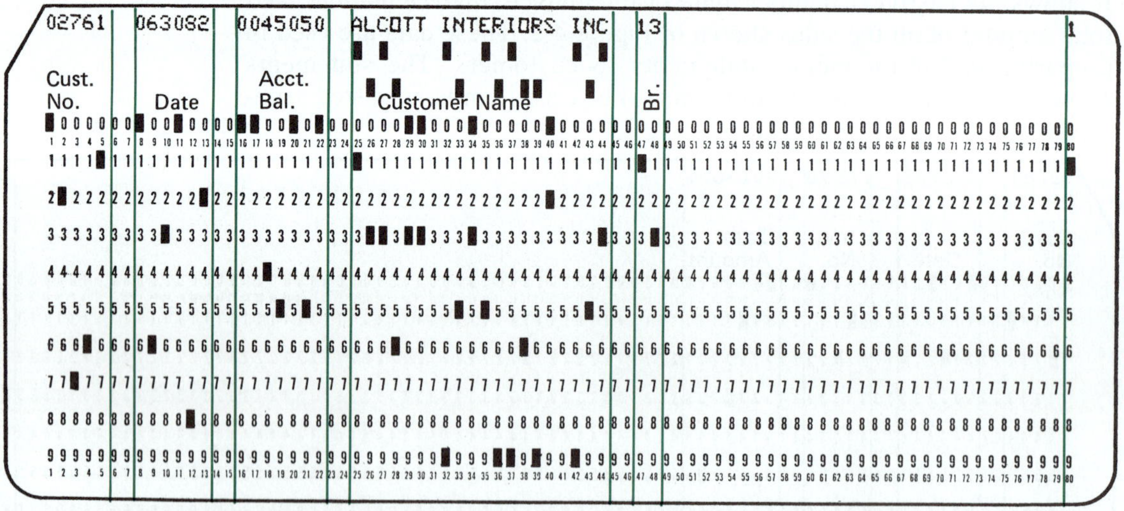

Figure 4-5. *The balance record shows the account balance on a given date.*

Balance records are used to prepare end-of-the-month statements. They are also used to prepare reports of accounts receivable, in which customer names and amounts owed by them are listed. Balance records could also be used to prepare a report showing the amount of each item of stock on hand or the amount of money in each account in a bank on a certain date.

Other files

If customers receive credit allowances for defective merchandise or items returned, another detail file is needed. The problems in this text will not use another detail file, however.

TRANSACTION CODES

There are several meanings to the word, transaction. In this book, a *transaction* is an act carried out while handling business. A transaction takes place between at least two people or two businesses. When you buy something, you, as the buyer, are having a transaction with the seller.

Many types of data records and files are required in preparing business reports of transactions. Master files, detail files, summary files, and balance files have been shown in this chapter. Because the records in the files are different, some method must be used to enable the computer to distinguish one kind of data record from another. Usually a transaction code is used for this purpose.

Using the transaction code, a programmer can write a program to direct the computer to perform the calculations needed to prepare a report and to print the results. In the records shown in this chapter:

(1) Master records have a zero punch in Column 80. This punch can direct the computer to have the customer's name and address printed on three lines or only one line, depending on the program.
(2) Balance records have a 1 punch in Column 80, which will direct the computer to print the data or to add or subtract, depending on the program.
(3) Sales detail records have a 2 punch in Column 80, which will direct the computer to add or subtract, according to the program. If the items are shipped to a customer, the amount could be added to a sales invoice. If, on the other hand, the computer is processing an inventory program, the items could be subtracted from the stock on hand.
(4) Sales summary records are identified by a 3 punch in Column 80. The 3 punch can direct the computer to add or subtract, depending on the program.
(5) Payments detail records have a 4 punch in Column 80. Again, according to the program, this punch could tell the computer to subtract the customer's payment from the amount still owed. On the other hand, the 4 punch could tell the computer to add the amount paid to a list of payments received from all customers for the month.

Sometimes the transaction code is in the last field in a record. Sometimes it is in the first. It can be anywhere the programmer wishes it to be. A *transaction code* may be defined as a code recorded in a specific field of a data card, tape, or disk record, which code makes it possible for the computer to distinguish one kind of record from another and to perform an operation according to program instructions.

CONTROL CODES

A transaction code should not be confused with a control code. As indicated earlier, transaction codes distinguish one data record from another. A *control code*, on the other hand, gives the computer special instructions about the program itself. Control codes will be described later in this book.

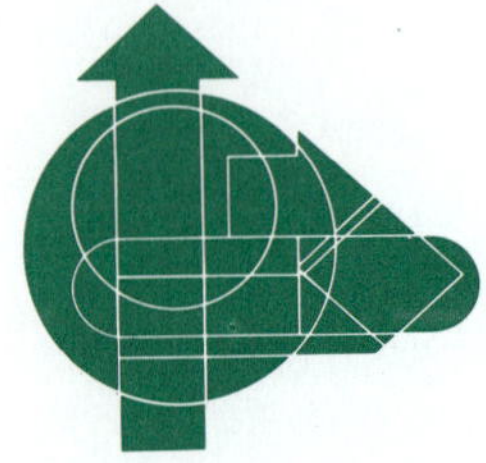

REVIEW QUESTIONS

1. What is a *file*?
2. Name three types of media that may be used for files in electronic data processing?
3. What is a *record*?
4. What is a *unit record*? Give an example of a unit record.
5. May a single card include information on more than one customer or student?
6. Name two ways in which the records in a customer file may be distinguished one from the other.
7. What is the *key* or the *key field*?
8. What is a *field* in a punched card record?
9. What kinds of fields or data items would be included in a master file of customer records?
10. What kinds of records are usually kept in detail files? Give an example of a field or data item in a payments detail record for customers.
11. What four fields of information are included in the sales summary file record shown in Figure 4-4, p. 71?
12. What is the purpose of a transaction code? In what card column must transaction codes be recorded?
13. Can transaction codes be used with tape and disk records?

REPORT PREPARATION

Many types of problems can be solved from the records in the master, detail, summary, and balance files. In business data processing, these problems are about the following:

(1) Keeping records of routine transactions.
(2) Preparing reports from these transactions.
(3) Updating the files.
(4) Preparing operating reports for management.
(5) Preparing communications.
(6) Preparing a variety of special reports.

Keeping records of routine transactions

An example of records that a business keeps for routine transactions are those used in reporting sales to customers and payments received from them. These records have been explained earlier. Other examples are the records that must be made for:

(1) Purchases of goods to be sold or used in the manufacture of a product.
(2) Various expenses incurred in running the business.
(3) Hours worked by employees so that payrolls, salary checks, and tax reports can be prepared.
(4) Purchase of equipment used in running a business.
(5) Costs incurred in remodeling office and plant facilities.

Preparing reports from transaction records

Many reports can be prepared from transaction records. The invoice shown in Figure 4-2 was prepared by combining the master customer file records with the sales detail records.

Preparing an invoice. Figure 4-6 shows a flowchart for a system for preparing an invoice. It is assumed in this flowchart that the customer's purchase order has already been approved by the system explained in Chapter 1. Note that cards will be keypunched for new customers. These cards will be sequenced in numeric order according to customer number and merged with the master customer card file in an updating operation. After the master customer file has been updated, the master records are combined with the sales detail records to produce an invoice similar to the one in Figure 4-2.

Output after processing will include the invoice, the updated master customer file, and the sales detail file. When the computer totals the amount of the invoice, a sales summary record will be produced as output also. This sales summary record will be used later in preparing the statement of account. Figure 4-6 is shown on p. 76.

Preparing a statement of account. A statement of account is prepared from the records of sales to customers and of payments received from them. A *statement of account* is a form that summarizes the charges to a customer's account, the payments made, and the balance due. This statement is usually sent to the customer monthly. The date of the statement is shown as well as the account balance at the beginning of the month. The statement also shows the charges made by the customer, along with the dates. Also shown are the payments received, with the dates. Finally, the balance due from the customer at the end of the month is shown.

See Figure 4-7, in which the records needed to prepare a statement of account are shown. The customer data at the top of the form is taken from the master record. The beginning balance record is the same record that was prepared at the end of the preceding month.

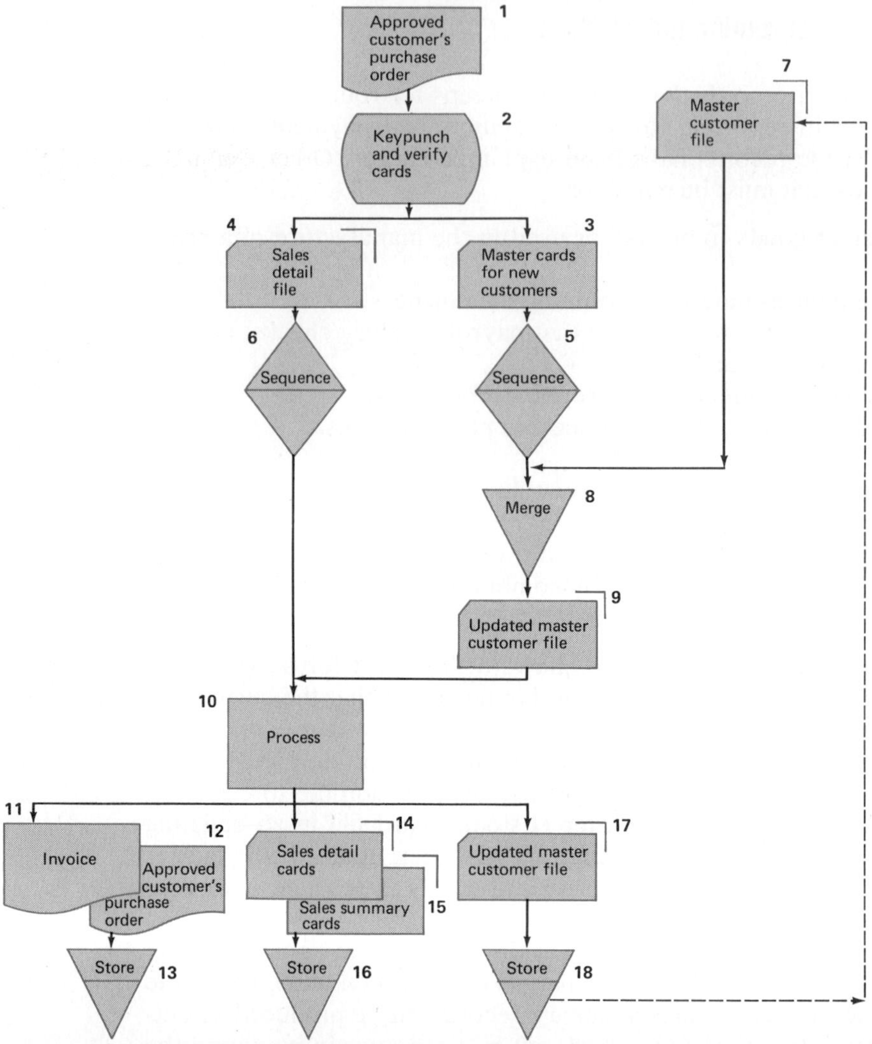

EXPLANATION

1. From the approved customer's purchase order,
2. cards are keypunched and verified, giving
3. a master card for a new customer and
4. a separate sales detail card for each item on each purchase order.
5. Master cards for new customers are sequenced in numeric order according to customer number.
6. Sales detail cards are sequenced in numeric order according to customer number.
7. The master customer file is then
8. merged with the master cards for new customers, producing
9. an updated master customer file, which is combined with the sales detail file.
10. Processing produces as output
11. an invoice showing all the items of stock purchased, with the total amount of each sale.
12. The approved customer's order is
13. stored temporarily.
14. Output also includes the sales detail cards for each item on each invoice and
15. sales summary cards, giving the total sales record on each invoice.
16. The sales detail cards and sales summary cards are stored temporarily.
17. The updated master customer card file is
18. stored temporarily until needed in this or some other data processing application.

Figure 4-6. *Customers' master cards are combined with sales detail cards to produce an invoice.*

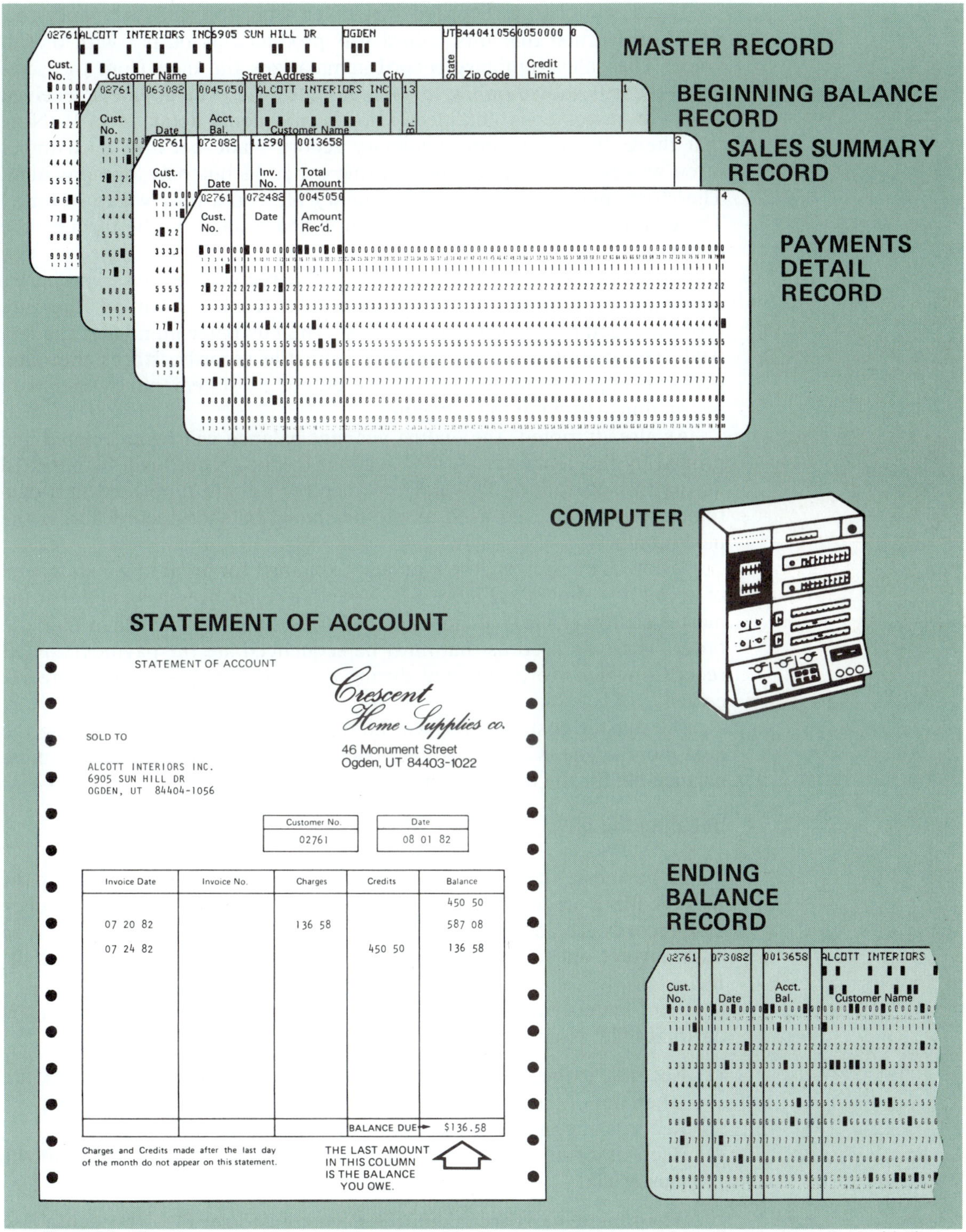

Figure 4-7. *The statement of account is prepared by the computer by combining the master record with the beginning balance record, the sales summary record, and the payments detail record.*

The single charge recorded was taken from the sales summary record. You learned that this record was produced as output with the invoice. The sales summary record summarizes the data from the sales detail records shown on the invoice in Figure 4-2. The payment received from the customer is obtained from the payments detail record. (Note that there is no payments summary record made because a customer often makes several purchases during a period but only one payment. Therefore, making a payments summary file could be a waste of time.) The ending balance would be calculated and printed on the form by the computer.

The customer number appears on all the records needed to prepare a statement of account. Therefore, the data from the various files are brought together by customer number. The customer number is the key field. The computer reads the data from the records, stores the data, performs calculations, and prints the output on statements by means of instructions stored in the computer.

As already noted, the ending account balance will be calculated and printed by the computer. A new account balance record will be punched during this operation. This new balance record will be placed in a customer balance file and used as the beginning balance record during the next month.

A flowchart showing the plan just explained for preparing a statement of account is shown in Figure 4-8. Note that it has been assumed that the master customer file, balance file, and sales summary file are in numeric order. The only records that must be sequenced are the payments detail records, which were punched during the month as payments were received.

The master customer file will be used again as necessary during the next month. The ending customer balance file will become the beginning balance file for the next month.

Updating the files

In business, data processing is often concerned with updating the files. A file is updated when the continuing records are kept and when new records are added. Also, records needing changes must be replaced with correct ones, and discontinued records must be taken out of the file.

See Figure 4-9, p. 80. It illustrates the process of updating a master customer file. Note that:

(1) Records to be changed and records of terminating customers are taken out of the master file.
(2) Records of continuing customers are kept in the file.
(3) Records of new customers and corrected records are added to the master file.

When these steps are taken, the master customer file is brought up to date. The flowchart of a system for solving this problem is shown in Figure 4-10, p. 81.

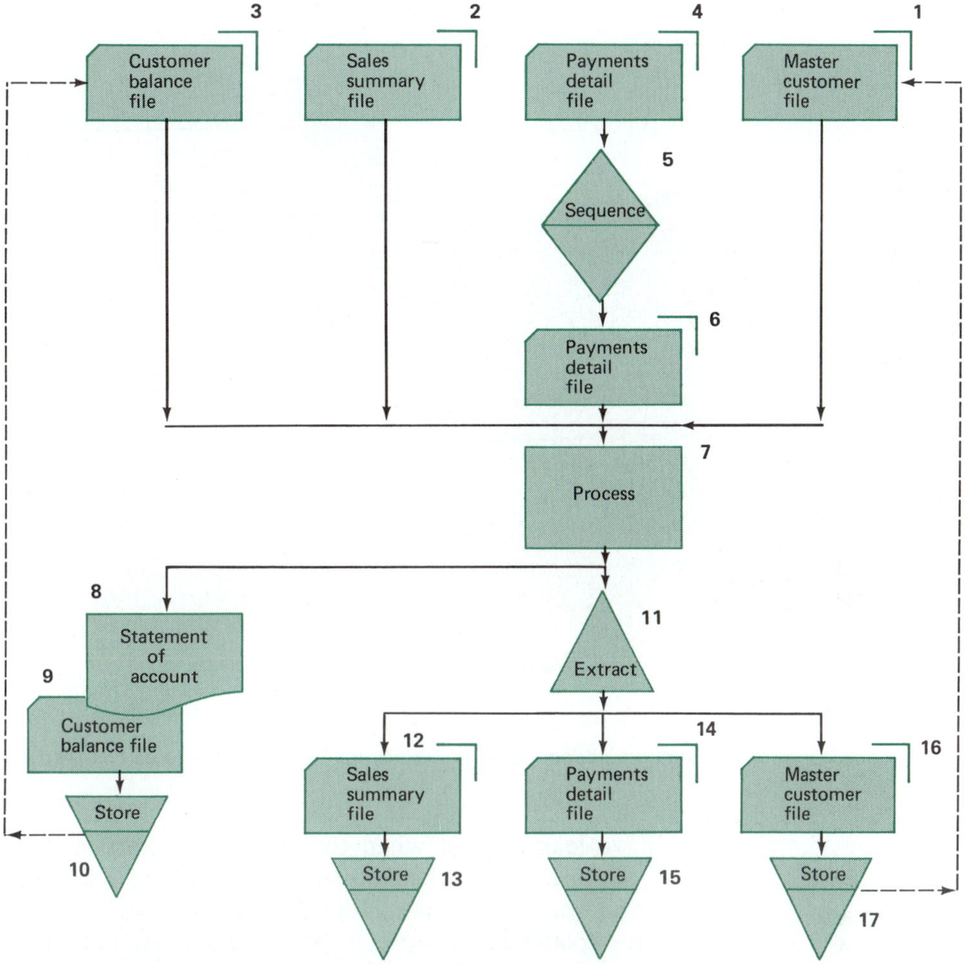

EXPLANATION

1. The master customer file and . .
2. the sales summary file have been in numeric order by customer number since processing to produce the invoices at different times during the month. (See Figure 4-6).
3. The customer balance file has been in numeric order since processing the statements of account from the previous month.
4. The payments detail file is made up of cards showing payments at different times during the month and is
5. sequenced into numeric order by customer number, giving a
6. sequenced payments detail file.
7. The master customer file is combined with the customer balance file, sales summary file, and payments detail file. Output consists of
8. the statements of account and
9. the customer balance file with the ending balances,
10. which is stored temporarily and which becomes the beginning balance file for the next month.
11. The files that have been combined to produce the output must be separated (extracted) again into separate files.
12. The sales summary file
13. is stored temporarily.
14. The payments detail file is
15. stored temporarily.
16. The master customer file is
17. stored temporarily and becomes the master customer file for the next time that the data must be processed.

Figure 4-8. *The master record is combined with the detail records to prepare a statement of account.*

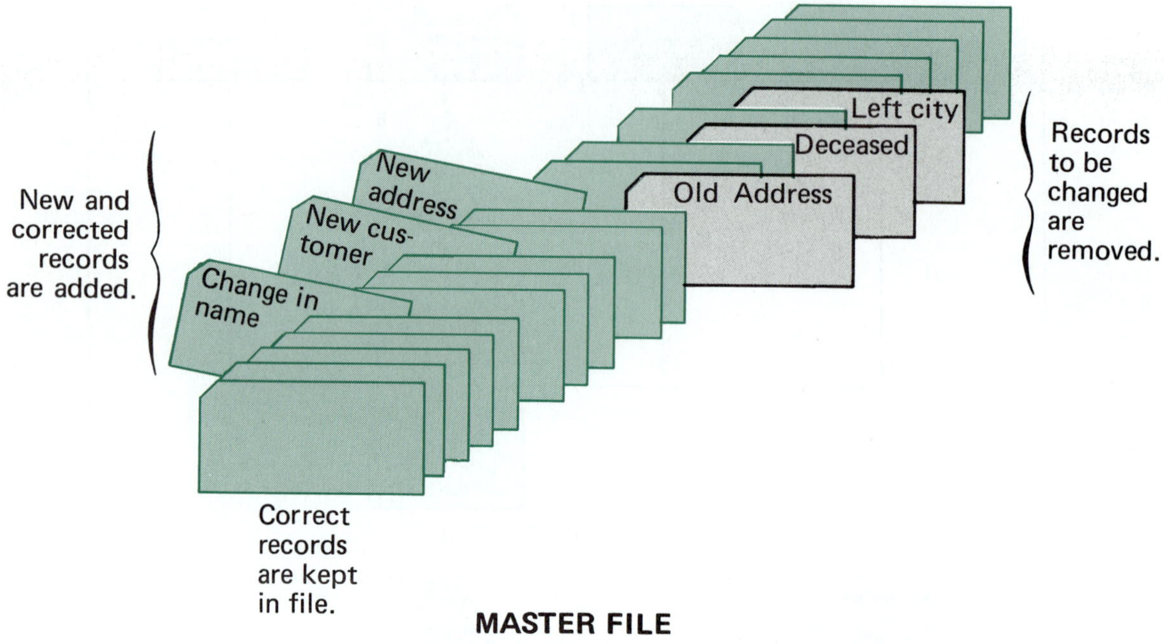

Figure 4-9. *New and corrected records are added. Current records are kept. Records to be changed are taken out of the file.*

You have learned that when the customer's purchase orders were received, the order clerk checked to see if there were any new customers. Order numbers were then assigned to the new customers. This procedure was explained in Chapter 1. These new customers were added to the master file at the time the invoices were prepared. However, there are other applications for credit received from people who have opened accounts and have not made any purchases as yet. The approved credit applications for these new customers as well as the notices of corrections are the source documents for the flowchart in Figure 4-10.

The system itself is shown in Figure 4-11. Note that each step in the system is shown in complete sentence form, not in the same form as the explanation that accompanies the flowchart. The explanation with the flowchart is shortened and is only given to make the flowchart clearer. An actual system would be written out in a manner similar to Figure 4-11.

Note that the output from the system includes the updated master punched card file. New punched card records replace the old ones when corrections are made. When a record is to be discontinued and "pulled" from the master file, the punched card in the corrections file will have the same customer number. A transaction code in the correction record will tell the computer that the customer's card should be taken from the file.

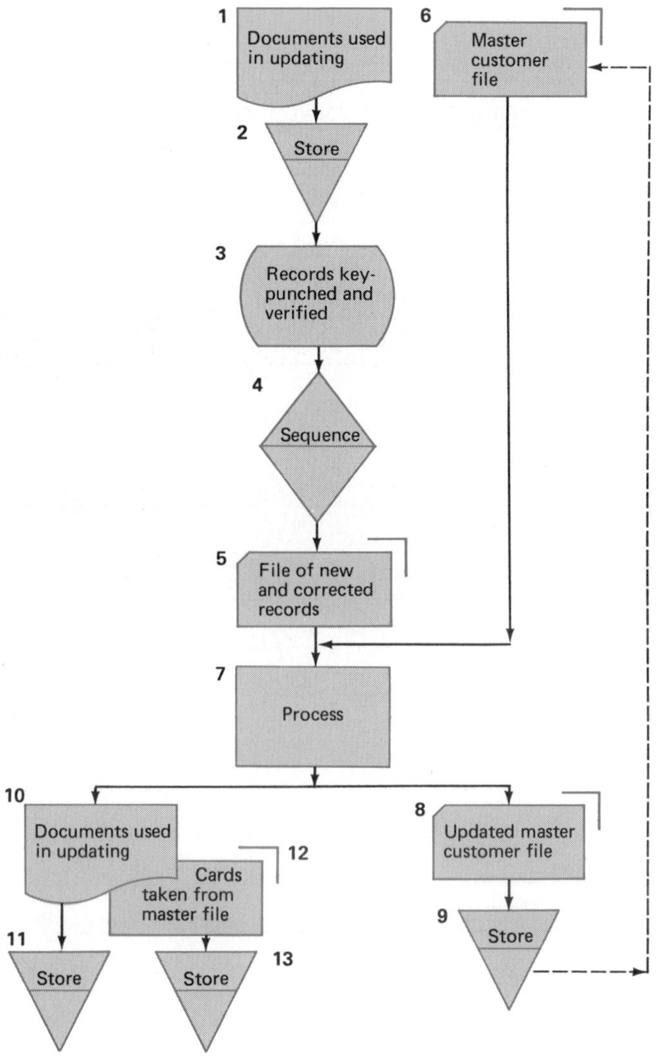

EXPLANATION

1. Source documents used in updating are
2. stored temporarily.
3. From these documents, punched card records are keypunched and verified.
4. The records are then sequenced in numeric order according to customer number, thus creating
5. a file of new and corrected master records.
6. The master customer file and the file of new and corrected records are
7. processed together. Processing includes the merging of the master customer file and the file of new and corrected records. Processing also includes extracting (selecting) from the file the records that have been discontinued or corrected.
8. Output includes the updated master customer file, which is
9. stored temporarily.
10. The documents used in the updating operation are
11. stored temporarily.
12. The discontinued and corrected card records are
13. stored temporarily.

Figure 4-10. *This flowchart shows how a master file is updated by adding new and corrected records and withdrawing discontinued and corrected records.*

Step No.	Procedure
1	APPROVED CREDIT APPLICATIONS OF NEW CUSTOMERS AND MEMORANDA CONTAINING DATA ABOUT CORRECTIONS AND TERMINATIONS ARE USED AS SOURCE DOCUMENTS.
2	THESE DOCUMENTS ARE FILED TEMPORARILY.
3	RECORDS OF ADDITIONS AND CORRECTIONS ARE KEYPUNCHED AND VERIFIED.
4	PUNCHED CARDS ARE SEQUENCED IN NUMERIC ORDER.
5	THE SEQUENCED CARDS BECOME A FILE OF NEW AND CORRECTED MASTER RECORDS.
6	THE MASTER CUSTOMER FILE OF RECORDS THAT ARE ALREADY IN NUMERIC ORDER ENTER THE SYSTEM ALONG WITH THE FILE OF NEW AND CORRECTED RECORDS.
7	PROCESSING INCLUDES EXTRACTING OR WITHDRAWING OF DISCONTINUED AND CORRECTED RECORDS AND ADDITION OF NEW RECORDS.
8	AN UPDATED MASTER CUSTOMER FILE IS CREATED.
9	THIS FILE IS STORED TEMPORARILY UNTIL NEEDED, WHEN IT BECOMES THE MASTER CUSTOMER FILE FOR THE NEXT DATA PROCESSING OPERATION.
10	REMAINING ARE THE SOURCE DOCUMENTS USED FOR UPDATING THE FILE.
11	THESE SOURCE DOCUMENTS ARE STORED TEMPORARILY.
12	THE FILE OF CARDS OF DISCONTINUED CUSTOMERS AND CORRECTIONS REMAINS.
13	THESE CARDS ARE ALSO STORED TEMPORARILY.

Figure 4-11. *The above is a system for updating a master customer file.*

A telephone directory is brought up to date by keeping the records of continuing users, by adding the records of new users, by taking out the records that have been changed and replacing them with corrected records, and by taking out the records of terminated users.

Two other examples of updating files were explained and shown in Chapter 2. In the first example, a master enrollment file was updated due to new enrollments. New enrollment forms were filled out and filed temporarily. From time to time, these forms were sequenced and merged with the forms in the master file. As a result, the master file was updated. A flowchart showing this process appears in Figure 2-11, p. 32.

In the second example, the employees' earnings file was updated by recording earnings and deductions for the pay period in each employee's earnings record. These data, when added to those entered in the records for previous payroll periods, updated the file. A flowchart illustrating this process is shown in Figure 2-18, p. 38.

Preparing operating reports for management

Operating reports keep management in touch with the financial condition of a business. A good example is a report of accounts receivable (amounts due on accounts.) This report lists alphabetically the name of each customer and the amount owed by each at the end of the period. At the end of the report is shown the total of all amounts owed.

This report can be prepared by using the customer balance file of records punched at the end of the period. This file contains the records of the customers' names and the amounts owed by each. A customer balance record was shown in Figure 4-5, p. 72. The customer balance file is in numeric order by customer number. The file of punched balance cards will have to be sorted into alphabetic order for this report. This time the cards will be sorted on the customer name field rather than the customer number field.

The flowchart of a system for preparing this report is shown in Figure 4-12, next page.

Operating reports that can be prepared from other records might show the sales by sales persons, by products, and by states. Inventory reports can be prepared which show the number of units of items of stock on hand.

Preparing communications

Computers can be programmed to type letters and memoranda of many kinds. Often many copies of the same message are typed to different persons whose names will appear in the letters. The letters appear to be tailored for each person. This type of form letter is often used in the promotion of a product or service. However, magnetic media instead of punched cards are generally used as the input media to prepare these communications. Magnetic tape and disk records are discussed in Chapter 5.

Special reports

A data processing system is also expected to give answers to a great many questions. In a real estate office, for example, punched card records may be used to provide answers to such questions as these: Do you have for sale a home with four bedrooms, two baths, and a family room? If you have homes of this type, are they within our price range? Where are these homes located? How are they heated? Do they have garages or basements? Answers to these and other questions must be readily available. Well-designed punched card records can provide answers to most of the questions that are asked.

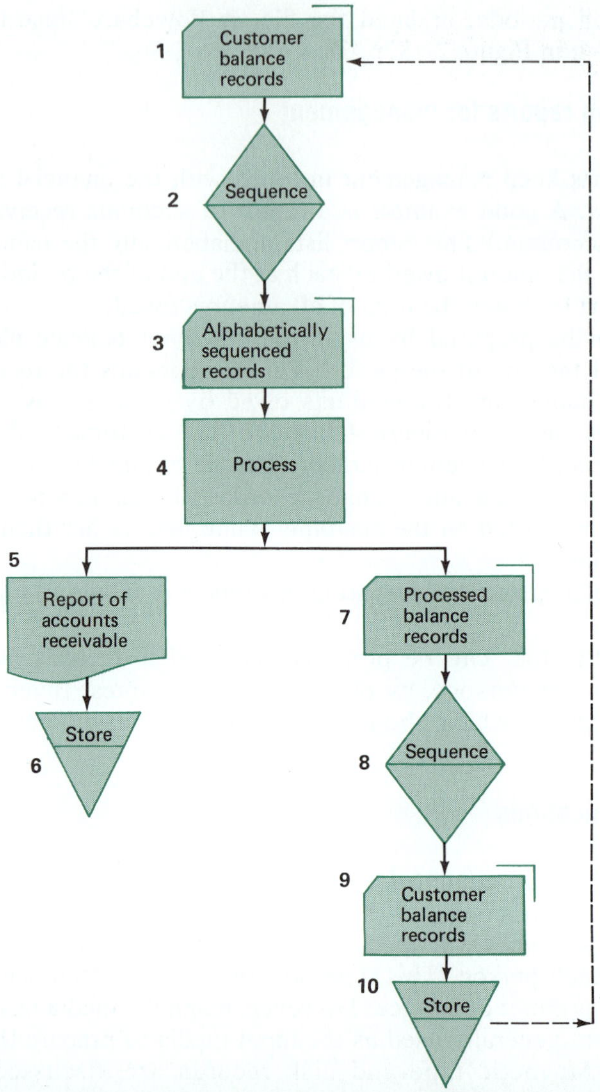

EXPLANATION

1. The file of customer balance records that has previously been kept by customer number in numeric order is
2. sequenced by customer name in alphabetic order, producing
3. a file of balance records arranged in alphabetic order by customer name.
4. Processing includes listing the names and amounts and accumulating a total of all the amounts.
5. Output includes the report of accounts receivable, which is
6. stored temporarily.
7. Output also includes the file of processed balance records.
8. The file of balance records is sequenced again in numeric order by customer number.
9. The file of customer balance records in numeric order is
10. stored temporarily and is used for the customer balance file at the beginning of the next period.

Figure 4-12. *This is a flowchart of a system for preparing a report of accounts receivable.*

A real estate office helps clients to sell or rent homes and other properties. It also helps buyers or renters to find the properties desired. The data needed for these two operations are controlled, in this example, by a system that is used in many areas. The system described is concerned with only the residential properties handled by real estate offices in a certain part of a state.

System for maintaining properties available file

The office maintains an alphabetic file of available residential properties that is updated weekly. The file is by address rather than by the name of the owner. People who wish to rent or buy property are more interested in the beginning with the neighborhood than they are with the owner's name. When a new listing is obtained, the agent secures important information from the client and manually records it on a Residential Properties Available form. This form, as a source document, is shown in Figure 4-13 next page. Figure 4-13 shows only part of the data that would be recorded on this kind of form.

The real estate office is a member of a multiple-listing service. This means that every week all real estate offices that subscribe to this service send to the central office a copy of the form shown in Figure 4-13 for each new piece of property listed by their agents. If a piece of property has been sold or if the listing has been canceled or has expired, a copy of the form is marked by the subscriber to show what has happened.

The important data about the questions asked most often are punched into a card for all new listings. The card file is maintained by the central office and processed by computer. The card layout form is shown in Figure 4-14. The cards are punched and added to the file by the central office. When a property is sold or withdrawn from the market, the card is removed from the file and stored temporarily. As a result, the file is constantly updated. Each week a printout of all multiple-listed properties available in the area is sent to each office belonging to the service. The printout lists all the data recorded in the punched card. A *printout* is a printed report prepared by a computer program.

Note that the address (Columns 1–10) is the first field in Figure 4-14 because people are more interested in neighborhoods than they are in the owners. The next field (Columns 11 and 12) is the location code, which shows in what geographic part of the city the property is located. (For example, property in the Highland Park subdivision within the boundaries of Park Avenue, Eaton Avenue, Gray Road, and Taft Place would have a code of 2M.) All sorting would be keyed to this location code field.

The address, city, and county are all abbreviated. The expiration date of the listing is shown in Columns 63–68. This record will be "pulled" from the other records when this date has passed. The asking price will be recorded in Columns 69–74. The agent (real estate sales

RESIDENTIAL PROPERTY FORM

Street Address	City	County	State	ZIP	Owner
495 Hill Top Ln	Wyoming	Ham'tn	OH	45215-1062	E & M Hansen

Construction	Style	Price	1/2-yr. Taxes	Date Listed	Date Expires
Brick	Colonial	84,900	560.00	11/1/19--	2/1/19--

ROOMS	First Floor	Second Floor	Third Floor	Lower Floor	Floor Type	Miscellaneous
Living Room	14x24'					W/B Fireplace
Dining Room	12x14'					
Kitchen	12x14'					Dshwshr/Disposal
Bath	1/2			1/2		Wshbl & Com.
Bath		10x10'				Shower & Tub
Bath		10x12'				Shower & Tub
Bedroom		12x19'				2 walk-in closets
Bedroom		12x14'				
Bedroom		12x14'				
Bedroom		10x10'				
Family Rm.	12x22'					
Utility Rm.						

TOTAL NO. OF ROOMS: 8

Basement Full Porch 1 Garage 2-car Carport 0 Patio 14x14'

Heat: Gas X Oil ____ Electric ____ Miscellaneous Forced air--humidifier

Air Conditioning: Central X Window A/C ____

Dishwasher Friq. Disposal Friq. TV Antenna Rotor Storm Windows and Doors No

Foundation Poured Water Heater Gas Wiring 220 Plumbing Copper

Wall Construction Brick Sewer X Septic Tank ____

Agent Kathy Burton (No. 14) Broker Sirk (605) Commission 7%

Mortgage $40,000 Mortgagor Eagle S & L Type of Loan Conv.

Figure 4-13. *A Residential Property Form is filled out by the real estate agent.*

person) has a code number that will be entered in Columns 75–76. The real estate office (broker) has a code number that will be entered in Columns 77–79. Column 80 will be used for a transaction code that will tell the computer whether to add this listing or withdraw it from the file.

Note also in Figure 4-14 that there are fields that will describe certain important points about a house. For example, a 4 punched in Column 31 indicates that there are four bedrooms. A 1 punched in Column 39 could mean that there is a dishwasher in the kitchen. A 2 could mean that there is a garbage disposal. A 3 could mean that there are both. The codes used in the program can mean whatever the programmer wants them to mean.

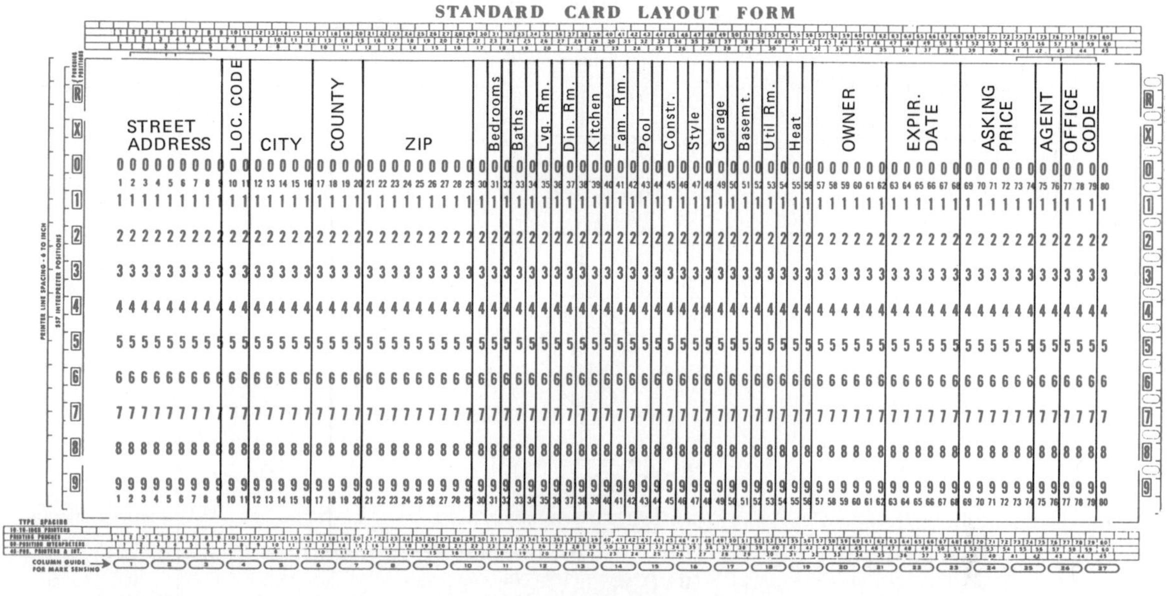

Figure 4-14. *This card layout form is designed to answer the questions most often asked about property.*

The flowchart of a system for recording and updating multiple listings is shown in Figure 4-15, next page.

Note that the source document shown in Figure 4-13 is the listing form of Residential Properties Available. From it a card is punched and verified. All the cards are then sequenced alphabetically according to address.

The computer processes this file of additions and deletions according to program instructions. The cards for new listings are merged, into the master file. The cards for listings to be deleted are removed from the file.[1] A transaction code in a card tells the computer when a card is to be extracted from the file. The program is written so that when the computer locates the record in the master file that has the same location code and address as the card in the corrections file, the record in the master file will be extracted from the file.

The computer is instructed to process the matching card in the master file according to the transaction code in the correction card. The deleted record from the master file leaves the system as output along with the correction card with which it was compared. This card file is stored temporarily.

Output includes the alphabetic list of all available listings. This list is distributed to all realtors subscribing to the service. Output also includes an updated master file of punched cards. This file will be stored temporarily and used when the file is updated on the following week.

Many reports could be prepared from data in punched cards similar to Figure 4-14. Some of the reports could show listings by neighborhood,

[1]Recall that listings that have been canceled, that have expired, or that are for property that has been sold must be removed from the updated file.

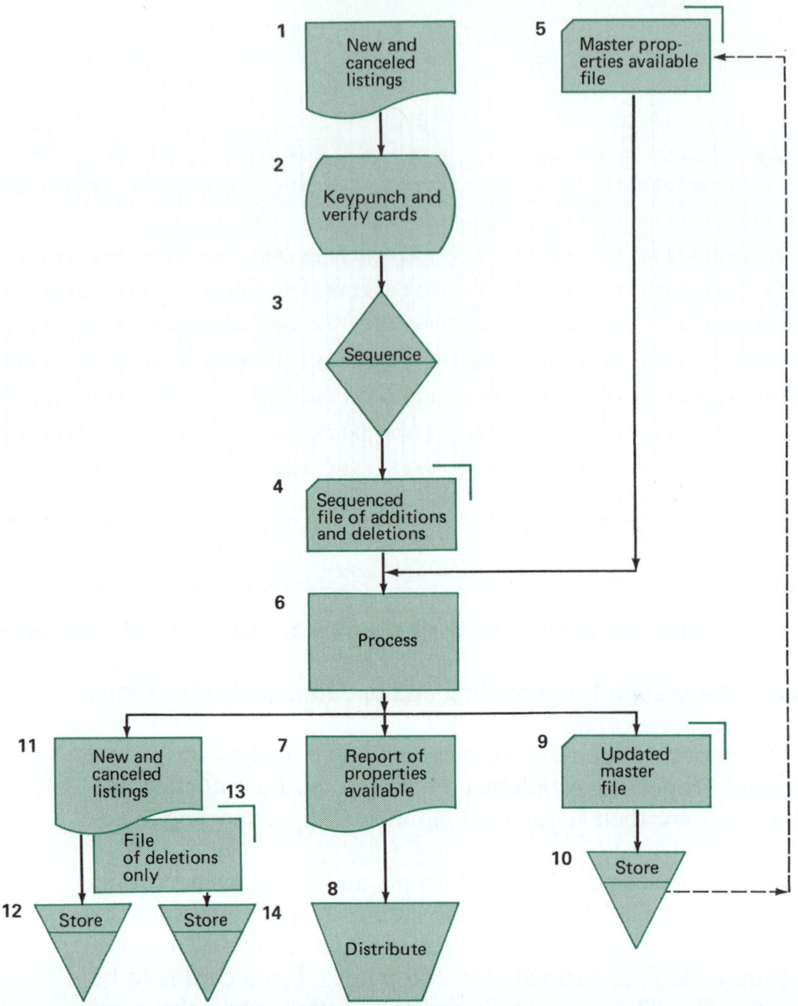

EXPLANATION

1. The source documents for the system are the new and canceled listing forms that have been received from realtors subscribing to the multiple-listing service.
2. Cards are keypunched and verified with selected data from the listing forms.
3. Punched cards are sequenced according to location code.
4. The sequenced cards make a file of additions and deletions.
5. The master properties available file and the sequenced file of additions and deletions are read into the computer.
6. Processing consists of merging the two files and of extracting the cards in the master file that have matching cards with a transaction code showing that the listings are canceled.
7. Output consists of a printed report of properties available, which is
8. distributed to all the realtors that subscribe to the multiple-listing service.
9. Output also consists of the updated master file of properties available. which is
10. stored temporarily and which becomes the master file for the next period.
11. New and canceled listing forms are
12. stored temporarily.
13. The punched card file of deletions only is
14. stored temporarily.

Figure 4-15. *This is the flowchart for a system to produce a list of addresses of residential properties available by location.*

by price range, or by number of bedrooms. Although the punched card system gives the realtors an up-to-date list each week, a great deal of time must be spent by them in studying the printout in order to be prepared for telephone calls and other inquiries.

In Chapter 6, you will learn more about storing data on magnetic disks. With disk storage, it is possible to search the master file and have an answer printed or displayed almost instantly. For example, the master file can be searched for a brick house with four bedrooms, two baths, and a family room or den, in a certain neighborhood, within a given price range. The computer can find the record while the person asking is still on the telephone. In many large cities, disk files are used for this purpose. It would not be logical, however, to make such a pointed search when using a punched card system. More about disk retrieval will be explained in Chapter 5.

SUMMARY

The vast amounts of data needed by business in order to take the guesswork out of decision making must be logically organized to be useful. Generally, the data are organized into files, records, and fields or data items.

A *file* is a collection of records treated as a unit. A file may have many records, but all the records in a file must contain the same kinds of data. A *record* is a single unit in a file. Each record or group of similar records is identified by a key or code. Also, each record consists of a number of data fields. The fields contain the data to be processed.

There are several kinds of files. Master, detail, summary, and balance files are explained in this chapter. A *master file* contains relatively permanent records that are updated periodically. A *detail file* is made up of records of day-to-day transactions. Separate records are required for each transaction. A great many reports can be prepared from these records.

Summary files are made up of records that summarize the transactions of a group of similiar detail records. When detailed records are not needed in preparing a report, summary records are used because they save processing time. *Balance files* are made up of records that show a balance of some kind for a certain date. They consist of records that show the balance owed by a customer on a certain date, the amount of cash in a bank, the amount owed for taxes, or the total assets owned by a business. All details are omitted.

When records from several files are used to prepare a document of some kind, transaction codes are used in the records. These codes make it possible for the computer, when properly programmed, to distinguish one record from another and to process the data.

Data processing produces records of day-to-day transactions, such as sales to customers and payments received from them. Data processing also produces a variety of reports from transaction records, such as an invoice or a statement of account. Also, data processing updates files, such as a master customer file, a master enrollment file, and an employee's earnings file.

Data processing also prepares operating reports for management, such as a report of accounts receivable, a report of sales made by sales persons, or a report of stock on hand. Finally, data processing prepares special reports which give answers to a great many questions.

REVIEW QUESTIONS

1. What four files are needed to prepare a statement of account?
2. How are master, balance, summary, and detail records used to prepare a statement of account?
3. How is a master customer file updated?
4. How is a telephone directory updated?
5. What information is listed in a report of accounts receivable? What file would be used to prepare this report?
6. What is the source document for a system to prepare a report of residential properties available? What are the two files that are used in a system to update a list of these properties? What are four outputs from the system?

NEW TERMS

- Balance
- Balance file
- Balance record
- Control code
- Data item
- Detail file
- Detail record
- Field (magnetic tape or disk)
- Invoice
- Item (data)
- Key
- Key field
- Master file
- Master record
- Payments detail file
- Printout
- Record
- Sales detail file
- Statement of account
- Summary file record
- Summary record
- Transaction
- Transaction code
- Transaction file
- Unit record

STUDY GUIDE

Complete Study Guide 4 by following the instructions in your STUDY GUIDES booklet.

PROJECTS

Complete Projects 4-1 and 4-2 by following the instructions in your PROJECTS booklet.

5

DESIGNING RECORDS for MAGNETIC FILES

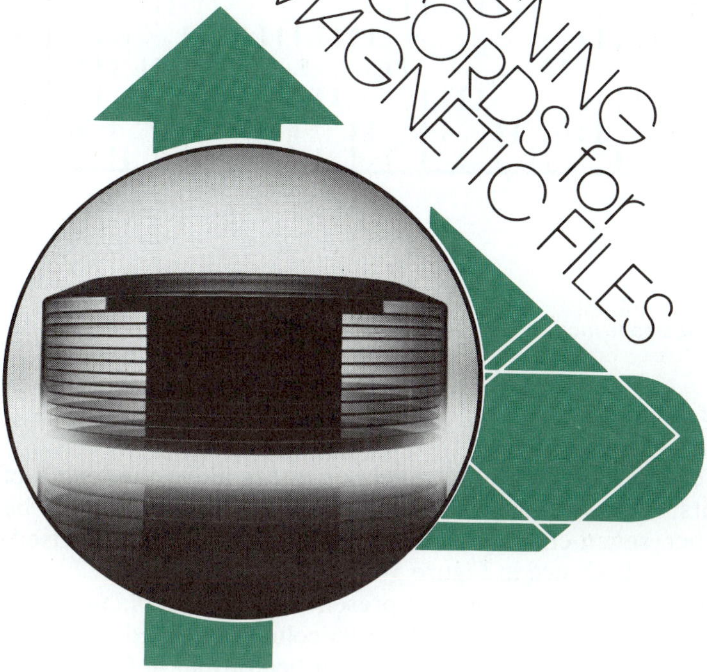

So far, you have learned that data punched into cards can be processed by the computer. Data recorded on magnetic tapes or disks can also be processed by the computer. The advantages of magnetic media are many, and they are used widely.

MAGNETIC TAPE FILES

Magnetic tape is a tape that has been coated with a magnetic material, on which data may be recorded in the form of magnetically polarized spots. Magnetic tape is like the tape used in an ordinary tape recorder found in many homes and offices. The tape is coated with a magnetically sensitive substance. The data are recorded on the tape as magnetized spots that create electronic impulses. The computer can read these impulses. One pattern of spots represents one letter or figure. Another pattern represents another letter or figure.

Although the spots on magnetic tape cannot be seen, Figure 5-1 shows how they might appear if they were visible.

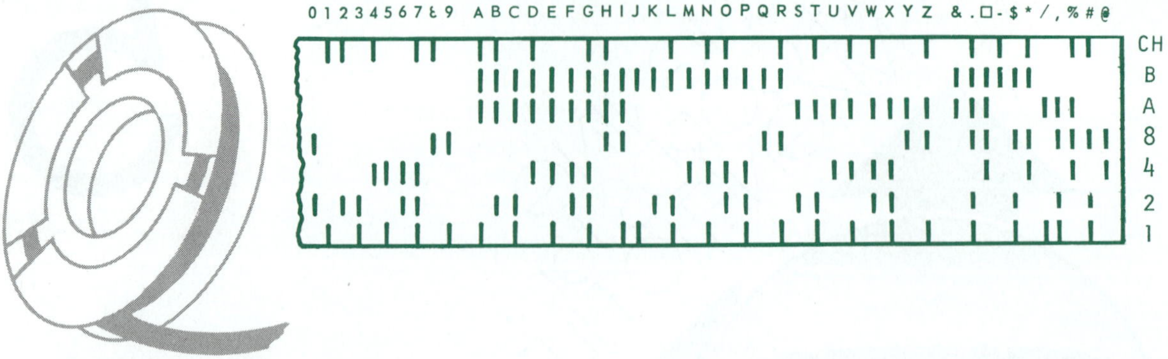

Figure 5-1. *The seven-channel magnetic tape code includes numbers, letters of the alphabet, and special characters.*

Magnetic tape codes

Data are recorded in parallel channels or tracks along the length of the tape. Digits, letters of the alphabet, or special characters may be recorded. Either seven-channel or nine-channel tapes may be used. Seven-channel tape is shown in Figure 5-1.

The binary coding on this tape to represent figures, letters, and some special characters is like that used in the 96-column punched cards described in Chapter 3. Binary code will be described further in Chapter 7.

A single character is recorded in each vertical row. Note how Digit 5 is recorded in Figure 5-2. The tape contains four numeric positions, two zone positions, and a C (parity bit or check) position. The numeric positions will record the digits 0 through 9. A combination of numeric and zone positions will record the letters of the alphabet and a number of special characters.

Figure 5-2. *This is a simulation of data recorded on magnetic tape.*

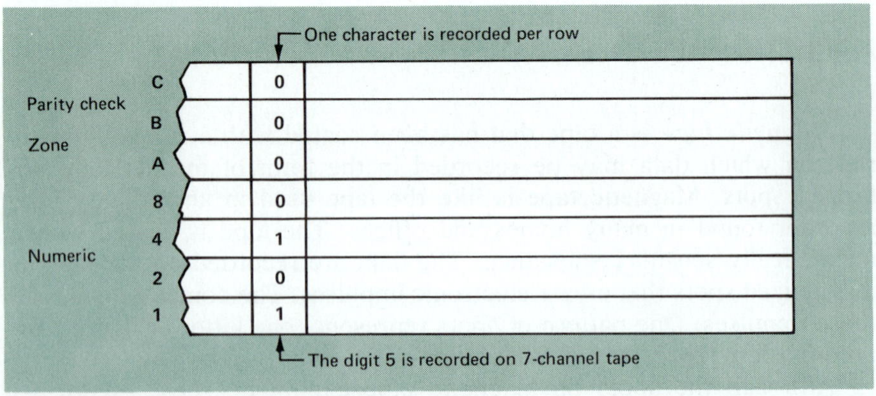

The parity check position (C) is used to check the accuracy of the storage of data on magnetic tape. Parity check is explained later in this chapter.

A read-write head is positioned over each channel in the tape input-output unit. The heads either read the data that are already on the tape and transfer them to the computer for processing, or they write the processed data coming from the computer onto a new reel of tape.

Writing on tape erases data previously recorded on it. The new data erase the old data as the new data are recorded. However, reading data on tape does not erase the data. (You can erase a tape on a tape recorder by recording over it. But, you can play a tape many times without erasing it. The idea is the same.)

Parity Check

Note in Figure 5-2 that on magnetic tape the channels run horizontally. Rows denote vertical positions, Note, also, that the C channel is shown as the parity channel.

Both the seven- and nine-channel tapes provide a parity-check channel. The *parity-check position* or channel is used by the recording mechanism to check its own errors. An electronic impulse is automatically added by the input device to maintain either an even or odd number of electronic impulses for each character on the tape.

In Figure 5-1, an electronic impulse is added in the parity-check position to maintain an even number of impulses for each character. This condition is referred to as even parity. For example, Digit 1 is represented by an impulse in the 1 channel. The input device added an impulse in the parity-check position to maintain even parity. On the other hand, Digit 5 is represented by impulses in the 1 and 4 channels, an even number. As a result, no impulse was recorded in the parity-check position.

Even parity, then, is the state of parity in which an electronic impulse is added in the parity-check position to maintain an even number of impulses for each character. *Odd parity*, on the other hand, is the reverse of even parity. An impulse is added to each character that is coded with an even number of impulses. In Figure 5-3, note that an electronic impulse has been added in the parity check channel (P) whenever the total of the magnetic impulses for a given character is even, thus maintaining an odd number of electronic impulses.

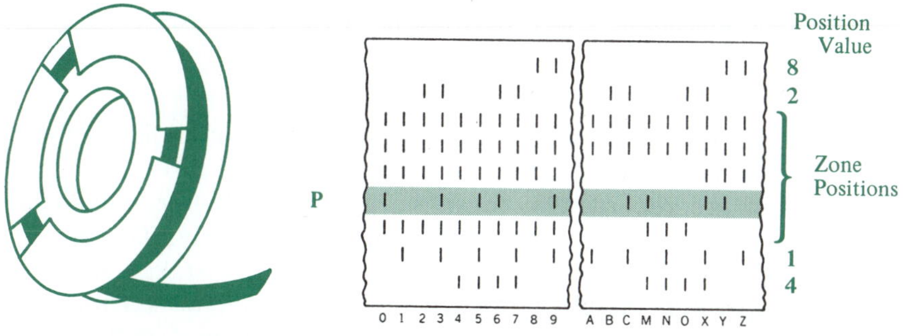

Figure 5-3. *This nine-channel magnetic tape uses an odd parity check.*

The parity-check impulse does not change the character that is coded. The impulse is automatically added as a check of the accuracy of the recording device. It does not check for mistakes in the actual data. Every time a character is addressed, moved, or used in a computation, the computer checks the number of impulses representing that character. If one of the impulses has been lost, the computer signals an error.

Recording data on magnetic tape

Data can be recorded on magnetic tape by a keyboard-to-tape machine. The machine has a typewriter-like keyboard. Data are keyed as digits, letters of the alphabet, and special characters. They are recorded on the tape as magnetized spots in a form of binary code. Some keyboard-to-tape machines have a cathode-ray tube (CRT) display. The transaction appears on the tube as it is recorded on the tape. The operator can read the information on the tube, check it, and correct any mistakes. See Figure 5-4 for a keyboard-to-tape recorder. Note that this recorder has a television-type screen (*cathode-ray tube*), also known as a *CRT*. A picture of all data being keyed is shown on the CRT. This picture helps the operator to see mistakes as soon as they have been made.

Figure 5-4. *This key-to-tape recorder is equipped with a cassette tape and CRT unit.*

Inforex, Inc.

Recording procedure. The procedure for writing records on magnetic tape varies from machine to machine. Generally, however, the procedure is as follows:

(1) The operator keys the data from a source document on the keyboard of the tape recording machine.
(2) The data are recorded in magnetic form in a *buffer*, which is a storage device designed to hold the data temporarily. The buffer is attached to the tape-recording machine. Keying mistakes, if noticed by the operator, may be corrected right away by backspacing to the point of error and keying the correct data over the incorrect data.

(3) After the data from a source document are recorded in the buffer, they are transferred on command to magnetic tape.

See Figure 5-5 for a flowchart of the steps taken to record data on magnetic tape. Note that a new symbol is shown for the first time. It is the *magnetic tape symbol*, which is used to show the use of a magnetic tape file in flow-charts.

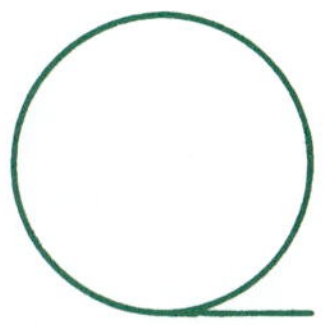

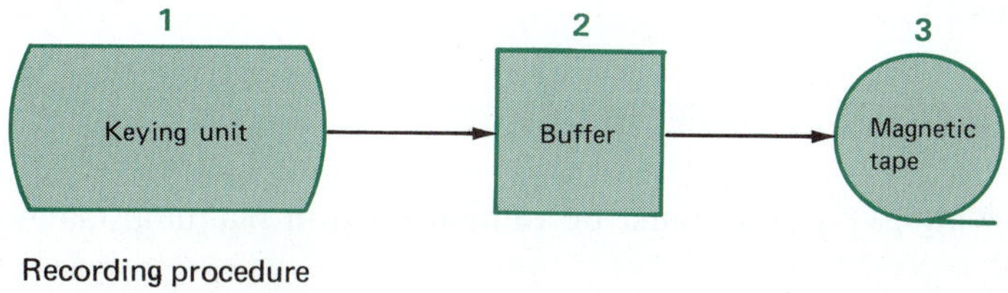

Figure 5-5. *There are three steps taken to record data on magnetic tape.*

Proofreading procedures. Again, the procedure for checking magnetic tape records for accuracy is different from machine to machine. Generally, however, the procedure is as follows:

(1) When all source documents have been processed as described, the tape is reversed to the beginning.
(2) The data from the tape enter the buffer again, one transaction at a time.
(3) The operator then rekeys the data into the buffer from each source document.
(4) As each letter or digit is keyed, it is compared by the machine to the corresponding character stored in the buffer memory. Verification continues in this way until a mistake is found. When it is, the keyboard locks. The mistake may be corrected by simply striking the correct key at the point of the error.
(5) From the buffer, the verified data are transmitted to magnetic tape and then to the computer for processing.

See Figure 5-6 for a flowchart of the steps taken to proofread data on magnetic tape.

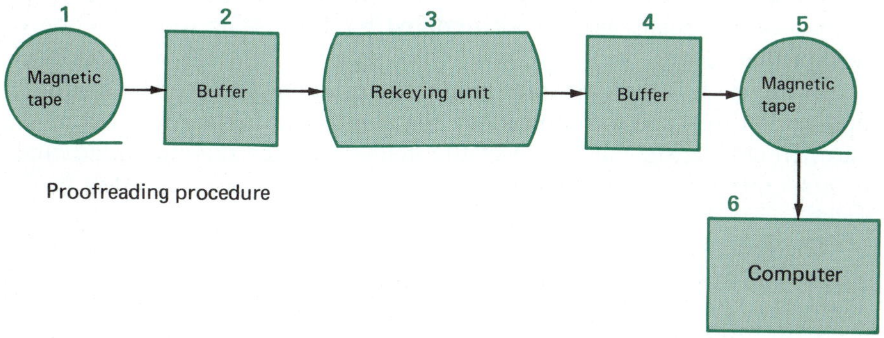

Figure 5-6. *Above are five steps taken to proofread data on magnetic tape.*

MAGNETIC TAPE RECORDS

A reel of magnetic tape records is typically a file. The records within a file are planned almost as they are with punched cards. With magnetic tapes, we refer to spaces instead of columns. Also, because magnetic tape is a continuous medium, a record does not have to be limited in length. It can be either longer or shorter than the 80 spaces used for punched cards.

PLANNING MAGNETIC TAPE RECORDS

The following five points must be remembered in planning magnetic tape records:

(1) The fields in the records on the tape must be written in a planned order, much as they are planned for a punched card.
(2) All records in a magnetic tape file must be of the same kind. (A master file will contain only master records. A detail file will contain only detail records.)
(3) The lengths of similar fields in like records must be the same. (The customer's name would use the same number of spaces in all the records in a file.)
(4) The number of spaces allowed for a field should equal the number needed for the largest item of data to be recorded in that field.
(5) All the records in a particular tape file must be the same length, but the records can vary in length from one file to the next.[1] (The records in a master file might require 110 spaces; the records in a sales summary file, only 40 spaces.) The records can be as long or as short as needed.

See Figure 5-7, in which an 80-column card record is compared to a magnetic tape record. Both records come from account balance files and represent the amounts owed by customers at the end of a period. Note that both the punched card and the tape records are identified by a key field or address associated with the records. In processing the record, the computer will use the key in order to locate the record. A particular record can be read, written, or updated by addressing the key code or field of that record.

In Figure 5-7, the customer number is used as the key. The customer number on the tape is followed by the same data items recorded in the card. In each case, the length of the fields has been planned in advance to hold the largest number of characters that might be recorded in the fields.

The records can be separated by short gaps on the tape, as shown in Figure 5-7, but this is not always the case. You learned that each

[1]The length of records within a magnetic file can vary with complicated programs, but in this text only fixed-length records will be discussed.

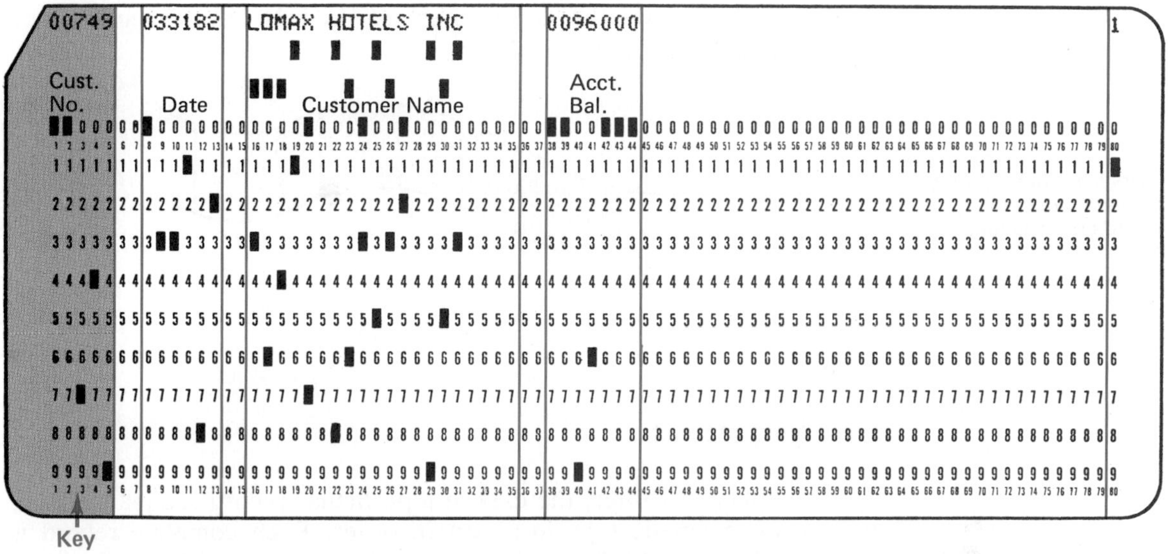

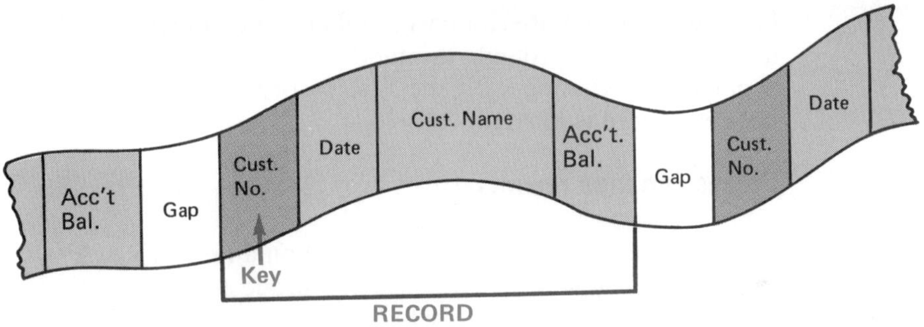

Figure 5-7. *Contents of a punched card and magnetic tape balance record are compared.*

punched card record in a file must be read into an input device separately. Magnetic tape, on the other hand, being a continuous medium, allows for faster processing. When an instruction to read data is given for a magnetic tape file, one data record may be read and the tape may stop briefly before it moves to the next record. However, tape records are usually read in a faster way.

The records on a tape file are greatly condensed because they do not have to use 80 spaces. Movement from record to record is very fast. A great many records can be stored on a reel of tape. Therefore, space and time can be saved by combining the tape records into blocks. For example, the blocks may be made up of five or ten records, with a gap before and after each block. A *block*, then, may be defined as a group of consecutive magnetically coded records that are separated by gaps from other blocks on a file. Each record is processed individually, however. These steps are taken so fast that passage from one record to another cannot be noticed.

Figure 5-8 shows the arrangement of records on a magnetic tape when five records make up a block.

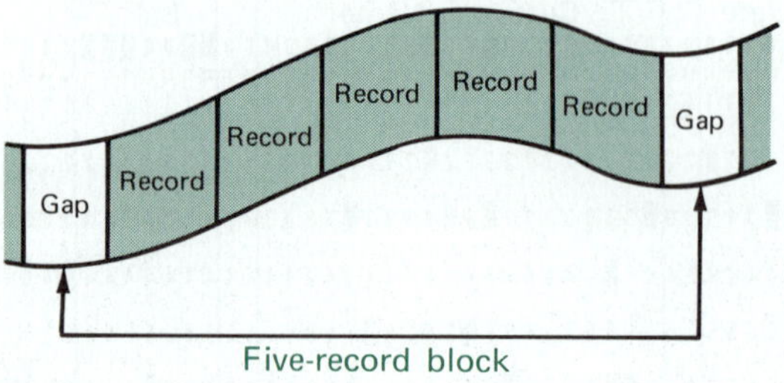

Figure 5-8. *There is a gap between blocks of records on magnetic tape.*

Identifying records

As explained earlier, the data in a particular record are planned and written on magnetic tape in a certain order. Each complete record is identified by a key field or code associated with the record. The key may be a customer number, a part number, an employee number, etc. When a record must be found, the tape records are read by the computer in sequence, beginning with the first record, until the key identifying the desired record is located.

Processing tape records

A reel of magnetic tape is mounted on a tape drive. A *tape drive* is an input/output device that is used for processing magnetic tape records. The tape is read by read-write heads attached to the tape drive. Figure 5-9 shows an operator mounting a reel of tape on a tape drive.

When reading, the read heads sense the magnetized spots on the tape and convert them to electronic pulses that are sent to the computer for processing. When processed data are recorded (written) as output on a magnetic tape, the heads convert the electronic pulses to magnetized spots. These spots are recorded (written) on the tape. The computer gives the READ and WRITE commands.

As explained earlier, when a certain record must be found on a tape, the computer reads all the records in order until the key identifying the desired record is located. The contents of the record can then be displayed on a cathode-ray tube or printed. *Sequential access* is the term used to describe this storage technique in which the stored items of data become available only in a one-after-the-other sequence, whether all the information in a record or only some of it is desired.

ADVANTAGES OF MAGNETIC TAPE RECORDS

The advantages of magnetic tape records as compared to punched card records are as follows:

Photo courtesy of IBM Corporation

Figure 5-9. *The computer operator mounts a reel of magnetic tape on a magnetic tape drive.*

(1) Data can be read into or written out of the computer much faster than is possible with punched cards.
(2) A reel of tape can hold data equal to that held by several thousand punched cards. Also, the tape is more compact and easier to handle.
(3) A reel of tape costs less than the cards it replaces. Also, the tape can be used again. Old data are erased as new data are recorded.
(4) Recording data on magnetic tape is faster than recording data in punched cards, resulting in better use of operator time.
(5) Magnetic tape wears better than punched cards.
(6) Any mistakes made by an operator in recording data on magnetic tape can be corrected during entry.
(7) A record can be either shorter or longer than the 80 columns of a punched card because magnetic tape is a continuous medium.

DISADVANTAGES OF MAGNETIC TAPE RECORDS

With all its advantages magnetic tape, as an input/output and storage medium, does have a number of disadvantages. They are as follows:

(1) Punched cards can be read by users and often serve as documents. Data on magnetic tape cannot be seen.
(2) Records on magnetic tape must be accessed sequentially. This means that all records leading up to the desired record must be checked before the correct record is found. For this reason, data stored on magnetic tape cannot be processed as fast as data on magnetic disks.

(Continued)

(3) There is a danger that data recorded on magnetic tape can be erased by accident.
(4) Key-to-tape recording units cost more than keypunch units.
(5) When magnetic tapes are used as files that must be updated, the updated files must be completely rewritten. The addition, deletion, or change of only a few records requires this procedure.

MAGNETIC TAPE FILE APPLICATIONS

Magnetic tape records, like punched card records, can be used to solve many kinds of business problems. Two common problems were explained earlier in this book. One was a problem for printing a report of accounts receivable. The other was a problem for printing a report of updated student enrollments. Both of these problems will be explained in this chapter with the use of magnetic tape files.

If the records in two tape files are to be merged, the records in each file must be in sequential order. Also they must both be sequenced in the same way, either numerically or alphabetically according to the key field used. It is easy to understand how punched card records can be sequenced into numeric or alphabetic order. However, it is harder to picture how records on tape files could be sorted into a new order because the tape records are not physically separated from each other. The methods used to sequence punched card and magnetic tape records will be described in detail in Chapter 6. However, both problems described here do include the sequencing of tape records.

Report of accounts receivable

A report is to be printed that lists alphabetically the name of each customer and the amount owed by each at the end of a period. There will also be a printed total of the amounts owed by all customers. The report is to be prepared from magnetic tape records in the customer balance file. Each record shows the account number, the name of the customer, the amount owed, and the date at the end of the period. The records in this file are arranged numerically by customer number.

The records will first have to be sequenced alphabetically by customer name and copied on another reel of magnetic tape. The computer can handle both of these jobs. The alphabetized tape is then used by the computer to prepare the printed report of accounts receivable, to accumulate a total of the amounts owed, and to print this total at the end of the report. Figure 5-10 shows the flowchart of the procedure that would be followed to prepare the report.

Note the difference between the flowchart in Figure 5-10 and the one shown in Figure 4-12, page 84, in which punched card records were used to prepare a report of accounts receivable. With the punched card file, the cards had to be sequenced again into numeric order after processing so that they could be used for invoices or monthly statements. With magnetic tapes, however, this is not necessary because there are two

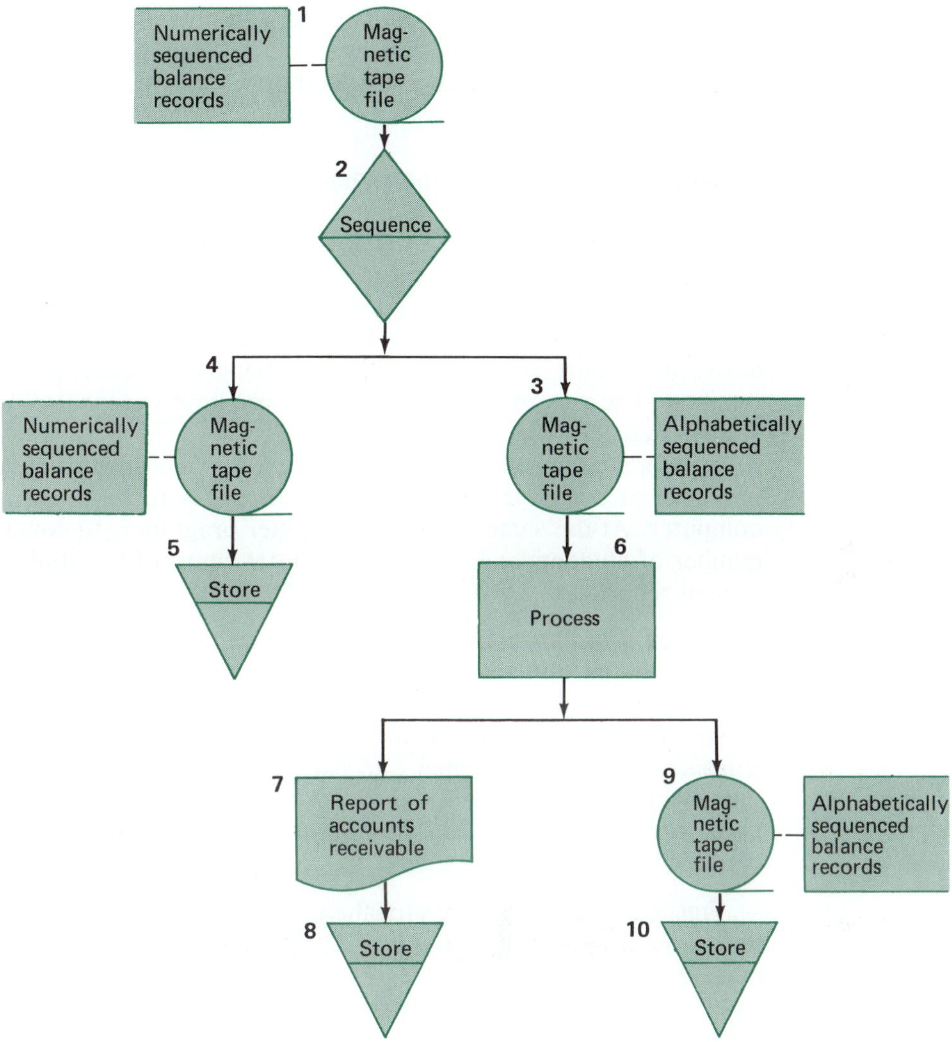

EXPLANATION

1. The tape file of customer balance records that has previously been kept by customer number in numeric order is
2. sequenced by customer name in alphabetic order, producing
3. a tape file of balance records arranged in alphabetic order by customer name and also
4. the original tape file arranged in numeric order by customer number.
5. The numerically sequenced file is stored until needed.
6. The new tape is used for processing, which includes listing the names and amounts, accumulating a total of all amounts, and printing the total at the end of the report.
7. Output includes the report of accounts receivable, which is
8. stored temporarily.
9. Output also includes the tape file of processed balance records that are in alphabetic order by customer name, which is
10. stored until needed.

Figure 5-10. *This is a flowchart for printing a list of accounts receivable.*

tapes after processing. The beginning tape of numerically sequenced records has not been changed. However, output also includes a new tape of alphabetically sequenced records. Both tapes may be stored and used as needed.

Updated report of student enrollments

Magnetic tape is often used for master file records. These records must be updated as new or corrected data are received. In the example shown here, a master student enrollment file on magnetic tape is updated from time to time as new enrollments are received, as students withdraw, or as addresses or other data are changed. Unchanged records are retained. The records in the master file are kept in alphabetic order by student name.

An updated master file is to be prepared by a computer program on a new reel of magnetic tape. A printed report is to be prepared by the computer. At the same time, the computer program is to count the total number of students and to record the total count of the students on the printed report.

Source documents. Enrollment and correction forms are prepared as changes in enrollment records are reported. These records are the source documents. They are saved (batched) until time to update the master file. The data from the forms are keypunched and verified. A transaction code is punched into each card in this file to tell the computer whether a record is to be added, deleted, or changed. The punched cards are then sequenced in alphabetic order, resulting in a punched card file of new records.

Processing the data. The alphabetized punched card file and the master magnetic tape file each enter the computer, one record at a time, as needed. The computer processes the records from the two files and enters the updated records on a new reel of magnetic tape. The records are in alphabetic order.

Processing consists of removing incorrect records as well as the records of students who have withdrawn from the school and adding correction records as well as the records of new students. Unchanged records are retained. The computer also prepares a printed report from the updated records. Also, the computer keeps a count of the processed records and enters the total count on the report.

Output. The combined file of records is the updated master student enrollment tape file. Output also includes a printed updated report. Figure 5-11 is a flowchart explaining this procedure. The flowchart differs from the one described in Figure 2-12, page 33, because that system was for a problem that added new students only, but made no corrections in the file.

The old master tape can be stored until needed. One of the advantages of magnetic tape is that an old tape can be kept for a while as a

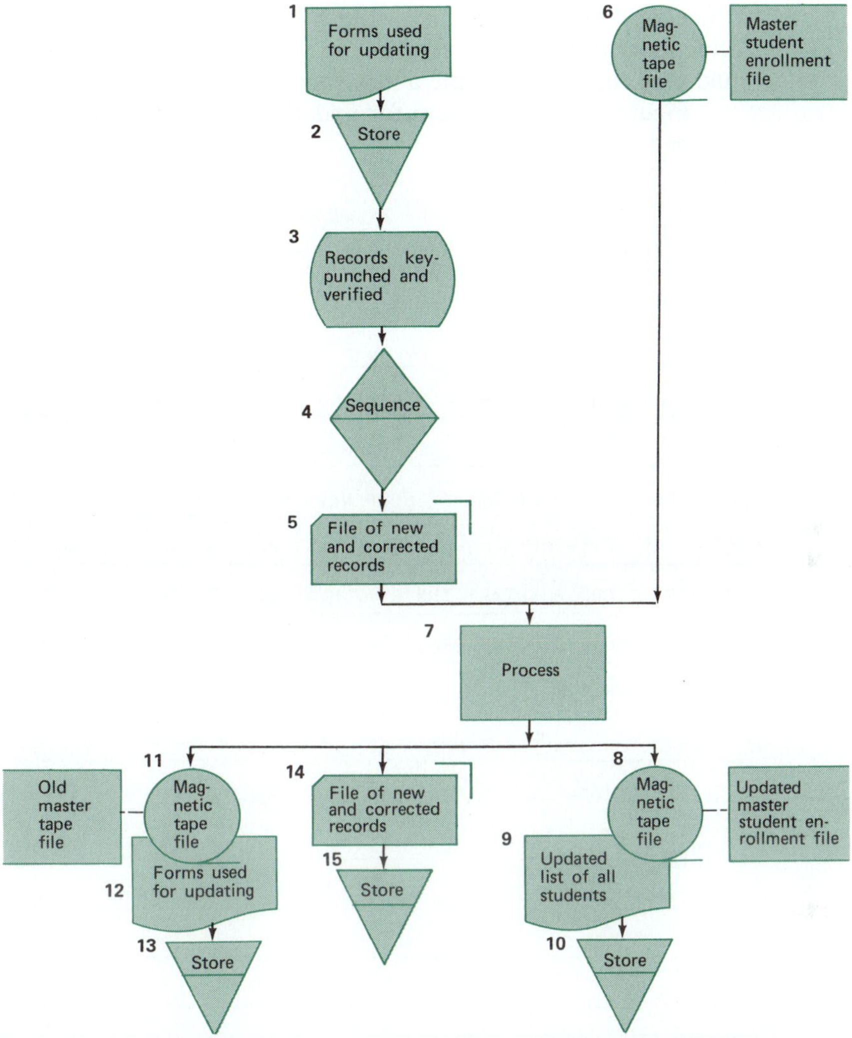

EXPLANATION

1. Source documents used in updating are
2. stored temporarily.
3. From these documents, punched card records are keypunched and verified.
4. The records are then sequenced in alphabetic order according to student number, thus creating
5. a file of new and corrected master records.
6. The master tape student enrollment file and the punched card file of new and corrected records are
7. processed together. Processing consists of creating an entirely new updated master tape file. The new student records will be merged with the old ones. The records of students who have withdrawn will not be copied on the new tape (will be deleted). The records that have changes of address, etc., will be replaced with corrected records on the new tape. Unchanged records will be copied.
8. Output consists of an updated master magnetic tape file and an
9. updated list of all students, showing the total number enrolled,
10. both of which will be stored temporarily.
11. The old magnetic tape master file and
12. the forms used in updating the file will be
13. stored temporarily.
14. The punched card file of new and corrected records is
15. stored temporarily.

Figure 5-11. *Above is a flowchart for updating a master enrollment file.*

"backup" file. In fact, it would be possible, if the new tape were accidentally erased or destroyed, to reprocess the punched cards and the old tape records to create a new tape.

Figure 5-12 is a system for updating the master enrollment file as described.

Step No.	Procedure
1	ENROLLMENT FORMS OF NEW STUDENTS AND MEMORANDA CONTAINING DATA
	ABOUT CORRECTIONS AND WITHDRAWALS ARE USED AS SOURCE DOCUMENTS.
2	THESE DOCUMENTS ARE FILED TEMPORARILY.
3	RECORDS OF ADDITIONS AND CORRECTIONS ARE KEYPUNCHED AND VERIFIED.
4	PUNCHED CARDS ARE SEQUENCED IN ALPHABETIC ORDER.
5	SEQUENCED CARDS BECOME A FILE OF NEW AND CORRECTED MASTER RECORDS.
6	MASTER TAPE FILE OF STUDENT ENROLLMENT RECORDS THAT IS ALREADY IN
	ALAPHABETIC ORDER ENTERS THE SYSTEM ALONG WITH PUNCHED CARD FILE
	OF NEW AND CORRECTED RECORDS.
7	PROCESSING CONSISTS OF PRODUCING ENTIRELY NEW MASTER TAPE ON WHICH
	ALL CORRECT RECORDS ARE RETAINED, NEW STUDENT RECORDS ARE ENTERED,
	CORRECTED RECORDS ARE REPLACED, AND TERMINATED RECORDS ARE WITHDRAWN.
	(TRANSACTION CODES IN PUNCHED CARDS TELL COMPUTER WHAT TO DO.)
8	OUTPUT FROM SYSTEM CONSISTS OF UPDATED MASTER STUDENT ENROLLMENT
	FILE.
9	OUTPUT ALSO CONSISTS OF UPDATED LIST OF ALL STUDENTS ENROLLED,
	SHOWING TOTAL NUMBER ENROLLED.
10	NEW TAPE FILE AND UPDATED LIST ARE FILED TEMPORARILY.
11	OLD MAGNETIC TAPE MASTER FILE REMAINS AFTER PROCESSING AS "BACKUP"
	TAPE.
12	ENROLLMENT FORMS USED IN UPDATING PROCEDURE REMAIN AFTER PROCESSING.
13	OLD MAGNETIC TAPE MASTER FILE AND ENROLLMENT FORMS ARE STORED
	TEMPORARILY.
14	PUNCHED CARD FILE OF NEW AND CORRECTED RECORDS REMAINS.
15	THIS PUNCHED CARD FILE IS STORED TEMPORARILY.

Figure 5-12. *This is a system for updating a master enrollment file.*

REVIEW QUESTIONS

1. How are data represented on magnetic tape?
2. What types of data may be recorded on magnetic tape?
3. How many read-write heads are needed to read or write data on seven-channel tape?
4. Do both writing and reading operations erase data previously recorded on tape?
5. What is the function of the parity check channel? Is the parity impulse added automatically?
6. In even parity, will a parity impulse be added when No. 5 is recorded?
7. What is the purpose of a buffer in a tape-recording operation?
8. How may keying errors be corrected if noticed by the operator?
9. What five requirements must tape records meet?
10. What is a *block* as it relates to magnetic tape records?
11. How are magnetic tape records identified? How does the computer locate a particular record on a reel of magnetic tape?
12. If the records in two tape files are to be merged into a single file, what requirements must be met regarding the arrangement of the records on both tape files?

MAGNETIC DISK FILES

Data to be processed by a computer are often recorded on magnetic disks. A *magnetic disk* is an input, output, and storage medium that is coated on both sides with a substance that can be magnetized. Data are recorded and stored as magnetic impulses or bits on the grooveless tracks of the disk. Each side of a disk has 200 to 500 such tracks. A great many records can thus be recorded on a single disk. Sometimes a disk file may consist of several disks.

Magnetic disk codes

Data are recorded on a track as invisible magnetized spots that create electronic impulses. Figure 5-13 shows an imaginary section of one track on one side of a disk.

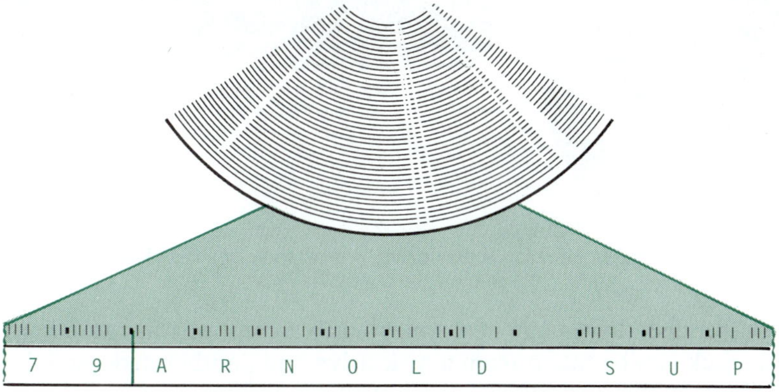

Figure 5-13. *This is a partial representation of how magnetic disk code might appear.*

Unlike punched cards and magnetic tape, which store data in vertical columns or rows, the magnetic disk has tracks that are narrow. For this reason, data are stored serially, bit-by-bit, along a track. The codes are like those used in recording data on magnetic tape.

The number of records that can be stored on a disk track depends upon the length of the records.

Types of disk systems

Two systems are in common use. They are disk packs and flexible disks.

Disk packs. A *disk pack* is a collection of two or more disks mounted on a common vertical shaft. A disk pack is mounted on an input/output device, known as a *disk drive*. A disk pack of six disks is shown in Figure 5-14. Some disk drives can rotate the disks at more than 3,600 revolutions a minute. Specified data stored on any one of the disks in the pack can be found and read, or new data can be entered.

Photo courtesy of Boise Cascade Corporation

Photo courtesy of IBM Corporation

Figure 5-14. *A computer operator mounts a disk pack on a disk drive. A disk pack of six disks is shown.*

Several disk drives can be connected to a computer at the same time. A disk pack can be taken from a disk drive and another disk pack loaded in its place, making additional disks available for processing data.

When new data are entered, the data previously recorded on the same area of a disk are erased. When data are read, on the other hand, there is no change. The data remain on the disk. A record can be located, read into, or written out of the computer at speeds so high that most people cannot begin to comprehend the rate.

The disks in a pack are separated from one another to allow space for access arms and read-write heads. As the disks rotate, the arms position the heads for reading or writing the data on a disk. The heads read or write data from both sides of a disk. Records are located almost instantly by their key codes, no matter where they are located on the disk pack. Figure 5-15 shows disks with access arms and read-write heads.

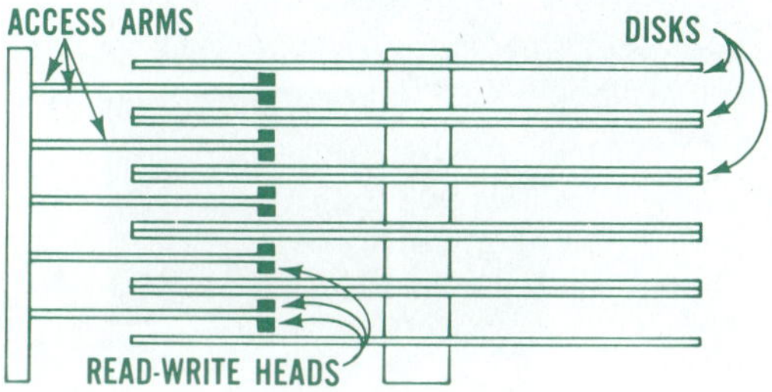

Figure 5-15. *Note how the access arms position the read-write heads between the disks.*

Flexible disks. A *flexible disk*, often referred to as a *floppy disk*, is a small, flexible magnetic platter that is something like a phonograph record. One disk can replace 3,000 eighty-column cards. The disk is easily stored or mailed. Data can be keyed on the disk and then processed directly by a computer. A floppy disk is illustrated in Figure 5-16.

Olivetti Corp. of America

Figure 5-16. *The operator inserts a floppy disk into a terminal. The data on the disk are recorded and read through the slits in the jacket.*

Recording and proofreading data on magnetic disks

Keyboard-to-disk units are available for recording data on disks in much the same way that data are recorded on magnetic tape. A keyboard-to-disk recorder is shown in Figure 5-17. Note that this recorder has a CRT as well. A key-to-disk recorder is also referred to as a terminal. This and other type terminals will be described in Chapter 8.

Figure 5-17. *This key-to-disk recorder has a CRT.*

To record the data, an operator first keys the data into a buffer or minicomputer, where they are stored temporarily.[2] If a mistake is found by the operator while entering the data, it can be corrected by backspacing and striking the correct key. When the first keying operation is completed, the data are rekeyed for verification. If a mistake is found, a light goes on and the keyboard locks. The mistake is corrected by keying the correct data over the error. When the mistakes, if any, are corrected, the data are entered automatically on the magnetic disk. See Figure 5-18 for a flowchart of the steps taken to record and verify data on magnetic disks. A *magnetic disk symbol* is used in the flowchart.

Some key-to-disk units display the entire transaction being entered on a CRT, just as was true in the case of keying data for entry on magnetic tape. Thus, the data can be checked for accuracy and corrected as they are recorded.

---

[2]Minicomputers will be described in Chapter 7.

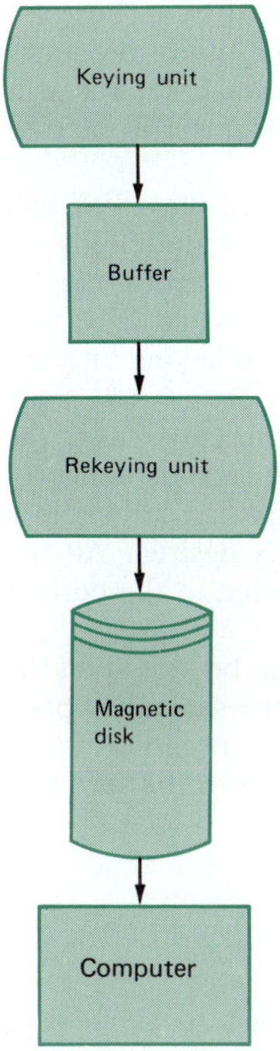

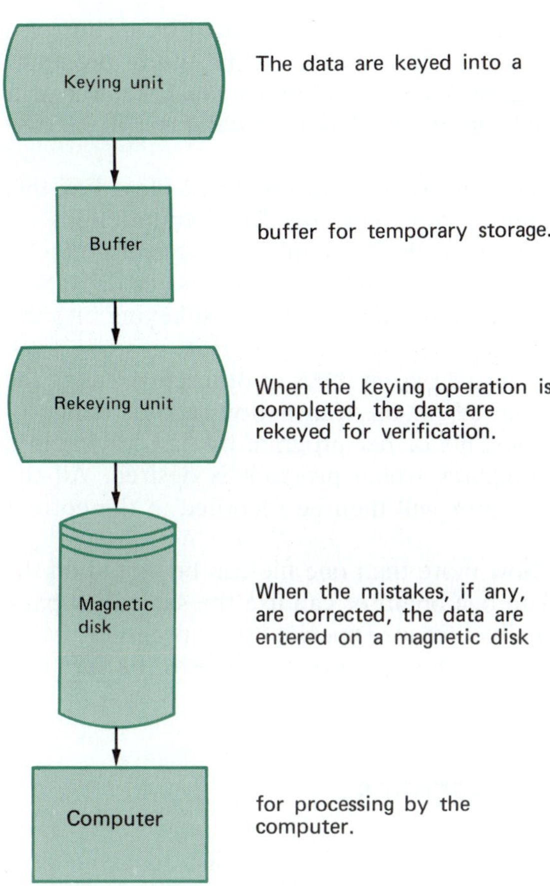

The data are keyed into a

buffer for temporary storage.

When the keying operation is completed, the data are rekeyed for verification.

When the mistakes, if any, are corrected, the data are entered on a magnetic disk

for processing by the computer.

Figure 5-18. *This flowchart shows the steps taken to verify and record data on magnetic disks.*

MAGNETIC DISK RECORDS

Magnetic disk records contain the data to be processed. They also contain a key code or address by which data can be found or recorded. Most often the key code is a data item or field in the record, such as the customer number, branch number, stock number, or invoice number. When the key code or field is entered into a terminal, the entire record is located. The key field identifies the record.

Like magnetic tape, a magnetic disk is a continuous medium. There is an important difference between the two, however. When magnetic disks are used, the computer does not have to search through a whole file in order to find a particular record. Direct access to data on a disk is possible. Any record can be reached directly without reading through the entire file.

A particular record can be read, written, replaced, or updated by addressing the key code of that record and processing it by the proper program instructions. This direct method of accessing data regardless of their position in a file is known as *random access*.

The key codes of data on magnetic disks are located by means of a complicated address system that is built into a special utility program. This utility program is purchased from the computer manufacturer or a seller who specializes in such programs. Utility programs will be discussed later in this text.

A magnetic disk pack may contain several unrelated files. For this reason, several operators may record many unrelated transactions on the same disk pack at the same time. For example, one operator can be recording employee data. Another one can be recording sales data. Still another one can be recording inventory data. All can be keying into the same disk pack at the same time.

All these data are entered into different disks or different areas of the disk pack that have been reserved for the transaction records being recorded. Each operator retrieves his or her program by first keying in a job number that tells the computer which program is desired. All the data being entered by the operator will then be recorded in the correct file on the disk pack.

It is not easy to picture how more than one file can be stored on the same disk pack and more than one operator can use the same disk pack at the same time. This is possible because special utility programs index the files and make it possible for the operator to retrieve the files and records as needed.

PLANNING MAGNETIC DISK RECORDS

Planning a record for a magnetic disk file is similar to planning a record for a punched card or magnetic tape file. The customer number or whatever is considered to be the key field is often planned for the first field in the record. The number of spaces allowed for this field should equal the number of spaces needed for the largest number of characters in the field.

Once the size of a certain field is decided, this field should be the same size on all the similar records in the file. For example, if six spaces are allowed for the customer number, six identical spaces should be allowed for the customer number in all the records in the file. See Figure 5-19.

When comparing punched cards and magnetic disks, the concepts of record planning are almost the same:

(1) The fields in the records on a disk must be written in a planned order, much as they are punched into a card.
(2) All records in a magnetic disk file must be of the same kind. (A master file will contain only master records. A detail file will contain only detail records.)
(3) The length of a given field in like records must be the same. (The customer name field would use the same number of spaces in all the records in a file.)

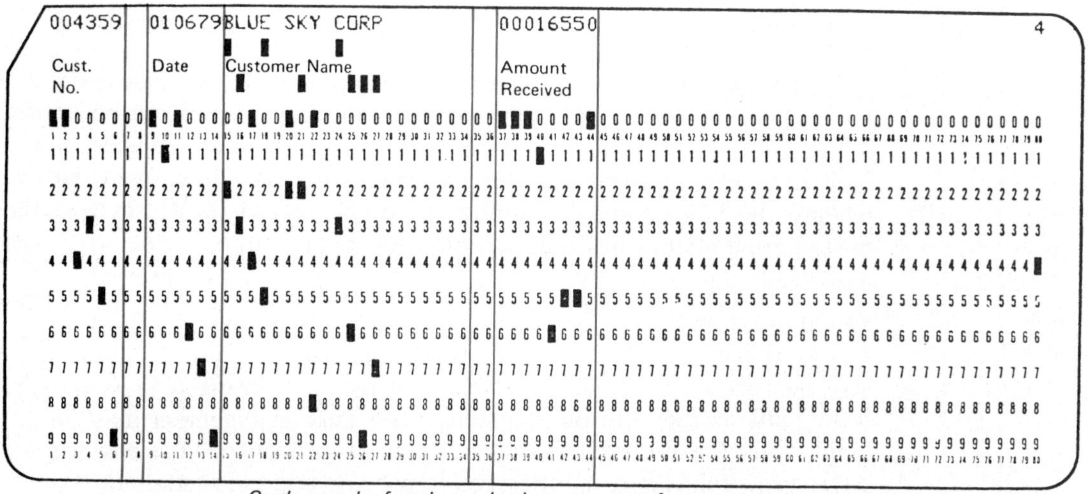

Card record of cash received on account from customer

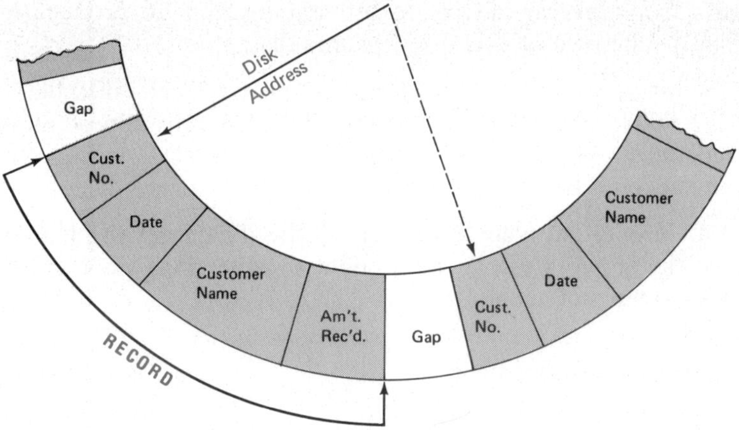

Disk record of cash received on account from customer

Figure 5-19. *Contents of a punched card and disk record are compared.*

(4) The number of spaces allowed for a field should equal the number needed for the largest item of data to be recorded in that field.

(5) All the records in a particular disk file must be of the same length, but the records can vary in length from one file to the next.[3] (The records may be as long or as short as needed. They do not need to have 80 spaces.)

Note that because a magnetic disk is a continuous medium, the records in a particular file may be longer or shorter than those in a punched card file.

[3]The length of records within a magnetic file can vary with complicated programs, but in this text only fixed-length records will be discussed.

Disk addresses

As stated earlier, each record in a magnetic disk file must contain a key field or address. The computer uses the key to locate a particular record on the disk. The record can then be corrected or replaced on the disk or read into the computer for processing. As mentioned earlier, usually the key code is a number from the record itself, such as the customer number, stock number, or invoice number.

Sequential files

The records in a magnetic disk file may be arranged in sequential order, just as they are on magnetic tape. This arrangement may be desired when the records normally appear in sequence, which is true of payroll records. There is little need to process them in random order.

Sequential order in magnetic disk files may also be desired when the records from several media are brought together to produce a report, such as a statement of account. Assume that:

(1) The master customer records appear on a magnetic disk file.
(2) The sales summary and payments detail records appear on magnetic tape files.
(3) The account balance records are in a punched card file.

With proper program instructions, the data from the matching records in the above files can be brought together in the computer to produce statements of account.

Random access files

Often magnetic disk records are not kept in sequence. In some cases, it is easier for a business to enter transactions just as they happen, Or, management may wish the records kept up to date at all times. Inventory records are a case in point. A company does not like to have large amounts of money tied up in stock. Neither does it like to run out of stock and not be able to fill its orders. Through the miracle of electronics, it is possible for the computer to enter records and to find them directly without reading through an entire file, as was done with magnetic tape files. As each item on stock is received, it can be added to the amount of stock on hand. As each item is shipped out, it can be subtracted from the amount on hand.

This direct or random access allows the instant adjustment of any amount. Any record can be printed or displayed on the CRT. If desired, a program can be written to print out or display only stock items that are in short supply. For this reason, magnetic disk files are often used for inventory records. Magnetic disk files are used when instant information is desired for making decisions.

ADVANTAGES OF MAGNETIC DISK RECORDS

The advantages of using magnetic disks for processing data are as follows:

(1) Locating a record is faster, and records can be read and written faster than on tapes.
(2) With disks, random access is possible because each record can be coded and located directly regardless of where it is in the file. When magnetic tape files are updated, the updated file must be completely rewritten. The addition, deletion, or change of only a few records requires that the whole file be written on a new tape.
(3) Transactions affecting a file can be processed as they happen, thus keeping the file up to date.
(4) Disks provide for more compact storage of data than tapes.

DISADVANTAGES OF MAGNETIC DISK RECORDS

The disadvantages of using magnetic disks, when compared with magnetic tapes, are as follows:

(1) Disk packs and disk drives cost more than tapes and tape drives.
(2) In updating a magnetic tape file, a new tape is created. The old master tape is not changed and can be stored for "back up." In updating a disk file, the record is read, brought up to date, and entered back on the same disk. Old data are erased. As a result, if there are mistakes, they are not as easily traced as they are when magnetic tapes are used.
(3) Many records, such as payroll records, appear in sequential order. There is really no need to process them in random order. When sequential processing is just as desirable, tapes may be better when costs are considered.

In summary, when rapid access is needed, it is best to use disk storage, but it is better to use less expensive media, such as magnetic tapes, for back up and long-term storage.

MAGNETIC DISK FILE APPLICATIONS

In some retail stores, it may be desirable to update records of customer accounts daily. When this is the case, a master disk file may be used. The records in this master file will most likely be kept in random order. A record in the master file will contain each customer's number, name, address, amount owed, credit limit, and other important data.

There are many ways to update this type of a master disk file on a daily basis. The method described here is one in which a terminal is used to update a record for charges and payments on account. In this method, detail files are not used, as was the case when magnetic tape files were used in the updating operation described earlier in this chapter.

A *terminal* is an input/output device consisting of a typewriter keyboard and often a CRT. It enables its user to have direct contact with a computer. The terminal is connected with a computer that has disk storage. (A terminal will be described in detail in Chapter 8.)

Retrieving a customer's account

A customer's account can be retrieved and shown on the CRT so the data in the account can be examined. The balance due from the customer can be seen. To retrieve an account, the operator first calls up the proper program by keying into the terminal a job number that tells the computer which program to use. The operator then retrieves a customer's record by entering in the terminal the key field of the record. The key could be the customer number. The computer will then find the record on the disk and display the data on the CRT. By this method, the amount owed by the customer can be determined almost instantly. (See Figure 5-20.)

Courtesy Mohawk Data Sciences Corp.

Figure 5-20. *A customer's account can be retrieved and shown on a CRT.*

Updating a customer's account

As sales are made, they are first recorded on sales tickets. Payments received on account are first recorded on payments received forms. These forms are the source documents from which input data are obtained. Most likely these forms would contain all the data needed to prepare statements of account. However, only the keys of the records, the total amounts of charges and payments, and the transaction codes would be used in this updating operation.

Direct access allows the operator to update a customer's record for charges and payments made on account. New charges can be added to the amount owed and payments received can be deducted by using the terminal to keep the account constantly up to date.

After the proper program is called up, as described earlier, the key of the record stored on the disk and total of the sale or payment are entered at the terminal. The key of the record tells the computer which record to update. Transaction codes can be keyed into the terminal to make it possible for the computer to distinguish one record from another. In some cases, they can also tell the computer to add or subtract the amounts in the records.

When a new record is added to the master file, the data would be keyed into the terminal for entry into the next available space on the disk file. The new record would contain fields for a customer's number, name, address, amount owed, credit limit, and other important data.

The flowchart of a system to update customer accounts on a random-access disk file is shown in Figure 5-21, next page. Note that there are three new flowchart symbols used in this flowchart. They are the manual input symbol, the display symbol, and the on-line storage symbol.

The *manual input symbol* is used for data input by on-line keyboards, such as the terminal.

The *display symbol* is used for data display by on-line devices, such as the CRT of the terminal.

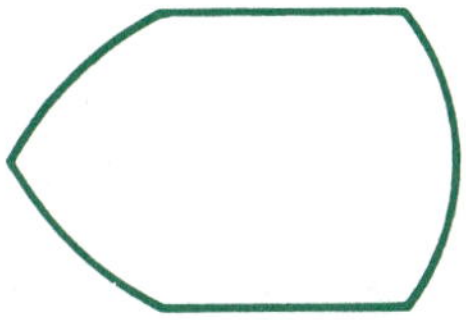

The *on-line storage symbol* shows that the magnetic disk is not removed from the disk drive and stored off-line as punched cards would be. Instead, the disk remains on the disk drive and is under the control of the computer. This means that the updating occurs on the same disk instead of a new one.

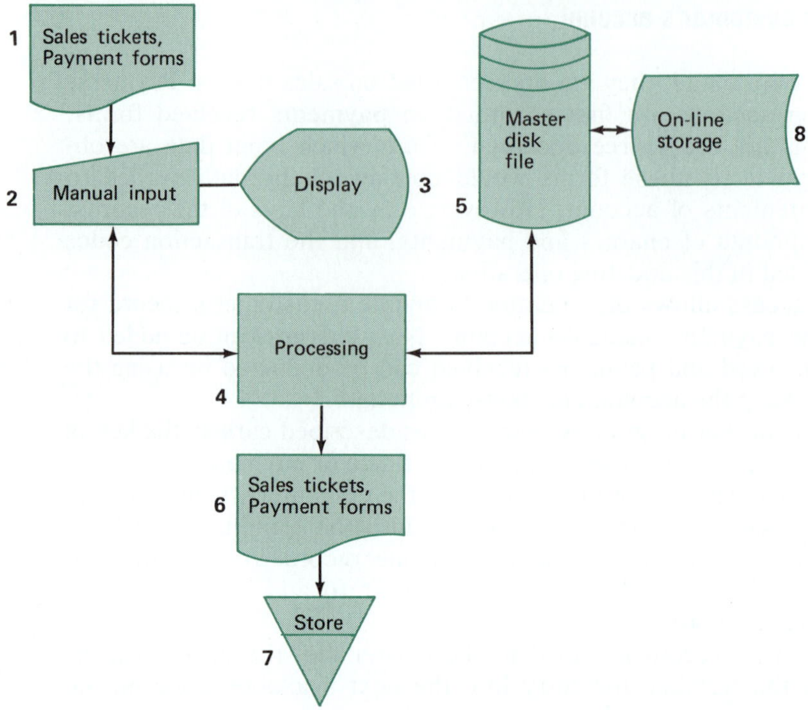

EXPLANATION

1. Source documents are the sales tickets and payments forms received. Data from these forms are
2. keyed into a terminal with a
3. CRT attached.
4. The keyed data enter the computer, which makes the necessary computations and records account balances on the
5. master disk file.
6. The source documents used in this operation are
7. stored temporarily.
8. The master magnetic disk file remains on-line at all times and is available for additional updating transactions.

Figure 5-21. *The master disk file remains on-line. Data from source documents are keyed into the computer at an on-line terminal. The computer updates the master disk file. Updated data may be displayed on the CRT.*

SUMMARY

Data are entered on magnetic tape records as invisible magnetized spots. The data are recorded in codes on either seven- or nine-channel tapes. Read-write heads are positioned over each channel. The heads can either read data into the computer or write processed information coming from it. New data erase the old data as the new data are recorded. Reading data already on the tape does not erase the data. Writing new data does.

Data can be recorded on magnetic tape by a keyboard-to-tape machine. The data can be checked for accuracy before they enter the computer. The records are written on the tape in a planned order, much as they are recorded in the fields of a punched card. Because magnetic tape is a continuous medium, the records can be either shorter or longer than the 80 columns of a punched card.

The chief advantages of using magnetic tapes are that data can be read into and out of the computer faster than is possible with punched cards. Also, the data are more compact and more easily handled.

A chief disadvantage of using magnetic tapes is that records must be addressed sequentially. This means that all records leading up to the desired one must be checked before the correct record is found. Also, when magnetic tape files are updated, the updated files must be completely rewritten.

When magnetic disks are used, the data are recorded as magnetic impulses or bits on the grooveless tracks of a disk. As the disks rotate, data can be located, read into, or written out of the computer by read-write heads positioned over and under each disk.

Planning records for disk files is like planning records for a punched card or magnetic tape file. Keyboard-to-disk units are available for recording data on disks. The data can be checked for accuracy before they are released to the computer for processing.

When magnetic disks are used, transactions can be processed as they happen, thus keeping a file up to date. Because random access is possible, records can be located and read, written, or corrected regardless of their placement in the file. When a disk file is updated, the record is read, brought up to date in the computer, and entered back on the same disk. As a result, if there are mistakes in the record, they are not easily traced.

REVIEW QUESTIONS

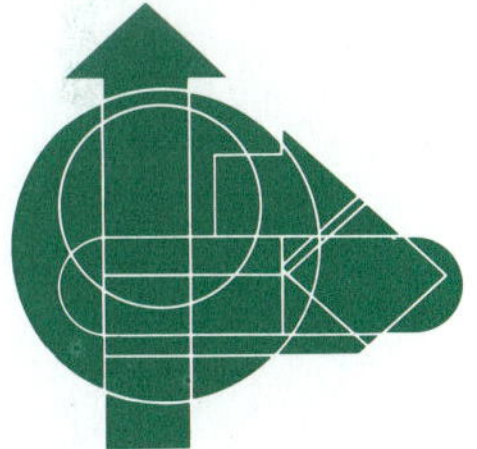

1. How are data represented on magnetic disks?
2. What is a *disk pack*?
3. How are data read or written on a magnetic disk?
4. What steps are taken to record and verify data on magnetic disks?
5. What is the unique function of a key field on a magnetic disk?
6. How does accessing records on disks differ from accessing records on tape?
7. What is *random access*?
8. Compare the planning of tape records with the planning of punched card records.
9. Can the fields in a record vary in length in a magnetic disk file?
10. Can a field allowed for a particular data item in all the records in a magnetic disk file vary in length?
11. Can the records in a particular disk file vary in length?
12. Which medium, tapes or disks, provides up-to-the minute data about the records in a file?
13. Which medium, tapes or disks, provides random access of records in a file?
14. Which medium, tapes or disks, allows for more efficient tracing of mistakes made in records?

NEW TERMS

- Block
- Buffer
- Cathode-ray tube
- CRT
- Disk drive
- Disk pack
- Display symbol
- Even parity
- Flexible disk
- Floppy disk
- Magnetic disk
- Magnetic disk symbol
- Magnetic tape
- Magnetic tape symbol
- Manual input symbol
- Odd parity
- On-line storage symbol
- Parity-check position
- Random access
- Sequential access
- Tape drive
- Terminal

STUDY GUIDE

Complete Study Guide 5 by following the instructions in your STUDY GUIDES booklet.

PROJECTS

Complete Projects 5-1 and 5-2 by following the instructions in your PROJECTS booklet.

6

ORGANIZING the FILES

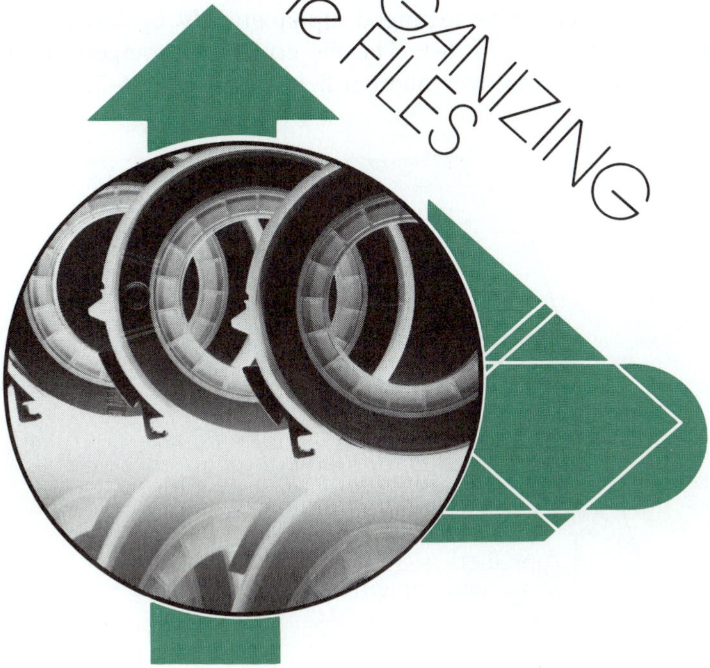

In data processing, much time is used in arranging and rearranging file records so many different reports may be prepared from them. In earlier chapters, you learned about sequencing and merging file records. In this chapter, you will learn how to use some new ways of arranging file records.

BASIC OPERATIONS

Sequencing and merging file records will be reviewed briefly. In addition, you will learn how to select, match, and match-merge file records to produce a number of reports.

Sequencing

Sequencing is the process of arranging records in either numeric or alphabetic order. If the records in a file contain a key field with numeric data, the records can be arranged in numeric order. If they contain a key field with alphabetic data, they can be arranged in alphabetic order. The records can be sequenced either one way or the other, depending on the report desired.

For example, an employee file containing records of the names and numbers of employees could be arranged alphabetically by keying the employee name field. See Figure 6-1. The file could be arranged in numeric order by keying the employee number field. See Figure 6-2.

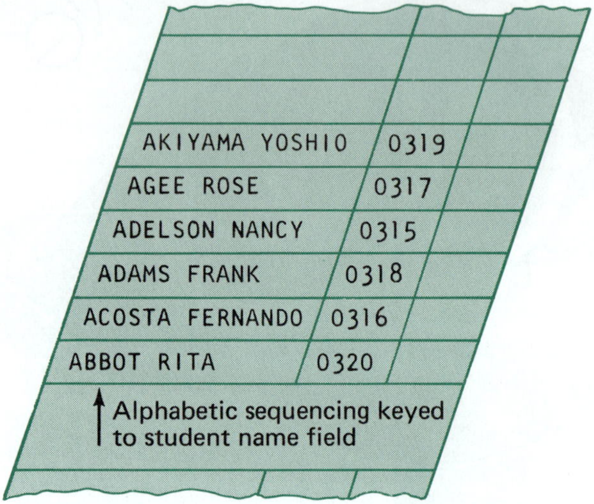

Figure 6-1. *Records are sequenced alphabetically.*

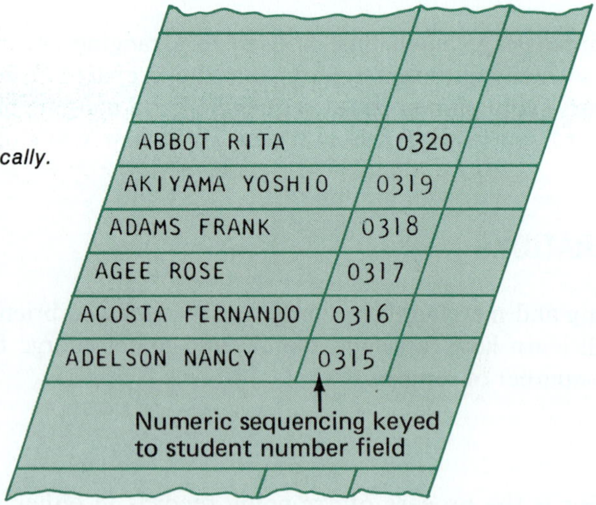

Figure 6-2. *Records are sequenced numerically.*

Often, file records are used to produce more than one report. If the records are arranged one way for one report and another way for a second report, two separate sequencing operations are needed. The sequencing operation simply arranges the records in the desired order. The computer is needed to process the data and produce the output in the form desired.

Selecting

Selecting is a process of separating from a file of records only those that have a particular name or number in a specific field. For example, assume that you wish to prepare a report for employees in the Sales Department only. They are identified with the Code 05 in the department field of the employees' records. The selecting operation would be keyed to the department number field, and a computer program would process only the records having Code 05 in this field. Figure 6-3 shows in color the records that would be selected from a tape.

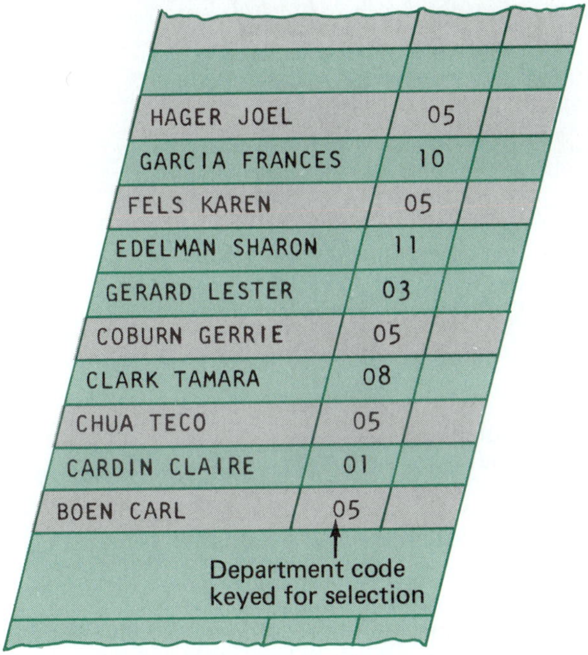

Figure 6-3. *Records are selected for processing by department code number.*

Merging

You learned earlier that merging is a process in which two or more files of records, each of which is in sequential order, are combined into one file. The records in the new file will appear in sequence. See Figure 6-4 for an example of merging the records of two tape files.

When tape records are used, the records from one tape can be merged with the records from another tape. The merged records will be recorded on still another tape. Three tape drives would be used for this merging operation.

With magnetic disks, merging is usually not done. Because of the random-access feature, new records are just stored at the end of the file and are retrieved in order, as needed.

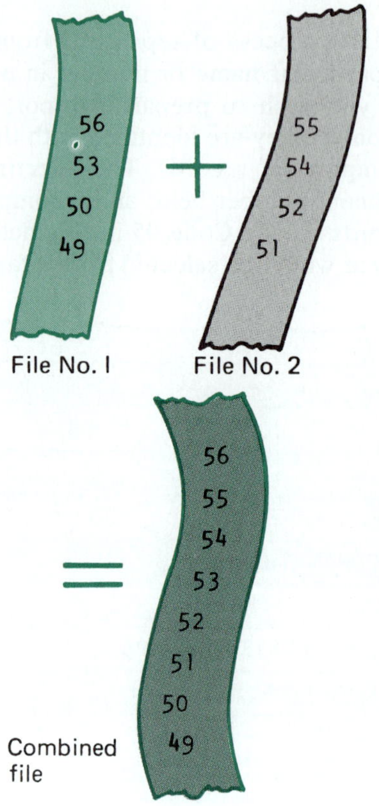

Figure 6-4. *Sequenced records from two files are merged to form a third file of sequenced records.*

Matching

Matching is the process of comparing the records in two files to see if key fields in the two sets of records are the same. If the fields are the same, a set of instructions will tell the computer what steps to follow to process the data in the records being compared. If the fields are not the same, the computer will follow another set of instructions.

Assume that you are a member of a stereo album club. You have been given an account number. Each month you are sent a letter describing the next album offered. You are also sent a refusal card to return if you do not wish to receive that particular record. If the refusal card is returned, you will not receive the album or a bill. If the card is not returned before a certain date, the album will be sent to you along with a bill.

A program will be written so that the account numbers on all refusal cards will be matched with the account numbers on the master records for all members of the club. If matches occur, the albums will not be mailed. If matches do not occur, the albums and bills will be mailed. See Figure 6-5. Note that albums and bills will be mailed to Numbers 35 and 37 because there is no match. No refusal cards have been received from them.

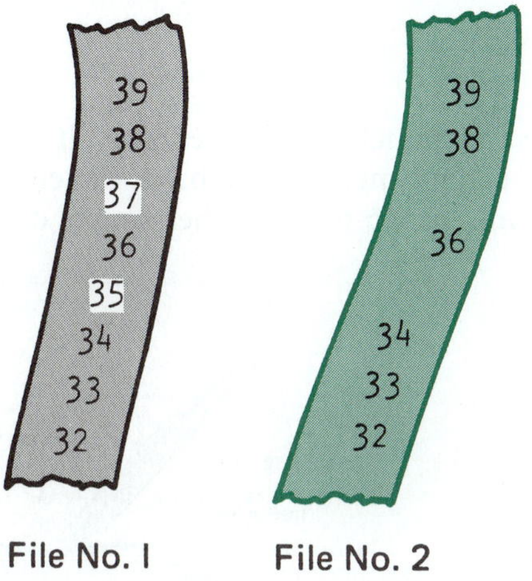

Figure 6-5. *In this example, the unmatched records, 35 and 37, will be processed.*

Match-merging

Match-merging is very much like the matching process. The difference is that matched records from two or more files are merged into a single file.

You learned in Chapter 4 that records from several files must be brought together to produce a statement of account. See Figure 4-7, p. 77. In preparing a statement of account, account numbers from records in the master, balance, sales summary, and payments detail files were matched. Then the detail records were match-merged with the master record. The computer processed the data to prepare the statement.

Sequence-checking

When properly programmed, a computer is able to check records to make sure that they are arranged in sequence. Sequence-checking is not the same as sequencing. Sequencing arranges the records in order. *Sequence-checking*, on the other hand, is the process of checking records that are already sequenced to be sure that the sequencing is correct.

PROCESSING AIDS

A mechanical sorter has long been used to handle the sequencing and selecting functions discussed earlier in this chapter. However, the sorter is used only for punched cards. Utility programs for magnetic media are of recent origin. With them, the sorting is done by a computer. Not only does the computer sequence and select data, but it also merges, matches, and match-merges. The computer performs these basic operations much faster than did the sorter and other machines once used. Utility programs will be discussed in detail later in this chapter.

Mechanical sorter

The sorter is limited to punched card records. It can sequence or select these records. It cannot merge, match, or match-merge them. A sorter, which is shown in Figure 6-6, is a rather simple device. It has the following parts:

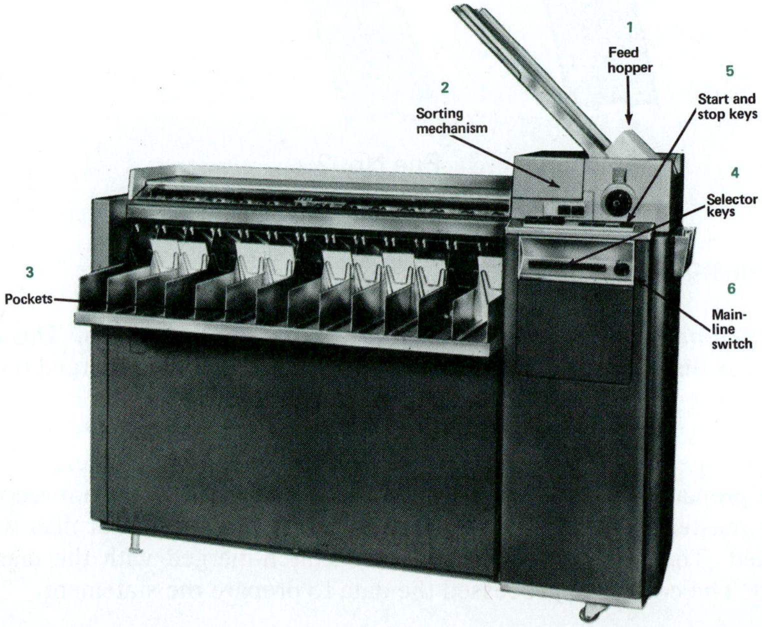

Photo courtesy of IBM Corporation

Figure 6-6. *A mechanical sorter can sequence or select punched card records.*

(1) A feed hopper for input cards.
(2) A sorting brush or photoelectric cell to sense the punches in a column of a card on which to sort.
(3) Thirteen output pockets for the sorted cards. Twelve of the pockets are for the 12 punching positions in a column of a punched card. The thirteenth pocket is for blanks or rejects.
(4) Selector keys for indicating the number of the column on which to sort.
(5) Start and stop keys for starting or stopping the sorting program.
(6) A main line switch for turning the power on or off.

Sensing device. A sensing device reads the punched data in a card. This device may be a metal brush that makes electrical contacts through the punched holes or a photoelectric cell.

The sensing device on the mechanical sorter illustrated in Figure 6-6 can be set to read the data in any of the 80 columns of a standard card. It can read the data in only one card column at a time, however. Thus, if the data being sorted are numeric and are punched in a field of six columns, the punched cards must be run through the sorter six times. On each pass, the sorting device must be set to read the data on another one of the six columns.

If the data being sorted are alphabetic, there will be two punches in each column. Each punch is treated separately. For that reason, the cards must be passed through the sorter twice for each column. The first time it must be set for the digit punch. The second time it must be set for the zone punch in the same column.

The selection mechanism on the sorter can be adjusted to sequence the cards or to select only certain ones.

Output sorting pockets. The sorter shown in Figure 6-6 has 13 pockets into which the sorted cards drop. The first pocket (R) is for rejects — usually those cards not having a hole punched in the column on which sorting is taking place. The remaining 12 pockets are for the 12 vertical punching positions on the card. Ten pockets are for digits 0 through 9 and two are for zone positions 11 and 12. See Figure 6-7.

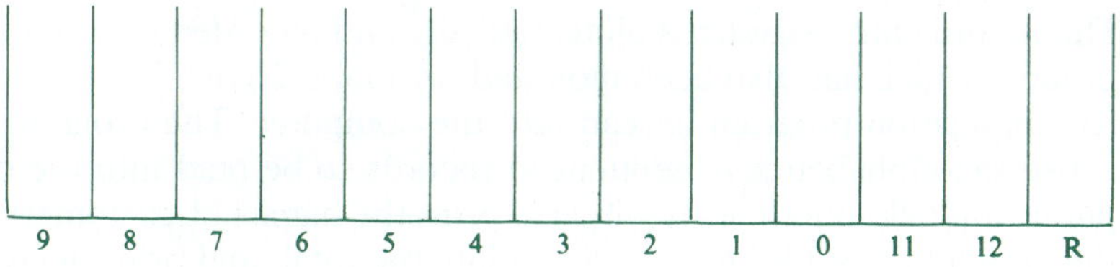

Figure 6-7. *The sorter has 13 pockets into which the sorted cards drop.*

Utility programs

Utility programs are furnished by computer manufacturers. These programs do many routine jobs, such as sorting, loading a program into memory, and writing out the contents in storage. They are widely used to sort magnetic tape and disk records. A utility program is loaded into the computer, where the program does the job for which it is made. In one case, it brings into the computer unarranged records from one magnetic tape or disk. It arranges the records in sequence and records them on another tape or disk.

A utility program can arrange records in sequence numerically that were previously arranged in sequence alphabetically, or the other way around. It can merge records from two or more tape files and enter them on another tape or disk file. It can match records from two or more files and record the matched records on a tape or disk file. It can match-merge records from several files and enter these records on another file.

Utility programs of the type described here can sort records and enter the sorted records on magnetic tape or disk files. They do not process the data in these records. That is the job of application programs, written by programmers for solving certain problems with the records. Application programs are not designed to do routine jobs, such as sorting. These jobs are done by utility programs. Application programs will be explained later in this chapter.

So that you will understand the part that utility programs play in solving a problem, assume that you have been asked to prepare a printed report of customers, the amounts owed by them, and the total of these amounts. The names of the customers are to be arranged in alphabetic order.

Customer numbers, their names, and the amounts owed by them appear on a magnetic tape file. However, the records are arranged numerically by customer number. To prepare the report desired, you must first arrange the records alphabetically. The procedure to solve this problem follows:

(1) A utility program to sequence the records alphabetically is loaded into the computer. The utility program appears on magnetic tape. It will continue to appear on the tape even though information from it is read into the computer.
(2) The tape file containing customer data is mounted on a tape drive.
(3) The customer data are read into the computer a block at a time.
(4) The records are sequenced alphabetically and recorded on a new reel of tape, which has also been mounted on a tape drive.
(5) An application program is read into the computer. The program will cause the alphabetically sequenced records to be read into the computer, a block at a time. It will also print the names of customers and the amounts owed by them, accumulate the total, and print the total.

Sorting by a utility program is not a simple job. The records must be run through the computer a number of times. One original and at least two output tape files are needed. Even with these handicaps, sorting by a utility program is much faster than sorting by a mechanical sorter.

Application programs

An *application program* is a program that is usually written by a programmer who works for the computer user, not the manufacturer.[1] This program is written to solve a certain problem. Application programs are not designed to do routine jobs such as merging and match-merging. These jobs are done by utility programs.

[1]Some general application programs can be bought by the computer user, but the programmer usually must make changes in them to fit the company's needs.

The selection of certain records from a file for processing can be handled by a program written by an application programmer. Assume that a student file is kept on magnetic tape. The records in this file contain the names of students and their code classifications. The first-year students are classified Code 1; sophomores, Code 2; juniors, Code 3; and seniors, Code 4. You have been asked to prepare a printed report of the names of only the junior students. The computer can follow instructions that have been written and stored in its memory to do this job. Writing instructions of this type in programming languages will be explained in later chapters. However, these instructions would tell the computer to take the following steps:

STEP 1: KEY TO THE STUDENT CLASSIFICATION FIELD.
STEP 2: READ EACH RECORD IN THE STUDENT FILE.
STEP 3: COMPARE THE DATA IN THE CLASSIFICATION FIELD OF EACH RECORD WITH THE DIGIT 3.
STEP 4: WRITE EACH RECORD WITH DIGIT 3 IN THE CLASSIFICATION FIELD ON A PRINTED REPORT OF JUNIOR STUDENTS.

The above is an example of a routine, which would be part of the application program. A *routine* is a set of instructions within a computer program for doing a certain task. The routine just explained is for processing one record in the student file.

REVIEW QUESTIONS

1. What is *sequencing*?
2. What is *selecting*?
3. If records are to be processed by department number, on which field would the records be keyed?
4. What is *merging*?
5. If records from two tape files are being merged, how many tape drives are needed?
6. What is the difference between sequencing and sequence-checking?
7. What device on a mechanical sorter makes it possible to read the data represented by the holes in the punched cards?
8. On how many card columns does a mechanical sorter read numeric data at one time?
9. When utility programs are used to sequence records, where does sequencing take place?
10. Do utility programs process the data in the records they sort?
11. What is an *application* program?
12. What is the difference between an application program and a utility program.

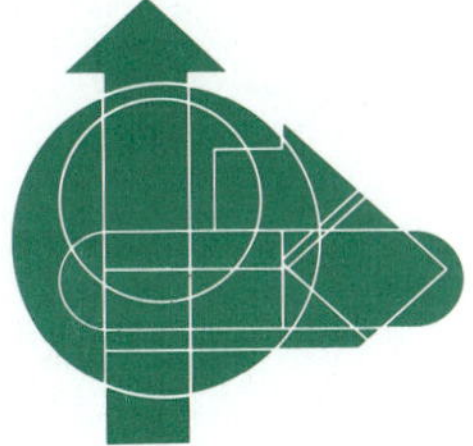

USING THE FILES FOR PREPARING REPORTS

Using the files of records for reports needed by business has been explained in Chapters 2–5. The principles developed have been applied to many problems. The following explanation is an extension of those principles that will reinforce your earlier study.

Updating reports prepared from sequential records

Business uses many kinds of reports that must be updated from time to time due to changes that take place. This means that the records in files used to prepare a report must be updated in order to print the report.

Reports in which there are few changes or in which updating delays are not too serious need not be updated as often as reports in which changes are common and in which up-to-the-minute information is vital.

Company telephone directories must be updated from time to time. Processing occasional changes, while important, is not essential. As a result, magnetic tapes are often used for this processing job.

The following steps must be taken in order to update the telephone records file. This file will be used to produce the updated directory.

(1) Records in which there are no changes are copied from the master file on the updated tape file.
(2) Records in which the data have changed since the last update are replaced on the updated file in order to show those changes.
(3) Records of employees who have left the company since the last update are deleted from the file.
(4) Records that have been created since the last update are added to the file.

You will recall that a file that must be updated from time to time is generally referred to as a master file. Files containing records that will update the master file are called detail files. In processing a telephone directory, the file from which the directory is printed is the master file. The changes that must be made in the master file to update it are recorded on a detail file. The different records needed to update the file are identified by transaction codes entered on the records in the detail file.

In this example, the master and detail files are on magnetic tape. The master file is arranged in alphabetic order according to the last name of the user of a telephone. Each record contains the name of the user, the department number, and the telephone number. The detail file must also be arranged alphabetically. Each record in this file will contain information needed to update the master file, as well as a transaction code. A program tells the computer what changes should be made, based on the transaction code in the record.

Updating routine, magnetic tape. The updating routine that follows gives important steps in a program to solve the problem:

(1) A record from the master file and a record from the detail file are read into the computer.
(2) The key field of the record in the master file is compared with the key field of the record in the detail file.

(3) If there is no detail file record to match an old master file record, no change in the master record is needed. The record will simply be copied on the updated master file. (No detail record is needed for retained records.)
(4) If the key field of a record in the detail file is *equal* to the key field of a record in the master file and if the transaction code indicates that the master record should be changed, the record in the master file will be replaced by the record in the detail file.
(5) If the key field of a record in the detail file is *equal* to the key field of a record in the master file, and if the transaction code indicates that it is a deletion, the old master record will be dropped from the updated master file.
(6) When there is no match and there is no existing record in the old master file, the record in the detail file is copied onto the updated master file. It is a new record.

Program instructions are written and stored in the computer. These instructions cause the records from both files to be read into the computer, which compares the two records and takes the steps needed to update the master file. The computer continues this routine until all the records from the old master file and the detail file have been processed and an updated file has been prepared. The printed master directory is prepared as output at the same time as the updated master file.

The flowchart in Figure 6-8 shows an updating routine when magnetic tapes are used for the master and detail files.

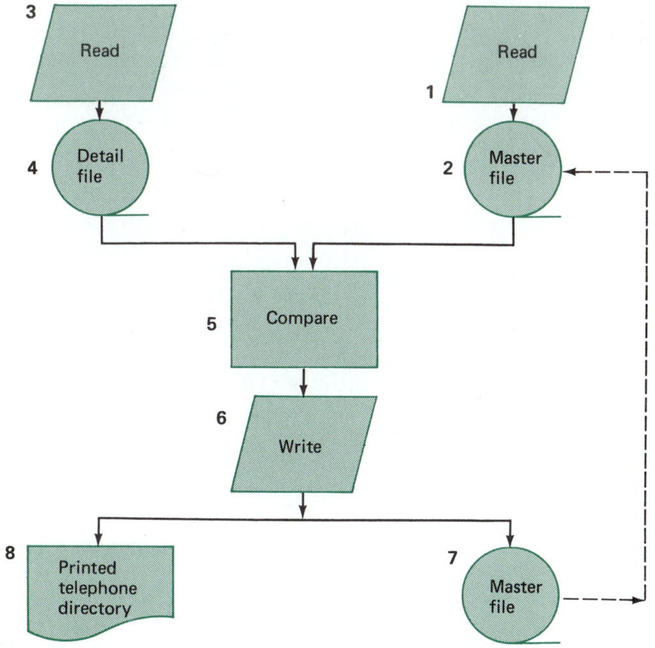

EXPLANATION

1. A read instruction reads a record from the
2. master file and
3. another read instruction reads a record from a
4. detail file
5. into memory for comparison of the key fields. The results of the comparison will determine what action is to be taken to update the records.
6. The updated records are written on the
7. updated master file, which becomes the master file for the next period.
8. Output also consists of a printed, updated telephone directory.

Figure 6-8. *Above is a flowchart of a routine in a program that is used when magnetic tapes are used for both master and detail files.*

Updating routine, magnetic disk with sequenced records. Magnetic disk files with sequenced records are updated in a manner similar to that used in updating files on magnetic tapes. The flowchart in Figure 6-9 shows an updating operation when a magnetic disk is used as the master file and a magnetic tape is used for the detail file. Note the few differences that exist between this figure and Figure 6-8.

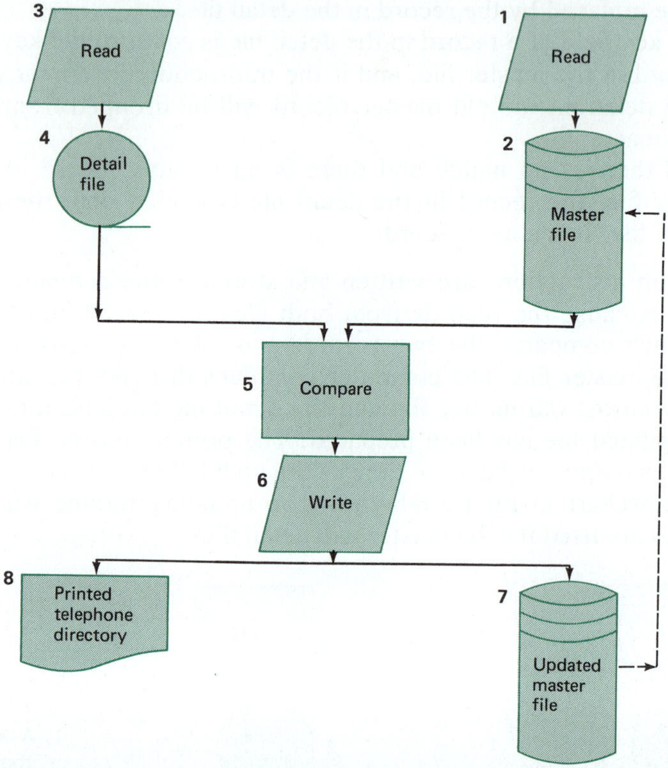

EXPLANATION

1. A read instruction reads records from a
2. master disk file, and
3. a read instruction reads records from a
4. detail tape file
5. into memory for comparison of key fields. The results of the comparison will determine which records will be updated and
6. written into the old master file as an
7. updated master disk file, which becomes the master file for the next period.
8. Output also consists of a printed, updated telephone directory.

Figure 6-9. *Above is a flowchart of a routine in a program used when a magnetic disk is used as a master file and a magnetic tape is used for a detail file.*

Batching records. A common way of updating a sequentially arranged master file is to prepare records when there are changes in the detail file or files. These changes are accumulated in the detail files until such time as it is decided to update the master file. Then the batches of records from the different detail files are sequenced and merged and used to update the master file. This method costs must less than updating the master file as each new record is prepared. *Batch data processing* is a method by which items to be processed may be coded and collected into groups before processing.

Coordinating the files. In an updating operation, if the master file is in sequential order, the supporting detail files usually are also arranged in that order. Keying must be on the same fields. If the master customer file is keyed to customer numbers, for example, the detail files must also be keyed to customer numbers.

Updating reports with random-access records

Records are usually arranged on magnetic disks in random order because faster input of data is possible. A given record on a disk can be read, written, replaced, or updated. The other records on the disk are not disturbed. This method of accessing data is also known as direct access.

Input records. The updating file records may be entered on any input medium that can be accepted by the computer. If punched cards are used, the data may first be transferred to a magnetic tape file for faster processing.

An on-line input terminal is usually used. It is connected by telephone or direct wire to the computer. Specific records on magnetic disks can be accessed and updated by an operator using the terminal. Detail records are not necessary with a random-access file. You will learn more about terminals in Chapter 8.

Random-access applications. Magnetic disks with random-access records are used for many different jobs. Inventories are a good example. Each item of stock is given a number. When a shipment is made from stock, a deduction is made from the inventory record. When stock is received, it is added. The transactions can be recorded and processed each day by the computer to give the balance of that item of stock on hand.

The *reorder point* for an item of stock is the lowest amount that can be on hand before ordering more of that item. When the amount on hand goes down to this amount or under this amount, more stock must be ordered. If this reorder point and the amount to reorder are included in each stock record, the computer can be programmed to print a report of stock numbers in short supply. The report will show the stock number, the reorder point listed in the record, the date of the last transaction, and the balance of that stock on hand. Also, the amount to reorder will be listed on the report.

A part of a stock record as it might appear on a disk is shown in Figure 6-10 in readable print. Note that it has a field for the stock number as the key field. A date field is included, and it will always give the date of the last transaction. The fields for the reorder point and the amount to reorder have amounts that are usually fixed. The balance on hand is updated every time a quantity of the stock has been received or shipped out.

Fields identified	Stock No.	Date	Reorder point	Amount to reorder	Balance
Record 1	19601	040582	500	200	600
Record 2	18769	100682	200	050	300
Record 3	51348	102182	700	250	650

Figure 6-10. *Shown are three simulated stock records as they would appear on a magnetic disk.*

If the balance of a stock on hand is lower than the reorder point, the computer will print a report of the data shown in Figure 6-10. Actually, Record 3 is the only one that would show a need to reorder. The balance on hand is 650, and the reorder point is 700. An order should be placed for 250 of this item. Record 3 is the only one that would be printed. However, any stock record on the disk can be accessed and displayed on a CRT.

Updating routine. The updating routine when random-access disk files are used is as follows:

(1) The operator enters the proper code and job number to retrieve the updating routine.
(2) A record from a detail disk file, which contains a key number or name and the updating data, is read into the memory of the computer.
(3) The utility program stored in the computer reads the input record and searches the master disk file for a record with the same key number or name.
(4) When the correct record on the master disk file is found, it is read into the computer memory. The additions or deductions to update the master file record are made.
(5) The updated record is then written into the same place in the same disk file. The updated record erases the contents of the original record that had been stored there, without disturbing the other records in the file.

The updated disk file can then be used to produce a reorder report and any other reports needed. A computer program reads the required data into the computer, directs computations, and prints or displays the processed information.

For an application of this routine, assume that 30 new electric motors, Stock No. 3478, have been received. An input record is created at a computer terminal, showing this information. The record is read into memory. The computer searches the disk file for the location of the record for Stock No. 3478. When the record is found, it is also read into memory. The program causes 30 units of stock to be added to the previous balance shown on the record. Assume that the balance is 170 units. The computer will add 30 to the 170 and write back the new record (200 units) into the same location on the disk file that was occupied by 170. This operation is shown in Figure 6-11.

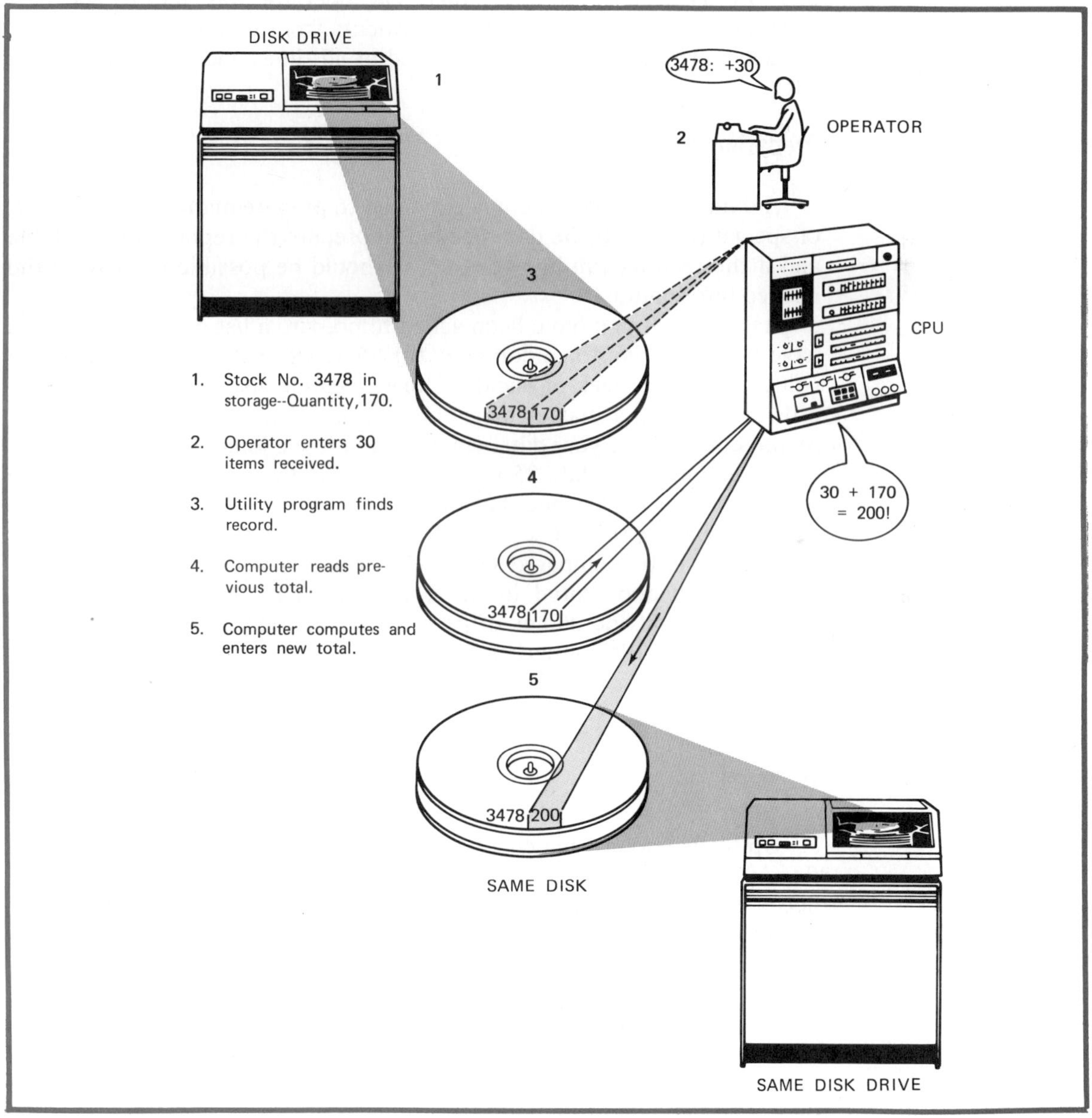

Figure 6-11. *Random-access records are used to update files.*

Other random access applications. The processing of requests for information is often handled by terminals connected to a central computer by telephone lines or direct wires. Usually the files are on magnetic disks and can be almost instantly retrieved and updated by these terminals. The transactions can be entered and processed as they take place. When a request is received through a terminal, the files are searched for the answer, which is sent to the inquirer by the terminal.

You learned in Chapter 5 how customers' accounts could be updated daily by using an on-line terminal. The operator was able to add new charges to an account or deduct payments from it. Using the terminal, the account balance could be checked at all times and displayed on the CRT.

Preparing special reports

A data processing system is expected to prepare many different kinds of special reports. If the data needed to prepare the reports are available and if the records can be accessed, it should be possible to provide the needed information.

Assume that you have been asked to prepare a list of employees who have been working for a company for 25 years or more. These persons will get an extra week of vacation time. Assume also that employee records are kept on a master magnetic tape file. One of the fields on each record contains the year date when the employee joined the company.

An employment date 25 years earlier than the current date will have to be determined. Assume that the current date is 1982. A date 25 years earlier would be 1957. The year of employment date field in each record in the file will be compared with 1957, which is written into an application program and stored in the computer. The computer will be instructed to print the names of persons whose records show the year of employment as 1957 or earlier.

Figure 6-12 shows a partial flowchart of this program when magnetic tape is used.

DATA BASE

Up to this point, this chapter has been concerned with the organization of different kinds of files in order to give management the reports it needs. The files always contained records. Each record was made up of a number of data fields or items. A file was designed to prepare a particular kind of report. Usually many different files were kept. As a result, there was much duplication of data items in the different files.

Another system has been developed that largely does away with files of records. Instead, the individual data items (fields) from those records are entered into a massive pool referred to as a data base. Each item of data is drawn from this pool as needed to prepare the reports manage-

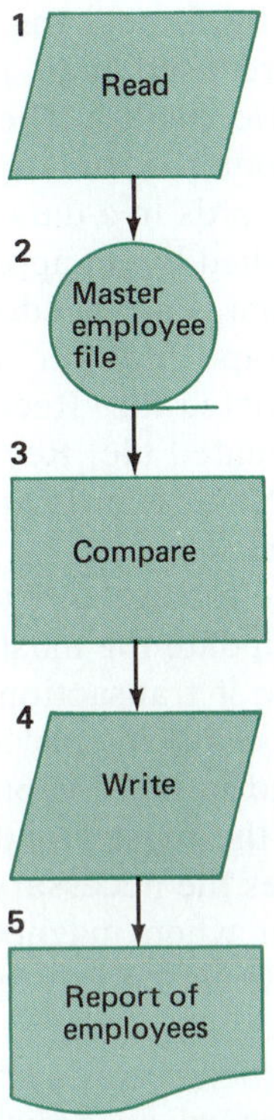

EXPLANATION

1. A read instruction reads a record from the
2. master employee records file
3. into memory for comparison of the year of employment field with a year date in the computer instruction.
4. A write instruction will record the name of the employees with 25 or more years of service in the company on
5. a special report.

Figure 6-12. *Flowchart of a routine that processes specific records from a magnetic tape file.*

ment wishes. While this concept will not be used in the applications described in the rest of this book, it is good for you to know that data base systems are available.

SUMMARY

Basic operations consist of sequencing, selecting, matching, and match-merging. Usually, one or the other of these operations must be used to arrange the records in a file so that they will be ready for further processing. More than one operation may be needed. Sorting operations can be performed manually, by a mechanical sorter, or by utility programs. Mechanical sorters are used with punched cards. Utility programs are used with magnetic media. The basic operations are performed very rapidly by a computer.

The selection of certain records in a data file that are needed to solve a specific problem can be handled by an application program, written by a programmer. A utility program is not needed.

In updating a magnetic tape file, records in which there are no changes are copied on the updated file. Records in which there are data changes are revised on the updated file. Records that have been terminated are taken from the file. New records are added to the file. A completely new file must be created.

The master file contains the records that must be updated. Detail files contain the changes that will update the master file. The changes may be recorded on a single detail file if transaction codes are used in the records to indicate the type of record being processed.

Program instructions stored in the computer cause the records to be read into the computer from the master and detail files. The computer compares the records and takes the necessary steps to update the master file. In an updating operation when magnetic tape files are used, the master and detail file records must be in sequential order. Keying must be on the same fields.

In an updating operation when records are arranged in random order on magnetic disks, a given record on a disk can be read, written, replaced, or updated without disturbing the other records on the disk. A new file is not created. The updating records may be entered on any input medium acceptable to the computer. On-line terminals are often used.

REVIEW QUESTIONS

1. In an operation to update a telephone directory on a magnetic tape master file, what four steps must be taken?
2. What input file will contain the records not requiring any changes in an updating operation?
3. May all the records needed to update a magnetic tape master file be recorded on one input file? What code is needed in these records?
4. What are the sequencing requirements for updating a master file on magnetic tape?
5. In an updating routine using magnetic tapes, what files will furnish the records that must be read into the computer? Must keying be on the same fields?
6. What is *batch data processing*?
7. Is an entirely new master file created when records are updated on a disk file?
8. In updating a master disk file, when an updated record is written into a location containing an old record, what happens to the old record?

9. In comparing the year of employment date with the present date, what field in the data record is read into the computer for comparison? How is the present date obtained for comparison?

NEW TERMS

- Application program
- Batch data processing
- Matching
- Match-merging
- Reorder point
- Routine
- Selecting
- Sequence-checking
- Sequencing
- Utility programs

STUDY GUIDE

Complete Study Guide 6 by following the instructions in your STUDY GUIDES booklet.

PROJECTS

Complete Projects 6-1, 6-2, and 6-3 by following the instructions in your PROJECTS booklet.

7 THE ELECTRONIC COMPUTER SYSTEM

Photo courtesy of Pitney Bowes

In terms of age, the computer can be thought of as a rather new development. Computers have been used in business and industry less than thirty years. Yet, there have been many great improvements in computer technology during this fairly short period of time.

COMPUTER GENERATIONS

Each major improvement in technology has led to the development of a new "generation" of computers. Since the use of the first computer in the early 1950s, three — some say four — different generations of computers have been developed. The announcement of the fourth generation of computers can be expected almost any time. In fact, some manufacturers already state that their latest computers are of the fourth generation. But, there is yet no industry agreement on this.

Each new generation of computers improved input/output and memory devices. The new input/output devices made it possible for the user to have much greater kinds of input media. Also, the data in these media could be recorded and processed at far greater speeds. The improved memory devices were not only smaller in size, but they were able to store more data in less space. (Input/output and memory devices will be described in detail later.) These changes made it possible to increase the internal processing speed of a computer about ten times with each new generation of computers.

First-generation computers

The first-generation computers used vacuum tubes for memory circuitry. For this reason, the machines were very large in size and fairly slow by today's standards. First-generation computers could make over 100 thousand calculations per second. Although this may seem extremely fast, the GUINESS BOOK OF RECORDS lists the speed of a modern Control Data Corporation computer at almost 100 million calculations per second in 1976. The large number of vacuum tubes in these early computers created many problems because of the amount of heat generated by the tubes. This heat problem made it necessary to install heavy-duty air conditioning units. The first-generation computers were mostly computational machines. Their input/output capabilities were usually limited to keyboard and/or punched card input and printer and/or punched card output.

Second-generation computers

The second-generation computers used transistors in place of the vacuum tubes. This change made it possible to reduce the amount of heat put out by the machines. The use of transistors also made it possible to reduce the size of the equipment. This change further increased the computer's computational speed. Also, the transistors proved to be much more reliable than vacuum tubes.

Removable disk storage units and magnetic tape input/output units were developed for use on these machines. The speed of the line printers was increased from 300 lines per minute, which was fairly common on first-generation computers, to 1,000 lines per minute. The speed of card readers and card punches was also increased, although not as dramatically as that of the printers. These changes in the computer made it more useful as a tool in business because of the large volume of data to be processed and the lengthy printed reports required.

Third-generation computers

The third-generation computers used very small electronic circuits called microcircuits rather than transistors. This change further decreased the size of the computer while increasing its speed. The speed of the first-generation computers was described in milliseconds (1/1,000 of a second). The speed of the second-generation computers was described in microseconds (1/1,000,000 of a second). The speed of the third-generation computers was described in nanoseconds (1/1,000,000,000 of a second). The speed of line printers on many third-generation computers was increased to 2,000 lines per minute. One computer manufacturer has developed a printer that has a rated speed of over 20,000 lines per minute. The electronic components used in different generations of computers are shown in Figure 7-1.

(Vacuum tube)
First Generation

(Transistor)
Second Generation

(Microcircuit chip)
Third Generation

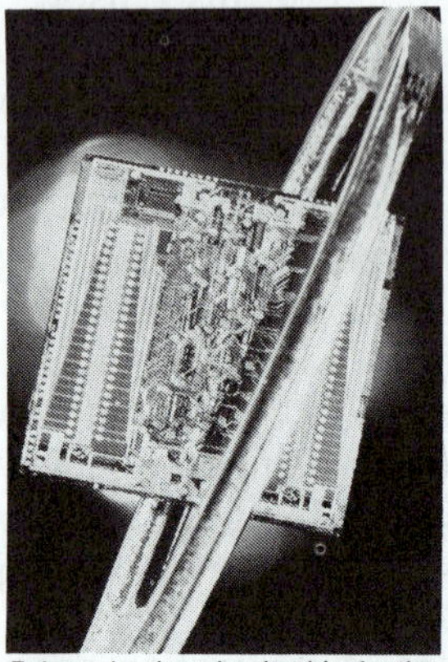

Enlarged microcircuit chip in the eye of a needle

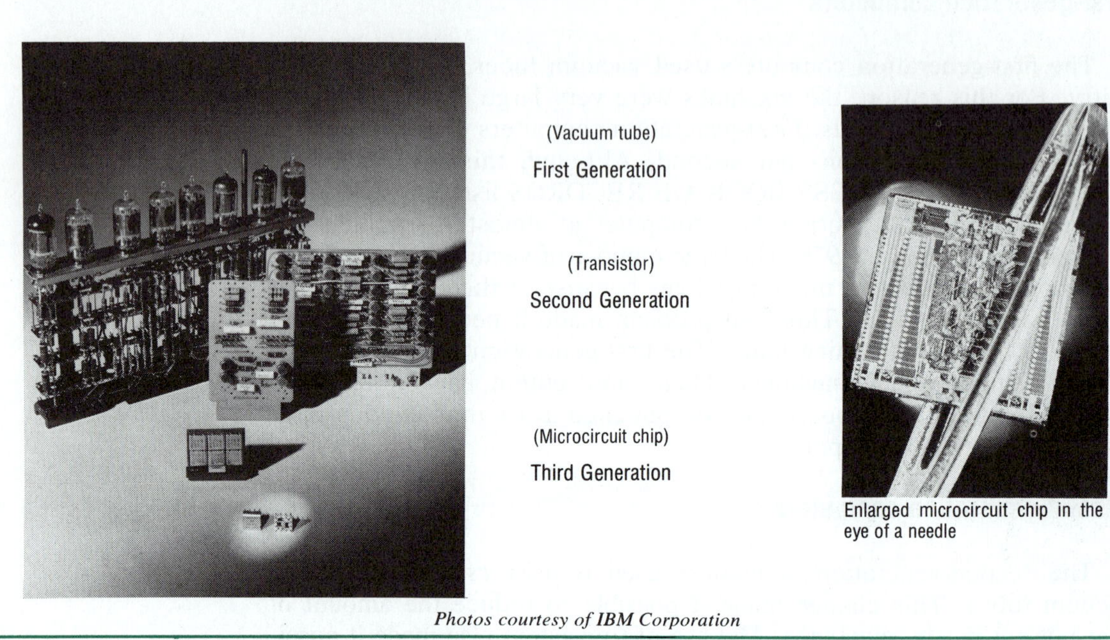

Photos courtesy of IBM Corporation

Figure 7-1. *Electronic components represent different computer generations.*

TYPES OF ELECTRONIC COMPUTERS

There are many ways to classify computers, but the basic division is between digital and analog computers. While these chapters are concerned entirely with digital computers, you should know that there are two basic types of computers.

The Digital Computer

The *digital computer* works with numbers or letters of the alphabet and special characters that can be coded numerically. It solves problems electronically by counting, adding, subtracting, multiplying, and dividing. An adding machine is a digital device, as is a cash register. Numeric data can be stored in digital computers until a total or result is desired. The answer represents units of something that can be counted. Digital computers are widely used in processing business and many kinds of engineering data. See Figure 7-2, which shows two typical digital computers.

NCR V8565 computer system *NCR Corporation*

Honeywell 68/80 Series 60 computer system *Honeywell Inc.*

Figure 7-2. *Two typical digital computers are shown.*

The Analog Computer

An *analog computer* is a type of calculating machine that uses numbers to represent quantities that can be measured (such as voltages, resistances, or rotations). Therefore, the analog computer is actually a measuring device. By means of gauges, meters, and wheels, the analog computer can measure and process physical variables such as amounts of electric current, speed of sound, temperature, pressure, and velocity. The speedometer, by means of a rotating wire, measures the speed at which a car is moving. The needles on a meter can show the amount of gas or electricity used in your home. The analog computer accepts these measures and processes them as directed. It is used mostly in scientific research.

The following comparison may help you to distinguish between the two types of computers. A digital computer can count the number of light fixtures in a building. It is not concerned with the amount of light in the building. An analog computer, on the other hand, measures the amount of light given off by each fixture and gives the answer in numeric form.

Analog computers accept data directly from gauges, meters, and other measuring devices. The data need not be converted to punched cards or other input media and entered into the computer. This feature makes the analog computer very fast and useful in such operations as controlling oil refineries, missile systems, and automatic pilot devices.

Many companies have found that the speed of processing can be stepped up in control kinds of tasks by using microprocessors. Analog-type measuring devices are still used to capture the data. The data are then converted to digitized impulses and used as input to a microprocessor. The microprocessor then is used to make all calculations needed. The output can be displayed in readable form, or it may be converted back to analog form by using a digital-to-analog converter.[1] See Figure 7-3, which shows an analog computer.

Figure 7-3. *An analog computer uses numbers to represent quantities that can be measured.*

Astrodata, Inc.

The Comcor 550

DISTINCTIVE FEATURES OF COMPUTERS

In Chapter 1, you were given a general description of a computer and what it can do. You learned that a computer is an information-handling device in which data and instructions for processing these data are represented as electronic codes or impulses. To this point, the discussion of computers has been mostly about hardware. *Hardware* is a term used to describe any of the physical equipment or components in an electronic computer system. The card reader, line printer, and magnetic tape drives are all hardware.

---

[1]Microprocessors are described on p. 159 of this chapter.

The term *software* is used to describe the programs (instructions) that cause the hardware to function. You have already learned about two kinds of programs — utility programs and application programs. A different application program is written for each new problem to be solved. The program is punched into cards or recorded on other input media and stored in the computer's memory. Data entering the computer are then processed according to the stored program.

Much of the software is provided by the manufacturer and comes with the computer. Other software can be bought as needed from the manufacturer or from a software house. Software houses are businesses that specialize in writing programs to make a computer do its job more efficiently. Software, such as application programs, can be written by a programmer who works for the computer user.

While new generations of computer hardware were being developed, software changes were being made too. New programming languages were being written all along. Many of these languages were designed to make the task of programming much easier. They allowed the programmer to communicate with the computer in a language that was much closer to human language than the language of the machine. Other languages were written to take advantage of the computer's new capabilities. However, most of the languages were designed with a particular application in mind. FORTRAN was designed for mathematicians and engineers. COBOL was designed for businesses. BASIC was designed for time-sharing. Many other languages have been developed over the years, but the number and names of each are not important at this time. Some of the languages used more often will be described in later chapters.

One of the features that make computers very versatile is the ease in which stored programs can be changed or modified. If a program is not doing the job desired, one or more instructions can be changed by entering only the changed instructions. The changes may be entered on an input medium acceptable to the computer being used.

All digital computers, regardless of size or make, have a central processing unit (CPU). This unit performs many different functions. It receives and stores instructions as well as the data to be processed. It moves and edits stored data. It makes arithmetic computations. It makes decisions of logic. It directs the action of the input and output units. At the same time, a control device located in the CPU makes these functions work in harmony with one another. The *central processing unit* (CPU) may be defined as that part of the computer that receives and stores instructions and data, performs arithmetic and logic operations, and directs the action of the input and output units.

In addition to the CPU, all computer systems are equipped with input and output units in a basic computer system. Most computer systems are also equipped with a console device, like a typewriter, and secondary storage devices. Figure 7-4 shows the three units in a basic computer system.

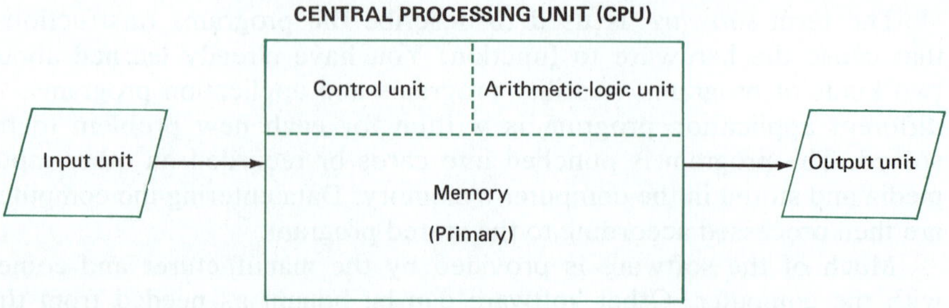

Figure 7-4. *The basic computer system consists of input and output units as well as a CPU. The CPU contains memory, arithmetic/logic, and control units.*

CENTRAL PROCESSING UNIT (CPU)

The CPU contains three smaller units. These units are: (1) internal storage (also referred to as primary memory), (2) arithmetic/logic, and (3) control. The CPU is the heart of the electronic computer system. Refer again to Figure 7-4.

Internal storage (primary memory)

The *internal (primary) storage unit* of the CPU is its memory. It is an integral part of, and under the direct control of, the computer. The internal storage unit can accept, hold, and release data as well as the instructions for processing these data. Depending upon their size, computers are able to store thousands or billions of characters of information, each of which can be reached almost instantly.

Data and instructions are stored as electronic impulses in specified locations in memory. Each of these locations is given an address. Generally, addresses start with zero and go up to the highest number needed. The locations are arranged in sequence. Any location may be reached in a fraction of a second. The data desired can be retrieved directly and used as many times as needed.

Data are erased from memory only when an erase or clear instruction is carried out or when new data are stored in memory locations in which data already appear. The new data will then replace the old. The way in which data are stored in a computer is explained later in this chapter.

Arithmetic-logic

All digital computers are equipped with an *arithmetic-logic unit*, which adds, subtracts, multiplies, and divides numeric data as directed by the program. This unit also makes it possible for the CPU to make certain logical decisions in regard to the data it is processing. It can compare two numbers. It can determine whether the numbers are equal or which one is larger if they are not equal. It can also compare two names to find whether they are the same or different names. Through its ability to compare two fields of data, the arithmetic-logic unit can make many decisions.

As an example of this feature of the computer, assume that a high school wishes to prepare a list of senior students who are on the honor roll. To qualify for the honor roll, a student must be taking at least four courses and have a grade point average of 3.5 or above, based on a 4-point scale. Figure 7-5 shows how the computer would select the cards of senior students who qualify for the honor roll.

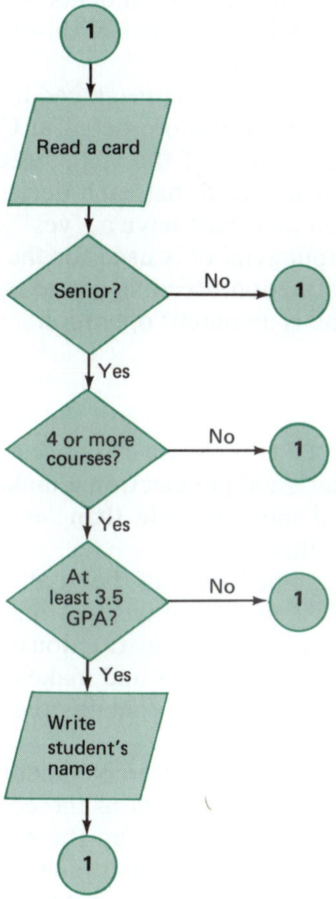

Figure 7-5. *This is a flowchart for a partial program showing typical decisions made by a computer.*

If a code number for a student in a punched card field equals the code number for a senior student which is stored in the computer for comparison purposes, the computer will go to the next instruction in the program. If the code number in the card is not for a senior student, the computer will return to Step 1 and read the next student's card. If the first card is for a senior student, the next instruction calls for the computer to compare another number stored in its memory with a number in a different field of the punched card just read into the computer. The number in this card field stands for the number of courses the student has completed. If the comparison shows that the student has completed four or more courses, the computer will go to the next instruction. This calls for a comparison of the number in a field representing the student's earned grade point average (GPA) for the term with a number stored in the computer.

The name of the student whose card meets all three tests is printed. The computer will repeat the procedure in Figure 7-5 until all cards have been processed. Any card failing one of the tests immediately causes the computer to stop further processing of data on that particular card. Instead, the computer automatically goes on to read the next student card in the file. As a result, when all the students' cards are processed, the printed report will show only the names of those meeting the three tests planned in the problem.

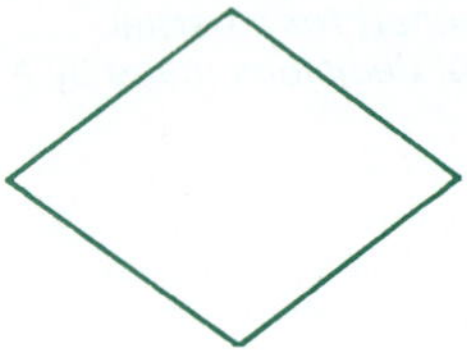

Note that the *decision symbol* is introduced in the flowchart in Figure 7-5. This symbol is explained in more detail in Chapter 9. Figure 7-5 is only a partial flowchart of some of the steps needed in a computer program to solve this problem. Note that each decision symbol in the flowchart has in it a question that must have a "yes" or "no" answer. Note, also, that the input/output symbol is used for the READ instruction and also for the WRITE instruction. Reading a card is an input operation and writing (printing) a name is an output operation.

Control

As you can see, the CPU is the heart of the entire computer system. Because of the computer's unique electronic makeup, the computer system is much faster and more flexible than any other data processing system developed up to this time.

So far, you have examined most of the vital organs of the CPU. One organ can arrive at decisions on the basis of name or number comparisons. Other organs store data and instructions used to make calculations. What gives life to these organs and makes them work in harmony with one another? The control unit contains the master clock that provides this unity.

The *control unit* regulates the different functions of the computer. It is here that the intricate timing system of the computer is located. It is here, too, that the instructions making up the programs are interpreted. The control unit also supervises the input and output devices. It works much as a police officer on a busy street corner, directing traffic. Figure 7-6 shows the path taken by data and instructions.

The program instructions to solve a problem are loaded in the memory of the computer first. The program is often punched into cards, although any available input medium may be used for this purpose. After the last instruction is stored in memory, the control of the entire computer system is turned over to the program. The control unit selects the first instruction, interprets it, and then directs the specific unit(s) needed to complete the necessary action. For example, if the first instruction is READ A CARD, the control unit causes the card reader to feed one card through its read mechanism. The data from this card are then read into the memory of the computer.

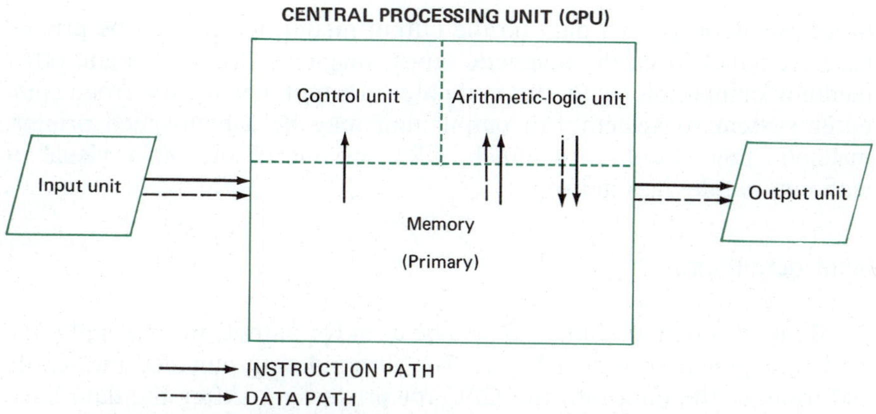

Figure 7-6. *The flow of data and instructions in a computer system is shown.*

The control unit constantly keeps track of the instruction sequence and always knows the address of the next instruction to be followed. In an arithmetic operation, the control unit directs the placement of the first number in the arithmetic/logic unit. Then it selects the second number and causes it to be added to (subtracted from, multiplied by, or divided into) the first number. Finally, the result will be stored back in the CPU's memory. Note that once data and instructions are in memory, they can be modified in the arithmetic/logic unit or transferred to an output unit as needed.

INPUT AND OUTPUT UNITS

All digital computers have one or more input and output units. These units, which are not part of the CPU, bring raw data to the computer and take processed information from it.

Input unit

The *input unit* is a device that receives the data and instructions needed to solve a problem and feeds the data and instructions to the CPU. An input unit is able to receive data from the punched card, magnetic tape, paper tape, electric typewriter attached to the computer, or any other input medium that is compatible with the computer being used.

Output unit

After the problem has been solved and the processed data have been stored, the computer must now send the answer in the form of electronic impulses to the output unit. The *output unit* is a device that records or displays the processed data on the output media, which may be printed reports, punched cards, magnetic tapes, magnetic disks, or some other medium compatible with the computer. Output units vary from computer system to system. An output unit may be a high-speed printer, magnetic tape drive, card punch, CRT, or one of the other visual or audio output devices in use.

Input/output unit

Many of the input units can also be used for output. For example, the card read-punch shown in Figure 7-7 can read data punched into cards and transfer the data into the CPU for processing. After the data have been processed, the results may be punched into a new set of cards if so desired. The CPU controls the action, but the card read-punch does the punching. The card read-punch is thus both an input and and output unit.

The magnetic tape drive also shown in Figure 7-7 can be used to read data into the CPU for processing. Another magnetic tape drive can receive the processed data out of the computer. Therefore, the magnetic tape drive also may be used as either an input or output device.

The high-speed line printer in Figure 7-7 is not used for input. The information printed by it must come from the CPU. The printer, then, is an output unit only.

There are many other input/output devices in the electronic computer system, which will be discussed later in this book.

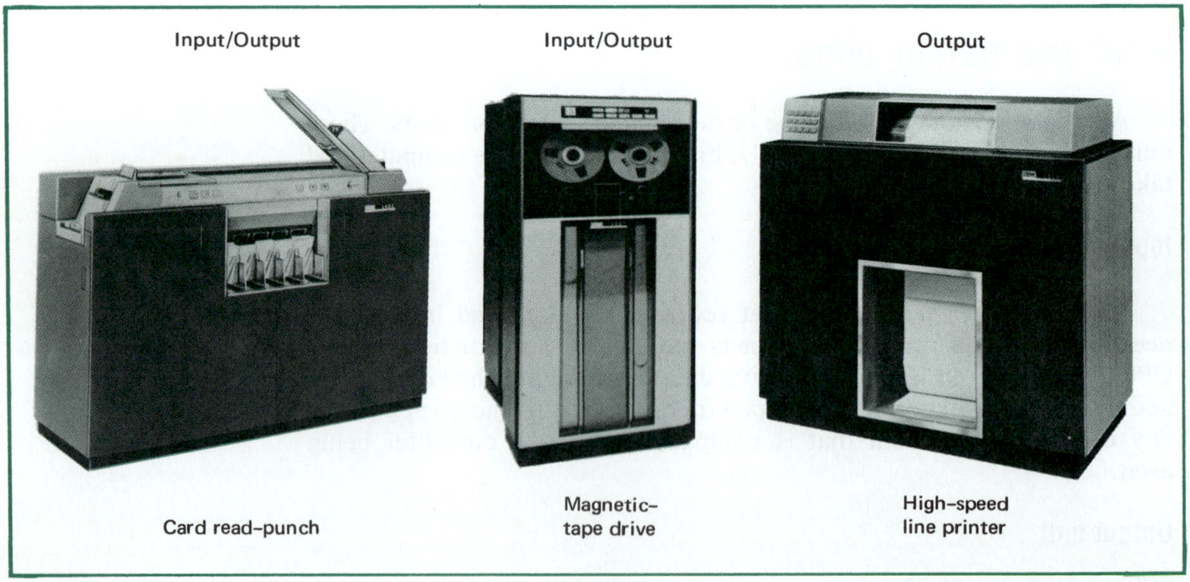

Photos courtesy of IBM Corporation

Figure 7-7. *Some common computer input and output units are shown.*

SECONDARY STORAGE

Supplementary storage devices that hold (store) data outside the memory of the CPU can be added to expand the memory capacity of the computer. These devices are called secondary storage devices. *Secondary storage* is storage on devices that are outside the CPU but that are connected directly to it. Data in secondary storage are *on-line*, which means that they are under the control of the CPU and accessible to it at all times. Secondary storage usually consists of magnetic tapes, magnetic disks, or other storage media that are mounted on the input/output devices.

A reel of magnetic tape that is connected to the computer by a magnetic tape drive is said to be on-line. When this reel of tape is mounted on the tape drive, the data stored on the reel of tape can be accessed (read) as needed. When the reel of magnetic tape is taken off the tape drive and stored it is said to be off-line. *Off-line* storage is the type of storage that is independent of the CPU. However, the data are always recorded in a form compatible with the CPU.

Secondary storage is designed to expand the memory of the computer system. Some secondary storage devices allow random access to data and are very fast. You learned in earlier chapters that random access means that the computer can go directly to an item of data and get it without looking at all the data in a file. Magnetic disks are examples of random-access media. Other media, such as magnetic tapes, access data sequentially and are much slower. You learned earlier that sequential access is a process by which each item of information on a file must be read one-after-the-other in the order in which they appear on the file. In other words, the reading of the last item on a reel of tape would require the reading of every other item on the whole reel of tape before getting to the desired item.

Secondary or on-line storage generally contains current operating data, such as customers' accounts, inventories, or subscription lists, which must be updated on a continuing basis. The program instructions and the data to be processed enter the memory of The CPU from input units. At this time they are said to be in primary storage. The processed data are returned to secondary memory. Output is produced on printed reports, updated tapes and disks, or displayed on CRTs or other output devices acceptable to the computer.

EXTERNAL CONTROL UNITS

The internal control of computer operations is handled by the instructions that have been written to solve a problem and that have been stored in the memory of the CPU. However, external control of operations by an operator is also possible. An operator can control the computer through the use of a console or console inquiry station with which computers are equipped. These are the glamor units of a computer because they are most often pictured in printed illustrations. The console panel has flashing lights, buttons, and switches, which tell the operator how the computer is reacting to the data being processed and any problems it may be having with the data or program.

Console

The *console* of the CPU, such as the one shown in Figure 7-8, is used to provide information to the operator about the performance of the system and to enter information into the system manually. The console is used to:

(1) Give information to the operator about the performance of the system.
(2) Enter information into the system by hand.
(3) Alter the data in storage when necessary.
(4) Start and stop the computer.
(5) Test for computer failures.
(6) Track down any malfunctions.

A console panel makes it possible for the operator to trace the movement of information through the system.

Figure 7-8. *This is a console of the UNIVAC 1100/80 System.*

Courtesy of Sperry Univac, a division of Sperry Rand Corporation

Console inquiry station

The console inquiry station extends the functions of the console. It may be part of the console or housed in a separate unit. Figure 7-9 shows it as a separate unit.

The *console inquiry station* is an input/output device that usually consists of a built-in or separate electric typewriter with a CRT. It is used by the operator to control computer operations. With it, the operator can enter new data or instructions into the CPU. This station can be used to ask the computer to furnish certain types of information. The request must appear in the exact form required by the computer. The program stored in the computer can determine from the request what information is desired. The reply (information asked for) will be typed out on the station typewriter, or it may be displayed on the CRT.

Figure 7-9. *This console inquiry station has a typewriter-like keyboard.*

REVIEW QUESTIONS

1. What are the distinguishing features of first-, second-, and third-generation computers?
2. What is meant by a microsecond? A nanosecond?
3. How does a digital computer differ from an analog computer?
4. What is meant by the term *software*? *Hardware*?
5. Why were new computer languages developed?
6. What units does a computer have, regardless of size?
7. What are the three units in the CPU?
8. What is another name for "internal storage"? What is the purpose of the internal storage unit of a computer? How are data stored in internal storage?
9. How does a computer make decisions? In what unit are the decisions made?

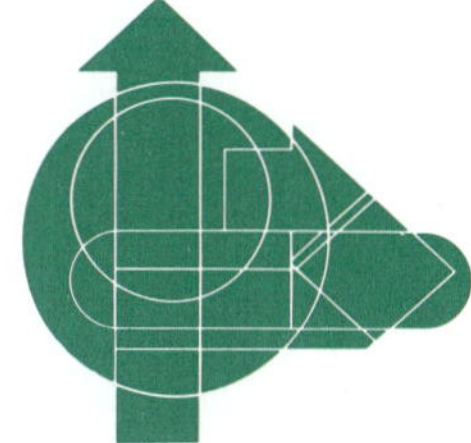

(Continued)

10. What is the purpose of an input unit? Of an output unit?
11. What is the difference between primary storage and secondary storage?
12. What is on-line storage? What is off-line storage?
13. What does the term *random access* mean? *Sequential access*?
14. How is internal control of a computer handled?
15. How is external control of the computer handled?

ELECTRONIC REPRESENTATION OF DATA

Nearly all computers use a form of the binary number system to represent data in memory. The *binary numbering system* is a full numbering system composed of just two symbols, 0 and 1. The binary numbering system is used by the computer because it is so simple to represent electronically.

Representation of Numbers in Binary Code

The computer can represent a 1 by magnetizing a core[2] in one direction (positively) and a 0 by reversing the direction (negatively). See Figure 7-10.

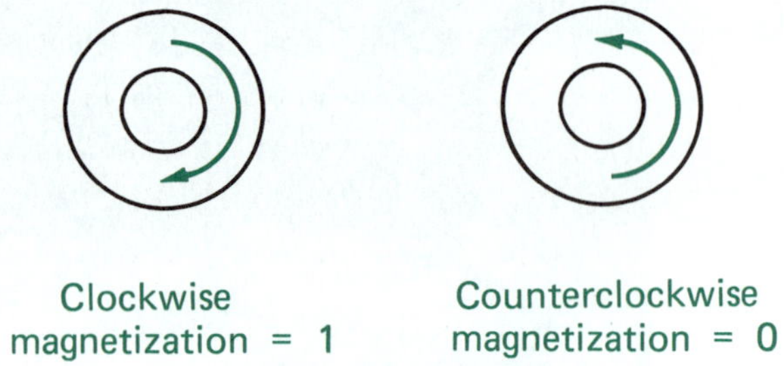

Figure 7-10. *A magnetic core can hold either 0 or 1.*

Each magnetic core can hold one *bi*nary digi*t* or electronic impulse, called a *bit*. If a core is magnetized in one direction, it is said to be "off" and to contain the Digit 0. If the core is magnetized in the other direction, it is said to be "on" and to contain the Digit 1. The binary numbering system (base 2) has the advantage of being the simplest numbering system because it uses only two symbols, 0 and 1.

Even though you may be familiar with other numbering systems, most of us are accustomed to the decimal system, in which numbers are built on a base of 10. We may find it hard to accept the fact that other systems are in use. The number of hours in a day, for example, is counted by 12s (the duodecimal system). The number of minutes in an hour is counted by 60s (the sexagesimal system).

A very familiar system that you use almost daily is based upon a binary number system. For example, two cups (glasses) of milk are referred to as a pint. Two pints equal one quart. Two quarts equal one-half gallon. Two half-gallons equal one gallon.

---

[2]Although many different types of memory devices are in use, the term "core" will be used in this book to represent all memory devices.

Comparison of Binary System and Decimal System

In the decimal system, using ten digits from 0 to 9, the value of a digit increases 10 times with each move of one space to the left. This is another way of saying that the number increases by the power of 10.

In the binary system, the value of a digit increases 2 times with each move of one space to the left. The number thus increases by the power of 2.

In pencil and paper figuring, the binary system uses only two digits, 1 and 0. The other digits, 2 through 9, are never used. In a computer, the 1 represents a circuit turned on. The 0 represents a circuit turned off. Study the following table. Note that a digit doubles its value each time it moves one place to the left.

Decimal Digit	*Binary Notation*
1	0001
2	0010
4	0100
8	1000

Next, note how the other digits are shown. The table below shows the on and off combinations for all the digits 0 through 9. Each horizontal row of four binary digits represents four core storage positions.

Decimal Digit	*Binary Notation*
0	0000
1	0001
2	0010
3 (2 + 1)	0011
4	0100
5 (4 + 1)	0101
6 (4 + 2)	0110
7 (4 + 2 + 1)	0111
8	1000
9 (8 + 1)	1001

Each position represents a binary digit in core storage. Each row of four horizontal cores shown stands for one unit of numeric data in the computer.

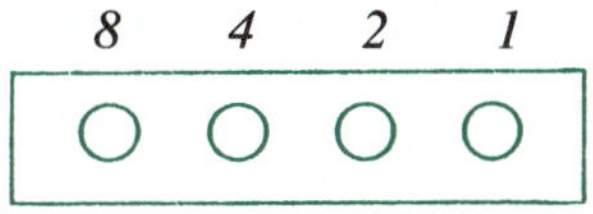

Note that four core positions are needed in a single storage unit in the computer to stand for all the digits, 0–9. Each core can be turned on or off. It follows that the storage capacity of the computer is determined by the number of cores that are present.

The above example shows how Digits 0 through 9 are represented. Storage of letters of the alphabet will be explained later in this chapter.

Often the question is asked: "Is information lost when the computer is turned off?" The answer is "No." It is the direction of magnetism in the cores that is important. Therefore, when the computer is turned on again, a core is magnetized exactly as it was before.

Pure Binary

Higher numbers may be expressed in binary by extending the digits to the left, just as higher numbers are expressed in the decimal system. Remember that in the binary system, the value of the digit doubles for each move of one position to the left. See the example of liquid measurements below.

GALLON (16)	*HALF GALLON (8)*	*QUART (4)*	*PINT (2)*	*CUP (1)*
		1	0	1 = 5 cups
	1	0	0	0 = 8 cups
1	0	0	0	1 = 17 cups
1	1	1	1	1 = 31 cups

There is no limit to the size of a number that can be represented in the binary number system. See the examples in the following table:

Decimal Digit	*Binary Notation*
1	00000001
2	00000010
4	00000100
8	00001000
16	00010000
32	00100000
64	01000000
128	10000000
66	01000010 (64 + 2)
40	00101000 (32 + 8)
45	00101101 (32 + 8 + 4 + 1)

The above method of expressing binary numbers is called the *pure binary* system.

Representation of Alphabetic Characters in Binary Code

To this point, the discussion of the binary code has been limited to representing numbers. Although the computer is referred to as a digital computer, it can store letters of the alphabet and special characters also. The earlier discussion has shown how decimal digits (0–9) can be represented by four binary digits. You also learned that the value of a digit doubles for each move from one position to the left in the pure binary system, which is used for numbers only. However, there are different kinds of binary systems, in which digits, letters of the alphabet, and special characters can be represented by adding additional bits called zone bits.

The Hollerith Code was explained in Chapter 3. It is used with the 80-column card. Refer to Figure 3-4, page 46. The top three rows in the card are zone rows. Punches in the zone rows are combined with punches in the digit rows to represent different letters of the alphabet. In many computers, zone bits are combined with digit bits in much the same way to represent digits, letters of the alphabet, and special characters.

One such code that is used with many third-generation computers is the *E*xtended *B*inary *C*oded *D*ecimal *I*nterchange *C*ode (EBCDIC). The *EBCDIC* coding system uses eight binary positions in the memory of the computer to stand for a single character. There are four zone positions and four digit positions. Refer to Figure 7-11, p. 156, to see how numbers and letters of the alphabet are represented in the EBCDIC coding system.

The leftmost four bits of the standard EBCDIC Code are called *zone bits*. The rightmost four bits are called *digit bits*. Each character requires the use of all eight bits in this system of coding. Note that Figure 7-11 compares the EBCDIC Code with the Hollerith Code. Note that even the numbers in EBCDIC have a zone code, 1111. Whereas the 12 punch is used as a zone punch in the Hollerith Code, the digits 1100 are used in EBCDIC. The 11 punch has a zone code of 1101 and the zero zone punch a code of 1110.

Some computers use the pure binary system, some use the EBCDIC system, and some use other numbering systems. They all use a code based upon the binary numbering system no matter what specific code is used.

Data enter the computer as coded digits, letters of the alphabet, and special characters that are punched into cards or recorded on some other input medium. The computer automatically translates this information into electronic signals. Data are moved around, used in calculations, and stored as signals based upon the binary code. Finally, when the information is processed, the electronic signals are translated into output that may be seen or heard and that can be understood by humans. Usually the output is in the form of printed reports; but it can be in the form of visual and graphic displays or limited audio responses. At the same time that the computer is producing this translated output for people to use, the processed information can also be recorded in punched cards, on magnetic tape, or on other output media. Keep in mind that all of this action is handled automatically by the computer.

	Hollerith's Punched Card Code	*EBCDIC*	
0	0	1111	0000
1	1	1111	0001
2	2	1111	0010
3	3	1111	0011
4	4	1111	0100
5	5	1111	0101
6	6	1111	0110
7	7	1111	0111
8	8	1111	1000
9	9	1111	1001
A	12-1	1100	0001
B	12-2	1100	0010
C	12-3	1100	0011
D	12-4	1100	0100
E	12-5	1100	0101
F	12-6	1100	0110
G	12-7	1100	0111
H	12-8	1100	1000
I	12-9	1100	1001
J	11-1	1101	0001
K	11-2	1101	0010
L	11-3	1101	0011
M	11-4	1101	0100
N	11-5	1101	0101
O	11-6	1101	0110
P	11-7	1101	0111
Q	11-8	1101	1000
R	11-9	1101	1001
/	0-1	1110	0001
S	0-2	1110	0010
T	0-3	1110	0011
U	0-4	1110	0100
V	0-5	1110	0101
W	0-6	1110	0110
X	0-7	1110	0111
Y	0-8	1110	1000
Z	0-9	1110	1001

Figure 7-11. *The EBCDIC Code for numbers and letters of the alphabet is compared with the Hollerith Code.*

HIERARCHY OF DATA

The nature and organization of data within a computer should be understood before learning how to program the computer. The electronic signals used to represent data and instructions in memory will be discussed from the smallest unit of memory to the largest classification of data within a computer system. Figure 7-12 shows the general hierarchy that will be explained briefly in this chapter.

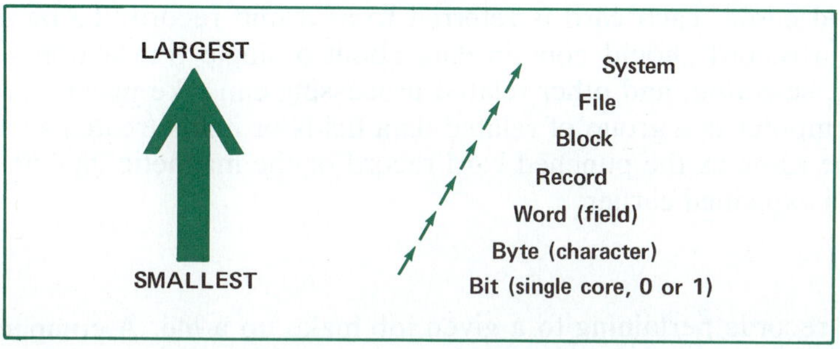

7-12. *The hierarchy of computer data is shown, from the bit to the system.*

Binary Digit

You learned earlier that a bit or binary digit is the contents of one magnetic core in a computer. A bit is also the smallest element of data in a computer memory system. A bit is one position (either 0 or 1) in the binary number system. A single bit has very little meaning or value. Bits, to represent some digit, letter of the alphabet, or special character, must be used in groups based upon some code.

Byte

A *byte* is a unit of computer memory, made up of eight bits, which can represent any digit, letter of the alphabet, or special character in binary code. Therefore, a byte stands for a single letter of the alphabet, special character, or digit in the EBCDIC coding system. In some computer systems, other coding is used to represent individual characters. In those systems, six, seven, or nine bits may be used to stand for each character. If that is the case, the term "character" is used rather than "byte." A byte is the smallest unit of memory that can have an address. Individual bits do not have addresses. Addresses in a computer will be described later in this book.

Word (Field)

You have learned that a field in a punched card is a vertical column or group of consecutive columns set aside to record a single fact. You also learned that on magnetic tapes or disks a field is a single space or group of consecutive spaces needed to record a single fact. When a field is read into computer memory, it is referred to as a word. A *word* is a unit of one or more bytes (characters) of computer storage, used to store one item (field) of data. These bytes (characters) are grouped to form a meaningful unit of data and are accessed as a single unit.

Record

Many words of memory can be grouped to form a record. With punched cards, each card is referred to as a unit record. To be of real value, a record should contain data about a single transaction so that sorting, selecting, and other related processing can take place. A record in a computer is a group of related data fields or items treated as a unit. It is the same as the punched card record or the magnetic tape and disk records explained earlier.

File

All records pertaining to a given job make up a file. A company has many files even if a computer is not used. Examples are payroll, personnel, accounts receivable, and balance files.

Block

When records are processed as a group for convenience, (primarily on magnetic tape), the group of records is addressed as a block. This concept was discussed in Chapter 4.

System

Many files are sometimes required to complete a particular task. In an accounts receivable system, many different files are required. For example, a customer name and address file, a balance forward file, a payments file, and a charge (current sales) file may be used. In other words, a system consists of one or more files.

There is one classification of data larger than a system. That is a data base. The term, "data base," is usually used in terms of a corporate data base, and it is used to reference all the data fields used by programs of an entire corporation. The term, data base, will not be discussed or used further in this book.

COMPUTERS CLASSIFIED BY SIZE

Computer generations were discussed earlier in this chapter. Another method of classifying computers is by size. Computers were available in a very limited range of sizes until a few years ago when production methods made it possible to produce very tiny computer components. Computers are now available in a wide range of sizes and capabilities.

The terms used to describe computer sizes today are (1) micro, (2) mini, (3) small, (4) medium, and (5) large. Like automobiles, the terms used to describe the size have not changed much, but the product that is described by the terms continues to change. For example, large automobiles today are about the same size as compact cars were just a few years ago. The use of plastic, aluminum and other lightweight metals has made it possible to make lighter and smaller cars that can be powered by small engines. Likewise, many computers classified as mini or small today have capabilities equal to or greater than those of large, first-generation computers.

Microcomputer

The *microprocessor* (CPU) of a microcomputer fits on a single silicon chip that is about the size of a fingernail. Although extremely tiny, the microprocessor has a control unit and an arithmetic/logic unit. The microprocessor chip is used alone in sewing machines, microwave ovens, automobiles, and many other devices to automate one or more functions. When combined with memory and input/output devices, it becomes a complete digital computer, costing between $500. and $2,000. See Figure 7-13, which shows an enlargement of a microprocessor held between two fingertips.

Figure 7-13. *The microprocessor chip combines a control unit and an arithmetic-logic unit.*

Minicomputer

Minicomputers have one or more input/output devices. The tape and disk drives used with a mini are usually smaller and slower than those used with a regular computer. The printer on minicomputers usually is much slower and is often a typewriter. A *minicomputer* is described as a small, inexpensive computer that has a CPU and one or more input/output devices. A minicomputer is often low enough in price that it can be purchased rather than rented. See Figure 7-14.

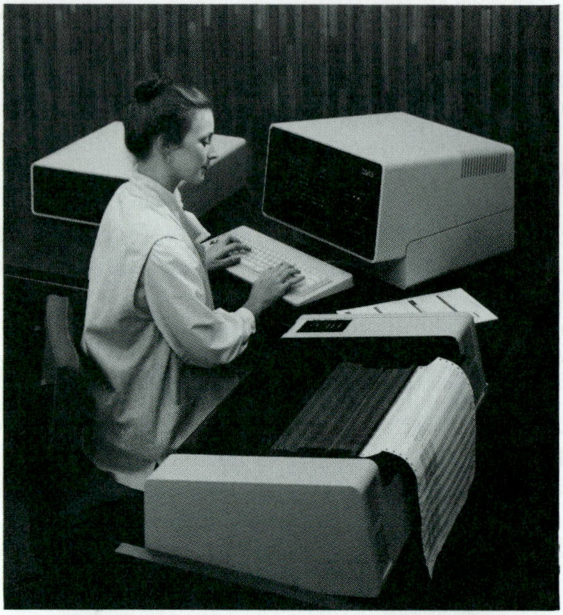

NCR I-8140 *NCR Corporation*

Figure 7-14. *A minicomputer has a CPU and one or more input/output devices.*

Small, Medium, and Large Computer

The terms, "small," "medium," and "large" are used to describe the different sizes of more traditional computer systems. There is no agreed-upon definition of these terms because the industry has been changing so fast. A computer that was thought to be medium-sized a few years ago might be considered small today. Computers that have only one or two input/output devices and 64,000 to 128,000 bytes of memory are thought to be small. The large computers are those that have many input/output devices, very large memory (500,000 to over one billion bytes), and the ability to process more than one computer program at the same time. It is quite possible for a small computer to become medium in size by adding input/output devices and/or memory. Likewise, medium-sized computers may be expanded to become large in size.

Most large-sized computer systems have the ability to be used for time-sharing. *Time-sharing* is the system by which more than one person can use a central computer at the same time by means of remote terminals. See Figure 7-15 for an illustration of a large, time-sharing computer.

IBM System/370 Model 168 computer system *Photo courtesy of IBM Corporation*

Figure 7-15. *A large, time-sharing computer can process more than one program at the same time.*

PROCESSING PLAN OF THE ELECTRONIC COMPUTER SYSTEM

Figure 7-16 shows a flowchart of the plan followed by the computer in processing data. The essential steps of this plan are as follows:

(1) Data originate in source documents, such as time cards, enrollment forms, membership applications, invoices, and score sheets.
(2) The data needed in solving problems are transcribed from source documents to punched cards, paper tape, magnetic tape, magnetic disks, or other input media that can be used by the computer.
(3) The data are checked for accuracy. The verification processes are described in Chapter 3.
(4) The punched cards are usually grouped and arranged in alphabetic or numeric order, as needed, to solve a particular problem. Data on magnetic tapes and disks may be sorted by the computer. However, data stored on magnetic disks are seldom sorted because the data can be accessed randomly.
(5) Detailed instructions (the computer program) are written to solve a particular problem. These instructions are usually written, one instruction to a line, on a program sheet, in the exact form required by the computer being used.
(6) The instructions are then recorded in punched cards or on other media acceptable to the computer.
(7) The instructions are verified for accuracy.
(8) These program instructions are read into the computer and stored in the CPU in the form of electronic impulses. The program instructions will be followed step-by-step as the computer carries out its work.

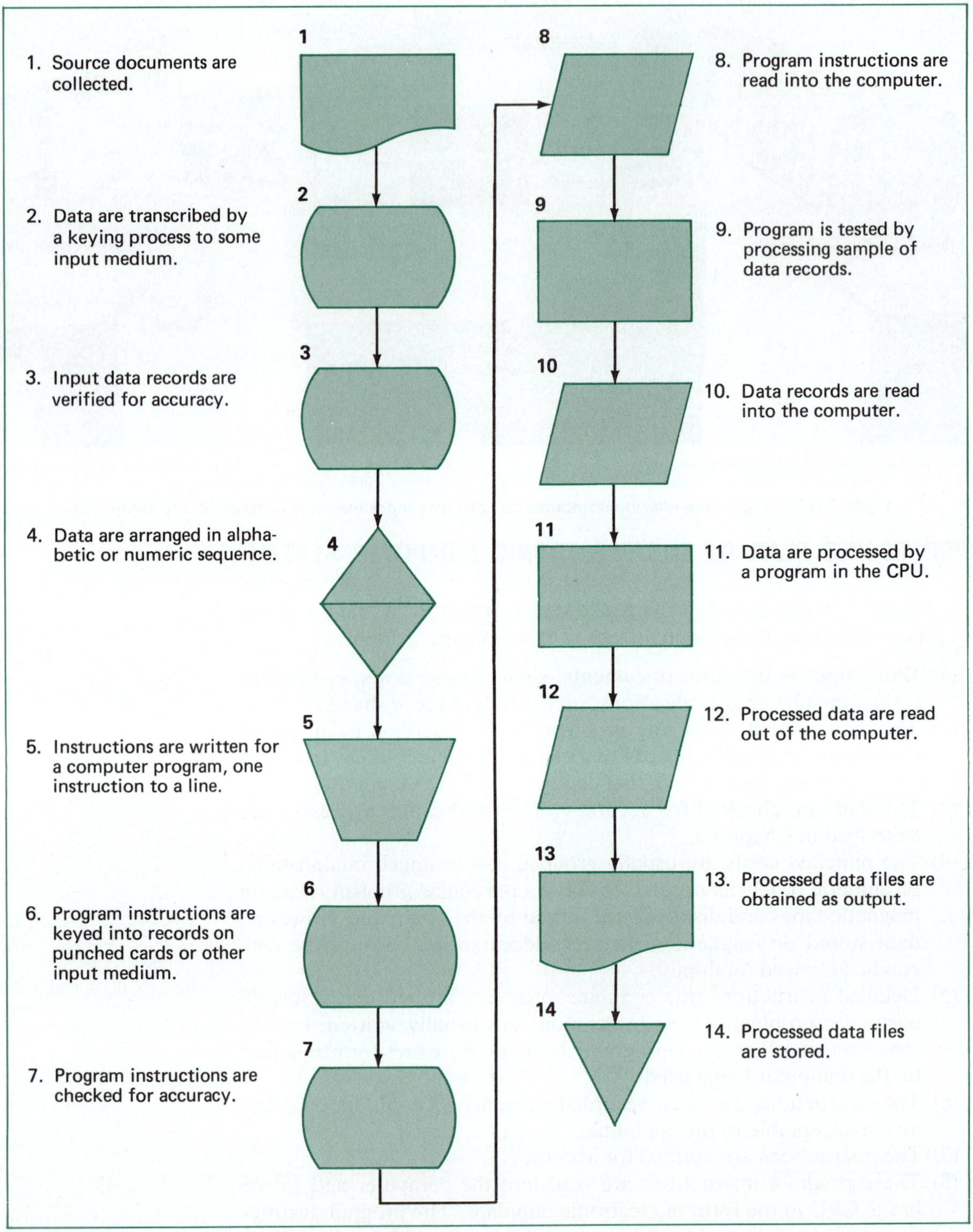

Figure 7-16. *Above is a flowchart of the steps followed in the electronic computer system when processing data.*

(9) The program is tested by processing a sample of the data records.
(10) The data records are read and translated into electronic impulses, in which form they enter the CPU.
(11) The data are then processed (moved, used in calculations, compared) as directed by the computer program.
(12) The processed data are then directed out of the CPU to an output device. The electronic impulses are then translated to the language of the output medium being used.
(13) Processing goes on until all data appearing on input media have passed through the foregoing plan and appear on output media. Then the program tells the computer to halt. Processed data files are obtained as output.
(14) Processed data files are stored.

SUMMARY

Three generations of digital computers have been developed since the early 1950s. First-generation computers used vacuum tubes and were fairly slow and large in size. Second-generation computers used transistors instead of vacuum tubes. Third-generation computers used microcircuits.

Each generation of computers became smaller in size while providing greater speed and reliability at less cost. Software changes were constantly taking place at the same time that hardware improvements were being made. New programming languages were written that were like human language and therefore much easier to use. Many of the new programming languages were developed to serve a specific group of users. For example, FORTRAN was written for mathematicians and engineers. COBOL was developed for business people. BASIC was created for time-sharing users.

There are two types of electronic computers: digital and analog. A digital computer counts. It uses numbers rather than physical variables such as temperature and velocity. It manipulates these variables according to a program or mathematical formula. An analog computer uses numbers to stand for quantities that can be measured.

A digital computer processes data by using a program that has been recorded on an input medium and stored in its memory. The computer follows in order the instructions in the program. It works at very high speeds.

All digital computers have a central processing unit (CPU). It receives and stores instructions as well as the data to be processed. It transfers and edits stored data. It makes arithmetic computations and decisions of logic. It also directs the action of the input and output units. In addition, the CPU has a control device that makes these functions work in harmony with one another.

All digital computers are equipped with one or more input and output units. These units bring new data to the CPU and processed information from it.

Secondary storage devices supplement the internal (primary) memory of the CPU. While these devices are outside of the CPU, they are connected to it and are under its control at all times. Secondary storage can be of two types: sequential access or random access. A magnetic tape is an example of a sequential-access medium. A magnetic disk is an example of a random-access medium.

External control of the computer is possible through the use of a console or console inquiry station. These devices make it possible for the operator to enter information into the computer manually. The operator can alter the data stored in the computer, start and stop the computer, track down failures, and perform other necessary duties.

The binary numbering system is a full numbering system using two symbols, 0 and 1, to represent all values. This code is used in some form in all digital computers. All computer coding systems are based on the idea that a core can be magnetized in either a clockwise or counterclockwise direction and made to represent a binary digit.

The *bi*nary digi*t* (bit) is also used in the coding of letters of the alphabet and special characters. One of the standard codes that is used with third-generation computers is the *E*xtended *B*inary *C*oded *D*ecimal *I*nterchange *C*ode (EBCDIC). This code uses four zone positions and four digit positions (8 bits) to represent each character.

The bit is the smallest item of data in computer memory, but single bits cannot be stored or retrieved separately. A group of bits (usually eight), depending upon the code system used by a particular computer, is called a byte or character. These bytes or characters can be combined to make a word (field). A field on the input medium will be stored as a word in the computer. Words can be grouped to represent records. Records can be grouped into blocks; blocks into files; and files into systems.

Computers are often classified into sizes as micro, mini, small, medium, and large. It is not easy to make these differences. As technology develops, you may find a minicomputer doing the job that was formerly done by a second-generation medium-sized computer. Computers do vary in size from the microcomputer that uses a single microcircuit as a processor to the large, time-sharing computer that can run more than one program at a time and have many terminals connected to it.

REVIEW QUESTIONS

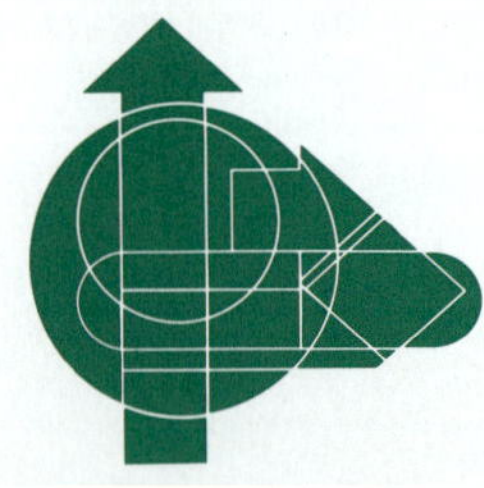

1. What two symbols are used in the binary number system?
2. What is the main advantage of using the binary number system in the computer?
3. Explain how the decimal numbers, 1 through 9, are represented in binary notation.
4. How are letters of the alphabet represented using the EBCDIC system?
5. How many cores (bits) are there in a byte?
6. What is the difference between a bit, a byte, and a word?

7. What is the smallest computer? What does it use for a processing unit?
8. What is a *minicomputer*?
9. Why is there no definition agreed upon today that can describe a small, medium, or large computer?
10. What is *time-sharing*?

NEW TERMS

- Analog computer
- Arithmetic-logic unit
- Binary numbering system
- Bit
- Byte
- Central processing unit
- Console
- Console inquiry station
- Control unit
- CPU
- Decision symbol
- Digit bits
- Digital computer
- EBCDIC
- Hardware
- Input unit
- Internal storage unit
- Microprocessor
- Minicomputer
- Off-line
- On-line
- Output unit
- Primary storage
- Pure binary system
- Secondary storage
- Software
- Time-sharing
- Word
- Zone bits

STUDY GUIDE

Complete Study Guide 7 by following the instructions in your STUDY GUIDES booklet.

PROJECTS

Complete Projects 7-1, 7-2, and 7-3 by following the instructions in your PROJECTS booklet.

8

INPUT and OUTPUT MEDIA and DEVICES

Earlier, you learned that an electronic computer is made up of three basic units: input, CPU, and output. Several different input and output devices may be used. For example, a computer may be equipped to accept input data from punched cards, magnetic tapes, and magnetic disks. It may record output on punched cards, magnetic tapes, magnetic disks, printed forms, or a CRT display. Input/output units are not considered part of the CPU. They bring raw data and instructions to the computer and take processed information from it.

INPUT UNIT

You know that the input unit receives data and instructions and communicates them to the computer itself. There may be one or more input devices that can receive data and instructions needed to solve a problem. As shown in Figure 8-1, different input media and devices may be used with these units.

Input begins with a command from the program instructions stored in the memory of the CPU. The CPU sends the command to the proper

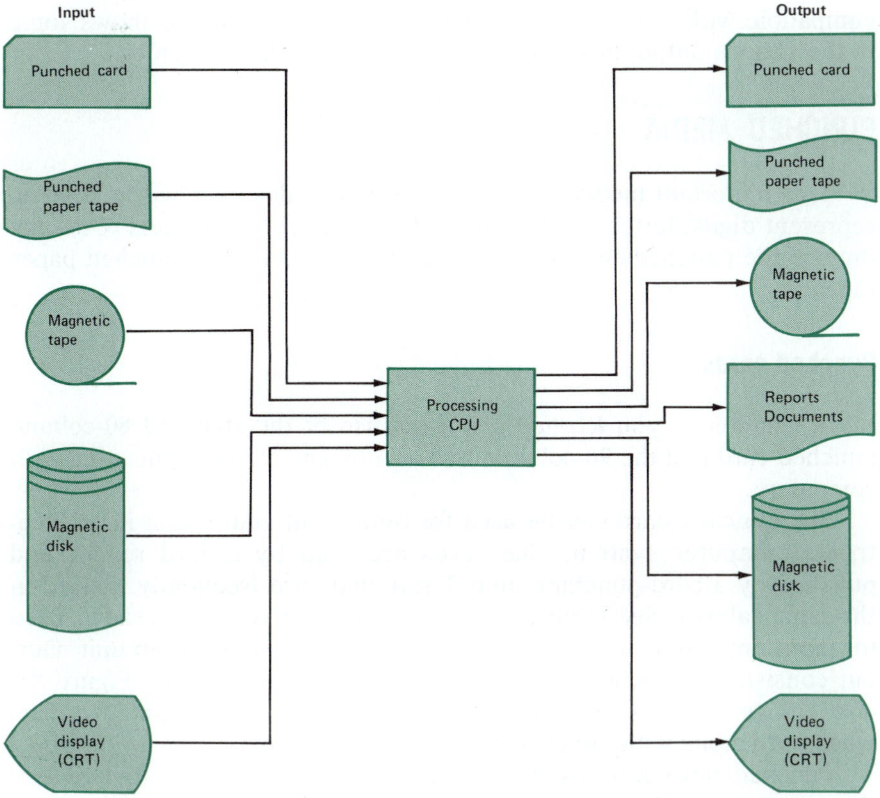

Figure 8-1. *Different kinds of input and output media and devices are used.*

input device to read a record from magnetic tapes, magnetic disks, punched cards, or any other input medium being used. The coded data on the input medium are sensed by the input device. These coded data are read and then converted to the code used by the computer. The data from the input record are then stored in memory and processed by the CPU in accordance with the stored program instructions.

OUTPUT UNIT

The work of the output unit is to record or display the processed data on output media that can be used with the computer. When data have been processed, the computer must reverse its opening procedure. A write instruction in the program in the CPU moves the processed data from the CPU to an output device. The data are translated from the language of the computer to the language of the output medium being used and are recorded on that medium. Printed reports, punched cards, magnetic tapes, magnetic disks, CRTs, or some other media or device compatible with the computer may be used. Figure 8-1 also shows some of the various output devices that may be used with a computer.

PUNCHED MEDIA

Two important media represent data with codes punched in holes to represent digits, letters of the alphabet, and special characters. One medium is the punched card, discussed earlier. The other is punched paper tape.

Punched cards

In Chapter 3, you learned about the use of the standard 80-column punched card and the 96-column card as a means of communicating with computers.

The punched card can be used for both input and output in an electronic computer system. The cards are read by a card reader and punched by a card-punching unit. These units are frequently housed in the same cabinet. See Figure 8-2 for an illustration of a card reader, used for input only, and a card read-punch, used as an input/output unit. Output consists of punched cards and usually a printed report. Figure 8-2 also shows a high-speed line printer, which produces printed output when used along with punched cards and other media.

Punched cards were used as the main input medium with first-generation computers. With the present greater kinds of input media, there has been less use for the punched card. In fact, the new microcomputers and minicomputers seldom use punched cards at all. Instead, data are entered directly from terminals or on one of the magnetic media available.

Input   Input/Output   Output

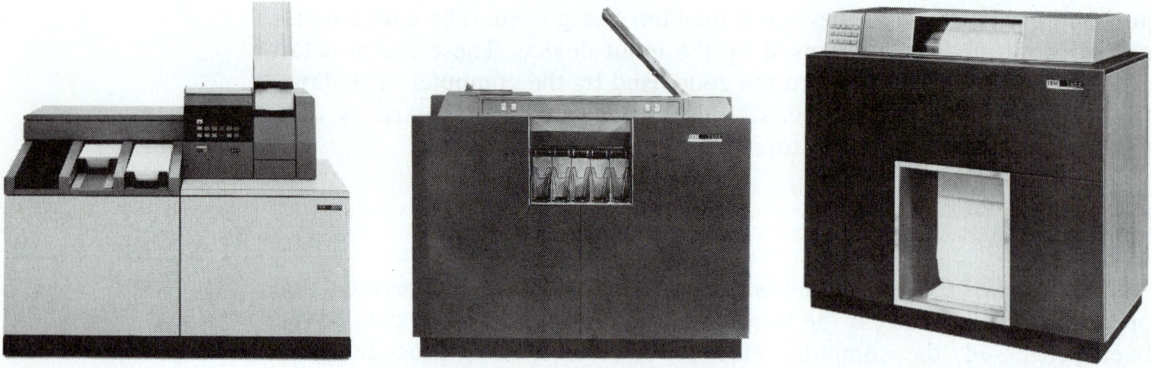

Photos courtesy of IBM Corporation

IBM 3505 card reader   IBM card read-punch   IBM high-speed line printer

Figure 8-2. *A card reader, card read-punch unit, and line printer are used to process punched cards.*

Although the punched card is used less and less with newer computers, the punched card has certain advantages that other media do not have. The punched card code is interpreted at the top so that it can be read by humans. The card can be used in manual operations and so is not limited to computers. Cards are used as checks, bills, voting proxies, and in many other applications. In Chapter 3, a punched card was shown when used for a voting proxy. Figure 8-3 shows a punched card used as a check and another one used as a ballot. With the ballot, the voter punches the choices with a stylus. The card is then ready to be processed by the computer.

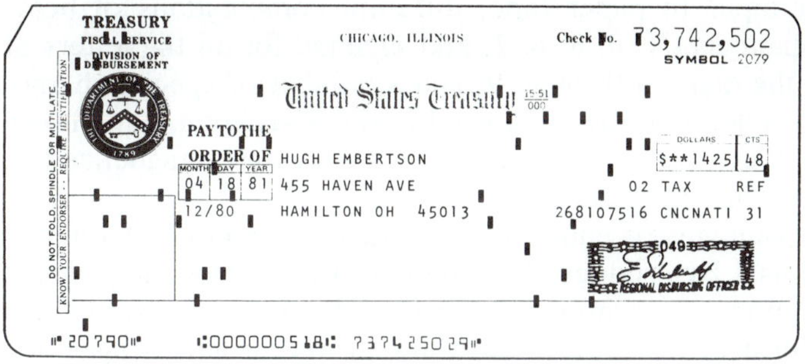

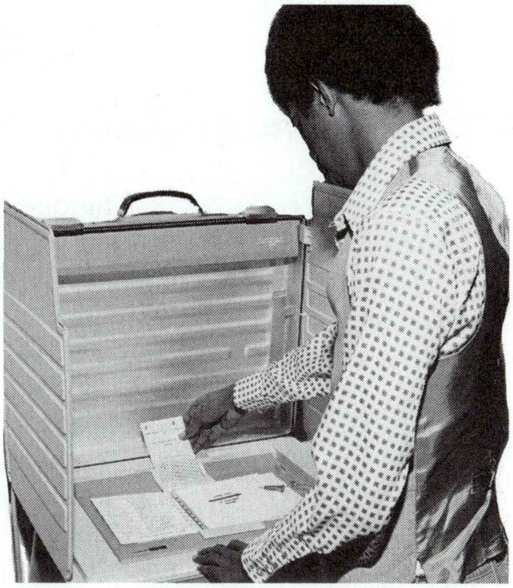

Butler County Board of Elections, Hamilton, Ohio

Voter, inserting punched card ballot into CES VOTOMATIC Vote Recorder

Figure 8-3. *One punched card is used as a check. The other is used as a ballot.*

Punched paper tape

Punched paper tape was a fairly common input/output medium for first- and second-generation computer systems. Paper tape, like punched cards, uses punched holes to represent numbers, letters, and special characters. Paper tape is a continuous recording medium, however. As a result, data enter and leave the computer faster than data punched into cards.

Data stored in paper tape are represented by punched holes in channels running the length of the tape. Each horizontal row of punches stands for one digit, letter, or special character. Most of the tapes have either five or eight channels. Because of this, the coding differs according to the width of the tape. Figure 8-4 shows eight-channel paper tape with an interpretation of the holes punched into the tape. Note the way in which digits, letters of the alphabet, and special characters are represented. Note also the machine functions that can be punched into the tape, such as tab, space, and carriage return.

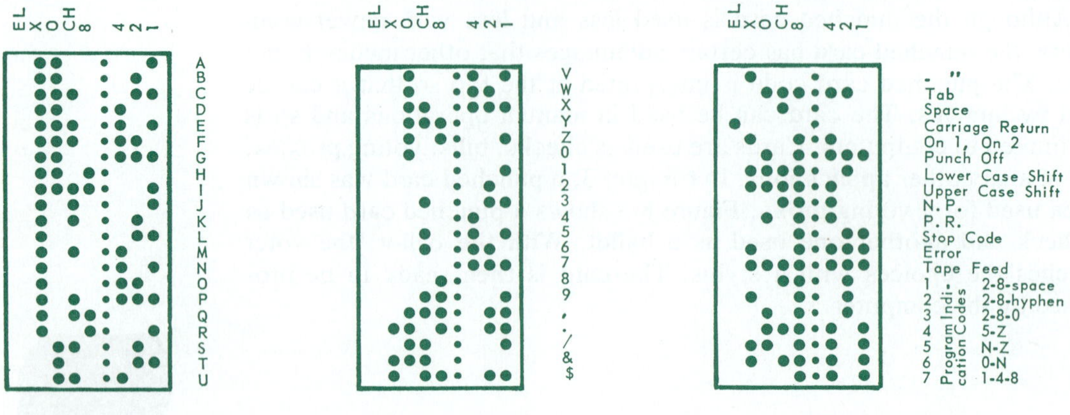

Figure 8-4. *This eight-channel paper tape shows the code for data and also for machine functions.*

The coding of data in the memory of the computer is like the coding of data in paper tape. In paper tape, different combinations of holes punched in six channels (X, 0, 8, 4, 2, and 1) stand for all the letters of the alphabet, all the digits 0 through 9, and a number of special characters. This is very much like the code used in the 96-column card shown in Chapter 3. In a computer, different sets of cores are magnetized to stand for alphabetic and numeric data.

One of the advantages of punched paper tape as an input medium is that it is created as a by-product of another operation. For that reason, the data entry step may be eliminated because the data are already in a machine-coded form in the tape. Figure 8-5 shows an adding machine that produces punched paper tape as part of its normal operation. It also shows a time-sharing telegraph terminal with a tape attachment.

While punched paper tape, as a continuous medium, is a faster means of input and output than punched cards, it has a number of disadvantages. Corrections are harder to make. The tape may be torn easily. Also, data punched in tape cannot be sorted as easily as data in punched

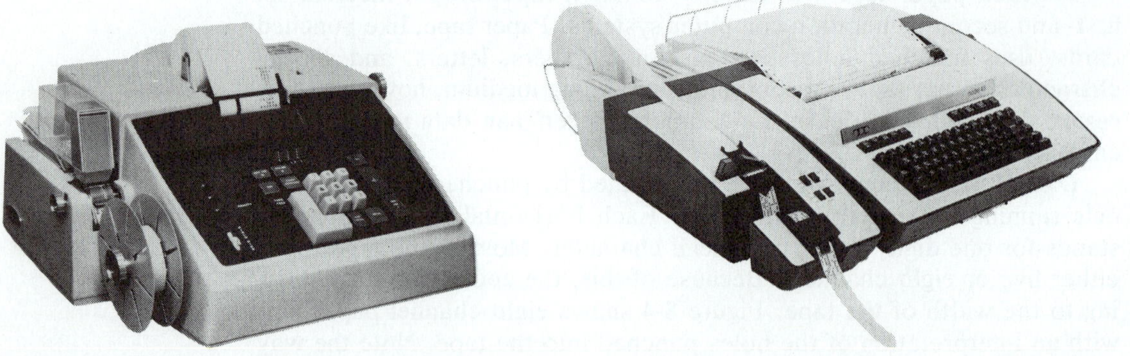

Courtesy of Friden, Inc. *Teletype Corporation*

Ten-key adding machine Model 43ASR uses the ASCII code.

Figure 8-5. *Paper tape is produced as a by-product of another operation.*

cards. Compared to other media, such as magnetic tapes and disks, processing data by punched paper tape is very slow.

MAGNETIC MEDIA

A number of input/output media use magnetized surfaces on which data are recorded.

Magnetic tape

Magnetic tape as an input/output medium has been described in Chapter 5. Data recorded on magnetic tape may be of two kinds. One kind contains the instructions that tell the computer what to do with the data it receives. The other contains the data that will be read into the computer and processed.

EBCDIC Code in magnetic tape. As described in Chapter 5, data are recorded in parallel channels or tracks along the length of magnetic tape. Seven-channel code is used with most second-generation computers. Nine-channel code is used with most third-generation computers. Figure 5-3 is repeated here as Figure 8-6. It shows the EBCDIC Code explained in Chapter 7. The EBCDIC Code is used in nine-channel tape.

Note in Figure 8-6 that four of the channels are used to record binary numbers. The zone positions are in the middle of the tape and the digit positions are at the top and bottom. You learned in Chapter 7 that there are four zone positions in EBCDIC. This feature allows for recording of more special characters as well as upper and lower case letters than could be recorded in seven-channel tape. A magnetic spot in any one of these channels will be read into the computer as a bit (binary digit). You learned in Chapter 7 that a bit is the smallest unit of storage in a computer.

The parity-check channel is shown with a "P" in color. Remember that the parity-check position or channel is used by the read/write mechanism to check its own errors. A check bit or additional electronic impulse is automatically added by the recording device to keep either an even or odd number of electronic impulses for each character on the

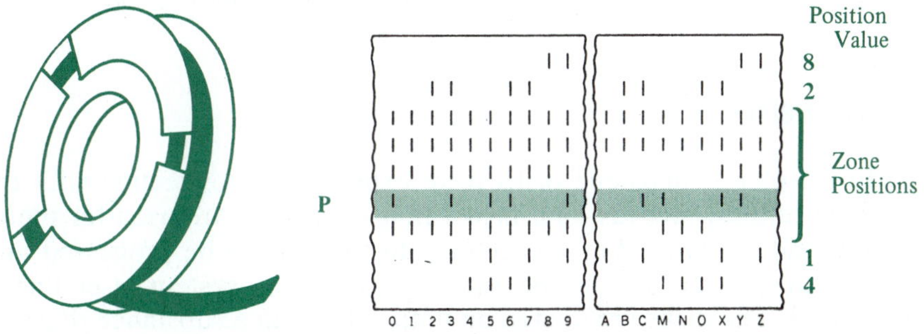

Figure 8-6. *Nine-channel magnetic tape uses the EBCDIC coding system.*

tape. In Figure 8-6 a check bit has been added whenever there is an even number of bits, in order to maintain odd parity. The parity-check bit has been added in the columns representing 0, 3, 5, 6, and 9. Whenever a character is accessed, moved, or used in a computation, the computer checks the number of bits representing that character. The number must be odd or even, depending on the computer. If one of the bits has been lost, the computer stops and signals an error.

Accessing magnetic tape records. As explained in Chapter 5, the data fields in a given record are planned much as they are in punched cards. The fields are recorded in a planned order. Each complete record of a transaction is identified by a key code (address) that belongs to that record only. The code may be a customer number, a part number, an employee number, etc. When a record must be found, the tape records are read by the computer in sequence. The computer begins with the first record and reads all the records until the code identifying the desired record is located. Although use of magnetic tapes does not allow access as fast as use of magnetic disks, the tapes are inexpensive. They are often used for master records that are updated only from time to time. The tapes take much less room than punched cards do, and access to data on tapes is much faster than access to punched cards.

Figure 8-7 shows a keyboard-to-tape recorder.

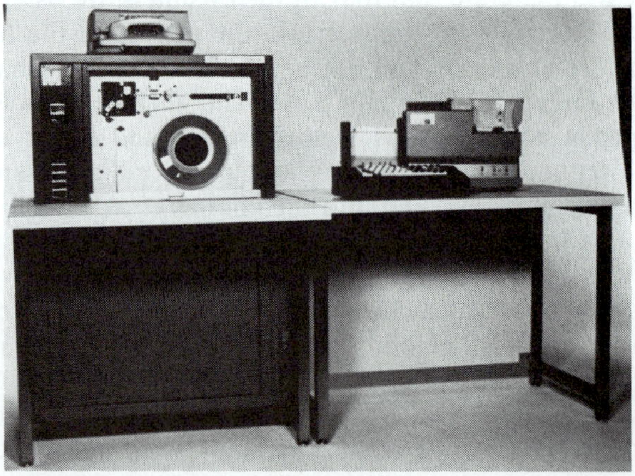

Mohawk Data Sciences Corporation

Figure 8-7. *This is a keyboard-to-tape recorder.*

Magnetic disks

In Chapter 5, magnetic disks were explained in connection with the planning of files, records, and fields. Magnetic disks are used for input, output, and storage. They can hold both the data to be processed and the instructions to process the data. The EBCDIC system of coding is often used. The disks are coated on both sides with a substance that can be magnetized easily. The data are recorded and stored as magnetic impulses or bits on the grooveless tracks of a disk.

Disk packs and drives. Disk packs and drives have also been explained in connection with planning files, records, and fields. A disk drive is the input/output unit on which magnetic disks are mounted. Figure 8-8 illustrates a disk drive with a removable disk pack.

Several disk drives can be coupled to a computer at any one time. This makes it possible for the CPU to have access to millions of characters of data. Also, disk packs can be removed from disk drives. As a result, a disk pack can be taken from a drive and another can take its place. Then additional data are available for processing.

Random (direct) access. You learned earlier that the most important advantage of magnetic disks is that there can be random or direct access to records. An entire file of records does not have to be read sequentially just to find one record, even if the records have been entered sequentially. A record is identified by a key code (address). The code may be a student number, a part number, an employee number, etc. Figure 8-9 shows a key-to-disk terminal with a CRT.

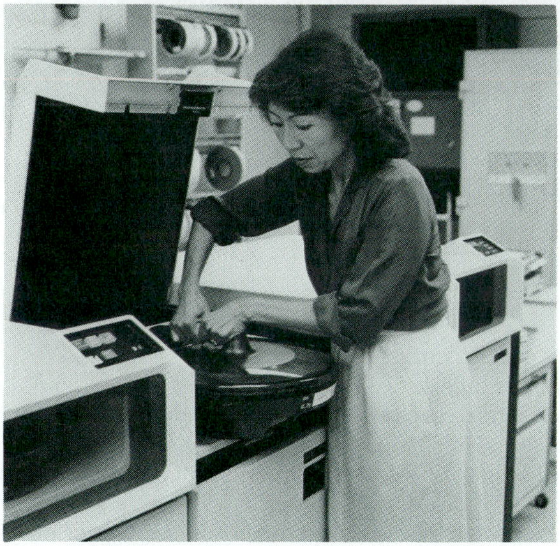

Figure 8-8. *A disk drive is shown with a removable disk pack.*

Figure 8-9. *This key-to-disk terminal has a CRT.*

Flexible disk

A small, compact, flexible diskette has come into wide use, usually with the microcomputer or minicomputer. This "floppy disk," as it is called by data processors, is really a small, flexible magnetic disk that is similar to a phonograph record. These floppy disks can be bought in different sizes. Although two different computers may use the same size floppy disk, the capacity of a disk may vary from about 250,000 characters to over 1 million. The disk is easily stored or mailed. Data can be keyed from a terminal onto the disk and processed directly by a computer. Or, the data can be transferred to other magnetic media, such as magnetic tape. Figure 8-10 shows a terminal of a microcomputer that uses a floppy disk. The floppy disks also allow random access to data.

In summary, when rapid access to data is needed, it is best to use disk storage to its fullest. Less expensive media, such as magnetic tapes, should be used for backup and long-term storage needs or for files that are not updated often.

Figure 8-10. *The operator is inserting a floppy disk into a microcomputer.*

Courtesy of Memorex Corp.

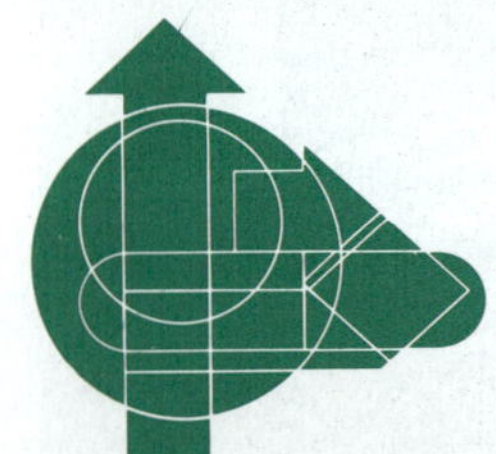

REVIEW QUESTIONS

1. What is the function of the input unit?
2. How are data stored in paper tape?
3. What are two advantages that paper tape has over punched cards? What are three disadvantages?
4. What is the advantage of using nine-channel magnetic tape rather than seven-channel tape?
5. How does the computer use the parity-check bit in nine-channel magnetic tape?
6. How is a data record identified on a magnetic tape?
7. How is a data record identified on a magnetic disk?
8. What is the main advantage of magnetic disks over magnetic tapes? What is the disadvantage?

OPTICAL-CHARACTER RECOGNITION (OCR) DEVICES

A device that could read numbers and letters of the alphabet directly from a typed, printed, or handwritten medium would be ideal. It would eliminate the keying of entry data. The problem of reaching this ideal has not been easy because of the many printing and handwriting styles that people use. Some progress is being made in this area, however. Optical-character recognition (OCR) devices are gaining favor as input devices of raw data. A number of OCR devices that are now being used are described in this section.

Optical-mark page reader

The *optical-mark page reader* is a device that can sense marks made by regular pencil or pen on specially designed forms. This reader is the simplest type of optical reader. It is used mainly for test scoring, data collection, inventory control, and other applications. The only items of equipment needed to create input data in a form that can be read by optical-mark page readers are a pencil or pen and standard-sized punched cards, forms, or full-page documents. A mark placed in a specified box or location on a card or form stands for specific information. Meaning to the marks recorded is thus given by the location of the marks on the input form.

In optical scanning, using the optical-mark page reader, there can be as many as 1,000 marks on an 8-1/2 by 11-inch piece of paper. Figure 8-11 shows one input medium used. The form is a multiple-choice test form on which a student marks the answers. Note that the fields are preplanned. There are locations for recording the student's name, identification number, and answer to each question. Note the boxes or spaces provided for the pencil or pen marks. The design of the form on which the marks are made can be changed to take care of special needs. An optical-mark page reader is shown in Figure 8-12, p. 176.

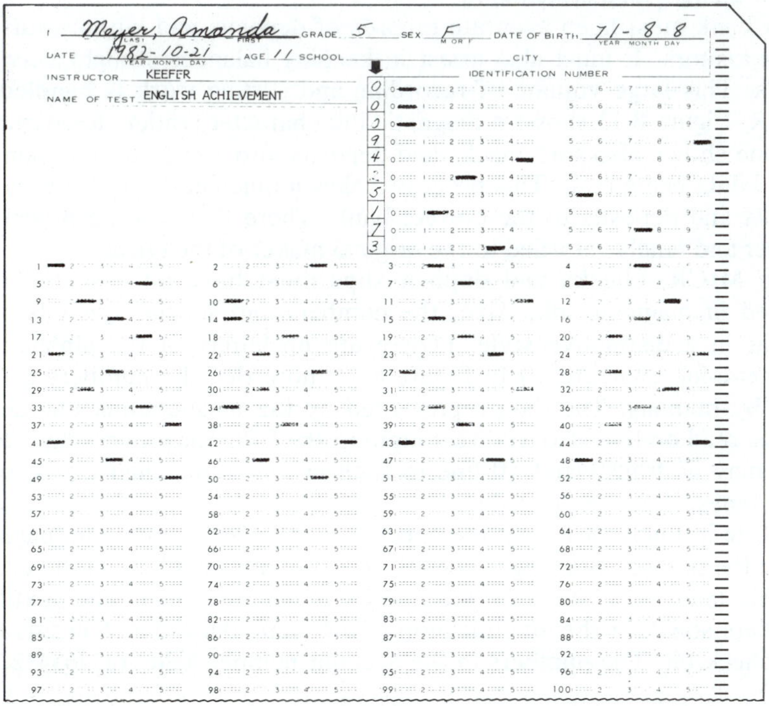

Figure 8-11. *This optical-mark page form is used for test scoring.*

Photo courtesy of IBM Corporation

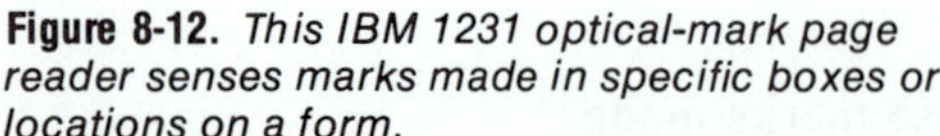

Figure 8-12. *This IBM 1231 optical-mark page reader senses marks made in specific boxes or locations on a form.*

Magnetic-Ink character reader (MICR)

The banks in the United States have adopted a *magnetic-ink character reader* (MICR). This is an input device that is used to process data printed in magnetic ink with specially designed numbers and symbols. A check written on a depositor's account in one bank is often deposited in another bank. Eventually the check must be returned to the bank on which it was drawn. Then, in canceled form, the check is returned to the maker along with a statement.

A bank must keep accurate records of deposits and withdrawals for its depositors. It must also assist in keeping balances straight between banks. This large volume of recording and sorting work is handled by MICR. Figure 8-13 shows a magnetic-ink character reader. Readers like the one shown also sort checks and deposits into groups based upon the coded data being read. This process makes it much easier to forward the checks and deposits to the correct bank. There they will be processed further and finally returned to the original maker of the check.

In MICR, checks and deposit slips must have all essential data printed in magnetic ink. Also, the numbers and special symbols must appear in a distinctive style. (There are no letters of the alphabet in magnetic-ink characters.) In Figure 8-14, note that the numbers can be read by humans. The data represented by the magnetic-ink characters can be read on-line also as direct input to the CPU for processing. These data may be transferred off-line to such media as punched cards, magnetic tapes, or magnetic disks.

Note in Figure 8-14 that the check has characters printed in magnetic ink at the bottom. Starting at the left, the first four numbers in the transit number field, 1211, stand for the Federal Reserve number. The next four numbers stand for the identification of the bank, 0322. The 6 in this field is a check bit. The numbers in the account number field, 123465432, are

Cummins-Allison Corp.

Figure 8-13. *The magnetic-ink character reader is used to process checks and deposits.*

those given to the depositor's account. All the numbers are printed on the checks and deposit slips in magnetic ink before they are issued to the account holder. The special symbols at the beginning and end of the two sets of numbers are punctuation marks. Just as a capital letter is used at the beginning of a sentence and a period at the end, these symbols alert the computer to the beginning and end of a group of numbers.

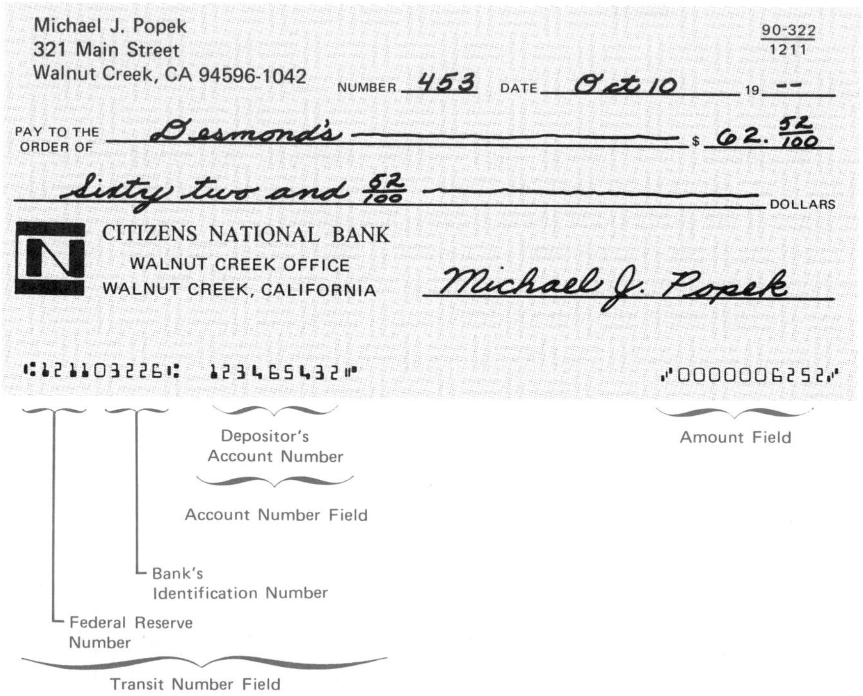

Figure 8-14. *Magnetic-ink characters are used on checks to indicate numeric data.*

The figures in the amount field, 62.52, stand for the amount for which the check is written. The figures in the amount field are imprinted at the bottom of the check on the right. They are imprinted after the check has been written, delivered to the recipient, and cashed or deposited in the bank. The bank will imprint the amount of the check in magnetic ink if it has the equipment. If not, the amount will be imprinted by the first bank that does have the equipment as the check is passed along in the clearing process. In the clearing process, checks are sent to a clearinghouse. The clearinghouse helps the member banks in settling claims against one another. If the amount has not been imprinted on the check up to this point, the clearinghouse will do so.

Figure 8-15 is a deposit slip with magnetic-ink characters. The data in the lower left of the deposit slip are the same as they are on the check. These data are imprinted at the time the deposit slips are printed. The amount of the deposit is shown at the lower right of Figure 8-15. This is added by the depositor's bank when a deposit has been made.

Michael J. Popek
321 Main Street
Walnut Creek, California 94596-1042

90-322
1211

PLEASE LIST ITEMS ON REVERSE SIDE
(OR ATTACH SEPARATE DEPOSIT SLIP)
AND SHOW THE TOTAL BELOW

NAME
(Show name as appears on statement unless printed above)

TOTAL DEPOSIT $ 125.00

DATE October 3, 19--
DEPOSITED FOR CREDIT TO THE ABOVE ACCOUNT

CITIZENS NATIONAL BANK

⑆121103226⑆ 123465432⑈ ⑇0000012500⑇

Figure 8-15. *This deposit slip is imprinted with magnetic-ink characters.*

The checks and deposit slips can be read and processed automatically. The instructions that tell the computer what to do with the figures are part of the program in the computer's memory.

The magnetic-ink method of handling checks and deposits makes it possible for a computer, with the aid of a magnetic-ink character reader, to do the following jobs automatically:

(1) Sort checks by Federal Reserve number.
(2) Sort checks by bank's identification number.
(3) Sort checks by depositor's account number.
(4) Provide data for clearance of checks among banks.
(5) Post checks and deposits to accounts of depositors, at the same time preparing monthly statements for depositors.

Bar-code readers

Bar-code readers are input units that can scan items on which bars or lines representing data have been recorded by a printer or recording machine. Generally, the bar codes cannot be read by humans. The Universal Product Code (UPC) symbol has been adopted by the food industry. It is made up of a series of vertical bars that reflect light from an optical scanner. The bars are a coded form of numbers. See Figure 8-16. The large zero to the left stands for the product as a grocery item. The first five digits at the bottom stand for the manufacturer or processor. The second five digits identify the product. The design of the symbol permits scanning in any direction.

0 12345 67890

Figure 8-16. *This bar code is the Universal Product Code used by the food industry.*

Bar-code readers can record input data directly into the computer. Retail stores use bar codes to automate cash register transactions. Bar codes are used in many grocery stores. Readers in check-out counters can scan coded data printed on items of merchandise or labels attached to the items. The information is read into a central CPU that is programmed with up-to-date prices. The customer gets a computerized sales slip for the purchases. The items are deducted from inventory. Store managers then have a system of instant inventory control.

Some bar-code readers can handle full-page forms, labels, or bar codes printed on objects. Bar-coded documents and readers are used in the automatic routing of the U.S. mail and in credit card applications. Figure 8-17 shows a bar-code reader in a grocery store.

NCR Corporation

Figure 8-17. *The item with the bar code is passed over the reader.*

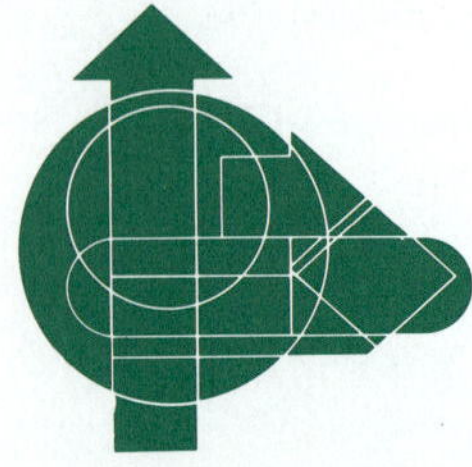

REVIEW QUESTIONS

1. What media are used to make the marks on optical-mark forms?
2. How does the optical-mark page reader give meaning to the marks recorded on the forms?
3. What input device is used by banks to process checks and deposits?
4. Is MICR able to identify alphabetic characters?
5. What four types of information are shown at the bottom of a check by magnetic-ink characters?
6. How are the magnetic-ink characters in the amount field entered on checks and deposit slips?
7. Besides identifying magnetic-ink characters, what additional data processing functions can a MICR unit perform?
8. What is a method used to read input data recorded on items of merchandise?
9. Can bar-code readers record data directly into the CPU for processing?
10. In addition to providing a computerized statement to a customer, what information is provided to managers when bar-code readers are used?

Optical-character reader (OCR)

The optical-mark, magnetic-ink, and bar-code readers have been described so far. They work with scanned data that have predefined characters. The *optical-character reader (OCR)*, on the other hand, identifies each character by comparing its distinctive features with those stored in the OCR's memory.

OCR scanning. Optical-character reading is like the reading method that humans use. When light is placed on a printed form, the human reader scans the form. The optical image of the letters, numbers, or marks is reflected on the retina of the eye. These images are transformed into nerve impulses and are transferred to the brain. The brain has been programmed through learning and experience to recognize these images. In the same manner, optical readers scan the characters and marks by laser or some kind of photoelectric device. The characters or marks are changed to video signals that can be analyzed by the recognition unit. The recognition unit compares these impulses with matching sets of stored impulses in order to identify them.

Figure 8-18 shows a piece work ticket for a payroll and also an invoice. These forms are used for recording optical characters in pencil. Note that the directions show the worker the proper way to print numbers so that the computer will accept them. The numbers scanned must have characteristics like those stored in memory.

The use of OCR forms makes it possible to have on-the-spot recording at low cost. A worker can record the amount of time it takes to complete a job. A customer's purchases can be recorded. A meter reader can record the meter readings for a certain date. The only equipment needed for this kind of recording is a pencil and an OCR form.

Some optical scanners read only data recorded in a special type. Figure 8-19 shows two of the types in common use with these scanners.

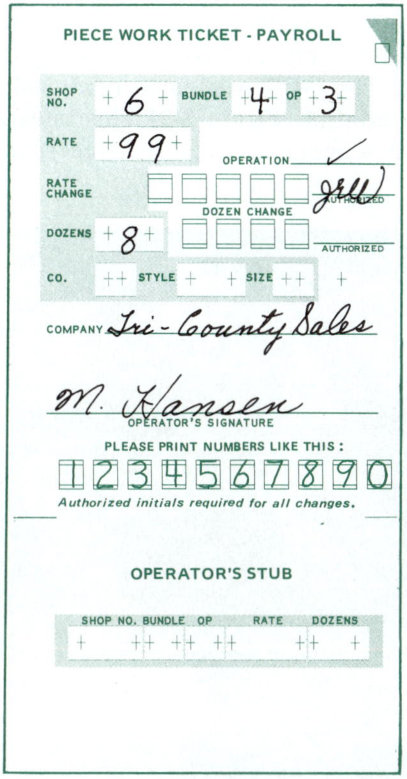

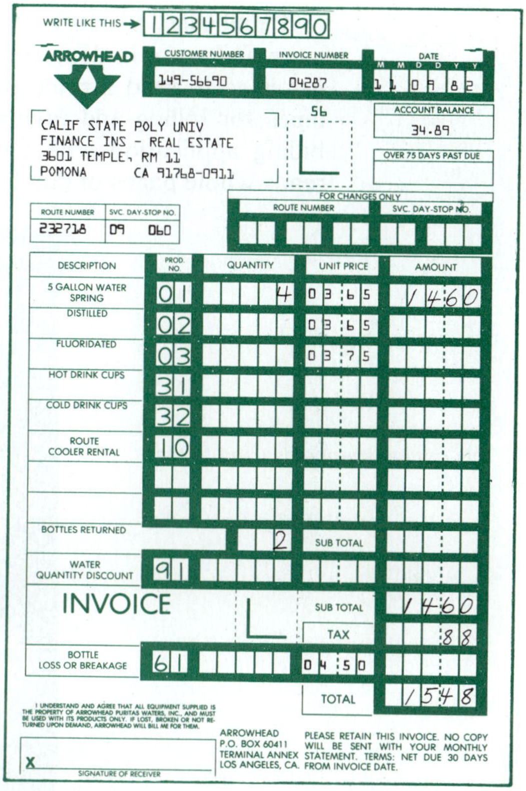

Figure 8-18. *These two forms must be filled in with numbers that are printed in such a way that the OCR unit will recognize them.*

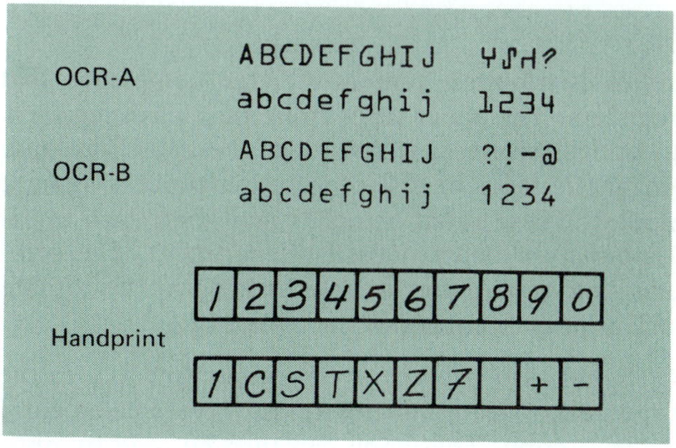

Cognitronics Corporation

Figure 8-19. *OCR-A and OCR-B upper/lower case letters and hand-print numeric and other characters are used with some OCR systems.*

OCR has been in commercial use for almost 20 years. Today, there are many systems available to meet the user's needs. OCR can be bought at a price from under $20,000 to over a million dollars, depending upon processing needs.

Retail uses. Because of recent improvements, OCR equipment is used more and more in department stores. Figure 8-20 shows an optical scanner used to read a price ticket. The OCR is used to read cash register tapes for billing and inventory control. Figure 8-21 illustrates an OCR billing application with a small scanner and also a large scanner that reads whole pages of data.

Figure 8-20. *This optical scanner is used to read a price tag.*

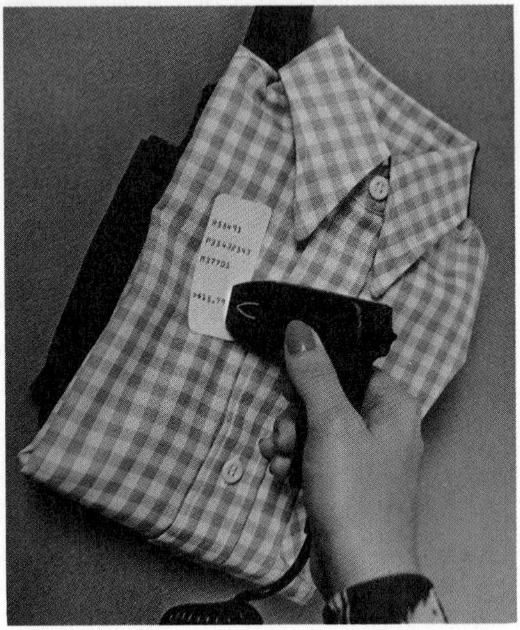

NCR Corporation

OCR-A reader

There are many retail distribution centers of large companies that have electronic cash registers. The paper tapes from these cash registers can be run through an optical scanner, which reads the data. The data are then recorded on magnetic tapes or disks for further processing by a large, centralized computer. These retail branches mail their cash register tapes daily to the company's data processing department. The computer in the data processing department is able to keep an up-to-date record of daily transactions in all branches of the company.

Word processing. OCR has also become a very important tool in the "electronic office." Typewriters, using several kinds of typing elements, are used to create first draft copy. That copy can then be read by optical-page readers and stored on magnetic disks or tapes. Once the data have been entered into the memory of the word-processing machines, editing of the data can take place. (Often these word-processing machines are microcomputer or minicomputer-based.) The corrected copy is then printed automatically without error and ready for mailing or distribution. Figure 8-22 shows a partial copy that was prepared on a type-

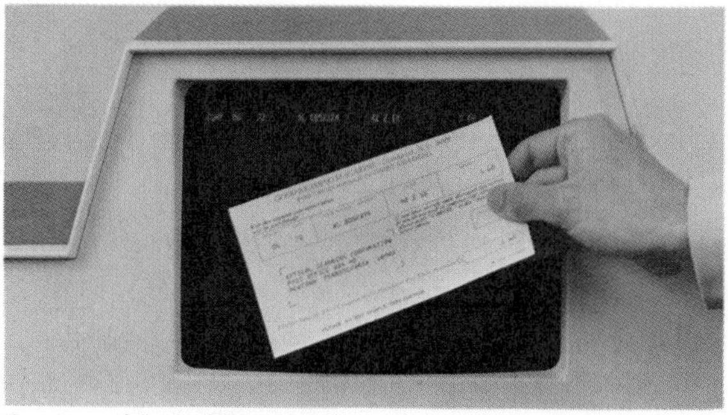

Courtesy of Optical Scanning Corporation, Newtown, Pennsylvania

OPSCAN 37 Optical Character Recognition System

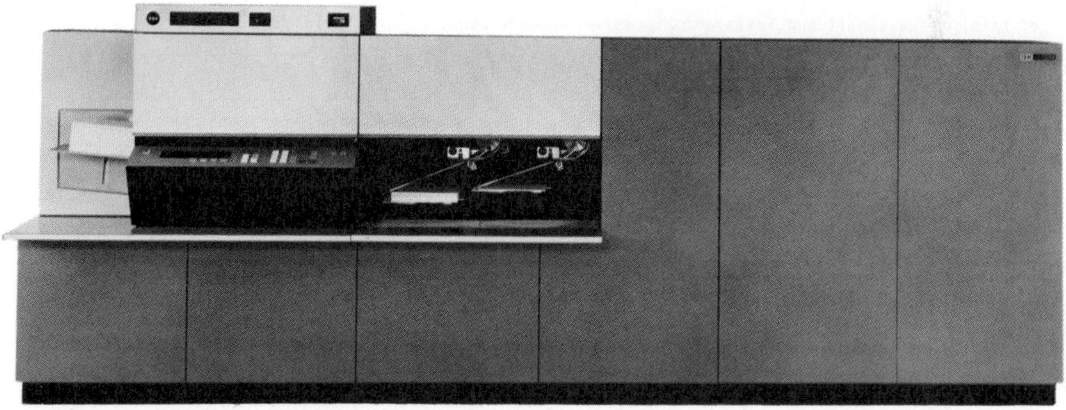

IBM 1288 optical page reader *Photo courtesy of IBM Corporation*

Figure 8-21. *Two types of OCR equipment are shown. The OPSCAN 37 OCR System is being used to process billing data. The IBM 1288 optical page reader scans large volumes of pages.*

writer and then read into a word processing machine by an OCR device, edited, and printed in final form. Figure 8-22 is on p. 184.

In Figure 8-22, the corrections were really written in red because the OCR scanner ignores that color. The entire page is read by the scanner and displayed on a CRT. The operator keys only the changes noted. The corrected document is then typed out at a ''stand alone'' printer.

Other OCR uses. Airlines use OCR to process airline tickets, bills to customers, and refunds. The Social Security Administration uses OCR to process the names, social security numbers, and quarterly earnings of about half the 70 million wage earners in the United States. The Postal Service is using scanners to sort mail. Schools use them when enrolling students. OCR is also used to grade tests and help in analyzing test results.

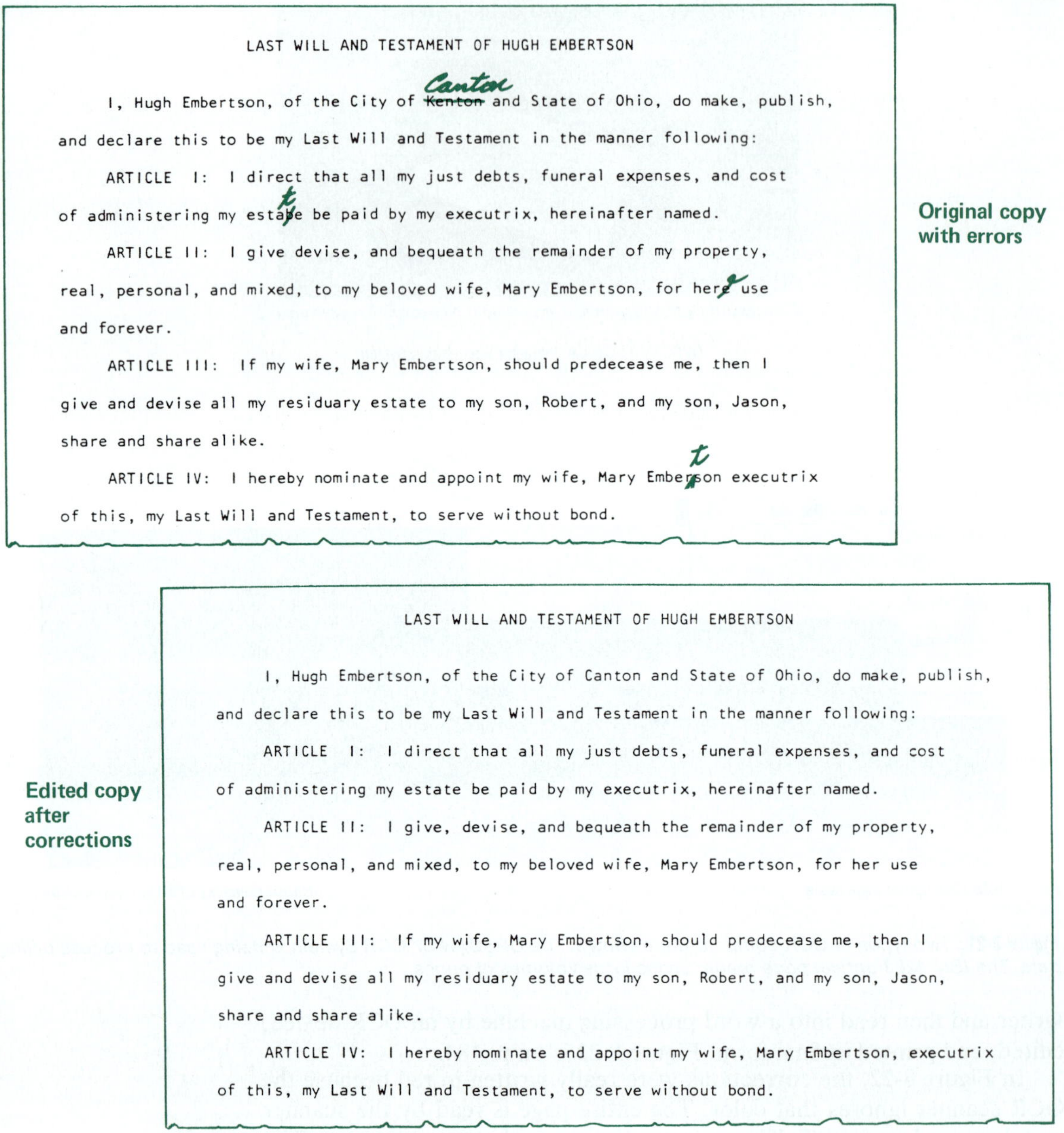

LAST WILL AND TESTAMENT OF HUGH EMBERTSON

I, Hugh Embertson, of the City of ~~Kenton~~ Canton and State of Ohio, do make, publish, and declare this to be my Last Will and Testament in the manner following:

ARTICLE I: I direct that all my just debts, funeral expenses, and cost of administering my estabe be paid by my executrix, hereinafter named.

ARTICLE II: I give devise, and bequeath the remainder of my property, real, personal, and mixed, to my beloved wife, Mary Embertson, for here use and forever.

ARTICLE III: If my wife, Mary Embertson, should predecease me, then I give and devise all my residuary estate to my son, Robert, and my son, Jason, share and share alike.

ARTICLE IV: I hereby nominate and appoint my wife, Mary Emberson executrix of this, my Last Will and Testament, to serve without bond.

LAST WILL AND TESTAMENT OF HUGH EMBERTSON

I, Hugh Embertson, of the City of Canton and State of Ohio, do make, publish, and declare this to be my Last Will and Testament in the manner following:

ARTICLE I: I direct that all my just debts, funeral expenses, and cost of administering my estate be paid by my executrix, hereinafter named.

ARTICLE II: I give, devise, and bequeath the remainder of my property, real, personal, and mixed, to my beloved wife, Mary Embertson, for her use and forever.

ARTICLE III: If my wife, Mary Embertson, should predecease me, then I give and devise all my residuary estate to my son, Robert, and my son, Jason, share and share alike.

ARTICLE IV: I hereby nominate and appoint my wife, Mary Embertson, executrix of this, my Last Will and Testament, to serve without bond.

Figure 8-22. *The copy is read by an OCR scanner, displayed on a CRT, edited at the word processing terminal, and printed.*

VISUAL DISPLAY AND AUDIO DEVICES

Visual display systems are widely used with computers. Audio systems, although still not in general use, are being improved.

Cathode-Ray Tube (CRT)

The CRT was first described in Chapter 4. It displays output data in much the same way in which the picture tube in a television set displays images. The advantage of the CRT is that an entire record is made available almost instantly. By way of contrast, a typewriter-like output device types the characters one at a time.

A CRT is often used as an input/output device in classrooms. A problem appears on the tube. The student may respond by typing an answer on a keyboard. The right answer may be indicated by touching the tube with a light pen. In either case, a message will appear on the tube, telling whether the answer is right or wrong. If a permanent record is needed of the data on the tube, the computer can respond to a write command. The desired information will then be printed on a typewriter or other printing device.

Terminal

CRTs are also used with computer terminals on a time-sharing basis. You learned earlier that time-sharing is a system by which more than one user shares a central computer at the same time by means of remote terminals. The users can be located at different points and at some distance from the computer itself. Direct contact with the computer is made through the terminal. It eliminates the need for having a computer physically near the user. This also reduces the cost of using the computer because each user shares in the cost. Time-sharing is cost-sharing.

CRTs offer many advantages over the traditional typed or printed output. The main advantage is that the output can be more than numbers, letters of the alphabet, and special characters. Instead, output can be line drawings, pictures, graphs, and charts. Some CRTs even make it possible to illustrate three-dimensional drawings. Some also provide color output.

Other advantages of CRTs over terminals with printed output only are speed and cost. CRTs can display entire pages of copy or complete illustrations almost instantly. The output can be displayed, analyzed, and then changed if needed before printing takes place. Paper costs have been rising at a very fast rate during the last few years, and the use of CRTs has helped to offset the increased cost of paper.

CRTs are used in many different occupations today. Figure 8-23 shows the use of terminals with CRTs in medicine, engineering, and education. These terminals have keyboards much like those of electric typewriters. The electronic keyboard of the terminal is connected by telephone or direct wire to the CPU. Inquiries and raw data are keyed into the terminal and transmitted to the CPU. Answers to inquiries as well as processed data are shown on the CRT screen. The data on the screen can be typed out automatically on the terminal typewriter. Some terminals are equipped with both a typewriter and a CRT, while others have only one or the other. Where both are available, the operator usually displays the data on the CRT first, reviews the data, and then decides if a hard copy (printed report) is needed.

Medical laboratory

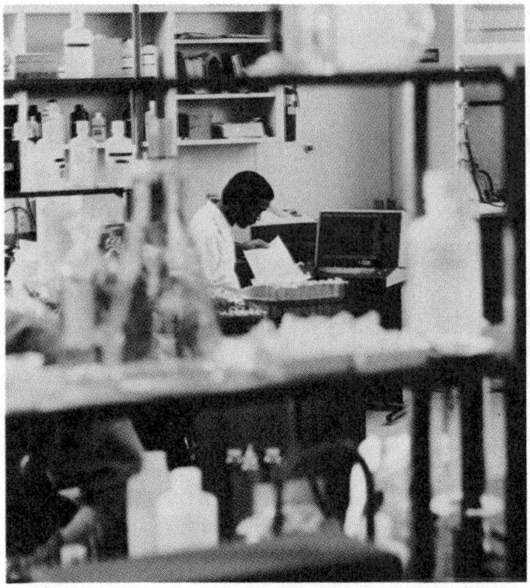

Photo courtesy of Tektronix Inc.

Engineering

Sanders Association, Inc.

Education

Photo courtesy of IBM Corporation

Figure 8-23. *Terminals with CRTs are shown being used in medicine, engineering, and education.*

In some jobs, printed copy is not often required. An example is the use of terminals in an airline reservation system. Persons wishing to make reservations can telephone the airline office. The reservations agent identifies his or her location to the computer by typing a code number on the keyboard of the terminal. The computer can identify each terminal connected to it. Upon proper identification, the agent receives a message on the CRT to feed the inquiry data into the machine. The data are processed, and the processed data are returned to the agent by the terminal and then displayed on the CRT screen. In a matter of seconds, the agent can learn what flights are available, times of departures and arrivals, connecting points, and cost of flights. That information can then be given to the customer making the inquiry. All of this can take place in just a matter of seconds.

Graphic Input and Output Units

In computer language, *graphic units* are those that represent data by use of pictures or graphs. With the coming of graphic systems in computers, the concept of direct communication between people and machines has taken on new meaning. Computer components have been developed that can process graphic data as well as letters and numbers.

A complete graphic system will link to a computer different input/output units, such as film scanners, film recorders, and display units. Information will be accepted in graphic form, converted to digital form for processing, and then stored. The system will convert the data from digital back to graphic form and will display it on a CRT screen, plotter, or some other output media. CRTs, graph plotters, and microfilm (microfiche) are the main graphic devices in use at this time.

Plotters

A *plotter* is used mostly as an output device that produces data in graphic form. A plotter uses paper and a printing device like a ballpoint pen with a large ink reservoir. The pen is controlled by instructions from the CPU. It can draw complex line drawings or simple digits and alphabetic characters. The output of a plotter is on paper instead of a CRT screen.

Like CRTs, plotters are used in many different occupations. They are used for mapping, weather forecasting, drafting, engineering, and in the garment industry. These are just a few of the applications. Figure 8-24, p. 188, shows several types of plotters.

Computer-Output Microfilm (COM)

Microfilm output is used where large amounts of data must be printed and stored for future use. Conventional paper output would be too bulky and would need very much space for storage. Also, much more time would be needed to search through the paper output to find a given record.

Computer-output microfilm (COM) is a medium in which computer output is recorded directly on a film quickly and automatically by a unit that converts computer signals to human language and records them on film. The image of each character is reduced greatly in size. the information

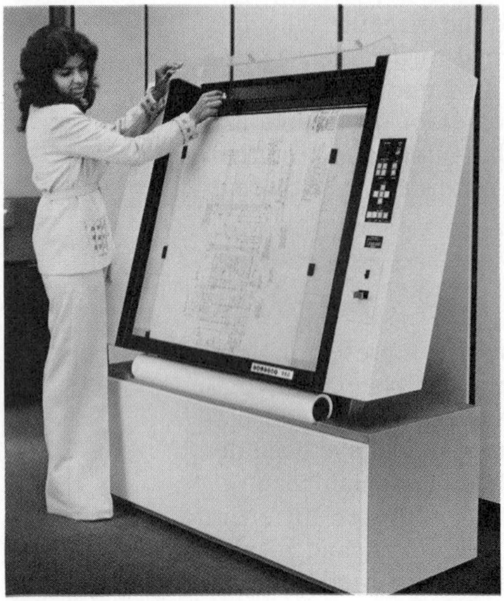

Photo courtesy of California Computer Products, Inc., (Cal Comp), Anaheim, CA

Cal Comp Model 960 Plotter

Photo courtesy of IBM Corporation

IBM 1627 Graph Plotter

Westvaco Corporation

Courtesy of Bausch & Lomb

Figure 8-24. *Plotters use a pen that is controlled by instructions from the CPU.*

can be recorded one character, one line, or one page at a time. The data are recorded on unexposed film. Processing of the film can be done on-line in some systems, off-line in others. The data on microfilm can be printed on some other output media if needed.

Microfilm strips. In some cases, information is recorded on a roll of microfilm. The roll can be placed in a viewer for reading as needed. Many libraries use microfilm strips and microfilm readers to make information available from copies of old books and periodicals. In some systems, the different records on the rolls of film can be indexed and coded so that a given record can be retrieved, enlarged, and displayed for reading quickly. Figure 8-25 shows a microfilm reader into which a roll of microfilm has been fed.

Bell & Howell Business Equipment Group

Figure 8-25. *The roll of film has been inserted in the microfilm reader and a record has been retrieved.*

Aperture cards. Aperture cards are also used in COM operations. An aperture card is a punched card with a microfilm inset. Data are punched into the card and also recorded on microfilm. The punched holes in the card provide a means of quick retrieval. When the desired card is retrieved, it is placed in a viewer for reading. See Figure 8-26.

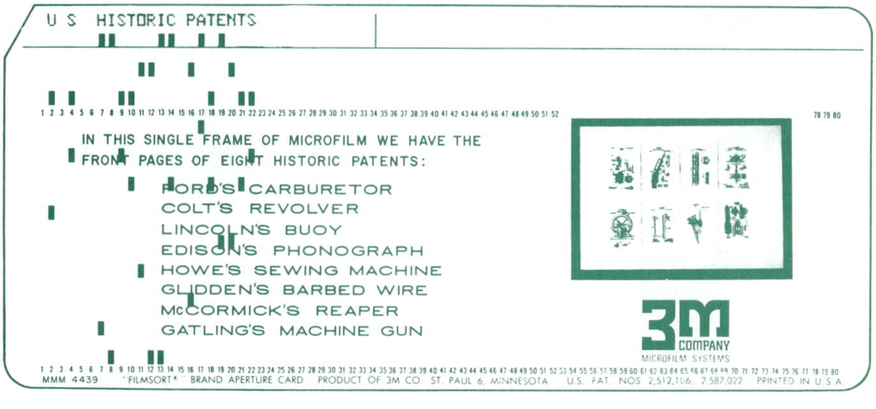

Courtesy of 3M Company

Figure 8-26. *This aperture card has a microfilm insert.*

Microfiche. *Microfiche* is a rectangular piece of film, on which images have been reduced and recorded. It is another form in which microfilm containing output data can appear. The film is usually 4 by 6 inches. It can contain many pages of information. A viewer is needed to enlarge and display the data. Figure 8-27 shows a microfiche reader as well as a microfiche card. One card can hold from 60 to 98 pages of copy. The exact number of pages a card will hold is based on how much the pages have been reduced.

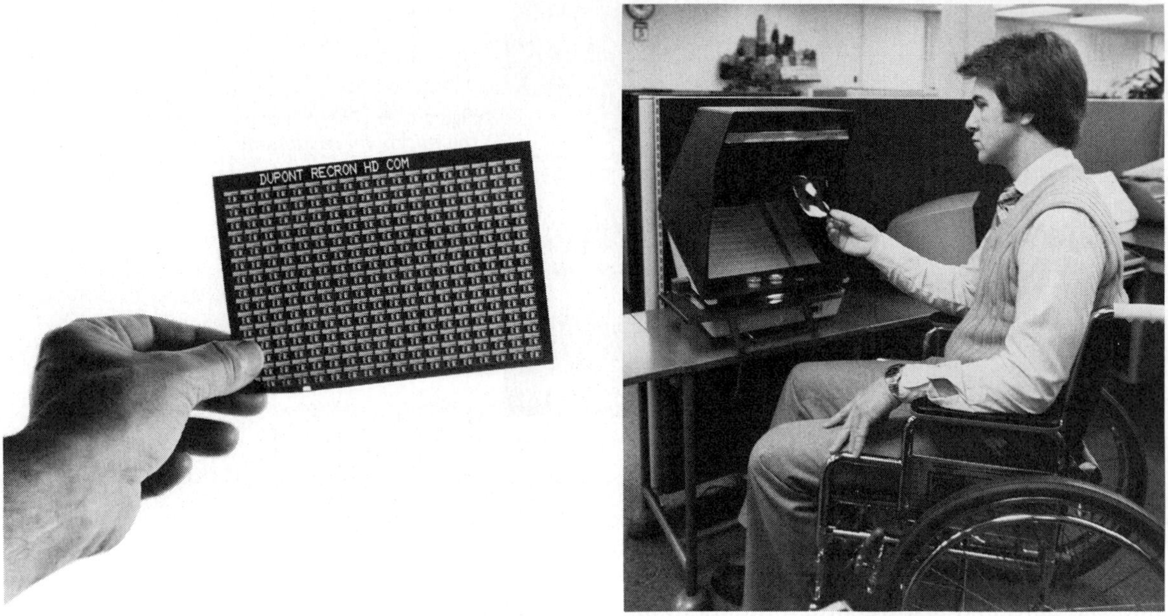

E. I. du Pont de Nemours & Co. Microfiche Microfiche reader

Figure 8-27. *A viewer is needed to enlarge and display the data on microfiche.*

Advantages and disadvantages of COM. COM provides a very fast way of recording human-readable output from a computer. COM is much faster than printing. The film itself is inexpensive and compact. However, complete COM systems are very expensive. The special equipment needed to enlarge and project the data in a form that can be used by humans is quite costly. Management must decide whether the benefits of a COM operation are worth the cost.

Some COM uses. Insurance companies, banks, utility companies, the federal government, and other businesses and industries that must store a large volume of computer-generated data can retrieve the data almost instantly when these are recorded directly on microfilm cartridges, microfiche, or aperture cards. Some of the many uses of COM are listed on p. 191.

(1) Customer and patient histories.
(2) Account records.
(3) Payroll records.
(4) Personnel Records.
(5) Transportation route and rate information.
(6) Credit information.
(7) Stock transfers.
(8) Inventory control.

Audio Devices

Audio systems are usually limited to voice output. Voice input is in the experimental state. The "talking computer" is a reality, but on a small scale. Audio systems are different in the way in which speech is duplicated and in the number of words a computer can use.

Some audio systems have vocabularies of from 100 to over 250 words. However, most audio systems have vocabularies of only about 50 words.

In some systems, human voice responses are recorded on magnetic tape and stored in the computer. When a question is asked, a stored response is matched to the condition of the data in storage. This response is then made to the inquiry. Some systems record parts of words or sounds. Then the systems assemble these syllables into complete words. Still other systems use electronic tones to synthesize the human voice.

Many users of talking systems are banks. The banks use them to give information on the status of loans, checking accounts, and mortgage transactions. Retail businesses use them to check the credit status of customers. They are also used by manufacturers to check the status of jobs in progress and stock inventories. The telephone company is a major user of audio devices.

ADDITIONAL INPUT/OUTPUT DEVICES

There are many other input, output, and storage devices that are used for general or specialized purposes.

Printed Output

You learned that terminals are often used to produce processed data in printed form. There are other methods for printing output that will be described along with terminals.

Printed output from terminals. Because the terminal is really a typewriter that is connected to the computer, the terminal can be used to print on paper whatever output is desired. The output can be numeric or alphabetic. An operator must make sure that paper is inserted in the terminal typewriter before the printing operation starts. Spacing of data on the paper is handled through the program instructions stored in the computer.

When a terminal is used for printed output, the speed of output is limited because only one key can print at a time. Also, the mechanical parts on the typewriter cannot move at high speeds. Whenever large amounts of printed output are desired, high-speed printers are used.

High-speed printers. High-speed impact printers are equipped with wheels, cylinders, or chains, on which are contained letters, digits, and special characters. Because each letter or digit appears in several places on the chain, more than one character can be printed at a time. Some of the faster models now in use can print up to 240,000 characters a minute. This is equal to 2,000 lines of print a minute.

Non-impact printing systems have come into being lately. They have increased printing speeds to over 20,000 lines a minute. Earlier printers have used mechanical impact devices, in which characters are formed by using type slugs to strike an inked ribbon against the paper. However, the new method uses a laser beam — a source of pinpoint accurate light. Printing is accomplished by the transfer of electrostatic charges directly on paper. There is a minimum of moving parts, making the printer much more reliable. This non-impact printer can make only one copy at a time, although slower printers can make carbon copies. But, the tremendous speed of the printer makes it possible to run extra copies, one at a time, and still finish the task in much less time than an impact printer. See Figure 8-28.

IBM 3811 impact printer

Photos courtesy of IBM Corporation

IBM 3800 non-impact printer

Figure 8-28. *An impact printer uses type to strike an inked ribbon against the paper. A non-impact printer uses a laser beam to cause electrostatic charges to be transferred directly on paper.*

Handwritten Input

A number of attempts have been made to perfect what is commonly called "talking" pen input. Most of these attempts have been only marginally successful. A recent entry in the field is a pen like an ordinary ball-point pen in size and shape. The pen is wired to a computer system. The CPU is programmed to receive signals as a person hand-prints characters with the pen. When this idea is fully worked out, the pen will have many uses. It could greatly speed up the rate at which data could be fed into a computer. Also, the pen can be used almost anywhere to input data. See Figure 8-29.

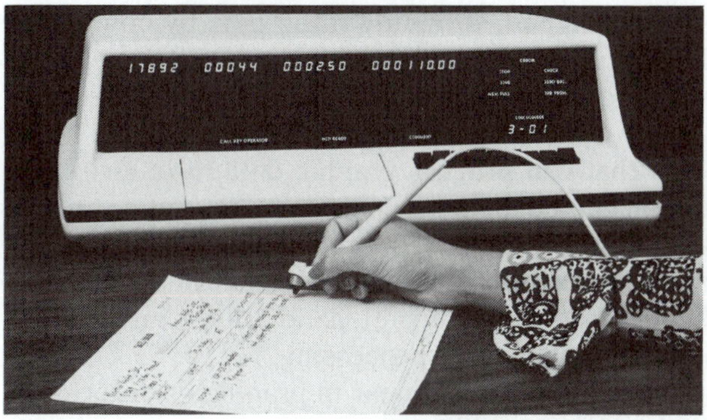

Alphabetic-70 Data Entry System

Figure 8-29. *The "talking pen" inputs hand-printed data directly into the computer.*

One rather interesting use of the talking pen is for signature analysis. A person is asked to "sign in" and the computer analyzes the signature to see if the person is who he or she claims to be. This system will be used more and more as a means of identifying persons who are trying to use credit cards or to cash checks.

SUMMARY

All digital computers have one or more input and output units. These units bring new data to and processed information from the CPU. The units are able to use many different media. Punched cards, punched paper tape, magnetic tape, magnetic disks, optical-character readers, electronic typewriters, high-speed printers, CRTs, and audio-response units are some of the input/output media and devices.

Punched cards, magnetic tapes, and magnetic disks were described in Chapter 3, 4, and 5.

Punched paper tape is like punched cards in that holes represent data. While paper tape, as a continuous medium is faster than punched cards for input and output, it has a number of disadvantages. Corrections are hard to make, and data cannot be sorted as easily as data recorded on punched cards.

There are a number of optical-character reading (OCR) devices that can provide input directly into the CPU. Data can also be transferred from the OCR devices off-line on other media such as magnetic tapes and disks. Optical-mark page readers sense marks made by a pencil or pen on specially designed forms. Meaning of the marks is determined by their location on the form. Magnetic-ink character readers (MICR) can sense the digits 0 through 9 and some special symbols printed in a distinctive style in magnetic ink. Checks and deposit slips can be read and processed automatically by this method. Bar-code readers sense data represented by lines or bars printed on forms or objects. This method is used mostly in the automatic routing of the U.S. mail, in credit-card applications, and in automating cash-register transactions in retail stores. OCRs identify printed, typed, or handwritten data by comparing the features of each character with those stored in the OCR's memory. OCRs are used to process data in airline offices, the Social Security Administration, and in many other business applications.

Computer components that can process graphic data have also been developed. The data are accepted in graphic form, changed to digital form for processing, and changed back to graphic form when the processed information leaves the computer. Some progress has also been made with an input device that can interpret handwritten information and relay it to the computer for storage or processing.

Computer input and output may also appear in graphic or descriptive form on a cathode-ray tube (CRT). CRTs are used extensively with terminals.

Large computers can process data from several different users on a time-sharing basis. The users may be located some distance from the computer. A user makes contact with the computer by means of a terminal connected to a computer by telephone lines. The user types a problem to the computer at the terminal. Processed information is then received on the terminal CRT or printer.

Computer-output microfilm (COM) is used in a process in which an output unit takes data from a computer and records it directly on film. The data can be recorded on film one character, one line, or one page at a time. Recording rates are very fast. Output is generally human-readable with the help of film viewers. While fairly new as an output medium, microfilm is being used in many different data recording applications.

Components have also been developed that allow the computer to understand verbal questions and to give verbal answers to the questions. As yet, the computer's vocabulary is quite limited.

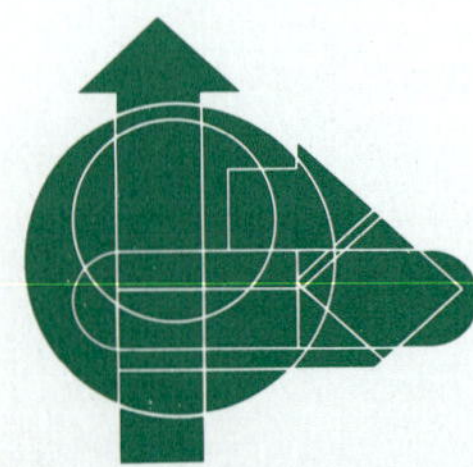

REVIEW QUESTIONS

1. Describe the manner in which optical character readers identify input data.
2. Tell how this method is different from that used by bar-code readers.

3. Describe how OCR is used in the "electronic office."
4. What are four main advantages of using CRT output rather than printed output with computer terminals?
5. Describe how graphic input and output are different from other types of input and output.
6. Describe the device that actually does the drawing (plotting) on a plotter.
7. How is retrieval of data achieved when they appear on a roll of microfilm?
8. What are the advantages of using computer-output microfilm?
9. Name three basic types of COM.
10. Describe two of the methods used by audio-response units in answering questions.
11. What is a disadvantage of using a terminal for printed output?
12. How is printing done with impact printers?
13. How is printing done with non-impact printers?
14. What success has there been in working out technology in which a computer can process handwritten characters as they are written?
15. Describe an application in which "talking pens" are used.

NEW TERMS

- Aperture card
- Bar-code reader
- Computer-output microfilm (COM)
- Graphic units
- Magnetic-ink character reader (MICR)
- Microfiche
- Optical-character reader (OCR)
- Optical-mark page reader
- Plotter

STUDY GUIDE

Complete Study Guide 8 by following the instructions in your STUDY GUIDES booklet.

PROJECTS

Complete Projects 8-1 and 8-2 by following the instructions in your PROJECTS booklet.

9

HUMAN LANGUAGE PROGRAMS and FLOWCHARTS

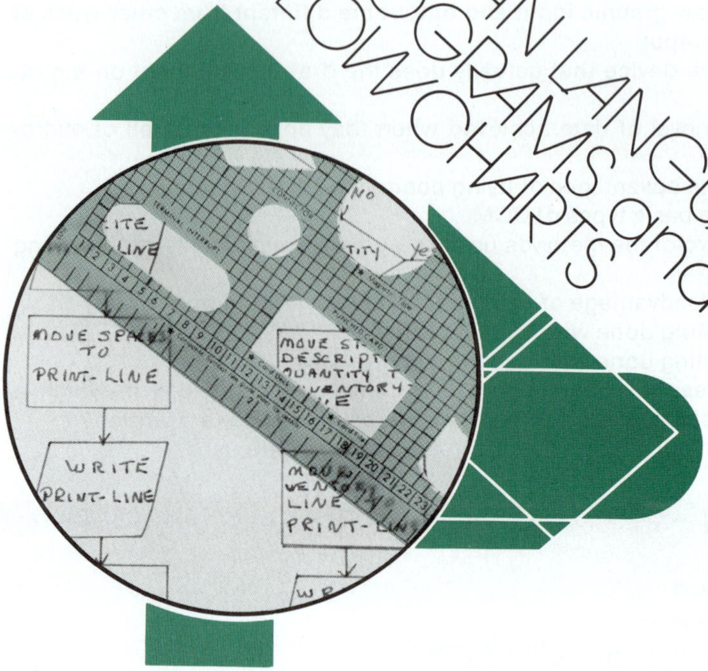

A computer system is made up of hardware and software. The hardware has been described in earlier chapters. The hardware consists of the CPU and all the input/output devices. The hardware cannot work properly without software, however. The software gives the instructions that direct the operations of the hardware in order to solve a given problem. Software includes the entire set of programs that are used with a computer.

You learned earlier that a program is a detailed set of instructions needed to solve a problem. A *computer program* is a detailed set of instructions needed to solve a problem on a computer. A computer instruction tells in code form what action is to be taken on what data. The code form is one that can be stored in the computer and understood by it.

The computer instructions are punched into cards, one instruction at a time, or recorded on some other input medium acceptable to the computer. The instructions are then changed by the computer to a form of binary code and stored in its memory until needed. When the data for a program are ready, the stored program takes over.

IMPORTANCE OF PROGRAMMING

An obvious fact stands out. Program writing plays an important part in processing data by a computer. A *programmer* is a person who plans, writes, and tests computer programs. The program must be logically written and clearly defined. It must give the computer step-by-step instructions on what course to follow.

A computer *instruction* is a coded program step that tells the computer what to do with certain items of data and where the data are stored. Even the simplest problem requires a number of detailed instructions that must be written and stored in the computer before processing takes place. A complex problem requires a great many detailed instructions, arranged in logical order. It is not unusual for complex programs to require many years of programming time. In fact, some systems may require the equivalent of one-hundred programming years of effort to complete. (This would be equal to one programmer working 100 years, ten programmers working ten years, or any combination totaling 100 years.)

Programming is an art that requires:

(1) A thorough understanding of the business in which you are employed.
(2) An intimate knowledge of the programming language and computer being used.

In this introductory course, you will not be expected to gain the programming skill of an experienced programmer. However, you will learn to write some simple programs in computer language systems. You will then become familiar with some of the different commands the computer can carry out. By writing these programs, you will also learn what decisions the computer can be programmed to make and how it makes them.

WAYS IN WHICH PROGRAMS MAY BE WRITTEN

There are many methods for writing computer programs. Some require a complicated knowledge of the inner workings of the computer. Other methods need only a basic knowledge of the console of the computer and of the input/output devices used.

There are four basic ways programs can be written, as follows:

(1) In human language (English).
(2) In the form of program flowcharts.
(3) In machine language — the basic language of the computer.
(4) In one of the synthetic languages especially developed for the computer. These synthetic languages consist of assembly-level languages and compiler-level languages. Both will be described in this chapter.

Generally, a computer program is written in flowchart form and then in one of the synthetic languages, such as COBOL, FORTRAN, or BASIC. The programmer may first write the instructions in English, however. In this form, they can be arranged in the logical sequence of a program. Also, it is usually much easier for the beginning programmer to "think" in English. In this manner, the programmer can concentrate on the logic required to solve the problem and need not worry about the peculiarities and rules of a computer language system.

Of course, the computer could not be expected to accept the instructions in human-language form. Each computer has a language of its own. Whatever information you want to tell the machine must be written in, or translated into, the language the computer uses. After the problem is defined and instructions are written in English to solve it, each instruction must be rewritten or coded in a language acceptable to the computer. *Coding* is the process of writing instructions in a language acceptable to the computer.

MACHINE-LANGUAGE INSTRUCTIONS

Each computer is built to understand a certain code or set of symbols and rules for each operation it performs. This code is built into the hardware of the machine and can be processed directly without further translation. For this reason, the code is referred to as machine language. At present, *machine language* is referred to as any language that can be understood and carried out by the computer without further translation. During the 1940s and early 1950s, machine language was the only type of computer language used.

Operation codes in machine language

You already know that a computer instruction tells in code form what action is to be taken on what data. The part of the instruction that tells the computer what to do is called the *operation code*. The operation code directs the computer to take steps such as reading a record, adding the contents of two memory locations together, or printing a line of data on a page. An operation code often represents an action verb such as READ, WRITE, ADD, and MOVE. Every instruction has an operation code.

Operands in machine language

The operation code tells the computer what action to take. The *operand* gives the location or address of the data to be processed or the next instruction to be used by the computer. Like people, computers must be told what to add when they are told to add. The designers of some older computers built the hardware so that when they received the operation code A, they would add two numbers together. Of course, the computer needed to know what two numbers were to be added.

All instructions and data are stored in certain locations of memory. Each of these locations has its own address. These addresses are specified in the operand part of the instruction. Figure 9-1 shows a typical ADD instruction in machine language.

A	1024	1092
Operation Code	A Operand	B Operand

Figure 9-1. *This is a machine-language ADD instruction.*

Note that the operation code A tells the computer to add the contents of the memory location with the address of 1024 (the A operand) to the contents of the memory location with the address of 1092 (the B operand). The operands in this example give the addresses of the two data fields to be added together. The addresses are not the same as the data. In this example, the total would be stored in Location 1092 (the B operand), replacing any previous total stored at that address. Although a machine-language instruction has only one operation code, it may have one or more operands.

Machine-language addresses

You learned in Chapter 7 how computers use a form of the binary code to represent data. Depending upon the computer used, each character (byte) has its own address. An *address* is a number given to each byte or to several bytes making up a computer word in memory. A unique address for a memory location in machine language is called a *machine* or *memory address*. Remember that the address tells the computer where to find the data or instruction, but the address is not the same as the data or instruction.

You learned in Chapter 7 that any character or group of characters treated as a unit by the computer is called a word. A word in a computer is equal to a field in a punched card. Although each byte in storage has an address, the computer usually accesses the data a word at a time. The computer manufacturer defines the maximum number of characters that can be stored in each word.

The memory of a computer is sometimes illustrated as a large group of mailboxes. A memory address is like a house address where the house numbers are assigned sequentially. Each house on a street has its own number for an address. Given a house number, you should be able to locate a certain house on a street. Given a computer memory address, the CPU can locate that certain storage unit within memory. Unlike houses, though, the computer memory addresses are always the same size in most computers. They also always have the same capacity. Depending upon the design of the computer, the capacity of each memory location is usually one byte (character) or one word. See Figure 9-2.

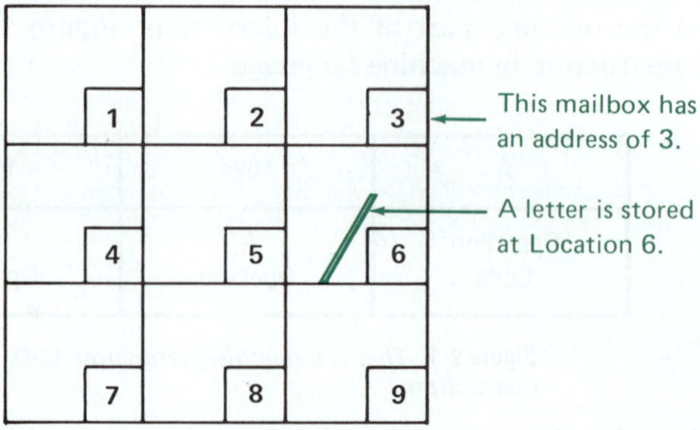

Figure 9-2. *Mailboxes with numeric addresses are like addresses in a computer.*

You have learned that a byte is the smallest unit in a computer that can have an address. However, most computers access data by the address of the entire word. Figure 9-3 shows a word of four bytes that contains a field of data in EBCDIC code, as it might appear.

Four-byte word

	P	A	R	T
Contents	1101 0111	1100 0001	110I 1001	1110 0011
Addresses	2125	2126	2127	2128

Figure 9-3. *A four-byte word is stored in EBCDIC Code. Note that the address of each byte is not the same as its contents.*

Note that the word PART is stored in this computer word. Each letter uses one storage location. Only one byte needs to be addressed by the computer to access the whole word. The word could be addressed by the first byte, 2125, or the fourth byte, 2128, depending upon the type of computer used.

Assume that each address can store one four-byte word. It is possible for a four-byte word to contain one, two, three, or four bytes of data, depending on the data in the field. For example, a 4 punched into a card as a code for a senior student could be stored in one byte of a computer. This single byte would be stored in a four-byte word. Although there would be three bytes of wasted space, the computer will still access the whole word, not the single byte. The address of the entire word is used in most computers, not just the address of a single byte. Moving four-byte words in a computer is so much faster than addressing single characters that the amount of computer and programmer time saved more than makes up for any wasted space.

Remember the machine-language ADD instruction in Figure 9-1, p. 199. The instruction tells the computer to add the contents of Address 1024 to the contents of Address 1092 and store the results at Address 1092. Assume further that 3333 is the amount actually stored at Address 1024 and that 5555 is the amount stored at Address 1092. The computer will add the two amounts and store the sum, 8888, at Address 1092. Figure 9-4 uses the mailboxes to demonstrate this concept. Note that there is a difference of four bytes between addresses. Each word has four bytes.

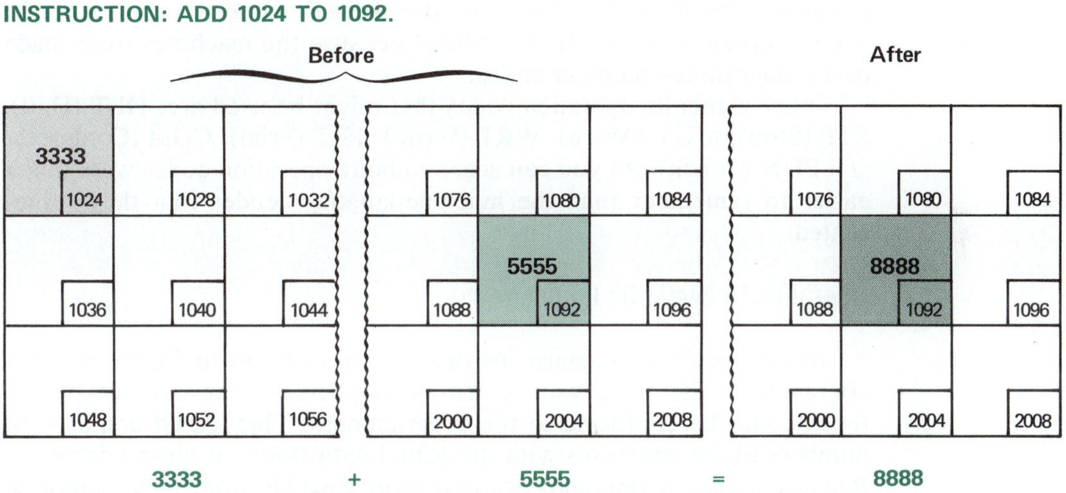

Figure 9-4. *The amount in Address 1024 is added to the amount in Address 1092. The results are stored at Address 1092.*

ASSEMBLY-LEVEL (SYMBOLIC) LANGUAGES

Machine language soon proved to be too hard to use for programmers who were not computer designers and engineers. There were too many different codes and addresses to remember. To make things even harder, each computer had different machine-language operation codes that had to be learned by the programmer.

In the early 1950s, several new languages were developed that made it easier to use the computer. These new languages were called symbolic or assembly-level languages. They were called *symbolic languages* because the machine-language codes were replaced by symbolic letter abbreviations or names for operation codes or addresses. A program written in symbolic language had to be translated by the computer into machine-language numeric addresses before processing could begin. Language translation will be discussed later in this chapter.

Operation codes in symbolic language

Each manufacturer decided upon machine-language operation codes for the computer it made. Some computers could understand and use only numeric codes. Others used a combination of letters or numbers. In the previous machine-language example, A was used as the operation code for ADD. Number 21 was used as the operation code for ADD in some computers. Number 60 was used in another computer. As you can see, programmers would have to learn a different set of codes for each machine. Symbolic codes were developed to make the job of programming easier.

The symbolic operation codes that were chosen were usually descriptive of the operation to be performed. For example, ADD, SUB, DIV, and MUL might be used for Add, Subtract, Divide, and Multiply. Some computers could accept the instruction READ. Other computers might use the operation code RED for Read because the machines were made to use only three-character codes.

Other symbolic operation codes that might be used are: HLT (Halt), STP (Stop), MUV (Move), WRT (Write), PRT (Print), COM (Compare), and PUN (Punch). As you can see, symbolic operation codes were much easier to remember than the machine-language codes that they represented.

Operands in symbolic language

In the machine-language instruction for addition in Figure 9-1, the operands or addresses were given as numbers. These numbers sometimes could be confusing to the programmers. They could confuse the numbers of the addresses with the actual data stored at those addresses. Because symbolic operands are in a short English form, they cannot be confused with the numeric data. For example, the operand can be AMT (Amount), TOT-SC (Total score), STU-NO (Student number), or TOT (Total). These symbolic names for memory addresses are called labels rather than actual machine addresses. A *label* may be defined as a name or abbreviation used in a program instead of a numeric address to identify the location of a computer word (field) in storage. See Figure 9-5.

ADD	AMT	TOT
Operation Code	A Operand	B Operand

Figure 9-5. *The above is a symbolic-language ADD instruction.*

The instruction in Figure 9-5 tells the computer to add the amount stored at the address named AMT to the amount stored at the address named TOT (total) and to store the total at the address named TOT. Again, if the number stored at the A operand (AMT) is 3333 and the amount stored at the B operand (TOT) is 5555, the total of 8888 will be stored at the B operand (TOT). The new total will replace any previous total stored at that address.

The computer keeps a record of the symbolic labels and the actual numeric addresses associated with these labels. Whenever a certain label is used in an instruction, the computer knows what address to go to. The labels are assigned by the programmer and must always be used consistently for the same memory addresses.

Symbolic languages are also called *micro-translation* languages because each symbolic instruction is translated by the computer into only one machine-language instruction. Translation is said to be on a one-for-one basis.

HIGHER-LEVEL (COMPILER-LEVEL) LANGUAGES

The development of symbolic or assembly-level languages was an improvement over machine languages. However, programming still required the programmer to have a complete understanding of the hardware of the computer. In trying to make programming less technical and more people-oriented, manufacturers kept on developing new languages.

Many of these newer languages were designed so that the programmer could instruct the computers in a code more easily understood by humans. The goal of the developers was to write a computer language to solve certain kinds of problems. These problem-oriented languages are called higher-level languages. A *higher-level language* is a problem-oriented language that is usually not limited to use on one kind of a computer. These higher-level languages are also referred to as *macro-translation languages* because one instruction written in the higher-level language may be translated into several machine-language instructions. The translation to machine language is not on a one-for-one basis, but is on a many-for-one basis.

Figure 9-6 gives two English-language examples of the logic in micro-instructions and the same logic in one macro-instruction. The examples are not related to any particular programming language or computer.

Macro-instruction (Many-for-one)	STEP 3	IF YEARS EQUAL TO OR GREATER THAN 15 AND LESS THAN 25 GO TO PRINT DETAIL.
Micro-instructions (One-for-one)	STEP 3	COMPARE YEARS WITH 15.
	STEP 4	IF YEARS EQUAL TO 15 GO TO PRINT DETAIL.
	STEP 5	IF YEARS GREATER THAN 15 GO TO STEP 6.
	STEP 6	IF YEARS LESS THAN 25 GO TO PRINT DETAIL.

Figure 9-6. *Only one macro-instruction is written to do the work of four micro-instructions. Macro-instructions save a programmer's time.*

Instructions in higher-level languages

Instruction formats in higher-level languages are less restrictive than those for assembly-level languages. Each higher-level language has been designed more like the language of a human than that of a computer. For example, some higher-level languages are designed to solve mathematical problems for engineers and scientists. The instruction formats used in those math-oriented languages are much like algebraic formulas. An example of a correct instruction written in one math-oriented language is:

```
GRPAY = RATE * HOURS
```

This instruction tells the computer to multiply the number stored at the address named RATE by the number stored at the address named HOURS. The computer is also instructed to store the answer at the address named GRPAY (Gross Pay). The same operation could be written in another higher-level language as follows:

```
MULTIPLY RATE BY HOURS GIVING GRPAY.
```

The above examples show how the programmer has much more liberty when writing programs in higher-level languages than in assembly-level or machine languages. The names chosen for the address can actually describe the contents of these addresses.

Compiler-level languages

Higher-level programming languages are sometimes called *compiler-level languages*. They are called compiler-level languages because they are translated into machine language by a compiler. A *compiler* is a translator program, usually furnished by the computer manufacturer. It translates each higher-level language instruction to one or more machine-language instructions. Compiler-level languages use more machine time and less programmer time. Assembly-level languages, on the other hand, use less computer time and more programmer time.

Among the many programming languages in the compiler-level group, some of those used most often are FORTRAN, BASIC, COBOL, RPG and PL/1. FORTRAN derived its name from the two words, FORmula TRANslation. BASIC stands for *B*eginners' *A*ll-purpose *S*ymbolic *I*nstruction *C*ode. COBOL stands for *CO*mmon *B*usiness *O*riented *L*anguage. RPG is an abbreviation for *R*eport *P*rogram *G*enerator, and PL/1, for *P*rogramming *L*anguage *1*.

Each compiler-level language has certain advantages and disadvantages. No one language is best for all purposes. Which programming language is the best depends upon the type of computer and the problems to be solved. In later chapters, two languages, BASIC and COBOL, will be discussed in detail. You will learn how to solve simple problems and then be able to see the advantages and disadvantages of using each language.

TRANSLATION OF SYNTHETIC LANGUAGES.

A *source program* is a coded program that is written in a language other than machine language. Any programming language other than machine language is called a *synthetic language*. All synthetic languages, assembly-level or compiler-level, must be translated into machine language before a computer can carry out the instructions. A different translator program is needed for each language and for each model of computer. The translator program is usually provided by the manufacturer of the computer. The program that results from the translation process is the *object program*. The object program, of course, is always in machine language.

Translating symbolic (assembly-level) languages

The process of translating a symbolic source program into a machine-language object program is called *assembly*. This job is done by a computer program called an *assembler*. The coded source program is recorded in punched cards or on some other input medium and loaded into the computer. The assembler reads the source program and translates each instruction on a one-for-one basis. An object program is produced as the result of this translation process. This machine-language object program is also in punched cards or on some other medium. The object program is read into the computer and is used to process data to solve a given problem.

Translating higher-level languages

Higher-level languages must also be translated into machine language before a computer can carry out the instructions. The program that translates a higher-level language into machine language is the compiler. The source program is recorded in punched cards or on some other input medium. The translation to the object program is done automatically by the computer under the control of the compiler instructions. The object program produced is also recorded in punched cards or on some other medium.

The compiler is stored in the computer first. The source program is read into the computer next. The source program is then translated by the compiler into a machine-language object program. See Figure 9-7.

	Operation Code	A Operand		B Operand
COBOL Instruction	ADD	AMOUNT	TO	TOTAL.

COMPILER PROGRAM

Machine-Language Instruction	A	1024	1092

COBOL language instruction is read by the compiler program and converted into machine language

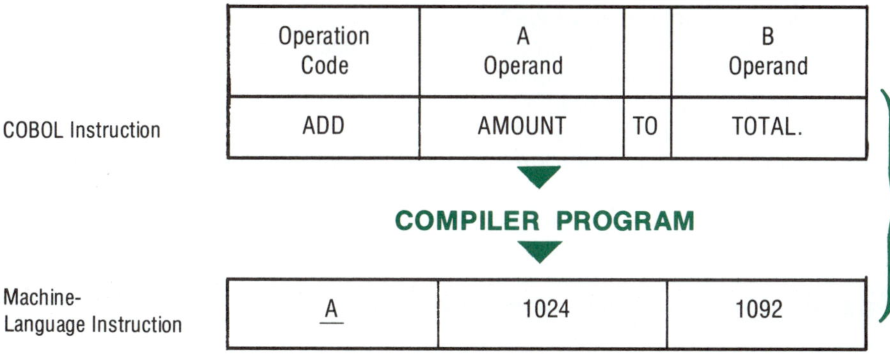

Figure 9-7. *The compiler translates a higher-level instruction into machine language.*

In Figure 9-7, note that the operation code in compiler-level language is ADD. The compiler will translate this code to machine-language A. The A operand, AMOUNT, will be translated to the machine address in memory, 1024. The B operand, TOTAL, will be translated to the machine address in memory, 1092. The computer will then add the amount stored at Address 1024 to the amount stored at Address 1092 and store the total at Address 1092. From Figure 9-4, you learned that the amount stored at Address 1024 is 3333. This amount will be added to the amount stored at Address 1092, which is 5555. The total, 8888, will then be stored at Address 1092.

The translation process for all synthetic languages is much alike. A coded source program is recorded in punched cards or on some other input medium and loaded into the computer. An assembler or compiler program reads the source program and translates it into a machine-language object program. The translation of compiler-level instructions is done on a many-for-one basis. The translation of assembly-level instructions is done on a one-for-one basis. The capability of creating many instructions from one higher-level instruction makes the computer work more and the programmer work less. Because compiler-level languages are easier to learn and use, most programs today are written in one of those languages.

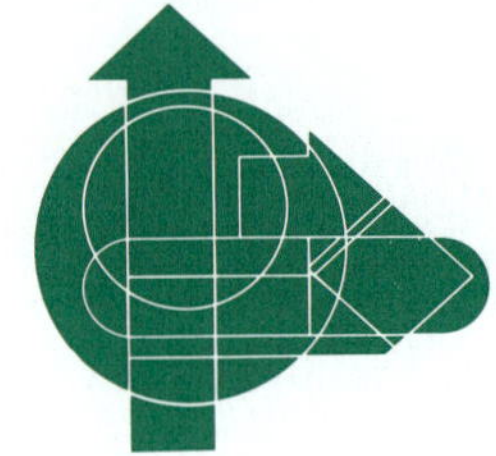

REVIEW QUESTIONS

1. What is a *computer program*?
2. What is the purpose of a computer instruction?
3. What are four ways in which computer programs may be written?
4. What is an advantage of writing a computer program in English before writing it in one of the languages acceptable to the computer?
5. What is *machine language*?
6. What are the two parts to a machine language instruction? What is the purpose of each?
7. What is a *symbolic language*?
8. Why were symbolic languages developed?
9. What is a *label*?
10. What is the difference between a micro-translation language and a macro-translation language?
11. What is the translator program that is used with assembly-level languages? With higher-level languages?
12. What is a *source program*?
13. What is an *object program*?
14. Describe the translation process from a synthetic language to machine language.
15. Why are compiler-level languages more widely used than assembly-level languages?

BASIC PROGRAMMING INSTRUCTIONS

The computer has proved to be a very versatile tool for processing data. It is very fast and accurate as long as the correct program instructions are written by the programmer. Some instructions are found in most all computer programs. They are instructions to:

(1) Read data into memory.
(2) Print data from memory.
(3) Clear memory locations.
(4) Repeat an instruction or series of instructions.
(5) Determine when the program has been completed.

Each of these basic instructions will be described. Then they will be used as part of a program to solve a sample problem.

READ Instructions

All data and instructions must be stored in the memory of the computer before processing can take place. Therefore, one of the first instructions in most programs tells the computer to read data and store it in a memory location, permitting the data to be used later in the program. Reading is done one record at a time. Every time an instruction is given to read data from a punched card, one entire card (record) is read and stored in the computer's memory. *Although the entire record is read into memory, the entire record is not always used in a problem.* The programmer will describe to the computer which fields to process and which to ignore. Figure 9-8 shows an input/output symbol used for a read instruction in a flow chart.

Figure 9-8. *This input/output symbol is used for a READ instruction.*

A programmer must remember that reading new data into memory automatically erases any data previously stored in the same location. This process is referred to as *destructive read-in*. If you have ever recorded something on a cassette tape, you learned that any old information on the tape is destroyed (erased or replaced) by the new information being read or recorded. If data from more than one record are to be read in and processed at the same time, different memory addresses must be used for each record. Or, the data on the first record must be moved before reading the second record.

PRINT (WRITE) instructions

After data are processed and the results are complete, these results must be printed on some medium that can be read by people. The output used most often by humans is the printed report, although output can be viewed on CRTs as well. In some languages and in some computers, certain locations of memory must be used for printing. In those cases, the programmer must write instructions to move data from one part of memory to the print area before printing can take place.

The programmer plans a line of printed output so that the necessary items of data may be printed on the line. Everything in the input record is not always printed. For example, a list of names and addresses of students could be printed without the telephone numbers and ages, which might be part of the input records. The programmer describes the fields that are to be printed and writes instructions for printing the data. Because printing is an output function, the input/output symbol is used in a program flowchart when data are to be printed.

In the example shown in Figure 9-9, a student's grade card is read, and the programmer is planning a program to print only the student's identification number and total score. The notation inside the symbol describes the fields to be printed.

Figure 9-9. *This input/output symbol is used for a WRITE instruction.*

This instruction will cause the computer to retrieve from memory the data at the locations named STUDENT-NO and TOTAL-SCORE and print them on a line with the printer or some other output device used with the computer system.

MOVE instructions

It is often necessary to move data from one area of memory to another. Movement of data may be needed before printing the data. This is often true in some computer languages. It is also true with some computers that have specific areas of memory reserved for use with a PRINT or WRITE instruction. The process symbol is used to represent a MOVE instruction on a flowchart. Figure 9-10 shows a process symbol used for a move instruction.

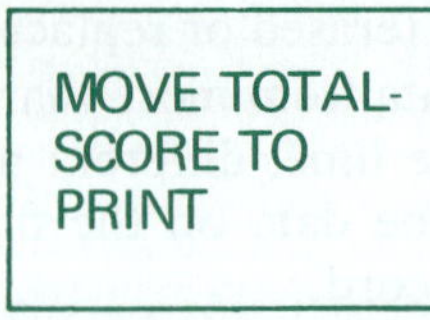

Figure 9-10. *This process symbol is used for a MOVE instruction.*

The MOVE instruction is possibly not well named. Data are not actually moved from one location to another. Instead, the data are copied from one memory address and duplicated at another address. Therefore, the data that have been copied are present in two different memory addresses after the MOVE instruction has been carried out. The term "copy" would be much more accurate in describing the function of a MOVE instruction.

CLEAR instructions

You learned that old data are erased in magnetic memory whenever new data are read into the same memory addresses. After one card has been processed, for example, a new card can be read into the same area. The new data replace the old data. If this were not true, a computer would waste space by holding data for thousands of records in its memory at the same time.

Sometimes it is necessary to clear memory locations before using them for other purposes. This is particularly true if memory locations will be used as work areas in which arithmetic computations will be temporarily stored. Zeros are used to erase previously recorded data in memory locations to be used for calculations. This clearing process is like the clearing of a previous total in an adding machine before keying in a new number.

After a line of data is printed, there must be some way to clear the print area so that the next record can be moved to it. The print area is not self-clearing as the read area is. Spaces are used to clear the print area of unwanted data.

Figure 9-11 shows the process symbol used to clear two different areas of memory. The symbol on the left is used to move zeros to an area used for accumulating a total. The symbol on the right is used to move spaces to a print area.

MOVE ZEROS
TO TOTAL
MOVE SPACES
TO PRINT-LINE

This MOVE instruction is used to clear unwanted data in a work area in memory for an arithmetic computation.

This MOVE instruction is used to clear unwanted data from a print area in memory.

Figure 9-11. *These MOVE instructions are used to clear storage areas.*

BRANCH instructions

A computer follows instructions written for it in a step-by-step order unless it is told to do otherwise. One of a computer's advantages is its ability to repeat an instruction or set of instructions over and over until it is told to do something else. Normally, the same processing must be done for every record in a file. It would waste time and computer memory to write a new instruction for each record.

Assume that you want the computer to figure the sales tax on a sales amount appearing in each card in a sales file. The same set of instructions must be repeated over and over for each card in the file. You need an instruction to bring the computer back to the READ instruction after each card is processed. An instruction that can cause the computer to branch back to the READ instruction is an unconditional branch instruction.

Unconditional branch. An *unconditional branch instruction* is an instruction that causes the computer to change the order of following instructions. It causes the computer to branch (jump) to another instruction regardless of conditions. See Figure 9-12.

Step No.	Statement
	START
1	READ A CARD.
2	MULTIPLY SALES AMOUNT FIELD BY .06 TO CALCULATE SALES TAX.
3	ADD SALES TAX TO SALES AMOUNT TO CALCULATE TOTAL SALES AMOUNT
	DUE.
4	WRITE SALES AMOUNT, SALES TAX, TOTAL SALES AMOUNT DUE.
5	GO TO STEP 1. Unconditional branch

Loop

Figure 9-12. *The unconditional branch at Step 5 causes the computer to loop back to the READ instruction, Step 1.*

GO TO STEP 1 will cause the computer to go back to the READ instruction every time the computer reaches Step 5 in the program. The unconditional branch has created a loop. A *loop* is the repetition of a set of instructions in a program until a certain condition is reached.

Note that the GO TO instruction will cause the computer to loop again and again to the READ instruction until all cards are processed. There must be some way, however, to tell the computer to break out of the loop and to end the program when the last data record is read. An instruction that can cause the computer to break out of the loop is a conditional branch instruction.

Conditional branch. A *conditional branch instruction* is an instruction that causes the computer to branch to another instruction if a certain test or condition has been met. A conditional branch is always the result of a decision.

In Figure 9-12, a decision is not made to see if there are more data cards to be processed. This decision should be made, however, because there must always be a way to end a loop. Otherwise, the computer will not know what to do when there are no more data cards to be processed. If there are no more cards, the computer should be told to stop. Figure 9-13 illustrates a last-card decision that will cause a branch, depending on the results of the test.

The branch to STOP shown in Figure 9-13 is a conditional branch because it is based on the condition that the last card must have been read. There are many other conditions and decisions that will be explained in later chapters.

Step No.	Statement
	START
1	READ A CARD.
2	TEST TO SEE IF THIS CARD CONTAINS THE LAST-CARD CODE. IF IT
	DOES, BRANCH TO STEP 7. IF IT DOES NOT, IT IS A DATA CARD--
	CONTINUE WITH NEXT STEP.
3	MULTIPLY SALES AMOUNT FIELD BY .06 TO CALCULATE SALES TAX.
4	ADD SALES TAX TO SALES AMOUNT TO CALCULATE TOTAL SALES AMOUNT
	DUE.
5	WRITE SALES AMOUNT, SALES TAX, TOTAL SALES AMOUNT DUE.
6	GO TO STEP 1. Unconditional branch
7	STOP

Loop

Conditional branch

Figure 9-13. *The conditional branch at Step 2 causes the computer to break out of the loop if the last data card has been processed. The branch is to Step. 7.*

Explanation of last-card test

In the older computers, there was a built-in last-card sense switch. This switch was designed to give an electronic signal when the last card had been read. The last-card test instruction in the program would be written *at the end* of a set of instructions, to tell the computer to check to see if the last card test signal were present. Based on the presence or absence of the signal, the branch to the next instruction in the program would be made.

In most modern computers, however, there is no last-card sense switch. Instead of testing for the last card *after* each data card has been processed, the test is done *before* each data card is processed. The computer operator places a special coded card at the end of the file of data cards. This special card has a predetermined code in one field of the card. The code may be $EOJ, /*, 99999, or any characters the programmer wishes to use. The code will be placed in a field that would ordinarily contain data. For example, if student cards were being read, the programmer could have 99999 punched in the Student Number field, knowing that no student would have this number. When the computer would sense this number, it would immediately branch to the instruction to which it was told to go

Instructions will be written so that when the first card is read, the card will be tested to see if it contains the last-card code. If the card does not contain the last-card code, the computer knows that it is a data card, and the card will be processed according to the program instructions. Each time another card is read, the new card will also be tested for the last-card code. If the code is not in the card, this card will be processed. If the code is in the card, a branch is made according to instructions.

Figure 9-14 illustrates a last-card decision in flowchart form.

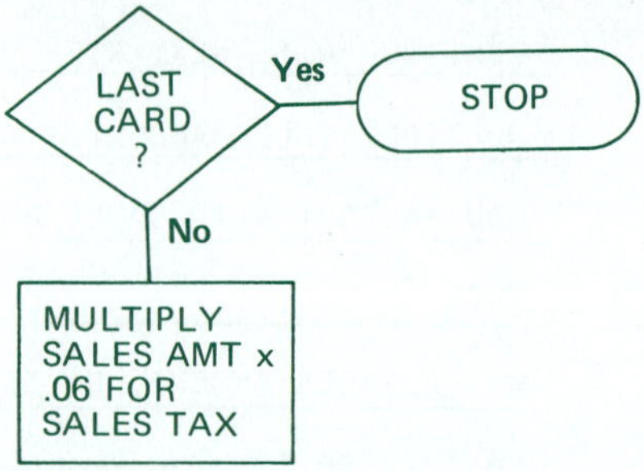

Figure 9-14. *This last-card test causes the computer to branch to STOP if the last-card code is in a card. If the code is not present, the computer goes on to the next step in the program.*

WRITING PROGRAMS IN FLOWCHARTS AND HUMAN LANGUAGE

Some of the computer instructions used most often have been explained, and corresponding flowchart symbols have been shown. A sample problem will be used to teach you how to draw a program flowchart.

Statement of the sample problem

In order to make this problem simple, assume that a sales amount will be punched into cards — one amount to a card. The purpose of this program is to figure the amount of sales tax due on each sale and then to print a report showing the sales amount, sales tax due, and total sales amount due on the sale, including the tax. The sales tax rate used is six percent (.06). This problem is an oversimplification of a real program for calculating sales tax. However, it does represent the basic parts of a flowchart and program. The sample includes input, a decision (conditional branch), processing (calculations), output, and an unconditional branch. These five main kinds of instructions make up most all program instructions.

Flowchart for solving the sample problem

Figure 9-15 is a flowchart for solving the sample problem. Note the conditional branch, the unconditional branch, and the loop. At Step 2 there is a branch to Step 7 if the last-card code is in the card. This is a conditional branch because it is based on a test. At Step 6, there is an unconditional branch back to READ instruction, Step 1. This unconditional branch sets up the loop, which will not be broken until the computer reads the last-card code in a data card placed at the end of the file. Note also that the terminal symbol is used for START and STOP.

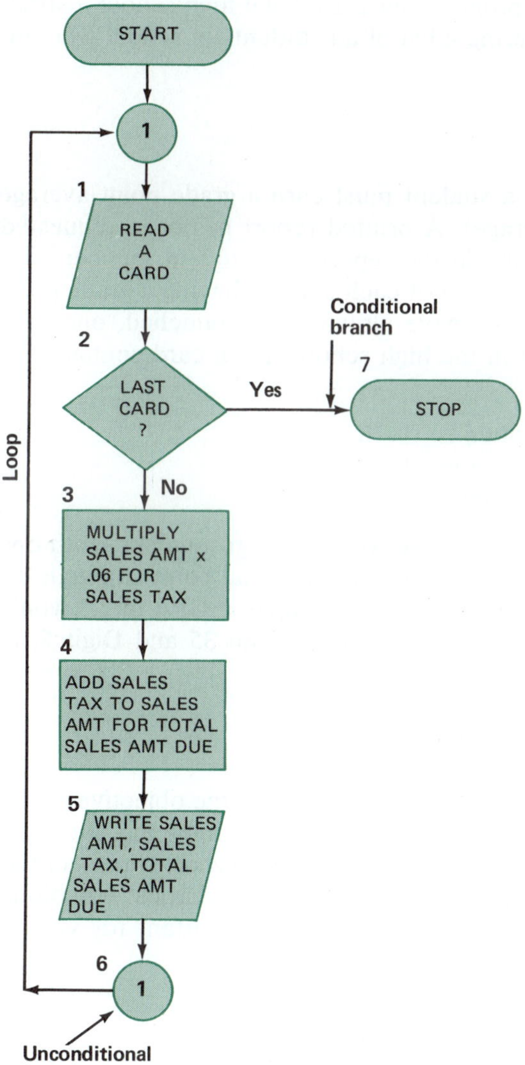

START

1. Read a card.
2. Is the last-card code in this card? If it is, branch to Step 7 and STOP. If it is not, continue to the next step.
3. Multiply the amount in the sales amount field by .06 to calculate the sales tax due.
4. Add the sales tax to the sale amount to calculate the total sales amount due.
5. Write (print) the sales amount, sales tax, and total sales amount due on a print line.
6. Go back to Step 1 and read another card.
7. STOP.

9-15. *Above is the flowchart to solve the sample problem.*

Human-language program for solving the sample problem

The human-language program to solve the sample problem has already been illustrated as Figure 9-13, p. 211. Note that the last-card test was made at Step 2. The unconditional branch that set up the loop was made at Step 6. Note that if the last-card code is in the card being tested, the computer will skip the instructions in Steps 3–6 and will branch to Step 7.

APPLICATION PROBLEM

Assume that you are the programmer for a local high school district. You are responsible for preparing a list of all students in school who are eligible for the honor roll.

Statement of the problem

To be on the honor roll, a student must earn a grade point average (GPA) of at least 3.0 (B average). A printed report has been requested that will list, on a separate line in the report, the student number, student name, and grade point average of each student having a grade point average of 3.0 or greater. Cards have already been punched, one card per student, for each student in the high school. Each card contains the following information:

(1) Student Number	Columns 1– 6
(2) Student Name	Columns 11–30
(3) Grade Point Average	Columns 35–36

The grade point average is punched as a two-digit number, with one of the digits assumed to be to the right of the decimal point although the decimal point is not actually punched. For example, a GPA of 2.5 would be punched as 25. Digit 2 would appear in Column 35 and Digit 5, in Column 36.

Flowchart for solving the application problem

Just as soon as you, the programmer, understand the objective of the program, the next step is to develop the logic. In programming, the logic of a program is represented in flowchart form. A flowchart shows all the necessary steps and the order of those steps. Mathematical equations are used to save space inside the symbols. It is important for you to understand the following symbols and their meanings:

$=$ EQUAL TO
$\neq$ NOT EQUAL TO
$<$ LESS THAN
$>$ GREATER THAN
$\leqslant$ LESS THAN OR EQUAL TO
$\geqslant$ GREATER THAN OR EQUAL TO

Figure 9-16 shows the flowchart for solving the problem. Note that the symbol ≥ is used for "greater than or equal to." Note also that this is a macro-instruction. The computer is instructed to make two comparisons in only one instruction.

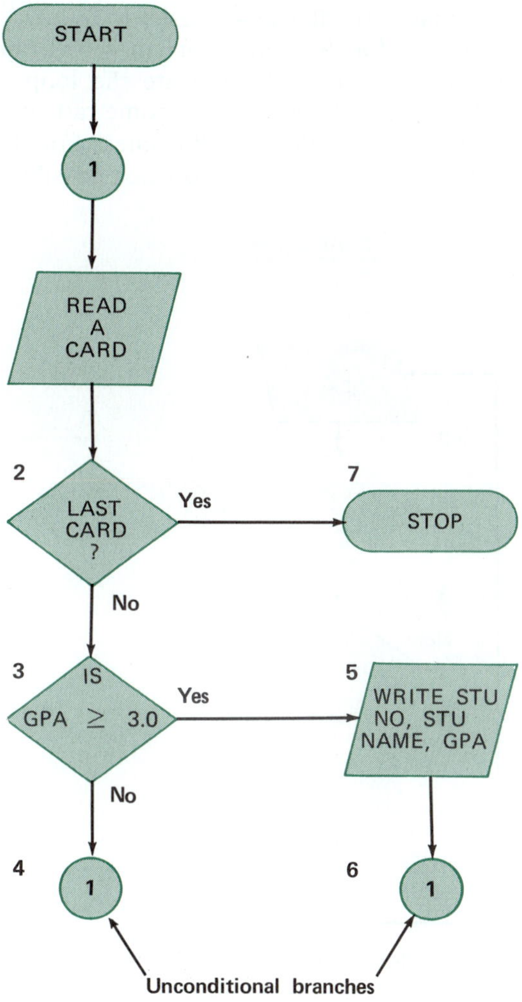

Figure 9-16. *This is a flowchart to print an honor roll. Note the use of on-page connectors.*

The flowchart in Figure 9-16 has four of the basic symbols used in program flowcharting. The terminal symbol is used to stand for START and STOP. The input/output symbol is used for the READ (input) operation and the WRITE (output) operation. The decision symbol is used twice in the flowchart. The first time it is used to test for the last card. If the last-card code is found in the card, the program is complete and the computer is told to stop. If the last-card code is not found, the computer is instructed to process the data card by going to the next instruction.

The on-page connector is used as a step identifier at Step 4 in the flowchart, to indicate that a conditional branch is to be taken whenever the grade point average is not greater than or equal to 3.0. The computer

is then instructed to go to Step 1 and read the next card. The on-page connector (Step 6) is also used after the WRITE symbol to indicate an unconditional branch back to the READ instruction. It is not really necessary to use an on-page connector above the READ instruction. However, it is a good idea to use it because the loop is usually back to the READ instruction. This use makes the flowchart easier to follow.

Figure 9-17 shows a flowchart for the same problem without on-page connectors. Reverse flowlines are shown to indicate the loops.[1] This flowchart is also correct. However, flowlines may become rather confusing to follow in a complex flowchart with many flowlines. For this reason, it is suggested that on-page connectors be used when possible.

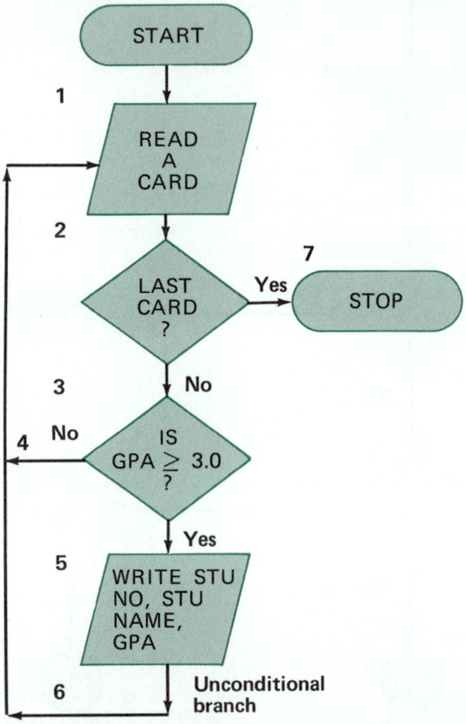

Figure 9-17. *This is a flowchart to print an honor roll. Note the use of reverse flowlines instead of on-page connectors.*

Two variations of the same flowchart have been presented. Both are correct. With on-page connectors, there is no danger of having overlapping flowlines. For this reason, the practice of using on-page connectors is preferred.

Human-language program for solving the application problem

The human-language program for solving this problem is shown in Figure 9-18. Note that the instructions are written much as they would

[1]You learned in Chapter 2 that the normal flow in a flowchart is from left to right and from top to bottom. When the flow of data is reversed, arrowheads must be used with the flowlines. In this text, arrowheads are used at all times.

be in a procedure manual written for humans to follow. This should not be surprising when you consider that both unskilled humans and computers must follow detailed instructions to complete a task.

```
        START
1       READ A CARD IN THE FILE OF STUDENTS' GRADE CARDS.
2       TEST TO SEE IF THIS CARD IS A DATA CARD BY CHECKING TO SEE IF
        THE LAST-CARD CODE IS IN THE CARD.  IF THE CODE IS IN THE CARD,
        THIS MEANS THAT THE LAST CARD HAS ALREADY BEEN PROCESSED, AND A
        BRANCH WILL BE MADE TO STEP 7.  IF THE LAST-CARD CODE IS NOT IN
        THE CARD, THE CARD CONTAINS DATA CONCERNING A STUDENT'S GRADES.
        THE CARD IS TO BE PROCESSED BY GOING TO THE NEXT INSTRUCTION
        (STEP 3).
3       CHECK TO SEE WHETHER THE STUDENT'S GPA IS GREATER THAN OR EQUAL
        TO 3.0.  IF IT IS, GO TO STEP 5.  IF IT IS NOT, GO TO STEP 4.
4       GO BACK TO STEP 1 AND READ ANOTHER CARD.
5       WRITE (PRINT) THE STUDENT'S NUMBER, NAME, AND GPA ON ONE LINE.
6       GO BACK TO STEP 1 AND READ ANOTHER CARD.
7       STOP
```

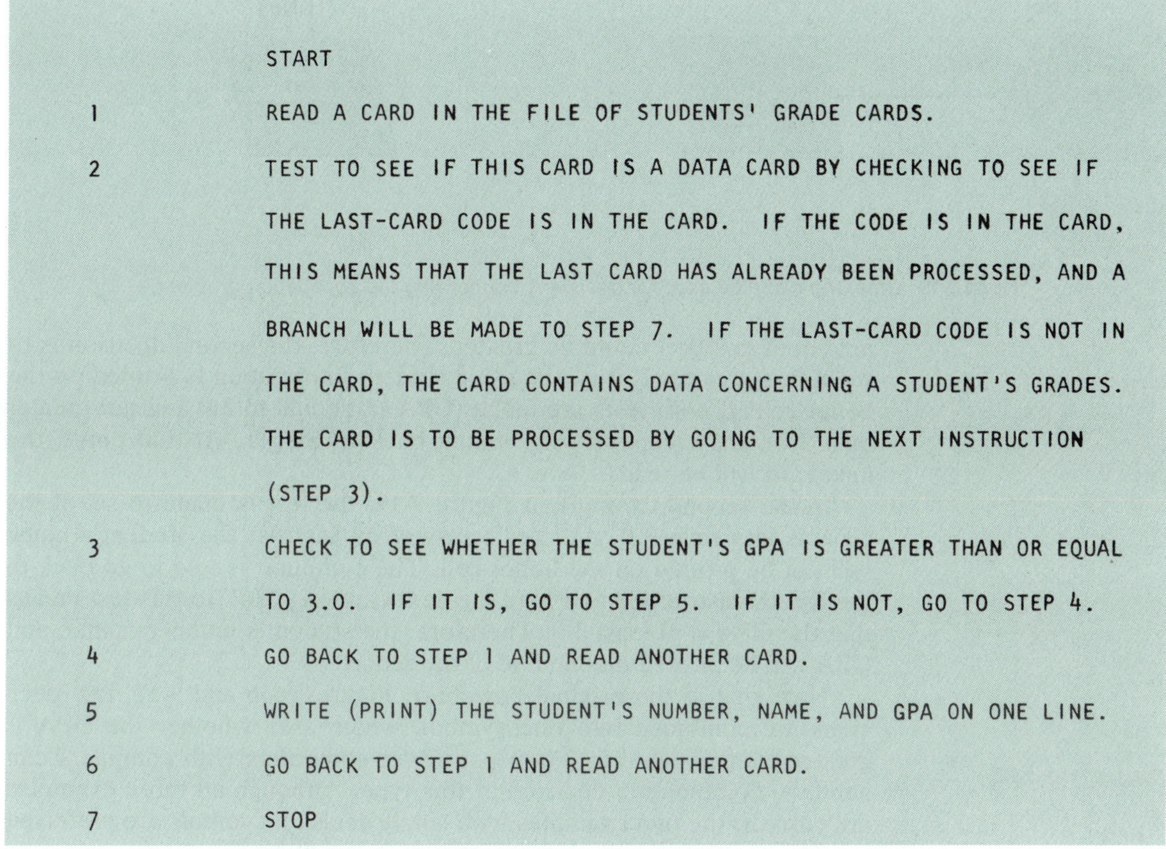

Figure 9-18. *This is a human-language program for the honor-roll problem.*

Different forms of logic in programming

Remember that flowcharts are drawn by humans. Humans think differently because of their own experience or training. There are also many ways to solve the same problem. Any flowchart or program that solves a problem is considered correct. An experienced programmer will flowchart and write programs with fewer steps than will an inexperienced one. Figure 9-19 shows partial flowcharts with differing logic concerning the second decision in the application problem flowcharted in Figures 9-16 and 9-17.

Example 1 has two decision symbols for testing for the GPA. The first test to see if the GPA is equal to 3.0. If it is, the student's number, name, and GPA will be printed on the honor roll report. If the GPA is

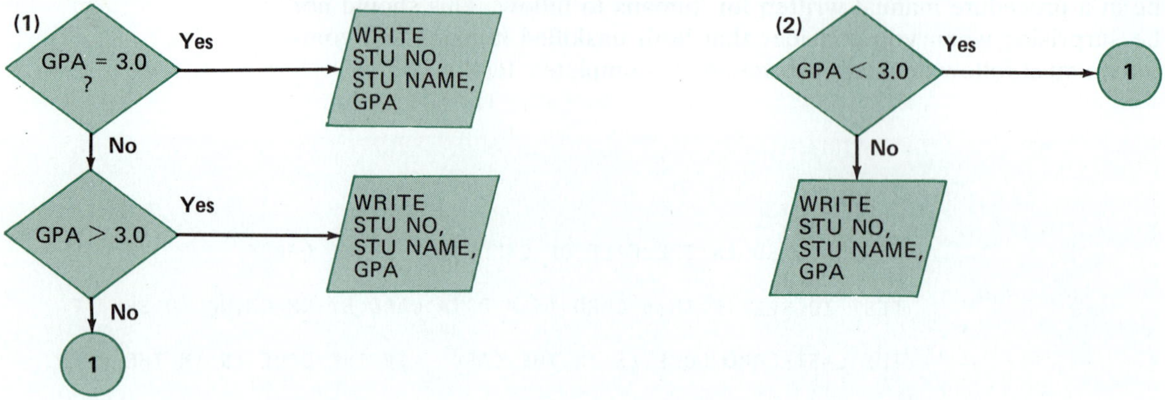

Figure 9-19. *Other logic can be used for decisions concerning the application problem.*

not equal to 3.0, it could be greater. Therefore, the second decision is to see if it is greater. If it is, the same student information is printed on the honor roll. If both tests are failed (GPA not equal to 3.0 and not greater than 3.0), the computer will branch back to Step 1. At that point, the next card will be read.

In the second example in Figure 9-19, the test is made to see if the GPA is less than 3.0. A "Yes" answer means that the student's name will not be printed on the honor roll. The computer is told to go back to the READ instruction and read the next card. A "No" to this test means that the GPA is at least 3.0. Therefore, the student's number, name, and GPA will be printed on one line of the report.

Note that in the original flowchart, Figures 9-16 and 9-17, two decisions are combined into one symbol, which asks whether the GPA is greater than or equal to 3.0. Most newer computers with compilers can handle a combination decision of this type. Although all three examples are correct, the two examples with single decision symbols are preferred because they get the work finished with fewer steps.

SUMMARY

A computer solves problems by following instructions that are written and stored in its memory. After the instructions have been stored in the memory, the stored program takes over and calls for the data as they are needed to solve a problem. Each step in a program must be correctly written. No detail can be omitted.

Computers vary in the form in which instructions must be written. A basic understanding of the art of program writing may be gained by writing instructions in human language first. Flowcharts are also very useful for learning how to think logically.

With the early computers, a programmer needed to write instructions in the hardware-oriented language of the computer being used. This language is referred to as machine language. It is the only language that a computer can actually understand. It is very complicated for humans to use, though, and other languages have been developed that are easier.

The human-oriented languages are of two types. The first type is the symbolic or assembly-level language. The second is the higher-level or compiler language. Machine language does not need to be translated because it can be understood by the computer as it is. However, symbolic language must be translated to machine language by a program called an assember. Higher-level language must also be translated to machine language by a program called a compiler.

Very few programmers use machine language or assembly language at the present time. Machine-language programming requires a thorough knowledge of the computer. It takes much more programmer time than does assembly or compiler-language programming.

A computer instruction is made up of an operation code and one or more operands. The operation code tells the computer what action is to be taken. The operand gives the address of the data or instruction to be used. Machine-language operands use the numeric address of the data or instruction. These addresses are not the same as the contents of the addresses. Symbolic labels or names are used as operands in symbolic and compiler languages. These labels or data names must be converted to machine-language addresses before they can be used. The translation is done by an assembler or compiler.

The original program that must be translated is called a source program. The resulting program, which is in machine language, is called an object program. The translator program is stored in the computer first. The source program is recorded in punched cards or some other input medium and is read into the computer next. The source program is then translated by the assembler or compiler to a machine-language object program. The object program is also recorded in punched cards or some other medium. The object program can then be read into the memory of the computer. Next, data records are read into the computer one at a time as needed by the program to solve the problem.

The computer is able to make a number of decisions on the basis of the program that is written and stored in its memory. A test to see if the last card or record has been processed is included in almost every program. It is used to see whether to repeat the instructions to process another card or to branch to a new set of instructions when the last card has been processed.

The computer can also test to see if two sets of data in a given field are equal or unequal. If they are unequal, a test can be made to see which field is larger or smaller than the other. The results of these tests determine what steps are to be taken next.

REVIEW QUESTIONS

1. Where are data and instructions placed before any processing can take place?
2. Can a portion of a record (card) be read and stored in memory? Explain.
3. What is meant by "destructive read-in"?

(Continued)

4. Why can the MOVE instruction be referred to as a "copy" instruction?
5. How is a work area in memory cleared for computations?
6. Is the print area of a computer self-clearing? How can it be cleared?
7. What flowchart symbol is used to represent a MOVE instruction?
8. What is an *unconditional branch instruction*?
9. What is a *loop*?
10. What is a *conditional branch instruction*?
11. What sort of branch is the result of a decision?
12. In modern computers, does the last-card test take place after a card is processed or before a card is processed? Explain.
13. What is the purpose of the on-page connector?
14. Are arrowheads needed on all flowlines?
15. What is the meaning of this decision? Is this a micro-instruction? Explain.

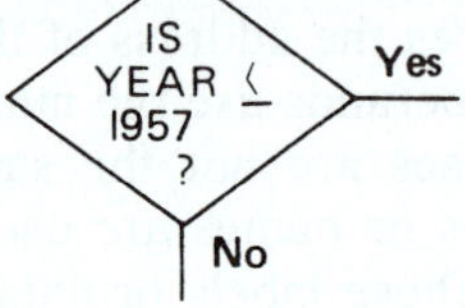

NEW TERMS

- Address
- Assembler
- Assembly
- Coding
- Compiler
- Compiler-level language
- Computer instruction
- Computer program
- Conditional branch instruction
- Destructive read-in
- Higher level language
- Instruction
- Label
- Loop
- Machine address
- Machine language
- Macro-translation language
- Micro-translation language
- Object program
- Operand
- Operation code
- Program (computer)
- Programmer
- Source program
- Symbolic language
- Synthetic language
- Unconditional branch instruction

STUDY GUIDE

Complete Study Guide 9 by following the instructions in your STUDY GUIDES booklet.

PROJECTS

Complete Projects 9-1 and 9-2 by following the instructions in your PROJECTS booklet.

10 PROGRAMMING in BASIC

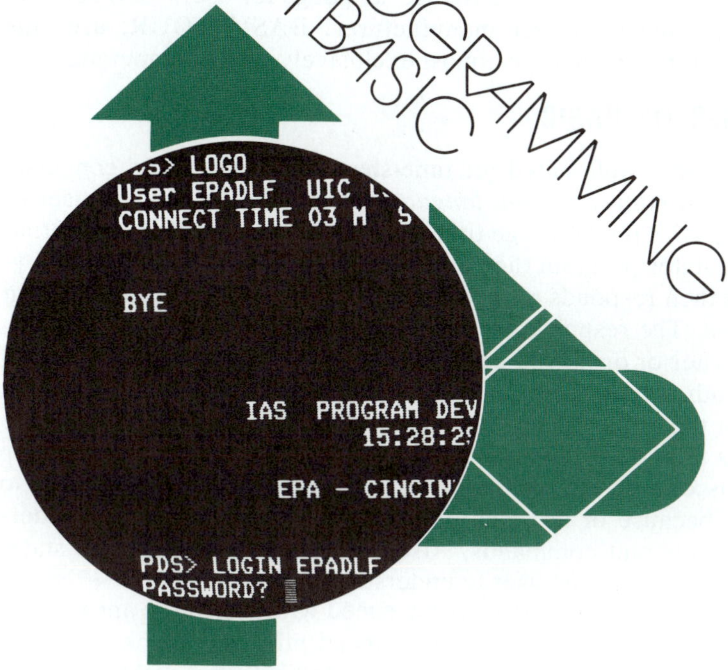

In the preceding chapter, you learned how computer programs can be written in human language. You also learned that computers cannot understand human-language instructions. Programmers must write commands or instructions in one of the many different programming languages that have been developed. The BASIC programming language can be used with many computer systems. It is often the first language taught in schools.

BASIC stands for *B*eginners *A*ll-purpose *S*ymbolic *I*nstruction *C*ode. This language was first developed at Dartmouth University as an easy-to-teach computer programming language. The language was originally used as a time-sharing language on a General Electric computer.

You learned earlier that time-sharing makes it possible for many users to share a computer at the same time. This time-sharing capability makes BASIC an ideal language for use in the classroom. Because of the computer's great speed, many students can use the computer during the same time span. The computer switches back and forth from one student to another so fast that each user is unaware that others are using the computer at the same time.

The BASIC language has gained almost universal acceptance as the industry standard for time-sharing. In fact, almost all computer manufacturers provide some form of the BASIC language for use with their computers today. One computer manufacturer, BASIC/FOUR, uses the BASIC programming language almost exclusively on its computers.

ADVANTAGES OF BASIC

BASIC is very well suited for time-sharing because of its conversational nature. A *conversational language* is one that allows the user to communicate with the language translator program by typing on a terminal. The translator program then evaluates each instruction on a line-by-line basis. It then responds to the operator if a mistake has been found in an instruction. The response to the operator may be printed on the terminal typewriter or displayed on the terminal CRT. Some BASIC terminals have both a typewriter and a CRT. However, most of them have either one or the other. Figure 10-1 shows a terminal with a CRT. Figure 10-2 shows a terminal with a typewriter.

BASIC is one of the most simple of all programming languages to use. This is because of its small number of powerful but easily understood statements and commands. Also, BASIC uses English-like statements that are easy for the user to understand.

Another advantage of BASIC is the speed with which the answer to a problem can be had if the program is planned properly. Some computer languages require that many steps be completed before a problem can be solved, as follows:

(1) A program is written.
(2) Each instruction is keypunched and verified.
(3) The program is then translated.
(4) After the program is translated, it is often necessary to correct mistakes in the instructions themselves.
(5) The object program (translated version of the program) is then run with a sample of test data to see if the program does the job it is supposed to do. (The process of correcting and testing a program before actually using it to process data is called *debugging*.)
(6) The object program is run with actual data, and the results become known.

In BASIC, however, the verifying and debugging take place on each instruction as it is entered at the terminal. In that way, the programmer can run test data just as soon as the last instruction has been entered.

The BASIC language allows instructions to be entered at any time and in any order. The translator program will arrange all the instructions in order and give the operator a corrected copy of the program upon request. All this will be explained later in this chapter. Creating and running a BASIC program can, and often does, take less than a half hour. Compare this time with that of an ordinary computer program that could take several days between its origin and final running.

Figure 10-1. *This BASIC terminal has a CRT.*

Figure 10-2. *This BASIC terminal has printed output only.*

DISADVANTAGES OF BASIC

One disadvantage of BASIC will soon become plain to those who have had exposure to other higher-level languages. It is that a printed line of output is much shorter than the usual printed line. The standard BASIC printed line is as short as 70 or 75 characters, and it is not much longer in some of the largest computer systems.

Another disadvantage to some forms of the BASIC language is that it is rather hard to plan printed output to fit preprinted forms.[1] The BASIC output statements used in this book will be limited to those that are available in most forms of the BASIC language.

[1] Many versions of BASIC have now overcome this disadvantage.

Probably the most important disadvantage of BASIC is that it is not designed to process large data files of any kind. As you know, most business reports are created by using data from one, two, and sometimes three or more files. Remember that four different files were used to produce the statements of account described in Chapter 4. BASIC is not designed to process data from many files. Instead, it is a conversational language. The operator usually enters the program and the data via a terminal keyboard rather than by using punched cards or other input media. BASIC is usually used to solve problems that:

(1) Require very low volumes of data.
(2) Need a rather quick response.
(3) May be one-time in nature.

The disadvantages of BASIC are not serious in a time-sharing environment because most time-sharing applications have minimal input. Also, output is mostly for immediate use and will not be forwarded to top management or to a customer.

You will soon learn that the disadvantages of BASIC are outweighed by the conversational nature of the language and the ease in which programs can be written. Besides, many of today's disadvantages are being corrected by computer manufacturers in later versions of the BASIC language. Many of the improved versions of BASIC have been given names such as Super BASIC, Extended BASIC, BASIC Plus, and Business BASIC.

This chapter will give you general rules for input and output in BASIC. The actual instructions for entering BASIC programs at a terminal will be given at the end of this chapter on pp. 248–250. Arithmetic statements and more advanced concepts will be explained in Chapter 11.

ELEMENTARY BASIC COMMANDS

This chapter will describe only the simplest commands for writing a BASIC program. You will not become an accomplished programmer. Instead, enough information will be given about some of the elementary commands to help you to interact successfully with the computer. Once these commands are mastered, you can try out more advanced applications of these statements if you wish. No attempt will be made to teach any advanced or specialized commands that are limited to one certain version of BASIC. All commands given in this text should work equally well on most computers using BASIC.

Any problem that can be solved with more advanced techniques can also be solved with the simpler statements given here, although the simpler solutions may not be as efficient. Once you have written a simple program in BASIC and have interacted with the computer, you can go ahead at your own pace to more sophisticated commands.

Even if you decide to stop after completing the problems in this chapter, you will find that you are able to relate to problems faced by computer programmers. This, in turn, will help you to become a better and wiser user of computing power in the future.

FIXED- AND FLOATING-POINT NUMBERS

Two different kinds of numbers are used to solve problems with the computer. They are fixed-point and floating-point numbers.

Fixed-point numbers

A *fixed-point* or *integer* number is a whole number, as opposed to a number containing a decimal. The decimal point is assumed to be "fixed" at the end of the whole number. All numbers of this type are said to be in fixed-point form. Examples of fixed-point numbers follow:

1984   71   483   594   52790

Fixed-point numbers will be discussed very little in this book because most of the computations will use floating-point numbers.

Floating-point numbers

A *floating-point (real) number* includes a fractional amount. All numbers having decimal points are said to be in floating-point form. This form automatically places the decimal point in the proper place according to the way in which the program is written. Examples of floating-point numbers follow:

1984.   78.5   399.00   18.333

Floating-point numbers are used very much in BASIC, especially for fields that may change from record to record. When they are printed out, however, all ending zeros that are to the right of the decimal point are dropped.

CONSTANTS AND VARIABLES

In order to understand computer programming, you must know the difference between a constant and a variable.

Constants

A *constant* is a value that is known in advance and which does not change during the processing of a program.

Numeric constants. Numeric constants can be positive or negative numbers. The following example is of a positive number. A constant can be used in figuring sales tax. Assume that the tax rate is 6%. Then, the value .06 could be used each time a certain set of instructions is carried out by the computer to calculate the actual amount of tax to charge. The value .06 would be a constant.

Other examples of constants are:

1 25 .000123 −1.75 1.5 −.5

Alphanumeric constants. The word *alphanumeric* is used in BASIC to describe data that consist of letters of the alphabet with any combination of spaces, numbers, or special characters. Examples of alphanumeric data are:

SALES TAX PROBLEM	(Letters and spaces)
MUSTANG 2	(Letters, space, and number)
J525/2	(Letter, numbers, and special character)
J52	(Letter and numbers)

An *alphanumeric constant*, then, is an alphanumeric value that is known in advance and which does not change during the processing of a program. Alphanumeric constants are used in BASIC for headings and for special phrases on other lines of a program. Examples of alphanumeric constants are:

```
10 PRINT "TAX PROBLEM"

20 PRINT "PROGRAMMED BY D. LUI"
```

Note that these two expressions are enclosed in quotation marks. Whenever alphanumeric constants are used in a BASIC program, the actual constant must be enclosed in quotation marks. The quotation marks will not be printed in the report, however. They only serve to tell the computer that everything between them, including the spaces, is to be printed on a certain line.

The quotation marks serve a similar purpose in BASIC as they do in a term paper. In a term paper, you would use quotation marks to show the exact words another person is using. In programming, the quotation marks are used to tell the computer the exact format of the data that are to appear on a printed line.

Constants will be explained further in this and the next chapter as they appear.

Variables

A *variable* is an item of data that is not known in advance and which changes during the processing of a program. A variable can be either numeric or alphanumeric.

Alphanumeric variables. Alphanumeric variables can consist of data items such as names of students. For example, the programmer can plan an alphanumeric field of 20 spaces for each student name. However, the actual name will not be known until it is entered at the terminal. For this reason, the names are considered to be variable data.

BASIC is more concerned with values and amounts than with long alphabetic lists, however. In this chapter, the BASIC programs will deal with numeric variables only.

Numeric variables. *Numeric variables* are numeric values that are not known in advance and which change as a program is processed. Examples of numeric variables are student numbers, tests scores, total test points for the term, and the student averages. A school may use a computer program to calculate grades earned by students during a given term. The program may be the same for each student, but the test scores of each student will be different. The BASIC program figures the entire problem for one student before going on to the next. Examples of numeric variables are:

Student No.	*Test 1 Score*	*Test 2 Score*	*Test 3 Score*	*Term Total*	*Average*
2350	94	89	90	273	91
2367	83	80	80	243	81
2399	90	79	89	258	86
2400	91	88	97	276	92

Variable names for addresses

You learned in Chapter 9 that higher-level languages use names instead of numeric addresses to describe storage locations. The names are then translated by the compiler program to the proper machine addresses. In BASIC, any data field that changes while a program is processed is a variable and must be given a variable name. *The name describes the address at which the data field is stored. The name is not the same as the data*. A *variable name* is a name given to an address at which a variable field of data is stored in the computer.

Variable names are assigned by the programmer. The translator program then assigns memory locations to each variable name. Certain rules that will be given to you must be kept in mind in assigning these names. In the previous example, note that the test scores vary from student to student. The total points for the term and the average also vary. A variable name must be assigned to each of these variable data fields in a computer program. The name assigned to a given variable must stay the same throughout the program so that the computer can always go to the same address for like fields of data.

For example, a name such as S1 could be given to Test Score 1. Each time a new value is entered, the amount stored at the location named S1 would be different. For Student No. 2350, S1 would contain 94. For Student No. 2367, S1 would contain 83. For Student No. 2399, S1 would contain 90, etc. S1 would describe the address, not the data.

Inventing names for floating-point numeric variables

Only the names for floating-point numeric variables will be discussed in this chapter. A *floating-point variable* is a field of data that contains a decimal point, the value of which field changes from record to record and is not known in advance. Numeric variables in BASIC must be given names because the actual data values are not known in advance. The rules for forming names for floating-point variables are as follows:

(1) No more than two characters are allowed in a variable name, the first of which must be a letter.
(2) The name may begin with any letter of the alphabet.
(3) Two letters may not be used together.
(4) The first character, which is a letter, may be followed by a single number.

These length limitations should make it clear that the variable names in BASIC cannot describe the data very well. In many other languages, variable names are not limited to only one letter or to one letter plus a single number. Names such as RATE, TOTAL, and ACCT-NUMBER might be used. In BASIC, these same names would be limited to such names as R, T1, and A9. Because of BASIC's length limitation, the programs usually include many remarks and comments to help the programmer remember the names assigned to each item of data.

Note the following names for floating-point variables:

R	Legal	Begins with a letter of the alphabet and has less than two characters.
T12	Illegal	Has more than two characters.
B4	Legal	Begins with a letter of the alphabet, is followed by a single number, and has no more than two characters.
27	Illegal	Must begin with a letter.
AA	Illegal	Can have only one letter of the alphabet.
A	Legal	Begins with a letter of the alphabet and has less than two characters.

REVIEW QUESTIONS

1. What do the letters in the name BASIC stand for?
2. Why is BASIC called a "conversational" language?
3. What are three advantages of BASIC?
4. What are three disadvantages of BASIC?
5. Why are the disadvantages of BASIC outweighed by the advantages?
6. What is a *fixed-point number*?
7. What is a *floating-point number*?
8. What are two differences between a constant and a variable?
9. How does a computer know what to do when it encounters an alphanumeric constant? What is printed on a line?

10. What do variable names describe?
11. Why must the name given to a particular variable stay the same throughout a program?
12. What is a *floating-point variable*?
13. What are the four rules for assigning names to floating-point variables in BASIC?
14. Why do the variable names in BASIC seldom describe the contents of the addresses they describe?
15. Identify each of the following variable names as "legal" or "illegal" and explain why:

T 4 S3 B27 4F

GENERAL RULES FOR WRITING BASIC STATEMENTS

The rules for operating the BASIC terminal are found on pp. 248–250 of this chapter. The following rules are for writing a BASIC program.

In BASIC, a program instruction is referred to as a *statement*. A BASIC program is made up of lines of statements, with each line representing one instruction. The following rules must be used:

(1) Each line of the program *must* begin with a line number. The line number identifies the statement and gives the order in which the statements must be processed. Even if the line numbers are not typed in sequential order in the program, the BASIC translator program will process the statements in numeric order according to line numbers.

(2) Each line number is followed by a BASIC statement.

(3) The lines are usually given numbers in multiples of ten (Line 10, Line 20, Line 30, etc.) so that additional statements may be added in between at any point whenever needed.

(4) Line numbers can range from 1 to 9999. Some computers can handle numbers larger than 9999, but the highest number taught in this book is 9999. If this number is not exceeded, the BASIC programs in this text should run on almost any computer using the BASIC language.

(5) More than one statement may be written on a single line as long as each statement (except the last) ends with a colon (:) or a back slash (\\).[2] For example:

```
780 READ N: PRINT N
```

(6) Each line is entered at the terminal and then followed by a carriage return (RETURN).

(7) A single statement may be continued to the next line. The LINE FEED key of the terminal keyboard must be depressed instead of the RETURN key. The LINE FEED key performs the carriage control, and a line-feed operation takes place. The next line does *not*

[2]Many programmers do not like to use this capability because it makes it harder to fit new statements into a program.

contain a new number in this case. A statement of more than one line cannot have more than 256 characters. The continuation break must be between names or words. A data name or word cannot be divided. For example:

```
790 READ S1, S2, S3, S4, S5, S6, S7, S8, S
    9, T1, T2
```

This is illegal because the variable name S9 is split.

(8) Spaces should be used freely in statements to make reading easier.

(9) The computer will follow instructions in line number sequence unless there is an instruction to branch (change the order of instructions). This can be done with an unconditional branch statement (GO TO 80) or a conditional branch statement (IF N = 9999 THEN GO TO 150).

REMARKS AND COMMENTS

Remarks and comments that explain the program are often used in a BASIC program. Because variable names are so short, it is helpful to use remarks and comments. They give information that will help the programmer or other users to understand what is being done. The name of the program, special instructions, and phrases explaining the instructions are often stated in the remarks.

Typical remarks and comments are shown in Figure 10-3. Two different methods of inserting remarks are shown.

```
10  REM  PROGRAM TO LIST TEST SCORES AND TOTAL OF SCORES
20  REM  "S1" WILL BE THE NAME FOR SCORE 1
30  REM  "S2" WILL BE THE NAME FOR SCORE 2
40  REM  "S3" WILL BE THE NAME FOR SCORE 3
50  REM  "T" WILL BE THE NAME FOR THE TOTAL SCORE
60  LET  T = 0               ! SETS T TO ZERO INITIALLY
```

Figure 10-3. *Remarks and comments in a BASIC program are shown.*

REMARK statement

The word REMARK can be abbreviated to REM for typing convenience. The actual message that follows the word REMARK or REM can contain any printing characters on the terminal keyboard. BASIC will ignore anything on a line following the words REMARK or REM. In Figure 10-3, Lines 10 through 50 contain remarks describing the purpose of a program and explaining the variable names, S1, S2, S3, and T. A remark may be continued to another line by entering another line number and the word REM or REMARK. A statement number must precede the continuing remark. For example:

```
110 REM THIS PROGRAM IS DESIGNED TO LIST THE STUDENT NUMBER AND
120 REM THREE TEST SCORES AND THE TOTAL OF ALL TEST SCORES
```

Exclamation point

Refer to Figure 10-3 again. Note that the statement on Line 60 contains an equation and a comment. The statement is LET T = 0. The comment is SETS T TO ZERO INITIALLY. The exclamation point is used to separate the statement from the comment. An exclamation point is used to separate the part of the program statement that will be processed from the comment part on the same line. BASIC will ignore the part of the statement after the exclamation point. The ! statement can also be used to begin a line. In that case, the entire line is treated as a comment. For example:

```
210 ! END OF PROGRAM
```

Use of REMARK statement and exclamation point

Messages in REMARK statements are usually called remarks. Messages after exclamation points are called comments. Remarks and comments are printed as part of the program, but they do not affect the processing of the program. They are not executable statements. An *executable statement* is one that directs the computer to perform a certain operation. It gives a command. A *non-executable statement* is a statement that does not specify action. It usually gives information to the programmer or the user of the program. The *REMARK* statement and the *exclamation point* are used to give information only. They are non-executable statements.

Remarks and comments are never written on the same line with a DATA statement, however. This rule will be explained in the discussion of DATA statements.

PROBLEM 1: PRINTING A LIST OF TEST SCORES FOR EACH STUDENT

Instead of giving a list of BASIC statements and their explanation, the BASIC statements presented in this book will be tied into a specific problem.

Statement of the problem

Assume that your teacher has asked you to write a program to create a four-column printed report. Each line of the four-column report should contain the student number, score for Test 1, score for Test 2, and score for Test 3, in that order. The program is to accept the student number and the three test scores for each student and then to print them in four columns. There will be no arithmetic calculations in this problem.

Analysis of the problem

The program must be written in such a way that the computer will read in the four values (student number, score for Test 1, score for Test 2, and score for Test 3) before printing any output. Important steps in the program are as follows:

(1) The assigning of variable names to the four different values to be used in the program. (Remember that the student number and three test scores are variable because they are not known in advance.)
(2) The creating of a conditional branch so that when the last set of scores has been read and printed on the report, the program will end properly. This is like the last-card test described in Chapter 9. A student number of 9999 will be used to tell the computer when the last student's scores have been processed.
(3) The writing (printing) of the information in four columns on the output. (This printout may be on paper in a terminal typewriter or on a display on the terminal CRT.)
(4) Ending the program.

Flowchart for solving Problem 1

Figure 10-4 shows the flowchart for solving Problem 1.

First READ instruction. The first flowchart symbol after START is an on-page connector (1). This on-page connector is used before the READ instruction to create a point to which an unconditional branch can be made later. You learned in Chapter 9 that the unconditional branch is used to create a loop. After each line of print has been completed, the computer will be told to go back to this READ instruction so that the next set of student data can be entered and processed.

Note that it is a simple input/output problem. It has no arithmetic calculations.

The input symbol is used for the READ instructions. There are two READ instructions in this program. At the first READ instruction, Symbol 1, the student number is read and stored in memory at a location given the variable name, N, for student *n*umber.

Conditional branch. Remember that in Chapter 9, the last-card test was explained. The computer read a record in a file of data cards. If the last-card code was not punched into a certain field in the card, the computer would recognize this card as a data card and would go on to process it.

In this case, there is no card. Instead, a value of 9999 will be entered at the terminal in the Student Number field at the end of all the data. A decision can be written to test to see if the first value read as N is equal

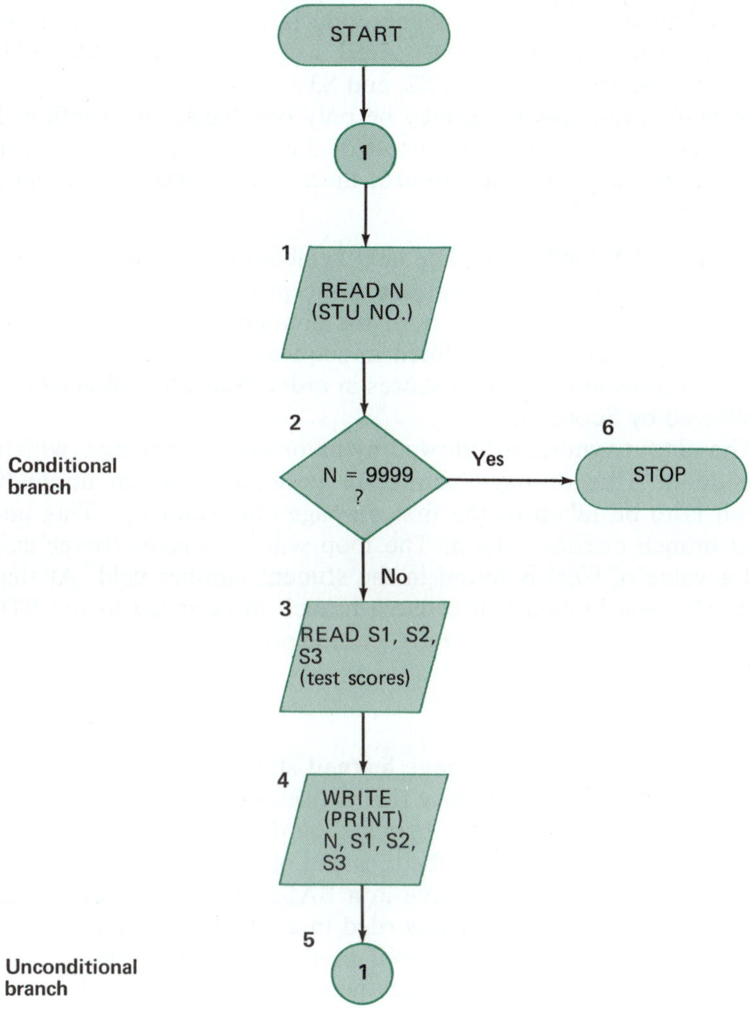

Figure 10-4. *This is the flowchart for solving Problem 1.*

to 9999. It has been decided that 9999 is a value that cannot possibly be encountered as a real student number. Therefore, if the value read as N is 9999, the computer will be told to stop. If, on the other hand, the value just read into the computer does not equal 9999, the computer will go to the next step in the program.

The decision symbol, (2) contains the conditional branch instruction, N = 9999? If N is not equal to 9999, the computer will go on the the next instruction, Symbol 3.

Second READ instruction

The input symbol is again used for the second READ instruction. The computer is now ready to read the three test scores into memory since it knows that the last-value code is not in the Student Number field. These test scores will be stored in the computer at the addresses having the variable names S1, S2, and S3.

In many programs there may be only one READ instruction. In this case, it is necessary to make a test of the student number field (N) before reading the scores. Therefore, there is a READ instruction before the test and one after the test.

Write (PRINT) instruction. The next symbol (4) is an output symbol. All of the data values (fields) that are to be printed on the line have been read and stored in the memory of the computer. This symbol indicates that the values should be printed in sequence with the student number (N) first, followed by the test scores in order (Score 1, followed by Score 2, followed by Score 3).

The output symbol is followed by an on-page connector, which has a 1 inside it. This on-page connector indicates that an unconditional branch is to be taken to the first on-page connector (1). This unconditional branch creates a loop. The loop will be repeated over and over until a value of 9999 is found in the student number field. At that time the conditional branch will cause a branch to be made to the STOP instruction (6), which ends the loop and the program.

Values in BASIC

Up to this chapter, you have learned about files, records, and fields. A *value* in BASIC is a quantity that is used for comparison or computation. It is equal to a field in a punched card or a word in a computer. In this chapter, values are described instead of files and records. For example, the tax rate may be a value in a BASIC program even though it is only part of the information recorded in a customer's sales record. The entire record need not be entered at the terminal keyboard and processed. In BASIC only the values needed from the record to complete certain computations or processing must be entered.

READ and DATA statements in BASIC

READ statement. The READ statement is one method used to enter data in a BASIC program. The READ statement must always be accompanied by a DATA statement. The *READ statement* tells the computer to read one or more variables that are listed in the READ statement and to give them the values listed in the DATA statement. The READ statement gives the variable names assigned by the programmer for the values in the DATA statement.

A READ statement must include the name of one or more variables. Refer to Figure 10-5 for the first part of the program to solve Problem 1. There are two READ statements, Lines 80 and 120. Line 80 tells the computer to read the first variable data value from the DATA statement and to store it in the memory address named N (student number). The

READ statement at Line 120 tells the computer to read three data values from the DATA statement. The first of these three variables will be stored at the address named S1. The next will be stored at the address named S2. The third will be stored at the address named S3.

```
10  REM  PROGRAM TO LIST TEST SCORES
20  REM  "N" WILL BE THE NAME FOR STUDENT NUMBER
30  REM  "S1" WILL BE THE NAME FOR SCORE 1
40  REM  "S2" WILL BE THE NAME FOR SCORE 2
50  REM  "S3" WILL BE THE NAME FOR SCORE 3
60  REM  A STUDENT NUMBER OF 9999 WILL BE USED TO
70  REM  TERMINATE THE PROGRAM
80  READ N
90  DATA  2350, 94, 89, 90, 2367, 83, 80, 80, 2399, 90, 79, 89
100 DATA  2400, 91, 88, 97, 9999
110 IF N = 9999 THEN GO TO 150
120 READ S1, S2, S3
```

Figure 10-5. *Above is a partial program for solving Problem 1.*

Note in Figure 10-5 that 2350 will be the value stored at the address named N. The score of 94 will be stored at the address named S1. The score of 89 will be stored at S2. The score of 90 will be stored at S3.

Because data must be entered into the computer before they can be processed, READ statements usually are placed near the beginning of the program. The variables in the READ statement are read in the order in which they appear in the statement.

DATA statement. The *DATA statement* assigns values to the variable(s) named in the READ statements. The READ and DATA statements for Problem 1 that are shown in Figure 10-5 are as follows:

```
 80 READ N
 90 DATA 2350, 94, 89, 90, 2367, 83, 80, 80, 2399, 90, 79, 89,
100 DATA 2400, 91, 88, 97, 9999

120 READ S1, S2, S3
```

The combination of the READ and DATA statements shown will cause the values listed on the right side of the equal sign (=) below to be stored in the locations named at the left of the equal sign.

N = 2350; S1 = 94; S2 = 89; S3 = 90	(First student)
N = 2367; S1 = 83, S2 = 80; S3 = 80	(Second student)
N = 2399; S1 = 90; S2 = 79; S3 = 89	(Third student)
N = 2400; S1 = 91; S2 = 88; S3 = 97.	(Fourth Student)
N = 9999	(Last-value test)

The READ and DATA statements are processed together. The values in the DATA statement are assigned storage locations at the addresses described by the variable names in the READ statement. These assignments are made in order. The first value in the DATA statement will be stored at the first address named in the READ statement. The second value in the DATA statement will be stored at the second address, and so on. Note that only four sets of student numbers and scores are listed in this program in order to make it easier to understand.

Writing the DATA statement in the program. Although every READ statement must have a DATA statement, the DATA statements do not have to be written immediately before or after the READ statement. In the program for Problem 1, the DATA statements are written below the first READ statement. If more than one DATA statement appears in the program, the DATA statements are processed according to line number sequence. This means that all the data values in the DATA statement with the lowest line number are processed before the data values from the next DATA statement.

Data block. The data values that are entered from more than one DATA statement in a program are combined into one data block before any actual processing takes place. If the line numbers are correct but are entered out of order, the translator program will sequence them properly before creating the data block.

When the program has been entered and before it is run, the translator program collects all the DATA statements in line number order. This collection of DATA statements is called a *data block*. Each time a READ statement is processed in the program, the next available data value is accessed from the data block.[3] It is important that the DATA statements be assigned line numbers in the proper order even if they are not placed with the READ statements.

In Figure 10-6, the statements on Line 90 and 100 constitute the data block. Note that the data values do not have to be on the same line to make a data block. In Figure 10-6, the data block is written with two DATA statements.

---

[3]If the data block has no more data at the time the READ statement is processed, it is usually assumed that there has been an error in the program and an error message is printed. The program execution is then ended. However, different computers may handle the out-of-data conditions in other ways.

Data block

```
 90 DATA 2350, 94, 89, 90, 2367, 83, 80, 80, 2399, 90, 79, 89
100 DATA 2400, 91, 88, 97, 9999
```

Figure 10-6. *This data block consists of values written in two DATA statements.*

The BASIC translator program will assemble the first value from Line 100 right after the last value from Line 90. The entire data block will be assembled as follows:

2350, 94, 89, 90, 2367, 83, 80, 80, 2399, 90, 79, 89, 2400, 91, 88, 97, 9999

This is true because data blocks are assembled in line number order. In this example, the two DATA statements could appear anywhere in the program as long as the two line numbers were in the proper order.

It is easy to see that because of the complexity of the data block, comments should never be written on the same line as a DATA statement.

Test for the Last Data Value

Remember that there must be some method for breaking out of a loop. This is done with a conditional branch. The conditional branch is used to see whether a predetermined value is present. In Problem 1, the predetermined value used is a student number of 9999. If the student number is not 9999, the computer will go on with the next statement in line number order. If the 9999 is detected, the computer is told to branch to a statement outside the loop. In this program, the branch is to the STOP statement on Line 150. This statement stops the processing of the program. See Figure 10-7.

```
110 IF N = 9999 THEN GO TO 150
120 READ S1, S2, S3
130 PRINT N, S1, S2, S3
140 GO TO 80
150 STOP
160 END
```

Conditional branch

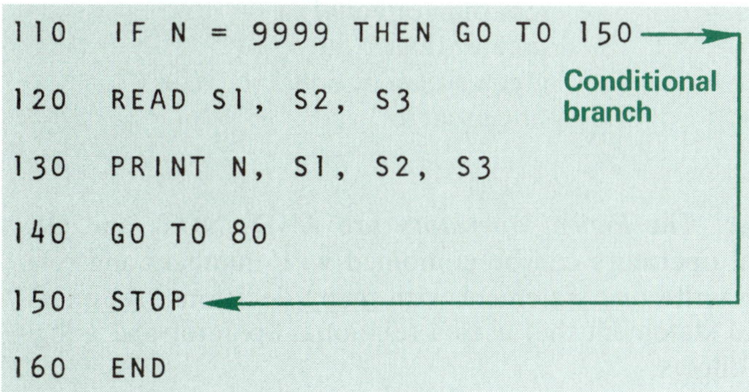

Figure 10-7. *The IF-THEN statement at Line 110 creates a conditional branch to Line 150 if the value stored at N does not equal 9999.*

IF-THEN statement

Conditional branching may be accomplished in BASIC programs by using the *IF-THEN* statement. This statement is written:

```
110 IF N = 9999 THEN GO TO 150
```

This statement is very easy to read and the meaning is clear. The statement could have been written as follows:

```
110 IF N = 9999 THEN 150
```

Note that the GO TO is missing in the second statement. The GO TO is not necessary but is used in this chapter to make the statement clear. In both examples, the computer is told to process the instruction at Line 150 if the value stored at the memory address called N is equal to 9999. If the value is *not* equal to 9999, then the next instruction in sequence (the one after Line 110) is executed. This is the instruction on Line 120 to read the three scores.

It is important to know that the IF must always be written before the GO TO. Otherwise, the computer would go to the instruction on Line 150 without ever making the test.

In order to write correct IF-THEN statements you should understand about relational and logical operators that are used in these statements.

Relational operators. *Relational operators* in BASIC are symbols on the keyboard of the terminal that are used when writing a statement that tests for equality, inequality, or the relationship of one value to another.[4] Relational operators are used by the programmer in statements to create conditional branches. Although relational operators may be used in other kinds of statements, they will be discussed only with the IF-THEN statements in this book. The relational operators used in BASIC are listed as follows:

Symbols	*Meaning*
=	equal to
<	less than
<=	less than or equal to
>	greater than
>=	greater than or equal to
<>	not equal to

Logical operators. The *logical operators* are AND, NOT, and OR. These three logical operators can be combined with numbers and relational operators to write one statement with many decisions. An example of a conditional statement that uses a relational operator and a logical operator is as follows:

```
660 IF A >= 80 and A < 90 THEN GO TO 710
710 PRINT "GRADE IS B"
```

This statement tells the computer that if the average is greater than or equal to 80 and less than 90, the computer should print GRADE IS B.

[4]Note that the symbols on the keyboard are not exactly like the mathematical equations shown on p. 214, of Chapter 9. For example, "greater than or equal to" is >= in BASIC instead of $\geq$.

The problems used in this book will not require the use of both logical and relational expressions.

Unconditional branch — GO TO statement

Unconditional branches appear in almost every program. You learned in Chapter 9 that an unconditional branch can be used to create a loop back to the beginning of the program to a READ instruction. In this BASIC program, there must be a loop back to the first READ instruction, Line 80, to read the next student number (N). This loop will be repeated until all values in the data block are processed. See Figure 10-8.

Unconditional branch

```
80   READ N
90   DATA  2350, 94, 89, 90, 2367, 83, 80, 80, 2399, 90, 79, 89
100  DATA  2400, 91, 88, 97, 9999
110  IF N = 9999 THEN GO TO 150
120  READ S1, S2, S3
130  PRINT N, S1, S2, S3
140  GO TO 80
```

Figure 10-8. *The unconditional branch at Line 140 creates a loop back to the first READ statement, Line 80.*

The *GO TO* statement in Line 140 gives the line number of the statement to which an unconditional branch must be made. The unconditional branch is used whenever the order of instructions is to be changed, whatever the condition that exists. An unconditional branch is written as follows:

```
140 GO TO 80
```

This is the branch that is needed to cause the computer to return to the first READ statement to read the student number.

Write (PRINT) statement in BASIC

The *PRINT statement* in BASIC is used to cause the computer to output data on the terminal CRT or typewriter. The PRINT statement tells the computer what data are to be printed on a line in a report or to be displayed on a CRT. This statement also tells the printer how the output is to be arranged.

Printing an alphanumeric constant. You have already learned that quotation marks can be used to identify an alphanumeric constant to the computer. You can order the printer to print exactly what you have typed within the quotation marks.

If you wished to have a heading printed, TEST SCORE REPORT, this could be done with the following statement:

```
20 PRINT "TEST SCORE REPORT"
```

The heading would be printed on one line without the quotation marks. The printer will print whatever is inside the quotation marks, but the quotation marks will not be printed.

If you were planning a program to find the class average, you might wish to plan a line of print at the end of a report that would say CLASS AVERAGE IS 83. Assume that you have chosen A as the variable name for the address of the average. You could have the line you wish printed with the following statement:

```
200 PRINT "CLASS AVERAGE IS  " A
```

Note that there is a space between IS and the second quotation mark. The computer will "print" this space. After printing the alphanumeric constant, CLASS AVERAGE IS , the printer will then print the value of A, which is 83. The printed space will keep IS and 83 from running together. All spaces within the quotation marks in an alphanumeric constant are always "printed," wherever they may appear.

Another way to "print" this space is to use a semicolon after the quotation marks. Using a semicolon, the same output would be produced with the following statement:

```
200 PRINT "CLASS AVERAGE IS"; A
```

The semicolon will create a space after the alphanumeric constant, CLASS AVERAGE IS. Figure 10-9 shows the two types of statements and the resulting printout.

BASIC PRINT statement	200 PRINT "CLASS AVERAGE IS " A
Printout	CLASS AVERAGE IS 83
BASIC PRINT statement	200 PRINT "CLASS AVERAGE IS"; A
Printout	CLASS AVERAGE IS 83

Figure 10-9. *Two ways to skip a space at the end of an alphanumeric constant are shown.*

In both examples shown in Figure 10-9, the printer prints the alphanumeric constant and then prints the amount stored at the address named A.

Printing variable data. In the partial program shown in Figure 10-8, p. 239, you wish the printer to print on one line the student number and the scores of the three tests. The PRINT statement is as follows:

```
130 PRINT N, S1, S2, S3
```

In this statement, four variable names are listed. N represents the student number. S1 stands for the first score; S2, for the second; and S3, for the third. The computer will go to the address called N and print the value stored there. It will do the same with the values at S1, S2, and S3, in sequence. The printout would appear as follows for Student No. 2350:

```
2350          94          89          90
```

The exact format for printing these values will be explained next.

Output format. You learned earlier that the output formatting in the original BASIC language is very limited. You also learned that the printed line is short and that there is a limit to the number of print zones.

The computer will perform a carriage return (line feed) at the end of each PRINT statement *that is not followed by a comma or semicolon*. Therefore, if you wish to have more than one data value printed on the same line, you can separate the data values by commas as shown:

```
130 PRINT N, S1, S2, S3
```

If four separate PRINT statements had been used, each data value would have appeared on separate print lines of the report. Using Student No. 2350 as an example, the program would appear as shown in the following two examples:

Example 1

```
130 PRINT N: PRINT S1: PRINT S2: PRINT S3
```

or

Example 2

```
130 PRINT N
140 PRINT S1
150 PRINT S2
160 PRINT S3
```

In either case, the printout would appear as follows:

```
2350
94
89
90
```

By using the colon after each PRINT instruction as shown in Example 1, more than one statement can be written on a single line, as explained in Item 5 of the general rules for writing BASIC statements, p. 229. However, the method used in Example 2 is preferred because it would be possible to enter an additional statement into the program if necessary.

Horizontal line spacing. Many computer languages allow for a printed line of at least 132 spaces. With BASIC, this is not the case. BASIC programming considers the terminal printer to be divided into five zones. With some computers, especially the smaller ones, each zone has 15 spaces. With others, each zone has 14. Some terminals also have greater capacity on each print line. They have additional zones in units of 14 or 15 spaces each. The programs in this chapter are written for a terminal printer that has five zones of 14 spaces each. If your terminal has more or less room on a print line, you can allow for this difference.

Comma. When an item in a PRINT statement is followed by a comma, the *comma* acts as a TAB key that immediately moves the carriage to the next print zone. The next value in the PRINT statement will be printed on the same line, but it will be printed at the beginning of the next print zone. Figure 10-10 shows how the PRINT statement in the program would appear if you wanted a printed line to show the student number, the scores of all three tests, and the average for Student No. 2350. It also shows how the line in the printout would appear. A is the variable name given to the average.

BASIC Program Statement

```
130   PRINT N, S1, S2, S3, A
```

Line in Printout

```
2350          94            89            90            91
```

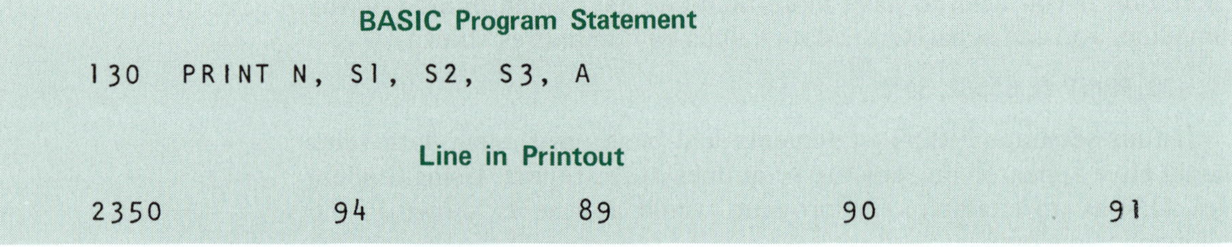

Figure 10-10. *Each print zone has 14 spaces. A comma in the PRINT statement will cause the printer to TAB to the next print zone.*

If all five print zones on the line are full, the carriage is returned automatically, and the next value to be printed appears in the first print zone of the following line. Figure 10-11 shows an example of the PRINT statement and the line as they would appear if you wished to print the student number, the scores of all three tests, the total of all scores, and the average for Student No. 2350. We shall assume that T is the variable name chosen for the address at which the total of all scores is stored and that A is the variable name for the address of the average.

BASIC Program Statement

```
130   PRINT  N, S1, S2, S3, T, A
```

Lines in Printout

```
2350          94            89            90            273
91
```

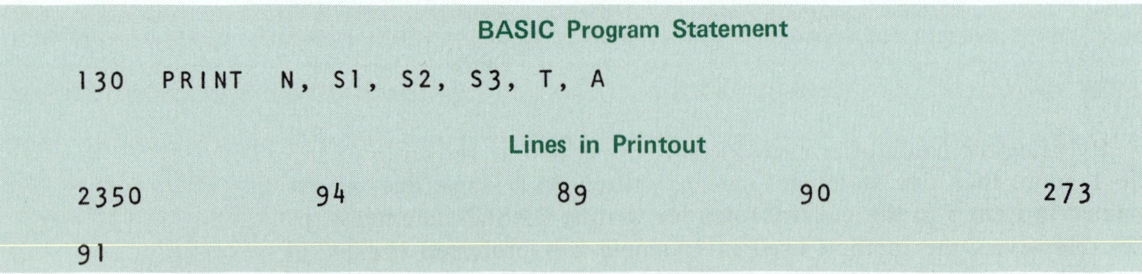

Figure 10-11. *The PRINT statement names the locations of six values. The printout prints five values on one line and the sixth value on the next line.*

Note that the sixth data value in Figure 10-11 is the first entry on a new line because the first line has all five print zones in use. Each comma serves the same function as that of the TAB key on a typewriter. In the case of standard BASIC computer terminals, the TAB stops are already set 14 or 15 spaces apart.

Two commas can be used together in a PRINT statement to cause a PRINT zone to be skipped. The computer is told to TAB twice before printing the next value. For example, if you wished the printer to print the student number and skip a print zone before printing the average, the PRINT statement could read as follows:

```
20 PRINT N,, A
```

The lines on the printed report with the student numbers and averages would appear as follows for the students listed in Figure 10-8, p. 239.

```
2350                           91
2367                           81
2399                           86
2400                           92
```

On the other hand, if you wished to indent the student number to the second print zone, the computer is told to TAB once before printing the first value. The PRINT statement could read as follows:

```
20 PRINT, N, A
```

The lines on the printed report would appear as follows for the students listed in Figure 10-8, p. 239:

```
               2350            91
               2367            81
               2399            86
               2400            92
```

In the first example, two commas are used to cause the computer to skip from the first to the third print zone. In the second example, the comma before N causes the computer to TAB to the second print zone to print the student number. The comma after N causes the computer to TAB to the third print zone to print the average.

If the last item in a PRINT statement is followed by a comma, no carriage return (line feed) takes place. This means that the next value to be printed by a later PRINT statement will appear on the same line and in the next print zone. Therefore, it is important not to place a comma in a PRINT statement, especially not at the end of a line, unless you want the printer to TAB to the next print zone and print another value.

Semicolon. It is possible to "pack" a printed line and to place more than five values on it, if desired. This can be done if a semicolon (;) is used instead of a comma. A semicolon causes the printer to skip only one space before printing the next value instead of tabulating to the next print zone. Figure 10-12 shows the effects of the same PRINT statement used with commas and then with semicolons.

BASIC Program Statements

```
10   READ  A, B, C, D, E, F, G

20   DATA  10, 20, 30, 40, 50, 60, 70

30   PRINT  A, B, C, D, E, F, G

40   PRINT  A; B; C; D; E; F; G
```

Printout for Line 30

```
10              20              30              40              50
60              70
```

Printout for Line 40

```
10 20 30 40 50 60 70
```

Figure 10-12. *A comma in a PRINT instruction causes a TAB to the next print zone. A semicolon causes only one space to be skipped.*

In the program for Problem 1, commas are used in the PRINT statement on Line 130, as follows:

```
130 PRINT N, S1, S2, S3
```

The print head on the terminal typewriter will TAB to the next print zone for each comma. This use of commas will create the four-column report requested.

It is important to remember that either a comma or a semicolon at the end of a PRINT statement will suppress the carriage return operation. These symbols should not be used unless you wish to enter another data value in the PRINT statement.

Skipping lines. The PRINT statement can also be used for skipping lines. You learned that a PRINT statement without a comma or semicolon at the end will cause a carriage return. So, if you wish to skip a line, you can write an extra PRINT statement with no data values. For example, if you wish to print a heading and then skip a line, the program might appear as follows:

```
130 PRINT "TEST SCORE REPORT"
140 PRINT
150 PRINT N, S1, S2, S3.
```

The command at Line 140 would cause the printer to "print" a line of spaces (skip a line). The printout would appear as shown in Figure 10-13.

```
TEST SCORE REPORT

2350         94          89          90
2367         83          80          80
2399         90          79          89
2400         91          88          97
```

Figure 10-13. *An extra PRINT statement causes a line to be skipped after the heading.*

STOP statement

The STOP statement is shown in Figure 10-15, p. 247. This statement is self-explanatory. The *STOP statement* tells the computer that (1) all statements needed to process data have been executed or (2) it is to stop processing data for some reason. In any event, the computer will terminate the program.

END statement

The *END statement* is the last statement in all BASIC programs. It must be present in every BASIC program and must have the highest line number. There are other statements the programmer will enter in order to run the program, store it, or recall it. These statements are not part of the programming logic and are presented on pp. 249 and 250.

Flowchart and program for solving Problem 1

The flowchart for solving Problem 1 was presented earlier as Figure 10-4. It is now repeated as Figure 10-14, p. 246. The complete program is shown as Figure 10-15. Line numbers from the program have been placed alongside the symbols representing the steps in the flowchart.

A quick review of the flowchart shows that a student number (N) will be read. As soon as the value is read, the computer checks to be sure that the value is not 9999, which would signal the end of the program. If the value is equal to 9999, the computer will branch to the statement on line 150 and stop. If the value is not equal to 9999, the computer will continue by going to the next statement in the program. In this case, the next statement is at Line 120.

The statement at Line 120 causes the computer to read the next three data values in the data block. The computer is then told on Line 130, to print a line of print with four data values. The commas appearing between the variable data names instruct the computer to TAB to the next

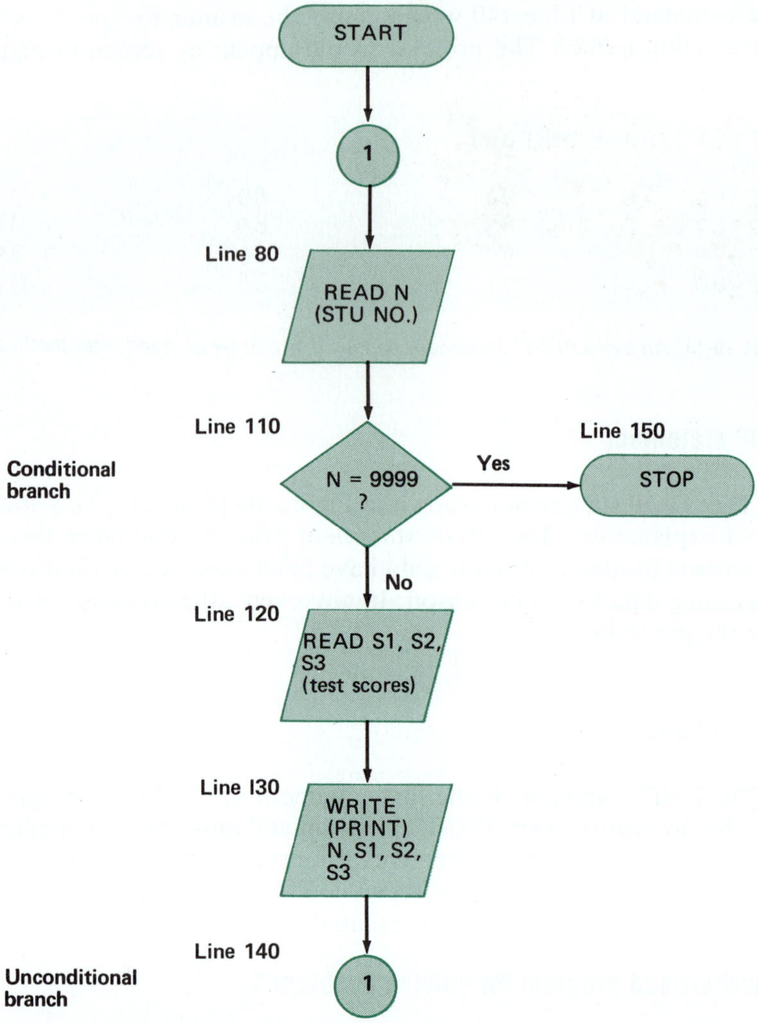

Figure 10-14. *The flowchart for solving Problem 1 is repeated.*

print zone after printing each value. Therefore, the student number (N) will appear in the first print zone. Test Score 1 (S1) will appear in the second print zone. Test Score 2 (S2) will appear in the third print zone. Test Score 3 (S3) will appear in the fourth print zone.

The next statement, Line 140, tells the computer to branch back to Line 80 and repeat the program. This loop is repeated until a 9999 is detected in the student number field.

The STOP statement at line 150 is executed only if the conditional branch is made from Line 110. This only happens if the student number is equal to 9999, indicating that the last data value has been processed. The next statement, END, is the last statement in every BASIC program and is required.

```
10  REM  PROGRAM TO LIST TEST SCORES
20  REM  "N" WILL BE THE NAME FOR STUDENT NUMBER
30  REM  "S1" WILL BE THE NAME FOR SCORE 1
40  REM  "S2" WILL BE THE NAME FOR SCORE 2
50  REM  "S3" WILL BE THE NAME FOR SCORE 3
60  REM  A STUDENT NUMBER OF 9999 WILL BE USED TO
70  REM  TERMINATE THE PROGRAM
80  READ N
90  DATA  2350, 94, 89, 90, 2367, 83, 80, 80, 2399, 90, 79, 89
100 DATA  2400, 91, 88, 97, 9999
110 IF N = 9999 THEN GO TO 150
120 READ S1, S2, S3
130 PRINT N, S1, S2, S3
140 GO TO 80
150 STOP
160 END
```

Figure 10-15. *The above BASIC program for Problem 1 will print the student number and three test scores on one line for each student number listed.*

REVIEW QUESTIONS

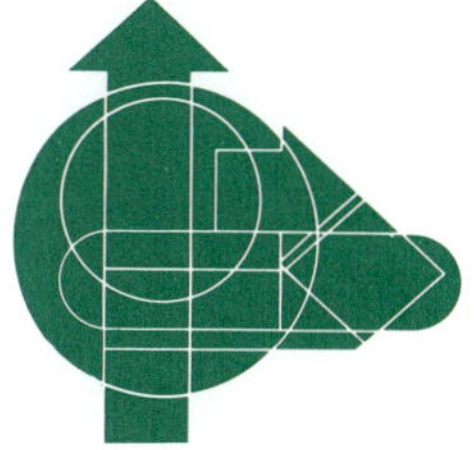

1. Why are line numbers often assigned in multiples of 10?
2. When would you use the LINE FEED key instead of the RETURN key?
3. Why is it important to use REMARKS and/or comments in BASIC?
4. How is a remark written in a BASIC program?
5. How is a comment written in a BASIC program?
6. What is the purpose of the READ statement in BASIC? What statement must always accompany a READ statement?
7. What is the purpose of the DATA statement in BASIC?
8. What assignments will be made by the BASIC translator program when the following three statements are processed?

```
210 READ A, B, C, D, E
220 DATA 15, 105.5, 97
230 DATA 18, -71
```

Continued

9. What is a *data block*? How are data in a data block accessed by the computer for processing?
10. What statement in BASIC can be used to create a conditional branch?
11. What statement in BASIC is used to create an unconditional branch?
12. What does the comma tell the computer when it is used in a PRINT statement?
13. What does the semicolon tell the computer when it is used in a PRINT statement?
14. How would you write the PRINT statements in a BASIC program if you wished to cause a line to be skipped in a printed report?
15. What is the last statement in a BASIC program?

USING TIME-SHARING TERMINALS

Terminals for use on computers come in many different styles and models. Two of the terminals used were shown in Figure 10-1 and 10-2, p. 223.

Figure 10-2 includes a keyboard and printer. The operator enters the program and the data via the keyboard. The information entered appears on the paper in the typewriter as it is being entered.

Figure 10-1 shows a keyboard and a CRT. The data entered appear on the screen rather than on paper. The CRT has the disadvantage of not giving any ''hard copy'' (printed output). Once the image is off the screen, there is no record that can be referred to without using the CRT terminal again. In trying to overcome this problem, manufacturers have made CRT terminals with printers. The addition of a printer allows the operator to request a printed report as well as the CRT display. The operator uses the printer only when a permanent copy is needed.

Terminals may be connected to the computer in two ways. One way is referred to as being hard-wired. *Hard-wiring* indicates that the terminal is close enough to the CPU that it can be physically connected by means of a cable. A second way that is used more often is the connection of the terminal to the CPU with telephone lines.

The actual procedures are different, depending upon which of the two methods is used. Other small differences exist depending upon what computer system is used. Typical procedures will be explained next for using the BASIC programming language on terminals.

Signing on

Most terminals are connected to a computer by a telephone line. Therefore, the telephone procedure will be described here. Minor changes to this procedure will have to be made, depending upon the computer and terminals used. The following steps are typical of *signing on* (getting connected to a computer with time-sharing).

(1) A telephone number must be dialed. (Use the number that is for your computer system.)

(2) Certain switches must be set properly. (These will be different from terminal to terminal and will not be described here.)
(3) Type "HELLO" and then depress the carriage return.
(4) The computer will respond by typing a message. It will then ask that you (the operator) identify yourself.
(5) Type your account number and return the carriage.
(6) Type your password and return the carriage.
(Steps 5 and 6 are necessary because many different users may be allowed to use the time-sharing computer. Each user is given a specific segment of the computer's memory and may have data and/or programs stored. The account number and password are used to keep from having unauthorized use of the computer, data, and programs that have been stored.)
(7) If the computer recognizes the account number and password as being correct (for an authorized user), the terminal will print READY, and the computer is ready to accept the instructions and data you will enter.
(8) The next step is to type either OLD or NEW. The word, NEW, is typed if the operator plans to enter a new program. The word, OLD, is typed if the operator plans to process a program that was entered earlier and "saved."
(9) The computer will respond by requesting the name of the file (program) that is to be used. The operator will type the name of an old program. In the case of a new program, the name typed in by the operator will be the name the operator wishes to give to the new program that will be entered.
(10) The computer will then answer by typing the word, READY.

Entering the program

(11) The operator can enter a new BASIC program, one line at a time. The RETURN (carriage return) key should be depressed after each line has been entered. The computer will then translate the line of code (BASIC statement). If there is any error, an error message will be typed immediately, telling what is wrong. The operator must then retype the entire line of code, beginning with the line number. If the line of code is correct, the operator may go on with the next line because no error message will be received.
(12) After the last line of the program has been entered properly (after the END statement), the operator can type one of the following commands.

SAVE — Causes the entire program to be stored in line number order, with all corrections made. All duplicate line numbers are destroyed except the last one entered. If there are several statements with the same line number, which may be the case if there have been corrections, only the last revision of the line number is saved.

LIST — Causes the entire saved program to be displayed in line number order. This statement is very useful if there have been many corrections and you wish to check the entire corrected program before running it. It is also useful when recalling an old program because you will wish to read and study the old program before entering new data.

RUN — Causes the program that you have entered to be processed, beginning with the lowest line number. The program cannot be executed without this statement.

REPLACE — Causes the entire program to be saved, thereby erasing (replacing) any other program with the same name.

(13) Whenever the program is through processing, the computer will type the message, READY. The operator can then request that the program be run again by typing RUN. Or, the operator may type NEW and enter another new program or OLD and request a different program from memory.

Signing off

(14) Sooner or later, the operator will have run all of the programs and/or data that have to be processed. At that time, the operator types the word BYE. The computer will then "log out" by telling the operator how many minutes of computer time have been used. Other messages may also be printed.

SUMMARY

BASIC is a programming language designed to be an easy-to-use language. It has become the industry standard for time-sharing applications. Many modern computer systems provide some form of the BASIC language. There are small differences in the BASIC language for the different computer systems. Those differences cause very few problems for the programmer who understands the language, however.

BASIC is called an interactive or conversational language because of its built-in ability to respond to the programmer on a line-by-line basis. The ability to respond so fast makes it appear as though the programmer and the computer are carrying on a conversation.

Numeric variables in BASIC can be of two types. Floating-point numbers are numbers that have a decimal point and may or may not have a decimal value. Floating-point numbers are also called real numbers. Fixed-point numbers are whole numbers. They have no decimal points or decimal values. They are also called integers.

Names are chosen to describe the memory addresses for variables in BASIC. These names must conform to a certain set of rules. Names for floating-point variables must start with a letter of the alphabet. The letter may or may not be followed by a single number. The entire name may not be over two characters in length. The first character must always be a letter. If there is a second character, it must always be a number. Fixed-point variable names are not described in this text.

Because of the short variable names, the use of remarks and comments is very important. The word REMARK or REM may be used to tell the translator program that the statement following is not to be processed as an instruction. Instead, it is to be printed with the program as a form of explanation.

The READ and DATA statements may be used together to enter data into the computer. The READ statement gives the variable names of the addresses of the values to be entered. The DATA statement gives the actual values stored at those addresses.

One or more data values may be entered with each DATA statement, and the BASIC translator program will establish a data block by combining all data values together in the order in which they appear in the program. The data in the data block are assembled according to the line numbers of the DATA statements. Every time a READ statement is processed, one or more data values are selected from the data block in the order in which they appear.

One disadvantage of BASIC is the limited formatting capabilities that are available for printing business reports. The printed line is short, and there is a limit to the number of standard print zones. This disadvantage is not serious, though, because the BASIC language and time-sharing are not used very often for formal business reports. Besides, many computer manufacturers have introduced more powerful versions of BASIC which do offer additional capabilities.

The programs in this chapter have been written for a computer system having five print zones that add up to a 70-space line. There are terminals available with additional print zones of 14 or 15 spaces on a line. The programs in this text have not been written for sophisticated terminals, but these programs should run on any computer system that has a BASIC language.

Each data item named in a PRINT statement will be printed in a different print zone if the variable names are separated by commas in the PRINT statement. A comma serves the same function as a TAB key on the typewriter. If semicolons separate the variable names, this tabulation does not take place. Instead, the print head skips only one space and begins printing. The use of semicolons allows the programmer to place more than five data items on a print line.

Decisions can be made in BASIC using the IF-THEN statement. If the answer to the test in the statement is "Yes," the computer will process the statement following the word THEN. Usually, an unconditional branch is used to cause the computer to branch to a new set of instructions. If the answer to the test is "No," the next statement in line number order will be executed.

Time-sharing terminals may be connected to the computer either by telephone wires or by "hard-wire." Hard-wire procedures are used when the terminals are in the same general area as the CPU and connected to it by cables. In most cases, the telephone dial-up procedures are used because they allow the terminals to be located any place in the world where there is access to a telephone.

There are certain procedures that must be followed in using time-sharing terminals. These procedures may change from computer to computer. Once an operator uses one system, however, it is easy to make the change to almost any time-sharing system.

REVIEW QUESTIONS

1. When communicating with a terminal, what is the first message you type after the proper telephone number has been called and the necessary switches set for your terminal?
2. Why must you type your account number and password before the program can be entered or recalled?
3. What do you type when recalling a previous program that has been stored?
4. When all of the early steps have been taken properly, what does the computer say to you that lets you know that you can now enter your program?
5. What happens if there is an error message indicating that the line just entered is incorrect?
6. If you wish the program to be stored in line number order with all corrections made, what message do you type to the computer?
7. If you wish to see the entire program in line number order before running it, what word would you type?
8. What message must you type in order to have the computer process the program?
9. What is the purpose of the REPLACE statement?
10. If you wish to rerun a program that you have just run, what do you type?
11. What message does the terminal type when the program is through executing?
12. What message does the operator type to the computer when there are no more programs to be run? What does the computer do in response?

NEW TERMS

- Alphanumeric
- Alphanumeric constant
- BASIC
- Comma
- Constant
- Conversational language
- Data block
- DATA statement
- Debugging
- END statement
- Exclamation point
- Executable statement
- Fixed-point number
- Floating-point number
- Floating-point variable
- GO TO statement

- Hard-wiring
- IF-THEN statement
- Logical operators
- Numeric variables
- Non-executable statement
- PRINT statement
- READ statement
- Relational operators
- REMARK statement
- Semicolon
- Signing on
- Statement
- STOP statement
- Value
- Variable
- Variable name

STUDY GUIDE

Complete Study Guide 10 by following the instructions in your STUDY GUIDES booklet.

PROJECTS

Complete Project 10-1 through 10-5 by following the instructions in your PROJECTS booklet.

11 ADDITIONAL BASIC STATEMENTS

In Chapter 10, you were introduced to the BASIC programming language. You learned some of the elementary principles that must be followed by programmers in the language. Finally, you were given a chance to use the principles learned by writing simple programs.

In this chapter, you will expand upon the knowledge gained. You will be able to draw flowcharts and to write programs of a more complex nature. This chapter explains BASIC arithmetic statements, constants, multiple decisions, clearing of work areas, and writing headings.

ARITHMETIC STATEMENTS IN BASIC

You learned in the last chapter how to read data into the computer and how to write (PRINT) data from its memory. The computer can handle simple input/output tasks easily. However, its greatest power is in its ability to perform arithmetic calculations very fast and accurately.

In the BASIC language, arithmetic statements are written as equations. Each *equation* in BASIC will contain a variable, an equal sign, and an expression. The arithmetic expression always appears to the right of the equal sign in an ARITHMETIC statement. The equal sign does *not* mean equal to. It means "replaces." For example:

```
LET T = T1 + T2 + T3
```

In this example, the amount stored in the memory address with the variable name T1 is added to the amount stored in Address T2 and the amount stored at T3. The sum of the three amounts is then stored in the address named T, replacing any number previously stored in T. Remember that any new data read into the computer's memory erases (replaces) any data previously stored at that address.

Arithmetic expressions in BASIC

An *arithmetic expression* in BASIC is made up of numbers (numeric constants), variables, mathematical operators, or a combination of these. The arithmetic expression is always written to the right of the equal sign. The results of the calculations performed by the arithmetic expression are always stored in the address named at the left of the equal sign. In the equation, LET C = P + T, the arithmetic expression is P + T.

Arithmetic operators in BASIC

The arithmetic operators in BASIC are:

Operator	*Interpretation*	*Sample Expression*
+	Add	A + B
−	Subtract	F1 − T1
*	Multiply	Q1 * A
/	Divide	R / 12
↑	Exponentiation (Raised to the power of)	T ↑ 3 (Same as T cubed)

Note that the symbols for multiplication and division in BASIC are not the same as those used in ordinary arithmetic. The asterisk (*) is used for multiplication because X is considered to be a letter of the alphabet. The diagonal (slash) is used for division. Exponentiation will not be used in this chapter, but it is important to know its symbol.

Order of execution of arithmetic operations

The general rules of mathematics are followed in evaluating a BASIC arithmetic expression. An arithmetic expression can be made up of more than one arithmetic operation. If it is, computations are made from left to right in the following order:

	Order of Operations
(1) ( )	Equations within parentheses
(2) ↑	Exponentiation
(3) * and /	Multiplication and division
(4) + and −	Addition and subtraction

Note that operations within parentheses are acted upon first. In the case of more than one set of parentheses, the expression in the innermost set is acted upon first. If there are no parentheses, the expression is processed from left to right in the foregoing order.

Examples of equations are as follows:

(1) 270 LET A = (B + C) * D
First the contents of B and C are added together. Next, this sum is multiplied by the contents of D. The answer is stored in A.

(2) 280 LET A = B + C * D
First the contents of C are multiplied by the contents of D. Next the product of C times D is added to the contents of B. The answer is stored in A.

This example may seem to be like Example 1, but the missing parentheses in Example 2 really changes the results. For example, assume that the beginning values were B = 5, C = 2, and D = 7. In the first example, B would be added to C (5 + 2). That result would be multiplied by D (7), with the answer, *49*, being stored in A. In Example, 2 on the other hand, C would first be multiplied by D (2 times 7). Then, the product (14) would be added to B (5). The answer, *19*, would be stored in A.

(3) 290 LET T = W * X / Y − Z
First, the contents of W and X are multiplied together. Next, the product is divided by the contents of Y. Then, the contents of Z are subtracted from the result of the previous division. The difference is stored in T.

(4) 300 LET H = J * (M + K) / L
First, the contents of M and K are added together. Then, since multiplication and division are of equal rank, the equation is worked from left to right. The value stored at J is multiplied by the sum of the two values stored at M and K. The product of the above multiplication is divided by the value at the address named L. The end result will be stored at the memory address named H.

LET statement

You learned in the last chapter that the DATA statement is used to assign values to variables named in the READ statement. You have probably noted by now that the arithmetic statements used as examples in this chapter all contain the term LET. The LET statement is also a means of assigning values to addresses identified by variable names.

Assigning values with a LET statement. The *LET statement* assigns a numeric value to a memory address that has been given a variable name. The LET statement may appear to be an algebraic formula. However, it is actually an order to the computer to carry out the computations on the right side of the equal sign and to store the results in the address with the variable name on the left of the equal sign.

Each LET statement will take one of the following forms:

(1) 610 LET A =B
In this example, *variable name A* = *variable name B*. The value in the address with the variable name B is stored in the address with the variable name A. The new value being stored in A replaces any value stored at that address before.

(2) 620 LET B = 5
In this example, *variable name* = *constant*. The value, 5, is a constant because it is known in advance. The value, 5, is stored in the address with the variable name B, replacing any value stored before at B.

(3) 630 LET C = (D −E) / 6
In this example, *variable name* = *expression*. The value of E is subtracted from the value of D. The difference is then divided by 6. The result is stored in the address with the variable name C. Any value stored before at C is replaced by the result of this calculation.

Note that in the three LET statements just explained, the variable name is always on the left of the equal sign. In the first example, there is a variable also on the right of the equal sign. In the second example, there is a constant on the right. In the third example, there is an arithmetic expression on the right. Note that two variables and one constant are used in the expression. In all examples, the value stored in the variable address named on the left of the equal sign is the result of the values or computations shown on the right of the equal sign.

Entering data with a LET statement. You learned that BASIC was first designed as an instructional language. As such, it has limited data-handling capabilities for most business applications. Printed reports are limited both in line size and format. Because of its interactive nature, BASIC is used mostly in applications in which input data are limited to a few variables.

Sometimes, new data are entered with the program itself. This method requires that one or more program statements be changed each time different values are to be used in the program. One method of entering data with the program is with the LET statement. For example, four different test scores could be entered as follows:

```
10 LET T1 = 78
20 LET T2 = 93
30 LET T3 = 81
40 LET T4 = 70
```

If these test scores were to be changed before processing the program a second time, four new LET statements would have to be entered. The same line numbers would be used. The translator program would cause the statements entered last to replace those statements with the same line numbers entered earlier.

If more than one variable were given the same value, it would be possible to use a single LET statement as follows:

```
50 LET A, B, C, D = 12
```

In this example, the value of 12 would be stored at the addresses named A, B, C, and D.

It is also possible to enter several LET statements on the same line, separated by colons. An example is as follows:

```
60 LET A = 5: B = 23: C = 17: D = 0
```

In the above example values are assigned to more than one address by just one LET statement.

Clearing storage with a LET statement. A LET statement can also be used to clear memory addresses for computations.

```
50 LET A, B, C, D = 0
```

In this example, the constant of zero (0) is stored in all four memory addresses. Any data stored before in the same addresses will be replaced by zeros. The memory addresses are cleared of any old data.

REVIEW QUESTIONS

1. What does an equal sign mean in BASIC?
2. What is an arithmetic expression? Why does an expression always have to appear on the right of an equal sign in an ARITHMETIC statement?
3. What are the five arithmetic operators in BASIC? Why isn't the letter X used to signify multiplication?
4. What symbols are used to show the order of mathematical operations in arithmetic expressions?
5. Refer to the following expression. What operation would be performed first?

   A = B * C − D / (E + F)
6. Write a LET statement that will assign the value of zero (0) to a variable named T. You may use any line number.
7. Write a LET statement that will cause the computer to figure the total cost of 15 items. The price of only one of these items is stored at Address P. The total cost will be stored at Address C. You may use any line number.
8. Can the same constant be stored in more than one memory location with a single LET statement? Give an example.
9. What is the purpose of the colon (:) in a LET statement?
10. What will happen if two statements are entered with the same line number?

BASIC PROGRAM TO CALCULATE SALES TAX

You learned how to write a human-language program for solving a sales tax problem in Chapter 9. The same problem will be repeated here and used to illustrate a simple BASIC program with ARITHMETIC statements.

Statement of the sales tax problem

The purpose of this problem is to figure the amount of sales tax due on each sale and then to print a report showing the sales amount, sales tax due on each sale, and the total amount due on the sale, including the tax.

Flowchart for solving the sales tax problem

The flowchart used in Chapter 9 (Figure 9-1) is repeated on the left of Figure 11-1, next page. The flowchart on the right is the flowchart for the BASIC program. The flowchart on the right has very minor changes to make it agree more closely to the BASIC language. It should be noted, however, that the logic to solve the problem is the same.

In the flowchart on the right, the variable name of S has been given to the address of the sales amount. T1 is the name given to the address of the sales tax. T2 is the name given to the address of the total sales price. Note that these names begin with a letter of the alphabet and have no more than two characters.

In the human-language program, it was assumed that the sales amounts would be entered on cards (Step 1). In the BASIC program, the sales amounts will be entered at a terminal with the READ and DATA statements. A sales amount of 99.99 will be used to signal the end of data. Note that in the flowchart on the right of Figure 11-1, the comment inside the decision symbol has been changed to "S = 99.99?" (Is sales amount equal to 99.99?) This comment gives extra information to the programmer. It states that the Sales Amount field is being used for the last-value code. Whenever a value of 99.99 appears in that field, the computer can be directed with a conditional branch statement to STOP.

Note, also, that the comments in the processing symbols have been changed. In the flowchart on the right, the instructions are written in the form of arithmetic equations. Some programmers prefer to use equations in flowcharts. Others prefer English-like statements. The use of arithmetic equations is shorter, but either method is correct.

In Symbol 5, the word PRINT is used instead of WRITE. PRINT is used in BASIC. WRITE is used in FORTRAN, COBOL, and many other languages.

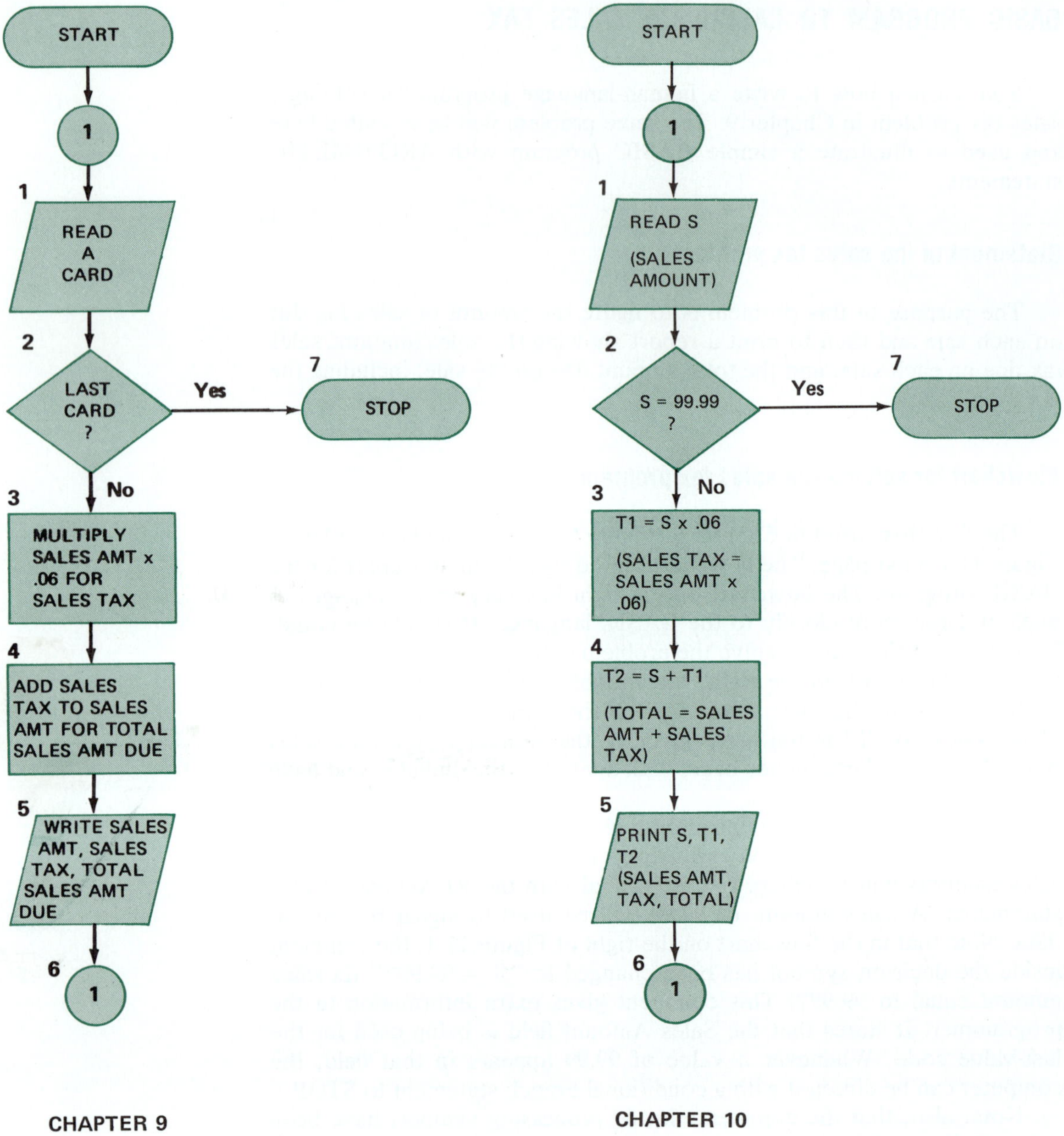

Figure 11-1. *Flowchart from Chapter 9 is compared with flowchart for sales tax problem to be solved in BASIC.*

Explanation of BASIC statements

The program to solve this sample sales tax problem will be explained in portions. The complete program will be shown after all statements have been explained.

REMARKS. Figure 11-2 shows the first six statements in the program. The remarks, Lines 10–60, explain what is taking place. The program would work the same without these remarks. This use of the REMARK statement is a form of documentation. It helps other programmers or users of the program because the variable names are too short to explain much. "T1" and "T2" would mean little to a user without the remarks.

```
10  REM  PROGRAM TO CALCULATE SALES TAX
20  REM  "S" WILL BE THE NAME FOR THE SALES AMT
30  REM  "T1" WILL BE THE NAME FOR THE SALES TAX
40  REM  "T2" WILL BE THE NAME FOR THE TOTAL SALES PRICE
50  REM  THE SALES TAX RATE USED WILL BE 6 PERCENT
60  REM  A SALES AMOUNT OF 99.99 WILL BE USED TO TERMINATE THE PROGRAM
```

Figure 11-2. *The first six statements of the BASIC program are REMARKS statements.*

Note that the statements are all numbered and are in numeric order. You learned earlier that if the statements are typed out of order, the translator program will arrange them in numeric order before processing the program. Numbering by tens is recommended because additional statements may be inserted without having to change the numbers of other statements.

Line 10 is used to identify the purpose of the program. This statement helps other users to tell whether this is the program they wish to use. Lines 20–40 explain the use of each variable name in the program. Line 50 states the sales tax rate that is used.

Line 60 explains that the test for the last value (similar to the last-card test) will be 99.99. It states:

```
60 REM  A SALES AMT OF 99.99 WILL BE USED TO TERMINATE THE PROGRAM
```

This is not the test itself. The remark only explains that the program logic calls for the value of 99.99 to be used as a test to see if all data values have been processed. This line actually tells the user what to enter as the last data value to tell the computer when to stop processing.

READ and DATA statements. You learned in Chapter 10 how the READ and DATA statements are used together to enter data. A READ statement must always be used with a DATA statement. The READ statement tells the computer to read one or more variables that are listed by name in the READ statement. The READ statement also tells the computer to take the first data value from the DATA block and store it in the first memory address named in the READ statement. The second data value will be stored at the second address, etc. The READ and DATA statements for the sales tax problem are shown in Figure 11-3.

```
70  READ  S
80  DATA 15.5, 9.5, 10., 3.5, 99.99
```

Figure 11-3. *These are the READ and DATA statements for solving the sales tax problem.*

READ statement. The READ statement in Line 70 simply orders the computer to read the sales amount, which has been given the address described by the variable name, S. Note that there is only one variable name in this READ statement.

Because data must be entered into the computer before they can be processed, READ statements usually are placed near the beginning of the program. If more than one variable name appears in a READ statement, the variables are read in the order in which they appear in the statement.

DATA statement. The DATA statement assigns values to one or more variables named in a READ statement. The READ and DATA statements in Figure 11-3 are as follows:

```
70  READ S
80  DATA 15.5, 9.5, 10., 3.5, 99.99
```

These two statements together cause the computer to assign an address in storage to a variable named S (sales amount). The first value to be read into this address will be 15.5 (15.50). The second will be 9.5 (9.50), the third will be 10. (10.00), etc., until all the values are read. The computer will cause the value 15.5 to be processed just as though it were a separate punched card field. After the 15.5 has gone through the steps in the program sequence, the computer will loop back to the READ statement and read the next value, 9.5. This process will go on until the computer reaches the last data value, 99.99, which has been chosen as a last-value-test code.

Test for the last value. Remember that the last value in the DATA statement on Line 80 is 99.99. An IF-THEN statement is used at Line 90. The computer is instructed to go to Line 140, which is the instruction to stop. See Figure 11-4.

If the data value does not equal 99.99, then the computer goes on to the next statement in numeric order, Line 100.

```
 90  IF S = 99.99 THEN GO TO 140
100  LET T1 = S * .06           ! CALCULATES SALES TAX
110  LET T2 = S + T1            ! CALCULATES TOTAL SALES PRICE
120  PRINT S, T1, T2
130  GO TO 70
140  STOP
```

Figure 11-4. *A conditional branch (IF-THEN) statement is used to test for the last value in the sales tax program.*

Arithmetic statements for calculating the sales tax and total. The arithmetic statements for calculating the sales tax and total sales price are shown in Figure 11-5:

The LET statement on Line 100 orders the computer to multiply the amount of sale, stored at S, by .06 (6 percent), the sales tax rate. The

```
100  LET T1 = S * .06          ! CALCULATES SALES TAX
110  LET T2 = S + T1           ! CALCULATES TOTAL SALES PRICE
```

Figure 11-5. *Arithmetic statements for the sales tax problem are shown.*

result is the sales tax, which will be stored in the memory address named T1.

The next statement, Line 110, causes the total sales price to be calculated. The sales amount, stored at S, is added to the sales tax, stored at T1, and the total is stored in the memory address named T2.

Comments. Up to this time, we have dealt mostly with remarks. However, on Lines 100 and 110, there have been comments inserted. Note that on Line 100 an exclamation point is used to insert the comment CALCULATES SALES TAX. On Line 110, an exclamation point is used with CALCULATES TOTAL SALES PRICE.

These comments explain to the user the purpose of each equation. The computer will stop processing when it reaches the exclamation point. Comments are not executable. They only give information to the user of the program.

Printing the desired output. The PRINT statement for printing the desired output for this sample program is shown below:

```
120 PRINT S, T1, T2
```

The PRINT statement on Line 120 tells the computer to print the three variables stored at S, T1 and T2 on one line. The commas between the variable names order the computer to place each variable in a different print zone. Remember that terminal printers use a print line that is divided into zones. A comma in the PRINT statement causes the terminal printer to skip to the next print zone before printing the variable named after the comma. In this problem, the sales amount will be printed in the first print zone, the amount of sales tax will be printed in the second zone, and the total (sales amount plus sales tax) will be printed in the third zone.

Unconditional branch. The statement on Line 130 is an unconditional branch, GO TO 70. See Figure 11-6. This statement causes the computer to branch back to the READ instruction at Line 70. This branch creates a loop that will be repeated over and over until the last value, 99.99, is read and detected.

```
 70  READ  S
 80  DATA  15.5, 9.5, 10., 3.5, 99.99
 90  IF  S = 99.99 THEN GO TO 140
100  LET  T1 = S * .06          ! CALCULATES SALES TAX
110  LET T2 = S + T1            ! CALCULATES TOTAL SALES PRICE
120  PRINT  S, T1, T2
130  GO TO 70
```

Loop

Figure 11-6. *The GO TO statement at Line 130 creates the loop back to Line 70.*

Final statements. Line 140 contains the single word, STOP. The IF-THEN statement on Line 90 directs the computer to go to Line 140 when a 99.99 is detected in the DATA block.

Line 150 contains the single word, END. The END statement is a required control statement that must appear as the last entry in every BASIC program. See Figure 11-7.

```
 70   READ  S
 80   DATA  15.5, 9.5, 10., 3.5, 99.99
 90   IF   S = 99.99 THEN GO TO 140
100   LET   T1 = S * .06            ! CALCULATES SALES TAX
110   LET T2 = S + T1               ! CALCULATES TOTAL SALES PRICE
120   PRINT  S, T1, T2
130   GO TO 70
140   STOP
150   END
```

Figure 11-7. *The statement at Line 90 directs the computer to the STOP statement at Line 140 after the last value has been processed.*

BASIC program for solving the sales tax problem

Figure 11-8 shows the complete BASIC program for solving the sales tax problem.

```
 10   REM   PROGRAM TO CALCULATE SALES TAX
 20   REM   "S" WILL BE THE NAME FOR THE SALES AMT
 30   REM   "T1" WILL BE THE NAME FOR THE SALES TAX
 40   REM   "T2" WILL BE THE NAME FOR THE TOTAL SALES PRICE
 50   REM   THE SALES TAX RATE USED WILL BE 6 PERCENT
 60   REM   A SALES AMOUNT OF 99.99 WILL BE USED TO TERMINATE THE PROGRAM
 70   READ  S
 80   DATA  15.5, 9.5, 10., 3.5, 99.99
 90   IF   S = 99.99 THEN GO TO 140
100   LET   T1 = S * .06            ! CALCULATES SALES TAX
110   LET T2 = S + T1               ! CALCULATES TOTAL SALES PRICE
120   PRINT  S, T1, T2
130   GO TO 70
140   STOP
150   END
```

Figure 11-8. *Above is the complete BASIC program for solving the sales tax problem.*

Lines 10–60 are REMARK statements that make the purpose of the program clear.

Lines 70 and 80 cause the computer to read a value from the DATA statement and assign it to the variable address named S. In the first case, S is assigned the value of 15.5. The DATA statement is not executable. It is always used with a READ statement.

Line 90 tells the computer to check the value just read, S, to see if it is equal to 99.99 (the last-value code). If S does not equal 99.99, the computer goes to the next instruction, Line 100.

Line 100 causes the sales tax, T1, to be figured. The sales amount, S, is multiplied by .06 (6 percent). The result is stored in the address named T1.

Line 110 causes the sales tax, T1, to be added to the original sales amount, S. The sum is stored at the address named T2, total sales price.

All three desired values are now stored in different locations of computer memory and are ready to be printed. Line 120 tells the computer to print the sales amount in the first print zone on a line. The comma following the S causes the printer to TAB to the next print zone before printing the value named T1. The comma after T1 causes another TAB to the third print zone before printing the last variable, T2.

The next instruction, Line 130, causes an unconditional branch back to the READ statement at Line 70. This branch creates a loop, and the next value will then be read. This loop will be repeated until the value, S, is equal to 99.99. At this time, a branch will be made to Line 140 to the STOP statement. The STOP statement indicates that all data have been processed. It is followed by the END statement, Line 150, which must be the last statement in any BASIC program.

Figure 11-9 shows how the data would be spaced in a report.

All columns are aligned on the left. All ending zeros after a decimal point are dropped. In fact, if there are no zeros after the decimal point, the decimal point is dropped also.

```
15.5          .93          16.43
9.5           .57          10.07
10            .6           10.6
3.5           .21          3.71
```

Figure 11-9. *This is a sample output report for the sales tax problem.*

This sales tax problem has been planned so that there would be no rounding problems. Some versions of BASIC take care of rounding; others do not. When working problems in BASIC that include dollars and cents, it may be necessary to round the results.[1]

PRINTING HEADINGS

Alphanumeric constants were explained in Chapter 10. An alphanumeric constant may include any letters of the alphabet, numbers, special characters, or spaces.

---

[1]If a fraction is more than a half-cent, use the next higher cent. (Example: 9.766 = 9.77.) If the fraction is less than a half-cent, use the next lower cent. (Example: 9.764 = 9.76.)

Alphanumeric constants used for headings

Alphanumeric constants must be enclosed in quotation marks. Examples of alphanumeric constants as they would appear in BASIC program statements are as follows:

```
62 PRINT "SALES TAX PROGRAM"
63 PRINT "PROGRAMMED BY MARCIA WILLIAMS"
```

Remember that the quotation marks enclosing the constant will not appear on the printed report. They are used only to tell the computer where to begin printing and where to stop. Everything between the quotation marks, including spaces, will appear on the printed report.

If the two alphanumeric constants just shown were inserted into the sales tax program, they would be processed before the READ statement at Line 70. The PRINT statement at Line 62 would cause the heading, SALES TAX PROGRAM, to be printed on the first line of the report. The quotation marks would not be printed. The next PRINT statement, Line 63, would cause the line, PROGRAMMED BY MARCIA WILLIAMS to be printed.

The printing of the two lines would begin in the first zone and continue across the page until everything within the quotation marks is printed.

```
SALES TAX PROGRAM
PROGRAMMED BY MARCIA WILLIAMS.
```

The two additional lines, 62 and 63, could be inserted into the program because the program was typed with line numbers in 10s instead of 1s.

One-Line Column Headings

Assume that the programmer wants to use column headings to identify the three values that are printed on each line in the sales tax problem. The heading, SALES AMOUNT, is to appear over the first column. SALES TAX will be over the second column, SALES PRICE will be over the third. The PRINT statement to print the three headings would appear as follows:

```
64 PRINT "SALES AMOUNT", "SALES TAX", "SALES PRICE"
```

The words, SALES AMOUNT, would be printed in the first print zone. The comma after the constant would cause a TAB to the second print zone. The words, SALES TAX, would be printed in the second print zone. The comma would cause a TAB to the third print zone. The words, SALES PRICE, would appear in the third print zone.

The heading would actually appear on the report as follows:

```
SALES AMOUNT      SALES TAX      SALES PRICE
```

Two-Line Column headings

The same heading could be printed in two lines by using the following statements;

```
64 PRINT "SALES", "SALES", "SALES"
65 PRINT "AMOUNT", "TAX", "PRICE"
```

In this example, the words SALES, SALES, and SALES would appear in the first three print zones of one line. The second PRINT statement would print AMOUNT, TAX, and PRICE in the first three print zones of the second line. The two lines of print would appear as follows:

```
SALES          SALES              SALES
AMOUNT         TAX                PRICE
```

The fourth and fifth print zones are not used on either line. Each new PRINT statement causes the printing to begin on a new line unless the last entry in the previous PRINT statement is followed by a comma or semicolon.

Skipping lines after headings

If you wish to skip a line between the heading and the body of the report, an extra PRINT statement may be added, as follows:

```
65 PRINT "SALES", "SALES", "SALES"
66 PRINT "AMOUNT", "TAX", "PRICE"
67 PRINT
```

The PRINT statement at Line 67 will cause a line to be printed with nothing on it. This is one way of skipping a line in order to double-space.

End-of-job message

Many programmers print an end-of-job message after the last line of print on a report. This tells the programmer and/or user that the program has arrived at a proper stopping point. In the sales tax program, a programmer might want to print an "end-of-job" message when the last-value code, 99.99 was reached. The conditional statement to test for the last value would have to be changed and one PRINT statement added to accomplish the printing of an end-of-job message. They could appear as follows:

```
90 IF S = 99.99 THEN GO TO 135

135 PRINT, "END OF DATA FOR SALES TAX PROGRAM"
```

The last line of print would now be END OF DATA FOR SALES TAX PROGRAM. It would be indented to the second print zone and continued across the page until the last character within the quotation marks had been printed. The comma after the word PRINT would cause the computer to TAB to the second print zone before printing.

Flowchart for solving the sales tax problem, with headings added

Figure 11-10 shows the flowchart for the revised sales tax program with headings. Note that there are extra input/output symbols used to show the printing of the report title, programmer name, the two heading lines, and the end-of-job message. (Symbols are not used for lines skipped.)

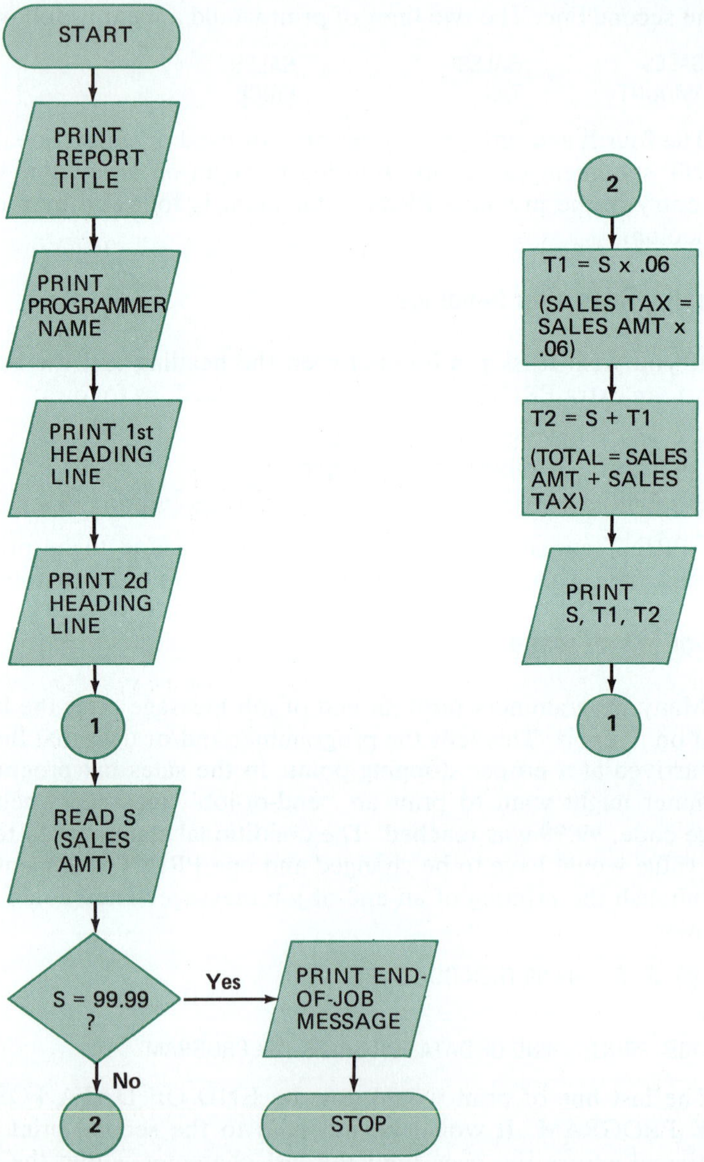

Figure 11-10. *This flowchart to solve the sales tax problem includes headings.*

There is an on-page connector with a 2 at the bottom of the flowchart. It shows that the flowchart is continued at the top right, where there is a matching 2. If the last-value code is not in S, the computer will continue to make the calculations and print the line before going back to read another value. If the 99.99 is in S, the computer will branch to the end-of-job message and stop.

BASIC program for solving the sales tax problem, with headings added

Figure 11-11 shows the BASIC program to calculate sales tax and print a report with headings.

```
10  REM  PROGRAM TO CALCULATE SALES TAX
20  REM  "S" WILL BE THE NAME FOR THE SALES AMT
30  REM  "T1" WILL BE THE NAME FOR THE SALES TAX
40  REM  "T2" WILL BE THE NAME FOR THE TOTAL SALES PRICE
50  REM  THE SALES TAX RATE USED WILL BE 6 PERCENT
60  REM  A SALES AMOUNT OF 99.99 WILL BE USED TO TERMINATE THE PROGRAM
62  PRINT  "SALES TAX PROGRAM"
63  PRINT  "PROGRAMMED BY MARCIA WILLIAMS"
64  PRINT
65  PRINT  "SALES", "SALES", "SALES"
66  PRINT  "AMOUNT", "TAX, "PRICE"
67  PRINT
70  READ S
80  DATA 15.5, 9.5, 10., 3.5, 99.99
90  IF S = 99.99 THEN GO TO 135
100 LET T1 = S * .06          ! CALCULATES SALES TAX
110 LET T2 = S + T1           ! CALCULATES TOTAL SALES PRICE
120 PRINT S, T1, T2
130 GO TO 70
135 PRINT, "END OF DATA FOR SALES TAX PROGRAM"
140 STOP
150 END
```

Figure 11-11. *This revised program for solving the sales tax problem will print a report with headings.*

Note in the program that two additional PRINT statements have been added at Lines 64 and 67. These allow for double-spacing after the name of the programmer and after the two-line heading. The PRINT STATEMENT on Line 135 has a comma after PRINT, which causes the end-of-job statement to be indented to the second print zone.

The logic in the program is the same as that in Figure 11-8, p. 264. The only difference is that the unconditional branch is to Line 135, the end-of-job message instead of to Line 140 (STOP).

Figure 11-12 shows a sample report for the sales tax program with the headings and an end-of-job message.

Note that the name of the program and the name of the programmer each begin in the first zone and continue across the page. A line is skipped between these two lines and the first line of the two-line headings. A line is skipped after the headings. The amounts are listed in the three print zones under the proper headings.

The end-of-job line has been indented to the second print zone. It could have been printed at the first print zone. Or, another line could have been skipped before it was printed. The programmer chooses the kind of spacing desired.

Again, in this report, note that all columns are aligned on the left. All ending zeros after the decimal point are dropped.

```
SALES TAX PROGRAM
PROGRAMMED BY MARCIA WILLIAMS

SALES            SALES            SALES
AMOUNT           TAX              PRICE

15.5             .93              16.43
9.5              .57              10.07
10               .6               10.6
3.5              .21              3.71
                 END OF DATA FOR SALES TAX PROGRAM
```

Figure 11-12. *Above is a sample report for the sales tax program.*

Printouts for sales tax program

Figure 11-13 shows a printout of the program for solving the sales tax problem and also of the problem itself. There is explanatory material above and below the printout. The computer has "logged" the date, the amount of time taken for the run, the name of the program, and has made several other comments. Note that the computer tells the user, "BYE," "GOOD AFTERNOON," and "DISCONNECTING."

REVIEW QUESTIONS

1. What is the purpose of the REMARKS statements at the beginning of a BASIC program?
2. Why are READ statements usually included near the beginning of a BASIC program?
3. What statement is always used with a READ statement?
4. What is the first word in a conditional branch statement?
5. Assume that the sales tax percentage rate is changed to 4%. Write the corrected statements to change the program. Refer to Figure 11-11.
6. How is a comment written on a line in a BASIC program? Does the computer process the entire line?
7. Write the statement that would cause the terminal to skip a blank line (double-space).
8. How does the computer identify an alphanumeric constant?
9. How does a programmer tell the terminal printer to skip to the next print zone before printing?
10. What statement must always appear as the last statement in a BASIC program?

```
NEW
NEW FILE NAME--TAX

READY

10  REM  PROGRAM TO CALCULATE SALES TAX
20  REM  "S" WILL BE THE NAME FOR THE SALES AMT
30  REM  "T1" WILL BE THE NAME FOR THE SALES TAX
40  REM  "T2" WILL BE THE NAME FOR THE TOTAL SALES PRICE
50  REM  THE SALES TAX RATE USED WILL BE 6 PERCENT
60  REM  A SALES AMOUNT OF 99.99 WILL BE USED TO TERMINATE THE PROGRAM
62  PRINT  "SALES TAX PROGRAM"
63  PRINT  "PROGRAMMED BY MARCIA WILLIAMS"
64  PRINT
65  PRINT  "SALES", "SALES", "SALES"
66  PRINT "AMOUNT", "TAX", "PRICE"
67  PRINT
70  READ S
80  DATA 15.5, 9.5, 10., 3.5, 99.99
90  IF S = 99.99 THEN GO TO 135
100 LET T1 = S * .06             ! CALCULATES SALES TAX
110 LET T2 = S + T1              ! CALCULATES TOTAL SALES PRICE
120 PRINT S, T1, T2
130 GO TO 70
135 PRINT, "END OF DATA FOR SALES TAX PROGRAM"
140 STOP
150 END

READ


RUN
TAX           13:39          02-NOV-82

SALES TAX PROGRAM
PROGRAMMED BY MARCIA WILLIAMS

SALES          SALES          SALES
AMOUNT         TAX            PRICE

15.5           .93            16.43
9.5            .57            10.07
10             .6             10.6
3.5            .21            3.71
               END OF DATA FOR SALES TAX PROGRAM
STOP AT LINE 140

READY

BYE
CONFIRM: X
SAVED ALL DISK FILES; 66 BLOCKS IN USE. 34 FREE
JOB 15 USER 10.12 LOGGED OFF KB8 AT 02-NOV-82  13:50
SYSTEM RSTS Y05B-95 CAL POLY POMONA
RUN TIME WAS 9.2 SECONDS
ELAPSED TIME WAS 44 MINUTES, 3 SECONDS
GOOD AFTERNOON

DISCONNECTING
```

Figure 11-13. *Above are typical computer printouts of a BASIC program and a printed report for the sales tax problem.*

HONORS PROGRAM

The next program will be a modification of the problem to print an honor roll from Chapter 9. In this problem, the school district has asked for a count of all students who qualify for the honor roll with a grade point average (GPA) of 3.0 or greater.

Statement of the honors problem

A BASIC program is to be written to cause the computer to count all students with a GPA of 3.0 or higher and to print the count on a report. The report will also show the name of the program and programmer.

Flowchart for the program to solve the honors problem

Figure 11-14 shows the flowchart for solving the problem in BASIC. Note that the first step in the flowchart is an instruction, PRINT PROGRAM TITLE LINE. The next step is an instruction, PRINT PROGRAMMER NAME LINE. These two instructions are written inside input/output symbols because a printed line is output.

The next step in the flowchart is LET C = 0 (CLEAR COUNT TO ZERO). Counting is done by adding one (1) to a previous total as each honor student's data are processed. As is true with adding machines, the user is never sure that the machine has been cleared of unwanted totals. With an adding machine, clearing is done by pushing a total key. In computers, clearing is done by moving zeros into the location for accumulating a total. Zeros replace any previous value stored at that address. The clear instruction in BASIC is written as follows:

```
80 LET C = 0
```

This means that the value on the right of the equal sign (0) will be stored at the address named C (Count). Now, a numeric constant of 1 can be added each time an honor student has been identified. The clear instruction must always be written outside the loop. If not, the total will be "wiped out" (cleared to zero) each time a new value is processed. That is why the clear instruction comes before the READ instruction in the flowchart.

The on-page connector, 1, is placed before the READ instruction, READ G (GPA). The READ instruction is in the input/output symbol.

There are two decisions in this problem. The first decision is used to check for the last-value code, 9.9. The test is made after each data value is read. A value of 9.9 has been chosen because no average could be that high. If the GPA is equal to 9.9, the last value has been processed. The computer is ordered to print out the count of the honor students and then to stop.

If the last value has not been processed (G is not equal to 9.9), the computer goes to the next step, which is also a decision.

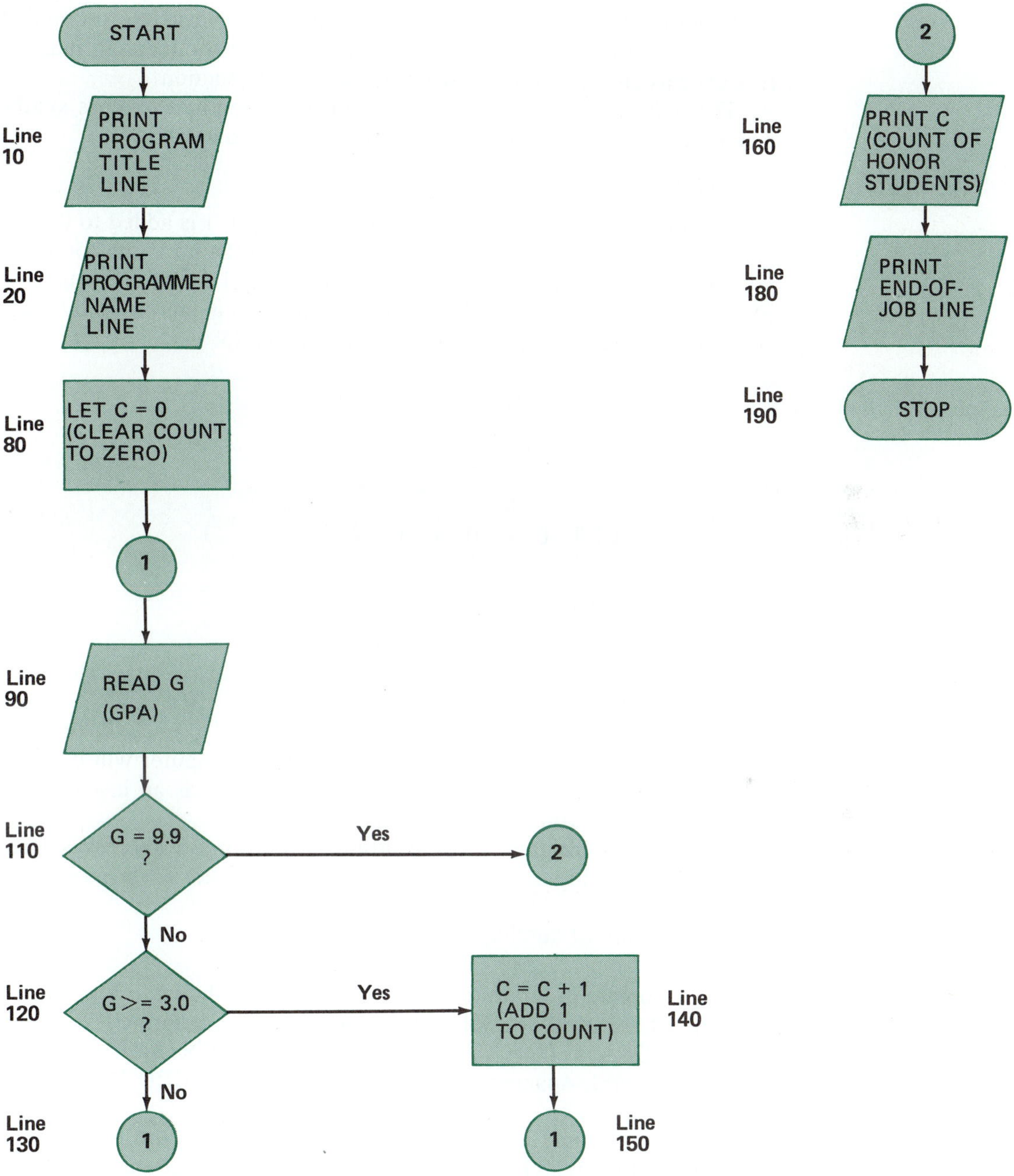

Figure 11-14. *This is a flowchart for the program to count honor students.*

The second decision is used to determine if the GPA is equal to or greater than 3.0. If it is not, the student will not be listed on the honor roll and will not be counted. The computer is ordered to branch back to the READ statement to read the next value in the DATA statement. The on-page connector (1) indicates this branch, which sets up the loop.

If the GPA is 3.0 or greater, the computer is instructed to count the student by adding 1 to the count. Remember that the location named C (count) was cleared to zero before the READ instruction.

The instruction to add 1 to the count is written in a process symbol. The BASIC statement for this addition of 1 is as follows:

```
140 LET C = C + 1
```

The first time that this instruction is processed, 1 is added to 0 (zero), giving a count of 1. The next time, 1 is added to the previous count of 1, giving a new count of 2. The next time, 1 is added to the previous count of 2, giving a new count of 3. The total count (C) is increased by 1 each time this instruction is processed. See Figure 11-15.

	C Before					C After
	0				=	0
LET C =	0	+	1		=	1
LET C =	1	+	1		=	2
LET C =	2	+	1		=	3
LET C =	3	+	1		=	4

Figure 11-15. *The equation C = C + 1 causes 1 to be added to the amount stored at C every time a new value is processed.*

After the last value has been processed, the computer will branch to the step shown with the on-page connector, 2. This is an instruction to print C (the count of honor students).

The next instruction is for printing an end-of-job line. This line is optional. It is included in a program if the programmer so desires.

BASIC program for solving the honors problem

The complete program to solve the problem is shown in Figure 11-16. Note that Line 20 allows for skipping a space after printing the program title, PROGRAM TO COUNT HONOR STUDENTS. Line 40 also allows for double-spacing after printing PROGRAMMED BY LESTER KUAI.

The remarks in Lines 50–70 state that G will be the name for the address used for the GPA; C will be the name for the count; and 9.9 will be the value used in G to test for the last value.

Line 80 clears the address named C to zero. Line 90 is the READ statement. There is only one variable name in this READ statement, G. Line 100 is the DATA statement. In real practice, of course, there would be many more values in the data block. Only seven GPAs were used in order to make the problem simple. Note that 9.9 is the last value on line 100.

```
 10  PRINT  "PROGRAM TO COUNT HONOR STUDENTS"
 20  PRINT
 30  PRINT  "PROGRAMMED BY LESTER KUAI"
 40  PRINT
 50  REM  "G" WILL BE THE NAME FOR GPA
 60  REM  "C" WILL BE THE NAME FOR THE COUNT OF HONOR STUDENTS
 70  REM  A GPA OF 9.9 WILL BE USED TO TERMINATE THE PROGRAM
 80  LET C = 0
 90  READ  G
100  DATA  2.89, 3.15, 3., 2.4, 4., 3.5, 2.73, 9.9
110  IF G = 9.9 THEN GO TO 160
120  IF G >= 3. THEN GO TO 140
130  GO TO 90
140  C = C + 1
150  GO TO 90
160  PRINT "TOTAL NUMBER OF HONOR STUDENTS IS " C
170  PRINT
180  PRINT "END OF HONOR COUNT PROGRAM"
190  STOP
200  END
```

Figure 11-16. *Above is the program to count the honor students.*

Line 110 directs the computer to go to Line 160 when the last value has been read. Note that Line 160 is not a STOP statement. It is a PRINT statement. If the last value has not been read, the computer goes on to Line 120, which is a decision statement. The computer is instructed to determine whether G is greater than or equal to 3.0. If it is, the branch is to Line 140.

Line 140 directs the computer to add 1 to the count (C) because the student is an honor student. The next step, Line 150 directs the computer to go back to Line 90 to read another value.

When the branch is made to Line 160 after the last value is read, the computer is told to print TOTAL NUMBER OF HONOR STUDENTS IS, to skip a space, and then to print the value of C. The space inside the ending quotation mark allows for spacing between the S in IS and the number that will be printed as the value of C. Otherwise, IS and the number would be run together.

Line 170 directs the printer to skip another line before printing the end-of-job statement, END OF HONOR COUNT PROGRAM. The next step, Line 190, is the STOP statement. Line 200 is the END statement, which must be the last statement in any BASIC program.

Refer again to the flowchart, Figure 11-14, and compare it with the program. Note that there are two unconditional branches back to the READ instruction, Lines 130 and 150. It is important to be sure that the branches in the flowchart logic are also entered into the program.

Note also that the CLEAR statement, Line 80, is written before the READ statement, Line 90. The loop is written from Line 90 to Line 150.

The corresponding lines of the program are printed next to the flowchart symbols in Figure 11-14. Observe how the IF-THEN statements are used on Lines 110 and 120 of Figure 11-16 to cause conditional branches.

Printout of honors problem

The completed report that would be created by this program would consist of only four lines of print, double-spaced as follows:

```
PROGRAM TO COUNT HONOR STUDENTS

PROGRAMMED BY LESTER KUAI

TOTAL NUMBER OF HONOR STUDENTS IS 4

END OF HONOR COUNT PROGRAM
```

SUMMARY

BASIC is a language that is simple to use but very powerful. BASIC gives the programmer the ability to perform all mathematical operations — addition, subtraction, multiplication, division, and exponentiation.

Arithmetic calculations can be made by using a LET statement. The word LET is written after a line number and is followed by a variable name, an equal sign, and an expression. The LET statement is an order to the computer to perform the calculations on the right of the equal sign and then to store the result in the address with the variable name on the left of the equal sign. The result of the calculation replaces any value that was stored at the address before.

Alphanumeric constants include any letter of the alphabet, number, special character, or space. Alphanumeric constants are enclosed within quotation marks and may be used to print headings. Everything, including spaces, that is contained within quotation marks will be printed when alphanumeric constants are used with a PRINT statement.

Double-spacing can be accomplished with a PRINT statement alone. The word PRINT is typed by itself after the line number. This causes the printer to print a blank line (skip a line).

No attempt has been made to introduce every BASIC statement. However, some of the statements used most often have been covered in this book. The reader should now be ready to create a BASIC program, using any of the statements presented. Every statement need not be used in each program. In fact, it would be unusual if a program did need all the commands that have been given. The user must decide what has to be done and how to accomplish it by using the instructions that have been presented.

REVIEW QUESTIONS

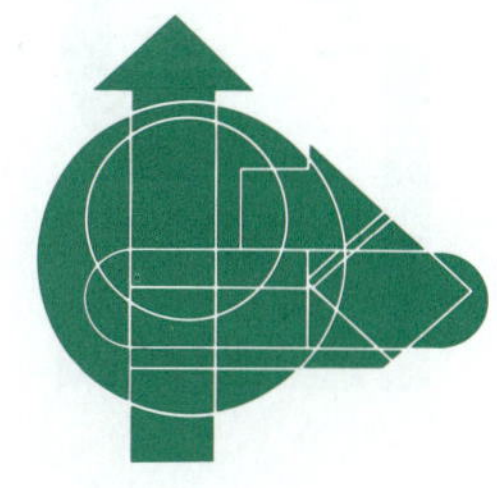

1. How are values separated in a DATA statement?
2. Why is it a good idea to clear storage areas that will be used for arithmetic results? How is this done?
3. What would be the order of computation in the following statement:

```
660 LET T = A * (B - C/D) + .5
```

4. What is the result of the following statement:

```
670 LET A = 0
```

5. Why should the statement in Question 4 never be written within a loop?

NEW TERMS

- Arithmetic expression
- Equation
- LET statement

STUDY GUIDE

Complete Study Guide 11 by following the instructions in your STUDY GUIDES booklet.

PROJECTS

Complete Projects 11-1 through 11-5 by following the instructions in your PROJECTS booklet.

12 INTRODUCTION to COBOL PROGRAMMING

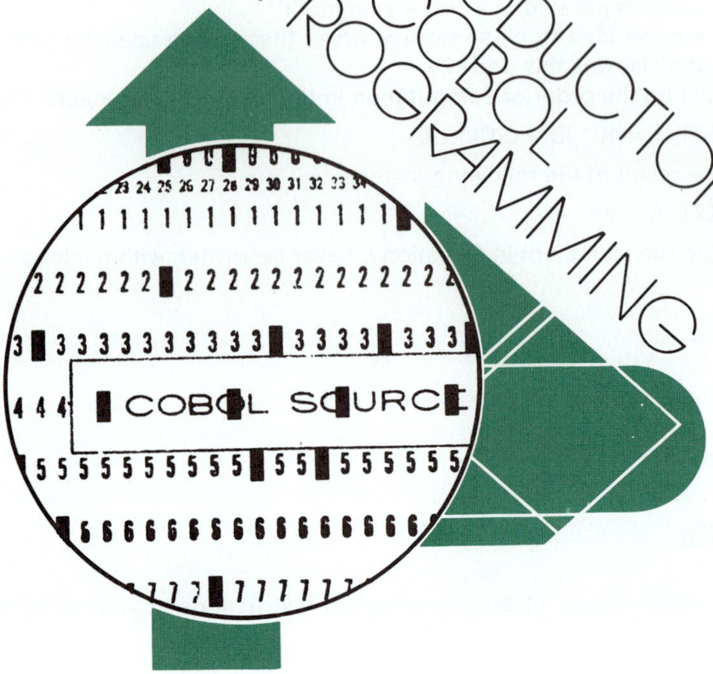

Since the first computer was invented, people have tried to find ways to make programming easier. There was a need for a programming language that would be easy to understand and that could be used with many different computers.

A commission was formed during the 1950s for the purpose of developing a standard business programming language. This commission was called CODASYL (*C*onference *o*n *D*ata *S*ystem *L*anguages.) Representatives from the federal government, computer manufacturers, and private industry served on CODASYL. The COBOL programming language was developed in 1959 as the result of the efforts of this group.

The name *COBOL* stands for *CO*mmon *B*usiness *O*riented *L*anguage. You learned in Chapter 9 that COBOL is one of the compiler-level source program languages. However, COBOL is a near-English language, in which English words are used to stand for the addresses of instructions and data. The concepts about language translation will be repeated in this chapter.

COBOL was designed to process and maintain large files. In fact, the word FILE is used many times in the programs. COBOL files can be recorded on any of the input/output media described earlier. However, punched cards will be used in this text for illustrations because you can not see the magnetic spots on tapes or disks. A file of punched cards related to a COBOL program is referred to as a COBOL file. Also referred to as a file is the printed report produced as output by the computer.

Magnetic tape and disk files will not be explained with the COBOL language in this text although many of the concepts are the same.

ADVANTAGES OF COBOL

COBOL has distinct advantages as a programming language. Some of them are described in the following:

(1) The steps of the program are stated in a near-English language. The word ADD orders the computer to add numbers. MOVE tells it to move data from one memory address to another. STUDENT-NUMBER can be used as the name for the actual address of the student number. The use of a near-English language makes COBOL easier for the programmer to understand than the short variable data names used in other programming languages such as BASIC. The logic of programs is easier to follow. Algebraic formulas are not used.

(2) COBOL is the most widely used business language. It can be used with almost any computer for which a COBOL compiler is available. Small changes may be made in order to adapt a program to a different computer system. As a rule, however, the COBOL programs that run on one computer can be easily changed to run on another computer. For this reason, COBOL is said to be a machine-independent language.

(3) COBOL programs can solve business problems that require long lists, many names and addresses, and descriptive sentences.

DISADVANTAGES OF COBOL

COBOL has some disadvantages. But, for business data processing the advantages far outweigh the disadvantages. Some of the disadvantages are as follows:

(1) COBOL compilers require more primary memory than many other compilers. For this reason, COBOL cannot be used with most small computer systems.

(2) COBOL programs are long. The near-English language that makes COBOL easy to read also creates long sentences and programs.

(3) COBOL is business-oriented. For that reason, it does not handle complex scientific or mathematical equations well.

(4) COBOL is harder to learn and use than languages like BASIC. However, once the rules are understood, COBOL's readability makes it easier to understand.

ORGANIZATION OF A COBOL PROGRAM

As is true with all high-level programming languages, COBOL must be translated into machine language before processing can take place. The translation is handled by a compiler program. The compiler program is furnished by the manufacturer and is part of the software for the computer.

Translation

Each line of the COBOL program is usually punched into a separate card. The original COBOL program is the source program. It is translated, one card or instruction at a time, into machine language. The resulting machine-language program is the object program. See Figure 12-1.

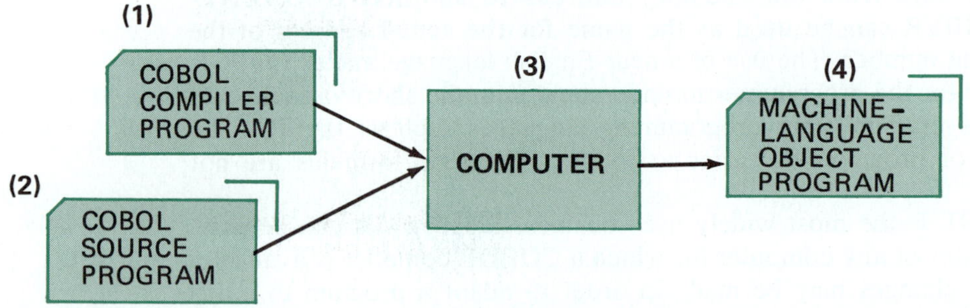

1. COBOL compiler program is read into the computer.
2. COBOL source program is read into the computer, one instruction at a time.
3. The compiler program translates each COBOL instruction into one or more machine-language instructions.
4. The resulting machine-language program is the object program.

Figure 12-1. *Translation process of a COBOL program is shown.*

As is true with most programming languages, a COBOL source program must be written according to a certain format. Otherwise, the compiler cannot translate the source program into an object program. Certain words have special meanings in COBOL. These words must be used in a very precise manner. These words are described briefly at this point. They will be explained in greater detail later when they are used.

Vocabulary

The words used in COBOL programs are of two types: those on a reserved word list of COBOL words and those invented by the programmer.

(1) Reserved-list words. A partial list of COBOL reserved words may be found on p. 317. *Reserved words* are certain words that have a specific meaning to a COBOL compiler. The compiler reserves these words for given purposes. There are reserved words in every COBOL program. The choice of words depends on the problem to

be solved and the type of computer used. Some of the words must be used in every COBOL program. The reserved words are explained in more detail on pp. 316 and 317.

(2) *Programmer-invented words.* Generally, all words other than the reserved words are invented by the programmer. Programmers are free to make up their own words as long as these words are not on the reserved list and as long as the same word is always used in a program to represent the address of the same item of data.

If a programmer-invented name consists of two or more words, there can be no blank spaces between them. The words must be joined by hyphens (STUDENT-NAME). There are other rules for the use of programmer-invented words. These rules are explained later in this chapter.

Program sheet

COBOL programs may be written on plain sheets of paper. In practice, however, a program sheet is used. See Figure 12-2.

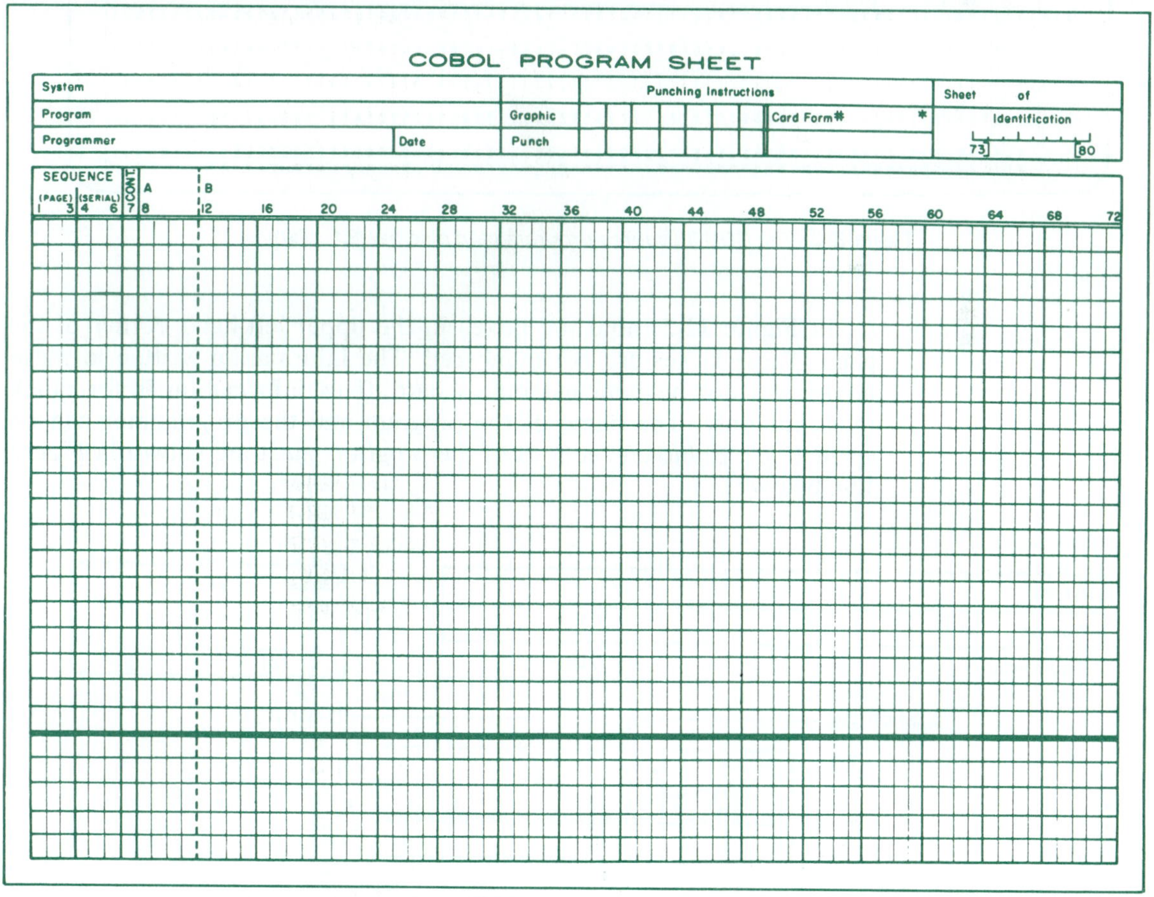

Figure 12-2. *The COBOL program sheet has 80 columns.*

The form shown is similar to one used by the IBM Corporation for IBM System/360 and System/370 computers. Note that the sheet provides space for 80 columns of information. These columns correspond to the 80 columns of a punched card. One source program card will be punched for each completed line of the COBOL program sheet. Information in one of the numbered spaces will be punched into the corresponding column of the card. Figure 12-3 shows an 80-column card that is used as the input medium for a COBOL source program. Note how the columns correspond with the columns in the COBOL program sheet.

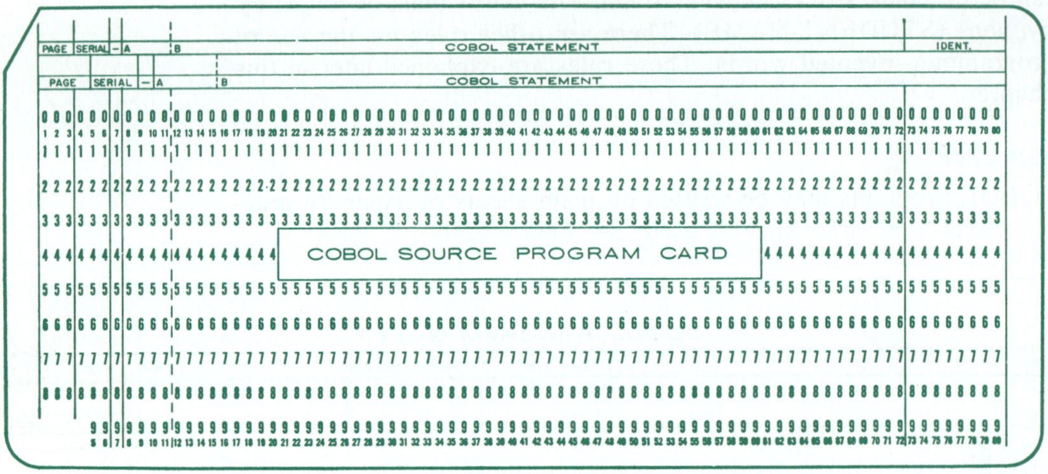

Figure 12-3. *The COBOL source program card also has 80 columns.*

In Figure 12-2, note the boxes in the upper left-hand corner of the page. These boxes are not numbered. The information written in these boxes will not be punched into a card. This information is for quick reference only. The name of the program and the programmer can be spelled out. Enlarged sections of the program sheet are shown in Figure 12-4 below.

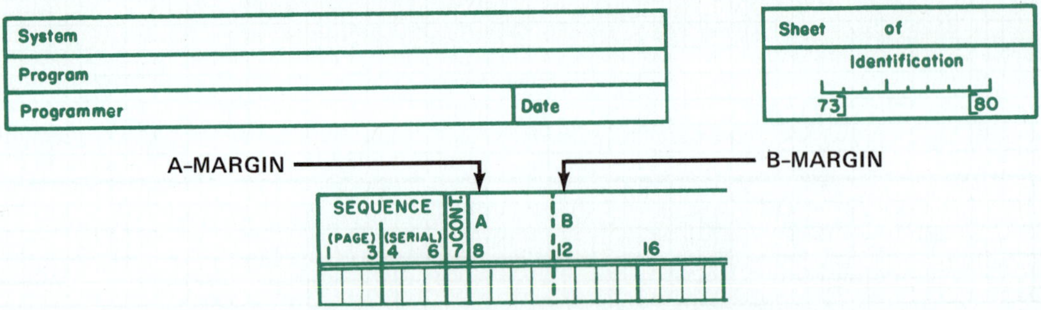

Figure 12-4. *Enlarged sections of the COBOL program sheet are shown.*

The box labeled "Identification" in the upper right-hand corner will contain information that will be punched into Columns 73-80 of the card. These spaces are for identifying the program if the programmer wishes. If so, the name will be punched into the source program cards. Note that the identification cannot be more than eight characters long. The box also has a place to show the sheet and page number.

The page number that will be punched into the source program cards is also written in Columns 1–3 of the program sheet under SEQUENCE. Columns 4–6 are used for the numbers of the instructions. Column 7 is used for a hyphen to indicate a divided word. The hyphen is placed in Column 7 of the line on which the word is continued.

In Figure 12-2, Columns 8–72 will be used for writing the statements making up the program. No line in the program may go beyond Column 72. Note the letters A and B appearing over Columns 8 and 12 of Figure 12-4. Column 8 is called the A-Margin. Column 12 is the B-Margin. You will learn how these columns are used as the different divisions and statements are explained on the program sheets in this chapter.

Program divisions

A COBOL program is made up of four divisions. These divisions and their titles *must* appear in every program in the following order.

(1) *IDENTIFICATION DIVISION.* This gives the title of the program, the name of the programmer, and the date the program is written.
(2) *ENVIRONMENT DIVISION.* This specifies the computer, the input/output devices, and input/output files.
(3) *DATA DIVISION.* This describes the data files to be used as the input before processing and the files and reports that will be the output. (This division also specifies the WORKING-STORAGE section reserved for constants, accumulating totals, and data developed during the program.)
(4) *PROCEDURE DIVISION.* This specifies the actual steps the computer is to follow in processing the data in order to solve a problem.

Each of the four divisions of a COBOL program may be written on a separate page, although this is a matter of choice.

REVIEW QUESTIONS

1. What is the meaning of the term COBOL?
2. What are the advantages of COBOL?
3. What are the disadvantages of COBOL?
4. Can a computer process data directly from a COBOL program? Why?
5. What two types of words are used in a COBOL program?
6. What must a programmer do when inventing a two-word name in a program?
7. How many columns are provided on a COBOL program sheet for entering information?

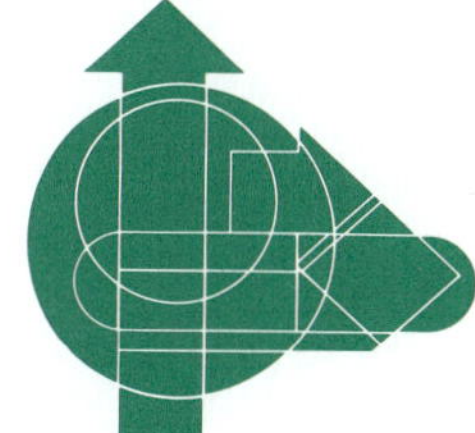

(Continued)

8. To which input medium does each line of the program sheet correspond?
9. What columns on a program sheet are used for recording the actual statements of a COBOL program?
10. What four divisions must be present in every COBOL program? In what order?

PROBLEM 1: PRINTING A REPORT LISTING STUDENTS' NUMBERS, NAMES, AND TEST SCORES

The explanation of COBOL programming will be applied to a specific problem to be solved in COBOL. On hand is a file of punched-card records. Each record contains the student number, name, class code, and three test scores. The format of the data card is shown on p. 293 with the explanation of the DATA DIVISION.

Statement of the problem

A COBOL program is to be written to cause the computer to print a list of students' numbers, names, and three test scores, using an input file of punched cards. Each line of the five-column report will be centered on a 132-space line.

Analysis of the problem

A program must be written to solve Problem 1 as follows:

(1) IDENTIFICATION DIVISION. The title of the program will be SCORES.
(2) ENVIRONMENT DIVISION. An IBM SYSTEM/360 computer will be used. A card reader will be used as the input device and a printer will be used as the output device.
(3) DATA DIVISION. The input and output files, records, and fields will be described.
(4) PROCEDURE DIVISION. The actual steps to be followed by the computer to solve the problem will be described.

WRITING A COBOL PROGRAM

Unlike BASIC and many other programming languages, COBOL has many statements (entries or instructions) that are required in every program. Four of the required entries are the names of the four divisions just listed. These four divisions must appear in every COBOL program in the order listed. They must also be spelled exactly the same in every program. Additional statements are required in each division. In this book, all required entires will be underlined to make them easier to find. *You do not underline these entries when writing a program. They are only underlined to make them easier to recognize.*

Each COBOL division will be explained in the order in which it must appear in a program. The examples used in the following paragraphs to show how statements appear will be those necessary to solve Problem 1.

IDENTIFICATION DIVISION

This division contains the following information:

(1) Name of the division: IDENTIFICATION DIVISION.
(2) Title of the program: PROGRAM ID (on the list of reserved words).
(3) Name of the programmer.
(4) Date the program was written.

The name of the division and title of the program are required. The name of the programmer and the date are helpful, but not required.

Example

The following example of an IDENTIFICATION DIVISION for Problem 1 shows how the entries would be written. The required entries are underlined.

```
010 IDENTIFICATION DIVISION.
020 PROGRAM-ID.
020         'SCORES'.
040 AUTHOR.
050         PEREZ.
060 DATE-WRITTEN.
070         OCTOBER 4, 1982.
```

The actual division is shown in Figure 12-5 as it would appear on a program sheet.

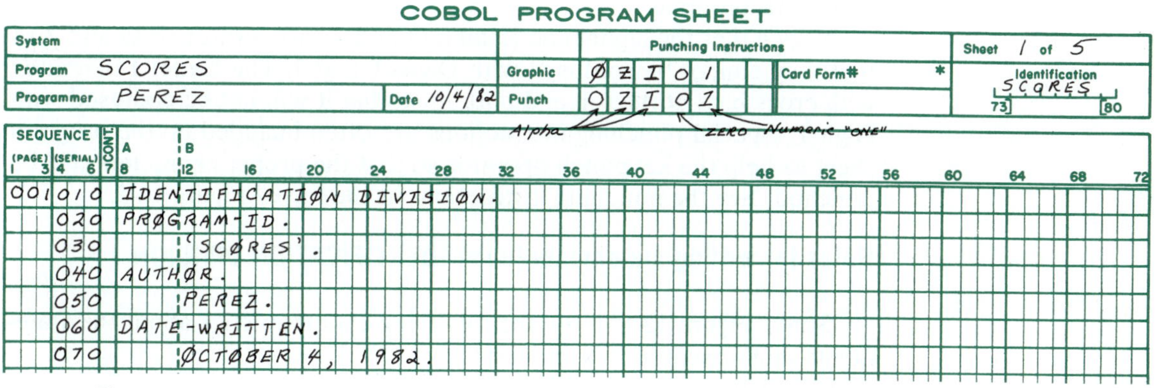

Figure 12-5. *Above is the IDENTIFICATION DIVISION for the program to solve Problem 1.*

Each page of a COBOL program is always numbered in the upper right-hand corner. Figure 12-5 shows that the IDENTIFICATION DIVISION is sheet (page) 1 of 5. The page number is also repeated in Columns 1–3 of the program sheet. Because all entries on a page are for the same page number, a page number may be written only once — usually on the first line. When the keypunch operator punches the COBOL program cards, the page and line numbers are punched into each card. Then, if the program cards are dropped accidentally or separated, they can easily be placed back into the proper order.

Each line in a COBOL program is numbered. In Figure 12-5, the line numbers could have been written in 1s (Line 001, 002, 003, etc.). However, the form used in 10s (Lines 010, 020, 030, etc.) helps to avoid confusion if changes must be made in the program. The zero following the numbers allows for insertion of additional lines when needed. Line 035 could be inserted between Lines 030 and 040 with no problems.

Explanation of the example

Line 010 in Figure 12-5 gives the name of the division.

Lines 020 and 030 give the name of the program. *PROGRAM-ID* is the abbreviation for program identification. The program name on Line 030 is alphabetic and cannot have more than eight characters. It must be enclosed in single quotation marks. A period must follow the ending quotation mark. Hyphens or spaces cannot be allowed in the name. The first character must be a letter of the alphabet.

Lines 040 and 050 give the name of the programmer (author).

Lines 060 and 070 give the date on which the program was written. (The date could have been written in figures: 10/4/82.)

Note that all items are written in capital letters. Each heading and each line of information is followed by a period. Some of the words in the examples are underlined. These words are required by the compiler and they must appear in every COBOL program in the exact order given. The underline itself is not part of the program. The underline is used in this text only as a key to words or statements that are required in a COBOL program.

Notice that the alphabetic letters, O and Z, are written as Ø and Ƶ so that they cannot be confused with Digits 0 and 2. The Letter I is written with cross bars at the top and bottom so that it will not be confused with Digit 1. Special punching instructions are often included on the program sheet to help the keypunch operator so that the proper characters will be punched. See the punching instructions at the top of Figure 12-5.

Rules for writing statements in the IDENTIFICATION DIVISION

Study Figure 12-5. Note the following characteristics about the statements that appear in this division:

Line 010:

The division name always appears first in a division. It starts at the A-Margin, Column 8, and ends with a period.

Lines 020, 040, and 060:

The IDENTIFICATION DIVISION contains paragraphs. The paragraph names or headings also start at the A-Margin, Column

8, and end with a period. Line 020, PROGRAM-ID, is a required paragraph heading, and it must appear in every COBOL program as the first entry after the name of the division, IDENTIFICATION DIVISION. Line 040, AUTHOR, is the heading for the identification of the programmer. Line 060, DATE-WRITTEN, is the heading for the date of the program. Note that PROGRAM-ID and DATE-WRITTEN contain hyphens. They are also listed as COBOL reserved words on p. 317.

Line 030:
The title used to identify the program is indented. It starts at the B-Margin, Column 12. It ends with a period. Column 12 is used because the program title is actually a part of the paragraph, PROGRAM-ID.

Line 050:
The author's name is indented. It starts at the B-Margin, Column 12. It ends with a period.

Line 070:
The date is indented. It starts at the B-Margin, Column 12. It ends with a period.

Note that only the main entries of the division start at the A-Margin. All entries that are a part of a main paragraph start at the B-Margin. This requirement helps to make a COBOL program easy to read and understand.

ENVIRONMENT DIVISION

This is the second division of a COBOL program. It must include the following information:

(1) Name of the division: <u>ENVIRONMENT DIVISION</u>.
(2) Names of the two sections in the division: <u>CONFIGURATION SECTION</u> and <u>INPUT-OUTPUT SECTION</u>.
(3) Names of the source and object computers: <u>SOURCE-COMPUTER</u> and <u>OBJECT-COMPUTER</u>. Remember that the original COBOL program is called a source program and the translated version of it is called the object program. The *source computer* is the computer that will be used to translate the program. The *object computer* is the computer that will run the machine-language object program. Often the same computer will be used for both operations, but this is not always the case.
(4) Name required by the COBOL program to identify the input and output files: <u>FILE-CONTROL</u>.
(5) Name that the programmer invents for the input file (data to be processed) and the name of the input device to be used.
(6) Name that the programmer invents for the output file (data that have been processed) and the name of the output device to be used.

All of the information in the ENVIRONMENT DIVISION discussed in Items 1–4 above are required in every COBOL program. All of the underlined entries are listed in the reserved words.

Example

The following example of the ENVIRONMENT DIVISION is for the problem explained earlier. Remember that the underlined words are required by the program.

```
010 ENVIRONMENT DIVISION.
020 CONFIGURATION SECTION.
030 SOURCE-COMPUTER.
040      IBM-360.
050 OBJECT-COMPUTER.
060      IBM-360.
070 INPUT-OUTPUT SECTION.
080 FILE-CONTROL.
090      SELECT SCORES-FILE, ASSIGN TO 'SYSIN' UNIT-RECORD.
100      SELECT PRINTED-REPORT-FILE, ASSIGN TO 'SYSOUT' UNIT-RECORD.
```

The actual division is shown in Figure 12-6 as it would appear on a COBOL program sheet. The page number of the program sheet is p. 2 of 5. The page number is given at the top of each program sheet in Columns 1–3. Note that the line numbers begin again with Line Number 010. The line numbers could be continued from the previous page. The line number could be 080 because the last line number on p. 001 was 070. However, the usual practice is to begin each page with a beginning line number.

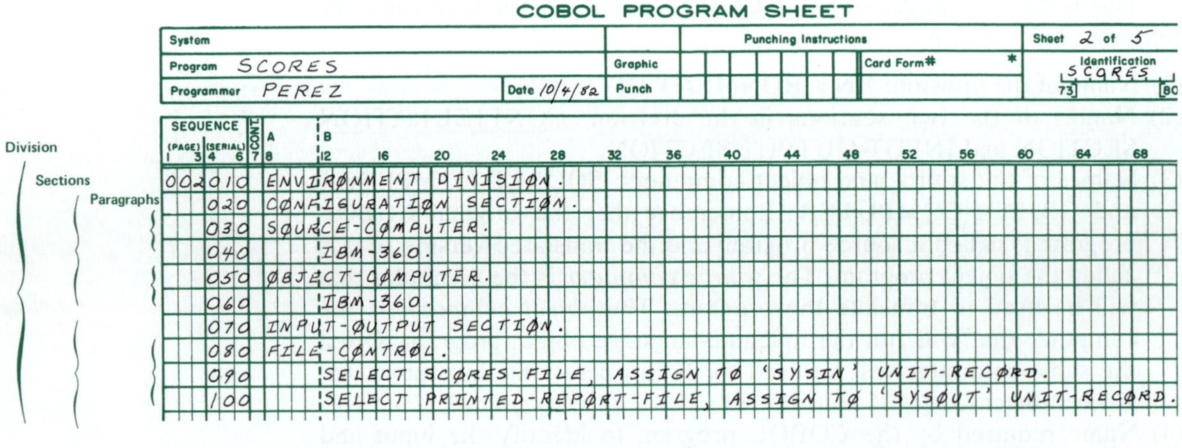
COBOL PROGRAM SHEET
System
Punching Instructions
Sheet 2 of 5
Program SCORES
Graphic
Card Form#
Identification
SCORES
Programmer PEREZ
Date 10/4/82
Punch
SEQUENCE
(PAGE) (SERIAL)
CONT.
A
B
Division
Sections
Paragraphs
002010 ENVIRONMENT DIVISION.
020 CONFIGURATION SECTION.
030 SOURCE-COMPUTER.
040 IBM-360.
050 OBJECT-COMPUTER.
060 IBM-360.
070 INPUT-OUTPUT SECTION.
080 FILE-CONTROL.
090 SELECT SCORES-FILE, ASSIGN TO 'SYSIN' UNIT-RECORD.
100 SELECT PRINTED-REPORT-FILE, ASSIGN TO 'SYSOUT' UNIT-RECORD.

Figure 12-6. *The ENVIRONMENT DIVISION describes the computers and the input and output files.*

Explanation of the example

Line 010 gives the name of the division.

Lines 020 and 070 give the names of the two required sections, CON-

FIGURATION SECTION and INPUT-OUTPUT SECTION. These two section headings must appear in every COBOL program.

Lines 030 and 040 give the name of the computer that will translate the COBOL source program into a machine-language object program.

Lines 050 and 060 give the name of the computer that will process the object program.

Line 080 gives the heading for the input and output files, FILE-CONTROL. This heading is required in all COBOL programs just before the names of the input and output files.

Line 090 gives the name of the input file (SCORES-FILE) and also the input medium to be used. In this example, the *programmer has assigned the name* SCORES-FILE to input file. The name SCORES-FILE refers to the entire file of punched data cards to be used as the input medium.

In COBOL, the name UNIT-RECORD is used to identify the punched-card reader as the input device for the IBM-360 computer. The words SELECT and ASSIGN are required words in the statements under FILE-CONTROL.

The IBM System/360 is used for the example in this text because this computer is available to many schools. The programs can be changed very easily to run on any other computer that has a COBOL compiler.

'SYSIN' in single quotation marks is a COBOL reserved word when used with the IBM-360 computer. *'SYSIN'* stands for *sys*tem *in*put. This word tells the compiler that SCORES-FILE is the name for the input data file.

Line 100 gives the name of the output file (PRINTED-REPORT-FILE). It also indicates which output device will be used (UNIT-RECORD), which is the printer. In the example, the programmer has assigned the name PRINTED-REPORT-FILE to the report containing the output data. This name refers to the entire report that will be printed as output. Note that in COBOL the name UNIT-RECORD may be used for the input device (card reader) or output device (printer).

'SYSOUT' in single quotation marks stands for *sys*tems *out*put. This term will appear in the FILE-CONTROL paragraph for all programs in this text.

Note that most of the entries in this division are required by the compiler. The only names invented by the programmer are:

(1) The name of the computer on which the program will be compiled.
(2) The name of the computer on which the program will be run.
(3) The names of the input and output data files.
(4) The names identifying the input and output devices.

All other information is prescribed by the COBOL language.

Rules for writing statements in the ENVIRONMENT DIVISION

Study Figure 12-6 again. Note the following statements that appear in the ENVIRONMENT DIVISION.

Line 010:

Again, the division name comes first. It starts at the A-Margin and ends with a period.

Lines 020 and 070:

Names of section headings start at the A-Margin and end with periods.

Lines 030 and 050.

Names of paragraph headings that fall under the section heading CONFIGURATION SECTION start at the A-Margin and end with periods.

Line 080:

Name of paragraph heading that falls under the section heading, INPUT-OUTPUT SECTION starts at A-Margin and ends with a period.

Lines 040 and 060:

The names of the source and object computers are indented under the proper paragraph headings. They start at the B-Margin and end with periods.

Lines 090 and 100:

The statements that assign names to the input and output files, as well as the names of the input and output devices and media are started at the B-Margin, Column 12. They fall under the paragraph heading FILE-CONTROL. These statements are followed by periods.

Commas may be used within lines to aid human reading, as they are in Lines 090 and 100 (SELECT SCORES-FILE, ASSIGN TO 'SYSIN' UNIT-RECORD. SELECT PRINTED-REPORT-FILE, ASSIGN TO 'SYSOUT' UNIT-RECORD.). The commas may be omitted, however. They have no effect on the object program. If commas are used, they must be followed by at least one space.

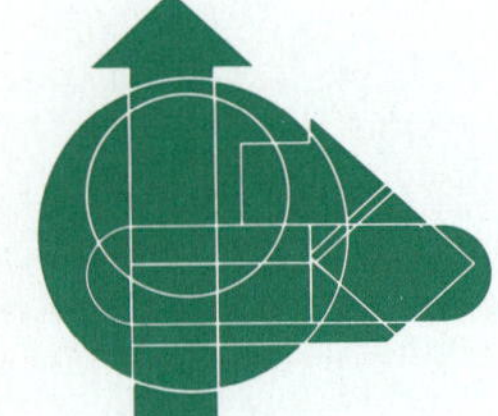

REVIEW QUESTIONS

1. What two items of information must be in the IDENTIFICATION DIVISION of every COBOL program?
2. What is the meaning of PROGRAM-ID?
3. What column of the COBOL program sheet is referred to as the A-Margin? B-Margin?
4. At which margin does the division name begin? The paragraph name? The statements within a paragraph?
5. Can the name invented by the programmer for the program be of any length? Explain.
6. What information does the ENVIRONMENT DIVISION contain?
7. Name the two sections in the ENVIRONMENT DIVISION.
8. What paragraph name is used to identify the input and output files in the ENVIRONMENT DIVISION?
9. Who assigns the names to the input and output files?

(Continued)

10. Explain the meaning of this statement in the ENVIRONMENT DIVISION:
    SELECT SCORES-FILE, ASSIGN TO 'SYSIN' UNIT-RECORD.
11. Which of the words in Question 10 are required in a COBOL program?
12. What information in the ENVIRONMENT DIVISION is supplied by the programmer?

DATA DIVISION

The DATA DIVISION is the first division in a COBOL program that changes much from program to program. The DATA DIVISION is also one of the longest divisions. In the DATA DIVISION the programmer must describe every file, record, and field that will be used in the program.

In COBOL, the programmer uses names instead of numbers to describe the addresses. A compiler will translate GO TO END-OF-JOB to an order to go to an address named END-OF-JOB. This makes the programmer's work easier because meaningful names are used to describe numeric addresses.

It must be remembered that the programmer-invented name stands for the address at which data are stored, *not the data stored at that address*. However, if the programmer-invented name does describe the data stored at that address, the program becomes easier to understand.

Files, records, and fields

You have already learned the difference between a file, a record, and a field. Figure 12-7 shows again this distinction when punched cards are used as the input medium. An input file is a deck of punched cards. A record is a single punched card. A field is a division of a single punched card.

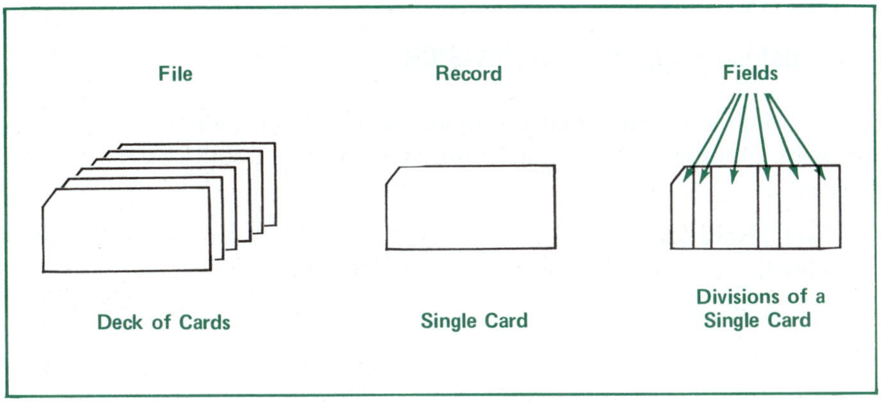

Figure 12-7. *An input file, a record, and fields on the record are shown.*

Note the difference between files, records, and fields when a printed report is used as the output medium. See Figure 12-8. Note that the printed report containing the output information is the output file. A record is a single line on the report. A field is a specific item of information on that line.

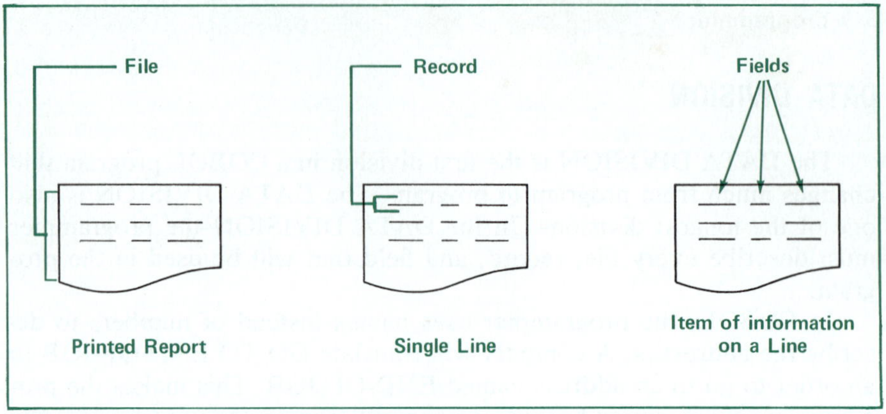

Figure 12-8. *An output file, a record, and fields on the record are shown.*

Purpose of the DATA DIVISION

The purpose of the DATA DIVISION is to describe the input file, records, and fields in such an exact manner that the compiler will be able to translate the names into memory addresses that it will assign. The output file, records, and fields should also be described exactly. The compiler will then be able to translate the names into memory addresses, to process the program commands, and to print the report just as desired. Although the step-by-step commands are given in THE PROCEDURE DIVISION, if the DATA DIVISION is not written accurately, the program will not work.

For convenience, the DATA DIVISION is discussed in two parts: (1) input statements and (2) output statements. Input statements are explained first.

Input statements in the DATA DIVISION

You learned earlier that the input file for this problem consists of a deck of punched cards containing information about students' test scores.

Data record for input. Refer to Figure 12-9 for a sample of the data card for this problem. The fields on the card are as follows:

Field	*Columns*	*Type of Data*
Student Name	1–20 (20 columns)	Alphabetic
	21–30 (10 columns)	None-blank
Class code	31 (1 column)	Numeric — 1 for 1st-year student
		2 for 2d-year student
		3 for 3d-year student
		4 for 4th-year student

Field	Columns	Type of Data
	32–40 (9 columns)	None-blank
Score 1	41–43 (3 columns)	Numeric
Score 2	44–46 (3 columns)	Numeric
Score 3	47–49 (3 columns)	Numeric
	50–80 (31 columns)	None-blank

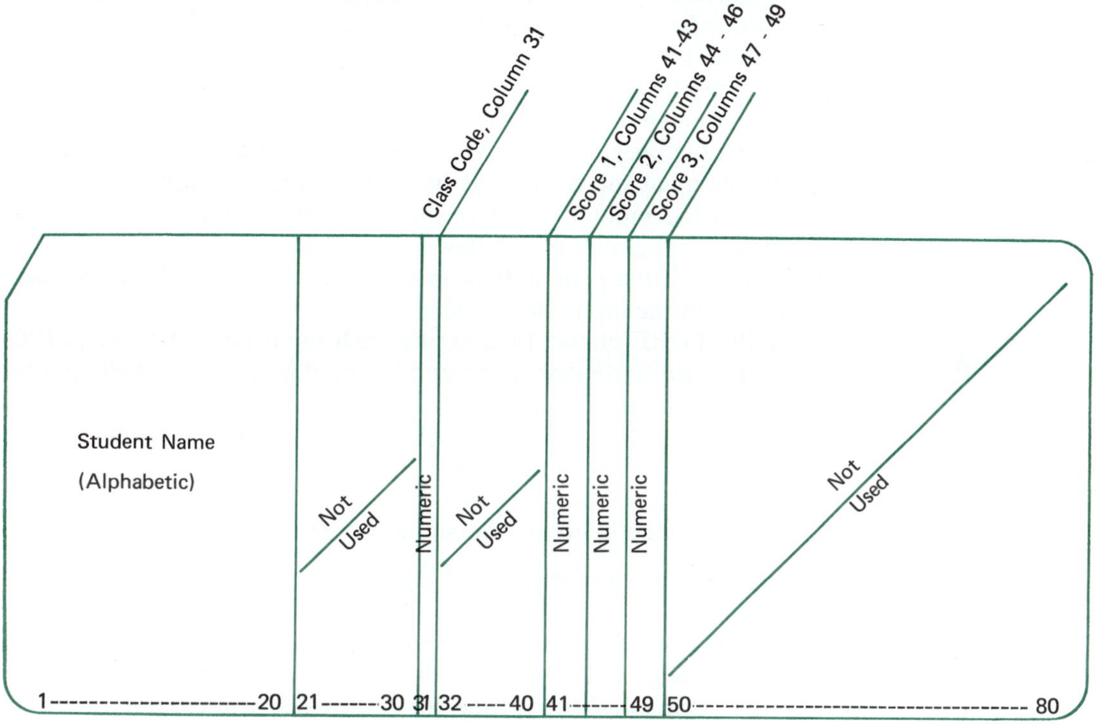

Figure 12-9. *Above is the format of the data card used for Problem 1.*

Required input statements. The input portion of the DATA DIVISION must include the following information:

(1) Name of the division: DATA DIVISION (on the list of COBOL reserved words, p. 317).
(2) Names of the sections in the division: FILE SECTION and WORKING-STORAGE SECTION (on the list of COBOL reserved words).
(3) Name that the programmer invents for each input file and several statements that will give the compiler needed information about the input file. The name used in the DATA DIVISION for each file must be the same as that used in the ENVIRONMENT DIVISION. (In this chapter, the input file has been named SCORES-FILE. The output file is PRINTED-REPORT-FILE.) Compiler programs vary in the number and wording of explanatory statements used. However, the following statements are usually included in the FILE SECTION of all DATA DIVISIONS.

a. A statement about the length of the recording mode. This statement tells the compiler whether the input record is of fixed, variable, or unspecified length. (The input record is of fixed length because a punched card always has 80 columns.)
b. A statement about the length of the input record. (Of course, it contains 80 characters if a punched card is used.)
c. A statement about the use of labels in the input record. Labels are used when magnetic tapes or disks serve as input or output media. Labels are not needed if punched cards are used. This statement about label records is required by the COBOL compiler even though no labels are used.
d. Name the programmer invents for each record in the input file.

(4) Restatement of the name that the programmer has invented for the record in the input file. There must also be statements to describe the fields on the record as follows:
a. Name that the programmer invents for each field of data on each record in the input file.
b. A PICTURE clause to describe each input field of data. A *PICTURE clause* describes the number of characters in a field and the type of characters: alphabetic, numeric, or alphanumeric (mixed). PICTURE clauses also describe the location of decimal points in numeric fields when needed. There are no decimal points in the fields in the records described in this chapter. PICTURE clauses are explained in greater detail on pp. 297 and 298.

Inventing names for addresses of input data. All input data to be processed must be named in the DATA DIVISION. The names given to the different kinds of data must be invented by the programmer. Once invented in the DATA DIVISION, these names must be referred to in exactly the same way every time they are used in the same program. They cannot be misspelled, changed, or abbreviated in any way. Remember that these names identify the addresses at which data will be stored, not the data.

In COBOL, the names of addresses can also describe the data stored at these addresses. Programmer-invented names are not limited to one alphabetic character with or without a number, as they are in BASIC. COBOL names may be as long as 32 characters with most COBOL compilers.

As you learned earlier, the programmer can invent any name as long as it does not appear on the reserved-word list, p. 317. If the programmer-invented name has two or more words, there can be no blank spaces. Instead, the words must be joined by hyphens. (Score 1 will be named SCORE-1.) A number or hyphen may not be the first character of a programmer-invented name.

Programmers invent names for files, records, and fields. It is usually safe to invent hyphened names because most names on the reserved list are not hyphened. A hyphened name can consist of words on the reserved word list, but the words may not be used singly. For example, both HEADING and LINE are on the list, but HEADING-LINE is not. (Programmer-invented names are discussed on p. 318. Only enough information is given here to explain the example.)

Example

Refer again to Figure 12-9, which shows the format of the input data card. Note the 20-column Student-Name field is alphabetic. The next ten columns are not used. The single column Class-Code field, Column 31, is numeric. The next nine columns are not used. Columns 41–43 contain Score 1. Columns 44–46 contain Score 2. Columns 47–49 contain Score 3. The next 31 columns are not used.

The following example is for the problem presented in this chapter. It describes the input data file, record, and fields.

```
010 DATA DIVISION.
020 FILE SECTION.
030 FD  SCORES-FILE
040     RECORDING MODE IS F
050     RECORD CONTAINS 80 CHARACTERS
060     LABEL RECORDS ARE OMITTED
070     DATA RECORD IS PUNCHED-CARD.
080 01  PUNCHED-CARD.
090     02  STUDENT-NAME           PICTURE A(20).
100     02  FILLER                 PICTURE X(10).
110     02  CLASS-CODE             PICTURE 9.
120     02  FILLER                 PICTURE X(9).
130     02  SCORE-1                PICTURE 999.
140     02  SCORE-2                PICTURE 999.
150     02  SCORE-3                PICTURE 999.
160     02  FILLER                 PICTURE X(31).
```

Explanation of the Example

Line 010 gives the name of the division: DATA DIVISION.

Line 020 gives the name of the section: FILE SECTION.

Line 030 contains the letters *FD*, which stand for *F*ile *D*escription. This line gives the name which was assigned to the input file in the ENVIRONMENT DIVISION. In this problem, the name SCORES-FILE was chosen for the file of input cards containing the data to be processed.

Lines 040 through 070 are statements that give the compiler general information about the input file. The COBOL statements required are different for different computers. Some compilers do not require the statements in Lines 040 and 050.

Line 040, RECORDING MODE IS F, is a required statement when an IBM System/360 is being used. This statement describes the recording mode of the input record. The input record, PUNCHED-CARD, contains a *f*ixed number of columns (80). (If magnetic tape or some other input medium is used, the recording mode or length may not be *f*ixed.)

Line 050 gives the length of the input record, 80 characters (columns) each. This statement is required by an IBM System/360 compiler.

Line 060 gives the required statement regarding the use of labels. None are used with punched cards, as the statement shows.

Line 070 gives the name assigned by the programmer to each record in the input file. In this problem, the name assigned to each record is PUNCHED-CARD.

Line 080 01 is a heading that restates the name assigned to the data record, PUNCHED-CARD. (The 01, which appears before the data record name, is a level number of the first order and will be explained later.)

Line 090 02 gives the name invented by the programmer for the first data field in the record. In addition, this statement describes the data that will appear in the field. (The 02, which appears before the first field name, is a level number of the second order and will be explained later.)

Line 100 02 indicates that there are 10 unused columns following the name field on the data card. The word *FILLER* describes columns or spaces that are not used.

Line 110 02 gives the name of the second data field on the card, CLASS-CODE, and describes the data in the field.

Line 120 02 shows that there are 9 more unused columns following the CLASS-CODE field.

Line 130 02 has the name of the third data field on the card, SCORE-1, and a description of the data in the field.

Line 140 02 gives the name of the fourth data field on the card, SCORE-2, and a description of the data in that field.

Line 150 02 gives the name of the fifth data field on the card, SCORE-3, and a description of that field.

Line 160 02 indicates that there are 31 columns on the card following SCORE-3 that are not used.

Note that the sum of the fields described in Lines 090–160 equals 80, which is the length of the data record, PUNCHED-CARD. The entire record must be described in COBOL even if part of it contains blanks or is not used.

Figure 12-10 shows the input statements in the FILE SECTION of the DATA DIVISION of the COBOL program for solving Problem 1.

Level numbers

The DATA DIVISION does not have paragraphs as do the other three divisions of a COBOL program. The DATA DIVISION has level numbers instead. *Level numbers* perform the same function in a program that Roman and Arabic numerals do in an outline. Level numbers show the relationship of the data names in a program. They are used in the DATA DIVISION only.

The division name and section are always written at the A-Margin. Because the file is the broadest classification of data, it is given a special

```
003010 DATA DIVISION.
   020 FILE SECTION.
   030 FD  SCORES-FILE
   040     RECORDING MODE IS F
   050     RECORD CONTAINS 80 CHARACTERS
   060     LABEL RECORDS ARE OMITTED
   070     DATA RECORD IS PUNCHED-CARD.
   080 01  PUNCHED-CARD.
   090     02  STUDENT-NAME                PICTURE A(20).
   100     02  FILLER                      PICTURE X(10).
   110     02  CLASS-CODE                  PICTURE 9.
   120     02  FILLER                      PICTURE X(9).
   130     02  SCORE-1                     PICTURE 999.
   140     02  SCORE-2                     PICTURE 999.
   150     02  SCORE-3                     PICTURE 999.
   160     02  FILLER                      PICTURE X(31).
```

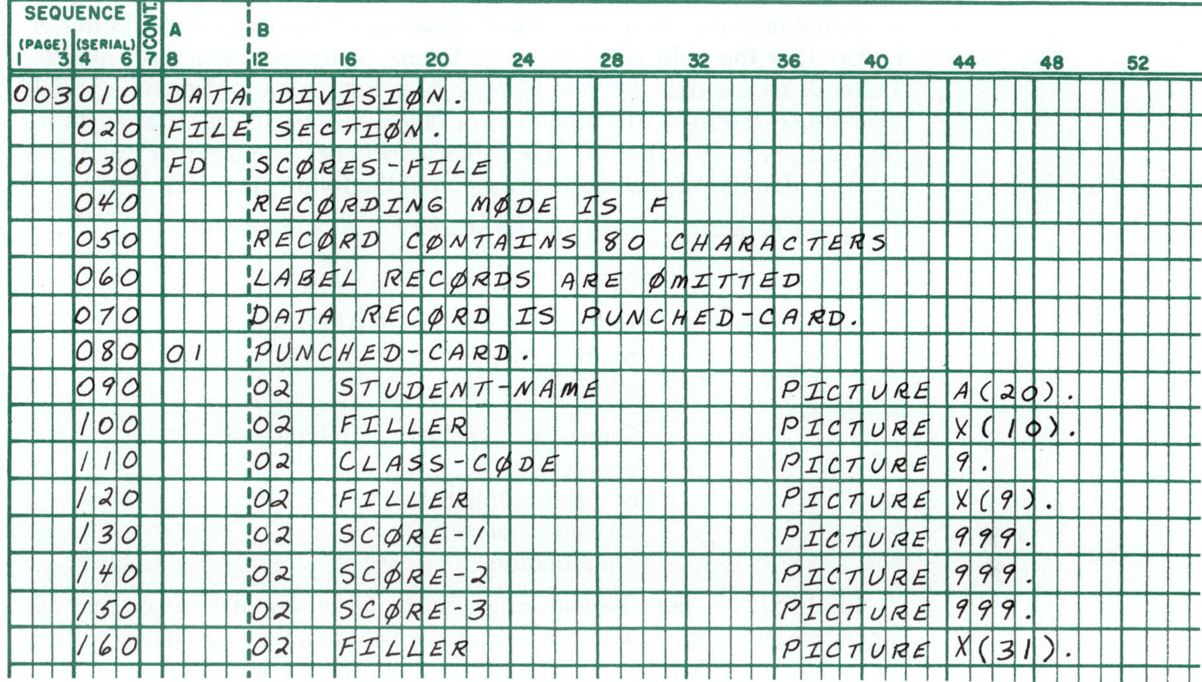

Figure 12-10. *Above are the input statements in the FILE SECTION of the DATA DIVISION.*

level indicator, FD, to place it at a primary level. The FD (*F*ile *D*escription) is also written at the A-Margin.

The record is at the next level of importance, and it is always assigned the level number 01. All the record descriptions are divided into levels according to their importance. Since the level 01 always refers to a record, the level 02 refers to a field within that record. The level 03 refers to an item within a field.

In the example of the partial program just shown, Level number 01 designates PUNCHED-CARD as the record (Line 080). Level 01 (PUNCHED-CARD) begins at the A-Margin. Level number 02 then names the different fields in the record (STUDENT-NAME, CLASS-CODE, etc.). Level 02 begins at the B-Margin, Column 12. If a field were subdivided; for example, the STUDENT-NAME field into last name and first name, these subdivisions would be shown by Level 03 and would be indented to Column 16.

Level numbers will also be used to designate the records and fields in the output statements and in the WORKING-STORAGE SECTION of the DATA DIVISION.

PICTURE clauses

You learned that PICTURE clauses indicate the number of characters in each field. These clauses also tell the compiler what type of information is contained in each field. PICTURE clauses are used only in the DATA DIVISION.

Number 9 means that a field is made up of numbers only. Letter A means that the field is made up of letters of the alphabet and spaces. Letter X means that the field is made of a combination of digits, special characters, letters of the alphabet, or blank spaces. If you refer again to Figure 12-9, p. 293, the PICTURE clauses will become clear to you.

The identifying characters are given in the following table:

Character	*Data Representation*	*Classification*
9	Numeric digits	Numeric
A	Letters of the alphabet with or without spaces	Alphabetic
X	Digits, special characters, letters of the alphabet, spaces, or any combination	Alphanumeric

In BASIC, a field having letters and spaces would be classified as alphanumeric only. In COBOL, the same field can be classified as either alphabetic or alphanumeric. The programmer has a choice in the matter.

Note that in Figure 12-10 all the PICTURE clauses begin at Column 36. The program was written in this manner in order to align all the PICTURE clauses on the program sheet. This makes the program easier to read. It also makes it easier for the programmer to add the characters in the PICTURE clauses to be sure they add up to 80 for the input record and 132 for the output record (printed line).

If the programmer decides to write the PICTURE clause just following the field name, there must be at least one space allowed between the two. Also, there is always one space between the word PICTURE and the rest of the clause. There must be no intervening spaces in the descriptive part of the PICTURE clause. For example, on Line 090, it is written PICTURE A(20). The parentheses are required. The number inside the parentheses gives the number of columns in the field. Note also that the PICTURE clause always ends with a period.

Note that the PICTURE clause for CLASS-CODE in Line 110 is PICTURE 9. Because there is only one character in CLASS-CODE, it is easier to write the 9 by itself. However, if the PICTURE clause is used to describe a larger numeric field, it can be written differently. For a student number field, for example, the PICTURE clause can be either 9(4) or 9999. They both mean the same. Parentheses are often used with the longer fields.

Rules for writing statements in the DATA DIVISION

Refer again to Figure 12-10, p. 296. Only the statements presenting new problems will be explained. Apply what you learned in the discussion of statements in the first two divisions.

Line 010:

The division name starts at the A-Margin and ends with a period.

Line 020:

The section name (FILE SECTION) also starts at the A-Margin and ends with a period.

The five lines that follow contain the five COBOL statements which name and describe the general nature of the input file. Only the last statement in the FD (Line 070) must end with a period.

Line 030:

The FD (*F*ile *D*escription) starts at the A-Margin. Note, however, that SCORES-FILE, the name assigned to the input file, starts at the B-Margin.

Lines 040 through 070:

The four statements describing the general nature of the input file, including the name assigned to the record within that file (PUNCHED-CARD) all start at the B-Margin. The period at the end of the statements (Line 070) is required. Some COBOL programmers insert commas or semicolons at the end of the descriptive statements, Lines 040–060. Because these commas or semicolons are not required, they will not be used in this text, in order to make the programs simple.

Line 080:

The level number 01 has been given to the input record (PUNCHED-CARD). The 01 is written at the A-Margin. PUNCHED-CARD is written at the B-Margin and must be followed by a period. Note that the name of the input record is first mentioned in Line 070 and that it is restated on Line 080. The ending period is required by the COBOL compiler for the Level 01 statements in the DATA DIVISION, because the 01 statements name the records.

Lines 090 through 160:

These lines describe each field in the punched card. These fields are subdivisions of the record. Therefore, the statements describing the fields are indented to the B-Margin because they are Level 02 statements. If there were any Level 03 numbers in this program, they would have been started at Column 16. Note that the codes, such as A(20), are written without intervening spaces. The parentheses are required. Note, also, that the period for the entire line follows the PICTURE clause. This period is required.

Lines 100, 120, and 160 describe the FILLER with the Code X. In this example, there are 10 columns not used between the first and second data fields. There are 9 not used between the second and third data fields. There are 31 not used at the end of the data card. The sum of all used and unused (FILLER) columns should equal 80, the length of the input record. Refer again to Figure 12-9, p. 293. See the relationship between the card format and the PICTURE statements in Lines 090 through 160 of the input statements in the FILE SECTION of the DATA DIVISION.

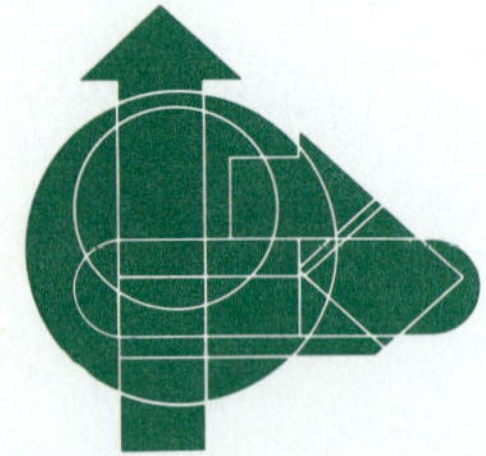

REVIEW QUESTIONS

1. Describe a file, a record, and a field in reference to a deck of punched cards.
2. Describe a file, a record, and a field in reference to a printed report.
3. What information must be included in the input statements of the DATA DIVISION?
4. For what types of information in the input statements of the DATA DIVISION must the programmer invent names?
5. Where is the programmer-invented name for the input file mentioned the first time in a COBOL program?
6. Assume that you have a deck of cards in which have been punched each customer's name and the sales amount representing the total cost of an order. Provide a name for the deck of cards, for a single card, and for each of the two data fields on the card. Which is the file? The record? The field?
7. Is the level number 01 associated with a file? A record? A field?
8. Is the level number 02 associated with a file? A record? A field?
9. What are PICTURE clauses used to describe: Files? Records? Fields?
10. What format requirements must be observed in writing a PICTURE clause?
11. Explain the meaning of the following three statements in the input portion of the DATA DIVISION:

```
01 PUNCHED CARD.
   02  FILLER                    PICTURE X(60).
   02  CUSTOMER-NAME             PICTURE A(20).
```

12. What is the meaning of Number 9 in a PICTURE clause? Letter A? Letter X?

Output statements in the DATA DIVISION

The output statements of the DATA DIVISION will now be explained. Input and output statements really appear together in the FILE SECTION of the DATA DIVISION. They have been separated in this chapter to make learning easier. It is important to remember that input statements describe a file of punched card records. Output statements describe a printed report file. The input record is a single punched card. The output record is a single line on the printed report. The input field is a field on the punched card. The output field is a specific item on a line of the printed report.

Required output statements. The output statements in the DATA DIVISION do not repeat the name of the division and the sections. This material has been covered in the input statements. The output statements must give the following information:

(1) Name that the programmer invents for each output file produced as a result of the program and statements describing the nature of the output file. The name used here for the file must be the same as that used in the ENVIRONMENT DIVISION. The *f*ile *d*escription statements are similar to those shown in the input statements, Lines 030–070, Figure 12-10.

(2) Restatement of the name that the programmer has invented for each record in the output file and one or more statements that describe the format of each record.

Inventing names for addresses of output data. All output data referred to in the same program must be named in the DATA DIVISION. The names assigned to the data being produced must be invented by the programmer. Once named in the DATA DIVISION, however, they must be referred to in exactly the same way every time they are used in the program. They cannot be misspelled, changed, or abbreviated. Otherwise, the compiler becomes confused, just as you might if there were two or more students in your class with exactly the same name.

If the same name is used for more than one item of data within a program, the compiler detects this error and the computer stops. The error must then be corrected before the COBOL program can be translated into an object program.

The programmer does not use the same name for an output field that has been used for an input field. Quite often the word PRINT is added to a name. For example, STUDENT-NAME in input would be changed to STUDENT-NAME-PRINT in the output description. This will be discussed in greater detail later in this chapter.

Example

The output statements of the DATA DIVISION includes Line 170–220, as follows:

```
170 FD  PRINTED-REPORT-FILE
180     RECORDING MODE IS F
190     RECORD CONTAINS 132 CHARACTERS
200     LABEL RECORDS ARE OMITTED
210     DATA RECORD IS PRINT-LINE.
220 01  PRINT-LINE                 PICTURE X(132).
```

Explanation of the example

Line 170 contains the letters FD (*F*ile *D*escription). This line gives the name that was assigned to the output file in the ENVIRONMENT DIVISION. The name PRINTED-REPORT-FILE was chosen.

Lines 180–210 correspond to Lines 30–70 of the input section, p. 297. They give the compiler general information. Line 180 states that the recording mode is *f*ixed. (A printed report can have only as many characters on a line as are built into the printer. The line length may be different from printer to printer. It is always fixed, however. In all examples in this text, a printer with a 132-space print line will be used with the COBOL programs.)

Line 190 states that the output record has 132 characters. Line 200 states that no labels are used. Line 210 gives the name that the programmer has chosen for the output data record, which is PRINT-LINE.

Note that the FD begins at the A-Margin of Line 170 and does not have a period until the end of the description on Line 210.

Line 220 repeats the name of the data record, PRINT-LINE, and describes the contents of the line. The statement is written at the 01 level because a record is always described at the 01 level. The 01 level statements must have periods at the end.

The PICTURE clause that describes PRINT-LINE is PICTURE X(132). The X tells the computer that the 132 characters are alphanumeric. Remember that on p. 298 you learned that alphanumeric data can consist of digits, special characters, letters of the alphabet, spaces, or any combination of these. Therefore, the description covers anything that could possibly be printed on a line in the report. Figure 12-11 shows the entire FILE SECTION of the DATA DIVISION.

```
SEQUENCE
(PAGE)(SERIAL) CONT. A   B
1    3 4    6  7     8   12  16  20  24  28  32  36  40  44  48  52
003010  DATA DIVISIØN.
   020  FILE SECTIØN.
   030  FD  SCØRES-FILE
   040      RECØRDING MØDE IS F
   050      RECØRD CØNTAINS 80 CHARACTERS
   060      LABEL RECØRDS ARE ØMITTED
   070      DATA RECØRD IS PUNCHED-CARD.
   080  01  PUNCHED-CARD.                                    ┐
   090      02  STUDENT-NAME            PICTURE A(20).       │
   100      02  FILLER                  PICTURE X(10).       │
   110      02  CLASS-CØDE              PICTURE 9.           │
   120      02  FILLER                  PICTURE X(9).        │ Input
   130      02  SCØRE-1                 PICTURE 999.         │ Record
   140      02  SCØRE-2                 PICTURE 999.         │
   150      02  SCØRE-3                 PICTURE 999.         │
   160      02  FILLER                  PICTURE X(31).       ┘
   170  FD  PRINTED-REPØRT-FILE
   180      RECØRDING MØDE IS F
   190      RECØRD CØNTAINS 132 CHARACTERS
   200      LABEL RECØRDS ARE ØMITTED
   210      DATA RECØRD IS PRINT-LINE.
   220  01  PRINT-LINE                  PICTURE X(132).        Output Record
```

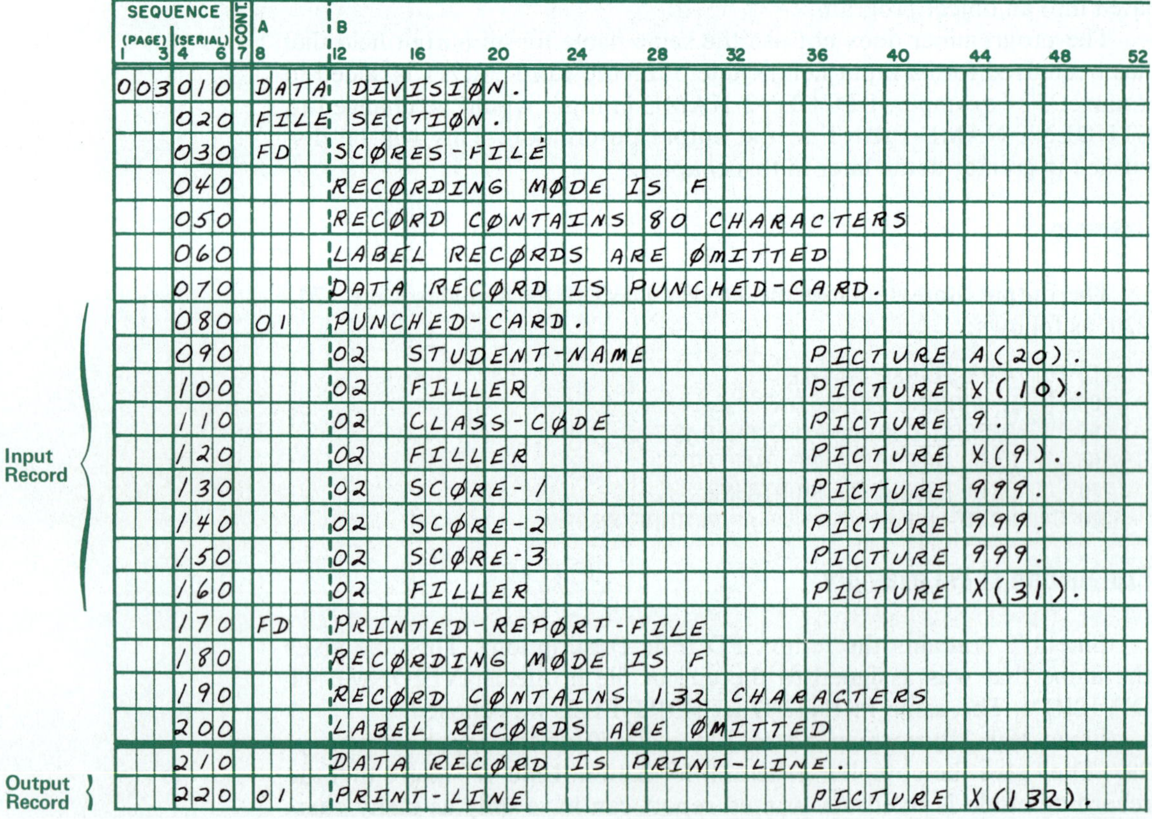

Figure 12-11. *Above is the entire FILE SECTION of the DATA DIVISION for the program to solve Problem 1.*

Note that Lines 080–160 describe the input record, PUNCHED-CARD, in detail. However, the output record, PRINT-LINE, has been described broadly with only one line. The individual fields in PRINT-LINE could be described in the FILE SECTION in detail, but it is easier to describe them with a "dummy" line, X(132), and to give the detailed description in the WORKING-STORAGE SECTION of the DATA DIVISION. This section will be described next.

Purpose of the WORKING-STORAGE SECTION of the DATA DIVISION

The *WORKING-STORAGE SECTION* is used to describe temporary storage areas for computer results or other information developed during processing. Therefore, that section is used to provide working areas in memory for items not described in the FDs in the FILE SECTION. In this problem, the WORKING-STORAGE SECTION will be used to describe the print line and each field on it. Other uses for the WORKING-STORAGE SECTION will be explained in Chapter 13.

WORKING-STORAGE SECTION used for line descriptions

Printed reports often have titles and column headings that make them easier to read and understand. Whenever many different lines are used, such as heading lines and total lines, each line must be described as a different record in the WORKING-STORAGE SECTION. The different print lines (records) are described in the WORKING-STORAGE SECTION at the 01 level. Then, all 132 characters on a single line of print are moved from WORKING-STORAGE to PRINT-LINE at the same time.

Although only one print line is required in Problem 1, the WORKING-STORAGE SECTION will be used here because it will be needed in all the problems in Chapter 13. Also, this is the way in which most COBOL programs are written.

The programmer-invented name for the output record, PRINT-LINE, describes a "dummy" record in the FILE SECTION. The broad description, PICTURE X(132), on Line 220, tells the computer to reserve 132 locations for any type of data.

In COBOL, only one name may be used for the input data record and only one name for the output data record. Therefore, it must be emphasized that before printing can take place, each line to be printed must first be moved out of WORKING-STORAGE to the area previously described as PRINT-LINE in the FILE SECTION. PRINT-LINE is the only output record name that the compiler will recognize because it is the name given in the record description on Line 210 (DATA RECORD IS PRINT-LINE.).

SCORES-LINE *is not the name of the output record*. It is the name of a detail line that is being described in WORKING-STORAGE. A *detail line* in COBOL is the name of a line described in WORKING-STORAGE that will be moved later to the address of the output record that was described in the FILE SECTION of the DATA DIVISION. In other words, SCORES-LINE must be moved to PRINT-LINE before printing can take place.

Format of the printed report for Problem 1. The printed report required as output is described on a printer spacing chart in Figure 12-12. The report is to be single-spaced. This is shown by the fact that the first two horizontal rows of Xs are not separated by a space. Vertical spacing will be discussed in detail in the next chapter. In COBOL, the reports will be single-spaced unless the computer is instructed otherwise.

SCORES

PEREZ

PRINTER SPACING CHART

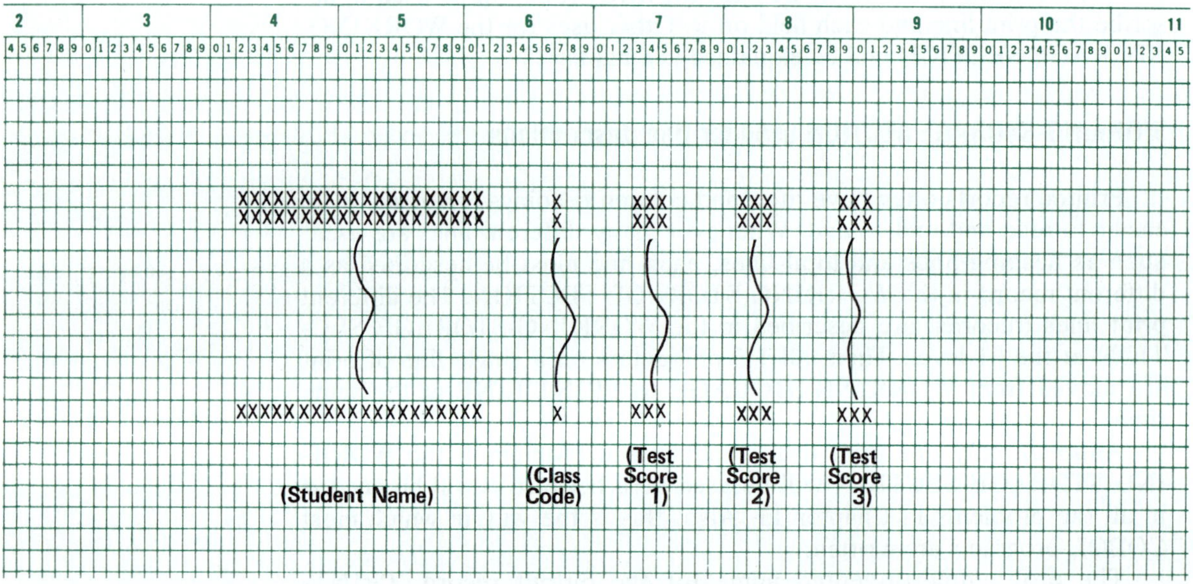

Figure 12-12. *Part of a printer spacing chart is shown.*

Designing a line of print. The horizontal position of the information on a print line is figured mathematically. In this problem, the report is to be centered on a 132-space line. The entire printer spacing chart is too large to be shown in Figure 12-12. The large numbers at the top of the chart stand for twenties, thirties, forties, etc. You can see from the chart that the first printing position used is Number 42.

Five columns of information will be printed. Five blank spaces will appear between each printed column. The number of spaces in each margin is figured by counting the total number of print positions that are needed on the line for the data. In this problem the fields require the following number of positions:

Field Name	*No. of Positions*
Student Name	20
Spaces	5
Class Code	1
Spaces	5
Test Score 1	3
Spaces	5
Test Score 2	3
Spaces	5
Test Score 3	3
	50 Total positions needed

When the 50 positions needed are subtracted from the 132 spaces in the print line, there are 82 spaces left, to be divided between the two margins. In this problem, 41 spaces are allowed in the left and the right margins (132 − 50 = 82 ÷ 2 = 41).

The first 41 spaces will be in the left margin. The name will be printed in 42–61 (20 positions). The five positions, 62–66, will be left blank. The class code will be printed in 67, followed by five more spaces (68–72). The first test score will be printed in 73–75 (three spaces). The next five positions (76–80) are blank. The second test score will be printed in 81–83. The next five positions (84–88) are blank. The third test score will be printed in 89–91. The remaining 41 positions (92–132) will be the right margin and will be blank.

Example

The following example is for the WORKING-STORAGE SECTION of Problem 1. The output format for the report was shown in Figure 12-12.

```
004 010 WORKING-STORAGE SECTION.
    020 01  SCORES-LINE.
    030     02  FILLER                   PICTURE X(41).
    040     02  STUDENT-NAME-PRINT       PICTURE A(20).
    050     02  FILLER                   PICTURE X(5).
    060     02  CLASS-CODE-PRINT         PICTURE 9.
    070     02  FILLER                   PICTURE X(5).
    080     02  SCORE-1-PRINT            PICTURE 999.
    090     02  FILLER                   PICTURE X(5).
    100     02  SCORE-2-PRINT            PICTURE 999.
    110     02  FILLER                   PICTURE X(5).
    120     02  SCORE-3-PRINT            PICTURE 999.
    130     02  FILLER                   PICTURE X(41).
```

Explanation of the example

Line 010 gives the name of the section: WORKING-STORAGE SECTION. The 004 shows that a new program sheet has been started. With a new page, the programmer will be able to see all the PICTURE clauses at one time. The characters will be easier to count.

Line 020 gives the name of the record, SCORES-LINE. This record is described at the 01 level. The 01 level statements must have periods.

All the other statements in the WORKING-STORAGE SECTION describe the fields in SCORES-LINE. The number of characters in these fields must add up to 132, the length of the print line. This entire line will be moved to the area described as PRINT-LINE (Line 220 of Figure 12-11) when the proper order is written in the PROCEDURE DIVISION.

The fields in the record are described at the 02 level. The 02 level statements have PICTURE clauses. The periods appear at the end of PICTURE clauses. Names must be invented for each output file, record, and field. These names must be different from those given to similar data in the input descriptions. Note that the word PRINT has been added to the name for each field. STUDENT-NAME in the input description has been changed to STUDENT-NAME-PRINT. CLASS-CODE has been changed to CLASS-CODE-PRINT. SCORE-1 has been changed to SCORE-1-PRINT.

Lines 030 and 130 describe the blank margins with the PICTURE clause X(41). Line 040 02 describes the student name field, STUDENT-NAME-PRINT, with a PICTURE clause of PICTURE A(20). This tells the compiler that there are 20 letters of the alphabet in that field. Lines 050, 070, and 090 have the descriptions PICTURE X(5). These statements describe the blank spaces between columns shown in Figure 12-12.

Line 060 02, CLASS-CODE-PRINT has a PICTURE clause, PICTURE 9. This shows that one position will be used by a number.

Lines 080, 100, and 120 describe the three test scores, PICTURE 999. This allows room for three numbers for each of the three test scores on the line (SCORE-1-PRINT, SCORE-2-PRINT, and SCORE-3-PRINT).

Figure 12-13 shows the entire DATA DIVISION for Problem 1 with the WORKING-STORAGE SECTION. Note that each of the five input fields shown on Lines 003 090, 110, 130, 140, and 150 have been described in WORKING-STORAGE on the detail line, SCORES-LINE. See Lines 004 040, 060, 080, 100, and 120. Note also that the word PRINT has been added to the data names because they represent output descriptions.

The record description for SCORES-LINE begins on Line 004 020. When the order, MOVE SCORES-LINE TO PRINT-LINE is given in the PROCEDURE DIVISION, everything described in Lines 004 020 through 130 will be moved to the area in print described as PRINT-LINE on Line 003 220.

```
SEQUENCE      A    B
(PAGE)(SERIAL)
1   3 4   6 7 8   12  16  20  24  28  32  36  40  44  48

003010 DATA DIVISIØN.
   020 FILE SECTIØN.
   030 FD  SCØRES-FILE
   040     RECØRDING MØDE IS F
   050     RECØRD CØNTAINS 80 CHARACTERS
   060     LABEL RECØRDS ARE ØMITTED
   070     DATA RECØRD IS PUNCHED-CARD.
   080 01  PUNCHED-CARD.
   090     02  STUDENT-NAME                PICTURE A(20).
   100     02  FILLER                      PICTURE X(10).
   110     02  CLASS-CØDE                  PICTURE 9.
   120     02  FILLER                      PICTURE X(9).
   130     02  SCØRE-1                     PICTURE 999.
   140     02  SCØRE-2                     PICTURE 999.
   150     02  SCØRE-3                     PICTURE 999.
   160     02  FILLER                      PICTURE X(31).
   170 FD  PRINTED-REPØRT-FILE
   180     RECØRDING MØDE IS F
   190     RECØRD CØNTAINS 132 CHARACTERS
   200     LABEL RECØRDS ARE ØMITTED
   210     DATA RECØRD IS PRINT-LINE.
   220 01  PRINT-LINE                      PICTURE X(132).
004010 WØRKING-STØRAGE SECTIØN.
   020 01  SCØRES-LINE.
   030     02  FILLER                      PICTURE X(41).
   040     02  STUDENT-NAME-PRINT          PICTURE A(20).
   050     02  FILLER                      PICTURE X(5).
   060     02  CLASS-CØDE-PRINT            PICTURE 9.
   070     02  FILLER                      PICTURE X(5).
   080     02  SCØRE-1-PRINT               PICTURE 999.
   090     02  FILLER                      PICTURE X(5).
   100     02  SCØRE-2-PRINT               PICTURE 999.
   110     02  FILLER                      PICTURE X(5).
   120     02  SCØRE-3-PRINT               PICTURE 999.
   130     02  FILLER                      PICTURE X(41).
```

Figure 12-13. *DATA DIVISION of COBOL program for Problem 1 with WORKING-STORAGE SECTION. The proper MOVE command in the PROCEDURE DIVISION will cause the entire SCORES-LINE described in WORKING-STORAGE to be moved to the area called PRINT-LINE.*

Distinguishing files, records, and fields

Study Figure 12-13. Note that the entire printed report is the output file. A single line on the report is a record. A single item (column of print) is a field. The output file was named in the ENVIRONMENT DIVISION as PRINTED-REPORT-FILE. A record (line on the printed report) is named PRINT-LINE.

The names for the fields are not the same in the output description as they are in the input description. The compiler must have one name for the field read into the computer and another name for the same field when it is to be moved and printed. Any names that are different can be used. The method shown in Figure 12-13 is often used by programmers because the names are easier to remember.

Field	*Input Name*	*Output Name*
Student Name	STUDENT-NAME	STUDENT-NAME-PRINT
Class Code	CLASS-CODE	CLASS-CODE-PRINT
Test Score 1	SCORE-1	SCORE-1-PRINT
Test Score 2	SCORE-2	SCORE-2-PRINT
Test Score 3	SCORE-3	SCORE-3-PRINT

Note how much easier it is in COBOL than it is in BASIC to give to an address a name that can be easily associated with the data stored at that address.

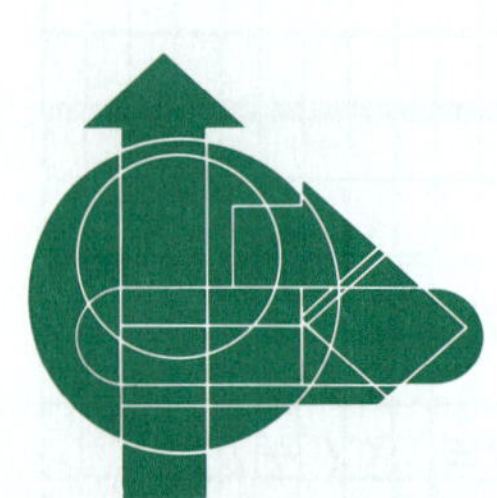

REVIEW QUESTIONS

1. What information must be included in the output statements of the DATA DIVISION?
2. What is the purpose of the WORKING-STORAGE SECTION?
3. Assume that you wish to produce an output printed report showing students' numbers in one column and the total test scores in a second column. Provide a name for the report, for a single line in the report, and for each of the two fields in the line.
4. Can the names assigned in Question 3 above be the same as those assigned to the corresponding input data? Why?
5. What is an easy way to assign names to the output fields that are different from those assigned to the corresponding input fields?
6. Explain the meaning of the following statement in the FILE SECTION of the DATA DIVISION:

```
220 01  PRINT-LINE              PICTURE X(132).
```

7. Explain the meaning of each of the following statements in the WORKING-STORAGE SECTION of the DATA DIVISION:

```
01      REPORT-LINE.
        02  FILLER                      PICTURE X(41).
        02  NAME-PRINT                  PICTURE A(18).
        02  FILLER                      PICTURE X(25).
        02  AMOUNT-SOLD-PRINT           PICTURE 9(7).
        02  FILLER                      PICTURE X(41).
```

8. When adding the characters in the PICTURE clauses in Question 7, to check for accuracy, what should the sum be? Why?
9. How is REPORT-LINE, described in Question 7, moved to PRINT-LINE before printing?
10. A punched-card record is read into the computer. A field called Amount Sold on the card is read into an address in computer memory that the programmer has named AMOUNT-SOLD. Why must this field be changed to AMOUNT-SOLD-PRINT or changed in some other way from the input description before it can be printed?

PROCEDURE DIVISION

The PROCEDURE DIVISION is the fourth and final division in a COBOL program. It contains the logic of the computer program. It gives the actual step-by-step commands the computer will follow in processing the data records. COBOL requires certain extra steps that are not needed in other programming languages. Many programmers do not include these extra steps in their flowcharts because the steps are not part of the actual logic to solve the problem. Those extra steps will be included in the flowcharts in this text, however. Using them will help the beginning programmer to write all the steps needed in the PROCEDURE DIVISION. Refer to the flowchart shown in Figure 12-14, p. 310. The extra steps are shaded to identify them more clearly. The symbols are also numbered in order to make the following explanation easier. The symbols are not normally numbered.

Opening and closing files in COBOL

Symbol 2 indicates that there are certain "get ready" or "housekeeping" steps to be taken at the beginning of a COBOL program. The symbol in the flowchart is a process symbol. It simply reminds the programmer to write a statement in the program to open the input and output files. This process is an operation that causes the input and output devices to be turned on.

Symbol No. 10, a process symbol, shows that there are like steps needed at the end of a COBOL program. This time, the operation is to close the two files. This symbol in the flowchart is a reminder to the programmer to write the statement needed to close the files. This operation causes the input and output devices to be turned off.

Clearing storage in COBOL

In Chapter 9, you learned that many computer programming languages require the programmer to write instructions for clearing work areas for computations in the computer. One type of clear instruction is for clearing work areas in the computer for computations. Zeros are used to erase previously recorded data. This clearing concept will be described in the next chapter.

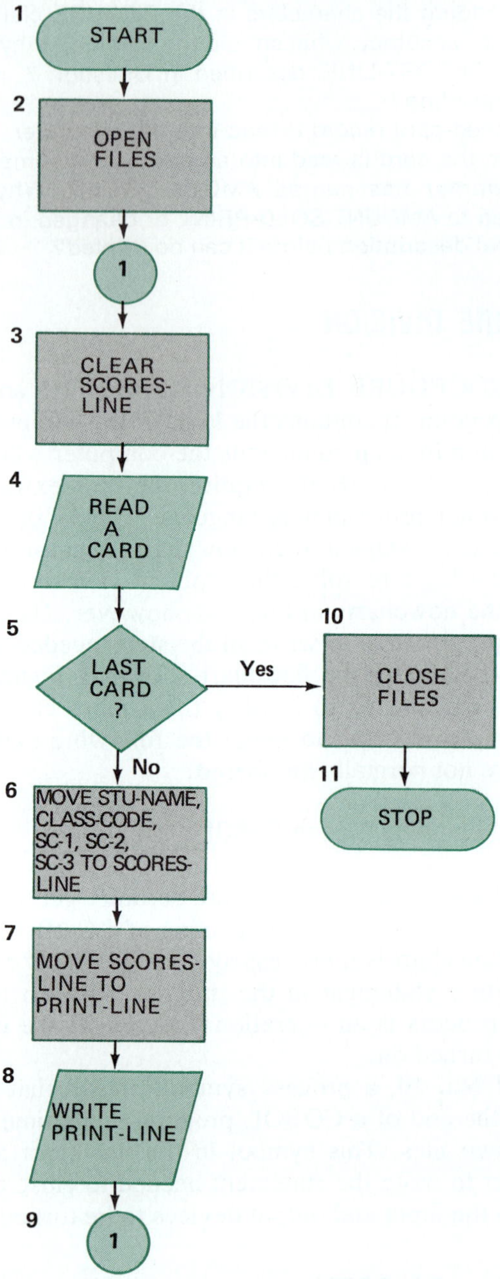

Figure 12-14. *Above is the flowchart for the PROCEDURE DIVISION of the program for solving PROBLEM 1.*

You also learned that there is another type of clear instruction. This is an order to clear old data from a storage location in the print area of the computer in order to make room for new data. This order is needed in COBOL. Old data must be erased from any output area before new data are recorded. One way in which this clearing can be done is by writing an instruction in the PROCEDURE DIVISION to MOVE SPACES TO SCORES-LINE, thus causing spaces to be moved to the detail line (SCORES-LINE) previously described in the WORKING-STORAGE SECTION of the DATA DIVISION. Remember that work areas for calculations are cleared by zeros; print areas are cleared by spaces.

Flowchart logic for Problem 1

Upon examining Figure 12-14, observe that the loop is always back to CLEAR SCORES-LINE before a data card is read. All data from an old record are cleared from the detail line in WORKING-STORAGE before a new record is processed. It is easier to write this instruction first. If it is written last, there could be old data that would not be erased before the first data card is processed.

After storage is cleared, the data card is read (Symbol 4). If the last-card code is in the data card, the computer branches to the instruction to close files (10). The program is then ended (11).

If the last data card has not been read, the five fields are moved *individually* to the print area in WORKING-STORAGE named SCORES-LINE (6). Remember, SCORES-LINE is not the name of the output record. It is the name of a detail line that is being described in WORKING-STORAGE. This line must be moved out of WORKING-STORAGE to PRINT-LINE before it can be printed.

Symbol 7 indicates that the entire SCORES-LINE is moved to PRINT-LINE. Then, the order, WRITE PRINT-LINE causes the line to be printed on the report (8).

The connector, Symbol 9, has a 1 inside. It shows that there is a branch back to the instruction to clear SCORES-LINE of the data just printed. A new card is then read and processed. This procedure goes on until the last data card has been processed.

The conditional branch is shown in the decision symbol for the last-card test (5). The unconditional branch is made after a line has been printed (9). The computer is ordered to go back to the clear instruction (3). This unconditional branch sets up the loop in the program.

Now that the logic in the flowchart has been explained, you are ready to learn how to write the PROCEDURE DIVISION of a COBOL program.

Writing the PROCEDURE DIVISION in a COBOL program

As you already know, the PROCEDURE DIVISION contains the actual logic needed to solve the problem. The logic in this division will follow the logic in the flowchart, Figure 12-14.

Inventing paragraph names

Because COBOL is a near-English language, the sequences of the procedures can be broken up into paragraphs. The paragraphs, in turn, are made up of statements or sentences. However, in the COBOL PROCEDURE DIVISION, the first line of a paragraph is not indented. The paragraph is given a name by the programmer, which is called a *paragraph name*. In Figure 12-15, p. 315, START-JOB, DETAIL-PROCESSING, and END-OF-JOB are paragraph names.

These names cannot be on the list of reserved words, p. 317, unless two or more words are joined with hyphens. For example, DETAIL and PROCESSING are on the list, but DETAIL-PROCESSING is not. Each sentence will be explained later in this chapter. Note that each paragraph name begins at the A-Margin and ends with a period. Also, each of the sentences in a paragraph is indented to the B-Margin and ends with a period.

Now the advantage of COBOL over many programming languages becomes clear. Because of its English-like nature, the programmer can:

(1) Write instructions to go to any of the paragraph names in the PROCEDURE DIVISION. The paragraph names can describe the steps that are listed in the paragraphs.
(2) Give names to memory addresses that actually describe the data stored in those addresses. The use of names instead of abbreviations makes it easier to understand the logic in a COBOL program.

Required statements in the PROCEDURE DIVISION

The PROCEDURE DIVISION includes the following information:

(1) The name of the division: PROCEDURE DIVISION.
(2) A paragraph name for the opening steps in the program.
(3) The opening steps needed for "getting ready" the input and output files.
(4) One or more paragraph names (depending on the problem) for the processing steps needed to solve the problem.
(5) A list of the steps needed to solve the problem.
(6) A paragraph name for the closing steps in the program.
(7) The closing steps needed to end the program and stop the computer.

Example

The following statements solve Problem 1. Note how these statements parallel the flowchart shown in Figure 12-14, p. 310.

```
005 010 PROCEDURE DIVISION.
    020 START-JOB.
    030     OPEN INPUT SCORES-FILE.
    040     OPEN OUTPUT PRINTED-REPORT-FILE.
```

```
050 DETAIL-PROCESSING.
060     MOVE SPACES TO SCORE-LINE.
070     READ SCORES-FILE, AT END GO TO END-OF-JOB.
080     MOVE STUDENT-NAME TO STUDENT-NAME-PRINT.
090     MOVE CLASS-CODE TO CLASS-CODE-PRINT.
100     MOVE SCORE-1 TO SCORE-1-PRINT.
110     MOVE SCORE-2 TO SCORE-2-PRINT.
120     MOVE SCORE-3 TO SCORE-3-PRINT.
130     MOVE SCORES-LINE to PRINT-LINE.
140     WRITE PRINT-LINE.
150     GO TO DETAIL-PROCESSING.
160 END-OF-JOB.
170     CLOSE SCORES-FILE.
180     CLOSE PRINTED-REPORT-FILE.
190     STOP RUN.
```

Explanation of the example

Again, Line 010 gives the name of the division, PROCEDURE DIVISION.

Line 020 (START-JOB) is the paragraph name for the "get ready" or "housekeeping" steps in the program. A paragraph name is required as the first line after the division name in the PROCEDURE DIVISION. The name of the paragraph is invented by the programmer. It may, therefore, be any name desired as long as the name follows the rules of COBOL. Remember, when naming data or paragraphs in COBOL, that no reserved words can be used. The list of reserved words is on p. 317.

Line 030 opens the input file (SCORES-FILE). Line 040 opens the output file (PRINTED-REPORT-FILE). These statements are required. The OPEN statements identify which file(s) are to be used for input and output. The names of the files are those that were invented by the programmer for the ENVIRONMENT DIVISION and described in the DATA DIVISION. The underlines are used to show that these are required entries.

Line 050 gives the paragraph name (DETAIL-PROCESSING) for the processing steps needed to solve the problem. This paragraph name is needed in the program because the branch is always back to this name. The paragraph name is also invented by the programmer and can be any name desired. Descriptive names are recommended to help a reader to understand the steps described in the paragraph.

Line 060 clears the storage locations for printing by moving spaces (blanks) to the detail line in WORKING-STORAGE (SCORES-LINE).

Line 070 indicates that a card from SCORES-FILE is to be read. This line also tells the computer that after the last card has been processed, a branch is to be made to the paragraph name END-OF-JOB. This, of course, is the conditional branch because the closing steps will only be processed if the last card in SCORES-FILE has already been read. Line 070 combines the READ instruction with the last-card test.

The combination of READ and AT END make up a last-card test in COBOL. This statement orders the computer to read a card. If the card contains the last-card code, the computer is to branch to END-OF-JOB on Line 160.

Line 080 moves the data in the first field read from the card (STUDENT-NAME) to STUDENT-NAME-PRINT, the first data field on the detail line in WORKING-STORAGE. The detail line has been named SCORES-LINE in the WORKING-STORAGE SECTION of the DATA DIVISION.

Line 090 moves the data from the second field on the data card (CLASS-CODE) to the second data field on SCORES-LINE, which has been named CLASS-CODE-PRINT.

Lines 100–120 move the test scores from the remaining three fields on the data card to the proper fields on SCORES-LINE.

Note that each input data field was moved separately to the proper position on SCORES-LINE. Now, Line 130 moves the entire detail line (SCORES-LINE) at one time from WORKING-STORAGE to the output record, PRINT-LINE. Line 140 writes the entire line of data on a line of the printed report.

Line 150 orders the computer back to DETAIL-PROCESSING. This step sets up the loop that causes a new record to be processed. Spaces are again moved to SCORES-LINE to clear the data just printed from the last data card. You learned in Chapter 9 that when data are moved with a MOVE instruction, they are merely copied. That is why there must be a CLEAR instruction to erase the data copied from SCORES-LINE before new data can be entered there. The name of the paragraph (DETAIL-PROCESSING) was assigned by the programmer. GO TO are words on the COBOL reserved word list.

Line 160 establishes the paragraph name (END-OF-JOB). This name is for the closing steps of the program. A paragraph name is required because of the conditional branch statement that appears on Line 070 (AT END, GO TO END-OF-JOB). This paragraph name is also invented by the programmer. It must follow the usual COBOL rules. END-OF-JOB was chosen because it describes what is taking place in the paragraph. Line 170 closes the input file. Line 180 closes the output file. The word CLOSE is required in both statements. The words INPUT and OUTPUT are not used again because the two files were already named in Lines 030 and 040. The names of the files (SCORES-FILE and PRINTED-REPORT-FILE) must be used, however.

Line 190 stops the run. The job is completed. The COBOL term STOP RUN is required and cannot be changed.

You can easily see that it is in the PROCEDURE DIVISION that the step-by-step directions for processing the data cards in the COBOL program are given. Names are used to stand for memory addresses. The compiler translates the names to numeric addresses in computer memory. The paragraph name is used to identify the beginning of a new step or sequence of steps in the PROCEDURE DIVISION. The statements or sentences are the single steps in these sequences.

Format of statements in the PROCEDURE DIVISION

Figure 12-15 is the PROCEDURE DIVISION for the program to solve Problem 1. The following requirements pertain to the statements.

Lines 010, 020, 050, and 160:

The name of the division and the names of the paragraphs of the opening, processing, and closing steps of the program start at the A-Margin and end with a period.

Lines 030 and 040:

The statements that open the input and output files start at the B-Margin and end with a period.

Line 060 is a statement that clears the print area. The statement begins at the B-Margin and ends with a period.

Lines 070 through 150:

Each step of the program written to solve the problem starts at the B-Margin. Each statement is a sentence, so each statement ends with a period. A sentence might be so long that it is continued on other lines. If so, continued statements will start at the B-Margin (Column 12). Or, if desired, the continuation can be indented to Column 16.

Lines 170 through 190:

Each of the closing steps starts at the B-Margin. Each sentence, of course, ends with a period.

```
SEQUENCE     C  A   B
(PAGE)(SERIAL)O
1   3 4   6  7  8   12  16  20  24  28  32  36  40  44  48  52  56
005   010       PRØCEDURE DIVISIØN.
      020       START-JØB.
      030           ØPEN INPUT SCØRES-FILE.
      040           ØPEN ØUTPUT PRINTED-REPØRT-FILE.
      050       DETAIL-PRØCESSING.
      060           MØVE SPACES TØ SCØRES-LINE.
      070           READ SCØRES-FILE, AT END GØ TØ END-ØF-JØB.
      080           MØVE STUDENT-NAME TØ STUDENT-NAME-PRINT.
      090           MØVE CLASS-CØDE TØ CLASS-CØDE-PRINT.
      100           MØVE SCØRE-1 TØ SCØRE-1-PRINT.
      110           MØVE SCØRE-2 TØ SCØRE-2-PRINT.
      120           MØVE SCØRE-3 TØ SCØRE-3-PRINT.
      130           MØVE SCØRES-LINE TØ PRINT-LINE.
      140           WRITE PRINT-LINE.
      150           GØ TØ DETAIL-PROCESSING.
      160       END-ØF-JØB.
      170           CLØSE SCØRES-FILE.
      180           CLØSE PRINTED-REPØRT-FILE.
      190           STØP RUN.
```

Figure 12-15. *Above is the PROCEDURE DIVISION for the COBOL program to solve Problem 1.*

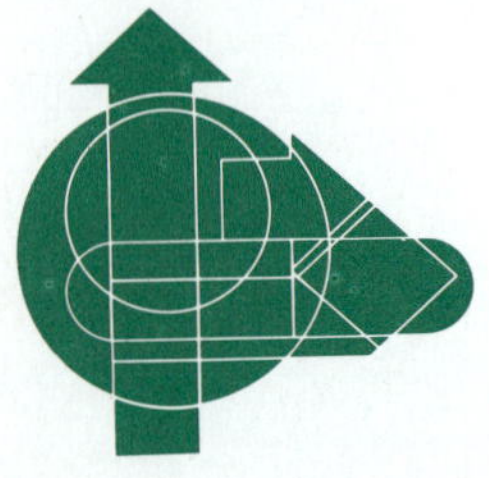

REVIEW QUESTIONS

1. What is the purpose of the PROCEDURE DIVISION?
2. How does the use of names make COBOL easier for the programmer than many other programming languages?
3. What information is included in the PROCEDURE DIVISION of a COBOL program?
4. What statements are included under the paragraph name for the opening or "get ready" steps in the program?
5. How can a print area be cleared in a COBOL program?
6. Why is the CLEAR instruction placed before the READ statement in the flowchart, Figure 12-4, p. 310?
7. What are the paragraph names in Figure 12-15, p. 315?
8. What is the order that causes the detail line to be moved out of WORKING-STORAGE to the print area? What is the order that causes the line to be printed?
9. What words combined with a READ statement cause a last-card test to be made?
10. What is the last statement in the PROCEDURE DIVISION? Is it the same statement in every COBOL program?

NAMES USED IN A COBOL PROGRAM

Each line of a COBOL source program is punched into a separate card. The computer reads each card. The COBOL program statements punched in the cards are then translated to machine-language statements by the compiler program, which is stored in the computer before the file of program cards is read. From the machine-language object program, the computer then processes the data cards prepared for a problem.

The COBOL names assigned to the data identify the addresses at which the data will be stored. Because COBOL is a near-English programming language, it is possible to give names to the data that describe the data and also identify the addresses. However, you must bear in mind that the names really identify the addresses, not the contents of the addresses.

Reserved COBOL words

A partial list of COBOL reserved words is given in Figure 12-16. Each word on this list has a very special meaning to the compiler and must be used in the prescribed manner every time. Some of these words are used in every program.

Note that many of the words that appear on the reserved word list are action verbs such as READ, WRITE, ADD, SUBTRACT, and MOVE. These words correspond to the operation codes in machine language or assembly language. Some of the other reserved words are used by the COBOL compiler as special control words. Many of the reserved words listed in Figure 12-16 have been used in the four divisions of the program to solve Problem 1. ASSIGN, DIVISION, ENVIRONMENT, FD, FILE-CONTROL, and FILLER are just a few.

ACCEPT
ACCESS
ACTUAL
ADD
ADVANCING
AFTER
ALL
ALPHABETIC
ALTER
ALTERNATE
AND
APPLY
ARE
AREA
AREAS
ASCENDING
ASSIGN
AT
AUTHOR

BEFORE
BEGINNING
BLANK
BLOCK
BY

CALL
CF
CH
CHANGED
CHARACTERS
CHECKING
CLOCK-UNITS
CLOSE
COBOL
CODE
COLUMN
COMMA
COMPUTATIONAL
COMPUTATIONAL-1
COMPUTATIONAL-2
COMPUTATIONAL-3
COMPUTE
CONFIGURATION
CONSOLE
CONTAINS
CONTROL
CONTROLS
COPY
CORRESPONDING
CREATING
CYCLES

DATA
DATE-COMPILED
DATE-WRITTEN
DE
DECIMAL-POINT
DECLARATIVES
DEPENDING
DESCENDING
DETAIL
DIRECT
DIRECT-ACCESS
DISPLAY
DISPLAY-ST
DIVIDE
DIVISION

ELSE
END
ENDING
ENTER
ENTRY
ENVIRONMENT
EQUAL
ERROR
EVERY
EXAMINE
EXHIBIT
EXIT

FD
FILE
FILES
FILE-CONTROL
FILE-LIMIT
FILLER
FINAL
FIRST
FOOTING
FOR
FORM-OVERFLOW
FROM

GENERATE
GIVING
GO
GREATER
GROUP

HEADING
HIGH-VALUE
HIGH-VALUES
HOLD

IBM-360
IDENTIFICATION
IF
IN
INCLUDE
INDEXED
INDICATE
INITIATE
INPUT
INPUT-OUTPUT
INSTALLATION
INTO
INVALID
I-O
I-O-CONTROL
IS

JUSTIFIED

KEY

LABEL
LABELS
LAST
LEADING
LESS
LINE
LINE-COUNTER
LINES
LINKAGE
LOCK
LOW-VALUE
LOW-VALUES

MODE
MORE-LABELS
MOVE
MULTIPLY

NAMED
NEGATIVE
NEXT
NO
NOT
NOTE
NUMERIC

OBJECT-COMPUTER
OCCURS
OF
OH
OMITTED
ON
OPEN
OR
ORGANIZATION
OTHERWISE
OUTPUT
OV
OVERFLOW

PAGE
PAGE-COUNTER
PERFORM
PF
PH
PICTURE
PLUS
POSITIVE
PRINT-SWITCH
PROCEDURE
PROCEED
PROCESS
PROCESSING
PROGRAM-ID
PROTECTION

QUOTE
QUOTES

RANDOM
RD
READ
READY
RECORD
RECORDING
RECORDS
REDEFINES
REEL
RELATIVE
RELEASE
REMARKS
REPLACING
REPORT
REPORTING
REPORTS
RERUN
RESERVE
RESET
RESTRICTED
RETURN
REVERSED
REWIND
REWRITE
RF
RH
RIGHT
ROUNDED
RUN

SA
SAME
SD
SEARCH
SECTION
SECURITY
SELECT
SENTENCE
SEQUENTIAL
SIZE
SORT
SOURCE
SOURCE-COMPUTER
SPACE
SPACES
SPECIAL-NAMES
STANDARD
STOP
SUBTRACT
SUM
SYMBOLIC
SYSIN
SYSOUT
SYSPUNCH

TALLY
TALLYING
TERMINATE
THAN
THEN
THRU
TIMES
TO
TRACE
TRACK-AREA
TRACKS
TRANSFORM
TRY
TYPE

UNIT
UNIT-RECORD
UNITS
UNTIL
UPON
USAGE
USE
USING
UTILITY

VALUE
VARYING

WHEN
WITH
WORKING-STORAGE
WRITE
WRITE-ONLY

ZERO
ZEROES
ZEROS

Figure 12-16. *Above is a partial list of COBOL reserved words.*

Required entries (names)

In all explanations of the four divisions of a COBOL program presented in this chapter, the required entries have been underlined as a teaching device. *Required entries* are words that must be used in every COBOL program. The names of the division and the sections are required. Examples are ENVIRONMENT DIVISION, CONFIGURATION SECTION, and INPUT-OUTPUT SECTION. Some others are SELECT, ASSIGN, and STOP RUN. All of these words appear on the list in Figure 12-16.

Programmer-invented Names

Generally, all words other than the reserved words are invented by the programmer. Any words can be invented as long as these words do not appear on the reserved word list and as long as the same word is always used throughout the program to stand for the same item of data. If a programmer-invented name has two or more words, there can be no blanks. The words must be joined by hyphens (SCORE-1-PRINT).

It is important that the programmer choose the names for paragraphs and data with care. Almost any name not on the reserved list may be used. However, common sense should suggest that a chosen name be meaningful. START-OF-JOB and END-OF-JOB are good examples. They explain themselves. The name chosen does not matter to the computer. It will process the program as long as the COBOL rules are followed. However, if the name means nothing, one of the main advantages of COBOL is lost — that of writing in English so that others can understand the program.

Certain rules must be followed in inventing names for a COBOL program. These names will be used by the computer to identify addresses in which data will be stored. The rules for inventing names for these addresses are as follows:

(1) The same name must be used in a program each time it stands for a certain heading, paragraph name, file, record, or field.
(2) Names appearing in the COBOL reserved list may not be used in exactly the same way in which they appear on the list.
(3) Letters of the alphabet, A through Z; digits, 0 through 9; and the hyphen may be used. However, a number or hyphen must not appear as the first character in the name. A hyphen also cannot appear as the last character.
(4) Names invented by the programmer may be made up of all alphabetic letters or a combination of alphabetic letters and figures. No name may consist of figures only or contain a space.

Study the following examples of programmer-invented names. Some meet the COBOL rules just stated; some do not.

STUDENT NAME	Incorrect	Space not allowed within name.
STUDENT-GRADE	Correct	Meets all rules.
TOTAL-$-SALES	Incorrect	Dollar sign not allowed.
-END-OF-JOB	Incorrect	Hyphen at beginning of name not allowed.
READ	Incorrect	READ is a COBOL reserved word.
AVERAGE-	Incorrect	Hyphen at end of name not allowed.
1234567	Incorrect	All numbers not allowed.
CLASS-4	Correct	Meets all rules.
PROCEDURE	Incorrect	PROCEDURE is a COBOL reserved word.
WORKING-STORAGE	Incorrect	WORKING-STORAGE is a COBOL reserved word.

PUNCTUATION RULES FOR COBOL

Punctuation marks appear in all COBOL programs. The following rules of punctuation must be followed at all times:

(1) At least one space must appear between two successive words (except programmer-invented words, which may be hyphened).
(2) A period, comma, or semicolon, when used, must immediately follow the word and must be followed in turn by at least one space.
(3) Commas and semicolons are used for readability only and are never required in a statement.
(4) Each division name, section name, and paragraph name must be ended with a period.
(5) Each FD must end with a period after the last word in the last line of the file description.
(6) Each statement or sentence in a paragraph must end with a period followed by a space.
(7) Each field description must end with a period at the end of the PICTURE clause. Several statements may be combined to form a sentence within the COBOL program. For example, you could write the following set of statements as a sentence: IF CLASSIFICATION IS EQUAL TO FRESHMAN-STUDENT, WRITE PRINT-LINE. ADD 1 TO SENIOR-STUDENT-COUNT.

COBOL PROGRAM FOR SOLVING PROBLEM 1

The explanation of the four divisions of COBOL programs in this chapter have been applied to Problem 1. Before presenting the entire COBOL program at this time, Problem 1 is restated.

(1) On hand is a file of cards having the names of students, their class codes, and three test scores for each student.
(2) Names of students are punched in Columns 1–20. Class codes are punched in Column 31. Test scores are punched as three digit fields in Columns 41–49. Test score 1 is in Columns 41–43. Test Score 2 is in Columns 44–46. Test score 3 is in Columns 47–49.
(3) A program is to be written that will cause a list of students to be printed. Each printed line in the report will contain the name of a

student, the class code, and the three test scores. The report will appear as a five-column report centered on a 132-space line. There will be five spaces between each column.

Complete program for solving Problem 1

The complete program to solve Problem 1 is shown in Figure 12-17. Each line of the program is punched into a separate card.

COBOL PROGRAM SHEET

System		Punching Instructions	Sheet 1 of 5
Program SCORES		Graphic: Ø Z I O 1 — Card Form # *	Identification SCORES (73–80)
Programmer PEREZ	Date 10/4/82	Punch: O Z I O I	

Alpha — ZERO — Numeric "ONE"

```
SEQUENCE  A   B
(PAGE)(SERIAL)
1    3 4   6 7 8   12  16  20  24  28  32  36  40  44  48  52  56  60  64  68  72

001010 IDENTIFICATIØN DIVISIØN.
   020 PRØGRAM-ID.
   030         'SCØRES'.
   040 AUTHØR.
   050         PEREZ.
   060 DATE-WRITTEN.
   070         ØCTØBER 4, 1982.

002010 ENVIRØNMENT DIVISIØN.
   020 CØNFIGURATIØN SECTIØN.
   030 SØURCE-CØMPUTER.
   040         IBM-360.
   050 ØBJECT-CØMPUTER.
   060         IBM-360.
   070 INPUT-ØUTPUT SECTIØN.
   080 FILE-CØNTRØL.
   090         SELECT SCØRES-FILE, ASSIGN TØ 'SYSIN' UNIT-RECØRD.
   100         SELECT PRINTED-REPØRT-FILE, ASSIGN TØ 'SYSØUT' UNIT-RECØRD.

003010 DATA DIVISIØN.
   020 FILE SECTIØN.
   030 FD  SCØRES-FILE
   040         RECØRDING MØDE IS F
   050         RECØRD CØNTAINS 80 CHARACTERS
   060         LABEL RECØRDS ARE ØMITTED
   070         DATA RECØRD IS PUNCHED-CARD.
   080 01  PUNCHED-CARD.
   090         02  STUDENT-NAME          PICTURE A(20).
   100         02  FILLER                PICTURE X(10).
   110         02  CLASS-CØDE            PICTURE 9.
   120         02  FILLER                PICTURE X(9).
   130         02  SCØRE-1               PICTURE 999.
   140         02  SCØRE-2               PICTURE 999.
   150         02  SCØRE-3               PICTURE 999.
   160         02  FILLER                PICTURE X(31).
```

Figure 12-17. *Above is the COBOL program to solve Problem 1.*

```
   170 FD  PRINTED-REPØRT-FILE
   180     RECØRDING MØDE IS F
   190     RECØRD CØNTAINS 132 CHARACTERS
   200     LABEL RECØRDS ARE ØMITTED
   210     DATA RECØRD IS PRINT-LINE.
   220 01  PRINT-LINE                      PICTURE X(132).

004010 WØRKING-STØRAGE SECTIØN.
   020 01  SCØRES-LINE.
   030     02  FILLER                      PICTURE X(41).
   040     02  STUDENT-NAME-PRINT          PICTURE A(20).
   050     02  FILLER                      PICTURE X(5).
   060     02  CLASS-CØDE-PRINT            PICTURE 9.
   070     02  FILLER                      PICTURE X(5).
   080     02  SCØRE-1-PRINT               PICTURE 999.
   090     02  FILLER                      PICTURE X(5).
   100     02  SCØRE-2-PRINT               PICTURE 999.
   110     02  FILLER                      PICTURE X(5).
   120     02  SCØRE-3-PRINT               PICTURE 999.
   130     02  FILLER                      PICTURE X(41).

005010 PRØCEDURE DIVISIØN.
   020 START-JØB.
   030     ØPEN INPUT SCØRES-FILE.
   040     ØPEN ØUTPUT PRINTED-REPØRT-FILE.
   050 DETAIL-PRØCESSING.
   060     MØVE SPACES TØ SCØRES-LINE.
   070     READ SCØRES-FILE, AT END GØ TØ END-ØF-JØB.
   080     MØVE STUDENT-NAME TØ STUDENT-NAME-PRINT.
   090     MØVE CLASS-CØDE TØ CLASS-CØDE-PRINT.
   100     MØVE SCØRE-1 TØ SCØRE-1-PRINT.
   110     MØVE SCØRE-2 TØ SCØRE-2-PRINT.
   120     MØVE SCØRE-3 TØ SCØRE-3-PRINT.
   130     MØVE SCØRES-LINE TØ PRINT-LINE.
   140     WRITE PRINT-LINE.
   150     GØ TØ DETAIL-PRØCESSING.
   160 END-ØF-JØB.
   170     CLØSE SCØRES-FILE.
   180     CLØSE PRINTED-REPØRT-FILE.
   190     STØP RUN.
```

Figure 12-17. *The COBOL program to solve Problem 1 is continued.*

If you study this program, you will note that the orders are given in the PROCEDURE DIVISION for the computer to act on the data described in the DATA DIVISION. These data, in turn, are contained in files that are named in the ENVIRONMENT DIVISION. These files are processed by hardware that is also named in the ENVIRONMENT DIVISION.

Two punched COBOL program cards are shown in Figure 12-18. The first card shows a single line from the DATA DIVISION. A single line in the PROCEDURE DIVISION is shown in the second card.

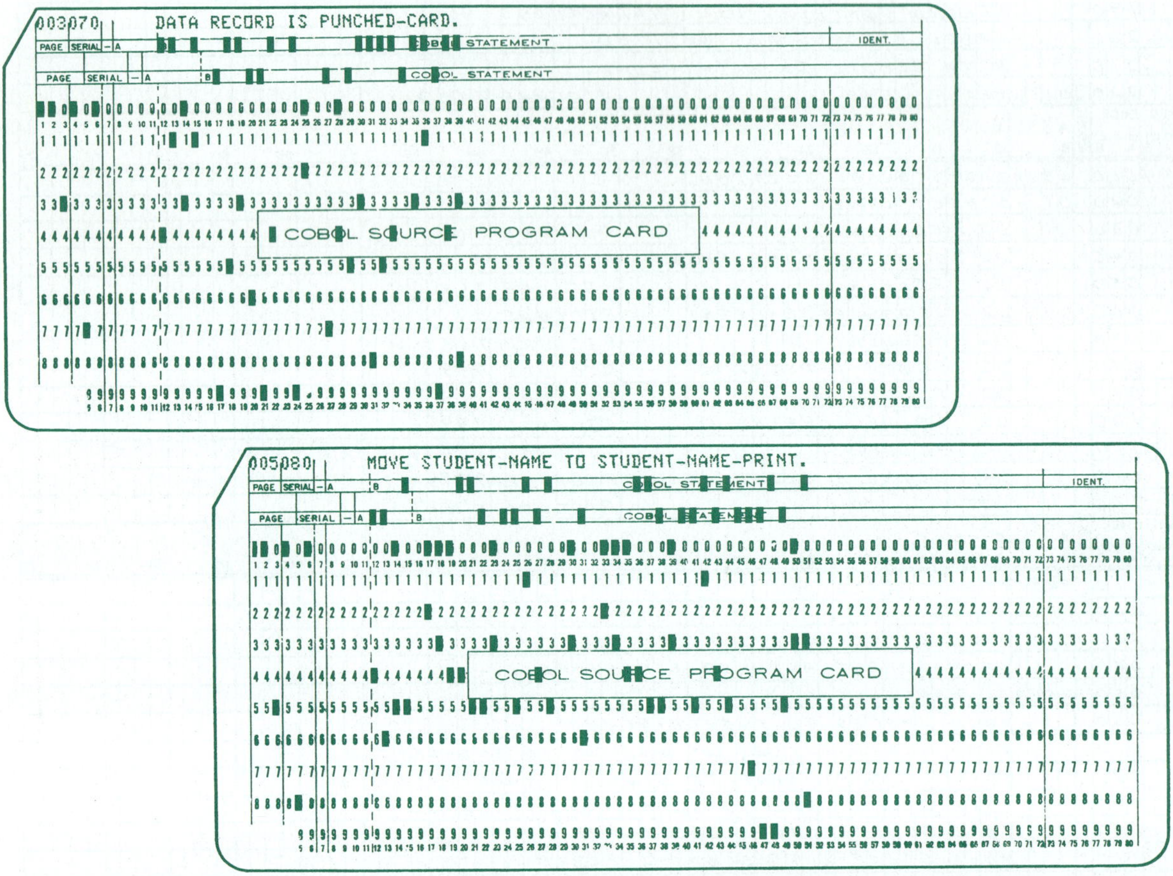

Figure 12-18. *Above are two sample COBOL program cards.*

You learned in Chapter 9 that after program cards are keypunched and verified, there must be testing and debugging of a program before it can be run with real data. The file of COBOL program cards is read into the computer along with any job control cards that may be needed. These job control instructions are not explained in this text because they change from computer to computer.

The compiler program causes the COBOL source program to be translated to a machine-language object program and prints a copy of the program at the same time. Next the file of data cards is read into the computer.

Shown in Figure 12-19 is a portion of a COBOL program as it would appear on printout. Figure 12-20 shows how the printed report would look for Problem 1.

```
005010 PROCEDURE DIVISION.
005020 START-JOB.
005030     OPEN INPUT SCORES-FILE.
005040     OPEN OUTPUT PRINTED-REPORT-FILE.
005050 DETAIL-PROCESSING.
005060     MOVE SPACES TO SCORES-LINE.
005070     READ SCORES-FILE, AT END GO TO END-OF-JOB.
005080     MOVE STUDENT-NAME TO STUDENT-NAME-PRINT.
005090     MOVE CLASS-CODE TO CLASS-CODE-PRINT.
005100     MOVE SCORE-1 TO SCORE-1-PRINT.
005110     MOVE SCORE-2 TO SCORE-2-PRINT.
005120     MOVE SCORE-3 TO SCORE-3-PRINT.
005130     MOVE SCORES-LINE TO PRINT-LINE.
005140     WRITE PRINT-LINE.
005150     GO TO DETAIL-PROCESSING.
005160 END-OF-JOB.
005170     CLOSE SCORES-FILE.
005180     CLOSE PRINTED-REPORT-FILE.
005190     STOP RUN.
```

Figure 12-19. *Above is a printout of the PROCEDURE DIVISION of the COBOL program to Solve Problem 1.*

DOROTHY FOSTER	4	92	89	96
STANLEY FRANKLIN	3	76	78	85
ANITA FRIEDMAN	4	89	91	92
TOBY GLANDORF	2	85	72	76
LUCY GONZALES	3	91	100	82
JOSEPH HAZLETON	2	77	72	73
CHRISTINA HILL	4	92	96	100
JOHN KATO	3	91	89	86
LAVERNE LYKINS	2	77	82	79
ANDERSON MEYER	2	88	92	94
TIEN SHEN	2	82	96	91
LOUISE SHUMARD	4	62	78	81
CATHERINE SMITH	4	78	69	72
MARY SILVERMAN	3	84	86	84
JONATHAN SPAULDING	2	81	79	83
MARCELLA SPIROS	3	69	78	82
JOSEPH STAUDENMEYER	1	69	78	81
LOUISE UNTHANK	2	76	71	70
BARRY VOLLMER	4	86	100	91
AGNES WAVERLY	4	72	76	73
MELANIE WILLIAMSON	3	88	89	92

Figure 12-20. *Above is a partial printout of the report resulting from the COBOL program to solve Problem 1.*

SUMMARY

COBOL is the name given to a symbolic language system for electronic computers. This system was developed by a committee representing the federal government, computer manufacturers, and private industry. The program statements are written in a near-English form.

Addresses for instructions and for data in storage are given names instead of numbers.

A COBOL program must be translated into machine language before the computer can process the program. The translation is handled by a compiler program obtained from the computer manufacturer. The compiler program is stored in the computer before the COBOL program is read into the machine.

Every COBOL program has four divisions, which must appear in the program. The IDENTIFICATION DIVISION gives the name of the division, title of the program, name of the programmer, and the date the program was written. The ENVIRONMENT DIVISION gives the name of the division and names of sections in the division. It also names the source and object computers as well as the names that identify the input and output media and devices to be used. In addition, the names the programmer assigns to the input and output files used in solving a problem are given in this division.

The DATA DIVISION includes the name of the division and the names the programmer gives to input and output files, records, and fields. Through PICTURE clauses the DATA DIVISION also shows how data are arranged on input cards and how the processed data will appear on printed reports.

The DATA DIVISION also may include a WORKING-STORAGE SECTION. In this section, the programmer describes temporary storage areas for computations. Also described are addresses for information developed during processing. Various printed lines can also be described in the WORKING-STORAGE SECTION.

The PROCEDURE DIVISION gives the name of the division, paragraph names, and sentences (statements) about the opening, processing, and closing steps in a program. This division gives the actual steps the computer will follow in processing the data records.

A COBOL program has some required names, some COBOL reserved words, and some names that are invented by the programmer. In inventing names, the programmer must use a number of rules. The punctuation and format of the statements are also subject to strict rules by COBOL.

When names are used properly and when the statements of a program are punched in the proper columns of program cards, a COBOL compiler can translate the source program into an object program that a computer can use in processing data.

REVIEW QUESTIONS

1. What is the purpose of the COBOL program for solving Problem 1?
2. May more than one line of the program be punched into a data card?
3. Which file of punched cards is fed into the computer first?
4. What is the second file of cards to be fed into the computer?
5. What is the purpose of the compiler program?

6. After the first two files of punched program cards are fed into the computer, what type of printed output is produced?
7. Which file of cards is fed into the computer last?
8. Which one of the four divisions of a COBOL program actually gives the step-by-step directions for processing the data cards in the program?
9. What are the three types of names used in a COBOL program?
10. Why must COBOL reserved words be used in a prescribed manner? Why must a programmer insert hyphens between words on the reserved word list if these words are to be programmer-invented names used in a program?

NEW TERMS

- COBOL
- CONFIGURATION SECTION
- DATA DIVISION
- ENVIRONMENT DIVISION
- FD
- FILLER
- IDENTIFICATION DIVISION
- Level numbers
- Object computer
- PICTURE clause
- PROCEDURE DIVISION
- Program ID
- Programmer-invented words
- Required entries
- Reserved words
- Source computer
- 'SYSIN'
- 'SYSOUT'
- WORKING-STORAGE SECTION

STUDY GUIDES

Complete Study Guide 12 by following the instructions in your STUDY GUIDES booklet.

PROJECTS

Complete Projects 12-1, 12-2, and 12-3 by following the instructions in your PROJECTS booklet.

13

COBOL APPLICATIONS

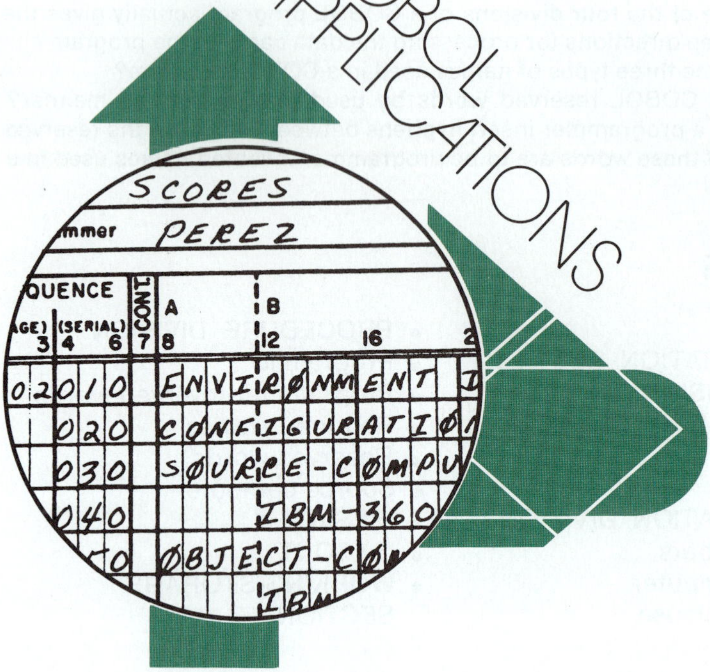

Most programs used in actual business situations are more complicated than that shown in the last chapter. However, almost all computer users want programs to perform simple listing operations like the one in Chapter 12. In fact, most programs are limited to very simple orders, such as READ, WRITE, CALCULATE, and basic decisions based upon the comparison of two values (fields of data).

What you have learned about COBOL up to this point will become the foundation on which will be added more commands until there is a fairly complete understanding of the basic COBOL language. Many of the required elements of a COBOL program have been explained in Chapter 12. These concepts will be reviewed as new programs are developed.

In this chapter the programs will be concerned with amounts as well as with lists. You will also learn about vertical spacing. New concepts will be presented as they are needed.

VARIABLES AND CONSTANTS

If you have studied the BASIC programming language, much of the following will be review.

Variables

A *variable* is an item of data that is not known in advance and which changes during the processing of a program. Most of the programmer-invented names for data fields in the first COBOL program have been variables because they represented student numbers and names that changed each time a new card was read.

The COBOL compiler uses programmer-invented names instead of numeric addresses to describe the locations in memory in which these variables will be stored. In the last chapter, STUDENT-NAME, CLASS-CODE, SCORE-1, SCORE-1-PRINT, etc. were all variables. Most of the programmer-invented names in the DATA DIVISION for fields on the punched card and on the printed line are variable names.

Variable names in COBOL have been used to represent addresses of numeric, alphabetic, and alphanumeric data fields. The numeric fields are described in the PICTURE clauses with 9s; the alphabetic fields, with As; and the alphanumeric fields with Xs.

Constants

A *constant* is a value that is known in advance and which does not change during the processing of a program. Constants, like variables, must be placed into the memory of a computer before they can be used. You do not need to invent names for constant data, however. The COBOL language allows the programmer to use the actual value of a constant rather than a numeric address or a programmer-invented name. Constants are of three types in COBOL, (1) numeric, (2) alphabetic, and (3) alphanumeric.

Numeric constants. A *numeric constant* is a numeric value that is known in advance and which does not change during the processing of a program. These constants can be positive or negative values. In this text, they are all positive. If the Digit 1 is added each time a certain set of instructions is carried out by the computer, the Digit 1 is a constant. Many programs require that a count be kept of the number of data cards processed or of lines printed. Counting can be done by adding 1 to a total each time a record is processed before looping back to the READ instruction to read a new record.

An instruction to accumulate a count could read:

```
ADD 1 to COUNT.
```

In this example, the 1 is a constant because it is known in advance and will not change during processing of the program. The value named COUNT is a variable because it changes every time a new card is processed and the Digit 1 is added to it.

Numeric constants can also be used in other instructions in the PROCEDURE DIVISION. This use will be described later in this chapter.

Alphabetic constants. An *alphabetic constant* is composed of letters of the alphabet and spaces. It is known in advance and does not change during processing of the program. You learned in the last chapter that in COBOL an item of data may be described as alphabetic with an A in the PICTURE clause. However, it may have only letters of the alphabet with or without spaces.

An example of an alphabetic constant is a heading such as CLASS CODE. In the program, the heading is placed inside single quotation marks. All letters and spaces are counted. When it is described to the computer, this alphabetic constant will read 'CLASS CODE'. It will be described with a PICTURE clause PICTURE A(10).

Alphanumeric constants. An *alphanumeric constant* consists of alphanumeric data that are known in advance and which do not change during processing of a program. When appearing in the program, the constant is also written inside single quotation marks. The constant may be made up of digits, special characters, letters of the alphabet, spaces, or any combination. Examples are:

July 24, 1982
478-34-8522
STUDENT NAMES

It is easy to see that the first two headings are alphanumeric. The first has letters, numbers, a comma, and a space. The second has numbers and hyphens (special characters). The third heading, STUDENT NAMES, has letters of the alphabet and a space. It can be classified as either alphabetic or alphanumeric, according to the programmer's wishes.

When describing a constant to the computer, all characters inside the single quotation marks are counted, even the spaces. The single quotes tell the computer that everything within them is part of the constant. Examples of alphanumeric constants as described to the computer are:

'July 24, 1982'	(13 characters including spaces) PICTURE X(13)
'478-34-8522'	(11 characters) PICTURE X(11)
'STUDENT NAMES'	(13 characters including space) PICTURE X(13) or PICTURE A(13)

Alphanumeric constants will be explained more fully later in this chapter.

PROBLEM 2: PRINTING A STUDENT REPORT LISTING STUDENTS' NAMES, CLASS CODES, AND TEST SCORES, WITH A TOTAL OF ALL TEST SCORES

On hand is a file of punched cards like the card used in Problem 1, except that there is only one test score in the card. Each punched card in the file contains the name, class code, and test score for each student in the class.

Statement of the problem

A program is to be written that will cause the computer to print a three-column report. The input file of punched cards will be punched as follows:

(1) The student's name is punched in Columns 1–20. The name field is alphabetic.
(2) The class code will be punched in Column 31. The class code field is numeric.
(3) The student's test score will be punched in Columns 41–43. The test score will be punched without a decimal point and will be numeric.
(4) All other columns of the input card will not be used.

A program is to be written that will cause the computer to print a three-column report as follows:

(1) The name of each student will appear in the first column of the report. The class code will be printed in the second column. The test score will be in the last column.
(2) The total of all test scores will be printed at the end of the report after the information from the last data card has been printed.
(3) The report will be centered on a page 132 spaces wide. Ten spaces will appear between the columns. The total of all test scores will be printed under the test score column. The total will be aligned to the right under the test score column.
(4) The report will be single-spaced. One blank line will appear between the last detail line (last student) and the total of all scores.

Analysis of the problem

The problem will be very much like Problem 1 in Chapter 12. A COBOL program will be written to print a list of students, their class codes, and test scores. Now, the computer will be instructed to add all of the test scores in order to accumulate a final total of all test scores for the class.

It will be necessary to write a program to solve Problem 2. The title of the program will be TEST. An IBM System/360 computer will be used as the source computer and the object computer.

IDENTIFICATION DIVISION of the program for Problem 2

The IDENTIFICATION DIVISION for the new program must be written first. Remember that the IDENTIFICATION DIVISION gives the name of the division, the title of the program (PROGRAM-ID), the name of the author, and the date the program is written. Special punching instructions are given on the first page of the program. Once they have been given in the IDENTIFICATION DIVISION, the punching instructions do not need to be repeated.

Figure 13-1 shows the IDENTIFICATION DIVISION for the new program.

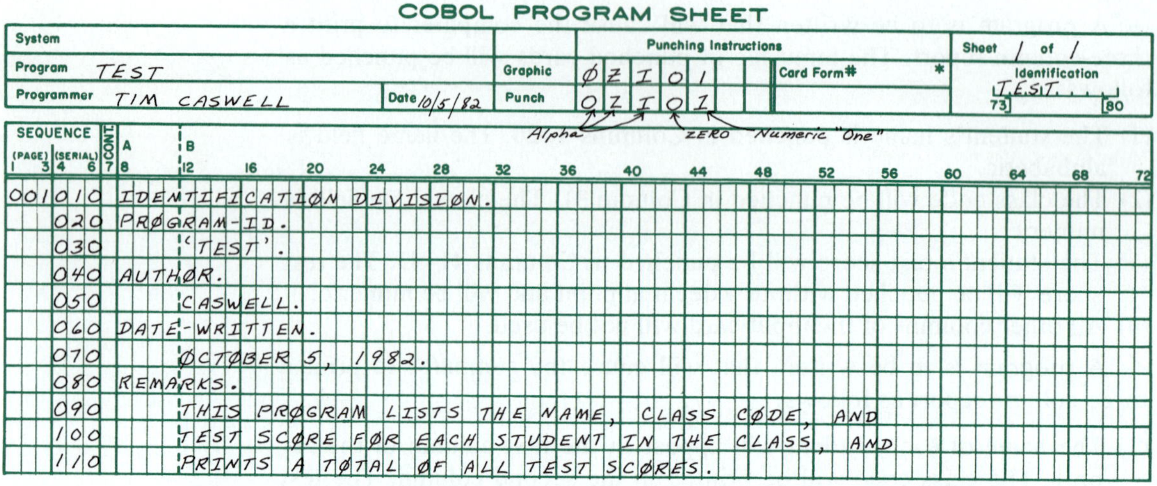
COBOL PROGRAM SHEET

System

Program TEST

Programmer TIM CASWELL Date 10/5/82

Punching Instructions: Graphic Ø Z I O 1 / Punch O Z I O 1 (Alpha, ZERO, Numeric "One"); Card Form #

Sheet 1 of 1

Identification T.E.S.T. (73–80)

SEQUENCE (PAGE) 1–3 (SERIAL) 4–6, CONT. 7, A 8, B 12

```
001010 IDENTIFICATIØN DIVISIØN.
   020 PRØGRAM-ID.
   030     'TEST'.
   040 AUTHØR.
   050     CASWELL.
   060 DATE-WRITTEN.
   070     ØCTØBER 5, 1982.
   080 REMARKS.
   090     THIS PRØGRAM LISTS THE NAME, CLASS CØDE, AND
   100     TEST SCØRE FØR EACH STUDENT IN THE CLASS, AND
   110     PRINTS A TØTAL ØF ALL TEST SCØRES.
```

Figure 13-1. *This IDENTIFICATION DIVISION has a REMARKS section added.*

Note that the name written in the upper right-hand corner under "Identification" is TEST. The name can have eight characters or less. This identification is not required, but it is helpful for documentation. The program name is also written out in the upper left-hand corner. Here the name can be over eight characters long. Information on this line is used for documentation only. It is never punched into cards or made part of the computer record. This name does not have to be identical to the name in the right-hand corner. However, in this case it is.

On Line 030, the PROGRAM-ID is written as 'TEST'. The limit of eight characters is required when using the IBM System/360 computer because the ID is also used as an identification label if the program is stored on magnetic tapes or disks.

The programmer may wish to add additional comments. For this reason, a REMARKS section can be added to the program, as in Figure 13-1. Note that in the REMARKS section, any remark you wish can be included to explain the program. There is no restriction for length. When REMARKS are used, the word REMARKS is written beginning at the A-Margin, Column 8. The word REMARKS must be followed by a period. The REMARKS are written beginning at the B-Margin of the next line. They can be continued on as many lines as are needed, beginning always at the B-Margin, Column 12. There is a period at the end of all the REMARKS.

The REMARKS are printed on the printout of the program, but they are not processed by the computer. They are used for documentation only. In Figure 13-1, Lines 080–110 are REMARKS.

ENVIRONMENT DIVISION of the program for Problem 2

Figure 13-2 shows the ENVIRONMENT DIVISION of the program as it would appear. All the entries in Figure 13-2 are required in every COBOL program. Lines 010, 020, 030, 050, 070, and 080 must appear in every COBOL program exactly as written. The information on Lines 040 and 060 may change if a different computer is used. The names of the files and devices used (090 and 100) may also be different. All programs use some input and output files. Therefore, the SELECT and ASSIGN statements appear in every COBOL program. However, the file names and devices may be different, depending upon the equipment used.

```
002010 ENVIRØNMENT DIVISIØN.
   020 CØNFIGURATIØN SECTIØN.
   030 SØURCE-CØMPUTER.
   040     IBM-360.
   050 ØBJECT-CØMPUTER.
   060     IBM-360.
   070 INPUT-ØUTPUT SECTIØN.
   080 FILE-CØNTRØL.
   090     SELECT TEST-FILE, ASSIGN TØ 'SYSIN' UNIT-RECØRD.
   100     SELECT PRINTED-REPØRT-FILE, ASSIGN TØ 'SYSØUT' UNIT-RECØRD.
```

Figure 13-2. *The ENVIRONMENT DIVISION of the COBOL program for solving Problem 2 is shown.*

Any name may be chosen for the input and output files as long as the name conforms to the COBOL rules. Remember that no name appearing on the list of reserved words, p. 317, may be used exactly as it appears on the list. Otherwise, any name may be used that has no more than 32 characters. No spaces are allowed in the name. Hyphens may be used instead of spaces in order to use names with more than one word. The first character of each programmer-invented name must be a letter of the alphabet.

In this problem, as in Problem 1 of Chapter 12, the assignments are made to UNIT-RECORD. That is the IBM name for the punched-card input device and the printer output device to be used. Like UNIT-RECORD, 'SYSIN' and 'SYSOUT' are names used with the IBM-360 computer.

DATA DIVISION of the program for Problem 2

The third division of any COBOL program is the DATA DIVISION. This division will be explained in two parts to make the explanation easier. The FILE SECTION with its input and output statements will be explained first. Then the WORKING-STORAGE SECTION will be described.

FILE SECTION. The FILE SECTION contains both the input and the output statements that describe the input record (punched card) and output record (printed line).

Input statements. The input statements will describe the punched card shown in Figure 13-3. Note that the name field is in Columns 1–20. It is alphabetic. Columns 21–30 are not used. Column 31 is used for the class code and is numeric. Columns 32–40 are not used. The next three columns, Columns 41–43, are used for the test score. The test score is numeric. The last 37 columns of the card are not used.

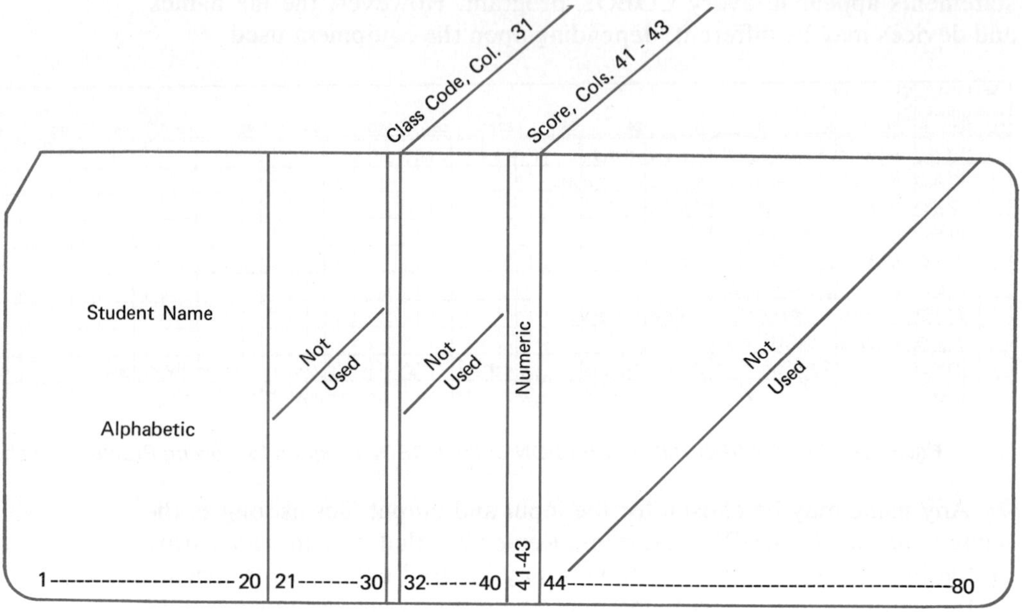

Figure 13-3. *This punched data card will be described in the input statements in the FILE SECTION of the DATA DIVISION.*

The required entries in the input statements of the DATA DIVISION are included in Lines 010–070 of Figure 13-4. They are the name of the division, the name of the section and the FD. The FD (file description) begins on Line 030 and ends with a period on Line 070. Note that the FD gives the following information:

(1) The recording mode is *fixed*.
(2) The record contains 80 characters.
(3) Label records are omitted.

All these entries have been explained in Chapter 12.

The name of the division and FILE SECTION begin at the A-Margin and end with a period. The FD begins at the A-Margin and ends with a period at the end of the description on Line 070. On Line 030 the compiler is given the name that was assigned to the file in the ENVIRONMENT DIVISION, TEST-FILE. Lines 040–060 describe the file. Line

```
SEQUENCE   A   B
(PAGE)(SERIAL)
003010 DATA DIVISIØN.
   020 FILE SECTIØN.
   030 FD  TEST-FILE
   040     RECØRDING MØDE IS F
   050     RECØRD CØNTAINS 80 CHARACTERS
   060     LABEL RECØRDS ARE ØMITTED
   070     DATA RECØRD IS PUNCHED-CARD.
   080 01  PUNCHED-CARD.
   090     02  STUDENT-NAME        PICTURE A(20).
   100     02  FILLER              PICTURE X(10).
   110     02  CLASS-CØDE          PICTURE 9.
   120     02  FILLER              PICTURE X(9).
   130     02  SCØRE               PICTURE 999.
   140     02  FILLER              PICTURE X(37).
```

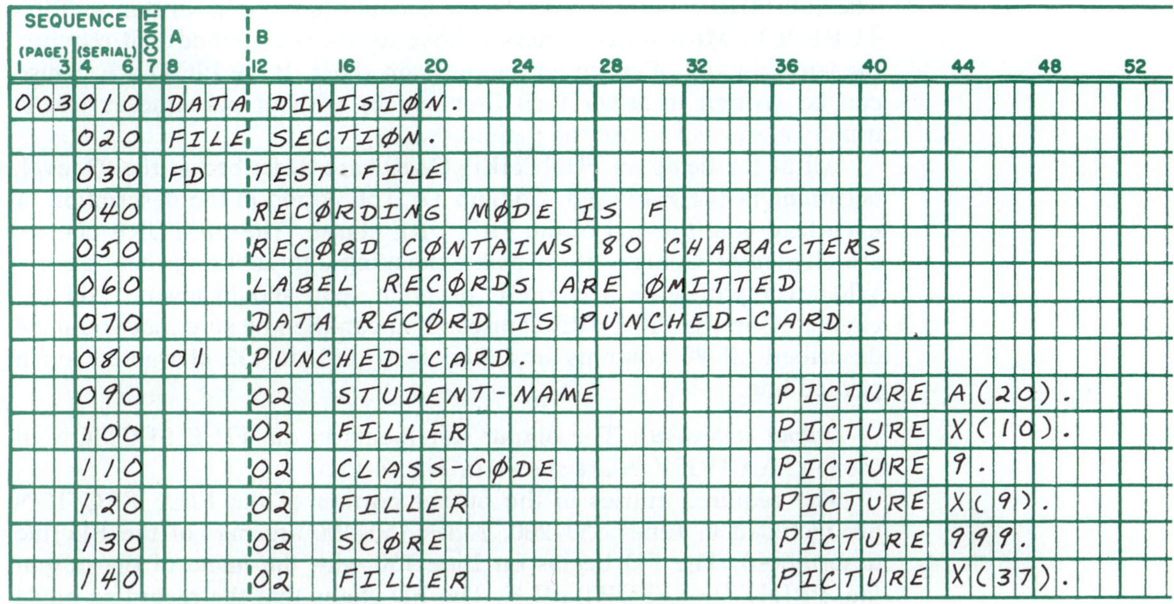

Figure 13-4. *The above statements in the FILE SECTION of the DATA DIVISION describe the punched data card.*

070 gives the names of the data record, which is PUNCHED-CARD. The period is used at the end of the FD statements.

The programmer-invented names in the input statements are:

(1) The name of the file, TEST-FILE, assigned in the ENVIRONMENT DIVISION, Line 030.
(2) The name of the record, PUNCHED-CARD, Line 070.
(3) The name of the record repeated on Line 080 at the 01 level. (It is the heading under which the fields or items are subheadings.)
(4) The names of all the fields on the PUNCHED-CARD (STUDENT-NAME, CLASS-CODE, and SCORE).

There are also FILLER statements that explain the length of the unused columns in the punched card. Compare the PICTURE clauses in Figure 13-4 with the columns in the punched card, Figure 13-3. STUDENT-NAME on Line 090 is described as containing twenty alphabetic characters, PICTURE A(20). CLASS-CODE (PICTURE 9.) is described as a numeric field of one digit. SCORE (PICTURE 999.) is described as numeric and three digits long. All columns not used on the card are described with FILLER statements. The X is used to describe the columns as alphanumeric. (Remember that letters of the alphabet, numbers, special characters, or spaces can be described as alphanumeric.)

Note that the PICTURE clauses for the SCORE field and the CLASS-CODE field do not have parentheses. The single 9 in the PICTURE clause describing CLASS-CODE tells the computer that it is numeric and that there is only one digit in that field. The three 9s (999) in the SCORE field tell the computer that there are three numeric digits.

The PICTURE clause for the SCORE could have been written as PICTURE 9(3). Most programmers choose to use the method that requires the least amount of space on the program sheet. If the PICTURE clause can be written in fewer than four spaces without parentheses, it is usually easier not to use the parentheses.

All of the fields on PUNCHED-CARD are described at the 02 level, beginning at the B-Margin, Column 12. The period in the description of each field is at the end of the PICTURE clause. The PICTURE clauses are aligned at Column 36 to make checking and counting them easier. Whenever you write a COBOL program, you should always add the characters in the PICTURE clauses. You can then be sure that you have described all 80 columns in a punched card or 132 characters on a printed line.

Output statements. The output statements in the FILE SECTION of the DATA DIVISION are shown in Figure 13-5.

The required entries in the output portion of the FILE SECTION are included in Lines 150–200. Lines 150–190 are part of the FD (file description). The FD begins on Line 150 with the name of the output file, PRINTED-REPORT-FILE. The FD states that the recording mode is fixed; that the record contains 132 characters; that label records are omitted; and that the data record is PRINT-LINE.

The programmer-invented names are PRINTED-REPORT-FILE on Line 150 and PRINT-LINE on Line 190. Note that the FD begins at the A-Margin on Line 150 and ends with a period on Line 190. Line 190 gives the name of the data record, PRINT-LINE.

Line 200 describes PRINT-LINE with the PICTURE clause X(132). Remember that this method of describing the output record in the FILE SECTION is used because there are often many line formats on the same report. PRINT-LINE is the only name the computer will recognize. Therefore, any lines described in WORKING-STORAGE must be moved to PRINT-LINE before printing can take place. X(132) is a description into which any detail line planned in WORKING-STORAGE can fit.

It is easier for the programmer to name the different detail lines and describe them in the WORKING-STORAGE SECTION of the DATA DIVISION. Then, each detail line can be moved to PRINT LINE with a

```
150 FD  PRINTED-REPORT-FILE
160     RECØRDING MØDE IS F
170     RECØRD CØNTAINS 132 CHARACTERS
180     LABEL RECØRDS ARE ØMITTED
190     DATA RECØRD IS PRINT-LINE.
200 01  PRINT-LINE                   PICTURE X(132).
```

Figure 13-5. *The output statements of the FILE SECTION of the DATA DIVISION describe the printed line.*

MOVE instruction in the PROCEDURE DIVISION. Remember that there are two different lines in the report for Problem 2. One will be the detail line with the student's name, class code, and test score. The other will be the line with the total.

WORKING-STORAGE SECTION of the DATA DIVISION for Problem 2. The first detail line described in the WORKING-STORAGE SECTION will be named SCORE-LINE. It will contain the name of each student, the class code, and the test score. The other line will be named TOTAL-LINE. It will contain only the total of all the test scores.

Each line of the printed report is to be centered on a 132-space line. Ten spaces are allowed between each of the three columns. The report is to be single-spaced. However, there will be one blank line between all the student data and the total. The total will be aligned on the right with the scores above it.

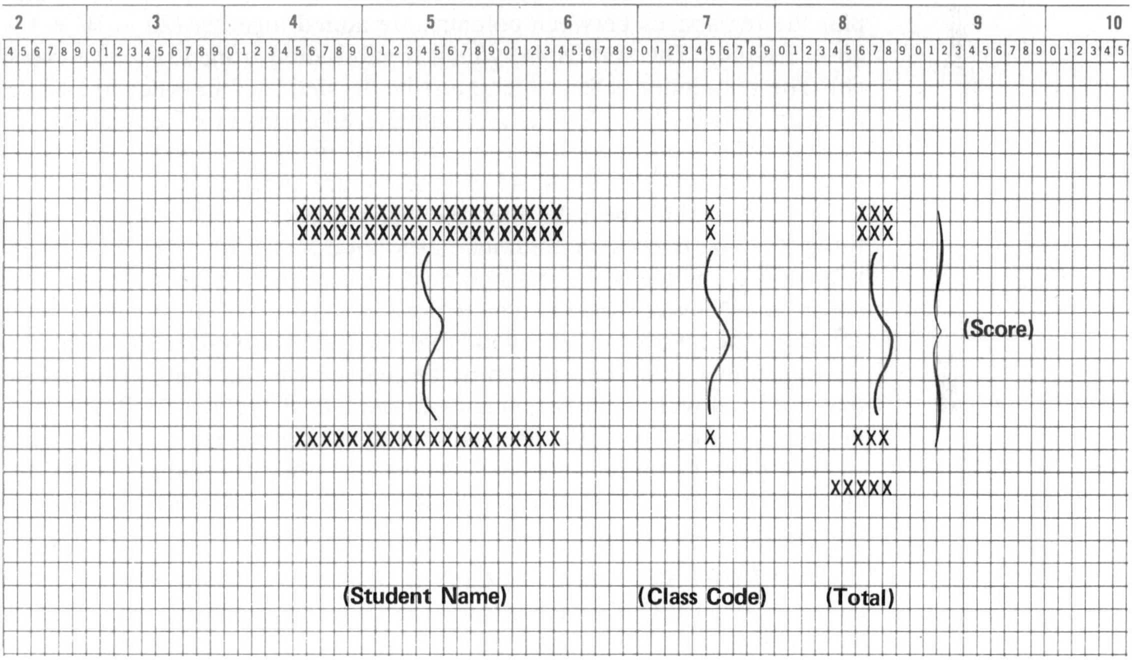

Figure 13-6. *The printer spacing chart shows the format for the printed report for Problem 2.*

Format of the printed report for Problem 2. The output format for this problem is shown in the printer spacing chart, Figure 13-6.

Note that the first line of print on the chart is shown on Line 7. That indicates that the first line of print on the report should start about one inch from the top of the report.

The form is too large to illustrate, but you can see that there are 44 spaces in the margin to the left of the student name. The Xs are used to indicate where the data fields will be printed. The number of Xs in each field indicates the largest number of characters allowed for each field. However, the actual data may not need all the spaces in every case.

At least two print lines should be shown on the printer spacing chart. In Figure 13-6, two print lines are shown at the top and one print line is shown below. These are connected by "squiggles" (wavy lines). These wavy lines indicate that all other lines will appear in the same format. The "squiggle" also indicates that the actual number of print lines may vary.

The two print lines next to each other at the top show that the report is to be single-spaced. Double-spacing would be shown by allowing one blank line between the two lines of Xs on the printer spacing chart. Note that one blank line appears between the last detail line of print and the total score. The blank line at this point shows that double-spacing is to take place before printing the total.

Designing the lines of print. In figuring the horizontal spacing on this chart, the number of characters needed for the three columns of data plus the ten spaces between columns are added together (20 + 10 + 1 + 10 + 3 = 44). The sum is 44, which is subtracted from 132 (132 − 44 = 88). The remainder is 88, which must be divided by 2 in order to find the number of spaces to allow in each margin. 88 divided by 2 equals 44, the number of spaces in each margin. Note in Figure 13-6 that the student name field begins at Column 45. The test score ends at Column 88.

Note also that the total has five Xs, but each single score has only three Xs. The two extra columns in the total allow for "carries." There is always a chance of having one or more numbers in a total than there are in each amount that is added. Reports should be planned to allow space for the largest possible total that can be generated by the data.

Remember that the total must be aligned on the right. This means that the total will begin two spaces to the left of the scores. The scores begin at Column 86, so the total will begin at Column 84.

The printer spacing chart will be used by the programmer in writing the line descriptions of the detail lines in the WORKING-STORAGE SECTION.

WORKING-STORAGE SECTION Illustrated. The WORKING-STORAGE SECTION begins on Line 010 of p. 4 of the program for solving Problem 2. See Figure 13-7.

This section is used to define temporary storage areas for computer results or other information developed during processing. In this problem, a total must be accumulated of all student test scores. This temporary storage area is described in the WORKING-STORAGE SECTION as follows:

```
004 010 WORKING-STORAGE SECTION.
    020 77  TOTAL-SCORE           PICTURE 9(5) VALUE 0.
```

The compiler is told that a location is to be reserved in the WORKING-STORAGE area of the computer for numeric data that will occupy a maximum of 5 positions. The name given to the address will be

COBOL PROGRAM SHEET

System		Punching Instructions		Sheet 4 of
Program TEST		Graphic	Card Form# *	Identification
Programmer TIM CASWELL	Date 10/5/82	Punch		TEST 73

```
SEQUENCE  C A   B
(PAGE)(SERIAL) 7 8  12  16  20  24  28  32  36  40  44  48  52  56  60  64
004010    WØRKING-STØRAGE SECTIØN.
   020    77 TØTAL-SCØRE                 PICTURE 9(5) VALUE 0.
   030    01 SCØRE-LINE.
   040          02 FILLER                PICTURE X(44) VALUE SPACES.
   050          02 STUDENT-NAME-PRINT    PICTURE A(20).
   060          02 FILLER                PICTURE X(10) VALUE SPACES.
   070          02 CLASS-CØDE-PRINT      PICTURE 9.
   080          02 FILLER                PICTURE X(10) VALUE SPACES.
   090          02 SCØRE-PRINT           PICTURE 999.
   100          02 FILLER                PICTURE X(44) VALUE SPACES.
   110    01 TØTAL-LINE.
   120          02 FILLER                PICTURE X(83) VALUE SPACES.
   130          02 TØTAL-SCØRE-PRINT     PICTURE 9(5).
   140          02 FILLER                PICTURE X(44) VALUE SPACES.
```

Figure 13-7. *The WORKING-STORAGE SECTION of the DATA DIVISION for Problem 2 uses VALUE clauses.*

TOTAL-SCORE. The compiler is also told to store the value of 0 at these five positions.

Note that the number of characters allowed in the WORKING-STORAGE area is larger than that in the actual test score field. Remember that in the printer spacing chart, Figure 13-6, there were two extra positions allowed for the total. In this problem, it is assumed that the total will never be longer than five digits. It is always safe to allow too many positions rather than too few when planning a field for a total.

Level 77 entries. For the first time in this text, Level 77 is used. See Line 020 of Figure 13-7. Entries for arithmetic computations in the WORKING-STORAGE SECTION are always assigned a level number of 77. When items appear in the WORKING-STORAGE SECTION at Level 77, *they must always precede other items with different levels*.

VALUE clauses. The *VALUE clause* is a method in COBOL for specifying the beginning value of a data item in WORKING-STORAGE. It is used as follows:

(1) To describe the beginning value of a numeric variable
(2) To describe the value of a constant.

In the program for solving Problem 2, the beginning value of the variable address named TOTAL-SCORE should be zero. TOTAL-SCORE is a variable because it is not known in advance and it changes during the processing of the program as each card is processed. One method of clearing an area of memory to use for computations is to write the order

MOVE ZEROS TO TOTAL-SCORE. However, by using the VALUE clause in the WORKING-STORAGE SECTION, there is no need to write a MOVE instruction in the PROCEDURE DIVISION to clear TOTAL-SCORE to zero. A value of zero is given to TOTAL-SCORE in the WORKING-STORAGE SECTION. See Line 020 of Figure 13-7.

The word VALUE is found on the COBOL reserved-word list. It must be used in a certain manner. The use of the word VALUE has a special meaning to the computer. You know that a PICTURE clause describes the size of a data field and the kind of data. But, the PICTURE clause never tells the computer exactly what the data will be. In order to give a starting value to a data item in WORKING STORAGE, the PICTURE clause can be followed by the word VALUE and the actual value.

```
004 010 WORKING-STORAGE SECTION.
    020 77  TOTAL-SCORE              PICTURE 9(5) VALUE 0.
```

The above VALUE clause gives the initial value of the numeric variable TOTAL-SCORE. If the value is numeric, it is usually cleared to zero as shown above. If there is a field of spaces, the word SPACES is used.

If the value is an alphabetic or alphanumeric constant that is to be printed, it is written within single quotation marks. This use of alphabetic and alphanumeric constants will be explained with Program 3.

FILLER statements in the output descriptions for Problem 2. FILLER statements were used in the last chapter to describe unused spaces on the data card and print line. In the WORKING-STORAGE SECTION, Figure 13-7, the FILLER statement is combined with the VALUE clause to give the actual value of the alphanumeric data described. All of the FILLER statements in Figure 13-7 tell the compiler that the margins and area between data fields will have spaces.

The VALUE clause can be used in the FILLER statement to describe the spaces because spaces are alphanumeric and they are constant. (They are known in advance, and their number will not change during processing of the program.)

The use of the VALUE clause makes the WORKING-STORAGE DIVISION a little harder to write. But, it will shorten the PROCEDURE DIVISION by eliminating two MOVE instructions. These two MOVE instructions would have been used each time a new card was processed. One instruction would have been MOVE SPACES TO SCORE-LINE. The other would have been MOVE SPACES TO TOTAL-LINE. By defining exactly where the spaces will be at all times, the programmer can be sure that there is no chance of unwanted data appearing on the print line.

Line description in the WORKING-STORAGE SECTION. Two detail lines are described in the WORKING-STORAGE SECTION, Figure 13-7. They are the same detail lines on the printer spacing chart, Figure 13-6.

The first line described is SCORE-LINE. It begins at Position 45 on the chart. There will be 44 blank spaces in the left margin of the report. Refer to Line 040 of the WORKING-STORAGE SECTION. The first field at the 02 level is described with the PICTURE clause, PICTURE X(44) VALUE SPACES. This tells the computer to skip the first 44 print positions which will be spaces (blanks). The VALUE clause is used here because SPACES is an alphanumeric constant.

Spaces in the margins and between fields of data are treated as constant fields of data. They are known in advance and will not change. Therefore, unused areas on a print line can be described as constants and given a beginning value of SPACES, using the VALUE clause.

Remember that the advantage of using VALUE clauses to describe spaces is that there are fewer MOVE instructions in the PROCEDURE DIVISION.

SCORE-LINE appears as follows:

```
01 SCORE-LINE.
   02  FILLER                   PICTURE X(44) VALUE SPACES.
   02  STUDENT-NAME-PRINT       PICTURE A(20).
   02  FILLER                   PICTURE X(10) VALUE SPACES.
   02  CLASS-CODE-PRINT         PICTURE 9.
   02  FILLER                   PICTURE X(10) VALUE SPACES.
   02  SCORE-PRINT              PICTURE 999.
   02  FILLER                   PICTURE X(44) VALUE SPACES.
```

Because SCORE-LINE is a record (line of print), it begins at the 01 level. The descriptions are written at the 02 level. Note that the word PRINT has been added to STUDENT-NAME, CLASS-CODE, and SCORE. There are no VALUE clauses for these variables. There are VALUE clauses for all the FILLER statements because SPACES is an alphanumeric constant.

The second detail line described is TOTAL-LINE (Line 110 of Figure 13-7). It also begins at the 01 level. Remember that in the printer spacing chart, Figure 13-6, the total begins at Position 84. Line 120 shows 83 spaces in the left margin. Line 140 shows 44 spaces in the right margin. Allowing 5 positions for the total, the print positions add up to 132.

```
110 01 TOTAL-LINE.
120    02  FILLER                 PICTURE X(83) VALUE SPACES.
130    02  TOTAL-SCORE-PRINT      PICTURE 9(5).
140    02  FILLER                 PICTURE X(44) VALUE SPACES.
```

Here again the word PRINT has been added to the output record (TOTAL-SCORE-PRINT).

Remember that each of these detail lines must be moved out of WORKING-STORAGE to PRINT-LINE before any printing can take place. PRINT-LINE is the name of the output record in the FILE SECTION. Both SCORE-LINE and TOTAL-LINE are detail lines. They do not become output records until they are moved to PRINT-LINE.

Figure 13-8 shows the entire DATA DIVISION for Problem 2, including the WORKING-STORAGE SECTION.

```
SEQUENCE
(PAGE)(SERIAL) CONT. A   B
1   3 4   6    7     8   12  16  20  24  28  32  36  40  44  48  52  56  60  64
003010 DATA DIVISIØN.
   020 FILE SECTIØN.
   030 FD  TEST-FILE
   040     RECØRDING MØDE IS F
   050     RECØRD CØNTAINS 80 CHARACTERS
   060     LABEL RECØRDS ARE ØMITTED
   070     DATA RECØRD IS PUNCHED-CARD.
   080 01  PUNCHED-CARD.
   090     02  STUDENT-NAME            PICTURE A(20).
   100     02  FILLER                  PICTURE X(10).
   110     02  CLASS-CØDE              PICTURE 9.
   120     02  FILLER                  PICTURE X(9).
   130     02  SCØRE                   PICTURE 999.
   140     02  FILLER                  PICTURE X(37).
   150 FD  PRINTED-REPØRT-FILE
   160     RECØRDING MØDE IS F
   170     RECØRD CØNTAINS 132 CHARACTERS
   180     LABEL RECØRDS ARE ØMITTED
   190     DATA RECØRD IS PRINT-LINE.
   200 01  PRINT-LINE                  PICTURE X(132).

SEQUENCE
(PAGE)(SERIAL) CONT. A   B
1   3 4   6    7     8   12  16  20  24  28  32  36  40  44  48  52  56  60  64
004010 WØRKING-STØRAGE SECTIØN.
   020 77  TØTAL-SCØRE                 PICTURE 9(5) VALUE 0.
   030 01  SCØRE-LINE.
   040     02  FILLER                  PICTURE X(44) VALUE SPACES.
   050     02  STUDENT-NAME-PRINT      PICTURE A(20).
   060     02  FILLER                  PICTURE X(10) VALUE SPACES.
   070     02  CLASS-CØDE-PRINT        PICTURE 9.
   080     02  FILLER                  PICTURE X(10) VALUE SPACES.
   090     02  SCØRE-PRINT             PICTURE 999.
   100     02  FILLER                  PICTURE X(44) VALUE SPACES.
   110 01  TØTAL-LINE.
   120     02  FILLER                  PICTURE X(83) VALUE SPACES.
   130     02  TØTAL-SCØRE-PRINT       PICTURE 9(5).
   140     02  FILLER                  PICTURE X(44) VALUE SPACES.
```

Figure 13-8. *Above is the entire DATA DIVISION of the COBOL program for solving Problem 2.*

Subdividing data items. Level numbers 01 and 02 were discussed in Chapter 12. These level numbers show the relationship of the data items to each other. Level numbers are required whenever a record is subdivided into fields.

There are two types of data items in the DATA DIVISION of a COBOL program:

(1) A *group item* is an item or field that can be "broken down" or subdivided into smaller items. A group item can be a date. It is possible to divide a date into a month, day, and year. A name could be a group item because it may be subdivided into first name, middle name or initial, and last name.

(2) An *elementary item* is an item or field that cannot be subdivided any further. For example, the class code can be considered an elementary item.

When a programmer is assigning level numbers, the facts are organized as they would be for any outline. Assume that a record consists of a student's name and test score only. The entire record will be referred to as PUNCHED-CARD. The levels might be arranged as follows:

```
01 PUNCHED-CARD.              (group item)
   02  STUDENT-NAME           (group item)
       03 LAST-NAME           (elementary item)
       03 FIRST-NAME          (elementary item)
       03 MIDDLE-INITIAL      (elementary item)
   02  TEST-SCORE             (elementary item)
```

The programmer is free to assign levels of 01 through 49, if needed, for any of the group or elementary items. In this introductory text, however, there will be no subdividing beyond the second level.

Page and line numbers. Many programs are quite long and may have more line numbers than would fit in the three-column spaces (Columns 4–6) on the COBOL program sheet. Therefore, most programmers do not continue the line numbers in numeric order from page to page. It would be correct to continue the DATA DIVISION from Line 250 of one page to Line 260 of the next. However, as long as each page is numbered in order, the program cards can be kept in proper order. (For example, 004 010 would logically follow 003 250.) In this text, the second page of any division will begin with Line 010 and a new page number.

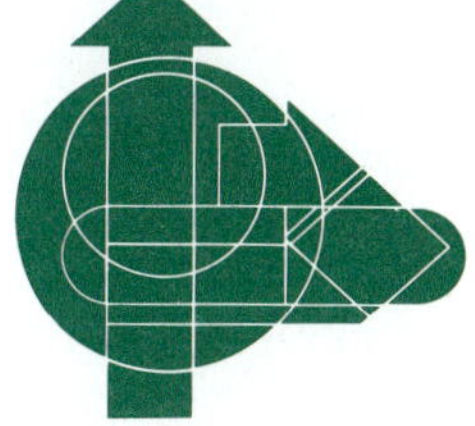

REVIEW QUESTIONS

1. What is a variable? What is a constant?
2. Which of the following are alphabetic constants? Alphanumeric constants? Both?

'ADDRESS'	'FIRST-YEAR STUDENTS'
'END OF PROGRAM'	'HONOR STUDENTS'
'PART NO.'	'INVENTORY AS OF MAY 30, 1983'

3. What new section has been added to the IDENTIFICATION DIVISION in Program 2? What is the purpose of this section? At what margin does the section begin?
4. Why is it a good idea to align the PICTURE clauses whenever possible?
5. How is single-spacing indicated on a printer spacing chart? How is double-spacing indicated?

(Continued)

6. When is the Level 77 used in the WORKING-STORAGE SECTION? What is the position of Level 77 entries in the WORKING-STORAGE SECTION.
7. What are two uses of a VALUE clause?
8. Where is the VALUE clause written in the DATA DIVISION? What instructions need not be written in the PROCEDURE DIVISION when VALUE clauses are used to clear storage in the DATA DIVISION?
9. What are two ways to continue a division of a COBOL program from one page to another?
10. In the following record description, which are the group items? The elementary items?

```
01 PUNCHED-CARD.
   02 EMPLOYEE-NUMBER
   02 EMPLOYEE-NAME
      03 LAST-NAME
      03 FIRST-NAME
      03 MIDDLE-INITIAL
   02 DATE-HIRED
      03 YEAR
      03 MONTH
```

Flowchart for solving Problem 2

Figure 13-9 is the flowchart that will be used for solving Problem 2. The process symbol (2) is used just after the start symbol to indicate the "housekeeping" steps, OPEN FILES.

In this flowchart, a symbol to MOVE SPACES TO SCORE-LINE is not needed. VALUE clauses were used in the WORKING-STORAGE SECTION to set up the beginning value of SPACES in both margins and between the three columns of print. A VALUE clause was also used to clear the area named TOTAL-SCORE to zero. If there were no VALUE clause here, an order would have to be written in the PROCEDURE DIVISION, MOVE SPACES TO SCORE-LINE.

The next step (3) is written in the input/output symbol. It is an order to read a data card. Just after this instruction is the last-card test (4). You learned in Chapter 12 that in COBOL a READ statement combined with an AT END statement creates a last-card test. If the last card has been processed, the computer is told to branch to a new instruction (9) that is shown with the on-page connector, 2. Step 4 creates the conditional branch if the last card has been processed. If not, the computer will go on to the next step in sequence.

The computer is then told to add the score in the input record to the TOTAL-SCORE (5). (This is the score that will be accumulated in WORKING-STORAGE in the area described for it and which has been cleared to zero in the beginning.)

After adding the test score to the total, the computer is told to move STUDENT-NAME, CLASS-CODE, and SCORE to SCORE-LINE (6). These fields are moved one at a time because they are variables and could not be described with VALUE clauses. After these three fields have been moved to the area described for them on SCORE-LINE in

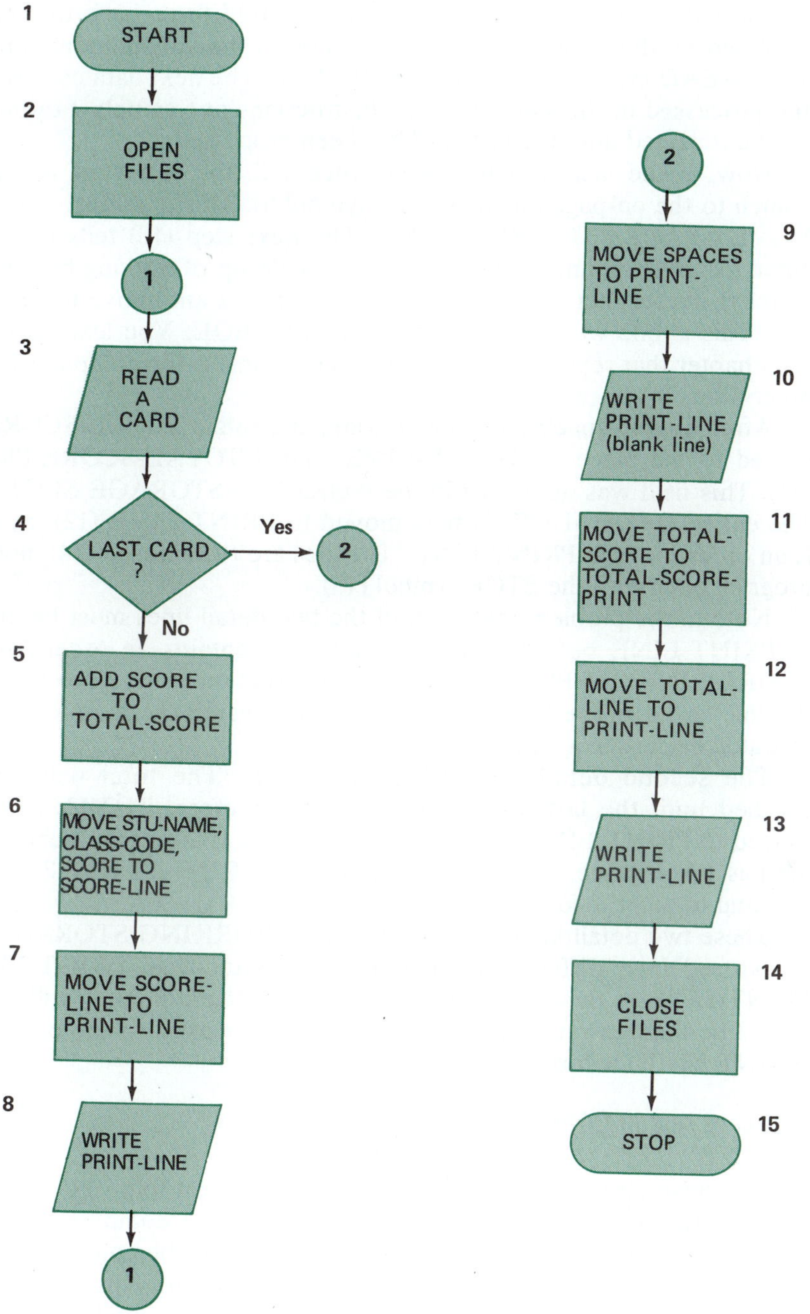

Figure 13-9. *Above is the flowchart for solving Problem 2.*

WORKING-STORAGE, the entire SCORE-LINE is moved to the print area (7). It is moved to PRINT-LINE, which is the output record described in the FILE SECTION and which is the only output record the compiler can recognize. The next step (8) is a WRITE instruction. It causes the entire PRINT-LINE to be printed.

After the line is printed, the computer is told to go back to the step identified by the on-page connector, 1. This is the unconditional branch to the READ instruction that creates the loop. The next data card is read and processed in the same manner. Instructions at Symbols 3 through 8 will be repeated until the last card has been processed.

Now, if the last card has been processed, the computer is told to branch to the on-page connector, 2 (Symbol 9). This is an instruction to MOVE SPACES TO PRINT-LINE. The next step (10) tells the computer to print the line. Since this line is made up of nothing but spaces (blanks), the printer will "print" a line of spaces and move to the next line. This is one way of double-spacing in COBOL. You learned in the last chapter that reports will be single-spaced unless the computer is told otherwise.

After double-spacing has been done, the total, TOTAL-SCORE, is moved to the place on TOTAL-LINE named TOTAL-SCORE-PRINT (11). This field was described in the WORKING-STORAGE SECTION. The entire TOTAL-LINE is then moved to PRINT-LINE (12). Step 13 is an order to write PRINT-LINE. The files are then closed (14), and the program ends with the STOP symbol (15).

Note in the problem that each of the two detail lines must be moved to PRINT-LINE before printing. Symbol 7 contains an order MOVE SCORE-LINE TO PRINT-LINE. The instruction in Symbol 8 causes the line to be printed. These two steps are inside the loop. They are repeated each time a new card is processed.

The second detail line is TOTAL-LINE. The total will not be reached until the last card is processed. Therefore, TOTAL-LINE is moved to PRINT-LINE only once (12), and that is after the double-spacing has taken place (11). The order, WRITE PRINT-LINE (13) causes the total to be printed.

These two detail lines were described in WORKING-STORAGE and are stored in a different area of the computer than PRINT-LINE. PRINT-LINE is the only output record name the computer will recognize. For this reason, each detail line must be moved to the print area (PRINT-LINE) before printing can take place.

Last-card test in COBOL

You have already learned that a READ statement followed by an AT END statement is a last-card test in COBOL. The computer operator must place an additional coded *test control card* at the end of the input file of data cards before running a COBOL program. This test control card may vary according to the kind of computer or compiler used. The card may be punched with a /*, a / /, the words END-OF-FILE, or one of many control codes or punches. When the computer reads this test control card, a branch is made to the final steps of the program. In COBOL, the branch is made to a paragraph name in the PROCEDURE DIVISION under which the final steps appear. In this text, the paragraph name is END-OF-JOB.

PROCEDURE DIVISION of the program for Problem 2

The PROCEDURE DIVISION is the division that gives the actual instructions to the computer on the steps to be followed in completing the job at hand. The PROCEDURE DIVISION will follow the logic in the flowchart to solve the problem.

The required entries in this division are few because this division contains the logic of the problem. The required entries in the PROCEDURE DIVISION shown in Figure 13-10 are as follows:

```
005 010 PROCEDURE DIVISION.
    030 OPEN INPUT
    040 OPEN OUTPUT
    200 CLOSE
    210 STOP RUN.
```

All names of data in this division have already been described in the DATA DIVISION. It is very important that the same names be used and that they be spelled exactly the same. Once assigned, a name is permanently given to the same area of memory and to the same kind of data in that particular program.

```
SEQUENCE        A   B
(PAGE)(SERIAL)
1   3 4   6   7 8   12   16   20   24   28   32   36   40   44   48   52   56   60
005010 PRØCEDURE DIVISIØN.
   020 START-JØB.
   030     ØPEN INPUT TEST-FILE.
   040     ØPEN ØUTPUT PRINTED-REPØRT-FILE.
   050 DETAIL-PRØCESSING.
   060     READ TEST-FILE, AT END GØ TØ END-ØF-JØB.
   070     ADD SCØRE TØ TØTAL-SCØRE.
   080     MØVE STUDENT-NAME TØ STUDENT-NAME-PRINT.
   090     MØVE CLASS-CØDE TØ CLASS-CØDE-PRINT.
   100     MØVE SCØRE TØ SCØRE-PRINT.
   110     MØVE SCØRE-LINE TØ PRINT-LINE.
   120     WRITE PRINT-LINE.
   130     GØ TØ DETAIL-PRØCESSING.
   140 END-ØF-JØB.
   150     MØVE SPACES TØ PRINT-LINE.
   160     WRITE PRINT-LINE.
   170     MØVE TØTAL-SCØRE TØ TØTAL-SCØRE-PRINT.
   180     MØVE TØTAL-LINE TØ PRINT-LINE.
   190     WRITE PRINT-LINE.
   200     CLØSE TEST-FILE.
   210     CLØSE PRINTED-REPØRT-FILE.
   220     STØP RUN.
```

Figure 13-10. *The PROCEDURE DIVISION of the COBOL program to solve Problem 2 is shown above. The paragraph name START-JOB is used only for clarity. The paragraph names DETAIL-PROCESSING and END-OF-JOB must be used because branches are made to them during the processing of the program.*

You have learned that only the division name and paragraph names begin at the A-Margin. All the statements in the paragraphs begin at the B-Margin. Paragraph names are useful for clarity at the beginning of each new set of steps. This is the reason for writing the first paragraph name, START-JOB, on Line 020. Paragraph names are *required*, however, at the beginning of any set of instructions to which a branch will be made from the normal order in the program.

In Figure 13-10, Line 130, the statement reads GO TO DETAIL-PROCESSING. Line 130 creates the loop back to Line 050, DETAIL-PROCESSING. The normal order of processing COBOL statements is changed by using the GO TO statement and naming the paragraph name of the new sequence to which the computer is to branch. Line 060 reads AT END GO TO END-OF-JOB. This statement will cause a branch to the paragraph name END-OF-JOB.

COBOL program for solving Problem 2

The complete COBOL program for solving Problem 2 is shown in Figure 13-11. Note that the program is identified in the IDENTIFICATION DIVISION. The files and equipment are named in the ENVIRONMENT DIVISION. All records and fields are described in the DATA DIVISION. The PROCEDURE DIVISION causes the input data to be read, processed, and prepared as output according to the descriptions in the DATA DIVISION.

COBOL PROGRAM SHEET

System | Punching Instructions | Sheet 1 of 1
Program TEST | Graphic Ø Z I O 1 | Card Form # *
Programmer TIM CASWELL | Date 10/5/82 | Punch O Z I O 1 | Identification TEST (73–80)
(Alpha — ZERO — Numeric "One")

```
SEQUENCE   A   B
001010 IDENTIFICATIØN DIVISIØN.
   020 PRØGRAM-ID.
   030     'TEST'.
   040 AUTHØR.
   050     CASWELL.
   060 DATE-WRITTEN.
   070     ØCTØBER 5, 1982.
   080 REMARKS.
   090     THIS PRØGRAM LISTS THE NAME, CLASS CØDE, AND
   100     TEST SCØRE FØR EACH STUDENT IN THE CLASS, AND
   110     PRINTS A TØTAL ØF ALL TEST SCØRES.
002010 ENVIRØNMENT DIVISIØN.
   020 CØNFIGURATIØN SECTIØN.
   030 SØURCE-CØMPUTER.
   040     IBM-360.
   050 ØBJECT-CØMPUTER.
   060     IBM-360.
   070 INPUT-ØUTPUT SECTIØN.
   080 FILE-CØNTRØL.
   090     SELECT TEST-FILE, ASSIGN TØ 'SYSIN' UNIT-RECØRD.
   100     SELECT PRINTED-REPØRT-FILE, ASSIGN TØ 'SYSØUT' UNIT-RECØRD.
```

Figure 13-11. *Above is the complete COBOL program to solve Problem 2.*

```
003010 DATA DIVISIØN.
   020 FILE SECTIØN.
   030 FD  TEST-FILE
   040         RECØRDING MØDE IS F
   050         RECØRD CØNTAINS 80 CHARACTERS
   060         LABEL RECØRDS ARE ØMITTED
   070         DATA RECØRD IS PUNCHED-CARD.
   080 01  PUNCHED-CARD.
   090     02  STUDENT-NAME            PICTURE A(20).
   100     02  FILLER                  PICTURE X(10).
   110     02  CLASS-CØDE              PICTURE 9.
   120     02  FILLER                  PICTURE X(9).
   130     02  SCØRE                   PICTURE 999.
   140     02  FILLER                  PICTURE X(37).
   150 FD  PRINTED-REPØRT-FILE
   160         RECØRDING MØDE IS F
   170         RECØRD CØNTAINS 132 CHARACTERS
   180         LABEL RECØRDS ARE ØMITTED
   190         DATA RECØRD IS PRINT-LINE.
   200 01  PRINT-LINE                  PICTURE X(132).
004010 WØRKING-STØRAGE SECTIØN.
   020 77  TØTAL-SCØRE                 PICTURE 9(5) VALUE 0.
   030 01  SCØRE-LINE.
   040     02  FILLER                  PICTURE X(44) VALUE SPACES.
   050     02  STUDENT-NAME-PRINT      PICTURE A(20).
   060     02  FILLER                  PICTURE X(10) VALUE SPACES.
   070     02  CLASS-CØDE-PRINT        PICTURE 9.
   080     02  FILLER                  PICTURE X(10) VALUE SPACES.
   090     02  SCØRE-PRINT             PICTURE 999.
   100     02  FILLER                  PICTURE X(44) VALUE SPACES.
   110 01  TØTAL-LINE.
   120     02  FILLER                  PICTURE X(83) VALUE SPACES.
   130     02  TØTAL-SCØRE-PRINT       PICTURE 9(5).
   140     02  FILLER                  PICTURE X(44) VALUE SPACES.
005010 PRØCEDURE DIVISIØN.
   020 START-JØB.
   030     ØPEN INPUT TEST-FILE.
   040     ØPEN ØUTPUT PRINTED-REPØRT-FILE.
   050 DETAIL-PRØCESSING.
   060     READ TEST-FILE, AT END GØ TØ END-ØF-JØB.
   070     ADD SCØRE TØ TØTAL-SCØRE.
   080     MØVE STUDENT-NAME TØ STUDENT-NAME-PRINT.
   090     MØVE CLASS-CØDE TØ CLASS-CØDE-PRINT.
   100     MØVE SCØRE TØ SCØRE-PRINT.
   110     MØVE SCØRE-LINE TØ PRINT-LINE.
   120     WRITE PRINT-LINE.
   130     GØ TØ DETAIL-PRØCESSING.
   140 END-ØF-JØB.
   150     MØVE SPACES TØ PRINT-LINE.
   160     WRITE PRINT-LINE.
   170     MØVE TØTAL-SCØRE TØ TØTAL-SCØRE-PRINT.
   180     MØVE TØTAL-LINE TØ PRINT-LINE.
   190     WRITE PRINT-LINE.
   200     CLØSE TEST-FILE.
   210     CLØSE PRINTED-REPØRT-FILE.
   220     STØP RUN.
```

Figure 13-11. *Complete program to solve Problem 2, continued.*

Printed Report for Problem 2

Figure 13-12 shows a partial printed report. The student name is in the first column. The class code is in the second. The test score is in the third. The total of all test scores appears under the third column. It is aligned on the right.

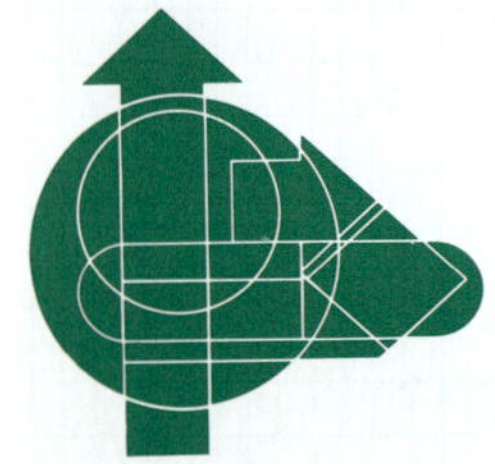

DOROTHY FOSTER	4	96
STANLEY FRANKLIN	3	85
ANITA FRIEDMAN	4	92
TOBY GLANDORF	2	76
LUCY GONZALES	3	82
JOSEPH HAZLETON	2	73
CHRISTINA HILL	4	100
JOHN KATO	3	86
LAVERNE LYKINS	2	79
ANDERSON MEYER	2	94
TIEN SHEN	2	91
LOUISE SHUMARD	4	81
CATHERINE SMITH	4	72
MARY SILVERMAN	3	84
JONATHAN SPAULDING	2	83
MARCELLA SPIROS	3	82
JOSEPH STAUDENMEYER	1	81
LOUISE UNTHANK	2	70
BARRY VOLLMER	4	91
AGNES WAVERLY	4	73
MELANIE WILLIAMSON	3	92
		12009

Figure 13-12. *Above is a partial printed report for Problem 2.*

REVIEW QUESTIONS

1. What is the programmer-invented name of the work area in the WORKING-STORAGE SECTION for accumulating a total in the program for solving Problem 2?
2. Which instruction causes an unconditional branch in the program shown in Figure 13-10?
3. What are the two detail lines described in WORKING-STORAGE in Figure 13-11? Why must these lines be moved to PRINT-LINE before printing can take place?
4. How may double-spacing be accomplished in COBOL?
5. Why are very few entries required in the PROCEDURE DIVISION of a COBOL program?
6. What is the purpose of the paragraph name on Line 050 of the PROCEDURE DIVISION in Figure 13-11?
7. What is the purpose of the paragraph name on Line 140 of this program?
8. In what division of Figure 13-11 are REMARKS written? In what division are the files named for the first time?
9. In what division are the records and fields described? Where in that division has a field been described for accumulating a total? At what level?
10. What is the name of the output line described in the FILE SECTION? At what level is it written?

ADDITIONAL COBOL STATEMENTS

So far, in Problems 1 and 2, you have learned about the READ, AT END, MOVE, and WRITE statements. They are all written in the PROCEDURE DIVISION of a COBOL program. There have been other statements mentioned while explaining the programs. These statements will be described in greater detail now.

GO TO statement

The *GO TO statement* tells the computer to branch to a step other than the next step in the order of a program. This statement is used only in the PROCEDURE DIVISION. By itself, the GO TO statement creates an unconditional branch, as in Figure 13-10 (GO TO DETAIL-PROCESSING). The GO TO statement, combined with the IF statement, creates a conditional branch. (IF CLASS-CODE NOT EQUAL TO 4, GO TO DETAIL-PROCESSING.)

IF statement

If you have studied BASIC, you already understand the IF statement. The IF statement is used in COBOL to create conditional branches. The IF statement can be written in many different ways. The *IF or conditional statement* is used to make certain tests and to direct further processing, based upon the results of these tests. One of the easiest tests that can be made is the relation test.

Relation test. Two values are compared in a *relation test*. The result of this comparison will decide the next instruction in a program that is to be followed. The IF statement follows English-language logic. The program may say IF _____ IS NOT EQUAL TO _____ GO TO _____. Relation tests can be performed to test EQUAL, NOT EQUAL, GREATER THAN, LESS THAN, GREATER THAN OR EQUAL TO, and LESS THAN OR EQUAL TO.

In BASIC, the operator would type on the terminal > =. In COBOL the words may be written out, which makes them easier to understand. (IF _____ IS GREATER THAN OR EQUAL TO _____ GO TO _____.)

In order to save space, when drawing a flowchart for a COBOL program, the relation symbols are used as they were in Chapter 9, as follows:

$=$ EQUAL TO
$\neq$ NOT EQUAL TO
$<$ LESS THAN
$>$ GREATER THAN
$\leqslant$ LESS THAN OR EQUAL TO
$\geqslant$ GREATER THAN OR EQUAL TO

The IF statement must always be written before the GO TO because the computer follows the instructions in logical order. If the programmer writes the GO TO first, the computer will go to the step mentioned and will never make the test. It would be as though the IF had never been written.

Options available with IF statements. The IF statement calls for a decision to be made. You learned in Chapter 9 that decisions may be written into a program in many ways. For example, in testing for seniors in a file of student cards, an IF statement could be written as follows:

```
IF CLASS-CODE NOT EQUAL TO 4 GO TO DETAIL-PROCESSING.
IF CLASS-CODE EQUAL TO 4 GO TO PROCESS-SENIOR.
IF CLASS-CODE LESS THAN 4 GO TO DETAIL-PROCESSING.
```

In these IF statements, a test is made for a 4-punch in CLASS-CODE in a data card. If CLASS-CODE contains a 4, the computer is told to branch to a set of instructions referred to by the paragraph name PROCESS-SENIOR. If not, the computer is instructed to branch back to the paragraph named DETAIL-PROCESSING to process a new record.

ADD statement

An ADD statement is shown on Line 005 070 of the PROCEDURE DIVISION in Figure 13-10, p. 345.

```
ADD SCORE TO TOTAL-SCORE.
```

This instruction will cause the value stored at the address named SCORE to be added to the value stored at the address named TOTAL-SCORE. The sum will be stored at the location named TOTAL-SCORE, replacing any value stored at that address before. This is much easier to understand than algebraic equations used in many other programming languages. For example, the same addition could be done with the following instructions in FORTRAN and BASIC.

```
TOTSC = TOTSC + SCORE      (FORTRAN)
    T =     T +     S      (BASIC)
```

In the COBOL example ADD SCORE TO TOTAL-SCORE, both SCORE and TOTAL-SCORE are variables. They are not known in advance. An ADD statement can also be used when adding a constant, such as 1 to a total count. For example, if a count were being made of all the records processed, an instruction could be written to add 1 to the count after each record was processed. The instruction would read:

```
ADD 1 TO COUNT.
```

REVIEW QUESTIONS

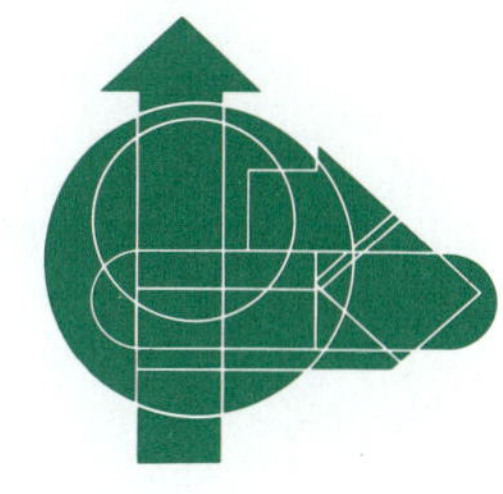

1. A GO TO used by itself forms what kind of branch?
2. What is a relation test?
3. What are six conditions that can be tested for in a relation test? How are these conditions stated in flowchart decision symbols?
5. What statement in COBOL is combined with a GO TO to form a conditional branch?
6. Should the GO TO be written first in the statement referred to in Question 5?
7. Explain the following ADD statement:
   ADD SALES-AMOUNT TO SALES-AMOUNT-TOTAL.
8. Can numeric constants be used in ADD statements? Give an example.

PROBLEM 3: PRINTING A REPORT WITH A HEADING AND MORE THAN ONE DECISION

The next problem will be a modification of Problem 2. The entire program will not be described — only the points that are new. The concepts introduced for the first time in this problem are the use of report headings and more than one decision.

The same file of cards will be used that was used for Problem 2. However, there will be only two columns of information on the printed report. There will be headings above these two columns. The computer will double-space between the headings and the first detail line of the report. Remember, double-spacing is not new. It is done by printing a line with nothing but spaces. This requires two instructions: (1) a MOVE instruction to clear the print area, and (2) an instruction to print (WRITE) the line of spaces.

Statement of the problem

A program is to be written that will cause the computer to print a two-column report, using the same input file of punched cards that was used in Problem 2. See Figure 13-3, p. 332. Details of the problem are as follows:

(1) A heading will be placed over each column of the report. The heading STUDENT NAME will be centered over the first column. The heading SCORE will be centered over the second column.
(2) A blank line will appear between the two column headings and the body of the report. Another blank line will appear between the last detail line of the report and the total score, which will appear as the very last line. The main body of the report will be single-spaced.
(3) A program is to be written that will cause the computer to print a two-column report. The student name should appear in the first column of the report and the test score in the second column.

(Continued)

(4) This report is to list the names and scores *for seniors only*. Therefore, it will be necessary to make an additional decision in the program to select only seniors (CLASS-CODE = 4?) for inclusion on the report.
(5) The printer will double-space before printing a total of all test scores for the seniors. The words TOTAL SCORE should appear to the left of the total with one space between TOTAL SCORE and the total.
(6) The entire report will be single-spaced and centered on a page 132 spaces wide. Ten spaces are to appear between columns. The total of all senior test scores will appear under the test score column, aligned on the right underneath the scores.

Analysis of the problem

There are four differences between Problems 2 and 3, as follows:

(1) There will be two columns instead of three on the printed report. (The class code will be part of the program for decision purposes. However, it will not be printed.)
(2) There will be column headings centered over each column, and double-spacing will appear at two different places in the report.
(3) The total score will be printed with the words TOTAL SCORE to the left of the total with one space intervening.
(4) Only senior students are to be listed in the report. The decision to test for senior students will compare the class code in the input record (punched card) with a constant, 4. Remember that the class code for seniors is 4. That is known in advance and can be used as a constant in the IF statement.

IDENTIFICATION DIVISION of the program for Problem 3

The IDENTIFICATION DIVISION for Problem 3 is shown in Figure 13-13. Line 030 is changed because of the change in the name of the program. Line 050 is changed because a different programmer's name is used. The REMARKS have been changed also to describe the purpose of this program. The required entries at Lines 010, 020, 040, and 060 are not changed.

ENVIRONMENT DIVISION of the program for Problem 3

The ENVIRONMENT DIVISION is the same as that for Problem 3. It gives the names of the source and object computers. In the FILE-CONTROL SECTION, it assigns the names of the input and output files. It also names the input and output devices. SELECT TEST-FILE, ASSIGN TO 'SYSIN' UNIT-RECORD. SELECT PRINTED-REPORT-FILE, ASSIGN TO 'SYSOUT' UNIT-RECORD.

COBOL PROGRAM SHEET

System | Punching Instructions | Sheet / of 6

Program SENIORS | Graphic Ø Z I O / | Card Form# | * | Identification SENIORS (73–80)

Programmer MINERVA THOMAS | Date 10/6/82 | Punch O Z I O I

Alpha — ZERO — Numeric "One"

```
001010 IDENTIFICATIØN DIVISIØN.
   020 PRØGRAM-ID.
   030     'SENIØRS'.
   040 AUTHØR.
   050     THØMAS.
   060 DATE-WRITTEN.
   070     ØCTØBER 6, 1982.
   080 REMARKS.
   090     THIS PRØGRAM LISTS THE NAME AND TEST SCØRE
   100     FØR EACH SENIØR ØNLY. CØLUMN HEADINGS WILL BE
   110     PRINTED AT THE TØP ØF THE REPØRT. A FINAL TØTAL
   120     ØF TEST SCØRES WILL BE PRINTED AT THE END.
```

Figure 13-13. *The IDENTIFICATION DIVISION for Problem 3 is very much like that for Problem 2.*

FILE SECTION of the DATA DIVISION of the program for Problem 3

Figure 13-14 shows the first part of the DATA DIVISION of the program for solving Problem 3.

The FILE SECTION, Lines 010 through 200, is the same as that for Problem 2. The same data card is used for input. It is described in Lines 030–140. The input record is PUNCHED-CARD.

```
003010 DATA DIVISIØN.
   020 FILE SECTIØN.
   030 FD  TEST-FILE
   040     RECØRDING MØDE IS F
   050     RECØRD CØNTAINS 80 CHARACTERS
   060     LABEL RECØRDS ARE ØMITTED
   070     DATA RECØRD IS PUNCHED-CARD.
   080 01  PUNCHED-CARD.
   090     02  STUDENT-NAME          PICTURE A(20).
   100     02  FILLER                PICTURE X(10).
   110     02  CLASS-CØDE            PICTURE 9.
   120     02  FILLER                PICTURE X(9).
   130     02  SCØRE                 PICTURE 999.
   140     02  FILLER                PICTURE X(37).
   150 FD  PRINTED-REPØRT-FILE
   160     RECØRDING MØDE IS F
   170     RECØRD CØNTAINS 132 CHARACTERS
   180     LABEL RECØRDS ARE ØMITTED
   190     DATA RECØRD IS PRINT-LINE.
   200 01  PRINT-LINE                PICTURE X(132).
```

Figure 13-14. *The FILE SECTION of the DATA DIVISION for Problem 2 is the same as that for Problem 3 because the data card is the same.*

PUNCHED-CARD is described exactly as it is for Problem 2. Note that CLASS-CODE is still part of the description in the input file. Even though it will not be printed on the report, the class code is used to make a comparison. Remember that the class code is used in the IF statement to determine whether the data card is for a senior student. For that reason, the computer must know where the class code is located. The computer must also be told whether the field is numeric, alphabetic, or alphanumeric.

The output file name is PRINTED-REPORT-FILE, the same name that was used in Problem 2. The FD is the same on Lines 150–190. Note that on Line 200 the output record is again named PRINT-LINE. It has the PICTURE clause X(132). You learned that this PICTURE clause tells the computer that there will be a print line of 132 alphanumeric characters. PRINT-LINE is the only name the computer will recognize for the output record. This means that all the detail lines described in WORKING-STORAGE must be moved to PRINT-LINE before they can be printed.

WORKING-STORAGE SECTION of the DATA DIVISION of the program for Problem 3

Before writing the WORKING-STORAGE SECTION, the format of the printed report must be determined.

Format of the printed report for Problem 3. A printer spacing chart showing the output format of the report is shown in Figure 13-15.

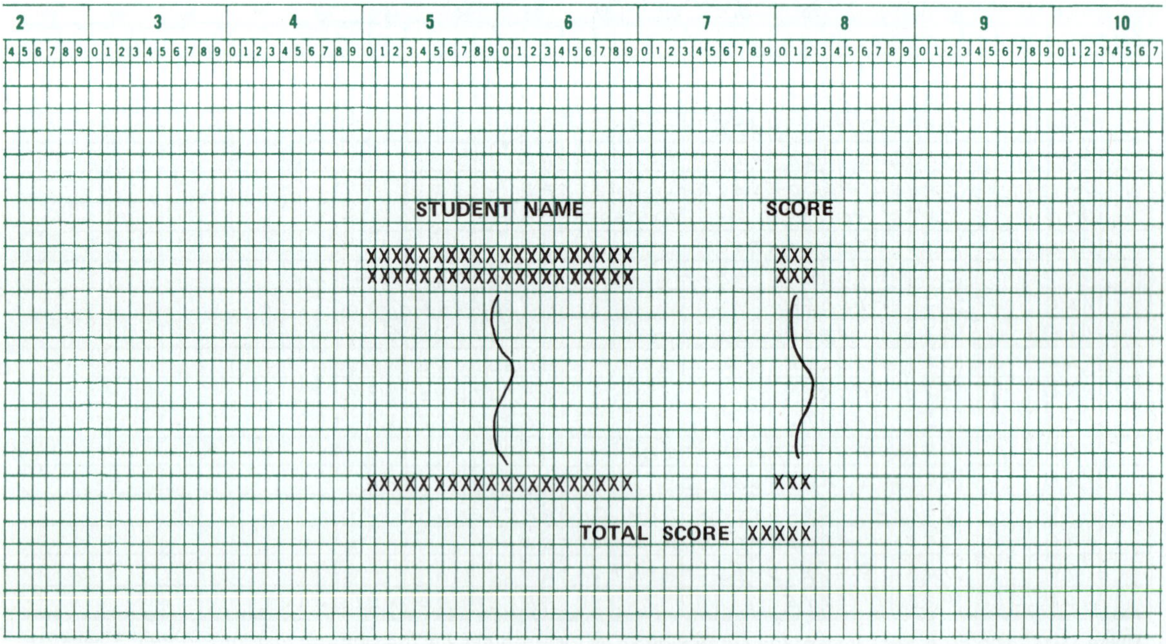

Figure 13-15. *The printed names in this printer spacing chart stand for constants; the Xs, for variables.*

Note that there are three different formats for detail lines on the report, as follows:

(1) The line for the headings will be named HEADING-LINE. The headings are centered over the two columns in the detail line name SCORE-LINE.
(2) All the lines in the body of the report use a second format. The name for each line in the body is SCORE-LINE. It will contain the student's name and score. SCORE-LINE will be centered on a 132-space line, with ten spaces between the two columns.
(3) The line for the total is named TOTAL-LINE. The total will have five characters as it did in Problem 2. It will be aligned on the right under the last score, with one blank line above it. This total will have a phrase to the left of it. It will be labeled TOTAL SCORE.

Note on Figure 13-15 that the headings are seven spaces from the top of the page (about an inch). There is a space between the headings and the body of the report. The report is single-spaced. That is shown by the two rows of Xs before the "squiggles."

The variable fields are shown with Xs. The constants represent themselves. The constants are STUDENT NAME, SCORE, and TOTAL SCORE.

SCORE-LINE format. In figuring the margins, it is easier to start with SCORE-LINE and then to center the headings later. The student's name uses 20 positions. The score uses three. There are ten spaces between columns (20 + 10 + 3 = 33). When 33 is subtracted from 132, the remainder is 99. 99 divided by 2 equals 49 spaces in one margin and 50 in the other. Note that the student name field begins at Position 50 in Line 9 of the chart. The score begins at Position 80.

HEADING-LINE format. STUDENT NAME, the first heading, has 12 characters including the space. It is to be centered over the 20-position name. 20 − 12 = 8 positions, to be divided by 2, to arrive at the number of positions to indent. The answer is 4. Therefore, STUDENT NAME is brought in four spaces and begins at Position 54 on Line 7.

SCORE is two characters longer than the score column. Therefore, SCORE is extended one space to the left. It begins at Position 79.

TOTAL-LINE format. The total is two characters longer than the scores. It is brought out two characters to the left of the score, which begins at Position 80. Therefore, the total begins at Position 78. Now, to the left of the numeric score must be allowed twelve spaces (eleven for TOTAL SCORE and one space between TOTAL SCORE and the actual total). This means that TOTAL SCORE will begin at Position 66 (78 − 12 = 66).

Use of numeric constants for comparisons. You have already learned how a numeric constant can be used to add 1 to a count. You have also learned that tests can be written in which a numeric constant is used.

The numeric constant is read into the computer in the form of an instruction. The constant in the instruction can be compared with a variable that has been read into the memory of the computer from a data card. For example:

```
IF CLASS-CODE EQUAL TO 4 GO TO PROCESS-SENIOR.
```

In the above instruction, the computer will read the Constant 4 and compare it with the number stored at the memory address named CLASS-CODE. Recall that this number is in Column 31 of the data card that has been read into the computer.

Why headings are used in reports. A heading is often written at the top of every page in a printed report. Headings identify the report itself. Often subheadings are used under the headings to identify the columns. The reports shown in this text are only one page long. However, most printouts needed by business have many pages. For that reason, you will learn how to plan a heading for a printed report.

Use of alphabetic and alphanumeric constants for headings. You have already learned how numeric constants are used in COBOL programs. You will now learn how alphabetic and alphanumeric constants may be used for headings in printed reports.

An example of an alphabetic constant used for a heading is CLASS CODE. This heading might appear over the same column on every page of a report. The heading is placed inside of single quotation marks. All letters and spaces are counted. CLASS CODE would be described with a PICTURE clause PICTURE A(10). It would be described in the WORKING-STORAGE SECTION of the DATA DIVISION with a VALUE clause. The entry would appear as follows:

```
02  FILLER              PICTURE A(10) VALUE 'CLASS CODE'.
```

However, it is often easier for the programmer to describe alphabetic data with an alphanumeric specification. When many headings are used in a report, some of the headings may have numbers or special characters. Often, the programmer will use alphanumeric descriptions, even for alphabetic material. For example, CLASS CODE has letters of the alphabet and a space. It could fit into an alphabetic or an alphanumeric class. The alphanumeric description would appear as follows:

```
02  FILLER              PICTURE X(10) VALUE 'CLASS CODE'.
```

On the other hand, a title such as FIRST-RUN MOVIES is alphanumeric only. It has a special character (hyphen).

It is always safe to describe alphabetic data with an X, but it is never correct to describe alphanumeric data with an A. Alphabetic data, with its letters and spaces, can fit into an alphanumeric (X) description. Alphanumeric data, on the other hand, may contain numbers or special characters as well. For that reason, the alphanumeric data cannot fit into an alphabetic (A) description.

Because report headings are known in advance and remain the same throughout the program, they can be described in WORKING-STORAGE with the use of the VALUE clause. In this text, all headings will be described with Xs.

WORKING-STORAGE SECTION of the DATA DIVISION for Problem 3 illustrated. The WORKING-STORAGE SECTION is shown in Figure 13-16.

```
SEQUENCE      A   B
(PAGE)(SERIAL)
004010 WØRKING-STØRAGE SECTIØN.
   020 77  TØTAL-SCØRE                 PICTURE 9(5) VALUE 0.
   030 01  HEADING-LINE.
   040     02  FILLER                  PICTURE X(53) VALUE SPACES.
   050     02  FILLER                  PICTURE X(12) VALUE 'STUDENT NAME'.
   060     02  FILLER                  PICTURE X(13) VALUE SPACES.
   070     02  FILLER                  PICTURE X(5) VALUE 'SCØRE'.
   080     02  FILLER                  PICTURE X(49) VALUE SPACES.
   090 01  SCØRE-LINE.
   100     02  FILLER                  PICTURE X(49) VALUE SPACES.
   110     02  STUDENT-NAME-PRINT      PICTURE A(20).
   120     02  FILLER                  PICTURE X(10) VALUE SPACES.
   130     02  SCØRE-PRINT             PICTURE 999.
   140     02  FILLER                  PICTURE X(50) VALUE SPACES.
   150 01  TØTAL-LINE.
   160     02  FILLER                  PICTURE X(65) VALUE SPACES.
   170     02  FILLER                  PICTURE X(12) VALUE 'TØTAL SCØRE '.
   180     02  TØTAL-SCØRE-PRINT       PICTURE 9(5).
   190     02  FILLER                  PICTURE X(50) VALUE SPACES.
```

Figure 13-16. *This WORKING-STORAGE SECTION uses a VALUE clause to set the beginning value of TOTAL-SCORE to zero. It also uses VALUE clauses for all the constants.*

VALUE clause used for numeric variable. You have already learned that temporary storage areas must be assigned when arithmetic computations are to be made. They are always assigned at the 77 level in WORKING-STORAGE. In this case, there is only one Level 77 item in Figure 13-16. It is TOTAL-SCORE, which is the same as it was in Program 2. The PICTURE clause, PICTURE 9(5) tells the computer that there will be five numbers in the total. The VALUE clause following the PICTURE clause tells the computer that the five positions will have a beginning value of 0 (zero). The VALUE clause clears TOTAL-SCORE to zero before processing the first data card.

VALUE clauses used for alphanumeric constants. Print areas are cleared of unwanted data by using a VALUE clause and the reserved word SPACES, as follows: VALUE SPACES. You learned earlier that spaces can be either alphabetic or alphanumeric in COBOL. In Figure 13-16, spaces are treated as alphanumeric and are described with Xs. The VALUE clauses tell the computer that the margins and the fields between printed columns contain blanks or spaces. Each blank field is treated as a constant field of data because its length and contents are known beforehand and the field will not change during processing of the program.

Other uses for alphanumeric constants. In the line named TOTAL-LINE, there is to be a label, TOTAL SCORE printed before the score. The words TOTAL SCORE can be described to the computer with the following:

```
PICTURE X(12) VALUE 'TOTAL SCORE '.
```

Note that there is a space between the word SCORE and the ending quotation mark. This will allow for a space between SCORE and the actual score so that the two do not run together.

Rules for the use of the VALUE clause. The VALUE clause is used only in the WORKING-STORAGE SECTION of the DATA DIVISION. It is used to give values to elementary items that cannot be subdivided further. It can describe the beginning value of a numeric variable or the actual value of a constant. A VALUE clause must have a PICTURE clause before it on the line. The period will then come at the end of the VALUE clause and not after the PICTURE clause.

When to use VALUE clauses. In order to describe heading lines, detail lines, and total lines with VALUE clauses as shown in Figure 13-16, you should remember four things:

(1) The description of PRINT-LINE in the FILE SECTION of the DATA DIVISION must be PICTURE X(132). This is a broad description of each kind of line.
(2) The detailed description of the fields on each line are given in the WORKING-STORAGE SECTION.
(3) All constants must have VALUE clauses. The PICTURE clause used with the VALUE clause for a constant must include a count of all characters, even the spaces.
(4) A numeric variable described at the 77 level must have a VALUE clause if it is used to set a beginning value of zero to an area for accumulating a total. All other variables should not have VALUE clauses because they will change automatically as new data are entered.

Advantage of the VALUE clause. The most important advantage of using the VALUE clause is that when VALUE clauses are used in the WORKING-STORAGE SECTION, the exact value of the fields is given. Unused areas on the print line are cleared with VALUE SPACES. This saves time and instructions in the PROCEDURE DIVISION because MOVE instructions are not needed for clearing print areas.

FILLER statements in the program for Problem 3. FILLER statements were used in earlier programs to describe unused areas on a punched card or print line. Another use of the FILLER statement is shown in the WORKING-STORAGE SECTION of the program for Problem 3, Figure 13-16. The statements are repeated here for easy access.

```
004 030 01  HEADING-LINE.
    040     02  FILLER               PICTURE X(53) VALUE SPACES.
    050     02  FILLER               PICTURE X(12) VALUE 'STUDENT NAME'.
    060     02  FILLER               PICTURE X(13) VALUE SPACES.
    070     02  FILLER               PICTURE X(5)  VALUE 'SCORE'.
    080     02  FILLER               PICTURE X(49) VALUE SPACES.

004 150 01  TOTAL-LINE.
    160     02  FILLER               PICTURE X(65) VALUE SPACES.
    170     02  FILLER               PICTURE X(12) VALUE 'TOTAL SCORE  '.
    180     02  TOTAL-SCORE-PRINT    PICTURE 9(5).
    190     02  FILLER               PICTURE X(50) VALUE SPACES.
```

Refer to Lines 050, 070, and 170. Note that these entries use the word FILLER instead of a programmer-invented name. The actual constant is set off in single quotes in a VALUE clause. Alphanumeric constants can be handled in this manner.

The word *FILLER* may be used instead of a data name whenever the data item will not need to be moved separately during the running of the program. Every item description entry in the DATA DIVISION must have either a programmer-invented name or the reserved word FILLER. The word FILLER has a specific meaning to the COBOL compiler. It cannot be referenced as a data field by instructions in the PROCEDURE DIVISION.

The reason for using the FILLER statements for all the fields in the heading line and the total line is that the computer can be told to move the entire line in each case to PRINT-LINE. Separate MOVE instructions are not needed for the column headings, STUDENT NAME and SCORE. The entire HEADING-LINE can be moved in one instruction in the PROCEDURE DIVISION because every field on the line is a constant. The detail line, SCORE-LINE, on the other hand, must have programmer-invented names for the variables, STUDENT-NAME-PRINT and SCORE-PRINT. For this reason, there must be a separate instruction in the PROCEDURE DIVISION to move STUDENT-NAME to STUDENT-NAME-PRINT and SCORE to SCORE-PRINT.

The use of the reserved word FILLER is preferred by most programmers when headings are being described with VALUE clauses. This practice makes for fewer MOVE instructions in the PROCEDURE DIVISION.

Note that each detail line is a record and must be written at the 01 level. Line 004 030 is written at Level 01 and states the name of the output record, HEADING-LINE. Lines 040–080 are fields within the record, HEADING-LINE. They are written at the 02 level. The elementary items (fields) on the record, HEADING-LINE, are all written at the

02 level. They are all FILLER statements and describe elementary items that are defined with VALUE clauses.

In Line 004 150, TOTAL-LINE is written at the 01 level. Each of the fields in the line is described at the 02 level. There are VALUE clauses used for the constants. The constants are the spaces in the margins as well as the words TOTAL SCORE. Note that there is a space between the words TOTAL SCORE and the single quote on Line 170.

On Line 180, TOTAL-SCORE-PRINT is a variable. It is the address to which the total score will be moved. The amount of the total score will not be known until the last card has been processed. Therefore, TOTAL-SCORE-PRINT does not have a VALUE clause. Remember that VALUE clauses are used either for constants or to set the beginning value of a numeric variable to zero.

Flowchart for solving Problem 3

Figure 13-17 shows the flowchart for solving Problem 3.
The first difference is in Symbols 3 and 4. In this problem, a heading line is needed. Symbol 3 causes HEADING-LINE to be moved from WORKING-STORAGE to the print area. It is then printed (4). A blank line for double-spacing is accomplished by moving spaces (blanks) to the PRINT-LINE (5) and then printing the line full of spaces (6).

The on-page connector (1) is placed just before the READ instruction (7). Steps 7 and 8 are used to READ and perform a test for the last-card code in a card in the data file. If the last-card code is in the card, the computer will branch to Step 14, shown with the on-page connector (3). If the last-card code is not in the card, the computer will go on with the program by moving to Step 9.

Step 9 is another decision symbol. A test is to be made to see if CLASS-CODE (Column 31 of the card) is for a senior (CLASS-CODE EQUAL TO 4). If there is a 4 in Column 31, the card is for a senior. The computer is ordered to continue processing the card by going to the step indicated by on-page connector (2). If the punch in Column 31 is not a 4, the card is not for a senior and should not be processed. The computer is then told to loop back to the on-page connector (1), Step 7, and read another card.

If CLASS-CODE is equal to 4, the student's score is added to the total score (10). The student's name and score are then moved separately to the areas described on SCORE-LINE for them, STUDENT-NAME-PRINT and SCORE-PRINT (11). The SCORE-LINE is then moved to the PRINT-LINE (12) and printed (13). After this, the computer is told to loop back to the on-page connector (1), Symbol 7, to read another card.

If the last card has been processed at Step 8, the computer is instructed to go to on-page connector (3) and perform the final steps in the program. Spaces are moved to PRINT-LINE (14) and printed (15). This causes double-spacing between the last student's score and the total

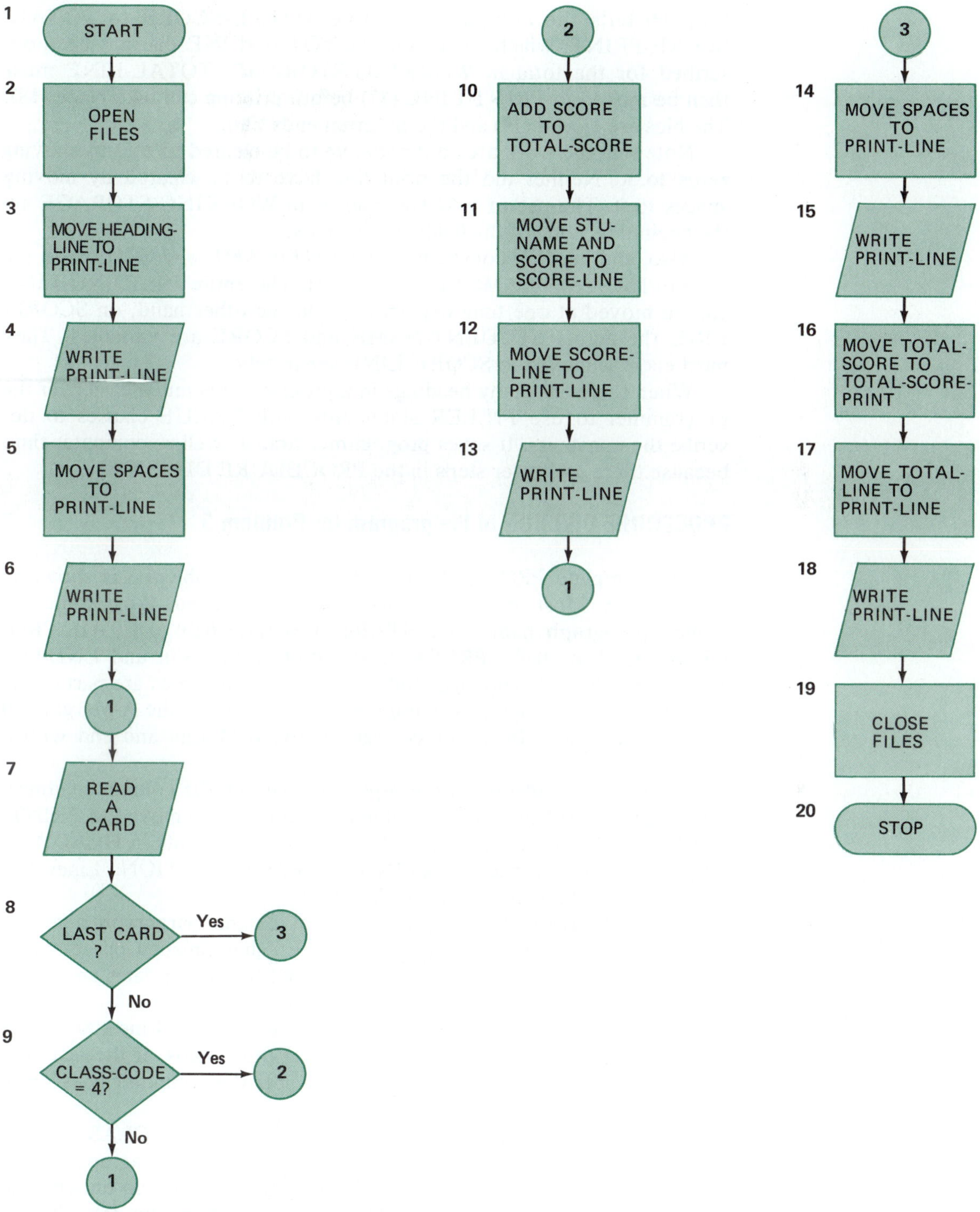

Figure 13-17. *The flowchart for Problem 3 has two decisions. It also allows for a heading line and a total line. There is double-spacing after the heading and before the total.*

Step 16 tells the computer to move TOTAL-SCORE to TOTAL-SCORE-PRINT, which is the area on TOTAL-LINE that has been described for the total in WORKING-STORAGE. TOTAL-LINE must then be moved to PRINT-LINE (17) before printing can take place (18). The files are closed (19) and the program ends (20).

Note that the work area did not have to be cleared to zero by moving zeros to it. Neither did the print line have to be cleared by moving spaces to it. The use of VALUE clauses in WORKING-STORAGE set the beginning value of the fields on the lines.

Also, the heading constants STUDENT NAME and SCORE do not have to have separate MOVE instructions. The entire HEADING-LINE can be moved at one time (Symbol 2). On the other hand, on SCORE-LINE the actual STUDENT-NAME and SCORE are variables. They must each be moved to SCORE-LINE separately.

When there are many headings in a program, it is much easier for the programmer to use FILLER statements with VALUE clauses to describe the constants. It saves programmer time as well as computer time because there are fewer steps in the PROCEDURE DIVISION.

PROCEDURE DIVISION of the program for Problem 3

The complete PROCEDURE DIVISION for Problem 3 is shown in Figure 13-18. Most of the steps need not be explained. Programmer-invented paragraph names are START-JOB (line 020), DETAIL-PROCESSING (Line 090), PROCESS-SENIOR (Line 130), and END-OF-JOB (Line 200). All sentences following paragraph names are part of the steps within the paragraphs. Paragraph names begin at the A-Margin and end with a period. Instructions begin at the B-Margin and end with a period.

Lines 050 and 060 begin the report by printing the column headings. Note that line 050 causes both column headings to be moved to PRINT-LINE at the same time because they are both constants in HEADING-LINE described in the WORKING-STORAGE SECTION. Lines 070 and 080 cause double-spacing to take place.

Line 090, DETAIL-PROCESSING gives the paragraph name to which the computer will branch each time it has finished processing a data card. Line 120, GO TO DETAIL-PROCESSING, creates an unconditional branch to set up this loop.

Line 100 is the READ and last-card test instruction. Line 100 creates a conditional branch to Line 200, END-OF-JOB steps, if the last-card code is in the data card just read. If it is not, the computer goes on in logical order to line 110.

Line 110 is another conditional branch instruction. If CLASS-CODE is equal to 4, the computer is told to branch to the paragraph named PROCESS-SENIOR, Line 130. If not, the computer will go on with the next instruction, Line 120. Line 120 is the unconditional branch, GO TO DETAIL-PROCESSING, that creates a loop back to the READ instruction.

```
SEQUENCE
(PAGE)(SERIAL)  A   B
005010 PRØCEDURE DIVISIØN.
   020 START-JØB.
   030     ØPEN INPUT TEST-FILE.
   040     ØPEN ØUTPUT PRINTED-REPØRT-FILE.
   050     MØVE HEADING-LINE TØ PRINT-LINE.
   060     WRITE PRINT-LINE.
   070     MØVE SPACES TØ PRINT-LINE.
   080     WRITE PRINT-LINE.
   090 DETAIL-PRØCESSING.
   100     READ TEST-FILE, AT END GØ TØ END-ØF-JØB.
   110     IF CLASS-CØDE EQUAL TØ 4 GØ TØ PRØCESS-SENIØR.
   120     GØ TØ DETAIL-PRØCESSING.
   130 PRØCESS-SENIØR.
   140     ADD SCØRE TØ TØTAL-SCØRE.
   150     MØVE STUDENT-NAME TØ STUDENT-NAME-PRINT.
   160     MØVE SCØRE TØ SCØRE-PRINT.
   170     MØVE SCØRE-LINE TØ PRINT-LINE.
   180     WRITE PRINT-LINE.
   190     GØ TØ DETAIL-PRØCESSING.
   200 END-ØF-JØB.
   210     MØVE SPACES TØ PRINT-LINE.
   220     WRITE PRINT-LINE.
   230     MØVE TØTAL-SCØRE TØ TØTAL-SCØRE-PRINT.
   240     MØVE TØTAL-LINE TØ PRINT-LINE.
   250     WRITE PRINT-LINE.
006010     CLØSE TEST-FILE.
   020     CLØSE PRINTED-REPØRT-FILE.
   030     STØP RUN.
```

Figure 13-18. *The PROCEDURE DIVISION for Problem 3 has a new paragraph PROCESS-SENIORS. It has two conditional branches and two unconditional branches.*

If there is a 4 in CLASS-CODE, the computer will branch to the paragraph name PROCESS-SENIOR. It will add SCORE to TOTAL-SCORE (Line 140). It will move STUDENT-NAME to STUDENT-NAME-PRINT (Line 150) and SCORE to SCORE-PRINT (Line 160). After these two variable fields have been moved to the areas on SCORE-LINE defined for them, SCORE-LINE itself must be moved to PRINT-LINE (Line 170). The computer will write PRINT-LINE (Line 180) and then branch back to DETAIL-PROCESSING (Line 190). Line 190 is another unconditional branch instruction.

When the last card has been processed, the computer branches to END-OF-JOB at Line 200. The next step consists of double-spacing before the total line (Lines 210 and 220). TOTAL-SCORE is moved to TOTAL-SCORE-PRINT, which is the area on TOTAL-LINE defined for it. TOTAL-LINE is then moved to PRINT-LINE. There is an order to write PRINT-LINE (Line 230). The input and output files are closed (Lines 006 010 and 020). The last line, 030, is the instruction, STOP RUN, which must be last in every COBOL program. The END-OF-JOB steps are the same as those in Problem 2.

COBOL program for solving Problem 3

Figure 13-19 shows the DATA and PROCEDURE DIVISIONS for the program. It is not necessary to show the other two divisions.

```
SEQUENCE  A   B
003010 DATA DIVISION.
   020 FILE SECTION.
   030 FD  TEST-FILE
   040     RECØRDING MØDE IS F
   050     RECØRD CØNTAINS 80 CHARACTERS
   060     LABEL RECØRDS ARE ØMITTED
   070     DATA RECØRD IS PUNCHED-CARD.
   080 01  PUNCHED-CARD.
   090     02  STUDENT-NAME        PICTURE A(20).
   100     02  FILLER              PICTURE X(10).
   110     02  CLASS-CØDE          PICTURE 9.
   120     02  FILLER              PICTURE X(9).
   130     02  SCØRE               PICTURE 999.
   140     02  FILLER              PICTURE X(37).
   150 FD  PRINTED-REPØRT-FILE
   160     RECØRDING MØDE IS F
   170     RECØRD CØNTAINS 132 CHARACTERS
   180     LABEL RECØRDS ARE ØMITTED
   190     DATA RECØRD IS PRINT-LINE.
   200 01  PRINT-LINE              PICTURE X(132).
004010 WØRKING-STØRAGE SECTIØN.
   020 77  TØTAL-SCØRE             PICTURE 9(5) VALUE 0.
   030 01  HEADING-LINE.
   040     02  FILLER              PICTURE X(53) VALUE SPACES.
   050     02  FILLER              PICTURE X(12) VALUE 'STUDENT NAME'.
   060     02  FILLER              PICTURE X(13) VALUE SPACES.
   070     02  FILLER              PICTURE X(5) VALUE 'SCØRE'.
   080     02  FILLER              PICTURE X(49) VALUE SPACES.
   090 01  SCØRE-LINE.
   100     02  FILLER              PICTURE X(49) VALUE SPACES.
   110     02  STUDENT-NAME-PRINT  PICTURE A(20).
   120     02  FILLER              PICTURE X(10) VALUE SPACES.
   130     02  SCØRE-PRINT         PICTURE 999.
   140     02  FILLER              PICTURE X(50) VALUE SPACES.
   150 01  TØTAL-LINE.
   160     02  FILLER              PICTURE X(65) VALUE SPACES.
   170     02  FILLER              PICTURE X(12) VALUE 'TØTAL SCØRE '.
   180     02  TØTAL-SCØRE-PRINT   PICTURE 9(5).
   190     02  FILLER              PICTURE X(50) VALUE SPACES.
```

Figure 13-19. *Above are the DATA and PROCEDURE DIVISIONS for the COBOL program to solve Problem 3.*

```
PROCEDURE DIVISION.
START-JOB.
    OPEN INPUT TEST-FILE.
    OPEN OUTPUT PRINTED-REPORT-FILE.
    MOVE HEADING-LINE TO PRINT-LINE.
    WRITE PRINT-LINE.
    MOVE SPACES TO PRINT-LINE.
    WRITE PRINT-LINE.
DETAIL-PROCESSING.
    READ TEST-FILE, AT END GO TO END-OF-JOB.
    IF CLASS-CODE EQUAL TO 4 GO TO PROCESS-SENIOR.
    GO TO DETAIL-PROCESSING.
PROCESS-SENIOR.
    ADD SCORE TO TOTAL-SCORE.
    MOVE STUDENT-NAME TO STUDENT-NAME-PRINT.
    MOVE SCORE TO SCORE-PRINT.
    MOVE SCORE-LINE TO PRINT-LINE.
    WRITE PRINT-LINE.
    GO TO DETAIL-PROCESSING.
END-OF-JOB.
    MOVE SPACES TO PRINT-LINE.
    WRITE PRINT-LINE.
    MOVE TOTAL-SCORE TO TOTAL-SCORE-PRINT.
    MOVE TOTAL-LINE TO PRINT-LINE.
    WRITE PRINT-LINE.
    CLOSE TEST-FILE.
    CLOSE PRINTED-REPORT-FILE.
    STOP RUN.
```

Figure 13-19. *The DATA and PROCEDURE DIVISIONS of the program to solve Problem 3, continued.*

Printed report for Problem 3

Figure 13-20 shows a partial printed report for the program to solve Problem 3.

```
STUDENT NAME          SCORE

DOROTHY FOSTER          96
ANITA FRIEDMAN          92
CHRISTINA HILL         100
LOUISE SHUMARD          81
CATHERINE SMITH         72
BARRY VOLLMER           91
AGNES WAVERLY           73

                  TOTAL SCORE 12009
```

Figure 13-20. *Above is a partial printed report for the program to solve Problem 3.*

Note that the column headings are centered over the two columns. Also, the printed total requires two more digit positions than are used for the test score. Also, the words TOTAL SCORE are printed to the left of the total.

VERTICAL SPACING IN COBOL

Vertical spacing in COBOL is usually single-spacing unless the computer is given other instructions. You have already learned how double-spacing is done by moving spaces to a print line and then writing an order to print the line. This method of double-spacing uses two instructions in the PROCEDURE DIVISION, as follows:

```
070 MOVE SPACES TO PRINT-LINE.
080 WRITE PRINT-LINE.
```

There is another way to cause double-spacing. This method makes it possible to double-space and write a line in the same instruction. The instruction can be written as follows:

```
070 WRITE PRINT-LINE AFTER ADVANCING 2 LINES.
```

This order causes the printer to advance (move the paper up) two lines instead of the usual one. It then writes a print line on the second line. This leaves one blank line and causes double-spacing.

Triple-spacing can also be done by either method. The first way would require three instructions, as follows:

```
070 MOVE SPACES TO PRINT-LINE.
080 WRITE PRINT-LINE.
090 WRITE PRINT-LINE.
```

Each print (WRITE) instruction will cause the printer to advance the paper one vertical print line. More blank lines could be had by repeating the WRITE statement as often as needed.

The same result can be had by the second method with the following order:

```
070  WRITE PRINT-LINE AFTER ADVANCING 3 LINES.
```

SUMMARY

The IDENTIFICATION DIVISION of a COBOL program may have a REMARKS section. In this section, the programmer can explain the nature and purpose of the program for documentation.

The data record to be processed is explained in detail in the DATA DIVISION. The programmer uses a printer spacing chart to plan the WORKING-STORAGE SECTION of the DATA DIVISION when describing output records. The chart is used to help describe the margins, spaces between columns, and data fields to the computer. The chart also shows whether the report is single-spaced or double-spaced and whether there are headings and totals. Variable data are represented in the spacing chart with the Letter X. Constants, such as headings, are shown as they will actually appear.

A work area in the computer must be cleared in order to accumulate totals. This is done in the WORKING-STORAGE SECTION. A programmer-invented name is given to this storage area. It is described with a PICTURE clause that must allow enough positions for the largest possible total. The line is described at the 77 level, beginning at the A-Margin. Level 77 entries are written ahead of all other entries in the WORKING-STORAGE SECTION. The value of zero can be given to the area with a VALUE 0. statement in the PICTURE clause.

Total lines, heading lines, and other detail lines can be described in the WORKING-STORAGE SECTION after Level 77 items. A total line is described with a FILLER statement preceding and following the total name with PICTURE clauses describing the number of spaces before and after the total. The total is given a name on the total line such as TOTAL-PRINT or TOTAL-SCORE-PRINT. The total is actually accumulated at an address in WORKING-STORAGE, such as TOTAL or TOTAL-SCORE. A MOVE instruction must be written in the PROCEDURE DIVISION to move the total to the area described for it on the total line. Another MOVE instruction must be written to move TOTAL-LINE to PRINT-LINE before printing can take place.

All detail lines to be printed must be moved from WORKING-STORAGE to PRINT-LINE before printing can take place.

The last-card test in COBOL consists of a READ statement combined with an AT END statement. This creates a conditional branch. The GO TO statement is used to create an unconditional branch. The IF statement is used for making a comparison or test. When combined with the IF statement, a GO TO statement will create a conditional branch. The IF must always be written before the GO TO, however, or the IF will never be reached.

Tests are made in COBOL based on relationships. Unlike BASIC, the relational operators can be spelled out. They are EQUAL TO, NOT EQUAL TO, LESS THAN, GREATER THAN, LESS THAN OR EQUAL TO, and GREATER THAN OR EQUAL TO.

An ADD statement causes a computation to be made. A statement such as ADD AMOUNT TO TOTAL causes a value stored at an address named AMOUNT to be added to a value stored at an address named TOTAL. The sum will be stored at the address named TOTAL, replacing any amount stored at TOTAL before.

Data processed in COBOL are of two kinds: (1) variable and (2) constant. Programmers invent names for variable data. The constant data are self-describing. For example, the Digit 1 can be added to a count each time a new record is processed. Digit 1 is a constant. Tests can be written in which a variable number that has been read into memory from a punched card is compared with a constant in an instruction. An example is CLASS CODE EQUAL TO 4?

Alphabetic and alphanumeric constants are described to the computer by enclosing them inside single quotation marks after a VALUE clause. All letters, numbers, special characters, and spaces inside of the quotation marks are counted as part of the field. The quotation marks are not counted. These constants are described in the WORKING-STORAGE SECTION of the DATA DIVISION by the use of FILLER statements combined with PICTURE clauses that contain VALUE clauses. The PICTURE clause describes the type and length of the data field. The VALUE clause states its actual value. An example is: FILLER PICTURE X(12) VALUE 'STUDENT NAME'. The FILLER statement is written at the 02 level. VALUE clauses can be used only in the WORKING-STORAGE SECTION for elementary items. They are used to set beginning values for numeric variables. They are also used to give a value to alphabetic and alphanumeric constants.

The input and output records are described in the FILE SECTION of the DATA DIVISION. However, when there are many print lines in a report, all print lines can be described in the FILE SECTION with a "dummy" line and a PICTURE clause PICTURE X(132). Each detail line can then be described in the WORKING-STORAGE SECTION with FILLER statements and VALUE clauses. Each line must then be moved out of WORKING-STORAGE to the print line with a MOVE instruction in the PROCEDURE DIVISION.

If an entire line contains nothing but constants that have been described with VALUE clauses, the entire line can be moved to PRINT-LINE with only one instruction. With variables, however, there must be one MOVE instruction for each variable data field to be printed.

COBOL usually allows for single-spacing unless the compiler is instructed otherwise. Double-spacing or triple spacing can be done with an order to MOVE SPACES TO PRINT-LINE and one or more WRITE instructions following. Another method is to write an instruction such as WRITE PRINT-LINE AFTER ADVANCING 2 LINES or WRITE PRINT-LINE AFTER ADVANCING 3 LINES.

REVIEW QUESTIONS

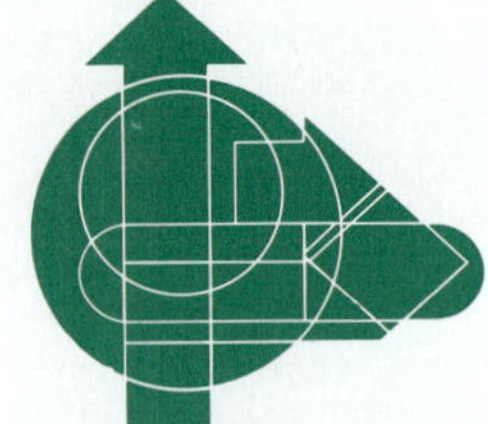

1. How are constants shown on a printer spacing chart? How are variables shown?
2. How is a numeric constant in a program instruction used to make a comparison with a variable field in a data card? Give an example.
3. How are print areas cleared of unwanted data with a VALUE clause?
4. How is a VALUE clause written for an alphanumeric constant? How are the characters counted?
5. Can a VALUE clause be used in the FILE SECTION of the DATA DIVISION?
6. What is the reason for using FILLER statements instead of data names when describing alphanumeric constants in WORKING-STORAGE?

(Continued)

7. Write a FILLER statement with a PICTURE clause and a VALUE clause for the following heading. You may use your own line number.

   STUDENT AVERAGES FOR FIRST SEMESTER

8. How do the directions in Symbols 4 and 5 in Figure 13-17 allow for skipping a line between the column headings and the first detail line of the report?
9. Explain why the use of VALUE clauses in the WORKING-STORAGE SECTION can save MOVE instructions in the PROCEDURE DIVISION.
10. Which lines in Figure 13-18 create the conditional branches? The unconditional branches?
11. How many lines will be skipped on a report with the following instructions?

```
060 MOVE SPACES TO PRINT-LINE.
070 WRITE PRINT-LINE.
080 WRITE PRINT-LINE.
090 WRITE PRINT-LINE.
```

12. How many lines will be skipped on a report with the following instruction:

```
100 WRITE PRINT-LINE AFTER ADVANCING 5 LINES.
```

NEW TERMS

- Alphabetic constant
- Alphanumeric constant
- Elementary item
- FILLER
- Group item
- IF statement
- GO TO statement
- Numeric constant
- Relation test
- Test control card
- VALUE clause
- Variable

STUDY GUIDES

Complete Study Guide 13 by following the instructions in your STUDY GUIDES booklet.

PROJECTS

Complete Projects 13-1 through 13-5 by following the instructions in your PROJECTS booklet.

14

SOCIAL IMPACT of the COMPUTER

American Micro Products, Inc.

Some people compare it to the discovery of the wheel or the invention of the printing press. Others say its effects on society are as important as those of the Industrial Revolution. Still others say that the very survival of the human race depends on it. A totally different opinion is that this device ignores human values — that individual differences and rights are not recognized. This device, of course, is the computer. It is apparent that its impact on society is great — whether good or bad. Why do these different opinions exist?

You have learned that the computer is a tool — a complex and powerful tool — but still a tool to do tasks that might also be done without it. These tasks might not be done as well without the computer. They might not be done as fast. As with any tool, however, its good or bad use depends upon the choices of the users. The computer gives people choices to use its power to help or to harm themselves or others.

BENEFITS OF THE COMPUTER TO BUSINESS DECISION MAKERS

Many people believe that American business could not operate today without the computer. The services and goods needed by the American public require many companies to supply them. The millions of people living in our communities are served by many companies that produce or sell cars, food, and other merchandise. Services, such as banking, telephone, gas, and electricity are supplied by many other companies. These goods and services could not be provided to so many people without the use of the computer. See Figure 14-1.

Figure 14-1. *Computers help banks to serve people.*

Source: Alabama Bancorporation, 1977 Annual Report

The computer helps business decision makers in the following ways:

(1) Information can be obtained quickly on the status of business operations. How many bills are due from customers? How much money is owed to other businesses? Is inventory low? What is the current profit or loss to the company? These are important questions to any business — with or without the computer to help get the answers. Having a computer makes the information available quickly. Then action can be taken before problems develop which cannot be corrected.

(2) Increased business can be handled easily. More customers can be served, and served better, by having the right products on hand, shipping the goods quickly, and billing customers promptly.

(3) Money is saved. Extra inventory does not have to be kept on hand. Just the right amount of raw materials is on hand for production. Manufactured items can be made to meet high standards by computerized control of production quality.

(4) Future operations can be planned with the help of the computer. Because of the computer's high speed, the outcome of several different future actions or decisions can be compared. Assuming that judgments about future events or conditions are correct, the best decision or plan can be chosen.

(5) Business operations can be controlled in part by looking at exception reports. An *exception report* is a report that tells when business events have not turned out as planned. Sales may be lower than expected; costs, higher; or profits, less. The manager needs to know what unusual events have taken place. Then actions can be taken to handle the problem. When business is going as planned, a report to the manager may not be needed. The report would only repeat details of earlier plans and contain no new information. With the aid of the computer, actual business events can be quickly compared with the planned or expected events. Then only the differences can be noted and reported to management. See Figure 14-2.

Figure 14-2. *A report to the manager may be needed when business events have not turned out as planned.*

ADVANTAGES TO BUSINESS EMPLOYEES

Computers are needed to perform business operations requiring the handling of a lot of data. Computers have made it possible for business to serve most customers and to earn profits by doing so. But, how have employees benefitted from the use of the computer?

Routine tasks eliminated

A major impact on employees has been the removal of routine record-keeping tasks. When the computer does the repetitive calculations, employees who have done routine tasks, such as adding and multiplying, can now do more interesting work. Some of the routine jobs which have been eliminated because they are no longer necessary in some companies have included payroll clerk, invoice clerk, accounts payable clerk, or accounts receivable clerk.

New jobs created

The computer has allowed businesses to operate better and to grow. New jobs have been created. Data-entry operators are needed to get data ready for the computer. Programmers are needed to write computer programs to process the data. Persons are needed to operate the computer and to take care of the magnetic tape and disk files. (See Figure 14-3.) Planners design the company procedures for using the computer. These job opportunities will be explained in more detail in Chapter 15, Data Processing Careers.

Modern Office Procedures

Figure 14-3. *A tape librarian is in charge of magnetic tape files.*

New computer-related jobs added

The jobs just mentioned are needed to use the computer within a business. Many other computer-related jobs have also been created that did not exist before the computer. Engineers make and repair the equipment. Sales persons sell computers to the growing number of businesses and individuals who are buying computers. Teachers train persons to fill the new data processing jobs. Researchers and scientists seek answers to questions that require complex calculations that could not be made without the computer.

BENEFITS TO INDIVIDUALS IN THEIR DAILY LIVES

Computers are changing the way society processes information to solve many kinds of problems. The following are just a few of the many uses of the computer that are going on right now to make life better or safer for all people.

Weather and environment

Weather forecasting makes use of computers to study conditions in different parts of the country and to predict the weather for the next day, week, or month. Trends can even be spotted to predict climate changes over the next several years. Long-range forecasting helps farmers in crop planting and harvesting. It aids towns in preparing for possible disasters — floods, tornados, or blizzards. Forecasting of hurricanes — their wind strength and directions — has saved thousands of lives. Computers have also been used, but with less success, to predict earthquakes.

Tracking oil spills and the flow of other pollutants in streams has helped to overcome environmental hazards. The path that water currents will take, the changes in the wind, and the changes in water temperature affect the direction in which pollutants will travel. When computers make these predictions, action can be taken quickly to clean up the mess.

Community service

Fire fighting and the saving of lives is helped by the computer. A fire department can keep a file of the names and addresses of sick persons. When an alarm sounds, fire fighters can then find out rapidly where a sick person lives and get to that person quickly. Stopping fires caused by arson can also be helped by the computer. A file can be kept in several fire departments to describe fires thought to be started on purpose by someone. By trading this information between departments, several fires that are alike can be noticed.

Crime control

Crime control is another area in which computers help to organize much information. States have agreed, for example, to share drivers' license records for persons whose licenses have been taken away. These people cannot go to a neighboring state for a license. Other records of crimes committed are kept by the FBI's National Crime Information Center. For example, this information has been used to find stolen cars that are driven across state lines. Society as a whole is protected when the computer helps in catching persons accused of crimes. Figure 14-4 shows a police officer checking a driver's license number.

Health promotion

People may be helped more directly by the computer in the medical field. The computer can be used to diagnose illnesses. It is possible in

Photo courtesy, Digital Equipment Corporation

Figure 14-4. *A computer helps in law enforcement.*

some cases for patients to sit at a terminal and answer common questions about how they feel and what illnesses they have had. These answers are looked at by the doctor, who continues with more detailed questions. Time is saved by busy doctors and nurses. More patients can be helped than if a doctor or nurse were needed to ask all the questions.

Computerized scanners are used to look for tissues that are not normal. These scanners aid in early diagnosis of serious diseases.

The computer can be used even more directly to help patients recover in hospitals. Monitoring devices can be attached to a person to tell if there are changes in temperature, heart rate, blood pressure, or other vital signs. The computer can check these measures against normal readings and send a message to nurses or doctors immediately if there is a change.

Persons with physical handicaps can be helped by the computer. It is possible with special printing devices to get computer output in Braille. Continuing work with voice synthesis is also of help to blind persons. Spoken sound can be used both as computer input and output. You learned earlier that the number of words that can be used for voice synthesis is still small, however.

Learning aids

An industry primarily concerned with sharing information is education. It is not surprising to learn that experimental work is going on to use computers for teaching. You learned in Chapter 8 that in some schools the students can sit at computer terminals as they are taught a subject. They use the computer keyboard to answer questions about what they have read on the CRT screen. The computer is very patient in checking answers and repeating information in different ways to help students understand. See Figure 14-5.

Figure 14-5. *Students use the computer terminal.*

Photo courtesy of IBM Corporation

Students who use computers directly for learning new subjects are taking part in *computer-assisted instruction*. The computer, rather than a human teacher, is presenting new information. A human teacher, of course, had to help write the computer program to teach the subject matter and give test questions. Preparing the program to teach a subject or to present a test in a subject is very time-consuming. But once the program is written, it can be used by hundreds of students. The teacher then has more time to work with students in other ways.

Using the computer to teach is not as common as using the computer to help manage student records. Just as in business applications, the computer can be used by schools to organize and store records. When the computer is used for planning lessons rather than for teaching, the process is known as *computer-managed instruction*.

Some schools allow students to learn by working on different materials in one classroom at the same time. With many activities going on in one class, the computer helps the teacher keep track of the lessons or units completed by each student. The computer may also score tests and plan future activities based on these test scores. The computer can be used for keeping class schedules and records of students' grades.

Electronic funds transfer

The computer is an important aid to people in managing their personal finances. They may not even be aware that the computer is handling the transfer of their money. Anyone who has a checking account at a bank receives a monthly statement. This statement is regularly updated by a computer. Without the computer, it would be impossible for banks to process large volumes of checks quickly and accurately.

The use of the computer to process personal financial transactions is likely to increase as the electronic funds transfer principle becomes more widely accepted. *Electronic funds transfer* is the process by which money can be exchanged electronically using the computer. A person does not have to start the process by writing a check or using another type of source document.

The electronic transfer of money can be made automatic because persons with bank accounts have done one of two things:

(1) Given earlier written authorization for money to be transferred into or out of their accounts automatically.
(2) Presented a coded *identification card (ID card)* to verify that they want their bank accounts to be changed.

The first type of authorization for automatic deposits and payments is used for the following kinds of transfers:

(1) Automatic deposits of payroll or Social Security checks into a checking or savings account. No trip to the bank is needed to deposit this money.
(2) Payment of bills that do not change from month to month. Examples are payments on home mortgages and car loans owed to the customer's bank. These amounts are deducted by the bank regularly from a savings or checking account. The person paying these bills would not have to remember to write a check each month. The bank has the use of the money sooner than if checks were sent through the mail.
(3) Payment of bills that vary from month to month. Examples are utility bills, telephone bills, and payments on charge accounts. The customer is given a list by the bank. The list has the code numbers of merchants and other companies who have money on deposit at the customer's bank. The customer uses a Touch-Tone phone to enter a code number for personal identification. When the ID has "cleared," the code numbers and amounts owed to each company are entered. The money is automatically transferred from the customer's account to the accounts of the companies listed. Again, no checks are written. Time is saved. The companies have the use of the money sooner than if checks were sent through the mail.

Electronic funds transfers using coded ID cards are carried out at terminals located outside the bank or in other public places. (Refer again to Figure 14-1.) These transactions include the following:

(1) Receipt of cash.
(2) Deposits of cash or checks into a checking or savings account.
(3) Payments by cash or check to the bank for loan payments.

The advantage of using the coded ID card in the terminal located outside the bank is that banking transactions can be carried out when the bank is closed. Banking terminals in other public places, such as airports, grocery stores, shopping centers, or university campuses, make it convenient to use banking services.

Persons using electronic funds transfer will get a written record of their transactions with their monthly bank statements.

As people become more familiar with electronic funds transfers, they may be more willing to use special ID cards to shop at retail stores. Goods can be paid for by presenting the plastic ID card. The money is transferred automatically from the customer's checking or savings account into the bank account of the retail store. This transfer eliminates the need for writing a check or making a charge account purchase at the retail store.

Electronic payment for items purchased, however, also means that the money will leave the customer's bank account almost immediately. Some people may wish to use regular checks, which take several days to "clear" the bank. They may also prefer to use charge accounts. They can then wait a month to be billed for the goods bought before writing a check. Persons who do use their plastic cards to purchase items electronically will surely buy fewer items on impulse.

Home use of the computer

All of the previous examples have focused on the use of computers by business, government, hospitals, and schools. Some people predict that computers will become household appliances. Many people use them now for amusement. They use microprocessors to play games on their TV sets. Microprocessors are part of newer cameras. They are even used in children's toys. See Figure 14-6.

Using the computer to play games makes people more comfortable with this technology. As the technology becomes less expensive, it is only one short step forward to the use of computers for other home applications. Ordinary people will be able to afford computers.

In the future, small computers may be used to keep home financial records, such as checking accounts and personal income tax data. More complex computer systems will be used to maintain the heating and lighting in the home. The temperature can be raised or lowered at different times to save energy. These computer-controlled thermostats are already here, but they are not in wide use at this time.

The telephone, as well as the TV set, may become part of a computer terminal for home use in the future. You already learned how the Touch-Tone telephone can be used to pay bills. However, when the phone is used to send data, it can do more than pay bills.

With a keyboard and a CRT terminal, persons may be able to do business at home rather than travel to an office. This could be of great help to handicapped people who may need to work in their specially equipped homes. Other persons may find the cost of driving to and from

AMP Incorporated

Figure 14-6. *Today's children have computerized toys.*

an office more costly than the use of a computer to send information to persons with whom they do business.

Already many appliances can be turned on and off to prepare meals that will be ready when families arrive home from school and work. The operation of many microwave ovens, dishwashers, washing machines, and clothes dryers are already controlled by microprocessors. The person using an appliance containing a microprocessor is probably not aware of the tiny computer and its parts in running the appliance. There are microprocessors in clock-radios, TV sets, and stereo record players.

Figure 14-7, p. 380 shows a combination microwave and conventional oven unit. The dials shown at the top of the picture control the semi-automatic oven at the bottom. The heat will be turned on and off at the times set. Cooking will be at the temperature selected.

The microwave oven is shown below the dials. Cooking can be programmed automatically by touching its surface on the right. A cooking time and temperature for the first stage of cooking can be entered into its memory as well as a cooking time and temperature for the second stage of cooking. The computer automatically switches to the second stage when the first stage is completed. Or, with the help of an electronic "probe," the microwave oven can be set to cook until a certain meat temperature is reached. At this time, it will turn itself off. After all cooking is completed, an electronic timer that has kept a "count-down" signals that the job is done.

Figure 14-7. *The microwave oven has touch control shown at the right. A microprocessor handles time and temperature for programmed stages of cooking.*

Courtesy: Sears, Roebuck and Co.

NEGATIVE ASPECTS OF COMPUTER USE

The use of computers has helped many people. It has also caused problems for others. Some people think that their special needs have not been noticed — that they are only numbers to a machine. Other people use the computer to hide crimes. Still others think that information about them has been given to the wrong people because the computer has made information easy to get. These problems will be explained along with some of the steps taken to overcome them.

Fear of automation

Over-mechanization or depersonalization has been blamed on the computer. Persons have been put into large groups and labeled with numbers so that the computer can process information about them. Treating all people in one group alike has meant that the special needs of individuals are ignored. All people in a group are not exactly alike. Sometimes persons ask for help with a problem, and they get a standard response from the computer. This may make them feel that the computer is more important than people.

Getting help for special cases can be very frustrating to people who do not know data processing jargon. The computer remains a mystery. People are kept from knowing how to solve their problems. The computer is seen as a magic, powerful box. It seems to ignore human needs, and it is a device people cannot control.

As people use computers more in their work, in schools, and at home, they begin to see that the computer is controlled by the persons who plan and write computer programs. (See Figure 14-8.) They begin to see that it is possible for the computer to handle many kinds of exceptions. People see that the special needs of different people can be handled by the computer if the programs are written properly. They begin to see, in fact, that the computer can handle many more personal cases than could be handled by manual data processing. The computer has the advantage of both logic and speed. What, in the early use of the computer, looked like mechanization is now seen as a way to serve the diverse needs of more people in less time.

Figure 14-8. *The computer is controlled by the persons who plan and write computer programs.*

Theft using computers

The use of complex computer programs has helped people as a whole. However, it has also helped criminals, who have used computers to commit and then to hide crimes. Computer programs have been changed to pay more money to some people than they were supposed to get. The money may be sent electronically from one account to another without any cash being involved. This money has been lost by the persons or businesses from whom it was taken.

Computer crimes include more than stealing money. Files of customer accounts or product information that are stored magnetically can be accessed by a person who knows how to get to these data. Having these records in magnetic files has made them easier to steal than if the data were in many large metal files that are locked.

Computer programs can also be stolen or changed by angry employees. Valuable computer programs may be wanted by competitors, and a disloyal employee might profit by selling these programs.

Many computer crimes are not noticed by the company until some time after the crime has occurred. When the crime is found, there may be no law on the books to deal with the computer theft. No physical property may have been taken — just magnetically stored information. Several states and the federal government are writing new laws to cover computer-related crimes. The Federal Computer Protection Act introduced in 1979 is such a law.

Loss of privacy

Another kind of computer loss has been the privacy of people who have personal information stored in a computer. Personal privacy begins to disappear when the first charge account is opened, when the first checking account at a bank is opened, or with the first filing of an income tax return. Personal privacy is lost when businesses collect too much information about a person. Privacy is lost when that information is given to people who do not have the right or the need to have it.

The problem of privacy is even greater when wrong information is passed on. Charge account billing errors can give people poor credit ratings. The credit ratings may not be changed after the billing errors have been corrected.

More harmful *mis*information is that relating to crimes. For example, persons have been arrested for stealing their own cars when police records are not up to date and do not show that the cars have been returned to their correct owners. The grand theft charge to the innocent owners may be very difficult to remove or explain after the information is passed along through different record systems.

Protecting information

To prevent personal information from being used without the knowledge of the individuals involved, the federal government has passed several laws. The Right to Financial Privacy Act of 1978, for example, has described the right of citizens to protect their privacy. This law says that:

(1) Persons should be able to get information about themselves in record-keeping systems. Individuals should be able to find out how this information is being used.
(2) There should be some way for persons to correct information about themselves that is wrong.
(3) Persons should be able to stop information from being used for anything but the intended purpose without their consent.
(4) Organizations should take steps to be sure that sensitive data are correct and are not misused.

The last statement above says that businesses should protect the data in their files. There are several ways in which computer centers protect the equipment and data that are stored in magnetic files.

One way is to limit access to the computer center. This means using special ID cards for persons who have limited access to the center. (See Figure 14-9.) It also means using locked doors and guards who can check IDs to prevent unauthorized persons from using terminals in top-security installations.

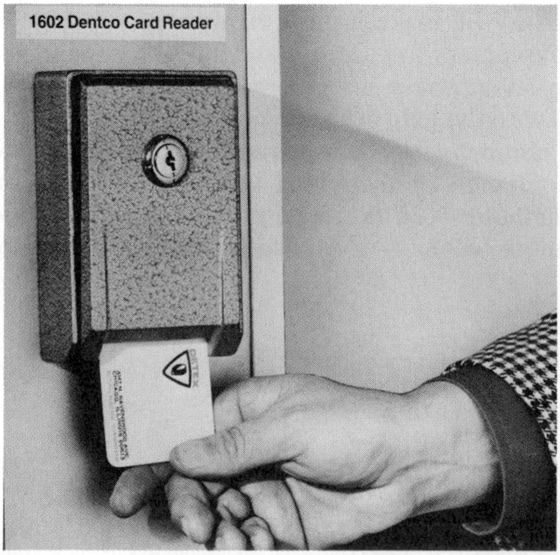

Photo courtesy of Data Terminal Systems

Figure 14-9. *In many computer centers, persons authorized to enter must have special ID cards.*

A second way of protecting stored data is to use passwords as part of the computer programs. In order for someone to use certain programs, that person must enter a password — a special number or name. These passwords are changed often to make sure that only the right people know them. (If you studied the BASIC chapters, you learned in Chapter 10 about using passwords to "sign on" when using a time-sharing computer.)

A third way to protect computer systems is to make sure that the people who know how to use the computer (the operators) are not the same people who write the instructions for the computer to follow (the programmers). By keeping these two jobs separate, there is less risk that the computer will be used improperly.

A fourth way to protect data is to code the data in a special way when it is to be sent by telephone lines outside the building. When data are sent to different locations, there is a risk that a competitor may "tap" the line and take important business information. One way to stop such thefts is by encryption. *Encryption* is the process of secretly coding data before they are sent across communication lines and of decoding these data after they are received by the correct people.

FUTURE TRENDS

The computer is probably one of the few items in our economy that is decreasing in price and increasing in the number of places in which it can be used. Increases in the price of many other goods and services might be even higher than they are if the computer could not be used to make business operations less costly. For these reasons, it is likely that people will see more and more uses for the computer in their daily lives.

More students may be using computers in their classes. The decreasing cost of microcircuits will make it more likely that schools will purchase several microcomputers for use by students. More students may then be able to learn about computer programming as well as to study other school subjects with the help of the computer.

Increased use of computers in business means that more and more employees will use computers on their jobs. See Figure 14-10. As people get to know what computers can do to help them learn and to earn a living, they may be more willing — even eager — to learn how to use a computer.

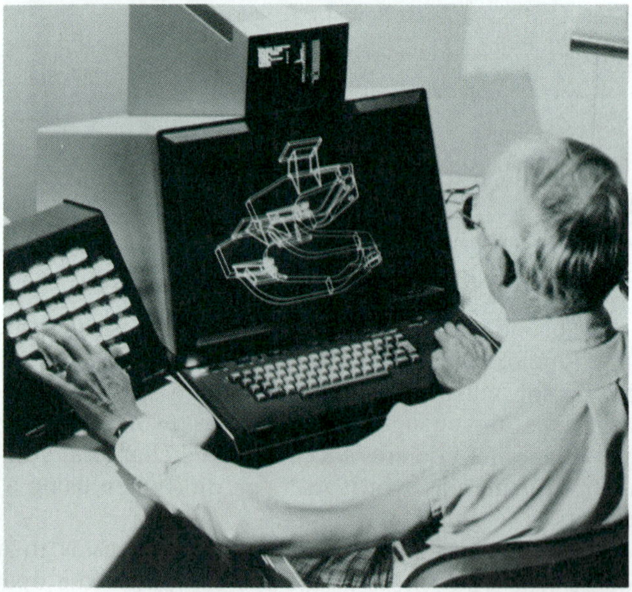

Figure 14-10. *This engineer uses a computer in his work.*

Several changes will continue to be made in computers to make them easier and more desirable to use. These are a few predictions:

(1) Color graphics will be used more in the output displays.
(2) Sound will become a common output option — both musical sound as well as spoken words. Voice input is also likely to become more available.
(3) Computer logic and storage devices will continue to decrease in size. This will permit their use in more and more appliances. These electrical appliances will be easier to repair than they once were. An

entire section or microcircuit will be replaced at a low cost. This will save hours of labor.

(4) The programming languages used will become simpler and more like the English language. The ease of learning a programming language will encourage more people to write their own programs.

(5) Computer programs that are already written will be easier to buy. This means that people who do not want to write their own programs will be able to buy software packages at low cost. This trend will apply to business computer users as well as home and recreational users.

It is safe to say that everyone's life will be affected by the computer in some way. Some people will be more directly involved with computers — using them in school, in work, and at home. Those who want to be even more involved can look to the computer industry as a place to find a career.

SUMMARY

Computers have had a major impact on society by the help they have given business managers. The computer has made it possible for larger numbers of customers to be served and a wider variety of goods to be manufactured and sold. The speed and accuracy of the computer also benefits people through improved weather forecasting, help in fire fighting and crime control, improved medical services, and assistance in learning. As people learn more about what the computer can do, the use of computers in the home may also increase.

While there are many advantages in using computers, there are negative features too. Increased automation may cause human needs to be overlooked. Crime may be easier to carry out or to hide. Privacy can be lost when too much information is collected by businesses or shared too widely.

Computer use will grow. As computers increase in their capabilities because of technological advances, they are also becoming less costly. More people will become familiar with computers and learn how to use them. This means that more people will be able to benefit from the power of the computer. They will also be able to take part in overcoming some of the negative outcomes of computer use.

REVIEW QUESTIONS

1. As the population in this country increases, the task of making products and services available to more people would not be possible without the use of the computer in business. Why is this true?
2. List four types of questions about business operations that computers can help a business to answer.
3. Name three new jobs that have been created by the use of computers in business.

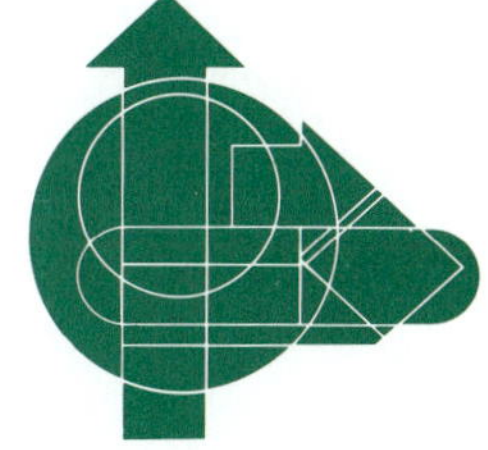

(Continued)

4. Name six areas in which computers are of benefit to individuals in their daily lives?
5. How could it be helpful to use the computer as an aid in teaching?
6. What are the two ways in which persons can authorize the electronic transfer of money into or out of their bank accounts?
7. Why are some persons now considering the use of computers in their homes?
8. Name seven household items or appliances that are already programmed with microprocessors.
9. What is meant by the criticism that the computer has "depersonalized" business transactions?
10. How has the computer made it possible for some persons to commit and to hide crimes?
11. What four rights do citizens have to protect their financial privacy as a result of the Right to Financial Privacy Act?
12. What four steps are normally taken by a business to protect computing equipment and data files from damage and theft?

NEW TERMS

- Computer-assisted instruction
- Computer-managed instruction
- Electronic funds transfer
- Exception reports
- Encryption
- ID card

STUDY GUIDES

There are no study guides for Chapter 14.

PROJECTS

There are no projects for Chapter 14.

15

DATA PROCESSING CAREERS in BUSINESS

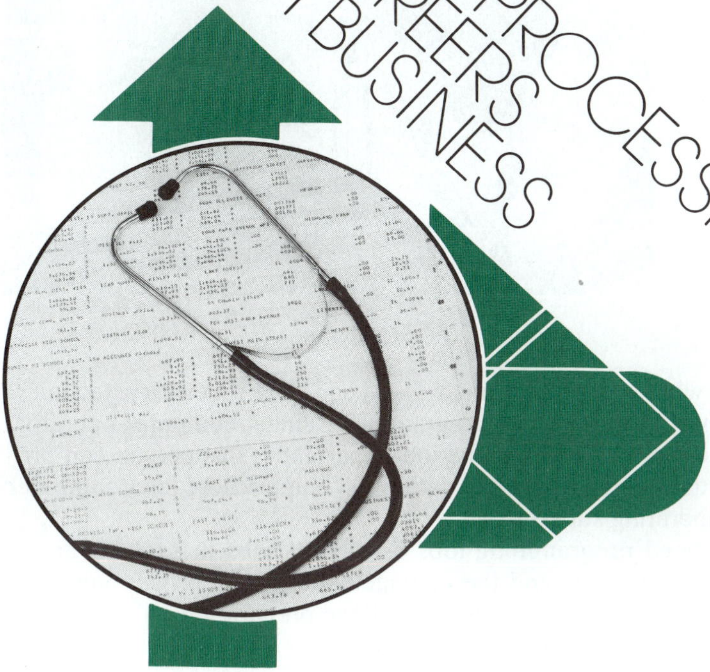

The need for qualified persons in business data processing has been so great that job seekers call it a "sellers' market." Job openings in this field now are greater than the supply of qualified persons. This has had the effect of pushing beginning salaries up as compared to those of other business and office jobs. Cities generally offer more job openings than do rural areas. But, as more small businesses acquire computers, this situation is likely to change. Persons interested in working with modern technology and willing to train in school and on the job will find many employment opportunities. Figure 15-1, p. 388, shows an on-line order/inventory control system in a large city.

JOB LEVELS

The entry-level jobs in business data processing include data-entry trainee, media librarian, and computer operator trainee. Some of these jobs are described in greater detail in this chapter. Entry-level jobs are those which persons may enter with either a high school or vocational-technical high school education, without job experience.

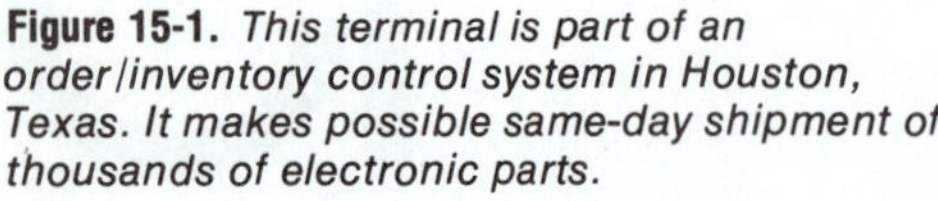

Figure 15-1. *This terminal is part of an order/inventory control system in Houston, Texas. It makes possible same-day shipment of thousands of electronic parts.*

Harris Corporation

A person with a degree from a two-year post-secondary technical school may enter at the level of programmer trainee, computer operator, or data-entry operator. With on-the-job experience, this person can progress to lead data-entry operator, data-entry supervisor, lead computer operator, or operating supervisor.

More advanced programming jobs as well as jobs in systems analysis, data communications, and the management of data processing operations all require four or more years of college preparation.

OBTAINING DATA PROCESSING JOBS

There are several ways in which a person can obtain a job in the data processing field.

Secondary education

Certain courses in high school can help you decide if you are interested in data processing as a career. Some of these courses could make it easier for you to learn once you are hired into an entry-level job. These courses include accounting, business machines, mathematics, typewriting, general business, introduction to business, and introductory data processing itself.

Post-secondary education

If you obtain more education at a community college or technical institute, you may be able to enter the data processing field at a higher level or at a higher starting salary than would be possible with a high school education alone. Two years or less of specialized training would let you know for sure if data processing interests you. You would also learn whether you have the abilities to succeed in this field. With data processing training beyond high school, you would also be prepared to accept such positions as data-entry operator, media librarian, computer operator, data clerk, data processing secretary, or programmer trainee.

Advanced education

Job opportunities in data processing will be wider if you complete a four-year degree in a major related to computers and the management of business information systems. This major might be called Computer Science, Business Data Processing, Management Information Systems, or perhaps just Mathematics or Business Administration with an emphasis on computers and data processing.

The advanced jobs in data processing that are open to persons with a four-year college degree might also be open to persons with less formal education but with more on-the-job experience in the data processing field. Some jobs at the higher levels of management require extensive on-the-job experience and perhaps formal education beyond a four-year college degree.

Career ladders

Figure 15-2, p. 390, shows some of the different job titles in the data processing field and the approximate amounts of education needed. This diagram shows that many different career ladders exist in data processing. Once people enter this field, they may advance to different or higher-level jobs. Advancement may depend upon their interests, education, experience, and willingness to learn on the job.

The amount of preparation may vary, depending on the size of the data processing installation. This ladder gives only a general idea of the education needed.

Many entry-level jobs are available in data processing that need little or no training beyond high school. However, almost all positions beyond the entry level do require specialized training and/or experience. Note that most entry-level positions are in the area of operations. This gives an opportunity for employment at night, making it possible for a worker to continue an academic program during the day. Many employees in computer rooms are part-time students.

The jobs shown at the bottom of Figure 15-2 show the entry-level jobs available with a high school or vocational high school education. The next division shows the jobs available with a post-secondary technical or junior college education. The third section shows the jobs that can be had with on-the-job training or additional education toward the bachelor's degree. The top section shows the jobs that require a bachelor's degree or more.

For the jobs in the top two sections of Figure 15-2, persons who have had on-the-job training while working toward a degree are more likely to be hired than are those who have had academic training only. Persons with on-the-job experience may be promoted by the companies that employed them while they were going to school. These persons are also of interest to any other company with a computer like the one they have

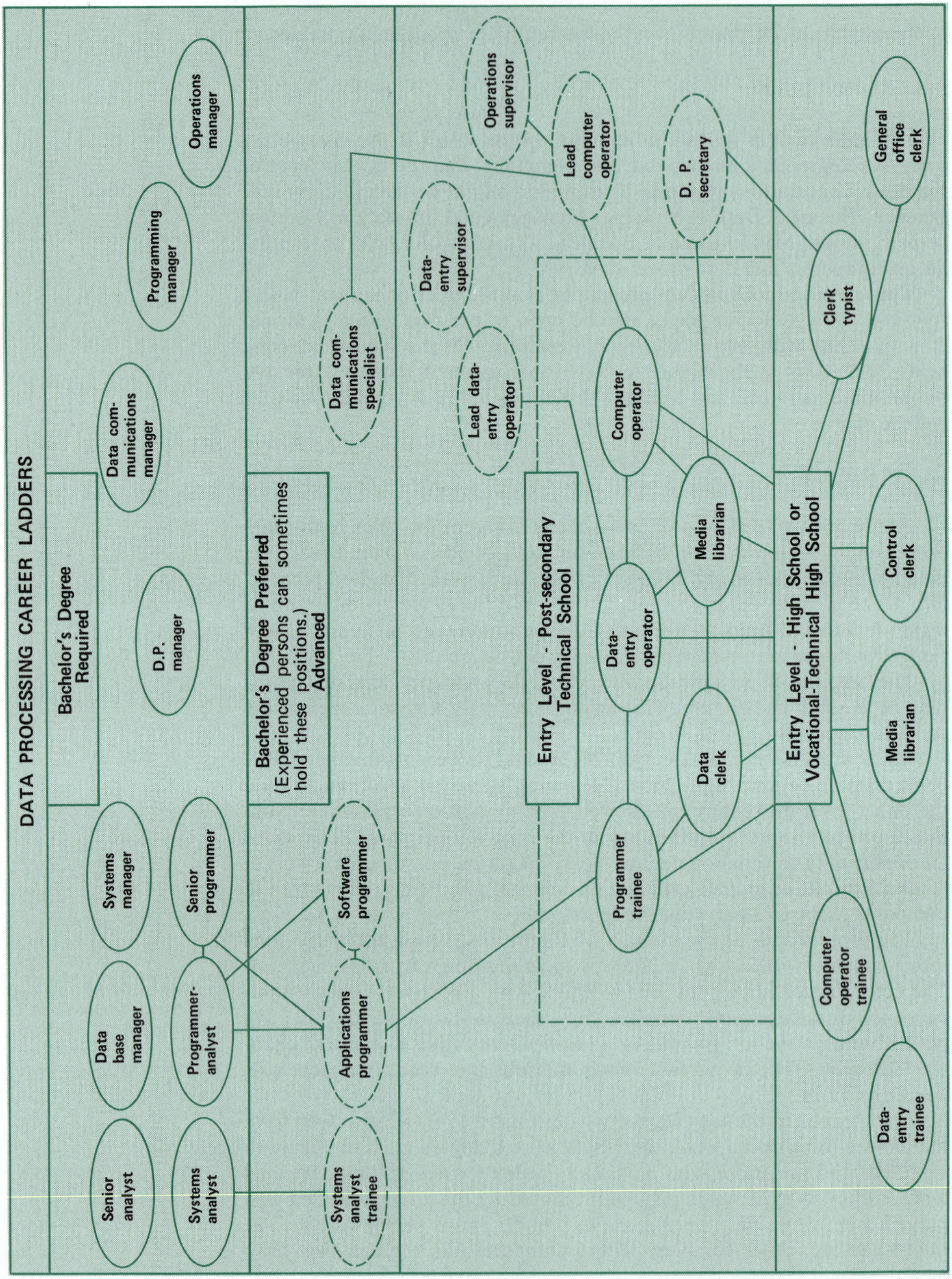

Figure 15-2. *Data processing career ladders*

been using. On-the-job programming experience in a particular language is also important to an employer.

In Figure 15-2, the jobs inside symbols with broken lines are possible promotions from another level. Symbols with solid lines are used for entry-level jobs. For example, a data-entry operator could become a lead data-entry operator or data-entry supervisor. A programmer trainee could be promoted to applications programmer with on-the-job training. The jobs of systems analyst, programmer analyst, and senior programmer in the top level are shown inside symbols with solid lines because a bachelor's degree is needed for these jobs at the entry level. However, these jobs are available as promotions to persons with on-the-job training.

DATA PROCESSING SALARIES

The salaries available to persons in data processing jobs vary considerably. Some of the factors affecting salaries are the following:

(1) Amount of education and job experience.
(2) Size of the company.
(3) Industry of which the company is a part, such as manufacturing of food, banking, retail sales, government, or others. (See Figure 15-3.)
(4) Geographic location of the company.

Photo provided by Data Terminal Systems

Figure 15-3. *Retail food stores pay above-average salaries to persons who operate computerized terminals like the one shown above. Little data processing experience is needed for this job.*

Because of inflation, or rising prices, and because of the shortage of qualified data processing employees, salaries in all data processing careers have been going up between seven to ten percent each year.

Figure 15-4 shows the ranges of typical weekly salaries received by data processing employees in 1980. The bottom figure is the average national low for the job. The top figure is the average national high. The middle figure is the national average salary for all persons having that particular job.

Notice the wide range of weekly salaries in each of the four job categories of data entry, operations, programming, and systems analysis. These salaries are the national averages reported by INFOSYSTEMS magazine. They should be adjusted upward about ten percent a year when updating the figures.

A LOOK AT FOUR DATA PROCESSING JOBS

Four data processing jobs will be described in more detail. The major tasks and the personal requirements to do these tasks will be described. These four jobs illustrate positions in data processing that are available to persons with different amounts of formal education.

Data-entry jobs are available to persons with high school training. The jobs in computer operations usually require training in a technical school. Programmer or systems training jobs may be available to persons with two years of technical school or community college training. Jobs in systems analysis or advanced programming usually require a four-year college degree as well as on-the-job experience.

These four jobs are important to examine for another reason. They show all the basic functions needed to plan, develop, and operate a data processing system using a computer. The starting point for using a computer in a business is planning the procedures used for solving a problem. Therefore, the systems analyst's job will be described first.

Once the information system has been planned, the detailed programming of the parts of that system must be done by the programmer. When the program is ready to be tested, the data-entry operator must key the program and the data into a form suitable for the computer being used. At the testing stage and later when the program is used, the computer operator comes into the picture to run the program.

Planning: the job of the systems analyst

In Chapter 2 you learned that a system is a group of items or actions that work together to perform a certain function. A data processing system makes information available to the user. Before this system or plan can be designed, the end product must be known and kept clearly in mind. A *systems analyst* is a person who is in charge of planning and carrying out a data processing system.

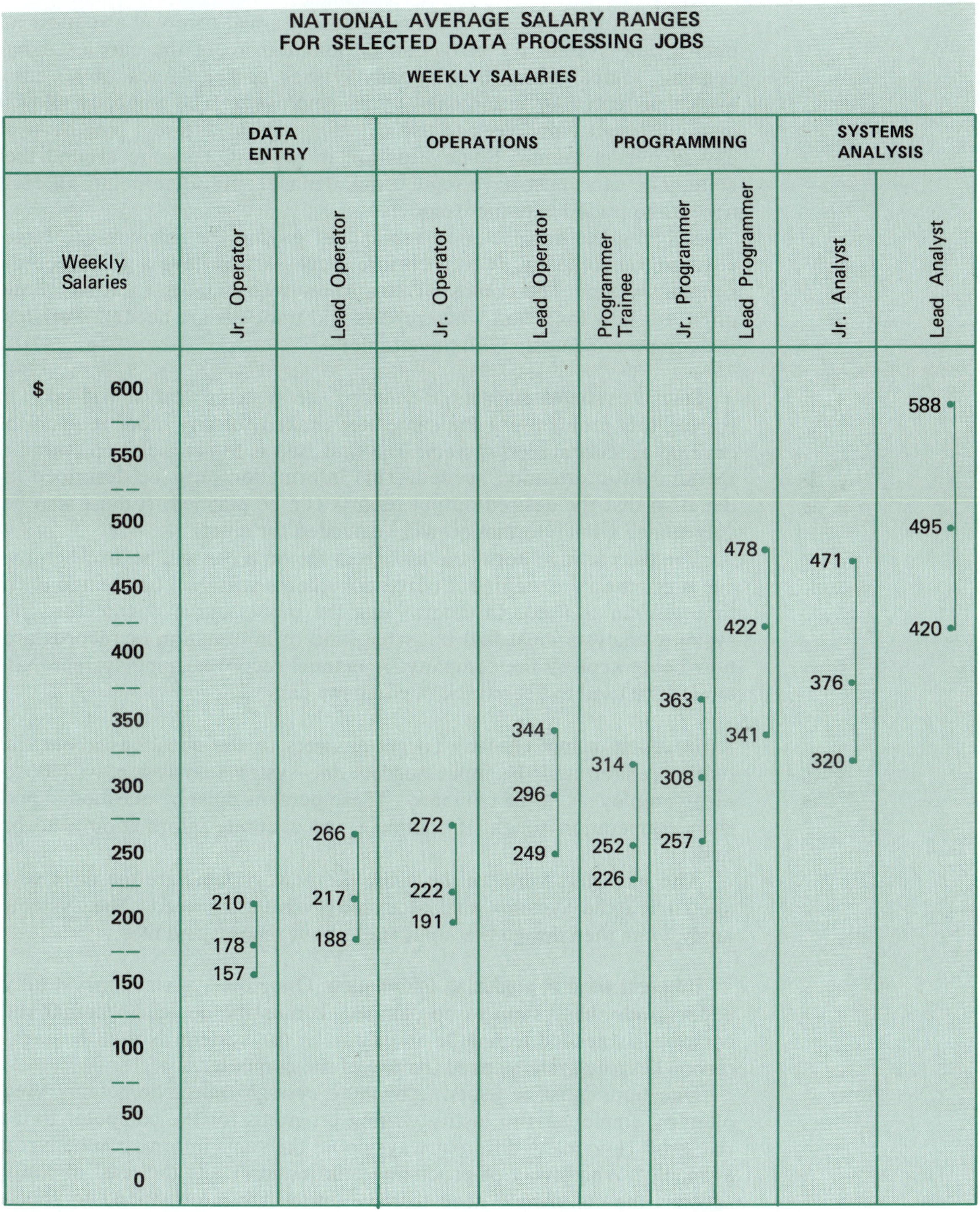

SOURCE: *Infosystems*, June, 1980, p. 46.

Figure 15-4. *The average weekly salaries vary according to the size of the installation and geographic location.*

Let's assume that the systems analyst has just received a request to plan a new system for providing information about the cars used by company employees. The company wishes to keep track of all cars owned or rented by it and used by its employees. The company allows many different employees to use cars for trips of different lengths — a day to over a month. Some trips are in town. Others are around the state. The cars must have regular maintenance. At some point, all cars need to be traded in on new models.

Keeping the cars in good repair and paying for gasoline are large costs to the company. It is, therefore, necessary to have a good record-keeping system. The company must know who is using each car, how often, for how long, and when repairs and trade-ins are needed. Perhaps the computer can help with this problem.

Steps in systems planning. The steps the systems analyst will take in solving this problem are the same steps taken for any other request to develop an information system. The first step is to get a clear picture of the kind of information needed. This information must be described in detail so that the desired output reports can be planned. It must also be determined what information will be needed for input.

For the car inventory, the historical file on a car will begin when the car is purchased or rented. Source documents will then be created each time the car is used. In determining the input source documents, the systems analysts must find out what kind of information or records are now being kept by the company. A manual record-keeping system may already be used to keep track of company cars.

Input and output needed. To get answers to the questions about the output desired and the input needed, the systems analyst must talk to many employees of the company. These persons must be questioned and their cooperation sought if complete and accurate information is to be had.

The managers who will be using the new systems are the ones who should tell the systems analyst exactly what they need. The systems analyst can then design the input and output records and files.

Different ways of producing information. Once the systems analyst fully understands the system to be planned, it must be decided whether the computer is needed to handle all or part of the system. Not all business record-keeping systems need the use of the computer.

Questions must be asked. Are there enough transactions (cars used often by employees) to justify writing programs for the computer to do the jobs? How many different ways could the same information be made available? Which way of producing information costs the least and still satisfies the company's need to have up-to-date information? In short, the systems analyst must look for several ways to solve the problem and then choose the best one.

Analyzing the system. If the computer is chosen to handle part of the car inventory record-keeping system, more detailed planning must be done:

(1) Source documents are identified and described.
(2) Input files of information are planned. The types of files are chosen — punched cards, magnetic disks, or magnetic tape.
(3) Decisions are made about the number and kind of computer programs needed to create and update these files.
(4) Output report files are planned in detail.
(5) Systems flowcharts are prepared to describe the car inventory system. (See Figure 15-5.)

Figure 15-5. *A systems analyst designs input and output records as well as flowcharts.*

Photo courtesy of IBM Corporation

Drawing systems flowcharts. You have already learned that a systems flowchart shows the media used for input and output and the flow of data through the various steps of a data processing system. The systems flowchart begins with the first source document for the purchase or rental of a car. The flowchart will show the history of the car inventory down to the summary report that tells how many cars are owned or rented, how often they are used, and so on. That part of the system that the computer will handle will then be ready to be assigned to a programmer, who will flowchart the programs and code them into a computer language.

Job requirements for the systems analyst. In order to plan how to use the computer, the systems analyst needs several knowledges and skills.

First, he or she needs to know about the overall operation of the company. Next, the systems analyst must understand what the computer system used in the company can and cannot do.

Educational background. A wide background in business and the technical aspects of data processing is needed. A four-year college degree in the business field is usually required. This degree may be in information systems. On the other hand, it may be in a related educational program that emphasizes a broad business management background.

A keen interest in solving problems and an ability to think logically are also needed. A creative mind is a must in order to see new ways to organize things. The analyst should be familiar with at least one programming language. He or she will then know the specific requirements for preparing a program for a computer using that language.

The systems analyst must also be able to compare the costs of several different ways of solving problems with and without the computer. These costs will include computer costs as well as costs for employees' time, supplies, and other business equipment.

Communicating skills. The systems analyst must be able to communicate well with users in order to plan a successful system. Once the system is designed, more communication is needed about what the completed programs can do.

It is important that the systems analyst should be able to communicate in speech and writing with different kinds of people. There must be contact with the technical staff who program and operate the computer. There must also be communication with other employees who will be using the computer output but who may know little about data processing.

Programming: The Job of the Computer Programmer

There are several kinds of programming jobs shown in Figure 15-2, p. 390. A software programmer works for the computer manufacturer or a house that furnishes ready-made programs to the user. The applications programmer is the one whose job will be explained here. You learned in Chapter 6 that an applications program is usually written by the user of the computer rather than by the manufacturer. Writing applications programs is one of the duties of the programmer that will be described.

Analyzing the program. The job of the *applications programmer* is to interpret the systems flowcharts and detailed plans received from the systems analyst and to prepare the program flowcharts and computer programs needed. The systems analyst plans the entire system. The applications programmer writes the programs within the system. (See Figure 15-6.)

The programmer must understand the source documents to be used, the processing to be done, and the output desired. The applications pro-

Figure 15-6. *The applications programmer prepares program flowcharts and codes the steps of the computer program.*

grams must first be flowcharted. Then the programmer must write or code these programs in a language that can be used by the company's computer.

Drawing program flowcharts. You learned earlier that a program flowchart outlines the step-by-step instructions to solve a problem with the computer. For example, it is concerned with reading all the records in a file, with branches made at the proper times, and with loops. The systems flowchart, on the other hand, is not as detailed as the program flowchart.

The entire car inventory system will first be flowcharted by the systems analyst. The programmer, on the other hand, will flowchart more than one program within the system. A few examples are programs for:

(1) Listing cars that have been driven over a certain number of miles.
(2) Listing cars according to age.
(3) Comparing miles per gallon of different makes of cars.
(4) Comparing miles per gallon according to geographic areas.

Coding programs. After the program has been flowcharted, the programmer codes it into a source language. The program is usually written in one of the higher-level languages, such as COBOL, FORTRAN, RPG, BASIC, or PL1.

If the program is complicated, the programmer may work with a team of programmers. In the car inventory example, several program segments might be identified for the complete program. Different source documents might be used for the purchase of cars than are used for the rental, sale, checking in or out, or maintenance of cars. Different sets of programming instructions may be written and then combined into one large program. Good planning and communications are needed if the programming team is to accomplish this task.

Documentation. When the program has been written, tested, and debugged, the programmer must document it. This means describing in written words and flowcharts just what the program requires for input, processing, and output. Instructions to the computer operator must also be included. Clear documentation is needed so that other programmers can understand the programs at a later time. It becomes easier to change the programs later if they need to be changed.

Job requirements for the programmer. A programmer needs to know at least one programming language. Because it is not always possible to predict the language a programmer will need when employed, the training for programmer often includes several of the common higher-level languages. A business applications programmer is more likely to study COBOL than is a scientist. BASIC is the most commonly used language for non-business applications, for interactive programming, and for programming on small computers.

Successful programmers think logically and like working with precise details. They can concentrate on a programming problem until it is solved. In the past, it was thought that programmers should be good mathematicians. However, logical thinking seems to be the essential asset.

Programmers may sometimes need to record their programs for input into the computer. To enter program statements, they may need to learn to typewrite and use the keypunch or input terminal. In small companies, the programmer may have to run the program on the computer. This would mean loading the input cards, tapes, or disks; starting the processing; and determining if the output is correct. Mixing the duties of programmer and computer operator is not wise, however, for security reasons. The danger of this practice was pointed out in Chapter 14.

Educational background. The background needed for writing programs usually requires training beyond the high school level. A programmer trainee should have graduated from a community college or technical institute. Many trainees are required to have a degree from a four-year college or university. If a trainee is a graduate of a two-year college, there is an opportunity for on-the-job training while securing more education. After becoming familiar with the programming language and programs of a particular company, the trainee may become a regular programmer.

Preparing Computer Input: The Job of the Data-Entry Operator

Getting data ready for input into a computer is an important job. No matter how carefully a program is planned by a systems analyst and programmer, if the input is not accurate, the output will not be correct. The data-entry operator plays a key part in preventing *GIGO* (''*G*arbage *I*n, *G*arbage *O*ut''). The *data-entry operator* records data on input media for processing.

Entering programs and data. First, the programmer completes the writing of the program. Then it is ready for testing on the computer. The first data-entry step begins. The data-entry operator must record the program on input media as well as the data that will be used to test the program.

When a program has been completely debugged, it can be used over and over without rekeying. Only the new data must be recorded each time the program is run. These data are keyed by the data-entry operator from the source documents in the format planned by the systems analyst.

The data-entry operator often works with different source documents — handwritten forms, typed forms, or specially marked sheets of paper. The data on these source documents will be keyed at a typewriter-like keyboard. The data-entry machine used may be a keypunch machine. It is more likely, however, to be a key-to-tape or key-to-disk terminal with a CRT. The operator sees what is typed on the screen, and the data are stored on magnetic tape, diskette, or disk. (See Figure 15-7.)

Photo courtesy of Hewlett Packard

Figure 15-7. *A data-entry operator needs to know the layout of the record and how to enter it from the source document.*

Whatever equipment is used, the operator will need to understand the layout of the record on the equipment and how to enter the data from the source document. Understanding the equipment and following directions carefully are important.

There is a high volume of data processed by most business data processing programs. Fast, accurate work by the data-entry operator is essential. The high volume of business data often makes data entry a 24-hour activity. For this reason, data-entry operators may have a choice of day or night working hours.

Job requirements for the data-entry operator. The main requirement for the data-entry operator is the ability to type or key data rapidly and accurately. Persons in this job like working with modern data-entry equipment and doing the same kind of work for long periods of time. They get satisfaction from producing a large volume of high-quality work.

Data-entry operators must be able to follow detailed instructions carefully and be able to work under time pressures when needed. Also, as equipment changes take place, operators must be able to adjust to these changes.

Educational background. Data-entry trainees can learn to use data-entry equipment in high school. Data-entry operators can be trained in technical school programs. Some businesses provide on-the-job training because the demand for qualified operators is greater than the supply. If a person knows how to typewrite, data-entry training on the job may take only three to six weeks.

Running the Computer: The Job of the Computer Operator

When programs have been written and data have been recorded for input, the next step is running these programs and the related data on the computer. The computer operator is responsible for sequencing the jobs and running them on the computer in the order of their importance. A *computer operator* is a person who monitors the operations of a computer, using routines that have already been set up.

Tape or disk files must be labeled and mounted for use by the computer when they are needed for a job. Punched cards must be loaded into the card reader. The printer must be loaded with paper for output. Figure 15-8 shows a computer operator at a magnetic tape drive.

Operating instructions for running programs must be followed closely. Messages will be received from the computer console during the running of a program. The computer operator will also type instructions at the console keyboard. If errors or problems occur during the running of a program, the operator must know how to handle them. Output must be checked to make sure that it is complete. The programmer or user must be informed if a "run" is not completed for some reason. Careful record keeping and attention to detail are required.

If the company is not large enough to hire different persons to "log in" the jobs for the computer or to manage the tape or disk library, the computer operator may have these duties as well. Also, the operator

NCR Corporation

Figure 15-8. *The computer operator mounts a tape file on a tape drive for use by the computer.*

may be expected to run other peripheral equipment, such as a card sorter, card reader, or card punch.

Job requirements for the computer operator. The computer operator must like working with equipment. Computer equipment is changing so often that operators must also be willing to learn new methods on the job. In small companies, an understanding of the accounting practices in the firm would also provide helpful background for operating the computer.

Most of the work will be done either standing or walking. There is a need to lift card files, paper, and other storage devices. Good physical condition is therefore important on the job.

The operator also needs appreciation for accuracy and attention to detail. Because this person must be able to interpret messages printed at the computer console and provide input at the console, an understanding of a programming language could be helpful. But, many large computer installations discourage their operators from knowing anything about programming for security reasons.

Educational background. Technical training in equipment operation and introduction to computer programming can often be learned at a two-year technical institute. This training can also be had on the job as an operator trainee. In some companies, the operator position might even be a training position for jobs in programming.

OPPORTUNITIES FOR CAREER ADVANCEMENT

All jobs in the data processing field have the possibility of leading to higher level positions in the same job area. New data processing areas can also be entered by acquiring additional training. Refer back to Figure 15-2, p. 390, for an illustration of these career paths.

Many entry-level jobs that need little or no training after high school are available in data processing. However, almost all jobs beyond the entry level do require specialized training and/or experience. Most entry-level positions are in the area of operations. This gives an employee a chance to work at night and go to school during the day.

Data-entry operators like the one shown in Figure 15-9 may wish to become computer operators or supervisors of the data-entry area.

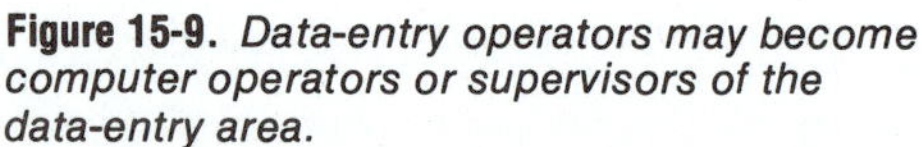

Figure 15-9. *Data-entry operators may become computer operators or supervisors of the data-entry area.*

Photo courtesy of Incoterm Corporation

Computer operators may advance to managerial jobs in the operations area. Programmers may move into different kinds of programming jobs. Or, they may prepare to become systems analysts. Both programming and systems analysis jobs offer advancement to the jobs of project leader or manager in the programming or systems development areas.

The data processing field is an exciting one for persons who like the challenge of changing technology. It is open to persons with wide ranges of education — from high school through advanced work in college. New equipment and new applications will continue to make many different job openings for well-trained people.

SUMMARY

A very high demand for data processing employees will continue to make jobs plentiful for persons interested in careers in this growing field. Entry-level jobs are open to persons with high school, technical school, or community college education. The jobs include data-entry trainee, data-entry operator, media librarian, data clerk, data processing secretary, computer operator trainee, computer operator, and programmer trainee.

It is possible for persons to obtain more specialized training on the job or at a four-year college or university. This training can qualify them for more advanced jobs in programming or systems analysis. On-the-job training and more education can also help a person to become a supervisor or manager in data-entry, programming, operations, or systems analysis.

The general shortage of data processing employees has caused salaries to rise in relation to other business and office jobs. This means that many people likely will be attracted to careers in data processing. The best jobs will go to those who are well prepared and who are willing to continue to learn as changes come. The persons who enjoy the challenges of working with computer technology will be able to find a satisfying career in business data processing.

REVIEW QUESTIONS

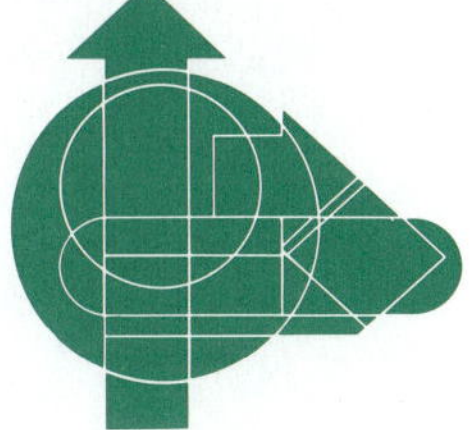

1. Explain why job opportunities in data processing have caused this field to be called a "sellers' market."
2. What high school courses could help prepare you for a data processing job?
3. What entry-level data processing jobs are available to persons completing high school?
4. What entry-level data processing jobs are available to persons completing a technical school or community college program?
5. What entry-level data processing jobs are available to persons completing a four-year college degree?
6. What are the promotion possibilities for a programmer trainee shown in Figure 15-2, p. 390.
7. Name four jobs for which a bachelor's degree is preferred, but for which experienced persons can sometimes qualify with on-the-job training.
8. What is a systems analyst? Name two job requirements for the job of systems analyst.
9. What education is needed by a systems analyst?
10. Why must a systems analyst have good communication skills?
11. What is an *applications programmer*? How does this job relate to the work of the systems analyst?
12. Name four duties of an applications programmer.
13. What are two job requirements of an applications programmer?
14. What are the educational requirements of an applications programmer?
15. What is a *data-entry operator*?
16. How does the job of data-entry operator relate to that of a computer operator in Figure 15-2, p. 390? To that of an operating supervisor?
17. What are the job requirements of a data-entry operator? The educational requirements?

(Continued)

18. What is a *computer operator*?
19. What are the job requirements of a computer operator?
20. How does the job of computer-operator trainee relate to that of operating supervisor in Figure 15-2, p. 390?

NEW TERMS

- Applications programmer
- Computer operator
- Data-entry operator
- GIGO
- Systems analyst

STUDY GUIDES

Complete Study Guide 15 by following the instructions in your Study Guides booklet.

PROJECTS

There will be no projects for Chapter 15.

APPENDIX

Many students may wish to experiment with additional BASIC and COBOL program statements. For this reason, an Appendix has been added to this text in order to teach additional programming concepts in both languages.

INPUT STATEMENT IN BASIC

You have learned how data can be entered into the computer by means of READ and DATA statements in a BASIC program. You know that all the data values are accessed one-by-one in sequential order until all values have been processed.

There is one disadvantage to a program of this type, however. All the data values must be known in advance. They must be entered at the beginning of the program and are part of the program itself.

There is another means of entering data, in which the values are not entered as part of the program. Instead, the INPUT statement is used.

Advantages of the INPUT statement

The INPUT statement may be used to enter data values at the terminal whenever needed during the execution of the program. It is possible to run the same program many times with different data values without having to change any of the program statements. Because the data values are entered during execution of the program, the program does not need to be changed in order to run it with new data.

Disadvantage of the INPUT statement

The INPUT statement should not be used for entering large amounts of data that are known in advance because it takes more user time. The operator must enter new data whenever the computer asks for it.

How the INPUT statement is used

Following is a variation of the program to solve Problem 1, Figure 10-15, p. 247. However, this time the computer will be instructed to compute the average. The printout will show the student number and the average, but not the scores.

Statement of the Average problem. Input includes the student number and three test scores. Output includes the student number and the average of the three scores. The average is obtained by adding the three test scores and dividing the total by 3. Each value will be entered at the terminal when the computer asks for it instead of being entered in advance in a data block.

Analysis of the Average problem. The student number will be N. The test scores will be S1, S2, and S3. The average will be A. The test to end the program will occur if N = 9999. Then the computer will branch to the instruction that "winds up" the program.

Program to solve the Average problem. The program to solve the Average problem is shown on the next page.

Note that the REMARKS, Lines 10-100, describe the program, the names given to the variables, and the value used to end the program, 9999. The operator first types the entire program at the terminal and then gives the command to "run" the program. The computer begins the program and continues until the word INPUT is reached. The terminal then prints the statement within the quotation marks and adds a question mark (?), which asks the user to enter the proper data.

Line 110 states: INPUT "ENTER NEXT STUDENT NUMBER OR 9999 IF ALL DONE" N. The terminal will print out:

ENTER NEXT STUDENT NUMBER OR 9999 IF ALL DONE ?

All processing stops until the user types in the needed value, the student number N, and strikes the RETURN CARRIAGE key.

```
10  REM  THIS PROGRAM CALCULATES THE AVERAGE
20  REM  OF THREE TEST SCORES
30  REM  "N" IS FOR STUDENT NUMBER
40  REM  "S1" IS FOR SCORE ONE
50  REM  "S2" IS FOR SCORE TWO
60  REM  "S3" IS FOR SCORE THREE
70  REM  "T" IS FOR TOTAL SCORE
80  REM  "A" IS FOR AVERAGE SCORE
90  REM  A STUDENT NUMBER OF 9999 WILL BE USED TO
100 REM  TERMINATE THE PROGRAM
110 INPUT  "ENTER NEXT STUDENT NUMBER OR 9999 IF ALL DONE" N
120 IF N = 9999 THEN GO TO 190
130 INPUT  "ENTER 3 SCORES SEPARATED BY COMMAS" S1, S2, S3
140 LET T = S1 + S2 + S3
150 LET A = T / 3
160 PRINT "STUDENT NUMBER IS " N
170 PRINT "AVERAGE OF SCORES IS " A
180 GO TO 110
190 PRINT "THERE ARE NO MORE SCORES TO AVERAGE"
200 STOP
210 END
```

If there should be more than one value, the values must be separated by a comma. If the values entered are not complete, the computer will print another question mark or an error message. For example, if the INPUT statement reads INPUT B1, B2, B3, and the user only types in the values of B1 and B2, the terminal will print another question mark or an error message, such as "NOT ENOUGH DATA — TYPE IN MORE" or "INCORRECT FORMAT — RETYPE." You can see why BASIC is referred to as a conversational language.

Refer again to Line 120 of the program. If the value of N is equal to 9999, the computer will branch to Line 190 and print the message within quotation marks, THERE ARE NO MORE SCORES TO AVERAGE. If there are more student numbers, the operator enters the next student number when the terminal requests the value of N.

The second INPUT statement is on Line 130:

INPUT "ENTER 3 SCORES SEPARATED BY COMMAS" S1, S2, S3

The terminal will print out:

ENTER 3 SCORES SEPARATED BY COMMAS ?

Line 140 causes the three scores to be added and the total to be stored at T (LET T = S1 + S2 + S3). Line 150 causes the total to be divided by 3, with the results being stored at A (LET A = T / 3).

Line 160 causes the printer to print the statement within quotation marks, STUDENT NUMBER IS, with a space after it. The student number (N) is then printed. Line 170 prints AVERAGE OF SCORES IS, with a space after it and before the average. For example, the last lines of printout could read:

```
ENTER NEXT STUDENT NUMBER OR 9999 IF ALL DONE
? 2400
ENTER 3 TEST SCORES SEPARATED BY COMMAS
? 91, 88, 97
STUDENT NUMBER IS 2400
AVERAGE OF SCORES IS 92
ENTER NEXT STUDENT NUMBER OR 9999 IF ALL DONE
? 9999
THERE ARE NO MORE SCORES TO AVERAGE
STOP AT LINE 200
READY
```

Note that after the first line, there was a new student number, 2400. After the student's number and average were printed, the computer asked for the next number or 9999 if there were no more student numbers. The operator entered 9999 and the computer branched to the end-of-job message (Line 190 of the program), THERE ARE NO MORE SCORES TO AVERAGE. The computer also showed that the STOP statement was on Line 200.

Statement of the Metric problem. Inches can be converted to centimeters and miles can be converted to kilometers with the proper INPUT statements. The following program converts inches to centimeters and then converts the centimeters into meters. To change inches into centimeters, the equation is LET C = I * 2.54 (with I being used for inches and C for centimeters). To change centimeters into meters, the equation is LET M = C / 100 (with M being used for meters). The program appears as follows:

```
 10  REM  PROGRAM TO CONVERT INCHES TO CENTIMETERS AND METERS
 20  REM  1 INCH EQUALS 2.54 CENTIMETERS
 30  REM  100 CENTIMETERS EQUAL 1 METER
 40  REM  "I" IS FOR INCHES
 50  REM  "C" IS FOR CENTIMETERS
 60  REM  "M" IS FOR METERS
 70  REM  INCHES OF -999 WILL BE USED TO TERMINATE THE PROGRAM
 80  INPUT "ENTER NUMBER IN INCHES OR -999 IF ALL DONE" I
 90  IF I = -999 THEN GO TO 150
100  LET C = I * 2.54      ! CONVERTS INCHES TO CENTIMETERS
110  LET M = C / 100       ! CONVERTS CENTIMETERS TO METERS
120  PRINT I, "INCHES", "EQUAL", C, "CENTIMETERS"
130  PRINT C, "CENTIMETERS", "EQUAL", M, "METERS"
140  GO TO 80
150  PRINT "THERE ARE NO MORE INCHES TO CONVERT"
160  STOP
170  END
```

The program is easy to follow. A last-value code of −999 is used because there will be no negative value of 999 entered into the program. The PRINT statments at Lines 120 and 130 will cause two lines to be printed, using all five print zones as follows:

200	INCHES	EQUAL	508	CENTIMETERS
508	CENTIMETERS	EQUAL	5.08	METERS

Other metric problems. Similar programs could be written, using the following equations:

LET K = M * 1.609	*(Converts miles to kilometers)*
LET M = K * .6214	*(Converts kilometers to miles)*
LET O = G * .035	*(Converts ounces to grams)*
LET G = O * 28	*(Converts grams to ounces)*
LET L = G * 3.8	*(Converts gallons to liters)*
LET G = L * .26	*(Converts liters to gallons)*
LET C = (F − 32) * .555	*(Converts Farenheit to Celsius)*
LET F = C * 1.8 + 32	*(Converts Celsius to Farenheit)*
LET Q = L * 1.06	*(Converts quarts to liters)*

The above equations use approximate conversion factors and should not be used where precision calculations are needed.

Alternate method of showing end of program. It is possible to tell the computer that the program is completed besides using a 9999 or −999 as a last-value test code. Some operators signal by entering a 1 or a 2. For example, Line 60 of the metric program could state REM ENTRY OF 1 WILL BE USED TO RUN PROGRAM, 2 TO STOP. Then the INPUT statement at Line 70 would read as follows:

```
70 INPUT "ENTER 1 TO RUN PROGRAM, 2 TO STOP" E
80 IF E = 1 THEN GO TO --- (INPUT statement)
```

In this case E is used for "entry." The message displayed would be:

ENTER 1 TO RUN PROGRAM, 2 TO STOP ?

The operator could enter a 2 if there were no more data values and a 1 if the program were to continue.

You can experiment with the codes you wish for ending a program.

DESCRIBING DECIMAL FRACTIONS IN COBOL

In the COBOL programs in Chapters 12 and 13, there were no dollar amounts or decimal fractions. Often, a number described in the DATA DIVISION of a program has dollars and cents or is a number that will be used in a computation. This number should be described with a decimal point, even if there is no decimal point in the punched card.

Assumed decimal point

You learned earlier that decimal points are not usually punched into cards. The programmer describes to the computer where the decimal point should actually go. If it is not punched into the card, it is said to be an *assumed decimal point*.

In planning the card layout, the programmer first describes the assumed decimal point with a *caret* (‸) that indicates that an insert is placed where the decimal point should be. See the partial card layout below. Note that the Sales Amount field will have six numbers (shown with Xs). Two of the numbers follow the assumed decimal point. Four are to the left of it. The description is XXXX‸XX.

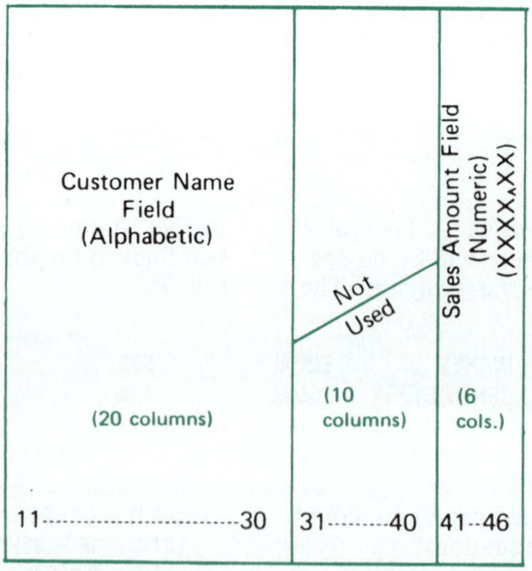

Use of the decimal point in accumulating a total

Input description. When describing the amount to the computer, the position of the decimal point is indicated with a V. The PICTURE clause would read as follows:

```
130 02 AMOUNT    PICTURE 9999V99.
```

The description of a punched card is shown below. Note that the "V" is not counted as one of the 80 columns because it is only assumed, but it is described to the computer.

```
070          DATA RECØRD IS PUNCHED-CARD.
080  01      PUNCHED-CARD.
090          02  ACCØUNT-NUMBER            PICTURE 9(6).
100          02  FILLER                    PICTURE XXXX.
110          02  CUSTØMER-NAME             PICTURE A(20).
120          02  FILLER                    PICTURE X(10).
130          02  AMØUNT                    PICTURE 9999V99.
140          02  FILLER                    PICTURE X(33).
150          02  TRANSACTIØN-CØDE          PICTURE 9.
```

The total to be accumulated will have one more position than the amount in order to allow for a carry. It is described at the 77 level of the WORKING-STORAGE SECTION as follows:

050 77 CHARGE-TOTAL PICTURE 9999V99 VALUE 0.

Output description. Part of a printer spacing chart is shown. Because the decimal point must appear in the printout, it is shown in the chart and is counted when arriving at a count of 132 positions for the print line. Note that the amount has seven positions, counting the decimal point. But, the total has one more position, allowing for a carry. The description of the amount is XXXX.XX and of the total, XXXXX.XX.

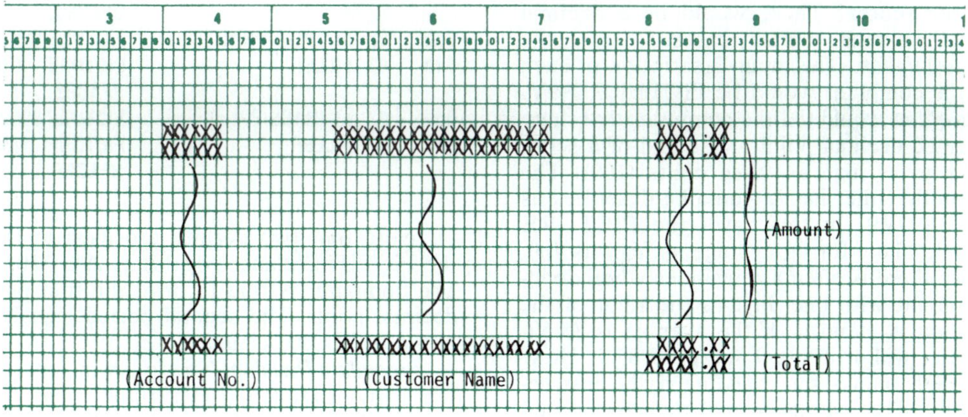

Below is shown the first entry in the WORKING-STORAGE SECTION for accumulating a total of charge sales:

The entry is written at Level 77 because all descriptions of areas for computations in WORKING-STORAGE are Level 77 entries.

```
220  WØRKING-STØRAGE SECTIØN.
230  77  CHARGE-TØTAL                    PICTURE 99999V99 VALUE 0.
```

The total is cleared to zero with a VALUE clause.

CHARGE-TOTAL is the name chosen for the total. It is described on the detail line named TOTAL-LINE as follows:

```
210 01  TØTAL-LINE.
220       02  FILLER                   PICTURE X(84) VALUE SPACES.
230       02  CHARGE-TØTAL-PRINT       PICTURE 99999.99.
240       02  FILLER                   PICTURE X(40) VALUE SPACES.
```

Note that the name used for the total on the printed line is CHARGE-TOTAL-PRINT. It has a decimal point shown after the fifth digit.

Procedure Division. An order in the PROCEDURE DIVISION, MOVE CHARGE-TOTAL TO CHARGE-TOTAL-PRINT must be followed by another order, MOVE TOTAL-LINE TO PRINT-LINE. An instruction can then be written, WRITE PRINT-LINE, to cause the total to be printed.

Use of decimal point in making calculations

Remember that in Problem 1, pp. 319–323 of Chapter 12, the computer was programmed to print a report with each student's name, class code, and three test scores. But, how would these test scores be described if you wished an average of the three scores? There would be a decimal fraction in the average in many cases.

Input description. The input description of each score to the computer would be PICTURE 999V. This description would tell the computer that there is an assumed decimal point at the end of a score that could go as high as three digits (100). The average, on the other hand, would be described as PICTURE 999V9. In this case, the PICTURE clause would allow for an average as high as 100, or, because there is often a remainder when dividing, an amount with one digit to the right of the decimal point is planned. If the average is 85.59, the computer will drop the 9 and print 85.5. However, COBOL allows for rounding if the instructions specify. The average would then be printed as 85.6.

An area in WORKING-STORAGE must be described for the total of the scores as well as the average. The three scores must be added together and then divided by 3 to obtain the average. These areas would be described at the 77 level as follows:

```
200 WORKING-STORAGE SECTION.
210 77 TOTAL-SCORE     PICTURE 999V VALUE 0.
220 77 AVERAGE         PICTURE 999V9 VALUE 0.
```

Output description. A line in the body of the printed report could be described as follows:

```
230 01 STUDENT-LINE.
240    02 FILLER               PICTURE X(36) VALUE
                               SPACES.
250    02 STUDENT-NAME-PRINT   PICTURE A(20).
260    02 FILLER               PICTURE X(5) VALUE
                               SPACES.
270    02 CLASS-CODE-PRINT     PICTURE 9.
280    02 FILLER               PICTURE X(5) VALUE
                               SPACES.
290    02 SCORE-1-PRINT        PICTURE 999..
300    02 FILLER               PICTURE X(5) VALUE
                               SPACES.
310    02 SCORE-2-PRINT        PICTURE 999..
320    02 FILLER               PICTURE X(5) VALUE
                               SPACES.
330    02 SCORE-3-PRINT        PICTURE 999..
340    02 FILLER               PICTURE X(5) VALUE
                               SPACES.
350    02 AVERAGE-PRINT        PICTURE 999.9.
360    02 FILLER               PICTURE X(36) VALUE
                               SPACES.
```

Note that two periods are used at the end of the PICTURE clauses on Lines 290, 310, and 330. The computer is told to print the first period as a decimal point. The second period signals the end of the PICTURE clause.

Procedure Division. The following instructions in the PROCEDURE DIVISION could cause the average to be figured and printed.

```
090 ADD SCORE-1, SCORE-2, SCORE-3 GIVING
      TOTAL-SCORE.
100 DIVIDE TOTAL-SCORE BY 3 GIVING AVERAGE ROUNDED.
```

Instructions to print the line would be written in the PROCEDURE DIVISION as shown in Lines 110–170 at the top of p. 411.

```
110 MOVE STUDENT-NAME TO STUDENT-NAME-PRINT.
120 MOVE SCORE-1 TO SCORE-1-PRINT.
130 MOVE SCORE-2 TO SCORE-2-PRINT.
140 MOVE SCORE-3 TO SCORE-3-PRINT.
150 MOVE AVERAGE TO AVERAGE-PRINT.
160 MOVE STUDENT-LINE TO PRINT-LINE.
170 WRITE PRINT-LINE.
```

The above instructions would cause all the variables to be moved to the detail line, STUDENT-LINE. One line of printout would show the student's name, all three scores, and the average.

There was no place allowed for the total of all scores on the print line. The total was placed in WORKING-STORAGE only for the purpose of computation. The average, on the other hand, had to be moved (LINE 150, MOVE AVERAGE TO AVERAGE-PRINT).

Variations in COBOL programs

With the foregoing instructions, you should be able to write more complicated programs that allow for accumulating dollar amounts, multiplication, or division.

Remember that the decimal point is indicated with a "V" in the input description and that it is not counted in the total of 80 positions. It is indicated with a decimal point in the output description and is counted in the total of 132 positions. An area may be cleared at the 77 level in WORKING-STORAGE for any computations. This entry should indicate with a "V" the position of an assumed decimal point. The area may be cleared to zero with a VALUE clause.

GLOSSARY of SPECIAL TERMS

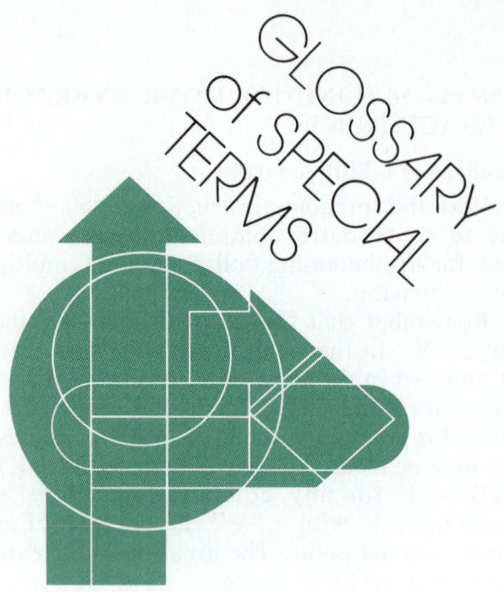

ADDRESS: Number given to each byte or to several bytes making up computer word in memory.

ALPHABETIC CONSTANT (COBOL): Value known in advance and which does not change during processing of program. Composed of letters of alphabet with or without spaces.

ALPHANUMERIC: Data consisting of letters of alphabet with any combination of spaces, numbers, or special characters.

ALPHANUMERIC CONSTANT: Alphanumeric data known in advance and which do not change during processing of program.

ANALOG COMPUTER: Calculating machine that uses numbers to represent quantities that can be measured.

ANNOTATION SYMBOL: Flowchart symbol used to give additional notes or comments. Broken line shows symbol being explained.

APERTURE CARD: Punched card with microfilm inset.

APPLICATION PROGRAM: Program, usually written by programmer who works for computer user, to solve certain problem. (Some general application programs can be bought, but user programmer usually must make changes in them to fit company's needs.)

APPLICATIONS PROGRAMMER: Person who interprets systems flowcharts and detailed plans received from systems analyst and prepares program flowcharts and computer programs needed.

ARITHMETIC EXPRESSION (BASIC): Made up of numbers (numeric constants), variables, mathematical operators, or combination of these.

ARITHMETIC-LOGIC UNIT: Part of CPU that adds, subtracts, multiplies, and divides numeric data as directed by program. Makes it possible for CPU to make certain logical decisions in regard to data it is processing.

ARROWHEADS AND FLOWLINES: Flowchart symbols used to show order of operations and direction of data flow.

ASSEMBLER: Computer program that translates symbolic source program into machine-language object program.

ASSEMBLY: Process of translating symbolic source program into machine-language object program.

ASSUMED DECIMAL POINT (COBOL): Decimal point that is not punched into a card, the position of which is described to the computer.

AUTOMATED DATA PROCESSING: Process, largely self-regulating, in which information is handled with a minimum of human effort and intervention.

BALANCE: Amount remaining at end of one period or beginning of another period.

BALANCE FILE: File made up of records that show balance of some kind for certain date.

BALANCE RECORD: Record in balance file.

BAR-CODE READER: Input unit that can scan items on which bars or lines representing data have been recorded by printer or recording machine.

BASIC (Beginners All-Purpose Symbolic Instruction Code): Compiler-level source programming language used for time-sharing purposes; conversational language that allows user to communicate with translator program by typing on terminal.

BATCH DATA PROCESSING: Method by which items to be processed may be coded and collected in groups before processing.

BINARY CODE: Two-digit numbering system used in computers.

BINARY NUMBERING SYSTEM: Full numbering system composed of just two symbols, 0 and 1.

BIT binary digit: Contents of one magnetic core in computer; smallest element of data in computer memory systems.

BLOCK: Group of consecutive magnetically coded records that are separated by gaps from other blocks on file.

BYTE: Unit of computer memory, made up of eight bits, which can represent any digit, letter of alphabet, or special character. Smallest unit of memory that can have an address.

BUFFER: Storage device designed to hold data temporarily.

CALCULATING: Process of computing in order to arrive at mathematical result.

CATHODE-RAY TUBE (CRT): Television-type screen.

CENTRAL PROCESSING UNIT: See CPU.

COBOL (Common Business Oriented Language): Higher-level source programming language, designed to process large files, in which programs are written in near-English language.

CODING (CLASSIFYING): Process of assigning system of symbols, letters, or words to data in accordance with set of rules.

CODING (PROGRAMMING): Process of writing instructions in language acceptable to computer.

COLUMN (CARD): Vertical division of a card that is marked with numbered scale above and below it. Column can hold one or more punches that stand for single number, letter of alphabet, or special character.

COM: See *Computer-Output Microfilm.*

COMMA (BASIC): Character that acts as TAB key in PRINT statement, immediately moving carriage to next print zone.

COMMUNICATING: Process of transmitting information to point of use.

COMPILER: Translator program, usually furnished by computer manufacturer, used to translate higher-level language into machine language on a many-for-one basis.

COMPILER-LEVEL LANGUAGE: Higher-level programming language that is translated by compiler program into machine language on many-for-one basis.

COMPUTER: Information-handling device in which data and instructions for processing data are represented as electronic codes or impulses.

COMPUTER-ASSISTED INSTRUCTION: Process by which students use computers directly for learning new subjects.

COMPUTER INSTRUCTION: Coded program step that tells computer what to do with certain items of data and where they are stored.

COMPUTER-MANAGED INSTRUCTION: Process of using computer for planning instruction rather than for teaching.

COMPUTER OPERATOR: Person who monitors operations of computer, using routines that have already been set up.

COMPUTER-OUTPUT MICROFILM (COM): Medium in which computer output is recorded directly on film quickly and automatically by unit that converts computer signals to human language and records them on film.

COMPUTER PROGRAM: Detailed set of instructions needed to solve a problem on computer.

CONDITIONAL BRANCH INSTRUCTION: Instruction that causes computer to branch to another instruction if certain test or condition has been met.

CONFIGURATION SECTION: Section of the ENVIRONMENT DIVISION of COBOL program that describes the source and object computers.

CONSOLE: Part of CPU used to: (1) give information to operator about performance of system; (2) enter information into system by hand; (3) alter data in storage when necessary; (4) start and stop computer; (5) test for computer failures and track down any malfunctions.

CONSOLE INQUIRY STATION: Input/output device that usually consists of built-in or separate electric typewriter with CRT. Used by operator to control computer operations.

CONSTANT: Value that is known in advance and which does not change during processing of program.

CONTROL CODE: Code recorded in specific field of card, tape, or disk record, which code gives computer special instructions about program itself.

CONTROL UNIT: Unit that regulates different functions of computer system. Contains the intricate time system of computer. Interprets program instructions and supervises input and output devices.

CONVERSATIONAL LANGUAGE: Computer language that allows user to communicate with language translator program by typing on terminal.

CPU (CENTRAL PROCESSING UNIT): That part of computer that receives and stores instructions and data, performs arithmetic and logic operations, and directs action of input and output units.

CRT (CATHODE-RAY TUBE): Television-type screen.

DATA: Term that means facts of all kinds.

DATA BLOCK: Collection of all DATA statements in BASIC program in line-number order. Each time READ statement is processed, the next available data value is accessed from data block.

DATA DIVISION: Third division in COBOL program. Describes data files to be used as input before processing and files and reports used as output. Also specifies WORKING-STORAGE section reserved for constants, accumulating total, and data developed during program.

DATA-ENTRY OPERATOR: Person who records data on input media for processing.

DATA PROCESSING: Converting facts into usable form.

DATA PROCESSING SYSTEM: Plan for making information available to user.

DATA STATEMENT (BASIC): Program statement that assigns values to variable(s) named in READ statement.

DEBUGGING: Process of correcting and testing program before actually using it to process data.

DECISION SYMBOL: Flowchart symbol that shows that test is to be made. There must be "yes" or "no" answer that will determine the next step to be taken in program.

DESTRUCTIVE READ-IN: Process by which new data read into memory automatically erases any data previously stored in same location.

DETAIL FILE: File that contains records of day-to-day transactions.

DETAIL RECORD: Record from detail file.

DIGIT: Any of numbers from 0 through 9.

DIGIT BITS: Rightmost four bits in EBCDIC Code shown in this text.

DIGITAL COMPUTER: Computer that works with numbers or letters of alphabet and special characters that can be coded numerically. Solves problems electronically by counting, adding, subtracting, multiplying, and dividing.

DISK DRIVE: Input/output device on which disk pack is mounted.

DISK PACK: Collection of two or more disks mounted on common vertical shaft.

DISPLAY SYMBOL: Flowchart symbol used to show data displayed by on-line devices, such as CRT of terminal.

DOCUMENT SYMBOL: Flowchart symbol used to show input/output using documents and reports of all kinds.

EBCDIC (Extended Binary Coded Decimal Interchange Code): Code that uses eight binary positions in memory to stand for a single character. There are four zone positions and four digit positions.

ELEMENTARY ITEM: Field that cannot be subdivided further.

11 POSITION: Same as 11 row, which is immediately below the top punching position on standard 80-column card.

ENCRYPTION: Process of secretly coding data before they are sent across communication lines and decoding after they are received by correct people.

END STATEMENT (BASIC): Last program statement in all BASIC programs.

ENVIRONMENT DIVISION: Second division in COBOL program. Specifies computer, input/output devices, and input/output files.

EQUATION (BASIC): Arithmetic statement that contains variable, equal sign, and expression.

EVEN PARITY: State of parity in which one electronic impulse is added in parity-check position to maintain even number of impulses for each character.

EXCEPTION REPORT: Report that tells when business events have not turned out as planned.

EXCLAMATION POINT: Used in BASIC to insert comment into a program. Statement following ! on line is non-executable.

EXECUTABLE STATEMENT: Statement that directs computer to perform certain operation. Gives a command.

FD: File description (COBOL).

FIELD (CARD): Vertical column or group of consecutive columns in punched card set aside to record single fact.

FIELD (MAGNETIC TAPE OR DISK): Single space or group of consecutive spaces needed to record single fact.

FILE: Collection of related records treated as unit.

FILLER: COBOL reserved word that has special meaning to compiler: (1) Used to describe unused spaces on data card or print line; (2) Used to describe fields that do contain data but which computer is to ignore; (3) Every field description entry in DATA DIVISION must contain either programmer-invented name or reserved word FILLER. (FILLER may be used as data name but it cannot be referenced as data field by instruction in PROCEDURE DIVISION.)

FIXED-POINT NUMBER (INTEGER): Whole number, as opposed to number containing decimal. Decimal point is assumed to be "fixed" at end of whole number.

FLEXIBLE DISK: Small, flexible magnetic platter that is something like phonograph record. One disk holds as much data as 3,000 eighty-column cards.

FLOATING-POINT NUMBER: Number that includes fractional amount; number having decimal point.

FLOATING-POINT VARIABLE: Field of data that contains decimal point, the value of which field changes from record to record and is not known in advance.

FLOPPY DISK: Same as *Flexible disk*.

FLOWCHART: Graphic representation of order of operations in data processing system or program, in which symbols are used to represent processing operations, media, equipment, and data flow.

FLOWCHART SYMBOL: Symbol used to represent processing operations, equipment, and data flow.

GIGO: "Garbage In, Garbage Out."

GO TO STATEMENT (BASIC): Program statement that gives line number of statement to which unconditional branch must be made.

GO TO STATEMENT (COBOL): Statement that tells computer to branch to step other than next step in order of program.

GRAPHIC UNITS: Units that represent data by use of pictures or graphs.

GROUP ITEM: Item or field that can be "broken down" or subdivided into smaller items.

HARDWARE: Term used to describe any physical equipment or components in an electronic computer system.

HARD-WIRING: State in which the terminal is close enough to the CPU to be physically connected by cable.

HIGHER-LEVEL LANGUAGE: Problem-oriented language that is usually not limited to use on one kind of computer.

ID CARD: (1) Identification card used for electronic funds transfer; (2) identification card used as key to gain access to computer.

IDENTIFICATION DIVISION: First division in COBOL program. Gives name of programmer and date program is written.

IF STATEMENT: Conditional statement used to make certain tests and to direct further processing based upon results of these tests.

IF-THEN STATEMENT (BASIC): Conditional branching statement.

INPUT: Data that enter system for processing.

INPUT MEDIUM: Form or material on which data are recorded for processing.

INPUT/OUTPUT SYMBOL: Symbol that refers to an input or output function. In systems flowcharting, this symbol refers to any type of medium bringing data into system for processing or any type medium on which processed information is recorded. Types of media are not shown.

INPUT STATEMENT (BASIC): Program statement that allows

operator to enter data values at terminal during execution of program.

INPUT UNIT: Device that receives data and instructions needed to solve problem and feeds data and instructions to CPU.

INTERNAL STORAGE UNIT: Memory of CPU.

INVOICE: Business form that lists all goods shipped, giving date, price, terms of sale, and other important information.

ITEM (DATA): Single position or group of consecutive positions needed to record a single fact. (Same as *Field*.)

KEY or KEY FIELD: Data field in a record used for identification.

KEYING SYMBOL: Flowchart symbol used to show operation using key-driven device, such as punching, verifying, and typing.

KEYPUNCH: Machine that records data in cards by punching holes to represent numbers, letters of the alphabet, and special characters.

LABEL: Name or abbreviation used in program instead of numeric address to identify location of computer word (field) in storage.

LET STATEMENT (BASIC): (1) Assigns numeric value to memory address that has been given variable name; (2) order to computer to carry out computations on right side of equal sign and store results in address with variable name on left side of equal sign.

LEVEL NUMBERS: Perform same function in program that Roman and Arabic numerals do in outline. Show relationship of data names in program. Are used in DATA DIVISION only.

LOGICAL OPERATOR (BASIC): AND, NOT, and OR. Used with numbers and relational operators to write one program statement with many decisions.

MACHINE ADDRESS (MEMORY ADDRESS): Unique address for memory location in machine language.

MACHINE LANGUAGE: Any language that can be understood and carried out by computer without further translation.

MACRO-TRANSLATION LANGUAGE: Higher-level computer language in which one instruction may be translated into several machine-language instructions, on a many-for-one basis.

MAGNETIC DISK: Input, output, and storage medium that is coated on both sides with substance capable of being magnetized. Data are stored as magnetic impulses or bits on grooveless tracks of disk.

MAGNETIC DISK SYMBOL: Flowchart symbol used to indicate magnetic disk file.

MAGNETIC-INK CHARACTER READER (MICR): Input device used to process data printed in magnetic ink with specially designed numbers and symbols.

MAGNETIC TAPE: Tape that has been coated with magnetic material, on which data may be recorded in form of magnetically polarized spots.

MAGNETIC TAPE SYMBOL: Flowchart symbol used to represent magnetic tape.

MANUAL: Done by hand.

MANUAL INPUT SYMBOL: Flowchart symbol used to show data input by on-line keyboards, such as the terminal.

MANUAL OPERATION SYMBOL: Any off-line process at human speed (without mechanical aid).

MASTER FILE: File that contains relatively permanent records. These files must be updated from time to time.

MASTER RECORD: Record in master file.

MATCHING: Process of comparing records in two files to see if key fields in the two sets of records are same.

MATCH-MERGING: Process like matching process. Difference is that matched records from two or more files are merged into single file.

MERGE SYMBOL: Flowchart symbol used to show combining of two or more sets of items into one set.

MERGING: Process by which two or more files of records, each of which is in sequential order, are combined into one file.

MICR: Magnetic-ink character reader.

MICROFICHE: Rectangular piece of film on which images have been reduced and recorded. One card can hold between 60 and 98 pages of copy.

MICROPROCESSOR: CPU of microcomputer, which fits on single silicon chip. Although tiny, microprocessor has control unit and arithmetic/logic unit.

MICRO-TRANSLATION LANGUAGE: Language that is translated into machine language on one-for-one basis.

MINICOMPUTER: Small, inexpensive computer that has CPU and one or more input/output devices. Often low enough in price that it can be purchased rather than rented.

9 EDGE: Bottom of standard 80-column card.

NON-EXECUTABLE STATEMENT: Statement that does not specify action. Usually gives information.

NUMERIC CONSTANT: Numeric value known in advance and which does not change during processing of program.

NUMERIC VARIABLE: Numeric value not known in advance and which changes during processing of program.

OBJECT COMPUTER: Computer used to run machine-language object program.

OBJECT PROGRAM: Program that results from translation of source program into machine language.

ODD PARITY: State of parity in which one electronic impulse is added in parity-check position to maintain odd number of impulses for each character.

OFF-LINE: Term used for storage that is independent of CPU. However, data are recorded in form compatible with CPU.

OFF-LINE STORAGE SYMBOL: Symbol showing storage of data off-line, regardless of medium used. Not directly accessible to computer.

OFF-PAGE CONNECTOR SYMBOL: Flowchart symbol that marks exit from and entry to flowline from one page to next.

ON-LINE: Term used to describe storage on devices that are outside the CPU but connected directly to it and under its control at all times. Same as *Secondary storage*.

ON-LINE STORAGE SYMBOL: Flowchart symbol used to show that an input/output medium is under direct control of computer.

ON-PAGE CONNECTOR SYMBOL: Flowchart symbol that denotes exit to, or entry from, another part of flowchart. Connection between two is shown by number placed in circle that marks end of flowline. Same number is then placed in another circle marking continuation of flowline.

OPERAND: Gives the location or address of data or of next instruction to be followed by computer.

OPERATION CODE: Directs computer to take steps, such as reading record, adding contents of two memory locations together, or printing line of data on page.

OPTICAL-CHARACTER READER (OCR): Device that identifies each character by comparing its distinctive features with those stored in OCR's memory.

OPTICAL-MARK PAGE READER: Device that can sense marks made by regular pencil or pen on specially designed forms.

ORIGINAL DATA: Data to be processed.

OUTPUT: Processed information.

OUTPUT MEDIUM: Form or material on which processed information appears.

OUTPUT UNIT: Device that records or displays processed data on output media, which may be printed reports, punched card, magnetic tapes, magnetic disks, or some other medium compatible with computer.

PARITY-CHECK POSITION: Used by recording mechanism to check its own errors. One electronic impulse is automatically added by input device to maintain either even or odd number of electronic impulses for each character recorded.

PAYMENTS DETAIL FILE: Detail file that contains records of payments on account received from customers.

PICTURE CLAUSE: Clause in DATA DIVISION of COBOL program that describes number of characters in field and type of characters: alphabetic, numeric, or alphanumeric (mixed).

PLOTTER: Output device that produces data in graphic form. Uses paper and a pen controlled by instructions from CPU.

PRIMARY STORAGE: Internal memory of CPU.

PRINT STATEMENT (BASIC): Program statement used to cause computer to output data on terminal CRT or typewriter. Also tells printer how output is to be arranged.

PRINTOUT: Printed report prepared by computer program.

PROCEDURE DIVISION: Last division in COBOL program. Specifies actual steps computer is to follow in processing data in order to solve problem.

PROCESS SYMBOL: Flowchart symbol that refers to processing operations or steps through which data must pass to produce desired output.

PROGRAM: Detailed set of instructions for solving problem.

PROGRAM, COMPUTER: Detailed set of instructions needed to solve problem on computer.

PROGRAM FLOWCHART: Flowchart that outlines step-by-step instructions in program to solve problem with computer.

PROGRAM ID: Program identification (COBOL).

PROGRAMMER: Person who plans, writes, and tests computer programs.

PROGRAMMER-INVENTED WORDS: All words other than reserved COBOL words are invented by programmer if they are not required entries.

PROXY: Document or form that gives one person power to act for another person.

PUNCHED CARD: Card in which pattern of holes is punched to represent data to be processed or stored. All digits (0 through 9), all letters of alphabet, and number of special characters can be recorded in single card.

PUNCHED CARD FILE SYMBOL: Flowchart symbol indicating punched card file as input/output.

PUNCHED CARD SYMBOL: Flowchart symbol indicating use of punched cards as input/output medium.

PURE BINARY SYSTEM: Method of expressing binary numbers in which value of digit doubles for each move of one position to left. There is no limit to size of number that can be represented in this system.

RANDOM ACCESS: Direct method of accessing data regardless of position in file.

RAW DATA: Data to be processed.

READ STATEMENT (BASIC): Program statement that tells computer to read one or more variables that are listed in READ statement and to give them values listed in DATA statement.

RECORD: Group of related data items treated as unit.

RECORDING: Process of writing, rewriting, or reproducing data by hand or machine.

RELATION TEST: Test that compares two values.

RELATIONAL OPERATOR (BASIC): Symbol on keyboard of terminal used when writing statement that tests for equality, inequality, or relationship of one value to another.

REMARK STATEMENT: Non-executable statement in source program that is inserted to make program clear.

REORDER POINT: Lowest amount of stock that can be on hand before ordering more of an item.

REQUIRED ENTRIES: Names that must be used in every COBOL program, such as names of divisions and sections as well as words such as SELECT, ASSIGN, and STOP RUN.

RESERVED WORDS: Certain words that have specific meanings to COBOL compiler. Are used for given purpose, must be used according to certain COBOL rules, and are named on list of COBOL reserved words.

RETRIEVING: Process of making stored information available when needed.

ROUTINE: Set of instructions within computer program for doing certain task.

ROW (CARD): Each horizontal line of punching positions across punched card. There are 12 horizontal rows in standard 80-column card.

SALES DETAIL FILE: Detail file that contains records of sales to customers.

SECONDARY MEMORY: Storage on devices outside CPU but under its control at all times. Same as *Secondary storage*.

SECONDARY STORAGE: Storage on devices outside CPU but connected directly to it and under control of CPU at all times.

SELECTING: Process of separating from file of records only those that have particular name or number in specific field.

SEMICOLON (BASIC): Character in BASIC program PRINT statement that causes one horizontal space to be skipped.

SEQUENCE-CHECKING: Process of checking records that are already sequenced to be sure that sequencing is correct.

SEQUENCING: Process of arranging records in either numeric or alphabetic order.

SEQUENTIAL ACCESS: Storage technique in which stored items of data become available only in one-after-the-other sequence, whether all information in record or only some of it is desired.

SIGNING ON: Getting connected to computer with time-sharing.

SOFTWARE: Term used to describe programs (instructions) that cause hardware to function.

SORT SYMBOL: Flowchart symbol showing arranging of set of items into some kind of sequence, using manual or computer methods.

SORTING: Process of arranging information in order or separating it into similar groups according to some predetermined plan.

SOURCE COMPUTER: Computer used to translate source program into object program.

SOURCE DOCUMENT: Document from which raw or original data are obtained.

SOURCE PROGRAM: Computer program written in language other than machine language.

STATEMENT: Computer programming instruction.

STATEMENT OF ACCOUNT: Form that summarizes charges to customer's account, payments made, and balance due.

STOP STATEMENT: BASIC program statement that tells computer that all statements needed to process data have been executed or that it should stop processing data.

STORING: Orderly safekeeping of information so that it may be used later.

SUMMARIZING: Process of converting processed data into concise, meaningful form.

SUMMARY FILE RECORD or SUMMARY RECORD: Record that summarizes transactions of similar detail records.

SYMBOL (FLOWCHART): Shape or outline drawn to represent certain medium, operation, piece of equipment, or direction of data flow.

SYMBOLIC LANGUAGE: Computer language that uses symbolic letter abbreviations or names for operation codes or addresses.

SYNTHETIC LANGUAGE: Any programming language other than machine language.

SYSIN: System input.

SYSOUT: System output.

SYSTEM: Group of items or actions that work together to perform certain function.

SYSTEMS ANALYST: Person who is in charge of planning and carrying out data processing system.

SYSTEMS FLOWCHART: Flowchart that shows media used for input and output and flow of data through various steps in data processing system.

TEMPLATE: Device used to draw symbols of different sizes and shapes in flowchart. Symbols appear as cut-out forms.

TERMINAL: Input/output device consisting of typewriter keyboard and often CRT. Enables user to have direct contact with computer.

TERMINAL SYMBOL: Flowchart symbol used for START and STOP in program flowchart.

TEST CONTROL CARD: Card placed at end of file of data cards, having in it predetermined value or set of characters that will indicate to computer that all data cards have been processed; (2) card containing last-card-test code.

TIME-SHARING: System by which more than one person can use central computer at same time by means of remote terminals.

TRANSACTION: Act carried out while handling business. A transaction takes place between at least two people or two businesses.

TRANSACTION CODE: Code recorded in specific field of data card, tape, or disk record, which code makes it possible for computer to distinguish one kind of record from another and to perform operation according to program instructions.

12 EDGE: Top of standard 80-column card.

12 POSITION: Punching position nearest top or 12 edge of standard 80-column card.

UNCONDITIONAL BRANCH INSTRUCTION: Instruction that causes computer to branch (jump) to another instruction regardless of conditions.

UPDATE: Act of changing file or program with current data according to specified plan.

UTILITY PROGRAM: Program furnished by computer manufacturer to do routine jobs, such as sorting, loading program into memory, and writing out contents in storage.

VALUE (BASIC): Quantity used for comparison or computation. Equal to field in punched card or word in computer.

VALUE CLAUSE (COBOL): Method for specifying beginning value of data item in WORKING-STORAGE. Used to describe beginning value of numeric variable and value of constant.

VARIABLE: Item of data that is not known in advance and which changes during processing of program.

VARIABLE NAME: Name given to address at which variable field of data is stored in computer.

VERIFIER (CARD): Machine much like keypunch, used for checking accuracy of previously punched data in standard 80-column cards.

WORD: Unit of one or more bytes (characters) of computer storage, which are used to store one item (field) of data. These bytes (characters) are grouped to form meaningful unit of data and are accessed as single unit.

WORKING-STORAGE SECTION: Section in DATA DIVISION of COBOL program, used to describe temporary storage areas for computer results or other information developed during processing. Used to provide working areas in memory for items not described in FDs in the FILE SECTION.

ZONE BITS: Leftmost four bits of standard EBCDIC code shown in this text.

ZONE PUNCH: Punch in 11 or 12 location of standard 80-column card. Zero punch is also considered zone punch when used with another punch in same column to represent letter or special character.

INDEX

R

S

T

U

V

W, Z